VOLUME

4

PLATO'S METAPHYSICS AND EPISTEMOLOGY

Edited with introductions by

T ERENCE I RWIN

Sage School of Philosophy
Cornell University

D0075264

GARLAND PUBLISHING, INC.
New York & London
1995

Library of Congress Cataloging-in-Publication Data

Classical philosophy : collected papers / series editor, Terence
Irwin.
    p.   cm.
    Includes bibliographical references.
    Contents: v. 1. Philosophy before Socrates — v. 2. Socrates
and his contemporaries — v. 3. Plato's ethics — v. 4. Plato's
metaphysics and epistemology — v. 5. Aristotle's ethics —
v. 6. Aristotle: substance, form and matter — v. 7. Aristotle:
metaphysics, epistemology, natural philosophy — v. 8. Hellenistic
philosophy.
    ISBN 0-8153-1829-4 (v. 1 : alk. paper). — ISBN 0-8153-1830-8
(v. 2 : alk. paper). — ISBN 0-8153-1832-4 (v. 3 : alk. paper). —
ISBN 0-8153-1833-2 (v. 4 : alk. paper). — ISBN 0-8153-1834-0
(v. 5 : alk. paper). — ISBN 0-8153-1835-9 (v. 6 : alk. paper). —
ISBN 0-8153-1836-7 (v. 7 : alk. paper). — ISBN 0-8153-1837-5
(v. 8 : alk. paper)
    1. Philosophy, Ancient.   I. Irwin, Terence.
B171.C53 1995
180—dc20
                                     95-5168
                                         CIP

Printed on acid-free, 250-year-life paper
Manufactured in the United States of America

CONTENTS

PROBLEMS AND DEVELOPMENTS IN THE THEORY OF FORMS

KNOWLEDGE, BELIEF, AND PERCEPTION

Series Introduction

The aim of this series is to collect some previously published work on Greek philosophy in a form in which it will be accessible to students and teachers. The pieces reprinted here were originally published in English and were almost all published in journals, though some appeared in collections of essays and a few as chapters of books. (I will refer to them, irrespective of their origin, as "papers" or "essays.")

The most difficult task for the compiler of such a collection is to decide what to exclude, since one has to choose from a large number of good essays published over the past 150 years. In this area of Anglophone scholarship, academic journals (as opposed to periodicals such as *Westminster Review* or *Athenaeum* aiming at a wider audience) began in the second half of the nineteenth century. The *Journal of Philology* (originally the *Journal of Classical and Sacred Philology*) was first published at Cambridge in 1854. *Mind* (originally a journal of both philosophy and psychology) began in Edinburgh in 1876. In the late nineteenth century these were followed by the *Classical Quarterly*. In the United States the first specialized journals began in the late nineteenth century, attached to universities; the *American Journal of Philology*, for instance, was founded at Johns Hopkins University and the *Philosophical Review* at Cornell University. In these journals, and the many other Classical and philosophical periodicals that have been founded in the twentieth century, essays on Greek philosophy have appeared regularly. The earliest essay chosen (by Henry Sidgwick) comes from the *Journal of Philology* in 1872. Also included are essays from the early 1990s and—though this was not part of my plan—essays from most of the decades in between.

The first journal devoted to ancient philosophy was *Phronesis* (not confined to English), which began in 1955. More recently *Oxford Studies in Ancient Philosophy, Apeiron, Ancient Philosophy* (all in English), *Revue de Philosophie Ancienne, Elenchos,* and *Methexis* have appeared. Some of the best recent work appeared in these specialized journals, and their growth indicates the increasing interest in Greek philosophy. It would be regrettable, however, if essays in this area were confined to the specialized journals.

Fortunately, important essays continue to appear in journals such as the *Classical Quarterly* and the *Philosophical Review*, which aim to reach a more general classical or philosophical audience.

The different journals publishing work in Greek philosophy tend, not surprisingly, to attract somewhat different essays and readers of this collection will notice different styles and approaches. Linguistic, literary, historical, and philosophical skills (and, no doubt, others) are all necessary for the full understanding, appreciation, and enjoyment of Greek philosophical texts, and it would be foolish to take the difference between "Classical" and "philosophical" essays too seriously. Included is an excerpt from the work of George Grote, whose contributions to the study of both Greek history (in his *History of Greece*) and Greek philosophy (in his books on Plato and on Aristotle) were of the highest importance. In Grote's time, of course, scholars in either of these areas did not need to read as much as now; moreover, the scholar had the benefit of a private income, and therefore did not hold a teaching position in a university. In practice most writers on ancient philosophy, having limited means, limited leisure, and limited knowledge, write primarily as Classicists or as philosophers.

Classical studies and philosophy have evidently not been static over the past 150 years; and the study of Greek philosophy has been deeply influenced by developments in its "parent" disciplines. A few examples will illustrate the point:

1. Nineteenth-century Classical scholars (here partly influenced by Biblical criticism) show a great deal of confidence in their ability to divide texts into "earlier" and "later" versions or sections and to recognize the work of "editors," or "redactors" or "interpolators." The sort of treatment given to the *Book of Genesis* and to the *Iliad* was also thought suitable for Plato's *Republic* and for Aristotle's *Ethics* and *Metaphysics*.

2. In the early twentieth century Classical studies were strongly affected by the latest trends in anthropology. These trends entered the study of Greek philosophy, and especially of the Presocratics, through the work of F.M. Cornford.

3. In the twentieth century Anglophone philosophy passed through the rise and fall of trends associated with logical positivism and its successors. These trends affected not only philosophers' views of which parts of Plato or Aristotle are deemed nearly true or hopelessly false but also their views of what, if anything, in the history of philosophy is worth studying.

4. Anglophone scholarship as well as Anglophone philosophy has been affected, to varying degrees, by the developments in

philosophy connected with Heidegger, Gadamer, Derrida, and their disciples. Greek philosophers play a central role as heroes or villains or both in these philosophers' views of philosophy and its history; and these views in turn have affected the questions raised about the Greek texts themselves.

These different trends in Classics and philosophy have caused the "Classical" and the "philosophical" aspects of the study of Greek philosophy to converge or diverge at different times. An extreme example of divergence is illustrated by Cambridge from (roughly speaking) 1900 to 1970. G.E. Moore, C.D. Broad, and Ludwig Wittgenstein were central figures in the development of Cambridge philosophy; but their conception of philosophy did not include any central place for the study of ancient philosophy. F.M. Cornford and W.K.C. Guthrie were the leading figures in the study of Greek philosophy in Cambridge; their conception of the right approach to ancient philosophy did not include any serious engagement with philosophy in general. Oxford between 1918 and 1945 presents a different picture; here the philosophers who took Plato and Aristotle seriously (for instance, H.H. Joachim, W.D. Ross, and H.W.B. Joseph) were regarded by some of their colleagues as intellectual dinosaurs.

No doubt these historical pictures are rather crude and exaggerated, but they may suggest the sort of thing that can happen when the relation between the study of Greek philosophy and its parent disciplines becomes unbalanced. It seems safe to say—without naive optimism—that the present situation is less unbalanced than it was in either of these extreme pictures. It would be wrong to suggest that the study of Greek philosophy has an assured and stable place in either parent discipline; since these disciplines are themselves developing, *nothing* has an assured place in them. It seems reasonable to claim, however, that a fairly wide range of Classicists and philosophers recognize a legitimate place within their disciplines for the study of Greek philosophy and that, conversely, most serious students of Greek philosophy recognize their obligation to learn from both Classics and philosophy.

The essays in this series were not chosen to illustrate anything in particular about the history of scholarship or about the different methods used in approaching Greek philosophy. I believe, however, that the essays in these volumes display the different skills and approaches of the philologist, the historian, and the philosopher. Some volumes are more heavily weighted in one direction than in the other; Volumes 1 and 2, for instance, contain more contributions that discuss historical and literary questions, while some of the essays on Aristotle are more evidently philosophical. One of the incidental but nontrivial benefits of studying Greek philosophy is the opportunity that it gives us to understand the approaches of these different disciplines and to see how they influence each other.

The general aim in selecting essays is quite vague: to collect some of the best work (so far as it is available within the limits mentioned above) on some important questions in Greek philosophy. I have, however, kept in mind (though probably not constantly or consistently) some slightly more precise criteria:

1. The essays naturally vary in the degree of difficulty and in the comprehension level that they presuppose in readers. I hope, however, that most of them are accessible to readers who are not already specialists in Greek philosophy, but rather students seeking aid in writing a paper, more advanced students beginning research, or specialists in other disciplines who want some idea of what has been going on in this area.

2. On the whole I tried to pick essays that raise issues of philosophical interest, whether or not the authors approach the issues from a primarily philosophical point of view. In doing this I was influenced by the twentieth-century tendency to bring the study of Greek philosophy closer to philosophy. This is not the only tendency (as I mentioned above), but it is prominent enough to affect the general character of essays published in journals.

3. The essays are not all recent. I sought some older essays—those that often are difficult to find, especially for students without ready access to old or well supplied libraries. Moreover, they often deserve to be read again and not simply to be cited in bibliographies and footnotes.

4. I collected some essays that examine different sides of a question to give readers some sense of the debate and dialogue that are characteristic of the best work in this area. In some cases I picked out one contributor to a debate and left it to readers to follow up the references that will acquaint them with the other sides of the issue.

5. In allotting space to different topics, I was guided by the quantity of good work available in journals in English. The allocation of space, therefore, does not reflect my own view about the relative importance of different topics in Greek philosophy; it reflects my view about the quantity and quality of the work done in different areas. Readers should bear this point in mind when they see, for instance, that this collection is heavily weighted toward Plato and Aristotle and that one whole volume (Volume 6) is devoted to questions related to Aristotle's doctrine of substance. If I had been thinking simply of the relative importance of different

topics, or seeking to point out directions for future research, I might have tried a different distribution of space.

6. Some readers may reasonably regret the fact that Greek philosophy after Aristotle is squeezed into one volume and that this volume does not go beyond the Hellenistic schools. Once again this decision reflects my view about the quantity and quality of material available for this collection. Some of the best work on Hellenistic philosophy, for instance, has appeared in collections of essays.

7. I made some effort to avoid reprinting essays that are easily accessible elsewhere. This criterion explains the absence of some deservedly well-known essays by, for instance, Gregory Vlastos, Harold Cherniss, and G.E.L. Owen; their work is available in the volumes of their collected essays. I have also tried to avoid extensive duplication of other useful and readily available collections, including those by Alexander Mourelatos and by D.J. Furley and R.E. Allen on the Presocratics, by R.E. Allen and by Gregory Vlastos on Plato, and by Jonathan Barnes, Malcolm Schofield, and Richard Sorabji on Aristotle. I have not been rigid in avoiding overlap, however; I have included some essays whose importance seemed to make them indispensable for a volume in this series, even if they were already reprinted elsewhere.

I am confident that by applying these criteria I have collected a body of important essays that, hopefully, will be useful to a fairly wide range of readers. I must disabuse readers, however, of any tendency to believe that these volumes collect the crème de la crème of work in Greek philosophy or that I suppose everything included here is superior to everything not included. The very fact that the collection is drawn entirely from work in English means that it cannot represent the full range of important work on Greek philosophy; some of the best work has been published in other languages—especially French, German, and Italian. The fact that the collection is confined almost entirely to journals also means that it misses some important work. Some of the most important contributions in several areas—especially in recent years—are in books rather than essays. Moreover, some important work—once again, especially in recent years—appears in collections of essays that have been published as books. These collections include the twelve volumes of Symposia Aristotelica published since 1957, and the five volumes of Symposia Hellenistica published since 1980. Other omissions from the present collection can be explained by the fact that some journals charge permission fees beyond the means of the publisher of this series.

In fairness to the authors of these essays readers should realize that the essays are reprinted in the form in which they appear in the journal or book from which they are taken. This means that they do not necessarily represent the current views of the authors. In many cases I picked essays that began or contributed to a discussion or controversy; in some of these cases authors may well have decided, in the light of later discussion, to modify some of their initial views. Readers should regard these essays as participants in a conversation. I hope that once readers listen to these earlier participants they also will want to continue the conversation.

INTRODUCTION

Plato's metaphysical and epistemological doctrines grow out of Socratic claims about inquiry and definition (see especially the essays by Richard Sharvy and Hugh H. Benson in Volume 2). It is often argued that "middle" Plato is distinguished from "early" Plato (identified with Socrates) primarily by a commitment to 1) a conception of knowledge as consisting in recollection of truths known in a previous existence, and 2) a conception of the objects of knowledge as separated, non-sensible Forms that are imperfectly embodied in the sensible world that is made in their likeness.[1]

Some interpreters claim that we should mark a sharp division not only between early and middle Plato, but also between middle and late Plato. They argue that the first part of the *Parmenides* raises severe difficulties for the Theory of Forms that is set out in the middle dialogues (especially in the *Phaedo* and *Republic*) and that dialogues later than the *Parmenides* (especially the *Theaetetus*, *Sophist*, and *Philebus*) abandon a set of claims that are both 1) essential parts of the Theory of Forms in the middle dialogues and 2) vulnerable to the objections raised in the *Parmenides*.

This attempt to show that Plato abandons the main elements in the middle-period Theory of Forms faces an apparent difficulty in the *Timaeus*—a dialogue normally taken to be one of Plato's later works—in any case later than the *Parmenides*—yet it maintains those claims about Forms that are held to be undermined by the arguments of the *Parmenides*. The choices open to us are 1) to argue that the *Timaeus* precedes the *Parmenides*, 2) to deny that the *Parmenides* undermines the claims maintained in the *Timaeus*, 3) to conclude that Plato did not realize the difficulties that he raised for himself in the *Parmenides*, or 4) to conclude that he realized the difficulties, but kept maintaining the same claims about the Forms nonetheless.

Among these options the first is maintained strongly by G.E.L. Owen in a series of essays that has stimulated a good deal of recent work on Plato's later dialogues.[2] The fourth option (or a position that combines elements of the third and fourth options) is defended by Gregory Vlastos. The second is maintained by H.F.

Cherniss in a reply to Owen,[3] and by several recent contributors to discussion of the later dialogues.[4] The different positions are not mutually exclusive; one might, for instance, claim that the main claims defended in the middle dialogues are invulnerable to the objections in the *Parmenides*, but that Plato saw how some of his ways of expressing these claims might seem to leave him open to the objections and so chose to modify his form of expression rather than the substance of his doctrine.[5]

These questions about Plato's philosophical development form the background for many of the essays in this volume. I did not, however, pick essays that directly take up the questions about development. I omitted such essays for two reasons: 1) the main ones are already easily available,[6] and 2) the dispute about development is interesting and important for its own sake, but also because it has provoked closer study of the relevant doctrines in the middle and late dialogues. I tried to pick some of the best examples of this closer study of texts and doctrines, whether or not they explicitly take up questions about development.

The order of the papers follows—in broad outline but not in detail—the probable lines of Plato's development. Plato neither systematically sets out the arguments that he thinks should convince a reader to believe in Platonic Forms nor gives a precise description of what is involved in such a belief. These unsystematic aspects of his presentation led some readers to accept two half-truths: 1) Plato does not argue for, but assumes, the existence of Forms, and 2) he has no real "theory" of Forms. These half-truths are true insofar as they emphasize the difference between Plato's presentation and the sort of presentation that a modern writer might find desirable. Aristotle apparently felt the need for a more systematic presentation than anything he could find in Plato; in his criticisms of the Theory of Forms he begins by stating his interpretation of the different arguments given and goes on to identify the features of Forms that seem to raise the most serious doubts about their existence.[7] I selected the following essays based on the assumption that Aristotle is right and that it is worth while to try to reconstruct a Theory of Forms. The volume begins with essays that discuss Plato's arguments for Forms and continues with the various features that need to be attributed to Forms if they are to carry out the various tasks that Plato assigns to them.

The *Meno* gives the clearest picture of the emergence of the Platonic distinction between knowledge and belief from Socrates's concerns with definition and inquiry. Plato argues that inquiry (or some sorts of inquiry) involves recollection and that the completion of a process of recollection counts as knowledge. Nicholas

White's paper gives an account of the argument that persuades Plato to connect knowledge with recollection.[8] The *Meno* itself does not mention Forms as objects of recollection, however in the *Phaedo* and *Phaedrus* mention Forms in this role. If, then, knowledge requires recollection and recollection must be of Forms knowledge must be of Forms. Questions about knowledge and Forms arise again in Part 2.

Aristotle claims that Plato believed in Forms because he believed sensible things are in flux and that knowledge requires objects that are not in flux. The next three papers in Part 1 (one by T.H. Irwin and two by White) deal with Plato's views about sensibles and their deficiencies as objects of knowledge. Comparing these papers with those in Part 4, which deal with some of Plato's later views on perception and on flux, will help readers determine how extreme a thesis about flux in the sensible world Plato actually maintains in different dialogues and what thesis is needed to support the contrast that Plato seeks to draw between sensibles and Forms.

A further role of Forms described in the *Phaedo* is their role in explanation. Plato claims that only Forms can be appropriately labeled "causes" or "explanations" (*aitia*) because other things provide inadequate explanations. Plato's appeal to Forms as causes was already criticized by Aristotle. (His criticism is discussed by Julia Annas in Volume 7.[9]) C.C.W. Taylor's essay gives a clear and sympathetic account of Plato's assumptions.

Part 2 is devoted to the treatment of Forms and related issues in Books V–VII of the *Republic*. Book V contains Plato's division between knowledge and belief, recalling the last part of the *Meno*, and his assertion that knowledge requires knowledge of Forms. This argument is often used to show that Plato denies the sensible world as a possible object of knowledge, claiming that we cannot have knowledge but can only have beliefs about such things as particular tables, chairs, trees, and people. Interpreting Book V in this way we can assume that the images of the Sun, Line, and Cave in Books VI–VII are understood in the same way. We can also assume that Plato, treats the sensible world as a realm of mere shadows or images of the Forms and believes that we can achieve genuine knowledge only by turning our attention away from the sensible world to the world of Forms.

The essays in Part 2 all raise some questions about this way of interpreting the metaphysical and epistemological doctrines of the central books of the *Republic*. J. Gosling's paper raises a basic question: what exactly are the things that Plato assumes to be matters of belief rather than knowledge? Gail Fine raises the same question, together with some further questions about the treatment of knowledge and belief. She argues that Plato's intent is not to assert the general claim that we can have beliefs only about sensible things. The next three papers—on the Line and the Cave—suggest ways of interpreting these images that do not imply the correlation of different cognitive states with different objects and so do not imply that if, for example, I have a belief about a particular sensible object, I cannot also have knowledge of that object. While these three papers are not intended to support Gosling's and Fine's view, and are certainly compatible with the rejection of it, they tend to remove some objections that might be derived from claims about the Line and the Cave.[10]

The type of interpretation suggested by Gosling and Fine was sharply criticized[11] and certainly did not become the standard view of these central Platonic doctrines. But readers who read through the essays in Part 2 and some of the related discussions will find themselves facing a series of important questions about the meaning and philosophical value of this section of the *Republic*.

Part 3 takes up the issues raised by the *Parmenides*. S. Marc Cohen and Sandra Peterson examine the "Third Man" argument, which Aristotle already notices as the basis of a possible objection to the Theory of Forms. Most modern interpreters supposed that the most obviously questionable premise in the Third Man argument is the one that affirms the so-called "self-predication" of the Forms—the claim that each Form is itself an instance of the property that it corresponds to, so that the Form of Equal is itself equal, and so on.[12] Cohen and Peterson suggest, for different reasons, that self-predication may not be the premise that needs to be questioned. Peterson argues that Plato is entitled to maintain a doctrine of self-predication.[13] Her conception of self-predication is one of those discussed by Alexander Nehamas in his survey of the different accounts given of the evidence which seems to commit Plato in the middle dialogues to self-predication.

If Plato accepts self-predication in the sense in which it is asserted in the relevant premise of the Third Man argument, it does not follow that he is vulnerable to the vicious infinite regress that *Parmenides* derives from this argument. He is vulnerable to the regress only if he is also committed to the other premises of the Third Man argument. Most interpreters have not scrutinized the Platonic credentials of these as carefully as they have scrutinized those of self-predication. Cohen's essay is an important discussion of the "one over many" premise. While this premise may appear innocuous and clearly Platonic Cohen's arguments suggest that this appearance may be misleading. If that is so then it is not obvious that Plato presents the objections in the *Parmenides* because he believes himself to be vulnerable to them. Whether or not we believe that Plato ought to have abandoned the Theory of Forms maintained in the middle dialogues the *Parmenides* does not give us any reason to believe that he actually does abandon it.

Some of the questions surrounding the *Parmenides* are connected with the apparent fact that Platonic Forms are treated both as properties and as instances of those properties. Aristotle describes this apparent fact by claiming that the Forms are treated as "universals," but also as "separable" (or "separate") and as "substances." According to Aristotle Plato is mistaken in assuming that he can consistently attribute all three features to the Forms; we can assume that this is the basic difficulty underlying the arguments in the *Parmenides*. This dispute between Plato and Aristotle is discussed in Fine's essay.

One late dialogue that was examined for signs of second thoughts about the Forms is the *Sophist*. Its references to the "greatest kinds" are sometimes interpreted as references to the Forms; others have argued that the greatest kinds are understood in ways that are incompatible with the view of Forms maintained in the middle dialogues.[14] The essays by Lesley Brown and John McDowell do not directly take up this question but do deal with some major issues in the *Sophist* that are also relevant to questions about Plato's development. Brown's discussion of uses of "to be" in the *Sophist* and McDowell's discussion of false belief should be compared with different possible views of the treatment of these topics in *Republic* V.[15]

Part 4 is devoted to the later dialogues; most of the essays are about the *Theaetetus* and most are about perception, though some cover other topics in the *Theaetetus* besides perception, and some cover other dialogues besides the *Theaetetus* on perception. The first part of the *Theaetetus*, which discusses the claim that perception is knowledge, seems to be connected with the claims about the senses that support Plato's arguments for Forms. Indeed, some interpreters have argued that the *Theaetetus* presents the view of the senses and the sensible world that is expressed in Plato's claims about the unreliability of the senses and the flux of the sensible world.[16] M.F. Burnyeat's essay presents an important alternative to this view of the *Theaetetus*; it examines the role of Heracleitean views of perception in developing the account of Protagoras that Plato seeks to refute. Further aspects of Plato's response to Protagoras are discussed by Sarah Waterlow Broadie. Her essay takes up some of the questions raised by G.B. Kerferd and Richard Bett in Volume 2; Burnyeat's paper in Volume 8 comes back to these questions. John M. Cooper's paper examines the conclusion of Plato's argument in the *Theaetetus*, discussing an important passage that is also examined in Michael Frede's essay on the senses.[17] This part concludes with Donald J. Zeyl's discussion of Plato's remarks on sensibles and flux in the *Timaeus*. I included this essay here because of its importance when compared with Frede's essay and the discussions of the *Theaetetus*; moreover, this is the right place for it chronologically, if the *Timaeus* is in fact one of Plato's later dialogues. It also, however, raises some of the questions that are raised by the arguments in the middle dialogues that deal with flux in sensibles. Readers who compare the essays in Part 1 with those in Part 4 may consider whether Plato's views on the senses develop in important ways, and if so, whether the development requires any repudiation or revision of his earlier views.

NOTES

1. See especially G. Vlastos, *Socrates* (Ithaca, 1991), chs. 2, 4.

2. Owen's papers are collected in M. Nussbaum, ed., *Logic, Science, and Dialectic* (London, 1986).

3. See Vlastos and Cherniss in R.E. Allen, ed., *Studies in Plato's Metaphysic* (London, 1965).

4. A survey of some discussions is W.J. Prior, *Unity and Development in Plato's Metaphysics* (London, 1985).

5. See, for instance, C.C. Meinwald, *Plato's Parmenides* (Oxford, 1991).

6. See Allen, ed., *Studies*; Owen, *Logic, Science and Dialectic*; and Vlastos, *Platonic Studies*, 2nd ed. (Princeton, 1981). See also Vlastos's forthcoming *Studies in Greek Philosophy* (2 vols., Princeton).

7. On Aristotle's criticisms see H.F. Cherniss, *Aristotle's Criticism of Plato and the Academy*, vol. 1 (Baltimore, 1944); G. Fine, *On Ideas* (Oxford, 1993).

8. On recollection see also G. Vlastos, "Anamnesis in the *Meno*," *Dialogue* 4 (1965), 143–67; D. Scott, "Platonic Anamnesis Revisited," *Classical Quarterly* 37 (1987), 346–66; G. Fine, "Inquiry in the *Meno*," in Kraut, ed., *Cambridge Companion to Plato* (Cambridge, 1992), ch. 6.

9. See also G. Vlastos, "Reasons and Causes in the *Phaedo*," in Vlastos, *Platonic Studies* ch. 4, from *Philosophical Review* 78

(1969), 291–325; G. Fine, "Forms as Causes: Plato and Aristotle," in A. Graeser A., ed., *Mathematics and Metaphysics* (Berne, 1987), 69–112.

10. See also Fine, "Knowledge and Belief in *Republic* V–VII," in S. Everson, ed., *Epistemology* (Cambridge, 1990), ch. 5.

11. For different views see G. Vlastos, "Degrees of Reality in Plato," in Vlastos, *Platonic Studies*; Annas, *Introduction to Plato's Republic*; N.P. White, *Plato on Knowledge and Reality* (Indianapolis, 1976); J. Hintikka, "Knowledge and Its Objects in Plato," in J. Moravcsik, ed., *Patterns in Plato's Thought* (Dordrecht, 1973), 1–30; F.C. White, "The 'Many' in *Republic* 475a–480a," *Canadian Journal of Philosophy* 7 (1977), 291–306, and "J. Gosling on *ta polla kala*," *Phronesis* 23 (1978), 127–32.

12. This emphasis on self-predication is clear in Owen's papers in *Logic, Science, and Dialectic*. It is somewhat corrected in Vlastos, "The Third Man Argument in the *Parmenides*, in Allen, ed., *Studies in Plato's Metaphysics*. For a recent discussion see J. Malcolm, *Plato on the Self-Prediction of the Forms* (Oxford, 1993).

13. Some of her ideas are developed, for quite different purposes, by Vlastos, "An Ambiguity in the *Sophist*," in *Platonic Studies*. They are used in a defense of self-predication by Fine, *On Ideas* (Oxford, 1993).

14. These opposed views are maintained by F.M. Cornford, *Plato's Theory of Knowledge* (London, 1935), who identifies the greatest kinds with Forms, and by M. Frede, *Prädikation und Existenzaussage* (Göttingen, 1967).

15. See also Brown, "The Verb 'To Be' in Greek Philosophy," in S. Everson, ed., *Language* (Cambridge, 1994), ch. 11.

16. See Cornford, *Plato's Theory of Knowledge*.

17. See also M.F. Burnyeat, "Plato on the Grammar of Perceiving," *Classical Quarterly* 26 (1976), 29–51.

INQUIRY

NICHOLAS P. WHITE

I

As some philosophers know, the paradox about inquiry at 80d–e of Plato's *Meno* is more than a tedious sophism. Plato is one such philosopher.[1] The puzzle is an obstacle to his project of discovering definitions, and is introduced as such (80d1–6). And it is met with an elaborate response: the theory of recollection, explicitly presented as an answer to the obstacle (esp. 81c–e). But then what of the famous conversation in which Socrates coaxes a geometrical theorem from a slave boy (82b*sqq.*) Is the theory not designed to explain the boy's ability to respond to the coaxing? It is, certainly, but that is not its only purpose.[2] The structure of the pasage is this: the theory is there to disarm the paradox, and the conversation is there to support the theory. To see this structure is to understand a notorious and otherwise troubling fact, that Plato is so very quick to take the slave's behavior—which he might have tried to explain in some other way—to be clear evidence for recollection. The reason why he so takes it is that the paradox has led him to think that only if recollection occurs is fruitful inquiry possible—and he is very anxious indeed to be assured that it *is* possible. He would not have been so enticed by explanations of the boy's behavior which did not also seem to him to dispose of the puzzle.

---

[1] A mistranslation of *"eristikon"* at 80e2 has helped to foster the idea that Plato does not take the paradox seriously. There is no reason to render the word here by "sophistical;" it means simply "contentious" or "obstructionist" (cf. *Lysis* 211b8, *Sophist* 225c9 with a2). Furthermore when Socrates is made to say at 81a1–3 that the paradox is "not well taken" (*ou kalōs legetai*), he does not mean that it is sophistical or foolish, but only that it does not establish what it claims to, namely that fruitful inquiry in all senses is impossible.

[2] See J. M. E. Moravcsik, "Learning and Recollection," G. Vlastos, ed., *Plato I: Metaphysics and Epistemology* (New York, 1970), pp. 53–69, esp. pp. 56, 63.

Here now is Plato's setting of the paradox:

Meno: But in what way will you inquire after (*zētēseis*) something such that you do not know what it is? What sort of thing, among those things which you do not know, will you set up beforehand as the object of your search? Or to put it otherwise, even if you happen to come right upon it, how will you know that it is that which you did not know?

Socrates: I understand, Meno, what you mean. Do you see how contentious the argument is which you are introducing, that it is not possible to inquire either after that which one knows or that which one does not know? He would not need to inquire after that which he knows, since he knows it and there is no need of inquiry for such a thing, nor after what he does not know, since he does not know what he is inquiring after.

His exposition is brisk, so we must try to see the nature of the difficulty which he faces.[3] As he presents the problem, we are engaged in an effort to "know" a thing, and the effort is pictured as, in a fairly literal sense, a search for the thing, i.e., as an attempt to *find* a thing and *recognize* it as what we were searching for.[4] But, we are told, if we do not already "know" the thing, we shall be unable to recognize it (80d7–8), whereas if we do already "know" it, then we have nothing further to do. Of course, an obvious reply is that we could be in a position of not yet having found the object, but of nevertheless being able to recognize it when we do. If you like, we might "know" it in one sense but

---

[3] I shall be unable here to treat the many rival accounts of the paradox and of Plato's theory of recollection—e.g., those of Moravcsik and of Vlastos, *"Anamnesis* in the *Meno,"* *Dialogue,* IV (1965), pp. 143–67. Also, the issues raised here are intimately connected with issues arising elsewhere in Plato's works, and to a large extent the present interpretation of the puzzle in the *Meno* cannot be argued for fully here, since much of its support lies in the way in which it links the *Meno* to other Platonic concerns. (I would not deny, moreover, that with varying degrees of exegetical latitude, any number of different puzzles can be read into 80d–e, taken in isolation.) I hope to fill this lacuna and others in this paper with a full-scale account of Plato's epistemology.

[4] It seems to me that no faithful interpretation can blink at this fact, which is ensured by 80d7–8. I do not think that we can rest content with interpretations, such as Moravcsik's (p. 57), which suppose that Plato intended a difference between Meno's formulation of the puzzle (d5–8) and Socrates's (e1–5), since this supposition leaves it quite unexplained why he never mentions the fact, and thenceforth acts as though he has only one difficulty to face. What Socrates does is simply to make clear that Meno's puzzle can be cast in the form of a dilemma.

not (yet) in another. Plato, however, does not take this way out, and we need to see why.

The essential point is that although Plato does think of the effort to "know" an object as a kind of search for it, that is not the only way in which he thinks of it. He is also thinking of it as an effort to say "what the object is," i.e., to produce a certain sort of definition or specification of it (esp. 79e5–6, 80d4). It is this sort of attempt that he has in mind when he says that if we can recognize the object, then we already "know" it. Accordingly, one line of interpretation is to say that Plato has inadvertantly conflated two projects: 1) the project of looking for something already specified, and 2) the project of discovering a specification of something. He supposes that we need to find a specified object, but then supposes that the need must have been fulfilled, provided merely that we possess a specification by which we may recognize what we are after. Nor is it impossible that Plato has made such a conflation. For both in early works like the *Meno* and later in the *Republic,* he tends not to mark a clear distinction between—so to put it—gaining a definition of an object (as he thinks of the matter), and getting the object itself somehow into one's "ken" or mental "view."[5] Moreover at 80d7–8, the crucial suggestion, that if you do not already "know" a thing you will not be able to recognize it, is presented utterly without argument or explanation.[6]

Such a conflation becomes more understandable when one realizes that specifications come in different varieties. Very roughly (cf. n. 10), we can say that some specifications are such that one can tell, simply by examining an object, whether or not it fits the specification. "The man sitting in the marketplace," e.g., might be taken to be such a specification. But other specifications, such as "my long-lost brother," are presumably not of this roughly demarcated sort. I can obviously initiate an effort "to

---

[5] See, e.g., R. M. Hare, "Plato and the Mathematicians," R. Bambrough, ed., *New Essays on Plato and Aristotle* (New York, 1965), pp. 21–38, and Vlastos, p. 165, and Moravcsik, pp. 68–69.

[6] Or is Plato to be acquitted of the conflation by the reply that Forms are of such a nature that somehow there is *no* distinction to be drawn betweeen acquiring a definition and "viewing" the corresponding Form? Even if this idea should appear in later works, it plainly does not figure in the *Meno,* and I shall ignore it here (cf. n. 3).

3

see my long-lost brother'' even if I do not yet know what he looks
like, and have no specification of the former type. What I hope,
of course, is that I can subsequently find a description of him by
which I *can* recognize him, and that can be shown to be co-referential with the specification, "my long-lost brother," with which I
began. Pretty clearly, however, Plato is leaving this second sort
of specification out of account, and if one does so, then it is perhaps not too difficult to fall into thinking that finding an object
is not much of a task once one has the specification (especially if
the object is thought of as being near at hand or readily "brought
to mind"), and thence into the conflation of search for object and
search for specification.

But is Plato subject to this degree of confusion? Perhaps
not, since he may have an argument up his sleeve for the crucial
move at 80d7–8. Though I shall not attempt to settle the question
here (cf. n. 3), the supposition that he does have such an argument
gives us more to deal with than a case of mere inadvertance on
his part. So let us turn to an interpretation based on that supposition. You are told that if you do not already "know" the
object of your search, you will not be able to recognize it. Why
not? Because, the argument goes, you must begin your search
with a specification of what you are trying to find, in order to
recognize it. But how do you know that the specification accurately describes the object in question? Only, the account continues, by examining the object to see that it does (cf. n. 8). But
to do this you must find the object. But for this you need the
specification. And so on. (Nor will it help to suppose that you
might begin without a complete specification, but with some information constituting part of one; for again the argument says
that you must examine the object to check on whether the information is correct.) So either you must already have examined
the object and can describe it, or you will never be able to do
either.

Although this argument raises obvious qualms, let us post-
pone them to consider why we might want to attribute at least a
dim awareness of it to Plato. First, it neatly explains, in an
obvious way, why recollection might have seemed to Plato such
an attractive response to the paradox. Second, it dovetails with
other facts about the early dialogues. As I have said, Plato be-

4

trays interest both in finding definitions and in "viewing" or "looking to" objects which he sometimes calls Forms.[7] But trouble threatens because of the way in which he connects these two projects. Sometimes he says that a purpose of finding a definition is to help us "look to" such an object (*Euthyphro* 6d–e). At other times (e.g., *Meno* 72c6–d1; cf. *Laches* 190c6), he appears to say that it is by "looking to" the object that we shall discover the correct definition.[8] Combining these two ideas obviously could lead to saying that we both need to look to the object before we have a reliable definition, and also need to have a reliable definition before we find the object. But this is just the trouble which the paradox, on this account, yields; so perhaps in *Meno* 80d–e Plato is attacking a problem arising out of his own work. Moreover the point can be strengthened by the reflection that the paradox can be seen as an extension of a similar difficulty already touched upon in the *Meno*. At 71b, Plato has distinguished between asking "what" (*ti*) a thing is and asking "what it is like" (*poion*), and has maintained that we cannot know what a thing is like until we know what it is—e.g., that we cannot know whether Meno is wealthy until we know who he is. But why not? Why could we not know on good authority (e.g., on Plato's) that Meno is wealthy without in any plausible sense knowing "who he is"? The answer is that Plato believes that to know that Meno is wealthy we have to find and examine him, so as to see that he is; for otherwise we are simply relying on hearsay, and thus on less

---

[7] "Look to" here renders "*apoblepein (pros)*," as in *Euthyohro* 6e4 and *Meno* 72c8; "view" represents "*theasthai*," not used in early works, but common in the *Republic* (e.g., 518c10, 526e6; cf. also 511a1, etc.). It has been observed to me by Prof. J. Hintikka that the issues which arise here are connected with matters which he discusses in, e.g., his "Knowledge by Acquaintance—Individuation by Acquaintance," D. F. Pears, ed., *Bertrand Russell: A Collection of Critical Essays* (New York, 1972), pp. 52–79.

[8] It is of both historical and philosophical interest that the idea of a need to examine a thing in order to check on the correctness of a putative specification or definition has its roots, as I believe, in the quasi-skeptical attitude apparently adopted by Socrates toward popular or received opinion, and toward any other information which is not gained somehow first-hand (see, e.g., *Crito* 47a–d; *Gorgias* 472b–c, 474a–b, 475e–476a; and, perhaps with more fully Platonic material, *Meno* 97b1–2; *Phaedo* 82e3–4, 83a–b). An analogous point applies to what will emerge *infra* concerning the *ti/poion* distinction.

than fully "direct" evidence.[9] But to find him, we need a specification enabling us to recognize him, and in that sense telling us who he is. But if this requirement is applied not only to *poion*-information but also to *ti*-information, then we have our paradox.

II

In the sort of inquiry concerning us, the inquirer is trying *inter alia* to bring an object into his "ken," in some sense, and to recognize it. The puzzle arises because he is said to need to examine the object to see whether his specification actually fits it. This need arises because the possibility is left open that his specification may be incorrect. So it is tempting to say right away that when one is seeking a thing in this manner, one's inquiry is, as it were, *defined* by the specification with which one begins, and that one is searching for *whatever* it is that fits that specification. One *could* not, then, be seeking something which does not fit it. This is, I think, the kernel of the solution of the puzzle. But this solution is not gained without a price, and we must see what that price is. I begin by developing this solution, and shall then explain what its cost is.

We must start with an account of what it is for a specification to be, as I shall say, an "initially usable specification" for the framing of an inquiry or search of our sort. We have seen that one's initial specification may not itself be one by which one can, in any reasonable sense, *recognize* the object when one encounters it. So our account must allow, e.g., for the case in which I begin an effort to see someone with the specification "my long-lost brother," unassociated initially with any description of his "visible" features, and then later discover that that specification picks out the same thing as some other specification which does describe

---

[9] This point can be taken to show that Plato views the context "knows that . . ." as referentially transparent—in the sense discussed by Quine, *Word and Object* (New York, 1960), pp. 141ff.—presumably because Plato is oblivious to the distinction between contexts which are referentially transparent and those which are not. For on this interpretation he is in effect imposing upon statements of the form "S knows that a is F" conditions similar to ones which some would place instead upon statements of the form "Concerning a, S knows that it is F."

"visible" features, and which I can use to recognize the thing when I see it. (But notice that the following account will not be limited to efforts to recognize things by sight, or even by sense; cf. n. 10.)

What we must say, I think, is roughly this. A singular term S is an initially usable singular specification for our sort of inquiry if and only if there is a singular term T which we can in some sense find, which denotes something which can be in some sense brought into one's "ken," and which satisfies the following conditions: T must be such that

a) we shall be able somehow to tell, upon examination (in the relevant sense) of a given object, whether or not T denotes it,

b) we shall be able to tell that T is co-referential with S.

In supposing, then, that "my long-lost brother" is an initially usable specification for an inquiry of this sort, we are supposing that somehow we may find a specification which is co-referential with it, and which we can determine to be met, or not to be met, by objects as they present themselves.[10] But there are also many inquiries which must be framed by means of expressions not of the form "*the* so-and-so," but of the form "*a* so-and so," i.e., by a general term. Thus, I can search for "a long-lost brother of mine," where I do not care which one(s), or how many, I find. By analogy to the foregoing, then, a general term S is an initially usable general specification just in case there is a general term T which we can find, that is true of something which one can bring into one's "ken," and which satisfies the following conditions:

---

[10] Pressed further, this account would presumably require something like a distinction between observational and non-observational terms (though I am unhappy with this distinction). Note, however, that I have left it *completely* open what counts as "observation" or "examination," and have insisted upon no limitation to *sensory* observation. The reason is that for our present exegetical purposes, we need to accommodate inquiries concerning such things as Platonic Forms. (This point prompts the remark that even a quite non-empiricist stance can require some distinction between "observable" and "non-observable" features, even though this distinction is generally thought of in connection with sensory observation.)

T must be such that

> c) we shall be able somehow to tell, by examining an object, whether or not T is true of it,
>
> d) we shall be able to tell that S is true of everything of which T is true.

I am well aware that numerous difficulties, requiring discussion all their own, are raised by these conditions, but I think that their basic thrust and motivation are plainly clear.[11]

These conditions are not meant to cover all inquiries. For clearly some inquiries are not naturally construed as efforts to bring objects into one's "ken." Thus, many would not think of an effort to, as we say, "discover a proof" of Goldbach's conjecture as literally an effort somehow to recognize an object which is the proof (cf. n. 10). I am willing to leave such recalcitrant inquiries aside (though remember that Plato allows more of them than others might). But notice that one could hope to claim that all inquiries *are,* or else in some sense, *are "equivalent to,"* inquiries which fall under the above conditions.[12] Someone might claim, e.g., that the effort to "discover a proof" of Goldbach's conjecture is, or is equivalent to, an effort to write down and recognize tokens of such a proof, where this effort is framed by

---

[11] Here are some of the problems. First, we need to know what it is to "examine" an object, and to "get it into one's ken." Next, the account employs modal notions requiring explanation. Third, it turns out on my account that "the present king of France" and "unicorn," e.g., are not initially usable specifications. Here, the appearance of problematicality is dispelled, I think, once one realizes that for a specification to fail of initial usability is not for it to be incoherent or meaningless. A fourth problem concerns objects which no longer exist, since my account presumably would not allow "the greatest philosopher of the fifth century" to be initially usable now, at least on a certain meaning for "can" in "can be brought into one's ken." But perhaps the most serious consequence of the account arises from the indeterminacy which will be discussed shortly. For on certain ways of treating that indeterminacy, it can be indeterminate whether or not a given term is an initially usable specification for a search or inquiry. While I think that *if* this is a problem, then it is an important and serious one, I am not inclined to think that it *is* a problem. But the question whether or not it is a problem *is* a problem, and too large a one to be dealt with here.

[12] This claim could be made for various reasons, and with various senses of "equivalent." This issue is plainly linked with questions surrounding verificationism, operationism, and related "isms."

the general term "token of a proof of Goldbach's conjecture." Of course this presentation is all very informal, but again the motivation and spirit are plain, and I shall not elaborate the idea further here.

Given our contentions (a)–(d), what shall we count as the successful completion of an inquiry? For brevity let me treat only inquiries which are framed by singular terms, since they present the most difficulty. Let us say roughly that the completion of an inquiry is the bringing into one's "ken" (the "finding," if you will) of an object denoted by some appropriate singular term T fulfilling conditions (a) and (b), recognizing it as such, and showing that T and one's original specification, S, are co-referential. The leading idea is that an inquiry is consummated by the finding of *whatever* object proves, whether directly or indirectly (in the cases, respectively, in which S and T are identical or distinct) to be denoted by one's initial specification. It is this idea which constituted our suggested way of avoiding Plato's puzzle.

III

But problems arise immediately. The first is best introduced by an example. Suppose that our current theory of the world admits a suitable notion of causation, and that we conceive an inquiry framed by a singular term S. Perhaps our current theory will itself provide our co-referential term T and allow us to recognize our quarry. But perhaps it will not. We may need what, by some reasonable standard for individuating theories, is a new theory, and indeed we may have good reason at the start to think that we will. Since we must deal with more than one theory, however, we shall then have to face the problems of inter-theoretic translation that Quine has made notorious recently.[13] In order to determine that we have successfully completed our inquiry, we shall have to pass on the co-referentiality of terms in different theories (or, in the case of inquiries framed by general terms, on the overlap of one extension by another). But if Quine is correct that such questions are in a sense indeterminate, and can be an-

---

[13] See, e.g., *Word and Object*, Ch. II.

swered only relative to a manual—arbitrarily chosen, to some extent—for translating one theory into another, then there will often be an indeterminacy in whether or not a given inquiry has been, or will be, successfully completed.

I would not myself want to claim that practical difficulty will generally arise on this account, though it might occasionally. Nor am I inclined, myself, to see here any crippling theoretical difficulty. For it is not clear to me just what the disadvantage is of being unable to say with utter finality that a certain discovery completes just *that* particular inquiry, and it is not clear that we cannot live with the idea that, in a certain sense, we make up our inquiries as we go along.[14]

But nevertheless the indeterminacy produces a sense of unease. For example, suppose that your inquiry is taken as framed by the phrase "my spouse," and that in the course of your search some radical change occurs in your general theory of the world. (You may imagine that the change is quite irrelevant to the search, or else that your spouse has been hidden by a physicist through the means of some ingenious new technology whose secret you must unravel.) Do we really want to say that whether you have found your spouse is indeterminate? Even if there is no practical difficulty, many will feel that even an indeterminacy in principle is undesirable. One might try to escape by denying our supposition that one's initial specification may be different from the one which one finally uses for recognition, but this course seems clearly wrong (and anyway troubles over inter-theoretic translation could still arise). The only course, then, unless one can rebut the relevant claim of indeterminacy, is to pin the blame on the supposition that inquiries are defined by specifications which frame them, and that whatever fulfills the specification is what the inquiry is after.

---

[14] Others would see worse consequences here, depending on their views about the relationship between old theories and theories which supersede them. E.g., see Feyerabend, "Explanation, Reduction, and Empiricism," H. Feigl and G. Maxwell, eds., *Minnesota Studies in the Philosophy of Science,* vol. III (Minneapolis, 1962), pp. 28–97. Notice, too, that a full treatment of these matters would have to deal more meticulously with the various problems and indeterminacies which can afflict inter-theoretic translation.

To deny this supposition is to say that when we search for something we search for, so to speak, *a particular thing,* and not for *whatever* satisfies a certain description. On this view, what defines an inquiry is its connection with a certain *object,* regardless of any specification, so that difficulties of translating specifications can be ignored. The idea can be developed further, too, by means of distinctions like Donnellan's between "referential" and "attributive" uses of definite descriptions.[15] For him, an attributive use of "the *F*" is one in which it refers, if at all, to whatever is uniquely *F,* while a referential use of it is one in which it may refer to something else. In this terminology, the notion of inquiry which we are considering says that inquiries are framed by referential uses of descriptions or specifications, and will thus be concerned "with the thing itself and not just the thing under a certain description."

But if we adopt this view of our sort of inquiry, then we seem certain to be caught in our paradox again. For this view allows the possibility that an inquirer may not "know what he is looking for," in the sense that he cannot be sure that his way of framing his inquiry correctly describes what he is allegedly after. But this fact raises the necessity for him (and, equally damaging, for anyone else) to somehow find the object of his search, to examine it, and to see whether or not the specification fits it. But if we need a specification to find the object, then we have our paradox.

Can we avoid trouble by denying that our inquiries must begin with a specification of what they are after? No, for then there would be nothing to distinguish between merely coming across something and finding something *for which one had been searching,* and this consequence could hardly be welcome to one who bridles at the problem of indeterminacy latent in the other view of inquiry. What gives sense to the idea that one has found what one was looking for is, at best, that there was previously a specification governing one's search. This is the reason why,

---

[15] See his "Reference and Definite Descriptions," *Philosophical Review,* LXXV, 3 (July, 1966), pp. 281–304, and "Putting Humpty Dumpty Together Again," *ibid.,* LXXVII (April, 1968), pp. 203–15, esp. the former, p. 303.

when a person enters a lost-and-found, the manager of the place is well-advised to ask what he is after, rather than simply letting him poke about and claim what he pleases. This is *not* to say that we must always insist that an inquirer be immediately ready to produce a specification. In many situations, where there is no need to be on guard, we may dispense with demanding one,[16] though the more we want to ferret out bogus findings, the more strict we shall be (cf. sec. V). Quite aside, then, from any questions about how we are to *tell* that there is a specification or what it is, the point is simply that somehow there must *be* one if there is to be a genuine inquiry of our sort.[17]

So paradox arises if we try to frame an inquiry with a description which is referentially construed in Donnellan's sense. What, then, about framing inquiries with proper names? Clearly there is no problem if names are construed as "disguised descriptions," in the manner of Russell and others,[18] so long as those descriptions are not referential in Donnellan's sense. But "logically proper names," as Russell thought of them,[19] cannot themselves frame an inquiry. For by themselves they provide no way of recognizing what they name, except on one condition, which is that one be in the presence of the object and somehow be told, as it were, "*That* is what the name stands for." But if one is in

---

[16] Cf. P. F. Strawson, *Individuals* (London, 1959), p. 85, n. 1, and p. 11.

[17] There are obviously further complications, since a person may begin an inquiry with more than one specification, which may perhaps be satisfied by different things, or of which only one may be satisfied at all; or he may begin with a specification, some parts of which are fulfilled by one thing and other parts by another. There are various ways of handling these situations, e.g., by saying that the person does not really have an initially usable specification (cf. n. 11), or by saying that he has more than one and thus is embarked on several different inquiries at once, or by seeing what specification he insists on keeping when his predicament is pointed out to him (this last expedient is similar to one pointed out in another connection by Brian Loar, which he says is similar to one suggested by Christopher Peacocke).

[18] See Russell, "On Denoting," *Mind*, 14 (1905), pp. 479–93, and Frege, "On Sense and Reference," P. Geach and M. Black, eds., *Translations from the Philosophical Writings of Gottlob Frege*, 2nd ed. (Oxford, 1960), pp. 56–78.

[19] E.g., in "Knowledge by Acquaintance and Knowledge by Description," *Proc. of the Arist. Soc.*, XI (1910–1911), pp. 108–28.

this circumstance, then search is pointless.[20] (Thus we have a new way of engendering paradox, by picturing inquiry as beginning with a term whose denotation can supposedly be recognized only by having it somehow pointed out to one—which shows that such terms cannot be used to frame fruitful inquiries.) And of course if there should be anything which can be specified *only* by a proper name, then one could never inquire after it in our sense.[21]

I emphasize, however, that I am not making, here, any general claim about *reference* or *denotation*.[22] Thus, I am not concerned now with the dispute between Russell and Donnellan, e.g., over whether a singular description may refer to something other than whatever may satisfy its encapsulated predicate, nor with the question whether an ordinary proper name like "Socrates" must be somehow "backed up" by a singular description.[23] I am simply concerned with what we must have on hand to launch an inquiry or search. I believe, however, that some advocates of construing descriptions roughly as Russell does, or of "backing up" proper names with descriptions, have been motivated in part by the consideration that it would be *desirable* to be able, in appropriate cases, to search successfully for the denotations of such expressions.[24]

The moral to be drawn, then, is that for inquiries of our sort we must choose between paradox on the one hand and indeter-

---

[20] This fact is reflected in Russell's view, *ibid.*, that identity-statements linking two logically proper names are "tautologies," along with the idea that "that" is a logically proper name.

[21] Whether Russell or Plato thought that there are such things is too large a question to be pursued here (cf. n. 3).

[22] Nor have I said anything directly about how to construe the "logical form" of such sentences as "Terpsion is searching for Eucleides" or "Diogenes is searching for an honest man," or about whether the context produced by "is searching for" is transparent or opaque (cf. n. 9). I have also left aside issues arising out of the views on reference of Donnellan, "Proper Names and Identifying Descriptions," *Synthese*, 21 (1970), pp. 335–58, and of S. Kripke, "Naming and Necessity," D. Davidson and G. Harman, eds., *Semantics and Natural Language* (Dordrecht, 1972), pp. 253–355. I do not believe that those views can be adapted to yield a satisfactory account of the framing of inquiry.

[23] See Donnellan and Kripke, *op. cit.*, as against Russell, "On Denoting," and Frege, *op. cit.*

[24] For possible signs of this motivation, see e.g., Strawson, pp. 3–19 and possibly Frege, p. 58, n. 1.

minacy on the other. I see no middle ground. Given these alternatives, the sensible choice seems to me to be the indeterminacy.
At least we can then console ourselves with the reflection that the
insistence on beginning an inquiry with a specification preserves
something of the notion of finding what one was looking for, and
I doubt that we can attain more.

IV

Although I have talked thus far quite generally about efforts
to bring objects into one's "ken" and recognize them, Plato is
concerned particularly with a special sort of inquiry, which has
to do with objects which he tended to think of as "Forms." This
concern has been inherited by modern philosophers, in the form
of a concern with "analysis" and the like. One sometimes hears
it suggested that certain sorts of analysis or definition are immune
to the paradox of the *Meno*, so long as they are cast in the formal
mode and are of the form "Expression E means the same as expression F" instead of the form "X is the same thing as Y." At
the same time, however, there is another paradox, the paradox of
analysis, which strikes one as similar to the paradox of the *Meno*,[25]
but which afflicts analyses which are squarely in the formal mode.
A brief comment on this state of affairs will bring issues into
clearer focus.

What reason is there for thinking that Plato's paradox is
avoided by the move to the formal mode? Simply that whereas
Plato's effort to discover what virtue is, say, can be relatively
easily construed as an attempt to find and recognize an object,
virtue, we have seen that other inquiries are not naturally so regarded (sec. II), and in the view of many modern philosophers the
effort to discover "what the *word* 'virtue' *means*" is one such.
But as long as we do not view inquiry as a search for an object,
then the paradox of the *Meno*, in its fully pristine form, cannot
arise.[26]

---

[25] See Moravcsik, pp. 63–64, and G. Nakhnikian, "Elenctic Definitions," Vlastos, ed., *Socrates: A Collection of Critical Essays* (New York,
1971), p. 129.
[26] Notice that further complications arise if we capitalize on an earlier
suggestion (sec. II), and decide somehow to construe the effort to say what

What, then, of the paradox of analysis? Is it the same problem as our paradox of inquiry? Two factors militate against a straightforward answer: the fact that there are many versions of the paradox of analysis, and the fact that standards of identity and distinctness for paradoxes are imprecise and probably not worth sharpening. Still, we can make a few observations.

One version of the paradox of analysis argues that a statement of the analysis can mean no more than something of the platitudinous form "A is A," and goes on to claim that analyses must therefore be trivial, and perhaps be known as soon as the corresponding platitudes are. Another version is directed against a notion of analysis which views its aim as the "grasping" or "apprehension" (or otherwise "bringing into one's ken" and recognizing) of an object which is the meaning of a certain expression, the *analysandum*. Such a version might say that the mere understanding of a request for analysis, or the claim that a particular analysis is needed, requires the very apprehension of that object which the analysis was supposed to provide. These versions involve certain notions, of meaning and understanding, which are absent from our puzzle as it stands, and that in itself is an important point of difference.

Another point of difference might appear at first sight to be the following. The crucial move in our puzzle is to raise an obstacle to our *recognition* of the thing at which, as it were, our inquiry was directed, and it tries to show that if we can *tell* that we are at the end of our search, then the search was unnecessary to begin with. Most versions of the paradox of analysis, on the other hand, have a slightly different structure. For although they usually argue, as does our puzzle that a certain effort is unnecessary if it is possible, their way of so arguing has not typically invoked a problem about how to *tell* when we have successfully concluded our analyzing, but rather a problem about what the conditions must be for the analyzing to get started, involving the understanding of the task, or of the meaning of what one must start with, or the like. Still, there can be exceptions, since one

---

a certain word means as the effort to bring into one's "ken" and recognize some object which is a token of an expression giving the meaning of that word.

may formulate the paradox of analysis by asking how one can tell that a putative analysis is correct, and go on to argue in one way or another that if one can tell this, then one had no need of the analysis in the first place.

V

Plato believes that his theory of recollection answers his puzzle. Let me now argue that he is wrong. I have two reasons for so doing. First, of the fair number of philosophers with whom I have discussed this issue, sober men all, about half have confessed to some amount of sympathy with Plato's belief. So the point is less controversial than one might think. But, second, Plato's view is of itself an ingenious one, deserving attention, particularly because it helps us to see some important and little noticed facts about both recollection and inquiry.

Plato seems to hold that what ordinarily appears to be successful inquiry is actually successful effort at recollection, i.e., inquiry concerning what we already know.[27] In fact, he goes a little farther, since he apparently believes not merely that all *successful inquiry* is recollection, but also that all *learning* must be so. But it is only the former to which his paradox is relevant. The whole difficulty there has to do with *recognizing* what one comes across to be *what one was after*. Nothing in 80d-e, under any possible interpretation, prevents us from saying that we can

---

[27] That it is what we already know is apparently disputed by Vlastos, p. 153, n. 14 (though cp. p. 164), but I do not agree with him in taking so lightly the wording of 86d6 (and of d9, 12, which he does not there mention), or in thinking that 86b1 "can only mean" something less than that we already know. His invocation of "*memathekuia(s)*" in 81d1 and 86a8 does not seem to help him, since it does not matter to the point in question whether the soul once learned things, so long as it learned them before its present incarnation. In saying earlier (e.g., at 84a) that the slave boy does not "know," Socrates is obviously speaking in accordance with ordinary usage, since he has not yet fully established his right to say that the boy is recollecting. Later on, when Socrates says that the boy only *believes* but does not yet *know* (98a), he is marking a new contrast, with a new use of "know," between the state in which the boy would be able to keep the geometrical theorem and its proof ready at hand, and the state in which he is liable to lose his grip on it (cf. 97e5–98a2); but there is no reason to take him to be going back on 86d. If we do so, then we cut the explicitly forged link between recollection and the paradox.

learn, or acquire new knowledge.[28] So perhaps Plato has fashioned an answer which is a bit too large for his problem.[29]

But does his answer really meet his problem at all? I have said that I do not think so, but let me make it quite clear what I am maintaining. I am not, I emphasize, quarrelling with the notion of recollection, or even, here, with the idea that we recollect Platonic Forms. For all that it concerns my present point, perhaps we do. But right now I am merely saying that the claim that we recollect, as Plato uses it, cannot, by itself, solve his paradox.

The first step is this: even given Plato's attempted solution, we are confronted with a new puzzle roughly analogous to his, which shows recollection to be no less paradoxical than *de novo* inquiry. Briefly, the problem is as follows:

> You will not of course attempt to recollect what you have already recollected, since you have no need to. But how will you attempt to recollect a thing of which you have merely unrecollected knowledge? What sort of thing, among those things of which you have only unrecollected knowledge, will you set up as the object of your search? Or to put it otherwise, even if you happen to come right upon it, how will you know that it is that of which you had merely unrecollected knowledge?

Not, of course, that this is a serious problem for us, since it rests on analogues of the moves which we have seen to be mistaken. Remember that we had two accounts of Plato's puzzle (sec. I). By analogy to the first, the mistake in this new puzzle would be a conflation of an attempt to recollect a specified object and an

---

[28] Cf. Moravcsik, p. 154. It is not certain, however, that Plato has gone so far as to deny the possibility of learning, particularly since 81d4–5 and 84c4–5 are phrased guardedly, and 85d12–13 and 86a1 *might,* in spite of 86b1–2, be an admission that knowledge can be acquired.

[29] Following most earlier commentators, both Vlastos and Moravcsik believe that for Plato, recollection has to do exclusively with *a priori* knowledge. Now this view may well be correct, but it is noteworthy that Plato does not say so in the *Meno.* Why not? Because he is primarily using recollection to solve the paradox, and can thus say merely that we recollect *whatever* we might be said to be able to come to know (through inquiry, *if* n. 28 is right). If he thinks that we can know only what we can know *a priori,* as he certainly believed later, then of course he must think that we can recollect only what we know *a priori.* But he need not pause here to say so (it would have involved a considerable digression), and the present interpretation allows us to see why he did not.

attempt to recollect a specification. By analogy to the second, the mistake would be the refusal to allow an attempt to recollect to be defined by the specification which frames it.[30]

The point to grasp is that there is neither more nor less reason to make either of these two mistakes in the case of recollection than there was in the case of *de novo* inquiry. In particular, there is no reason to allow an attempt at recollecting to be defined by a specification while withholding the same privilege from inquiry. But if recollection and inquiry are treated analogously, then either recollection is subject to the new paradox and so cannot be used to avoid the old one, or else there is no difficulty over inquiry which recollection can be invoked to solve. Recollection, therefore, helps to solve no pertinent puzzle. Notice the structure of this argument. It is *not* that we can defend inquiry in such a way that we do not *need* to identify it with recollection. (Thus, it is not analogous in structure to a certain one of Locke's arguments against innate ideas, that they are not necessary to explain the data; see the *Essay Concerning Human Understanding*, I, i, 1 and 3.) Rather, it is that granted the parallelism between recollection and inquiry, *if* recollection is immune to the new paradox, then by parity of reasoning, inquiry is immune to the old paradox, and therefore *there is no* paradox of inquiry for recollection to be called upon to solve.

But *should* we be granted the analogy between recollection and inquiry? According to Plato's defender, we should not. For he says that unlike inquiry, recollection does not require a specification at the start. His reason—and he might, as we shall see, claim that it is supported by the facts of experience—is that in the case of recollection both the object recollected *and* the specification can be recalled simultaneously, as when you cannot remember what you were looking for, but suddenly and simulta-

---

[30] It may be objected that on this interpretation, Plato fails to tailor the conversation with the slave boy to the paradox, since the conversation, unlike the paradox as here pictured, seems to have to do with "propositional" knowledge rather than knowledge "of" an object. But we have also seen that Plato slurs over this distinction elsewhere (n. 5). Moreover in 84a4–6 and 84c5 he writes in such a way as to suggest explicitly that he thinks that there is indeed an object of the boy's inquiry, namely "*the side of the eight-foot square.*"

ncously both come upon what you were seeking and remember that it was what you were seeking. Surely there is no specification here, beyond the plainly quite vacuous "the thing for which I was looking." But since you cannot correspondingly go hunting *de novo* for "the thing for which I *am* looking," therefore we must, the defender concludes, admit an irreducible difference between recollection and *de novo* inquiry, so that the former may be possible even where the latter is not.

This is wrong. There is no justification for such a double standard. We have already seen why inquiry must start with a more or less fixed specification, and the same reasons apply to recollection and serve the same ends: to allow a distinction between purposed and merely adventitious recollection, and between genuine and bogus claims of purposed recollection. (Note that the case of the dishonest visitor to the lost-and-found involves a certain sort of claim of recollection: "Those are my diamonds—I remember them perfectly!") But the point here is not even that specifications are always required. It is the weaker point that they are required for recollection *neither more nor less than* for inquiry, and that if one does not want a way of distinguishing between genuine and bogus recollection, it would seem overly demanding to insist upon an analogous distinction for *de novo* inquiry.

But the defender's point is perhaps not that we *ought* not to want a single standard for both recollection and inquiry, but rather that applying such a stringent standard to recollection would make it, as we know it, impossible. For specificationless recollection often *seems* to occur. Thus, suppose that you are in the market place, knowing that you were to meet one of your acquaintances, but not remembering who it was. Thus, it seems, no specification. But suddenly a familiar figure approaches; your mind "clicks;" and you say to yourself, "Socrates!" If we insist on an initial specification, are we not in danger of denying that this familiar sort of case is in fact a case of reliable recall?

One point in reply is that this sort of case is not one which Plato could envision as providing an answer to his puzzle. For this case presupposes that a project of inquiry has *previously* been framed, by means of some such specification as "the snub-nosed philosopher." This fact was recovered by recollection.

19

But in Plato's sort of case, there is no earlier specification to be retrieved.[31]

Much more important, however, is that in fact we do *not* in this case start out without a specification. For there are *two* attempts to recollect going on here. In one, which began some time before, the aim is, speaking loosely, Socrates. In the other it is, loosely again, a correct answer to the question "For whom was I looking?". Certainly the latter is framed by a specification. Moreover it is what I have called an initially usable specification, which can be determined to be satisfied. For we know from past experience that our sudden feelings or "clicks" of recollection are usually accurate, especially when accompanied by a memory of the circumstances in which the inquiry was earlier formulated. Moreover our feelings can be confirmed, in those cases in which we have earlier confided our project to another. It is largely thus that we have any faith in this sort of feeling, since we would have lacked faith had people generally said, "*That*'s not what you said you were looking for!" in those cases when the "click" of recollection occurred. At any rate, once this recollection has been performed, we have recalled the specification framing the other effort, the search for Socrates, that we can proceed to carry out forthwith. And of course it may take no time at all to carry out if he is present (as he will be in the case in which the sight of him helps to cause the recollection of the specification framing the search for him). So no specificationless recollection is required here.

I see one further potential line of defense of Plato's position. It is to say that since recollection is a "private," "mental" sort of thing, there is *no point* in requiring a specification in order to distinguish between genuine and bogus efforts at recall. For a person may *say* that he has called up an image of his kindergarten teacher, though he has actually brought to mind an image of, say, John Dewey; and no amount of specifying in advance what he was going to recollect will ever help us to detect the fraud. This fact, says the defender, jibes with the fact that we often, quite without

---

[31] This is because *ex hypothesi* the inquiry was not yet launched at any earlier time. But if it had been, then we can pick the time at which it was, and reinstate the paradox at that point.

anyone else's corroboration, can be utterly certain that we have correctly remembered a certain face.

But the defense fails. Quite aside from broader issues over the notion of the "mental" and the "private," there are two replies. The more limited one is that inquiry too may involve the calling up of something "private." Take, for example, a person's attempt to call up a mental image—his first ever—of an octagon, where he has never seen an octagon before, and must extrapolate from what he has seen of hexagons, squares, and the like. There is neither more nor less difficulty in checking up on him here than in the case involving the recollection of the kindergarten teacher, and ordinary standards accord equal right to subjective feelings of certainty in both. So we have here no defense of recollection *per se* as against inquiry *per se*.

Still, the defense makes us realize that there are two types each of recollection and inquiry. In one sense, I can "recollect Socrates" by calling up a "mental picture" of him and recognizing it as a mental picture of him; in another sense, I can recollect him by seeing him on the street and recognizing him as Socrates. Likewise, I can try to think what, on the basis of my information, Socrates will look like; or I can go trying to find the man himself.[32]

But even if we say that recollection can involve calling up something "private," we have a second reply to the defense, which is that in the cases which plainly interest Plato, and which normally interest us, the *object* which we are to recollect is *not* "private." In the case involving the kindergarten teacher, the recollection must, if successful, be *accurate*. (Saying what the accuracy consists in, of course, is a general problem about the mentalistic notions which we are employing, and we may leave it aside.) And of course in theory there are checks upon its accuracy, since in theory we could find the teacher, or photographs, or whatnot. But the possibility of checking obviously depends upon the existence of a specification, since it alone can tell *us* what to find to check against what the putative recollector tells us about

---

[32] Though I cannot develop the point here, Plato does not always make clear which sort of inquiry or recollection he has in mind; see, e.g., *Phaedrus* 254b5–7.

the image which he has called up. Thus, the specification is still crucial to distinguishing successful attempts to recollect, and both of these from the random flow of memory-images. Of course, the same point applies to inquiries of the analogous sort, since they too aim at accuracy. Once again, recollection and inquiry are on a par. Moreover even if one admits cases in which the object to be recalled *is* a "private" object (e.g., the mood I was in last Sunday), there are analogous cases of inquiry having to do with equally "private" objects (e.g., in the case of my attempt to put myself into, and recognize, the most befuddled state I have ever been in).

I therefore see no grounds for treating recollection and inquiry differently from each other, and thus no grounds for thinking that recollection can provide a solution of Plato's puzzle.

The University of Michigan.

THE
PHILOSOPHICAL
QUARTERLY

Vol. 27   No. 106   JANUARY 1977

PLATO'S HERACLEITEANISM

By T. H. Irwin

In his account of the origin of the Theory of Forms (*Metaphysics* 987a 32-b 7, 1078b 9-1079a 4, 1086a 31-b 11), Aristotle comments that Plato separated the Forms as objects of knowledge because sensible things are always in constant change, Heracleitean flux, and so unknowable. Some readers have believed Aristotle. Others have insisted that Plato's arguments for Forms display no concern with constant change or flux in the physical world, as commonly understood, and have inferred that Aristotle must be wrong. I want to show that Aristotle is right, but only if we reject the most common interpretation of his remarks on flux.[1]

I. Aristotle's Evidence and Plato's Dialogues

When we seek support for Aristotle in the dialogues, five main points in his account should be noticed.

(1) This is the original reason for the separation of Forms, apart from later doctrinal accretions (1078b 9-10).[2]

(2) Socrates' search for definitions in his ethical inquiries prompted (ἐκίνησε, 1086b 3) the doctrine of separation.

(3) Plato accepted Heracleitean arguments claiming that all sensibles are in constant flux.

---

[1]Earlier versions of this paper were read at the meetings of the American Philosophical Association, Eastern Division, in December 1973, and at Cornell University in November 1974. I am grateful to Robert Bolton for his dissenting comments, written and oral, on the first version, and for showing me his paper, "Plato's distinction between being and becoming". I have also benefited from the comments of Norman Kretzmann, and from detailed discussion by Gail Fine.

[2]A capital letter in 'Form', and in the names of individual Forms, indicates the Platonic separated Form, as opposed to the non-separated Socratic object of definition.

(4) He inferred that because of this flux there could be no knowledge of sensibles.

(5) Since he supposed none the less there was knowledge about something, it had to be about things separate from sensibles.

How well are these points confirmed by arguments and assumptions in the dialogues? Some have thought there is ample evidence that Plato believes the sensible world is constantly changing and therefore unknowable, just as Aristotle appears to say.[3] But this alleged evidence is faulty.

1. The last part of the *Cratylus* has been taken to argue from flux in sensibles to the existence of Forms (439c-440d). But it does not. (a) Plato is not concerned with *separated* Forms, but with the "stable natures" mentioned earlier in the dialogue, which Socrates too had recognized (386d 8-e 4, 389a-b).[4] (b) Plato does not *argue* for, but assumes, the existence of forms, and argues only about their characteristics (439c 7-d 1). (c) He does not say that sensibles are in flux, but only that *even if* they are, the forms are not (439d 3-6). Separated Forms are never mentioned or implied. Plato argues only that 'white' must always refer to the same colour; it follows, not that the referent exists independently of transitory white things, but that it always refers to their whiteness, not to some other quality of them. One crucial passage is 439d 3-4: "Let us then consider that very thing, not whether some face is beautiful or any of such things, and all these appear to be in flux." It is most natural to take "and all these . . ." as part of the "whether" clause. Others (see Gulley, p. 72) take it as a parenthetical categorical statement, "for all such things appear to be in flux" (Jowett, ed. 3). But the argument needs only a hypothetical concession to the Heracleiteans; *even if* all particulars are in flux, words must refer to the same things on different occasions, or we could not even describe change in the world. (d) Plato does not argue that forms must be separate from particulars; he argues that if particulars change their properties, the properties themselves cannot change their properties. The argument does not support Aristotle.

2. The *Theaetetus* discusses and rejects the extreme Heracleitean doctrine of flux. Plato never accepts its view of sensible objects. He never argues for separated Forms. *Tht.* 182c-d argues that if we say some sensible thing is something which changes, then the thing itself cannot be always changing in every respect. The different accounts of Owen, [1] p. 323, and McDowell

---

[3]See, among many, Cherniss [1], p. 211, who quotes *Tim.* 51b-52a, *Rep.* 477e-480a, *Cra.* 439d-440b, *Phil.* 58a-59d. See also p. 218n, quoting *Symp.* 207d-e, *Phil.* 59a-b, *Tim.* 52a-c. Aristotle's account, so interpreted, is also accepted by Ross, pp. 19 ff., 155-7, relying on *Symp.* 207d-e, *Phd.* 78c-79a, *Tht.* 155d-157c, *Tim.* 45b-d, 67c-68b; by Gulley, relying on *Cra.* 439c ff., *Phd.* 78c ff., 83b; and by Brentlinger, pp. 132-7, relying on *Cra.* 439c ff.

[4]Contrast the references to non-identity of Forms and sensibles in *Phd.* 74a 11, b 6-7, c 4-5, 7-8, *Rep.* 476c 9-d 3, *Symp.* 211a 8-b 5, *Parm.* 130b 1-5, *Tim.* 51b 7-c 5. Aristotle says the sensibles are παρὰ ταῦτα (the Forms, *Met.* 987b 8), and that Forms are ἕτερα, 987b 5; cf. παρὰ ταῦτα πάντα (the sensibles) ἕτερόν τι, *Phd.* 74a 11. He says the Forms are χωριστά, 1078b 30; cf. χωρίς *Parm.* 130b 2.

both require stability in sensibles, with no reference to Forms. Cherniss, [2] p. 9, finds an appeal to separated Forms. (I do not believe, as both Owen and Cherniss seem to, that *Cra.* 439c ff. and this *Tht.* argument aim at the same conclusion.) But even Cherniss's view of the argument would not by itself prove that Plato accepts extreme Heracleiteanism about the sensible world. Plato says he discusses that doctrine because it follows from the truth of "Knowledge is perception", and (whether or not it really follows) this reason explains the presence of the doctrine in the *Tht.* The claim that it is Plato's own view depends on the alleged evidence of the *Cra.*, *Phil.*, and *Tim.*

3. The *Philebus* claims that objects in the world which are subject to becoming exclude the best kind of knowledge (59a 7-b 8). But the sensible world suffers none of the Heracleitean flux described in the *Theaetetus*; and Socrates' ethical interests are not mentioned to justify the separation of Forms.[5]

4. The *Timaeus* claims that knowledge is of what is exempt from becoming (27d 5-28a 4); since sensibles are not exempt from becoming, there can be no knowledge of them (52a 4-7), and any knowledge must be of separated Forms (52d 3-7). But there is no extreme Heracleiteanism. Particular sensible objects need not suffer change in every respect all the time; only sensible fire and certain other constituents suffer change in *some* respect all the time. *Tim.* 49a-c does not show that "phenomena cannot be distinctively denominated, because no part of the phenomenal flux is distinguishable from any other" (Cherniss [3], p. 358). 49a 6-b 5 mentions sensible samples of the four elements; the impurity of these samples makes us unsure what to call them. Nothing implies the *Tht.*'s doctrine that objects are always changing from (e.g.) black to white or large to small; 49c 7-d 3 again mentions only problems about samples of the elements. Plato is silent about Socrates' ethical interests.[6]

Aristotle's five points are not to be found in any of these passages. The first two do not allude to separated Forms. The last two do not allude to Socrates' ethical interests; and so none supports Aristotle. These passages do not reflect the original arguments prompted by Socrates for the separation of Forms. If Aristotle relies on these passages, his claims are unjustified.

References to flux in arguments for separated Forms are hard to find. The separation-arguments in the *Phaedo* rest on Socrates' ethical interests

[5]*Phil.* 59b 1 mentions sensible things, "of which none either ever was, nor will be, nor is at the present in the same condition". Cherniss, [3] p. 350, quotes the passage, and (p. 356) takes it to show that "all γιγνόμενα are in *perpetual change in every respect*" (italics original). The passage implies no more than that they always change in some respect; it does not imply the Heracleiteanism of the *Tht.*

[6]The *Phil.* and *Tim.* claim that what changes cannot be an object of knowledge. I have not discussed why Plato believes this, since these dialogues are not good evidence for the arguments prompted by Socrates' interests. We should not simply assume that the *Phil.* and *Tim.* arguments must have been the original arguments for separation; we can decide only by studying the arguments apparently prompted by Socratic ethical interests.

(65d 4-e 5, 74a-c, 75c 10-d 3); similar arguments are used in *Republic* V (479a-d) to show that sensible things cannot be the primary objects of knowledge. The arguments rest on the compresence of opposite properties (equality and inequality, justice and injustice) in sensibles, a frequent concern of Plato's (cf. *Hippias Major* 289c 1-5, 293b 10-c 5); they do not depend on assumptions about constant change. Aristotle seems to misrepresent the origins of the Theory of Forms.

But it is not so easy. For though Plato does not mention flux in his argument for the Forms, he seems to mention it later; the Forms are exempt from change, while sensibles always change (*Phd.* 78d 10-e 3), or suffer becoming and perishing (*Rep.* 485a 10-b 4, 508d 4-9, 521d 3-4, 534d 2-3, *Symposium* 210e 6-211a 1). These comments do not vindicate Aristotle, since he finds appeals to flux in Plato's arguments, not in conclusions from the arguments. But they show that Plato, like Aristotle, apparently confuses the implications of the Theory of Forms with a doctrine of flux. Why should this apparent confusion seem attractive?

The right answer to this question will show that neither Plato nor Aristotle is confused. We thought we could easily identify Heracleitean claims about flux; but we should be less confident.

II. Types of Flux

The *Theaetetus* presents one view of flux; everything undergoes constant local movement and qualitative alteration (181b 8-182c 8), constantly gaining properties it previously lacked and losing properties it previously had. Let us call this kind of change *self-change* (*s*-change):

> *x* *s*-changes iff at time *t*1 *x* is F and at time *t*2 *x* is not-F, and *x* itself is not in the same condition at *t*2 as it was at *t*1 (e.g., at *t*1 it is hot, and at *t*2 it has become not-hot, by becoming colder than it was).

This is not the only kind of change associated with Heracleitus. His "unity of opposites" includes not only the things which *s*-change, but also things with compresent opposite properties—the road up and down, the straight and crooked writing, the food which is good (for some people) and bad (for others) (Heracleitus, B59-61).[7] Let us call this *aspect-change* (*a*-change):

> *x* *a*-changes iff *x* is F in one aspect, not-F in another, and *x* is in the same condition when it is F and when it is not-F (e.g., *x* is big in comparison with *y*, small in comparison with *z*).

The intuitive difference between *s*-change and *a*-change is that in *s*-change the changing object is being compared with itself at some previous time, and the reference to different times is essential to the explanation of its different properties. *a*-change, like *s*-change, involves the presence of opposite properties in different situations, but the reference to different times is not needed to describe the different situations, and the changing

---

[7]On flux and the unity of opposites in Heracleitus see Guthrie, pp. 439-46. B91 clearly associates compresence of opposites with flux; "or rather, neither again nor later, but at the same time it comes together and ebbs away".

object is not compared with itself at a previous time. We can speak temporally of *a*-change, and say that food is sometimes healthy and sometimes unhealthy; but we can equally explain the different properties non-temporally, by reference to the different consumers of the food. We may think that *a*-change is not genuine change at all, and that Plato and Heracleitus must be confused when they treat it as change, perhaps because they think of relative properties as intrinsic properties. But to show the confusion, we must show not only that they speak of both conditions as change, but that they mistakenly draw conclusions about the one which should only be drawn about the other. I see no evidence that Plato is confused in this way, but I do not claim he could *clearly* distinguish the two kinds of change. Talk of "aspects" allows widespread *a*-change (it corresponds to Plato's very broad use of μέρος or κατὰ ταὐτόν, *Rep.* 436b 8 ff.). The interest of the result depends on the aspects Plato selects.

Now Plato and Aristotle count *a*-change, not only *s*-change, as Heracleitean flux.

1. Both recognize that Heracleitus is concerned with the compresence of opposites (*Soph.* 242e 2-3, *EN* 1155b 4-6), and especially with the compresence resulting from dependence on different situations (*Top.* 159b 30, *Phys.* 185b 20, *EN* 1176a 5-8).

2. Plato refers to Heracleitus on the monkey for an example of something both beautiful (in one comparison) and ugly (in another) (*Hipp. Ma.* 289a). Later he extends this Heracleitean observation to types of action; an action-type can be called "beautiful and ugly" or "no more beautiful than ugly" because some of its tokens are beautiful and others ugly (293b 10-c 5).

3. The *Cratylus* mentions a Heracleitean etymology of some moral terms. People are confused about the truth in questions of justice, wisdom, knowledge, virtue and so on, and their dizzy confusion causes them to think that the things themselves are always shifting and changing (411a 1-c 6). Plato perhaps means that the apparent dependence of justice and virtue on particular situations, and the apparent exceptions to rules about them, encourage people to believe that there is no single account of justice, that justice includes opposite kinds of actions in different situations, and therefore undergoes *a*-change.

4. The flux-doctrine in the *Theaetetus* mentions compresence of opposites as a clear example of flux (152d 2-6). Plato does not accept the whole doctrine; but he does not find it odd to talk of *a*-change as a kind of flux. *Tht.* 155b-c argues from *a*-change to *s*-change; our belief that Socrates is bigger than young Theaetetus and smaller than older Theaetetus, because Theaetetus has grown and Socrates has not changed, is rejected because it conflicts with our alleged belief that Socrates cannot have become small without having become smaller than he was. The passage recalls *Phd.* 102b 3-6, which, however, avoids the *Tht.*'s conclusion. The conclusion depends on the Protagorean view that there is no Socrates "in himself"

remaining unchanged, apart from the Socrates in different situations who is always different. For a Protagorean (Plato argues) a-change implies s-change, and eventually implies even more, the dissolution of Socrates into a series of Socrates-stages, 159b-c. The passage is no evidence of Plato's own views.

Though neither Plato nor Aristotle definitely says that Heracleitean flux includes a-change as well as s-change, this evidence suggests that they do sometimes refer to a-change when they speak of flux.

III. POSSIBLE APPEALS TO FLUX

If we keep these options in mind, we can look for a clear appeal to flux in Plato's arguments.

1. Plato might argue, as the *Theaetetus* does, that if all sensible objects are in constant s-change, we cannot identify anything in the world or describe it coherently (*Tht.* 182 c-d); and he might infer, as the *Theaetetus* does not, that separated Forms solve this problem. But he never endorses the Heracleitean doctrine. In the *Symposium* Diotima shows how someone remains the same man throughout his lifetime; s-changes are regular and maintain a close qualitative similarity between the man at one time and at another, 208a 7-b 2. Contrast *Tht.* 159b, where the dissimilarity of Socrates at different times is taken to be a reason for treating him as several different Socrateses. Plato never endorses this analysis.

2. If particulars undergo some s-change, and eventually go out of existence, Plato might deny that there can be knowledge of them; perhaps he believes that knowledge must be of what is always true, and therefore about objects which do not change, not about objects which change and so falsify previous truths about them. No such assumption about knowledge is mentioned in any arguments for the separation of Forms.[8] If Plato relies on it, he will generate more Forms than those he argues for in the Middle Dialogues. The *Phaedo* argues for separated Forms only of relative properties and of the moral properties discussed in the Socratic Dialogues (75c 7-d 5).[9] He even contrasts the properties for which his arguments find Forms with those for which they find none (*Rep.* 523 a 10-e 1, *Phdr.* 263a). If he were

---

[8] *Tim.* 51c 5-52a 7 argues that if knowledge and belief are different, they must have different objects, unchanging, imperceptible Forms and changing, perceptible particulars. This is professedly a summary, and does not make clear Plato's grounds for demanding unchanging objects for knowledge. The grounds must be sought in his other arguments.

[9] Plato uses his separation-arguments to yield only a restricted range of separated Forms; these may not be the only Forms he believes in. At *Phd.* 75d 1 he argues for Forms "for all the things on which we set the seal 'the thing itself which is'" both questioning and answering in our questions and answers". The mention of questions and answers alludes to the forms which Socrates asks about in the elenchos. Socrates *recognizes* forms for bees (*Meno* 72c) and shuttles (*Cra.* 389b); but he *asks about* moral properties—and so Plato mentions here the admirable, the good, the just and the pious (75c 11-d 1), adding relative properties, the equal, the greater and the smaller (75c 9-10). These are the only Forms justified by the argument from compresence of opposites. *Rep.* 596a 6-8 seems to license a separated Form corresponding to every common name; but while the *M.* and the *Cra.* license unseparated forms for predicates not mentioned in the *Phd.*, Plato does not justify the *separation* of these extra forms.

primarily concerned with s-change, he ought not to rely on these restricted arguments. Sensible particulars are no more likely to change in their problematic properties (as Plato thinks), their justice, beauty, largeness and so on, than they are to cease being men or horses or tables; appeal to s-change does not explain Plato's interests.

3. An appeal to a-change in sensible particulars sounds much nearer to Plato's explicit concern; he says that sensible equals are both equal and unequal, and we need a Form which is always equal and never also unequal. But if the properties F and not-F are both present in something, we may still know what F is and what not-F is if we can distinguish the ways the thing is F from the ways it is not-F. Mere compresence does not justify a separated Form.

Perhaps Plato fails to see this, if he believes we can learn what it is to be F only from confrontation with a sample of F which is not also not-F; since the sensible world provides no such sample of some problematic properties, separated Forms will be needed.

Does Plato rely on this argument? If he did, he ought to show that for every property which concerns him, every sensible particular which has the property also has the opposite property. But he cannot show this. For some cases, explicitly relative or attributive properties, it is easy; every large mouse is also a small animal. A relative predicate like 'large' requires completion—'large for a mouse', 'large for an animal'—before we can see how it is true or false of a particular. But not all the properties of interest to Plato are relative or attributive. A particular just or brave action is (or may be) entirely just or brave, and not equally unjust or cowardly. And so, even if Plato does demand an ostensive sample of F when observable particular Fs are F and also not-F, his demand does not justify separated Forms for all moral properties. The demand for a perfect sample is meant to explain the argument for Forms. But it does not explain the argument, since it does not justify the Forms Plato wants. Perhaps he accepts the demand and is confused; alternatively, a-change in particulars may not be his main interest, since it will not support his case.[10]

IV. THE DEFICIENCY OF SENSIBLES

We will now consider Plato's arguments, and see what conclusions or assumptions about what kinds of flux they imply.

1. The finger passage in *Republic* VII explains why some properties do not provoke thought, because they are adequately judged by the senses, and others do provoke thought, because the senses reveal nothing sound (523a 10-b 4). We are not compelled to ask what a finger is; but the senses'

[10]The connexion between "incomplete predicates" and "ostensive samples" is used to explain Plato's argument by Owen [3], p. 346, Owen [2], p. 307, Strang, pp. 195-9. Owen recognizes, [2] p. 305 n4, that *Rep.* V implies, not that token-actions are both just and unjust, but only that the same action-type has some just and some unjust tokens; but he does not discuss the problem for the "ostensive sample" view.

confusion of hardness and softness compels us to ask what these properties are. The senses do not simply ascribe opposite properties to the same particular object. We can say without trouble that a centaur is a man and not a man; but the senses tell us that the same thing is hardness and softness, and make us look for an account of these properties, to show that they are different (524b 3-c 11). If we expect largeness, say, to be some observable property—a definite size, such as being three inches long—we will find that this property is "the large" or "largeness" in some things, since it makes them large, but is "the small" or "smallness" in other things, or in the same thing in different comparisons. Those properties accessible to the senses confuse largeness and smallness for us, as Plato says.

2. The deficiency of sensible properties supports Plato's rejection of mistaken efforts at explanation. If someone tries to explain why things are larger than other things by reference to some observable property (e.g., "by a head", *Phd.* 96d 7), he will fail; for many things are larger than other things without being larger by a head, and things may be smaller, as well as larger, by a head. Observable operations (e.g., "add two") equally fail to explain what makes one set more numerous than another (96e 1). These accounts are meant to be ridiculous—no one would try to explain largeness and numerousness that way. But Plato uses them to suggest that some apparently less ridiculous explanations are no more defensible. He rejects accounts of the beautiful referring to bright colours, shapes, "or anything else of this kind" (100c 9). He does not reject all attempts at a non-tautological account of the Forms, but only those which mention sensible properties which confuse us in our search for an adequate account.

3. The contrast between sense and intellect (*Rep.* 524c 13) and their areas of competence underlies the brief and controversial argument for separation in the *Phaedo* (see 74b 4-6, ἰδόντες . . . ἐνενοήσαμεν; cf. 65d 4-11). Plato might be taken to argue only that since any particular equal things are both equal and unequal, and the equal itself is only equal, the equal itself must be separate from the particulars. This argument would suggest the demand for perfect samples. But if the role of the senses is stressed, the argument rests on different grounds. If someone relies on the observable properties of equal sticks and stones as a good guide to what equality is, he will find, as in *Republic* VII, that the senses confuse equality and inequality; for the same dimensions will make the sticks both equal and unequal, making their equality (in some comparisons) into inequality (in others).[11] Plato need not mean that a perfect sample is needed, and unavailable in the sensible world;

[11]The talk of sticks and stones is an attempt to answer the question "What is the equal?". This is not foreign to Plato; at *Hipp. Ma.* 287e 3 Hippias says that a beautiful girl is (something) beautiful, to answer the question "What is the beautiful?". Hippias is not just ignorantly misunderstanding Socrates' question as a request for examples (since the question has just been distinguished from such a request, 287d 10); he supposes that he can generalize from features of an example to know what the beautiful is. Similarly in the *Phd.* Plato imagines someone appealing to the observable features of pairs of equals to say what the equal is.

he may mean that the right account of equality or "the equal" cannot be found by reference to sensible properties.[12] The argument is extended to the just, the pious and all the other properties for which Socrates sought definitions (75c 10-d 5). An argument from compresence of opposites in particulars could not be extended, since Plato does not think that every particular which has justice or piety also has the opposite property. But the argument from deficiency of sensible properties can be extended; for all sensible properties will fail to give an account of moral properties, as well as relative properties—this is Plato's later claim about beauty (100c 9-d 8).

4. The argument about the equals demanded separated Forms because of the deficiencies of sensible properties. *Republic* V defends that claim, by arguing that concentration on sensible properties will yield no knowledge of justice, beauty and so on. Plato's opponents are "lovers of sights and sounds", who deny the existence of a single form, the beautiful, besides the many sensible properties, each of which is alleged to be "the beautiful in" various things, houses, temples, institutions.[13] To find the beautiful in something, what makes something beautiful, the sight-lovers must find a property which is always beautiful, never not-beautiful (cf. *Phd.* 102d 5-8). But any of the sensible properties alleged to be the "many beautifuls" will also be not-beautiful (478e 6-479a 10); the bright colour (cf. *Phd.* 100d 1) alleged to be the beautiful in temples will be not-beautiful in some temples; debt-paying, alleged to be justice in actions, will also sometimes be unjust (cf. *Rep.* 331c-d, 538d 6-e 3); the pleasures which are alleged to be the good will sometimes be bad—some will be good and others bad (505c 10-11). These properties allow no knowledge of the beautiful, the just or the good; for knowledge, we must describe a separated Form irreducible to sensible properties.

V. INFERENCES ABOUT FLUX

These arguments all rely on the failure of sensible properties to answer the Socratic 'What is it?' question for certain difficult properties; and the *Phaedo* and *Republic* infer that we must appeal to separated Forms, not described in sensible terms, to answer the Socratic question and know what

---

[12]I take 74b 8, "appear equal to one, not to another", to mean "appear in one man's view equal (and really are), in another man's view unequal (and really are)". If 'appear' means 'appear to be' in a non-veridical sense, and the point is concerned with perceptual illusions, the argument is invalid. I think "equal to one thing, not to another" (suggested by Murphy, p. 111 n1, Owen [2], p. 306 n2, Crombie, II. p. 309) is less likely (cf. *Hipp. Ma.* 291d 2 for the reference to different people). But the main point is not much altered, as long as 'appear' is veridical. Different people consider these equals in different comparisons, and reach different correct results; for the same dimensions will make the sticks equal and unequal in different comparisons, just as they made the finger in *Rep.* VII large and small in different comparisons.

[13]I take the "many beautifuls" in *Rep.* V to be types or properties rather than particular token actions or objects; see Murphy, p. 110, Owen [2], p. 306 n4, Gosling, Crombie, II, p. 70. Talk of "types" or of "properties" will, for these purposes, be equivalent. We can say either "bright colour is beautiful and ugly" meaning that it is sometimes beautiful in things (i.e., makes them beautiful), sometimes ugly; or "bright-coloured things, *qua* bright-coloured, are beautiful and ugly".

these properties are. The arguments explain several points in Aristotle's comments:

(1) Plato clearly begins from Socrates' ethical interests and concern with definitions. He uses the failure of the senses with relative properties to illustrate their less obvious failure with moral properties.

(2) The argument is concerned with the deficiency of sensibles, which allow no correct answer to the Socratic question.

(3) The deficiencies of sensibles prevent them from being sources of knowledge about the relevant properties.

(4) Knowledge must be sought in separated Forms, not describable in sensible terms.

We have omitted only the reference to flux in sensibles. Can it be justified?

Plato can fairly claim that sensible properties are in flux, because opposite moral properties are compresent in them, and they a-change from being beautiful (e.g.) to being ugly in different situations—bright colour changes from being beautiful in this temple to being ugly in that one. Similarly, sensible things, in so far as they are bright-coloured, always change from beautiful to ugly—some are beautiful and others ugly. Do these kinds of flux justify Plato's specific claims that there is flux in the sensible world?

1. The strongest apparent statement of general flux follows the argument in the *Phaedo* about the equals. Plato contrasts the changeless Forms with the many beautifuls and equals—men, horses, cloaks and so on—which are never the same in relation to themselves or to each other (78d 1-79a 4). Objects, rather than properties, are said to be in flux. Plato's argument for separation claims that classes of sensible objects, in so far as they have sensible properties, are in flux; and he may mean the same here. He does not say that *each* man or horse is in flux, but that each of the many beautifuls, men, horses, and so on, is in flux. One of the many beautifuls will be, not a particular man, but the class of (e.g.) dark-complexioned men; and under this description they will change from being beautiful to being ugly (as Plato says, "never the same in relation to themselves") and from being more beautiful than pale men to being less beautiful ("never the same in relation to each other"). The phrase 'the many Fs' can refer as well to F-making properties or classes of Fs as to particular Fs (cf. *Eu.* 6d 10, *Meno* 72a 1, c 6).[14] Only flux in classes follows from Plato's earlier arguments, and no more is needed here.

2. Plato suggests that when Simmias is larger than Socrates but smaller than Phaedo, then the large in Simmias departs and the small enters (*Phd.* 102d 5-e 3). The *Theaetetus* infers that Simmias undergoes bewilderingly rapid s-change, becoming all the time in different comparisons larger or

---

[14]At *Eu.* 5d 8 Euthyphro says "The pious is what I am doing now", meaning "the kind of thing I am doing now"—and offers a general description of a type of action, 5d 9-e 2. Socrates regards this as one of the "many piouses", 6d 10. Similarly, Meno's "many virtues", *M.* 72a 1, b 2, c 6-7, are different types of action (see Murphy, p. 110).

smaller *than he was* (cf. *Tht.* 155b 4-c 5). But here Plato also says that Simmias has both largeness and smallness in him (102b 4-6); this compresence allows *a*-change, not *s*-change. In different comparisons Simmias undergoes *a*-change from large to small; *a*-change occurs in particulars with 'large', 'small', or 'equal', though not with all predicates yielding separated Forms. No extravagant conclusion about *s*-change follows from this talk of *a*-change; and there is no reason to believe that Plato draws any such conclusion.

3. Plato infers from his arguments in *Republic* V that the many beautifuls (etc.) suffer becoming and perishing, and so are objects of belief rather than knowledge (485a 10-b 4, 508d 4-9, 521d 3-4, 534d 2-3 ; cf. *Symp.* 210e 6-211a 1 —even if these passages were evidence of an interest in *s*-change of sensible particulars, they would not assert extreme Heracleitean flux). Now he has not argued in Book V that the perishability of this table or this chair prevents knowledge about it. He has argued that the many beautifuls, the sensible properties, are sometimes beautiful, sometimes ugly; when they gain and lose their beauty in different situations, the beauty in them comes to be and perishes (cf. *Phd.* 102d 9-e 2). Plato can justifiably claim that the many beautifuls suffer *a*-change, and therefore suffer becoming and perishing.

4. Aristotle's *Peri Ideōn* reports an argument from relatives for the separation of Forms, which repeats the main points of the *Phaedo*'s argument about equals. If we want an account of the equal itself, what makes things equal, and we predicate this equal itself of "things here", we predicate it only homonymously; for the same account (*sc.*, of the equal itself) will not apply to them all (since different sensible properties make different things equal), nor do we signify the really equal things (Alexander *in Met.* 83. 6-8). As in *Republic* VII, sensible properties allow no single account of equality or the equal, "for the quantity in sensibles changes and fluctuates constantly, and is not determinate" (83. 8-10). *s*-change is not relevant; if *s*-change in sensibles required a Form, it would require one for every predicate applying to sensibles, whereas this argument depends on special features of some predicates, including 'equal', not shared by other properties, such as 'man'.[15] And anyhow *s*-change is not mentioned in the *Phaedo*-argument reproduced here. But a reference to *a*-change is perfectly suitable. Aristotle thinks this is one of the "more exact arguments" (*Met.* 990b 15); if it is sound, it really proves what is sought, the existence of a separated paradeigmatic Form, not just of an Aristotelian common universal, which was the most required by any other argument for Forms (Alex. 83. 17-22).

5. In our *Metaphysics* passages Aristotle refers to the flux which supports the separation of Forms; in the *Peri Ideōn* he believes the best argument for Forms rests on *a*-change, and never mentions *s*-change; the *Metaphysics* recalls the comment in the *Peri Ideōn* (cf. 1086a 37-b 1 with Alex. 83. 8-10).

---

[15]Alex. 82.11-83.6 establishes the contrast between predicates like 'man' and predicates like 'equal', so that only the second kind figure in the argument. See Owen [2], p. 309.

There is good reason to believe, and no reason to deny, that the *Metaphysics* too is concerned with *a*-change and not *s*-change. It is far more plausible to suppose Aristotle refers here, as in the *Peri Ideōn*, to the arguments we have discussed than to suppose that here he suddenly thinks of general *s*-change and of the *Theaetetus*. The talk of flux does not require reference to *s*-change; the relevant kind of flux both in Plato and in Aristotle is *a*-change.

6. We have even less reason to find *s*-change in these *Metaphysics* passages if we consider Aristotle's discussion of extreme Heracleitean *s*-change, in *Metaphysics* IV. He argues against Cratylus and the Heracleitizers (1010a 1-15), relying on the *Theaetetus*; there must be some stability in the world for anything in it to be a subject of change (1010a 15-b 1). Now if Aristotle ascribes to Plato this extreme Cratylean view on *s*-change, why does he not attack Plato too? He never suggests that Plato abandoned the doctrine of sensibles in flux and separated Forms; and he would hardly agree that the incoherence of extreme Heracleiteanism about the observable world is avoided by the postulation of unchanging Forms separated from the particulars in total *s*-change. Aristotle never says or implies that the *Theaetetus* defends this pseudo-solution, or that its extreme Heracleiteanism is Plato's view, supporting the arguments for Forms.[16] If Aristotle's comments on separation refer to *s*-change, his failure to criticize Plato in *Metaphysics* IV is uncharacteristically and mistakenly charitable. But if only *a*-change appears in the comments on separation, the failure is justified; Plato's argument for Forms did not rely, and Aristotle knew it did not rely, on *s*-change in the sensible world.

Aristotle's comments are a fair account of the arguments for Forms in Plato's Middle Dialogues; the references to Socrates' interests in ethics and definitions, to sensibles, to flux, to knowledge and to separation can all be justified from the dialogues. Plato and Aristotle may not clearly distinguish *a*-change and *s*-change, though we have found no reason to believe that they conflate the two. Aristotle may not be aware of the right interpretation of his comments—though I see no reason to deny it, and reason in the *Peri Ideōn* and *Metaphysics* IV to believe it. Perhaps Plato's claims about the Forms and their separation cannot all be justified by the arguments we have examined; they may prove something, but not all he wants. But at least

---

[16]Cherniss [1], p. 217, believes that *Tht.* 181-3 is meant to show that ". . . the very "processes" into which all phenomenal existence is resolved by this hypothesis (cf. *Tht.* 156-157c) imply the existence of immutable determinate entities", which Cherniss takes to be separated Forms. He comments on *Met.* IV: "Aristotle himself puts the same argument in his attack on the relativists . . . the reason for the rise of the doctrine is said to be the failure to recognize non-sensible entities (1010a 1-5) and to distinguish between change of quantity and change of quality, the latter alone of which concerns the essence and the form in accordance with which we all know things (1010a 22-5, cf. 1063a 22-8)." Cherniss omits an important point; 1010a 22-5 (cf. *Tht.* 172c 9-10) implies that the things alleged to be undergoing flux must *themselves* have some stability. I believe this is the *Tht.*'s argument. If Aristotle derives his argument from the *Tht.*, he is unlikely to be reading the *Tht.* the way Cherniss reads it. Aristotle believes (this passage suggests) that Plato rejected extreme Heracleiteanism about the *sensible* world, not that he relied on this doctrine to postulate separated Forms.

Aristotle does not make the Theory of Forms rest on *s*-change in the sensible world. Those who think the arguments for Forms depend on general *s*-change must find the clear Platonic evidence which has eluded us; they cannot appeal to Aristotle for unambiguous support. Those who deny that Plato's arguments and concerns reflect belief in general flux and *s*-change need not be embarrassed by Aristotle's testimony, and can even welcome it; properly understood, it confirms the most plausible account of Plato's arguments derived from the dialogues themselves.

Cornell University

REFERENCES

Brentlinger, J. A., "Particulars in Plato's Middle Dialogues", *Archiv für Geschichte der Philosophie*, 54 (1972), pp. 116-52.

Cherniss, H. F., [1] *Aristotle's Criticism of Plato and the Academy*, Vol. I (Baltimore, 1944).
    [2] "The Philosophical Economy of the Theory of Ideas", in *Studies in Plato's Metaphysics*, ed. R. E. Allen (London, 1965), pp. 1-12. From *American Journal of Philology*, 57 (1936), pp. 445-56.
    [3] "The Relation of the *Timaeus* to Plato's Later Dialogues", in Allen, pp. 339-78. From *American Journal of Philology*, 78 (1957), pp. 252-66.

Crombie, I. M., *An Examination of Plato's Doctrines*, 2 vols. (London, 1962, 1963).

Gosling, J. C. B., "*Republic* V; *Ta Polla Kala* etc.", *Phronesis*, 5 (1960), pp. 116-28.

Gulley, N., *Plato's Theory of Knowledge* (London, 1962).

Guthrie, W. K. C., *A History of Greek Philosophy*, Vol. I (Cambridge, 1962).

McDowell, J. H., *Plato's Theaetetus* (Oxford, 1973).

Murphy, N. R., *The Interpretation of Plato's Republic* (Oxford, 1951).

Owen, G. E. L., [1] "The Place of the *Timaeus* in Plato's Dialogues", in Allen, pp. 313-38. From *Classical Quarterly*, NS 2 (1953), pp. 79-95.
    [2] "A Proof in the *Peri Ideōn*", in Allen, pp. 293-312. From *Journal of Hellenic Studies*, 77 (1957), pp. 103-11.
    [3] "Notes on Ryle's Plato", in *Ryle*, ed. O. P. Wood and G. W. Pitcher (New York, 1970), pp. 341-92.

Ross, W. D., *Plato's Theory of Ideas* (Oxford, 1951).

Strang, C., "Plato and the Third Man", in *Plato*, Vol. I, ed. G. Vlastos (New York, 1970), pp. 184-200. From *Proceedings of the Aristotelian Society*, Supp. Vol. 37 (1963), pp. 147-64.

Weerts, E., *Platon und der Heraklitismus*, *Philologus*, Supplementband 23 (1931).

PHILOSOPHICAL TOPICS
Volume XV, No. 2, Fall 1987

Forms and Sensibles: <u>Phaedo</u> 74B-C

NICHOLAS P. WHITE
University of Michigan

In *Phaedo* 74b6-c6 Plato offers an important argument for the proposition that such things as "the equal itself," i.e. such things as are often called "Forms," are distinct from sensible objects. The argument is especially important because it is one of a very small number of explicit arguments—perhaps only two—that Plato gives for this proposition.[1]

I wish to isolate this argument to concentrate on what I take to be its philosophically most interesting features as an argument for the existence of Forms distinct from sensibles. I am not here concerned with its other interesting features, such as its role in Plato's argument for the kind of *a priori* knowledge that he calls "recollection."

I am especially interested in what must be presupposed if the argument is to be thought cogent (though I certainly do not believe that it is in fact cogent), and what is likely to have been presupposed by Plato. I am also concerned to show just how narrow a basis Plato wishes to use for the argument. In particular, I would like to make it clear how little of his view about Forms is presupposed in the argument, and how little of that view one can infer simply from interpreting the argument itself, as contrasted with the surrounding context.

1. In 74a9-12, Plato writes as follows (translations are my own):

> We say that there is some equal,—I don't mean a log to a log or a stone to a stone or anything else of that sort—but something else different from all those, the equal itself. Shall we say it is something or nothing?

Plato's interlocutor, Simmias, agrees emphatically and without argument. His agreement is not surprising, in view of the fact that earlier at 65d4-e5

197

it has been said, with just as little controversy, "We say that there is something, [the] just itself," as well as "[the] beautiful [itself], [the] good [itself], size, health, strength, and the being of all of the others, what each is," and it has also been said that people have "not seen any such things with [their] eyes."

On the basis of these passages it is often thought that Plato is taking his theory of Forms for granted.[2] Some scholars used to infer even that a belief in Forms was held by the historical Socrates and indeed went back to the Pythagoreans, but that view is rarely enough held nowadays that I propose to pass over it. Others wonder whether Plato can perhaps have thought that the existence of Forms needed no argument at all to the ordinary person or the ordinary philosopher, though other Platonic passages, such as *Republic* 476-480 and *Sophist* 246a-b show that that is not the case. Another possibility is that he knew that the matter was controversial, but simply never had a cogent argument to give, perhaps believing either (though it is not at all clear that he would ever endorse such a form of inference) that belief in the existence of Forms could be justified indirectly, by some overall fruitfulness or reasonableness of the conclusions issuing from it,[3] or (something that he sometimes seems to suggest) that people to whom the existence of Forms is not obvious are too obtuse to be worth bothering with.

It is important, however, to be clearly aware of just what he is taking for granted, and what he is prepared to try to justify. He does take for granted that *there is such a thing as* "the equal itself," "the beautiful itself," and so on. He does not, however, take for granted that such things are *distinct from sensible, physical objects*, although he does state this claim before he actually argues for it. He states it in 65d-e, where it is agreed that one has "never seen with one's eyes" or "touched with any other of the bodily senses" any such things as "the beautiful itself" (65d9-12). It is also stated in 74a9-12 that "we say" that there is some equal that is not "a log to a log or a stone to a stone or anything else of that sort, but something else different from all those." But in 74b6-c6 Plato explicitly addresses the possibility that someone may not agree that Forms are distinct from sensible objects, and provides an argument to try to meet this view. "Or do they not appear different to you?" he says, and proceeds to argue that they are.

But before we take up this argument, let us ask what, after all, the claim Plato *has* taken for granted amounts to, if not that Forms are distinct from sensibles. Clearly, that there is such a thing as "the equal," "the

198

beautiful,'' and so on. However, this can easily seem in itself to be a relatively uncontroversial claim, when divorced from the further claim that these things are distinct from sensibles. ''Is there such a thing as equality?'' Plato probably expected interlocutors to respond affirmatively without hesitation, so long as the response was deemed compatible with denying that there exist any objects beside sensible ones, and with saying that equality is in fact a sensible object itself. ''Certainly there is such a thing as equality,'' he might expect them to say, ''but it isn't something distinct from sensible equal things, and perhaps it isn't any single thing (cf. *Rep.* 479a4-5, e.g.); rather, it is just different sensible equals, depending on the context of discourse, or else it is somehow all of them taken together.''

To this way of dispensing with Forms and the like there is of course a well-known alternative, exploited by Russell in another connection, of saying that all contexts of discourse containing explicit talk of ''equality,'' as purporting to refer to an object, ought to be regarded as a misleading manner of speaking, to be paraphrased *en bloc* into discourse not containing any expression seeming to designate such an entity. But although I think Plato could have constructed an argument against this alternative, he does not seem to me at all likely to have had it in mind, or expected his opponents to. For this reason, I think that he in no way intends here to be taking any controversial metaphysical claim for granted. Instead, as he and his opponents view the matter, the really controversial and substantive part of what he has to say here comes when he argues, in 74b6-c6, that the equal is distinct from sensible equal things.

2. That argument is in one way less interesting than it has sometimes been taken to be, but philosophically I think it is more interesting than is usually realized. It is less interesting because it gives us rather less information than we might have hoped to gain from it concerning Plato's views about Forms, or what I shall speak of, with many others, as his theory of Forms.[4] The argument rests on a claim that Forms have a certain feature that sensibles do not have, and therefore must be distinct from sensibles. The question is, what exactly is that feature. If it is important for delineating Plato's theory, then the argument may tell us something interesting about it.

Unfortunately, what the property is lies obscured in some exegetical problems, which we shall have to examine briefly. The passage, 74b6-c6, runs as follows:

199

. . . Or doesn't it [the equal itself] appear (φαίνεται) to you different [*sc.*, from sensible sticks and stones]? Consider thus. Don't equal (ἴσοι) sticks and stones sometimes, being the same (ταὐτά ὄντα), appear (φαίνεται) to one person equal and not to another?

Certainly.

Well, then, have the equals themselves (αὐτὰ τὰ ἴσα) ever appeared (ἐφάνη) to you unequal (ἄνισα), or equality (ἰσότης) inequality (ἀνισότης)?

Never yet, Socrates.

So these equals (ταῦτα τὰ ἴσα) and the equal itself (αὐτὸ τὸ ἴσον) are not the same.

They don't appear (φαίνεται) so to me at all.

On this translation of the passage, Plato seems to think that there is a difference between Forms and sensibles with regard to how it is possible for them to appear to us, and so we shall have to see what that difference is.

3. But the translation is controversial in one way that would conflict with this understanding of the argument.[5] For under a suggestion made by N. R. Murphy and developed by G. E. L. Owen, the passage should be taken to mean that "equal sticks and stones sometimes, being the same, appear equal to one thing and not to another."[6]

Although there is something to be said for this interpretation,[7] it seems to me now that it cannot be sustained as a reading of the present passage. Three points against it are noted by David Gallop.[8] One is that since any equal thing is inevitably equal to some things and not to others, it would seem very strange to say only that this happens "sometimes" (b8). Second, the interpretation makes Plato hold that the equal itself somehow is free from this feature of sensible equals, which appears to make little sense, since it involves supposing that the equal itself is somehow equal but not equal *to* anything.[9] Third, it is awkward, verbally at least, to apply the argument framed in terms of "equal", to the other terms ("beautiful", etc.) that Plato gives in 75c-d (as well as, one should add, 65d-e).

A fourth objection to the Murphy/Owen interpretation is that it makes little sense of Plato's repeated use of the word "appears" (φαίνεσθαι). If Plato's point were that equal sensible objects *are* equal to one thing but not to another, then he might be expected to have said just that.[10] It might be replied that φαίνεσθαι need not mean "appears" but can also mean

200

"is evidently or apparently". But this reading of the word fits awkwardly onto the present passage. The only contrast that is natural to see in 74b8, in the phrase "*being* (ὄντα) the same," is a contrast between how things are and how they appear, not one between how things are and how they evidently are. Moreover, when the conclusion is reached in c4-5, an emphatic "is" (ἐστίν) is used (which contrasts naturally with φαίνεται in b7, which deals with how things seemed before the argument was given).[11]

Of the objections that Gallop lists, the third seems relatively weak,[12] but the other two are weighty, as is the fourth objection just expounded. The first strengthens the observation just made about what the natural contrast is to see in the passage. The second would require an essay in itself to deal with, but seems to me extremely strong. Although Plato has been accused by philosophers since Russell of being confused about relations and relational predicates, it seems to me to require far more than such a philosophical confusion to explain how Plato could have thought, straightforwardly and consciously, that anything, sensible or not, could be equal but not equal to anything, or equal to some one thing but not unequal to other things that are themselves equal to that first thing.[13] Moreover there is strong evidence, from such passages as *Symp.* 199d*sqq.*, that Plato did indeed understand that relational predicates in general, or at least binary relational predicates, do not hold just of isolated single objects without regard to others, as nonrelational predicates do.[14] At any rate, the present case, "equal" does not seem to me to be one about which he could have been so ludicrously confused.[15]

4. So let us take our translation as provisionally given and try to understand its implications.

Remember that even though Plato is talking to people who, as we saw from 65d-e and 74a, are willing to accept the view that the equal itself is distinct from all sensible objects, he is in 74b6-c6 temporarily arguing against doubts about that thesis. For that reason, we may expect that his argument will use premises that will be plausible to those not accepting the thesis or special theses associated with it.

Let us look at those premises. I shall first expound them briefly, under what I take to be the natural and correct interpretation, and explain how they are supposed to yield the conclusion that Plato wishes. Then I shall take up a number of difficulties that have led commentators to interpret them otherwise.

201

Premise (A): Don't equal sticks and stones sometimes, being the same, appear to one person equal and not to another? What phenomenon is Plato alluding to here? The initially most natural interpretation, which is also supported by reasons that I shall be laying out, is that he is alluding, as W. D. Ross and R. Hackforth suggested,[16] to the familiar fact that any pair of visible objects, which are in fact equal, can appear equal to a person looking at them from one perspective, but appear unequal to a person simultaneously looking at them from another perspective. ("Sometimes," because of course at other times a pair of equal objects may well seem equal to all observers who are looking at them.) There have been objections to this interpretation, but I shall deal with them in due course.

Premise (B): Well, then, have the equals themselves (αὐτὰ τὰ ἴσα) *ever appeared* (ἐφάνη) *to you unequal* (ἄνισα), *or equality* (ἰσότης) *inequality* (ἀνισότης)?—*Never yet, Socrates.* What is being alluded to here is something much more complicated and problematical, though at first sight it may well seem to be the straightforward fact that Plato presents it as being. If one considers the question that one might formulate by asking whether equality could ever appear to one to be inequality, it seems very easy to reply that it obviously could not. For it seems hard to imagine, in any straightforward way, a circumstance in which one could say that equality appears to be inequality, or in which one thinks that equality is inequality.[17]

These two premises together are designed to demonstrate that the equal itself must be distinct from any sensible equal object or objects by showing that a certain feature possessed by the former is not possessed by the latter.[18] This feature is, to speak loosely, a kind of incapacity to be the subject of a certain sort of error or perhaps misapprehension. The crucial question is, exactly what is this resistance to error? As commentators have observed, this question is quite difficult.[19]

The main difficulty with the argument, as construed in this way, is that of finding one and the same sort of resistance to error that can reasonably be attributed to Forms but withheld from sensibles. It seems somewhat plausible to say that *equality* never appears to be *inequality*, but it seems doubtful that any equal objects ever appear to be *inequality* either. Similarly, it seems plausible, as we saw, to say that sensible equals sometimes appear unequal, but it sounds very strange to say that equality never appears unequal, since that makes it sound as though equality is some sort of object with dimensions that can be measured against others by the mind's eye. Equally, as David Bostock points out, it does not seem possible for Plato

202

to argue that whereas equality can never appear to be its contrary, sensible equals can appear to be "their contrary," since two different senses of "contrary" would be involved here, one for a property (or the like) that is contrary to another property, and another for a thing possessing the contrary property to that possessed by another thing.[20] So what is it that, according to Plato, is true of the equal but not of sensible equals?

It seems to me that this problem is solved once one correctly interprets the way Plato understands the supposition being argued against, that the equal itself might be sensible. Sensible equals, we agree, are capable of appearing unequal to people looking at them. Now if it is to be supposed that the equal itself might be a sensible equal thing or pair of sensible equal things, clearly it would have to be supposed *also* that the unequal, or alternatively inequality, was also a sensible object. For plainly the idea that motivates the supposition about the equal is that there are no objects other than sensibles, and there is no question that here—whatever may be the case elsewhere in Plato's works—Plato claims existence as much for the unequal as for the equal.[21] So if the equal were sensible, and if accordingly the unequal were also sensible, then since any sensible equal is capable of appearing unequal, it would turn out that the equal was capable of appearing, in respect of equality or inequality, just like the unequal and in the relevant way indistinguishable from it.[22] So the feature that equality possesses and that it would not possess if it were sensible is that of being incapable of appearing, from any point of view, indistinguishable from inequality.

To this perspectivalist line of interpretation Alexander Nehamas has raised an objection, that it does not allow the generalization of Plato's argument from "equal" to other predicates.[23] According to Nehamas, although Plato might conceivably hold that a given *type* of action, for example, would always have both just and unjust instances (see, e.g., *Rep.* 331c-d), he would never say that numerically one and the same *particular* action either (*a*) *is* both just and unjust or, given the circumstances in which it actually occurs, even (*b*) *appears* both just and unjust from different perspectives. As to (*a*), Nehamas is of course quite right, though it is not relevant to the present issue. But not about (*b*), which is. Plato agrees here that the sticks *are* equal (see ἴσοι, "equal," in b8, and n. 10). What he claims, on the perspectivalist interpretation, is that they appear unequal from different perspectives. Nehamas disputes this for other cases, such as "just". But it seems to me that on examination the case fails to hold up. The perspectives that Nehamas thinks are lacking in such

203

cases are provided precisely by the sources of that very disagreement among people—their own interests and mistaken or confused views about what justice is—that Plato thinks is rampant. From the viewpoint of the madman in *Republic* 331c-d, who knows that he has been promised a weapon and who believes that it is just to return what one owes, it will *appear* just for the weapon to be returned, even though in what Plato takes to be the correct view it *is* not just. He never suggests that viewpoints are lacking from which such correct judgments will appear false, or from which incorrect judgments will appear true. What makes it possible for us sometimes to adjudicate such cases correctly, he holds, is the use of calculation and measurement (cf. *Euthyphro* 7b-d), and also a knowledge of the Forms (e.g., *Rep.* 540a-b). But as the very example in the present argument shows, even when measurement shows that two things are equal it is possible for them to appear otherwise. So the perspectivalist interpretation seems to me to generalize quite as well as Plato could hope.

5. But even if this interpretation is conceded to be initially plausible, it faces some severe difficulties concerning Premise (B) that need to be confronted.

The first matter that needs to be disposed of concerns 74c1-2, where Plato asks, "Well, then, have the equals themselves (αὐτὰ τὰ ἴσα) ever appeared (ἐφάνη) to you unequal (ἄνισα), or equality (ἰσότης) inequality (ἀνισότης)?" And why does he use both the plural expression, "the equals themselves", and the singular, "the equal itself"? Do these expressions refer to different things or is Plato pleonastically raising one issue about one thing? Now in spite of some dissenting opinions, it seems to me impossible to make his argument hang together if we take him to be making distinct claims about distinct entities, since obviously c4-5 announces only one conclusion about one thing, "the equal itself."[24] Given that, we are obliged to say that in c1-4 he is using all three expressions, "the equals themselves", "equality", and "the equal itself", as different designations of the same item.

Let us first ask, then, why Plato uses the plural form, "the equals themselves", instead of the more common singular expression, "the equal itself", at c1-2? Here it seems to me that Owen had a reasonable initial answer: the plural form is a grammatically natural way of following up on the plural forms in the preceding lines (b7-9).[25] This answer is sufficient to dispose of any grammatical oddity in the shift of terminology. But it

204

leaves unanswered the further question whether there is any significance for Plato in the distinction between the singular, "the equal itself", and the plural, "the equals themselves", as designations of the Form, and, if so, what that significance is. Here it seems to me that the right response, insofar as our argument is concerned, is that there plainly is no significance at all, and that is why Plato moves so casually between the two expressions. Further issues within the theory of Forms might indeed require Plato to determine which expression, if either, is the more apt, and we are free to search other texts for more evidence on the question. But the present argument requires no such determination, and it seems to me a mistake to read one in.

The next question receives an answer similar to the previous one. If we assume that there is no significant difference between the designations "the equal itself" and "the equals themselves", we must then ask whether there is any significant difference between the phrases "the equal itself" and "equality" in Plato's formulation of Premise (B). (As Gallop points out,[26] both are of the sort that Plato frequently uses as variant designations of Forms.) Once again, it seems to me that there cannot be, because Plato clearly presents the argument as yielding a single conclusion concerning a single sort of object (c4-5 with b2, 4-6).

But what is the explanation of Plato's having used these two expressions? For they carry quite different suggestions. Notoriously, the phrase "the equal itself" suggests what Gregory Vlastos once called "self-predication," the idea that the Form of equal is itself equal, i.e., some sort of equal thing (or, perhaps, equal things), whereas the term "equality" seems to convey no such idea. Must we not understand the argument in one of these ways or the other?

Once again, the reasonable thing to say is that Plato does not settle this issue here, and casually allows both designations of the Form of equal, precisely because his argument here does not require that the issue be settled. The crucial thing for his argument is that the Form never appears to be its contrary, which it would do if it were a sensible object, as explained above at the end of sec. 4. Plato allows us to put this point in two different ways. One, which seems perhaps the less problematical, is to say that equality never appears to be inequality. The other is to say that the equal never appears to be unequal, which is to say that the Form never appears to have the distinguishing characteristic of its contrary (cf. n. 22). I see little doubt that Plato was in a position to ask himself which formulation was theoretically the more apt, and that he neatly sidestepped the question here because it seemed to him to have no bearing on this argument for the distinctness of Forms from sensibles.[27]

For this reason there seems no justification for reading the argument as if it requires for its cogency a "self-predicationist" picture of the Forms. Some commentators assume that it must, probably because they read it in the light of the ensuing passage, 74c7-75a4, in which Plato says that sensibles "fall short of" being just like Forms (74d5-7 with e1-2, 75a1-2, b1-2, 7-8). I myself think that it is very unclear whether that passage forces a self-predicationist account of the Forms,[28] but even if it does, that by no means entails that the present argument requires a premise either entailing or presupposing self-predication.

6. But even if we keep the argument unencumbered by special metaphysical assumptions, we still must ask what it means to say that equality never appears to be inequality.

A first possibility is this. By analogy to the case of the equal things that can appear unequal from some viewpoints, one might think of the equal itself as something that one is somehow "aware" of or with which one is "acquainted." And one might hold that one can never be aware of it in such a way as to make one believe that it is, while it is so presenting itself, inequality.

On a second view, one might take it that what is being said is solely that a certain proposition, that equality is inequality, is one that we are not capable of believing, or differently that a certain sentence, "Equality is inequality", is not one that we are capable of sincerely asserting. On this view, the notion of a relation between the object, equality, and the person or mind in question, would be eliminated.

Now it is clear, on the one hand, that there is no justification in the passage for saying that Plato's argument itself requires any substantial notion of awareness of equality by the mind. True, Plato often talks elsewhere in such a way as to suggest such a notion,[29] but even if he might accept it in the *Phaedo* too, he does not indicate at all that the argument in 74b6-c6 must make use of it. And although Premise (A) deals with the way in which one can be aware, through sensation, of equal physical objects, that by no means implies that Premise (B) does something analogous for the equal itself.

On the other hand, the second view as stated obviously will not serve the purposes of the argument in 74b6-c6. As we have seen, that argument

206

must proceed by citing a feature *of the object, equality,* which is shown not to attach to equal sensibles. So no property of a sentence or proposition will serve Plato's purposes *unless* it somehow implicates a feature of equality itself.

Now there is a way of introducing a feature of equality into this discussion of appearances without at the same time injecting a notion of awareness. This can be done through something like the notion of what has been called "belief *de re*."[30] The sentence, "Plato believes that the equal is a Form", need not be taken simply as saying that Plato stands in a certain relation to a particular proposition without involving a relation to the object, the equal. It can also be taken as ascribing to the equal a certain relation to Plato, namely, that of being believed by Plato to be a Form. In the same way, one can ascribe or deny to the equal another feature, that of being believed by Simmias to be the unequal. Now Plato does not here use the word "believe" but uses instead the word "appear". But it seems entirely possible that he has in mind, under the expression "(does not) appear to be the unequal", a feature that might be expressed equally by the phrase, "is (not) believed to be the unequal". If that is so, then he would be saying that the equal does not have the feature of being believed by anyone to be the unequal.

The difficulty with this proposal, however, is that it seems to make Premise (B) turn out to be obviously false. For even if it is true that no one would ever hold a belief that he represented to himself by the sentence, "The equal is the unequal", it is well known that there are other propositions, that arguably produce the same effect. For the equal can be referred to in other ways than by "the equal", e.g., "the Form referred to at *Phaedo* 74c5", and there seems no impossibility in someone's believing something expressed by the (false) proposition, "The Form referred to at *Phaedo* 74c5 is the unequal". But Plato's premise will be falsified if this fact licenses us to infer that the equal has the feature, being believed to be the unequal.[31] If (B) is to be plausible, examples of this sort have to be ruled out as expressing features of the equal. The question is whether Plato would have had any way of doing this.

Obviously what the argument needs is a denial that any and all ways of designating an object can generate beliefs implicating a feature of the object of the relevant sort, which as we have seen are features having to do with how things "appear" (φαίνεσθαι). For example, Plato must be able to deny that when someone believes falsely that—in these words—"the Form referred to at *Phaedo* 74c5 is inequality," that shows that equality has "appeared" to him to be inequality. To put the matter in a loose and slightly cumbersome way, Plato must be able to hold the thesis,

> (D) Not all designations of an object (or other ways of thinking about an object[32]) that can be used to refer to that object in the formulation of a belief concerning it generate *"appearances"* of the object.

If this thesis can be sustained, then it may perhaps turn out that Premise (B) can be sustained as well. That is, it may turn out that there are no designations of equality under which anyone could hold an *appearance-belief*, as we may call it, to the effect that equality is inequality.

Plato himself in this passage uses an expression that may convey the necessary idea. The verb (ἐννοεῖν), often translated "to have in mind" or "consider", occurs a number of times in a way allowing one to say that one has a particular object in mind (74b6, d1, e2, 75a5-6).[33] Perhaps we can say, as a rough approximation, that in Plato's view, someone's using the expression "the Form referred to at *Phaedo* 74c5" in a normal way would not *eo ipso* show that he "had equality in mind," whereas someone's using the expression "equality" in the normal way would show that he had equality in mind.

I have no idea how this distinction can be generally drawn in a clear and philosophically satisfactory way, but I think that from a naive point of view there does *seem* to be a distinction between designations that, properly used or possessed, implicate a person's having the designatum in mind and those that do not. Typically, people using the word "equality" can reasonably be said to have equality "in mind," and people using the phrase "the Form referred to at . . ." cannot (though by now the reader of the foregoing probably does). So if Plato is using such a distinction, he is using something that at least has some appeal.

Moreover it seems plain, as I have indicated, that—and this is a point to be emphasized—Plato's argument *must* presuppose *some* such distinction as this, in order to meet the obvious counterexamples to Premise (B), whether or not the distinction was clearly or explicitly in his mind, and whether or not he had any fixed way of explaining it. As I have already said, the distinction does not require him to hold that one can be "aware" of Forms in any full-blooded sense, though of course he might elsewhere have wished to use that notion (and I think he did). But it does require some notion of "having in mind" that will exclude the sort of counterexamples mentioned.

208

7. Let us briefly consider what lends Premise (B) the initial plausibility it seems to have.

The vague sense that one has about such abstract entities as equality is that any grasp of them must consist solely or almost solely in a grasp of their ''logical'' relations to other such objects and their roles in various necessary-seeming ''conceptual'' facts. That is indeed why such objects have sometimes been held to be nothing but ''logical constructions,'' not genuine entities at all. But if one sticks to a realistic view of the objects and takes this feeling seriously, one gets a picture of objects whose nature consists in, and can be grasped only through a grasp of, certain ''logical laws,'' possibly some ''mathematical laws,'' and various other ''conceptual truths.'' It is seen as part of thinking about equality that one simply cannot somehow take it to be the same as those other objects from which it is distinguished by a crucial difference of ''conceptual role.''

It is surely this sense that leads to the feeling that there is no way both to have equality in mind and nevertheless to take it to be inequality. If equality is for present purposes understood to be sameness of some spatial dimension, then inequality seems to amount to nothing but lack of sameness of that spatial dimension. Thus, equality and inequality seem to stand to each other as merely the possession and the lack, by things within the same domain, of one and the same feature. A person to whom equality appears to be inequality seems accordingly like a person who is not capable of realizing that the having of a certain feature and the lacking of it are distinct. And such a person might well seem to be someone who is incapable of having equality, or inequality, in mind.

In the *Theaetetus*, as is well known, Plato tries to fend off some argumentation for a much stronger thesis, that it is impossible to have in mind any object of the sort ''that one can only think about'' and nevertheless believe that it is *any* other such object (see 188a-d and 189c-200c, and esp. 195e-196a).[34] That thesis is stronger than our Premise (B) in at least two ways. For one thing, it deals not merely with the relation between a property and its contrary, but with a relation between an object that can be thought about and *all* other such objects. Secondly, it says not merely that an object of the relevant sort cannot ''*appear*'' to be a different object, but that it is impossible to *believe* that the one object is another. What the considerations are that motivate that thesis, and what Plato thinks he can do to combat it (his attempt in the *Theaetetus* to rebut it is a self-confessed failure), are things that I cannot explore here. My only point is to emphasize that the claim that he makes in the *Phaedo*, though perhaps related to that

209

thesis, is much weaker. It is also more plausible. As we have seen, some plausibility can be generated for the claim that it is impossible to have equality in mind and nevertheless have it appear to be inequality. It is far more difficult to generate any comparable plausibility for the contention that it is impossible to believe any abstract object, say, to be any other abstract object. Probably the reason is that because the relations among various abstract objects are as complicated as they are—far more complicated than the relation of simple contrariety between equality and inequality—it does not offhand seem impossible to have one abstract object "in mind" and not realize that it is distinct from another abstract object that stands in similar but different complicated relations to various other such objects. But of course much more would have to be said to get to the bottom of this issue.

8. Let us now briefly consider the contrast between sensibles and Forms that emerges from Premise (A) along with the foregoing considerations about Premise (B).

At the end of sec. 4 above, we saw that the feature possessed by equality that it would not possess if it were sensible, according to Plato, is that of being incapable of appearing to be inequality. We have just seen that Plato *must* put some sort of restriction on the notion of equality's "appearing" thus-and-so if he is to be able to uphold this claim.

It is of course not to be denied that a sensible object can be designated in such a way as to imply that it possesses a certain property and could not consistently actually possess the contrary property. For example, one can designate "that pair of equal sticks over there," and by that designation one implies that the pair of sticks is not at that time unequal. But the difference between sensibles and Forms to which Plato is pointing is this. It is impossible, he claims, for someone to "have" equality "in mind," or have an "appearance" of equality, and at the same time take it that equality *is* inequality. On the other hand it is not impossible, he holds, for someone to have equal sensibles in mind and take it that they are unequal, for the reason that equal sensibles are capable, though *being* equal at a particular time (cf. n. 10) of nevertheless *appearing* unequal at that same time. Indeed, equal sensibles are capable of *appearing* unequal *even when* one is aware explicitly that they are equal, because the knowledge of their equality is not capable of wiping away the sensory appearance of their inequality.[35] In the particular respect at hand, that is, he holds that

210

equal sensibles are capable of presenting misleading appearances in a way in which equality and inequality are not. Unlike sensibles, Forms are "cognitively reliable," as Vlastos has put it (though I would disagree with his way of explaining the matter).[36]

A common modern reaction to Plato's view, of course, is to contend that he has taken for a feature of equality something that is really only a feature of certain sentences, like "Equality is inequality", or of our ways of using such sentences, or of certain beliefs or other such states of the human mind, like the belief that equality is inequality. (This contention is compatible with the claim that there is such an object as equality, and with its denial.) I think—though I cannot defend the claim here—that Plato was led to his view by more than a mere failure to consider the alternatives, and that he had reasons for rejecting them.

A good deal of Plato's metaphysical thinking goes into trying to explain this difference between Forms and sensibles. As I understand his position, he takes the fact that sensibles exist in space and time to be what allows them to present contrary appearances to different perspectives. Forms, on the other hand, do not have a place within any "manifold" that allows different perspectives or anything of the kind. But the defense of this line of interpretation of the rest of Plato's view lies far beyond the scope of the present paper, and his metaphysical explanation is certainly not presented or used in the argument at hand. Rather, that argument leaves the resistance of the Forms to this particular sort of error at the level of a commonsense observation, on which Plato might hope for agreement from the persons at whom the argument is aimed.

NOTES

1. I myself would include with it only the argument at *Rep.* 476-480.
2. J. L. Ackrill and David Gallop hold that the "theory of Forms" is accepted by all parties in the *Phaedo* itself. See Ackrill, "*Anamnesis* in the *Phaedo*," in Lee *et al.*, eds., *Exegesis and Argument* (Assen, 1973), pp. 177-195, esp. p. 191, and Gallop, *Plato, Phaedo* (Oxford, 1975), p. 97.
3. Gallop, p. 95, perhaps attributes something like this line of thought to Plato. I myself think that Plato did regard the general capacity to help solve certain philosophical difficulties as commending a belief in the Forms, but I do not think that he regarded that as sufficient by itself to establish that belief (it would not exclude alternative ways of solving those difficulties). Instead, I think he believed that a more direct argument was required, such as we find in the present passage.
4. Many have thought that Plato's works are only fragmentary or inconclusive explorations of philosophical ideas, and some have misgivings about calling what he says about Forms a "theory" (see e.g., Julia Annas, *Introduction to Plato's Republic* [Oxford, 1981], p.

211

217). I myself think that it is correct to speak of Plato's dialogues as expounding a "theory" in some reasonably substantive sense of that word, but here I use it in a very broad and loose way carrying very little freight.

5. The text is mildly problematic too, but I think that what Burnet prints is clearly right, and that attempts to make sense of the alternative reading are clearly unsuccessful: see the discussion by Gallop, p. 122, of Verdenius' interpretation of the variant. I think that Gallop is also quite correct that the Greek will not bear the sense assigned it by his interpretation (c) of the usual text.

6. See N. R. Murphy, *The Interpretation of Plato's Republic* (Oxford, 1951), p. 111, n., and G. E. L. Owen, "A Proof in the *Peri Ideon*," *Journal of Hellenic Studies* (1957), Pt. 1, 103-111, reprinted in R. E. Allen, ed. *Studies in Plato's Metaphysics* (New York, 1965), 293-312, esp. p. 306, n. 2. (This article will be cited here in the latter pagination.) See also K. W. Mills, "Plato's *Phaedo* 74b7-c6," *Phronesis* 2 (1957), 128-148, and 3 (1958) 40-58, and the discussion in David Gallop, pp. 121-125, as well as Alexander Nehamas, "Plato on the Imperfection of the Sensible World," *American Philosophical Quarterly*, 12 (1975), 105-117.

7. And although I must admit that I once accepted it myself, in my *Plato on Knowledge and Reality* (Indianapolis, 1976), pp. 66-67 with n. 16.

8. Gallop, pp. 122-123.

9. The strongest considerations in favor of the Murphy/Owen reading are developed by Owen's arguments that Aristotle took Plato to believe such things, and argued against his theory of Forms partly on that score. See Owen, pp. 309-312.

10. I disagree with Bostock's strategy, pp. 75-77, of trying to support the view that this *is* what Plato meant by adducing *Rep.* 479a-c. To present my full reason for disagreeing would require a discussion of that passage, for which I do not have space here. However, Plato's use of the word "equal" ('ίσοι) at 74b8, with its plain implication that the sticks *are* equal, seems to me to make the present interpretation so much more natural than the other that one should accept the present interpretation if it allows—as I think I can show here that it does—clear sense to be made of Plato's argument.

11. Nehamas maintains (p. 111, n. 30), adducing *Rep.* 597-598 in support, that because Plato is drawing an ontological distinction, differences in appearance from different perspectives are unlikely to enter into the drawing of it. That seems to me a mistake. For Plato, one manifestation of the ontological distinction is precisely a difference between Forms and sensibles with regard to what appearances they are capable of presenting. See sec. 8.

12. Indeed, Nehamas (pp. 115-116) bases his defense of the Murphy/Owen interpretation (or something extremely like it) on the claim that it helps us understand Plato's willingness to generalize the argument of 74b-c to other Forms. See sec. 4, end.

13. As Owen observes, pp. 309-312, Aristotle accuses Plato of introducing a "nonrelative class of relatives," in the sense of somehow nonrelational cases of relational predicates. Although I cannot here adequately expound the issue, I think that Aristotle's remarks do not involve the relations that Owen thinks they do.

14. A partial list of passages in which Plato deals with relations is given—alas, to little effect—at my *op. cit.*, p. 79 (n. 16). See also E. Scheibe, "Ueber Relativbegriffe in der Philosophie Platons," *Phronesis*, 12 (1967), 28-49, and H.-N. Castaneda, "Plato's *Phaedo* Theory of Relations," *Journal of Philosophical Logic*, 1 (1972), 467-480. Though Castaneda's interpretation has raised controversy, he shows at the very least that later passages of the *Phaedo* can be interpreted in such a way as to explain why Plato sometimes talks as though relational predicates are monadic, without attributing to him the view that a relation can hold of a single object without regard to any others.

212

15. This objection seems to me crippling to the account of Plato's theory of Forms that is advanced by Alexander Nehamas, *op. cit.*, which is a version of the account developed by Owen (in line with the Murphy/Owen intepretation of this passage) and also, in a slightly different version, adopted by Gregory Vlastos, "Degrees of Reality in Plato," Renford Bambrough, ed., *New Essays on Plato and Aristotle* (New York, 1965), pp. 1-19. For Nehamas' account seems clearly to require that the Form of equal possess the property of equality "completely" and "in itself" (p. 116), by which Nehamas evidently means "nonrelationally." With this idea Nehamas seems to combine another one, that the Forms possess their properties *essentially, not accidentally* (*ibid.*). (For this idea see also Vlastos, *op. cit.*, p. 17, "All of [a Form's] properties must stick to it with logical glue.") Nehamas seems to be relying tacitly on the idea that there is some sort of connection between possessing a property essentially and possessing it nonrelationally. Perhaps he takes this connection to lie in the often-alleged impossibility of a thing's bearing an essential relation to some other thing (which is the denial of the traditional so-called Doctrine of Internal Relations). Unfortunately, he does not explain what he has in mind. In general, it seems plain that unless the connection is shown, essentiality is one thing and nonrelationality is quite another. It might be plausible to say that Plato took the Form of equal to be equal essentially, but this plausibility cannot be transferred to the idea that he took the Form of equal to be equal nonrelationally, as Nehamas' line of thought here seems to require.

    Independent of Nehamas' positive account there are also objections that he raises to the sort of account offered here. To those objections I turn in sec. 4.

16. See W. D. Ross, *Plato's Theory of Ideas* (Oxford, 1951), p. 23, and R. Hackforth, *Plato's Phaedo*, (Cambridge, England, 1955), p. 69.

17. To such interpretations as this Nehamas objects (p. 111) that it requires the equal to be "an impossible-object construction," something that appears equal from all angles. Not so (to pass over the fact—cf. n. 15—that an equal not equal to anything is quite as impossible). Plato's point is not that unlike sensibles, the equal appears equal from *all* angles. Rather it is that unlike sensibles, the equal does *not* appear *un*equal from *any* angles, because it doesn't, so to speak, *have* any angles. See further sec. 8.

    Nehamas seems to me clearly right, however, in rejecting the "approximation interpretation" of this passage, according to which only the Form of equal is exactly equal whereas sensible equals are only approximately equal. The approximation interpretation was also rejected by Owen, "A Proof," and Gregory Vlastos, "Degrees." See more recently Bostock, p. 73-74.

18. See Mills, p. 128; Gallop, p. 124-125; and Bostock, p. 83.

19. See for example Mills, p. 128; Gallop, p. 121; Mohan Matthen, "Forms and Participants in Plato's Phaedo," *Nous*, 18 (1984), 281-297; and Bostock, pp. 83-85.

20. Bostock. p. 84.

21. I think myself that Plato usually allows "contrary Forms," in spite of the fact that they seem to raise difficulties for his theory, as Gallop points out (p. 125). See Vlastos, "Degrees of Reality in Plato," pp. 7-8.

22. The person claiming that equality and inequality are both sensible will presumably claim that they are different sensible objects, but it is hard to imagine what the difference between them will then be said to be. That one is on Fourth Avenue and the other on Fifth Avenue? I think, in fact (though I cannot pursue the matter here), that Plato has in mind an opponent who believes that neither equality nor inequality is "a single thing," but that each, so to speak, is "many," i.e., equality is the many equal sensibles and inequality is the many unequal sensibles (see e.g., *Rep.* 479a4-5). The idea is probably that, for example, equality can be taken, depending on the circumstances, as any given

213

sensible instance of equality you like (comparison of this view with, say, Berkeley's is suggestive).

23. Nehamas, *op. cit.*, pp. 115-116.

24. Matthen, *op. cit.*, advances an interpretation that, like Bluck's earlier account (R. S. Bluck, "Plato's Form of Equal," *Phronesis*, 4 [1959], 5-11), finds in the argument not only Forms and sensibles but additional entities as well. Aside from points of detail (which I attempt to cover below), I think that both Matthen's interpretations and Bluck's introduce far more complexity into the argument than the text justifies (for example, Matthen, p. 291, requires the introduction of a complicated, non-trivial "unspoken lemma"). Plato presents his argument as a simple, brief, and straightforward one, not involving complicated background assumptions. It seems to me that that is how we ought to take it if we possibly can. (This does not, however, settle whether Plato *elsewhere*, as in *Phaedo* 102ff., introduces such entities as "Form copies" into his metaphysics.)

25. See G. E. L. Owen, "Dialectic and Eristic in the Treatment of the Forms," in G. E. L. Owen, ed., *Aristotle on Dialectic* (Oxford, 1963), pp. 103-125, esp. p. 114-115.

26. Gallop, pp. 123-124.

27. It is not clear that the same can be said of the argument for the same conclusion at *Rep.* 476-480.

28. Many interpreters have denied that that passage, and in general those passages that hold that sensibles are copies of Forms, support a strictly self-predicationist interpretation. See for example R. E. Allen, "Participation and Predication," Allen, ed., *op. cit.* pp. 43-60, esp. pp. 45-47. Gallop's view on the present passage (pp. 92-93, 125) is that Plato had not yet distinguished the descriptive and designative roles of such phrases as "the equal". Perhaps not (as I once agreed, *op. cit.*, pp. 64-65, 78 [n. 7], 86 [n. 54]). But *Meno* 73e-74b suggests otherwise (cf. *Rep.* 509a3). At any rate, my point here is that the present argument does not require for its cogency any implicit self-predicationist assumption, and our interpretation of the force of the argument itself should not incorporate one.

29. See e.g., *Phdo.* 109d-e, 11c; *Rep.* 515-516, 532b-c.

30. The recent discussion of this sort of matter goes back to Quine's paper, "Quantifiers and Propositional Attitudes," *Journal of Philosophy*, 53 (1956).

31. See, for example, Matthen, p. 285.

32. I add "ways of thinking about an object" to allow for the possibility that an object may be introduced into a belief by some means other than a strictly linguistic designation. Though important in other connections, this qualification is unimportant here.

33. Note that there is a distinction at work after our argument between ἐννοεῖν and ἐπίστασθαι, which is relevant to Plato's views about recollection.

34. I take this to be the import of 195e-196a, esp. 195e1-3, 196a2, though the matter is complex.

35. See, e.g., *Rep.* 602e and *Soph.* 235e-236a.

36. "Degrees of Reality," p. 7. The reason why I would disagree with his way of explaining the matter is that he accepts something rather closer to the Murphy/Owen account of Plato's attitude to predicates like "equal" than I would (cf. sec. 3).

214

Perceptual and Objective Properties in Plato

Nicholas P. White

This paper synoptically expounds an interpretation of Plato's views about how we understand the terms that we apply to sensible objects and that he also thinks we can apply to Forms.[1] The exposition is condensed, omits many relevant issues, and lacks many references that I would include in a longer presentation. One of my aims here is to explain an important feature of Joan Kung's work.

I

Since Russell, Plato has often been accused of being confused about relations.[2] The most direct form of the charge has been discredited, but it persists in a different form, derived from Aristotle by G. E. L. Owen. Even this form, as I shall show here, is mistaken. But it is not merely mistaken. It misses the point of Plato's treatment of the notions he is accused of being confused about. It makes us focus on a simple distinction between properties and relations instead of the much more complex problems about reality and objectivity with which he was concerned.

---

1 The exposition is a summary of some work that I did years ago. It has been impossible for me to revise it to take full account of various things that have been published since.

2 See Bertrand Russell, *A History of Western Philosophy* (New York 1945), 150.

The extreme form of the charge says that Plato ignored all distinction between properties and relations. But Plato explicitly attends to relational predicates, e.g., to the fact that a sensible object cannot be a brother without being a brother of something (*Symp* 199e). This fact is now generally recognised.[3]

The other form of the accusation, leveled by Owen, says that the predicates Plato was primarily interested in, which Owen calls 'incomplete' predicates, are really disguised relational terms that Plato mistreats by sometimes regarding them as monadic.[4]

Owen adduces various instances of this mistreatment. For one thing, Plato mentions Forms like the Form of Large, without saying clearly that as we use the word, 'large' expresses a comparative relation, not a property. For example, in *Phaedo* 102b-c he says that the sentence, 'Simmias is larger than Socrates', reveals the facts less accurately than the sentence, 'Socrates has shortness in relation to Simmias's largeness'.[5] Moreover he repeatedly makes use of simple predications like 'Simmias is large'.

Hector-Neri Castañeda has denied that this manner of speaking shows confusion.[6] For even though Plato often speaks as though largeness and smallness are properties, Castañeda points out that he can be interpreted as holding that they are 'tied' to each other in a way that makes his view substantially equivalent to a more orthodox way of construing relations.

Even so, Plato's view raises questions. For even if his theory of 'tied' Forms is in one way equivalent to the view of relations that we now accept, what makes him claim it more revealing to say that Socrates has shortness in comparison to Simmias's largeness than it is to say that Socrates is shorter than Simmias? This claim clearly indicates that

---

3 See for example E. Scheibe, 'Über Relativbegriffe in der Philosophie Platons', *Phronesis* 12 (1967) 28-49; H. N. Castañeda, 'Plato's *Phaedo* Theory of Relations', *Journal of Philosophical Logic* 1 (1972) 467-80.

4 G. E. L. Owen, 'A Proof in the *Peri Ideon*', R. E. Allen, *Studies in Plato's Metaphysics* (New York 1965) 293-312, reprinted in Owen, *Logic, Science and Dialectic* (Ithaca 1986) 165-79, esp. pp. 177-9.

5 The present issue is independent of whether Plato is saying that heights are accidental rather than essential properties.

6 Castañeda, 'Plato's *Phaedo* Theory'

Plato would not regard his view of relations as a mere notational variant of ours, but rather thinks – as Castañeda emphasises – that it more accurately represents the structure of things. Moreover, why does Plato so persistently refer to Forms by using positive terms like 'large' rather than comparative terms like 'larger'?[7] And what can be the basis of Aristotle's charge that Plato posits 'a non-relative class of relatives,' which seems to mean, Owen argued, that in associating relative terms with Forms, Plato treats them as if they were non-relative?[8] Plainly there are indications here of a view of relations different from our own.

Owen took these indications to be signs of confusion partly because he believed that Plato accepted what Gregory Vlastos called a 'self-predicational' view of Forms, according to which the Form of F is predicatively *F*.[9] For instance, the Form of Large is large, the Form of Equal is equal, and so on. Owen's view involves treating the terms as nonrelational when they are used to describe Forms, so that even if every equal *sensible* object is equal *to* something, the Form of Equal is taken to be equal but not equal *to* anything.[10]

Quite apart from self-predication (on which I shall have a little to say, in Sec. V), Owen's interpretation imputes to Plato a confusion about relations, namely, the belief that even if every equal *sensible object* that is equal must be equal to something, it still makes sense to conceive of *something* as equal but not equal to anything, and in general of something as bearing a relation R without bearing R to anything.

This seems such an eccentric view that one wonders how anyone could hold it.[11] But as we have seen Plato's propensity to use relational-seeming terms in a nonrelational-seeming way is strong enough to require explanation.

The scope of this discussion, however, will include more than just a limited class of predicates. Plato does not deal only with ones we

---

7 Similarly, there is a related question why he formulates the Principle of Non-contradiction in the way that he does in *Rep* IV 436a *sqq.*

8 Owen, 'A Proof in the *Peri Ideon*', 177-79

9 Gregory Vlastos, 'The Third Man Argument in the *Parmenides*', *Philosophical Review* 63 (1954) 319-49, reprinted in Allen, ed. 231-63

10 Owen, 'A Proof in the *Peri Ideon*', 310-12

11 See, e.g., Terry Penner, *The Ascent From Nominalism* (Dordrecht 1987), 48-9.

would immediately classify as relational. He treats many others as well, and is concerned with broader issues about reality and objectivity.

II

A predicate like 'hard', used as an example at *Republic* 523e-4a, illustrates Plato's view well. Consider the notion of hardness and our way of judging that a thing is hard by feeling it. Later I shall introduce judgments other than perceptual ones (sec. III), but here shall treat just these. Now a thing that would be said in one context to be hard would in another context be said to be not hard but soft. A day-old loaf of bread might, in a context in which it is being compared to a fresh doughnut, be thought of as being hard, but when it is compared to a block of steel, it might be thought of as being soft.

Consider what conscious reflection suggests is the content of the judgment that a thing is hard. Plainly the acceptability of the judgment varies with circumstances. Nevertheless when one reflects on what one seems to have in mind when one makes such a judgment, it is clear that no relativity enters into the notion expressed by the term 'hard'. Does one seem to have it in mind, when one feels the loaf, that it is, e.g., 'harder-than-the-doughnut,' or 'hard-in-comparison-to-these-baked-goods-? Reflection does not indicate any such thing. What one does think, it appears, is that the loaf is *hard*, period.

It may well be that such reflection is not a reliable guide to the real 'contents' of our thoughts or judgments. But my attention for now is confined only to the facts that reflection seems to reveal.

A similar response seems appropriate to the idea that a term like 'hard' expresses a relation to a kind or type rather than to particular members of it. Positive terms often seem to be tied to 'base predicates.' We speak of a 'tiny hippo', or a 'gigantic gnat' or, similarly, 'soft iron' or 'hard cheese'. These phrases suggest that even if 'hard' is not replaceable by 'harder than such-and-such', it might be replaceable by 'hard such-and-such' or 'hard for a such-and-such' or 'hard in comparison to (the class of) such-and-suches'. Other words that Plato associates with Forms, like 'beautiful' and 'good', might seem to call for similar treatment.

But if we take reflection as our guide it seems that base predicates need no more enter into the content of judgments about hardness or goodness than a reference to particular individuals does. A judgment that *a* is beautiful does not by any means always present itself as a judgment that *a* is a beautiful *F*. Likewise, even if a thing can be taken to be hard-for-a-loaf-of-bread, still a loaf can also be taken to be just plain hard.[12]

The same point holds for many terms that might ordinarily be taken to be 'covertly' comparative, such as 'heavy', 'soft', 'large', 'thick', and so forth, and that are used by Plato in illustrating his views about Forms (see, e.g., *Rep* 479b, 523e-4b). When a person makes an ordinary perceptual judgment using one of these terms, what often presents itself to one's mind is a judgment that lacks any relational or comparative element, and seems to be a straightforward ascription of a property to an object. Judgments like these are completely ignored in interpetations of Plato, but are an important part of what he was examining.

Republic 523a-4b, for example, shows his outlook clearly. Speaking of the limitations of perceptual judgments, Plato says that it is 'outlandish' (see ἄτοποι, 524b1) that perception can present the same thing as having 'contrary' properties (ἐναντίον, 523c3). Sight can present a finger as simultaneously both large and small, and the senses can also indicate that the same thing is both thick and thin, hard and soft, or heavy and light. Plato's description and argument show that he is thinking of the content of a perception as not containing any relativisation. Otherwise there would obviously be no 'contrariety' and nothing 'outlandish' about the pairs of judgments mentioned.

In my view, Plato focused on the positive terms that I have described, and used them as the basis of his account of Forms.

Owen's view was that Plato was confused because he missed the fact that many of the terms he was examining really *are* relational because they are comparative.[13] Owen seems to have assumed that there is some now-obvious way, which Plato missed, to replace the positive terms by comparative ones.

---

12 For some cases one may feel that Owen was clearly right and that Plato was indeed confused. Many would say that this is true of terms like 'one' and 'many', which he treats as one-place predicates. It seems clear that, as Frege argued, that sort of treatment leads to devastating difficulties. Some might further urge that even by the test of conscious reflection, there is no way to think of an object as just 'one,' for example, without thinking of it, quite explicitly, as one such-and-such. I doubt that that is right, but since these cases seem to be to be in doubt, I shall put them aside and confine myself to the other sorts of cases, which dominate his discussions.

13 Owen, 'A Proof', 174, takes some terms to be 'concealed comparatives.'

It is a mistake, though, to think that Plato was missing something straightforward. For it turns out to be far more difficult than Owen supposed to explain the positive forms in relational terms.[14]

Even a term like 'large' — whch at first sight seems somehow to involve a comparison but which Plato often uses in a nonrelational form — turns out to be surprisingly resistant to relational paraphrase. When one calls an elephant or a flea large, then even when a base predicate like 'elephant' or 'flea' is supplied to indicate a reference class, it is not at all easy to identify informatively either which particular thing one is saying the elephant or the flea is larger than, or what rank within the reference class the thing must occupy. This point is made clear by helpful recent philosophical literature on this issue, which the reader should consult. It will not do, for example, to say that a large flea is a flea larger than the average flea. Nor does any other straightforward paraphrase of 'large *G*' seem to be possible.[15]

In the absence of a paraphrase there are other ways of treating the positive notions as fundamentally comparative and relational. For one thing, we could say that the positives are disguised comparatives but that the standard of comparison is determined 'pragmatically' by the context in a way that permits no general account. Other ways might be also suggested, though there is no space to pursue them here.

Or we could dispense with the positive forms altogether and say only what can be said with the comparatives alone.[16] But that would be to hold that in a sense all of the sentences in which we use the positive forms are misguided. This seems counterintuitive, especially since these forms are so thoroughly entrenched in our judgments.[17]

The conclusion so far is that there is a genuine and unquestionable phenomenon of our judgments that Plato was attempting to deal with,

---

14 Owen thinks that Plato sometimes takes the positive notion, as applied to a Form, to be equivalent to the superlative ('A Proof', 178-9). Although I cannot discuss this matter here, I think that Owen's view is unwarranted (the reason will be glanced at in sec. V).

15 See John Wallace, 'Positive, Comparative, Superlative', *Journal of Philosophy* 69 (1972) 773-82; Samuel Wheeler, 'Attributive and their Modifiers', *Nous* 6 (1972) 310-34; and Philip Kitcher, 'Positive Understatement: the Logic of Attributive Adjectives', *Journal of Philosophical Logic* 7 (1978) 1-17.

16 The superlatives can obviously be defined in terms of the comparatives — see Wallace, 775.

17 See Kitcher.

and that the phenomenon cannot be whisked away, even today, by any obvious paraphrase. The phenomenon and Plato's way of dealing with it are concealed by Owen's suggestion that Plato's failure to treat the terms in question as 'incomplete' was a blunder. Whether Plato's treatment is ultimately acceptable is of course quite another matter. I am not here going to try to defend it. But I am going to try to discover what it was.

III

Even if no relativisation enters into the *content*, as it appears to reflection, of the perceptual judgment that a thing is hard, we can still allow that *something* about such judgments is indeed relational. This something can be vaguely called 'conditions of acceptable use'. It is important to sidestep for now the question whether 'acceptable' is tantamount to 'true'. Otherwise more issues will crowd in than we shall be able to cope with here. The kind of acceptability in question can be illustrated as follows. As we saw, if you press a loaf of bread just after pressing a block of steel, it will typically be unacceptable for you to judge that the loaf is hard. It will typically be acceptable, however, to judge that it is hard just after you have pressed a feather pillow.

If we accept these facts at face value, then we need to conclude that whereas the content expressed by the sentence, 'This loaf is hard', makes no reference to the surrounding circumstances, a statement of its conditions of the acceptability must make such a reference. In and of itself this difference between content and conditions of acceptability is perhaps not terribly surprising. It makes such sentences in some ways like demonstrative expressions. It also raises questions about their interpretation that I shall have to ignore here. In addition, however, it prompts a question about how Plato viewed them that we shall have to address.

That question is, what in the circumstances is the acceptability of such a judgment relative to? I wish to argue that in Plato's opinion what is relevant about the circumstances is the *perspective*, either of perception or thought, from which the judgment is made.[18] The way to

---

18 For present purposes I need to help myself to an unexplained notion of perspective that covers both perception, in an obvious way, and also thought, in a less obvious but nevertheless intuitively familiar way having to do with what one is thinking about in making a judgment.

make it acceptable to judge that Simmias is *large*, for example, is to look at him or think about him in a certain context, next to or in comparison with someone shorter. The judgment will be acceptable to the judger if he is looking at or thinking about Simmias in the right way, and will be acceptable to others if they are doing so too.

The relativity of such judgments to the judger's perspective seems to me to be hinted at in certain ways that English has of formulating them. Sometimes we might say, for example, 'Compared to a block of steel, this loaf is soft', or 'Compared to a feather pillow, this loaf is hard'. One could take these as just meaning, respectively, 'This loaf is softer than a block of steel', and, 'This loaf is harder than a feather pillow', but it does not seem that that conveys the same idea. Instead these judgments might be classed with 'This loaf is soft' and 'This loaf is hard' as explained above but with modifying clauses indicating the points of view from which the judgments are taken to be acceptable.

At the same time, it should now be noted, such judgments need not and usually do not contain a relativisation to perspectival circumstances as part of their content. 'Compared to a block of steel, this loaf is soft' is in some circumstances an amplification of 'This loaf is soft', not an articulation of its full meaning. Although in a given case the acceptability of '*a* is soft' may depend on the judger's adopting a certain perspective, that does not mean that the content of the judgment that he makes contains a reference to that perspective or its circumstances. Certainly it does not if we take conscious reflection as our guide, and, as before (sec. II), it is not evident what paraphrase would be adequate.

Once we recognise that the contents of such judgments are also unrelativised to perspective, we see how to apply the foregoing observations to far more than simply the positive terms that are associated with comparatives. Whether a book can acceptably be called red very often depends on perspectival circumstances—not just on the circumambient light, but on such things as whether, if the book is a bit toward the orange side, it is physically near, or thought about in conjunction with, other books that are slightly less so.[19] So it is in point to remark that in such cases the reference to those circumstances may

---

19 I owe this example, and very helpful conversation on this topic, to David Hills.

well not enter into the content of the judgment at all: usually one simply judges that the book is red, just as one judges that the loaf is hard.[20]

Let us turn back to Plato. Whatever may be true of the aforementioned English sentences, I think that an interpretation involving relativity to perspective yields the only way of accounting for his way of treating perceptual judgments. To begin with, I would cite a set of passages in which he persistently directly infers claims about how things are from claims about how they appear. In *Republic* 479a-c he concludes, from the fact that a thing can appear or be called both beautiful and ugly or both double and half, that it *is* no more the one than the other. And at *Phaedo* 74b-d, as commentators have often complained, he infers that things can fail to *be* unproblematically equal from the fact that sometimes they can *appear* unequal.

It has often seemed tempting to object that such an inference of 'is' from 'appears' is too obviously invalid for Plato to have accepted it. Owen tries to obliterate it by suggesting that Plato's point has nothing to do with appearances, but is merely that a thing can be equal to one thing but not another.[21] Aside from ignoring the repeated occurrence in the passage of the word 'appears', φαίνεσθαι, this interpretation also forces the result that the Form of Equal is equal without being equal *to* anything. Owen embraces this bizarre consequence, but others rightly take it as too outlandish—far more outlandish than an inference of 'is' from 'appears'!—to be attributed to Plato on such slim evidence.[22] As others have held and as I have argued elsewhere, the passage itself is better interpreted otherwise than Owen takes it.[23] Its

---

20 It is relevant here, I think, that many terms (including 'red') that may seem not to be associated with comparatives really are so, or, in other words, are 'matters of degree' in the sense recently explored by Rayme E. Engel, 'On Degrees', *Journal of Philosophy* 86 (1989) 23-37.

21 Owen, 'A Proof', 177-9.

22 Owen held that this strange idea could be attributed to Plato on the ground that, as Owen thought, Aristotle seems to attack Plato for just such an idea in *Sophistici Elenchi*, c. 31. I think Owen is probably wrong about what Aristotle meant, but even if he were right, I do not think that the attack would be a fair one.

23 'Forms and Sensibles', *Philosophical Topics* 15 (1987) 197-214. Earlier, however, I wrongly accepted Owen's interpretation: *Plato on Knowledge and Reality* (Indianapolis 1976), 66-9. Owen does note the possibility of the perspectival interpretation, at p. 306, n. 2.

contention—the contention that Plato needs for his argument there—is that there is always a perspective from which equal things can acceptably be said to *be* unequal, for example when they are viewed obliquely.

One must not mistake this contention for a thoroughgoing relativism. The contention does not mean that whenever two things appear from some perspective to be unequal, a measurement of them must justify the conclusion that they are in fact unequal. Measurement is quite another matter.[24] But the contention does mean that a perceptual judgment can yield a certain sort of nonrelational judgment about how a thing is. This sort of judgment, however, can come into conflict with a judgment from another source of judgments about sensible objects, namely, reason. This fact is obscured for some readers by *Republic* 476-480, which is often taken to say that sensible objects can be cognised only by perception.[25] But Plato also indicates clearly that some of our judgments about sensibles are arrived at partly by thinking and not by perception alone.

Clear examples of this sort of judgment appear in passages where Plato says that measurement can deliver well-founded judgments about sensibles. For example, *Euthyphro* 7c-d says that measurement can determine which of two lengths is greater when there is a dispute (a dispute that must be taken to have arisen from estimates made by eye), and that a scale can determine (better than mere feel) which of two things weighs more. The same idea crops up in *Republic* X. At 602c-3a Plato says that measuring and weighing can help us correct the deliverances of perception, *even though* if A is closer to the eye than B, the perception that A is longer than B persists in the face of the considered judgment, based on measurement, that B is longer than A. There are two conflicting judgments here, which Plato locates in different parts of the soul. He then goes on to apply the same idea to evaluative judgments. He contrasts the man who meets the death of his son simply with the grief-stricken reaction that the only thing for him to do is to

---

24 One of the main points of the *Theaetetus*, I think, is precisely to show that Plato's own views about perception did not commit him to a relativistic position like Protagoras's.

25 I made this mistake in *Plato on Knowledge and Reality*, 106. The mistake is criticized by Gail Fine, 'Knowledge and Belief in *Republic* V', *Archiv für Geschichte der Philosophie* 60 (1978) 121-39.

break down, with someone who, in addition to feeling grief, also reasons out exactly what is bad about his situation and which actions will ameliorate it (603e-4d). Again there are two conflicting judgments about what to do, Plato holds, and two parts of the soul that make them (604d).[26]

Although Plato does not analyse the procedures of weighing and measuring as fully as one would like,[27] he clearly thinks of them as involving more than simple perceptual judgments. Likewise the rational judgments in *Republic* X, by contrast to those of the grief-stricken man, plainly involve some kind of calculation of benefits and harms caused by different actions—an idea that also surfaces in *Theaetetus* 184-6. These are judgments of rational prudence, comparable to those that are contrasted in the *Gorgias* with the thoughtless reactions of Callicles, the hedonist of the present moment.[28] But Plato also allows for ascriptions about goodness that involve more than one individual.[29]

In general, evaluative predicates like 'good', 'just', and 'beautiful', as they figure in ordinary people's evaluations, provide good illustrations of Plato's treatment. He believes that the terms carry unrelativised contents, but that people often misguidedly take them so as to apply and withhold them on the basis of perspectival circumstances alone. The contents of judgments in which people ordinarily ascribe these features are unrelativised because people often judge that things are 'good' or 'just', not that they are 'good-for-X' or 'just-by-such-and-such-standards'. In *Republic* 505d-e, for example, Plato says that people seek what really is good, and although he agrees that people often think that justice is relative to local interests or standards, as *Republic* I-II makes evident, he holds that some people, like Glaucon and Adeimantus, think that there is such as thing as nonrelative justice whose nature they would like to discover. At the same time, however, he recognises that generally people accept or reject evaluations depending on their point of view.[30] Here too the acceptability of these types

---

26 See my *Companion to Plato's Republic* (Indianapolis 1979), 256.

27 The *Philebus* may be attempting such an analysis.

28 See my 'Rational Prudence in Plato's *Gorgias*', Dominic J. O'Meara, ed., *Platonic Investigations* (Washington 1985) 139-62.

29 See my 'Rulers' Choice', *Archiv für Geschichte der Philosophie* 68 (1986) 22-46.

30 E. g., *Euthyph* 6e-7d; *Phdr* 263a; *Alc I* 111a-12c; *Rep* 524a.

of evaluative judgments depends, in some sense, on the judgers' perspectives, even when the contents of the judgments are not relational. Here the perspectives involve more than perception in the narrow sense of 'sense-perception'. They include, in particular, such things as reactions of pleasure and pain to a thing, which Plato often calls αἰσθήσεις and regards as standing to many ordinary judgments about goodness or justice as tactile experiences stand to judgments about hardness or hotness.[31]

Beside these passages there is another reason for interpreting Plato as holding that the acceptability of the relevant judgments varies with perspective. In this way we come to understand his uniform treatment of certain terms that he associates with Forms. These are the terms that Owen calls 'incomplete predicates,' i.e., predicates that require some 'completion' in their application to sensibles.[32]

Owen had to regard these as merely a grab-bag collection, because he thought—mistakenly, as we have seen—that the relativity had to enter into the *contents* of the judgments, and could not see any unifying thread running through all of the appropriate-seeming 'completions'. On his interpretation, an 'incomplete' predicate applies to sensible objects only when actually supplemented by a 'qualification', which could be, e.g., a reference to something to which a comparison was being made, or to an evaluative standard, or in still other cases such as 'one', a principle of division. On this interpretation, no single philosophical consideration could motivate Plato's concern with these particular predicates.

But the set of predicates that Plato typically cites is in fact unified by his consistent concern with the way in which perspectival variation affects the acceptability of our perceptual judgments about sensible objects. In each case, I would maintain, Plato turns out on examination not to be concerned with the judgment whose content is that *a* is *F* relative to *b* while it is non-*F* relative to *c*—e.g., with the judgment whose content is that Simmias is taller than Socrates but shorter than Phaedo. Instead, he is focusing on the fact that when it is considered from a particular vantage point, *a* may be acceptably judged to be *F*, but when it is considered differently, it is acceptably judged to be non-*F*. So, by the standards that are applied to such judg-

---

31 See *Companion to Plato's Republic*, 252-53, 256.

32 See generally Owen, 'A Proof', 172-9.

ments, when we see Simmias standing next to Socrates it is acceptable to judge that Simmias is *tall*, whereas it is acceptable to judge that
he is *short* when we see him standing next to Phaedo. Likewise, when
considering something from a particular perspective (say, that of someone having certain interests), a person acceptably judges it good,
whereas one acceptably judges it bad when one regards it differently.
Even though 'tall' and 'good' are different sorts of predicates, Plato
justifiably treats them alike in the respect indicated.

IV

Plato's views about change in the the sensible world are notoriously
hard to interpret. The foregoing line of interpretation, I think, also
has the advantage of allowing us to integrate those views into the
rest of this account of sensible objects and our judgments about them.

We have seen that no sensible object can always be acceptably said
to be hard because each such object that may in one context be taken
to be hard may be taken in another to be soft. In addition, Plato seems
to think that no sensible object can always be acceptably said to be
a triangle, or golden, or a house, because anything that is a triangle,
say, at one time is differently shaped at some other time (e.g., *Tim*
49a-51b). The trouble is that although these two issues seem to be
quite different from each other, Plato treats them as if they were on
a par. For—one wants to say—before something ceases to be a triangle it *is* a triangle, and after it turns into a square it *is* a square, whereas it is wrong to say that a thing *is* tall at some times but *is not* tall
at others.

According to Owen, Plato's theory of Forms did not initially deal
much with change at all. Rather, Owen thinks, Plato was first concerned only with 'incomplete' predicates and then later decided, because of 'a greater preoccupation with mutability,' that all predicates
are incomplete as applied to sensibles, since 'all apply at one time and
not at another.'[33] In spite of what Owen says, though, earlier dialogues
such as the *Phaedo* show just as much preoccupation with mutability
as later works (see, e.g., 70d-1d, 78d-80b). And Owen himself admits

---

33 Owen, 'A Proof' 175-7

that the issue of change arises in the *Republic* and the *Symposium*, where the 'incomplete' predicates are prominent too.[34]

This, however, is a superficial feature of Owen's interpretation. If one puts it aside, one is left with the view that Plato holds that every predicate, including ones that are not overtly 'incomplete', applies to sensibles only with 'qualification'. As I have said (Sec. III), this collection of qualifications seems like a grab-bag and it is difficult to see any clear philosophical motivation that would have led Plato to thinking that it yields a clear way of thinking about how sensible objects possess their properties. One would certainly prefer a more unified interpretation.

One of the rare interpretations that deserves mention for trying to face this issue, the interpretation offered by Terence Irwin, is subject to similar difficulties.[35] Irwin sees two different kinds of 'change' in Plato, which he calls A-change and B-change. A-change is what is at issue when one says that the same thing can be now large, compared to Socrates, and now small, compared to Phaedo. B-change is at issue when the same thing is first red and then blue, or itself grows. But Irwin does not explain why Plato would have regarded these two kinds of 'change' as at all on a par with each other or why both deserve the title 'change'. In fact, what Irwin calls A-change does not seem a kind of *change* at all. As before, one would prefer to interpret Plato in a more uniform way. Indeed, it seems to me a reasonable condition of adequacy on any interpretation of Plato's view that it be capable of explaining his emphatic tendency to lump these two phenomena together.

I think that the interpretation that I have been suggesting will do that. When Plato considers change he is once again concerned with an issue about the contents of our perceptual judgments and the perspectives from which we make them. And as before, he recognises a difficulty in hastily construing our ordinary judgments as relational.

---

34 Owen, *Logic* ..., 307. In view of *Symp* 206-8, it is difficult to see why Owen classes that dialogue as not interested in change. Moreover Owen is clearly wrong when he says (p. 308) that the argument from the *Peri Ideon* that he is examining 'ignores this extension of the theory.' In fact, the argument explicitly raises the issue of change, in the section that Owen labels II(b) — a fact that Owen has to go to some lengths to minimize 308-9).

35 Terence H. Irwin, 'Plato's Heracliteanism', *Philosophical Quarterly* 27 (1977) 1-13

Suppose that you give a name to an apple, say 'Pom', and then you look at it and say, 'Pom is red'. But earlier the apple was green and later it will be rotten and brown, so when taken in some contexts, past and future, the judgment that it is red is unacceptable. One response is to say that 'Pom is red' really has a relational content, with a tacit indication of time. This is like saying that 'Simmias is large' is a disguised comparative, except that this time the paraphrase seems easier to come by: 'Pom is red' means 'Pom is red *now*'. A less plausible paraphrase, but a possible way of regimenting the sentence, might be 'Pom is red on August 11, 1988'. (There are other ways of coping with this situation, but I leave them aside as unlikely to have been dreamed of by Plato.)

But just as there was reason to be uneasy about relational paraphrases of 'Simmias is large', there is also reason to be uneasy about any paraphrase of the content of 'Pom is red'. To conscious reflection it is not at all clear that they actually contain any indication of relativity to time.[36] In particular, it seems to me very unlikely that the content of one's judgment in this case is simply that of 'Pom is red at the present instant'. Clearly one does not ordinarily mean to be restricting the scope of one's judgment as radically as that. Nor does one seem to have in mind anything quite like 'Pom is red roundabout now', as if one had a vaguely demarcated interval in mind but not quite pinned down, such as the 'specious present' or something a bit longer. Nor, of course, does one have any precisely specifiable interval in mind either. The same remarks seem to hold for 'Pom is an apple'. So I think that there is some reason to believe that there is no obvious temporally relational paraphrase of the contents of such judgments, just as there was no obvious one for 'This loaf of bread is hard' or 'Simmias is large'.

If the present tense in these judgments appears to indicate that the time in question includes the present, that indication can be eliminated by the use of so-called 'tenseless' verbs, which seem to be recognised by Plato at *Timaeus* 37c-8b,[37] and are common coin nowadays. The idea of tenseless verbs is similar to the one being discussed here.

---

36 For related observations a propos of problems about adverbs in general see, e.g., John Wallace, 'Some Logical Roles of Adverbs', *Journal of Philosophy* 68 (1971) 690-714.

37 See Owen, 'Plato and Parmenides on the Timeless Present', *Logic, Science and Dialectic*, 27-44.

But more than just *tense*lessness is involved in Plato's idea. As the same passage of the *Timaeus* makes clear, he is saying (as many others have said since) that there is a class of facts that are *time*less, i.e., not *in* time at all, and that judgments about them can be made in which any idea of position in time at all is completely absent (37e3-5 and ff.). *Not* that these facts hold at *all* times: Plato says explicitly that time is only an 'image' of the 'eternity' in which these facts hold (37d5-7). Rather, when we think of something as timelessly red, we can as it were *put aside* all thought of there being such a thing as a temporal dimension at all in which the fact is embedded. Moreover the predicates themselves express properties like redness or roundness, not temporal relations like red-at-*t*-ness or round-at-*t*-ness.

V

Plato's construal of ordinary perceptual judgments leaves us with a set of predicates whose standards of application in the sensible world are relative to perspectival circumstances but whose contents themselves are taken not to be so. We must now see briefly how he thinks these nonperspectival senses are to be understood.

According to Plato, anyone who makes such judgments about sensibles adequately must have knowledge or understanding of the appropriate Forms. Here I make a long story short. In *Republic* 522-5, for example, he argues that the clear understanding of any term that applies to sensibles only if its contrary does too requires some kind of grasp of the corresponding Form. And the whole *Republic* is the story of why it is necessary to have knowledge of the Forms if one is to rule a city adequately and tell which arrangements are just (see esp. *Rep.* 540-1).

One role of Forms in Plato's theory is to help explain what it is for us to understand the terms that we use. To understand the term F is to cognise, in some sense, the Form of F. But remember that the notion expressed here by F does not include a reference either to relata or to the circumstances of acceptable application; rather, it is the unrelativised, 'objective' notion that I have been explaining. To cognise the Form of F in the relevant sense, then, is to grasp the notion *of something that is* an F, period, and to which the application of the term F does not depend on perspectival circumstances in the way that applications to sensible objects do. We can call this use of 'F' an 'objective' use, i.e., a use that allows it to be applied under standards of acceptability that are not constituted, as the standards of acceptability that seem to govern perceptual judgments are constituted, by any particular relation of the judger to his perspective.

Plato believes, as we have seen, that the content of a perceptual judgment about sensibles is positive, unrelativised, and 'objective'. This means that even though we may often recognise the role that circumstances play in its acceptability, in a sense it attempts to apply to a sensible a term whose actual content does not apply to it. The content of the judgment conveys the misleading impression that its conditions of acceptability are different from what they in fact are.

Moreover the sensible objects and the spatio-temporal manifold containing them collaborate with us in producing the impression that the objective senses of these terms *do* apply to those objects. This is how sensibles, in the language of *Phaedo* 74e-5a, 'try' to be like Forms but do not succeed. It is also how Plato thinks we can mistake sensibles for Forms. He does not have in mind a straightforward case of believing that a sensible object is a Form.[38] Rather, he thinks that we make certain judgments about sensible objects whose contents are in a sense inapplicable to those objects. To call a sensible object hard, for example, is to treat it as something that it could not be, namely, as capable of being acceptably judged by perception to be hard *in a sense* to which the perspectival circumstances were irrelevant.

The important question that Plato's view raises is whether these 'objective' notions actually can be made sense of. Can we understand the idea of something's being in the relevant sense objectively, e.g., hard or large or hot or thick or, on the evaluative side, good or just or holy or beautiful (*Rep* 479a-b, 523e-4a)? The nature and severity of the problem varies depending on the predicate one picks and one's views about it. Philosophers differ, for example, on whether there is a coherent notion of beauty with standards of acceptability independent of facts about the beholder's perspective. Some predicates, however, seem clearly problematical. For instance it is hard to see what anyone could make of the idea of something's being 'objectively large', even if it is admitted — as seemingly it must be (cf. sec. III) — that 'large' in some uses seems irreducible in any straightforward fashion to a comparative relational term. The notion of objective hotness presents

---

38 See Alexander Nehamas, 'Confusing Universals and Particulars in Plato's Early Dialogues', *Review of Metaphysics* 29 (1975-76) 287-306.

problems that are in some ways the same and in some ways different. At any rate, all of these notions raise difficulties. His discussion of them is obviously a part of his overall discussion of the nature of the Forms.

But this problem is not to be confused with the problem about 'self-predication' mentioned earlier (Sec. II). Plato finds himself on the verge of being committed to the *intelligibility of the notion* of something's being objectively hard, just, etc. The important question about Forms is not whether they themselves *instantiate* such notions but whether the notions themselves are intelligible. Aristotle criticizes Plato in ways that certainly suggest that one account of the Forms in the Academy was a self-predicational one.[39] But even Aristotle does not dwell on self-predication nearly as much as recent scholarly literature has, or nearly as much as he himself dwells on other issues concerning the Forms— as a glance at *Metaphysics* I 9, e.g., clearly shows. Moreover although Plato frequently uses the language of paradeigmatism to describe the relation between sensibles and Forms, it is often rightly urged that that language can be taken as both highly metaphorical and free from literal self-predicational implications. Accordingly I am inclined to regard the whole issue of self-predication as peripheral. The problem that Plato focused on, and that we should focus on too, is the problem of making sense of the objective notions that he seemingly is committed to.

In some cases, particularly the evaluative ones, it is clear what his response was. The *Republic* is a sustained attempt to defend an objective notion of justice under which a city-state or a person can be acceptably called just independently of one's point of view or even one's own self-interest. It also adumbrates similar notions of goodness as well as moderation and courage and holiness,[40] as the *Symposium* points to one of beauty (esp. 211a). Even if one does not think that any such accounts are possible or agree with his, at least it is clear what he is trying to obtain.

VI

But in many of the non-evaluative cases, as just noted, Plato's task looks much more difficult. Most commentators have not seen that he had

---

39 See Owen, 'A Proof', and 'The Platonism of Aristotle', *Logic, Science, and Dialectic* 200-20, esp. 207-11.

40 See my 'Rulers' Choice', esp. 41-6.

such a task to begin with, because they have not taken seriously his positive, noncomparative notions. But once one does take them seriously, something else important about Plato's work starts to fall into place, namely, the point of the *Timaeus* in his overall philosophical project. And here we are indebted to Joan Kung for emphasising more than anyone else recently that the *Timaeus* is a philosophically serious work, not simply a piece of scientific or cosmological speculation.[41]

The first way in which the *Timaeus* is important emerges from the point raised at the end of section IV about timelessness. Although Plato had sometimes spoken – in the *Symposium* for example – as though the Forms possessed their natures for all time, the *Timaeus* revises and clarifies his view on this matter. In 37-38, as we saw (sec. IV), he insists that the Forms are not in time at all, and possess their natures not always but timelessly. On the interpretation that I suggested, this means the following. The Form of F represents the notion of something's being F apart from any notion of a temporal dimension within which it is judged to be F. Thus, to grasp the notion of something's being F is to grasp something in which the idea of a place in a temporal order does not figure. A god, so to speak, could grasp all of the notions that Plato treats without grasping any notion of time whatever. To the extent that we grasp these notions adequately, Plato thinks, we approximate that state.

The other way in which the *Timaeus* shows Plato doing important work on his own theory is connected with an important insight of Kung's, who realised that Plato's explanations of characteristics like hotness, lightness, hardness, roughness, and the like (61d sqq., 62c sqq., 63e-4a), as well as features like pleasantness and painfulness (64a sqq.), color properties, olfactory properties, and so on (64a sqq., 65-8), are intended not simply as explanations of phenomena but as *identifications* of perceptual or quasi-perceptual properties with microstructural features of physical bodies. She also noted that they were treated as identifications in the Academy and were, as such, frequently opposed by Aristotle.

Her insight suggests the following view of Plato's aims in the *Timaeus*. If the earlier parts of this paper are correct, then Plato

---

41 See esp. Joan Kung, 'How Learning Mathematics Helps Us Be Virtuous', John Anton and Anthony Preus, eds., *Essays in Ancient Greek Philosophy*, III (forthcoming).

sorely needed to explain how there could be objective, perspective-independent properties corresponding to terms like 'hard', 'heavy', and so on. It makes sense to think that in the *Timaeus* he undertook to do this. There are plenty of grounds for questioning the success of his effort. Just for one thing, in spite of what Kung points out about his intentions, some of his suggestions seem more defensible as replacements for properties than as identifications of them—for example, his account of hardness as the physical property of being something to which 'our flesh yields.' Nevertheless the enterprise is an important effort on his part, exhibiting a recognition of a difficulty to which his previous dialogues had paid virtually no attention.[42]

The same line of thought may help us with the well-known problem about the date of the *Timaeus*. Owen attempted to show that it came in the middle of Plato's career, shortly after the *Republic*. Most scholars have declined to accept this view. Owen's strongest argument probably always was his contention that the seemingly frank paradeigmatism of the *Timaeus* was incompatible with the evidence that Owen thought he saw in the *Sophist* and elsewhere that Plato had given up self-predication. But once self-predication is recognised to be a side issue on which Plato never thought much turned (cf. this section, supra), that argument loses its force, and indeed its special appeal to those who were anxious to rescue Plato, at least in his later life, from what seemed like a central absurdity in his theory. But it is important that no account was ever forthcoming from those who opposed Owen of something that clearly needed explanation all along, namely, why Plato should have undertaken the project of physical theorising that the *Timaeus* presents, and how it might have fitted into his overall philosophical enterprise.

I think we now have the explanation we need. The gap that the *Timaeus* was meant to fill is the gap left by Plato's need to posit both objective senses for the terms that he initially examined in the context of perceptual judgments. The motivation for the *Timaeus*'s identifications of these properties is the natural motivation that came from realising that if he was going to construe perceptual judgments as involving non-perspective-relative notions, he had to show how to understand them. In many works he attempted to do that for evaluative notions.

---

42 I suppose that the same might be urged for the identification of Forms with numbers that Aristotle reports in *Metaph* XIV. But that is another story.

In the *Timaeus*, late in his career, he does it for the non-evaluative notions too.

The picture that results makes sense. Plato was right to take seriously the nonrelative predications that he emphasises. His way of regarding the predicates that they introduce, as introducing objective notions not relative to point of view, is problematical but profound and suggestive. His appreciation that they demanded explanations was clearsighted. And his attempt to provide explanations – of the evaluative ones in various works and of many nonevaluative ones finally in the *Timaeus* – was well-motivated. Whatever the ultimate philosophical moral of this story may be, the story is not one of confusion.

Department of Philosophy
University of Michigan
Ann Arbor, MI 48109
USA

IV.—FORMS AS CAUSES IN THE *PHAEDO*

C. C. W. Taylor

I WISH to discuss two questions in this paper : (*a*) What sort of explanation did Plato think he was proposing in the *Phaedo* when he offered explanation in terms of the theory of Forms as an alternative to earlier methods of scientific explanation? (*b*) What relation does this kind of explanation bear to Aristotle's explanation in terms of formal causes?

The first important point is that Plato's method is of quite unrestricted application. It arises out of dissatisfaction with certain hitherto accepted ways of answering questions beginning ' Why . . .? ' At 96a 8-9 Socrates says that it seemed to him a wonderful thing to know the causes of each thing, why it comes to be and why it perishes and why it is. Mention of coming to be and perishing indicates that Socrates' interests included natural change (as is confirmed by his examples, *e.g.* inquiry into the causes of the generation of animals) and in general all phenomena which fall within the scope of natural science. But other questions are involved too : besides his scientific examples Socrates cites such questions as ' Why is ten greater than eight? ' and ' When one unit is added to another, is it one of the units which becomes two, and, if so, which one, or do both units become two? ' The latter question, at least, is clearly a conceptual question, in that it has to be answered by considering the meanings of terms used in talking about numbers, and by considering the logical relations of propositions formed from those terms. The first question ' Why is ten greater than eight?' is less easy to characterise ; it is clearly not an empirical question, but it is not recognisably a conceptual one either. It just isn't clear what question is meant to be posed in these words. But the answer which Socrates says he had held, and which he later rejected, that ten is greater than eight because it contains two units more than eight, indicates that the question is to be interpreted as ' What feature of the number ten explains or accounts for its being greater than eight? ' Thus interpreted the question is a conceptual one, to be answered by showing how the relation between the numbers ten and eight is a particular case of the succession of numbers which constitutes the natural number system. The method of explanation in terms of Forms, therefore, provides answers to all questions of causation in the natural world, and to all conceptual questions which can be introduced by the word ' Why . . .? ' It is, therefore, anachronistic to

45

understand that question as specifically a request for a causal explanation of a phenomenon, since it can be raised in areas where there is no question of causation ; rather it is an undifferentiated request for an explanation which will render a phenomenon intelligible. It is the ' Why? ' which introduces the child's question ' Why do the leaves fall from the trees in autumn?' and his question ' Why does Wednesday always come after Tuesday and never before? ' It is remarkable that Plato should have believed that there is a single kind of answer to so wide a range of questions.

It is not indeed clear whether there is any restriction on the range of questions to which the method is to provide answers. We can determine this by asking whether there was any kind of answer to any ' Why? ' question which, though not expressed in terms of Forms, was nonetheless exempt from the faults which vitiated earlier scientific explanation. Socrates isolates as the main fault of such explanatory theories their failure to recognise the necessity of a teleological explanation of all events and states of affairs, and says that to ignore that kind of explanation is as absurd as to purport to explain a human action in purely physiological terms, while saying nothing about the true cause of the action, *viz.* that the man acted so because he judged that it was best so to act. Here then we seem to have one kind of explanation which is in no way inadequate, but which yet seems to make no explicit reference to Forms, *viz.* explanation of human action in terms of a choice by the agent of the course which he judges to be the best. If this in fact represents Plato's position he is in effect singling out human action as a unique class of phenomena, which require an ultimately different kind of explanation from all other events and states in the physical world and from all necessary states. As far as the first contrast goes his view would bear a certain resemblance to that of a modern defender of free-will who argues that causal determinism holds universally in the physical world except in the sphere of human action ; he would, of course, differ from such a theorist in holding that all states and events other than human actions, including necessary states, have a single form of explanation. It may, however, be that Plato thought that even the explanation of human action depends ultimately on the Forms, in that every action gives rise not to a single explanatory proposition stating that the agent acted because he thought it best to act in that way, but to a chain of explanations terminating in a reference to Forms. An example of such a chain might be ' Why is Socrates sitting in prison instead of escaping to Megara? ' ' Because he judged it best to stay in prison.' ' Why did he judge it best to stay in prison? ' ' Because he is a good man.' ' Why is he a good man? ' ' Because he participates in the Form of the Good. ' Alternatively one might ask why a good man should judge that it is best to stay in prison, to which the answer might be that staying in prison in a situation like that of Socrates' is a case of keeping one's obligations, and that keeping one's obligations is good through sharing in the Form of the Good. I do not think that there is sufficient evidence in the *Phaedo* itself to determine which alternative represents Plato's view of the explanation of human action. On the whole I am inclined to guess that he thought that in that area too explanation must ultimately refer to the Forms, but the only support for that opinion which occurs to me is the reference at *Rep.* 511b 6-7 to the ' unhypothetical first principle of everything ' which implies that there is a single pattern of explanation for all phenomena, depending on a single principle which seems either to be identical with or to be some proposition concerning the Form of the Good. Either of the chains of explanation which I suggested might be constructed about an action would fit naturally into such a universal pattern. But that is admittedly speculative ; as far as the *Phaedo* we must admit human action as a possible exception of explanation which we are proposing to investigate.

What, then, is the method? In the *Phaedo* we are apparently given two accounts of it, or perhaps accounts of two stages of it. First of all we have the ' safe ' answer to every question of the form ' Why is x ϕ? ', *viz.* ' x is ϕ through sharing in the Φ ', which we interpret as ' x is ϕ through sharing in ϕ-ness '. The safe answer to the question ' Why does x become ϕ? ' will presumably be ' x becomes ϕ through coming to share in ϕ-ness ', or perhaps, in the language used later in the dialogue, ' x becomes ϕ through the approach of ϕ-ness to x '. This answer is safe in that it states a necessary and sufficient condition for the possession of the property of being ϕ ; nothing can be ϕ without sharing in ϕ-ness, nor share in ϕ-ness without being ϕ. Presumably the rejected answers are held to state conditions for the possession of a property which, though at least in some cases necessary, are not sufficient (99b 2-6). But the safety of the answer seems to lie just in its total lack of information ; one could as well say that ' x is ϕ because x is ϕ ' states a necessary and sufficient condition for being ϕ, since nothing can be ϕ which is not ϕ. If this answer is to have any explanatory force at all, much less provide a universal pattern of explanation, some independent specification of ϕ-ness must be given, which will enable one to discern the nature of the explanatory link between x's sharing in ϕ-ness and x's being ϕ.

Plato seems to have grasped this point, as he describes the safe answer as ' perhaps simple-minded ' (100d 4) and as ' stupid ' (105c 1), in contrast with another kind of answer which is ' more elaborate ' or perhaps ' more sophisticated ' ($\kappa o\mu\psi\acute{o}\tau\epsilon\rho o\nu$) (105c 2). This second kind of answer, which I have suggested may be regarded as a second stage of the pattern of explanation in terms of Forms, is represented by the following explanations : something is hot through the presence of fire in it, a body is sick through the presence of fever in it and alive through the presence of soul in it, a number is odd through the presence of the unit in it. The general form of explanation is that something is ϕ by having in it some substance or entity S, the presence of which in an object entails the possession of ϕ-ness by that object. The general kind of substance or entity, and the nature of the presence are left uncharacterised, and indeed it seems that Plato is lumping together quite different kinds of things and ' presences'. Thus fire is presumably thought of as a physical element, lots of little bits of fiery stuff, and as being present in objects as part of their physical structure (*cf. Tim.* 61d-62a) ; the unit, on the other hand, seems to be thought of as a kind of arithmetical building-block, which one uses to construct other numbers, and the sense in which it is present in odd numbers but not in even is far from clear (see below, p. 49). We might expect then, to find different kinds of explanation concealed in Plato's rather vague description ; further examination will make it clear that we do in fact find certain differences.

The first question which arises is how Plato conceived the link between the presence of S in x and the possession of ϕ-ness by x ; is the former a necessary and sufficient condition for the latter or merely a sufficient condition? One might well imagine that what made the safe answer attractive was its universality, *i.e.* its application to all and only cases of being ϕ ; if that feature is to be retained in the second stage the link between the presence of S and the possession of ϕ-ness ought to be that of a necessary and sufficient condition. The second stage would then amount to a filling out of the safe answer by giving an explanatory account of ϕ-ness ; to say that all and only things with fire in them are hot is in effect to say what heat is, in the sense in which one says that water's boiling really is a certain energy level of the molecules. It might reasonably be conjectured that Plato's intentions would be fulfilled by this programme of explaining the possession of a property by participation in a Form whose nature is then explained, and the example of life and soul fits this pattern perfectly. All and only bodies with souls are alive ; hence we explain what it is for a body to be alive by saying that for a body to be alive is for it to have a soul. The other examples, however, fit this pattern less clearly. At 103e-105b the link between the presence of S and the possession of φ-ness is illustrated by examples : 3 (ἡ τρίας, τὰ τρία) is always odd, 2 (ἡ δυας, τὰ δύο) always even ; hence anything in which 3 is present (*i.e.* any collection of three things) is not only three in number but also odd (104d 5-7), and (Plato leaves us to add) every pair is not only two in number but also even. Here the possession of the explanatory entity is clearly a sufficient but not necessary condition for the possession of the property. At 105c Socrates gives a general account of the arithmetical application of the method, as follows : ' If I am asked what it is that makes any number odd I shall not say the presence of oddness, but the presence of a unit, and similarly in the other cases.' A natural way to take this is in the sense of the examples above, as saying ' If any collection consists of one member, it is odd through the presence of the unit, and similarly in the other cases (*i.e.* if it consists of three members, it is odd through the presence of 3, and so on).' Another interpretation was, however, proposed by Hackforth (*Plato's Phaedo*, p. 158), *viz.* that Socrates is here alluding to the fact that the division of an odd number into two equal parts leaves one extra unit, which may be regarded as accounting for the oddness of the whole. This requires a lot to be supplied from the context, but is not to be excluded on that ground alone. A more serious objection is that it offers, without the least indication of the fact, a quite different explanation of oddness from that given in the preceding examples. On the other hand, Hackforth's interpretation gives a better sense to καί τἆλλα οὕτως (105c 6), which is better taken as summing up the method as a whole than as merely continuing the numerical examples. Moreover, there is some evidence that the account of odd numbers which it requires was an accepted one (Ar. *Met.* M8, 1083b 28-30 ; Stobaeus I, pr., 6 and 10). If it is accepted, then to give the better explanation of the oddness of a number will be to give necessary and sufficient conditions for its being odd, and the explanation of oddness will resemble the explanations of being alive and being hot, in so far as in each case the better explanation specifies what the phenomenon really is. But here we should notice a difference in the ways in which these explanations specify the nature of the phenomenon, a difference which will be important when we compare Plato's model of explanation with Aristotle's (see below, p. 57). In the case of oddness the necessary and sufficient conditions for a number's being odd provide an analysis of the concept, *i.e.* of what the word ' odd ' really means, while in the cases of heat and life they provide a causal explanation of the phenomenon in terms of entities which are accepted as more fundamental in the explanatory scheme. If the other interpretation is accepted, then the presence of the unit, etc., specifies a sufficient condition only for a collection's being odd in number. I do not propose to attempt to decide between the interpretations, and for the rest of the discussion shall keep both alternatives in mind.

Do the other examples throw any light on the question whether the presence of S is a necessary and sufficient, or merely a sufficient condition for the possession of ϕ-ness? As we have seen, it is reasonable to think that Plato means at 105c that the presence of fire is a necessary and sufficient condition of something's being hot, since fire is an element present (in the right amount, no doubt) in all and only hot things. On the other hand, at 103c-e and at 106a it is implied that the relation of fire to heat is parallel to that of snow to coldness ; Plato appears here not to be thinking of something's being made hot by having fire in it (as at 105c) or cold by having snow in it, but of something's being cold because it *is* snow, and hot because it *is* fire. Obviously, in that sense the relation of fire to heat is merely a sufficient condition, since other things may be hot than fire itself. It appears, then, that Plato has in mind not a single relation of fire to heat, but two relations, (*a*) that of the fiery element in a hot body to the heat of the body, (*b*) that of fire to the heat of the fire. In (*a*) the presence of fire is a necessary and sufficient condition for heat, in (*b*) the hot thing's being fire is merely sufficient. Finally, the fever-disease relation, like that between snow and cold and fire and heat in sense (*b*) above, is merely sufficient, as fever is classed by Plato (*Tim.* 81e-86a) as one among many diseases.

We find, then, that the general picture of the relation between the presence of S and the possession of ϕ-ness is somewhat complicated. In one case, that of soul and life, it is clearly required that the presence of S be a necessary and a sufficient condition for the possession of ϕ-ness, since the presence of S gives a causally explanatory account of what ϕ-ness is. In another case, that of fire and heat, Plato appears to have in mind two distinct relations, one sufficient only, the other necessary and sufficient ; in the latter case the explanation is of the same kind as the explanation of life by the presence of soul. In a third case, that of the unit and oddness, the interpretation of the relation as a necessary and sufficient condition is plausible, but not decisively more plausible than its interpretation as a sufficient condition only. If it is a necessary and sufficient condition, the explanation is of a different type from that in the first two cases, being an analysis of the concept of the phenomenon rather than a causal account of it. In the two remaining cases, those of snow and cold and of fever and disease, the relation must be a sufficient condition only. We have, then, no alternative to admitting that Plato gives a set of examples of different logical types without calling attention to or perhaps without even noticing the distinctions between them. Since, then, it is impossible to attribute to Plato the programme which I suggested earlier, *viz.* explaining the possession of a property by giving an account of the nature of that property in terms of its necessary and sufficient conditions, is it possible to give any coherent general account of the kind of explanation which he offers ?

It will not be enough to say simply that Plato's method is that of finding sufficient conditions for the possession of any property, since that fails to single out any particular method of explanation. Any explanation whatever must be of the form ' P because Q ', which is to single out Q as a sufficient condition, given other constant conditions, for P ; the rejected explanations of pre-Socratic science exemplify that pattern as well as do Plato's own. We must say something more, *viz.* that Plato thought that an object's having a property was explained by the presence of some entity which is at least sufficient to account for the object's possessing that property. But this gives a general description of Plato's method only if ' entity ' is stretched to the point of vacuity ; thus fever is a kind of disease, not some observable entity like a virus whose presence accounts for the occurrence of disease. Plato here confuses ' This is an A of type B ' with ' The fact that this is a B accounts for its being an A ' ; the former says nothing about the cause of the thing's being an A, but merely classifies it as an A of a certain kind. Again, to say that snow accounts for cold, or fire heat, in the sense that no snow can fail to be cold or fire fail to be hot is not to account for any phenomenon in terms of any explanatory entity. It is merely to say that snow must be cold and fire hot, which is itself a phenomenon in need of a causal explanation. Further, the explanatory ' entities ' account for the phenomena in radically different ways ; we have seen how Plato lumps together logically necessary and sufficient conditions with causally necessary and sufficient conditions, and the same assimilation may be observed in his sufficient conditions too. Thus it is only causally necessary that fire produces the sensation of heat ; given a different set of causal laws the same physical events might produce a different sensation. But it is logically necessary that any collection of three things must be odd in number. There is, however, no indication that Plato distinguished these kinds of explanation from one another ; for him heat was a necessary attribute of fire in just the same sense as oddness of any collection of three things. This is not to say that Plato thought it logically necessary that fire should be hot ; rather he did not clearly distinguish logical from causal necessity. He would regard it as absurd (ἄτοπον) that fire should not be hot, or that a collection of three things should be even in number, without any clear idea of whether the kind of absurdity varies from case to case.

This makes it extremely difficult to see what distinguishes Plato's method from those of his predecessors. We can't say that he substitutes logical for causal necessity, since he fails to distinguish the two. We have to be content with saying that he thought that the possession of the property to be explained had to be shown to be necessitated by the presence of some explanatory entity, in a quite undifferentiated sense of ' necessitate ' and ' entity '. But this is insufficient to distinguish Plato's method from those of his predecessors, since the authors of the cosmological and physiological theories which he mentions would no doubt claim that the causes which they cite necessitate their effects in just as strong a sense as that which Plato requires (see *D.-K.* III, 41-2 for attributions to Thales, Empedocles, Parmenides, Leucippus and Democritus of the view that everything happens according to necessity), while their causes, *e.g.* love, strife, the four elements, the atoms, have just as much right to be called entities as Plato's own examples. The main criticism which Socrates makes of their theories is their neglect of teleological explanations, which give the true cause of any phenomenon, while any other explanation (*e.g.* a mechanistic one) gives only a necessary, never a sufficient condition (99b 2-6). Yet Plato's own method contains no explicitly teleological element, while some of his examples, *e.g.* that something is hot because of the presence of fire in it, may as reasonably be called mechanistic as some of those explanations which he rejects.

On this point Socrates says (99c 6-d 2) that failing to find or to devise a satisfactory teleological account of phenomena, he resorted to the method of explanation in terms of Forms as a δεύτερος πλοῦς ; the best-attested sense of this nautical metaphor (see LSJ s.v. πλόος 3) is that it means rowing the ship when there is no wind, which involves getting eventually to your original destination by a longer and more laborious method. But what is the destination which he is to reach by this method? Is it 'giving a teleological explanation' or just 'giving an explanation'? Plato's practice in the *Phaedo* would imply the latter, while his theoretical statements imply the former; for it is difficult to see how, having castigated his predecessors for confusing the true cause (*i.e.* a teleologically-expressed one) of any phenomenon with its necessary conditions he could go on to expound a theory which takes no account of the true cause, but gives a variety of causes, some of them similar in type to the rejected ones. How could he avoid the charge of committing just the confusion of which he had accused his predecessors? I am inclined to believe that Plato did cling to the notion of the final cause as the true cause, and that the method of the *Phaedo* was intended to be a more laborious method of arriving at the final cause of any phenomenon, in that the teleological explanation was reached, not immediately, but at the end of such a chain of reasons as I have already posited (p. 46-7). Each of my two versions of the chain concerning Socrates' staying in prison ended at the Form of the Good; I think that all chains of explanations were supposed to end there, *e.g.* 'Why is this body hot?' 'Because it has a certain proportion of fire-atoms in it.' 'Why does the presence of fire-atoms in it make it hot?' 'Because the sharp edges of the atoms cause a piercing sensation in anyone who comes into contact with the body, and this sensation we call heat.' 'Why do the atoms have sharp edges?' 'Because they are pyramidical.' 'Why are they pyramidical?' 'Because that is the best arrangement.' 'Why is that the best arrangement?' 'Because the nature of goodness determines that it is.' In this example, which is derived from the *Timaeus*, I believe that we see in action the method which is sketched in the *Republic*, according to which all knowledge can be put on a basis of complete certainty by being derived ultimately from some proposition about, or perhaps a specification of the nature of the Form of the Good. I believe it likely that Plato had some idea of this in mind when he proposed his alternative method of explanation in the *Phaedo*. But it must be admitted that there is no hint of this in the text. Instead of insisting that all chains of explanation must lead back to the Good, Socrates allows that for the purposes of any particular argument a chain may be held to be complete when the ultimate explanatory hypothesis is accepted by the parties as adequate (101d 5-e 1), and himself exemplifies this practice by giving as complete explanations the examples we have already quoted, *e.g.* something is hot because there is fire in it. It is, therefore, inadmissible to assert that what distinguishes the method of explanation expounded in the *Phaedo* from the methods of Socrates' predecessors is that the former is a method of teleological explanation. The most that we can say is that the kinds of explanation given in the *Phaedo* were probably intended to form part of a teleological scheme, but the dialogue itself gives no account of that scheme nor any suggestion of how the particular types of explanation there given were to fit into it. It may indeed be that the complete scheme was merely a programme which Plato was as yet unable to carry out ; that would account for the tentative methodology and for the apparently incomplete character of the examples.

It appears, then, to be impossible to discover any coherent method underlying Plato's examples. All that we can say is that his method consists of two stages, first giving the ' safe ' (*i.e.* uninformative) answer ' x is ϕ through sharing in ϕ-ness ', and secondly giving the better answer ' x is ϕ through the presence in x of S, since anything in which S is present necessarily shares in ϕ-ness ' ; in the latter case S is an ' entity ' (in the widest possible sense) whose presence is in one or more of a number of ways a sufficient condition of the possession of ϕ-ness. These ways include being a merely sufficient condition either logically or causally, and being a necessary and sufficient condition either logically or causally ; none of these different kinds of condition are clearly distinguished from one another. This pattern of explanation, though not in itself teleological, was probably intended to fit into a teleological scheme of explanation.

I turn now to my second main question, an investigation of the relation which the explanations given in the *Phaedo* have to the role assigned by Aristotle to the formal cause in his explanatory scheme. This question is raised by Aristotle's acceptance of the *Phaedo* as providing examples of his type of explanation in terms of the formal cause (*Met.* A9, 991b 1-4, repeated at M5, 1079b 35-1080a 3). Since we have been unable to find any single principle of explanation in the *Phaedo*, it is natural to inquire just what the similarities are between the kinds of explanation found there and Aristotle's explanation by means of the formal cause.

In his summary of the four causes at *Phys.* II, 3 Aristotle describes the formal cause as ' the form and the pattern, that is the definition of what the thing is, including the genus to which the thing belongs and its differentiae ' (194b 26-9). His example is that the formal cause of the octave is the ratio 2/1, which is a species of number. Other examples make the notion clearer ; the form of a bronze sphere is its shape (*Met.* Z6, 1033b 5-10), the form of a threshold is its position, the form of breakfast is the time of day at which it is eaten (*ibid.* H2, 1042b 15-28). The best general characterisation of the formal cause seems therefore to be that it is that which answers the question ' Given a certain matter, *e.g.* a quantity of bronze, what are the characteristics whose possession by that matter is a necessary and sufficient condition of its being a thing of a certain kind, *e.g.* a statue? ' It is not sufficient to say, as Miss Anscombe does (*Three Philosophers*, p. 49), that ' The form . . . is what makes what a thing is made *of* into that thing '; that definition fails to distinguish the efficient from the formal cause, since in our example the sculptor too may properly be said to make what the statue is made of, *viz.* bronze, into the statue. Our definition remedies this deficiency by specifying that the form of anything is a characteristic or set of characteristics of that thing, not an external causal agency operating on the matter of that thing. In comparing the explanatory role of the Aristotelean formal cause with the method of explanation of the *Phaedo* we should notice these two points in particular : (*a*) that explaining a phenomenon in terms of a formal cause involves giving necessary and sufficient conditions for the phenomenon, and (*b*) that the notion of a formal cause is correlative with that of matter.

On the second point, the method of the *Phaedo* conforms reasonably closely to Aristotle's criteria. This may be seen from the way in which Socrates gives his examples at 105c :

> ' If you were to ask me what, when present in its body, will always make a thing hot, I shall not give you that safe, foolish answer " heat ", but, after what we have just said, a more subtle answer, " fire ". And if you ask what, when present in a body, will always make it ill, I shall not say " illness " but " fever "; and if you ask what, when present in a number, will always make it odd, I shall answer not " oddness " but " oneness ", and so on.' (Bluck's tr.)

Here in each case we have the specification of a subject which the presence of a certain characteristic causes to be a thing of a certain kind. This is precisely the sense in which in the Aristotelian scheme every formal cause is correlative to a certain matter. Bronze is made to be a statue by having a certain shape, a man is made to be a healthy man by having a certain kind of functioning of his bodily parts. Not all of Plato's examples fit easily into that pattern, *e.g.* snow's being the cause of cold is not very readily expressed by saying that some substance is made cold by being snow, but we have enough examples to allow us to say that in general a cause of the type specified in the *Phaedo* presupposes a certain definite matter in the same way as does an Aristotelian formal cause. On the first point, however, we seem to have a marked difference between Plato and Aristotle, since we have noticed that some of Plato's examples are cases of sufficient but not necessary conditions, whereas Aristotle's formal cause is a necessary *and* sufficient condition, or a set of such conditions, for something's being a thing of a certain kind. Can we see how Plato's examples of sufficient but not necessary conditions may be fitted into Aristotle's scheme? If, for instance, fire is a sufficient condition of heat, or snow of cold, in the sense that something will be hot if it *is* fire, or cold if it is snow, though there are hot things other than fire and cold things other than snow, how would Aristotle classify the relations between fire and heat and cold and snow?

In *De Gen. et Corr.* II, 2-3, Aristotle treats Hot and Cold as primary elements, and fire and ice as kinds of Hot and Cold respectively : ' fire is an excess of heat, just as ice is an excess of cold . . . ice is a freezing of moist and cold, fire . . . a boiling of dry and hot (330b 26-9).[1] This seems to assimilate these causes to that where fever is a sufficient condition of disease, in that fever is a species of disease. Aristotle's account of the relation of species to genus is that the species causes the genus, which in itself exists only potentially, to exist actually, *e.g.* anything which is an animal is so in virtue of being a man, a horse etc. (*Met.* Δ28, 1024b 8-9 ; Z13, 1038b 30-4 ; H6, 1045a 22-b 7). This relation is not covered by any of Aristotle's four causes ; we can't say that fever is the formal cause of disease, since if that were so ' fever ' would be the definition of disease. On the other hand it is very close to the formal cause, since fever is the formal cause of *this particular disease, i.e.* one says what this particular disease is by saying that it is fever. Plato's examples of threeness causing oddness and twoness causing evenness are perhaps to be regarded in this way also, taking twoness and threeness as species of evenness and oddness respectively. If that is so, we can see why Aristotle might have been willing to allow that the causes of the *Phaedo* are formal causes, even when they state only sufficient conditions. On the other hand there is another way of taking two of Plato's examples which fits the model of formal causation much less closely. On this view, heat and cold are viewed not as genera of which fire and snow are species, but as attributes necessarily belonging to fire and snow. However the relation

---

[1] I assume that, if Aristotle regarded ice as a species of Cold, he regarded snow as another species.

between substance and attribute is to be characterised in Aristotelian causal terms, a substance certainly cannot be the formal cause of one of its attributes, for the statement of the formal cause states what it is for some matter to be a certain thing, and one can't say what it is to be an attribute, *e.g.* cold, by specifying some substance, *e.g.* snow. If, then, this is allowed as a possible interpretation (and it is perhaps more likely than its alternative to have been Plato's own view), we must admit that Aristotle has overlooked a major departure from his model of formal causation.

We must now turn to those examples which it was plausible to regard as citing necessary and sufficient conditions for the phenomenon to be explained, *viz.* the soul-life relation, the strong interpretation of the fire-heat relation, that all and only fiery things are hot, and Hackforth's interpretation of the oneness-oddness relation, *viz.* that what makes a number odd is the fact that when it is divided into two equal parts there is a unit left over. In each of these cases the cause specifies the real nature of the phenomenon, which is what the Aristotelian formal cause does. But as we saw earlier (p. 49), the sense in which it does so differs in the last case from the other two ; in the case of oddness it does so by providing an analysis of the concept, while in the cases of heat and life it offers a causal explanation. It seems that it is only the first sort which Aristotle regards as giving the formal cause ; accounts of the second sort may be reckoned as forming part of a formal cause, but only if they accompany an analysis of the concept. The distinction between the two kinds of explanation is elucidated in the discussion of anger at *De An.* I, 1, 403a 29-b 19 ; a physiologist would define it as the boiling of blood round the heart, which he would presumably regard as saying what anger really is in the sense of giving an explanatory account in terms of a causal theory. But according to Aristotle it is the analysis of the concept, *viz.* desire for retaliation, which gives the formal cause. Yet in the same passage he says that the natural scientist, as opposed to the metaphysician, should include both elements in the definition,[1] while at *Met.* H4, 1044b 12-15 he says that just giving the formal cause of eclipse ' deprivation of light ' is uninformative unless the efficient cause is also specified, so that the best definition is ' deprivation of light through the interposition of the earth '. This is in fact the kind of definition which is said in the *Posterior Analytics* (*e.g.* II, 2) to be fundamental to scientific explanation. Since Aristotle

---

[1] His model definition of anger in fact does so: τὸ ὀργίζεσθαι κίνησίς τις τοῦ τοιουδὶ σώματος ἢ μέρους ἢ δυνάμεως ὑπὸ τοῦδε ἕνεκα τοῦδε (a 26–7).

holds that the term 'hot' is disjunctive in sense, in that things are called hot in virtue of a variety of criteria (*De Part. An.* II, 2, 648b 12-649b 7), he would presumably accept as the formal cause of heat the complete statement of these criteria, together with the specification of the presence of fire as their efficient cause (assuming that that is his view of the efficient cause of heat). But it does not appear that he could accept the presence of fire as itself the formal cause.

I have assumed in this discussion that in the *Phaedo* Plato regards the soul as a separate entity causally productive of the life of the body, and that the relation between soul and life is therefore parallel to that between fire and heat in the case where fire is a physical element causing heat in bodies where it is present. This view of the soul is required by the separation of soul and body which is so much emphasised in the *Phaedo*. Aristotle's view of the soul is quite different ; it is not a separate entity, but ' the first actuality of an organic body which potentially has life ' (*De An.* II, 1, 412a 27-8), *i.e.* it is identical with that actual activity of a body which constitutes that body's actually being alive, as opposed to merely being able to be alive. That is to say, for Aristotle soul and actual life are identical. The soul is thus the formal cause of the living body, since the answer to the question ' What makes this body, *i.e.* this collection of muscles, bones, etc., into a living body? ' is that it is made to be alive by the soul, or, which is the same answer, by the performance of those activities which make up its actually being alive. But if soul and actual life are thus identical, can we say that soul is the formal cause of life as well as of the living body? I find myself unable to give any confident answer to that question, but suggest that with some hesitation that Aristotle regards ' life ' as a term which covers both actuality and potentiality, that soul is identical with the actuality of life, and that the relation of actualisation to potentiality is not subsumed under the ordinary fourfold causal scheme. But, as we saw in the cate of genus and species (see above, p. 56) that relation is so close to formal causation that Aristotle may be pardoned for taking the two together. While, therefore, the actual account of the soul-life relation given in the *Phaedo* is that the soul is the efficient cause of life, which figures only as an element in a full formal explanation, Aristotle may have taken that relation in terms of his own theory of the soul, and so have assimilated it even more closely to his own formal causation.

To sum up, we are now able to see how, despite the diversity of Plato's examples, most of them can be accommodated, given a little stretching, to Aristotle's model of formal causation. We have indeed only one perfect example of formal causation, depending on a disputed interpretation of the text; that is the oneness-oddness relation on Hackforth's interpretation. On the other interpretation that example, along with the fever-disease relation, and possibly the fire-heat and snow-cold relations, becomes an example of the actualisation of the genus by the species, which is very closely related to formal causation. The relation of soul to life and that of fire as an element to heat are probably to be seen as examples of efficient causation, which forms part of formal causation for scientific purposes, but I have suggested that Aristotle may have regarded in the former in the light of his own theory as another case of the actualisation of potentiality. It is only if we adopt another interpretation of the fire-heat and snow-cold examples that we find a case which stands quite apart; that is the interpretation on which heat and cold are not genera of which fire and snow are species, but attributes of those substances. Though this is little more than a guess, I am inclined to think that that interpretation in fact represents Plato's own position rather than the other, and that if Aristotle meant explicitly to include those examples we have another case where he re-interprets Plato in terms of his own views. It is, however, perhaps more likely that Aristotle overlooked some of Plato's examples, and may be calling attention to the general similiarity which we have observed, rather than fitting every example in detail into his causal scheme.

University of Oxford

Republic

Book V : τὰ πολλὰ καλά etc.

J. GOSLING

THE THESIS of this paper is that when in Book V. of the *Republic* at
479A Socrates talks of τὰ πολλὰ καλά, δίκαια etc., he is not talking
about particular beautiful objects or just actions and saying that you
will never find an instance of either that you could not equally well, in
some sense or other, call ugly or unjust; but rather that there is no type
of characteristic or description of action [1] commonly said to be beautiful
or just which could not equally well be said to be ugly or unjust. In fact
"τὰ πολλὰ καλά" means not "the many particular beautiful objects" but
"the many kinds of colour, shape etc. commonly held to be beautiful".
As this may at first sight seem to be straining the text a little, I feel
constrained to argue for it; but it may be as well first to criticise the
view that it is particular objects that Plato has in mind, for no alternative
interpretation will seem really plausible while this one remains unscathed.

It is remarkable how readily the view finds acceptance.[2] It is assumed by
Field (*Plato*, in The Home University Library), and more strikingly,
because the book is more detailed, by Ross in *Plato's Theory of Ideas* c. IV.
Ross, indeed, does not seem to think it necessary to argue for his view:
he expounds it as what is obviously meant. This is the more noteworthy
in that he remarks on the peculiarity of the argument on this interpretation, puts forward as what Plato "must have been thinking of" what
it seems to me he in fact meant, and consequently stigmatises the whole

---

[1] This is possibly a little too precise. Mr. Crombie, of Wadham College, has pointed out
to me that it can be argued e.g. on the basis of the *Hippias Major* that the people Plato
had in mind would equally well have given types of object (peacocks, leopards) as καλά;
but I have kept to one kind of opponent in the hope that it makes the point clearer. A
good example of the kind of thing that Plato was combating as it appeared among
philosophers can be found in the Δισσοὶ Λόγοι (usually dated c. 400B.C.), though it must
be admitted that when a good case is to hand the author will shift from talking of types
of action etc. to talking of particular cases.

[2] An exception would seem to be Mr. Murphy in *The Interpretation of Plato's Republic*, who
on the main question appears, though not always by the same arguments, to hold the
conclusion put forward here. I say "appears" because while at times his view seems quite
clear it becomes obscured by his remarks on being and not-being, by his way of distinguishing ἐπιστήμη and δόξα, and by his talk of the straightness of sticks being imperfect, which seems to be a different use of the abstract noun form that in earlier remarks
about the beauty of Helen. I am hesitant, therefore, about claiming his support.

116

passage as a confusion, as a result of which, until the *Sophist*, Plato indulged in a "false and dangerous disparagement of all particulars, in the supposed interest of Forms".

It is worth wondering why it should be felt not to need arguing that Plato is in this passage concerned with the status of particular physical objects. In the first place, we are inclined to assume that when Plato contrasts τὸ ἕν with τὰ πολλά he is contrasting the one form with the indefinitely many particulars which are instances of it, or which partake in it. This, after all, – the distinction of forms and particulars, – is both his great discovery and his great problem. When, therefore, at the beginning of this discussion, at 476A, we find the contrast between the one (form) and the many, we feel that we are on familiar ground. We find confirmation in the fact that οἱ φιλοθεάμονες are said to make particular things their interest, as distinct from philosophers who seek after forms, – and this fits in nicely. Then, there are similarly worded passages both in the *Republic* and elsewhere in which particulars seem clearly to be in question, and it is natural to assume that the same point is being made here. Finally, in Book VI 507A-C Socrates recalls what was said in Book V and it is there made quite clear that the distinction is between visible (audible etc.) objects and intelligible forms.

There are doubtless other minor supporting considerations, but these, I think, are the main points. I do not pretend to know what exactly Plato is supposed to be saying on this interpretation, nor how what he says is supposed to be relevant to the argument, – or alternatively what the argument is to which they are supposed to be relevant; but the fact remains that these points might be adduced to support the claim that, whatever he meant by it, it is forms and particulars that Plato is in fact talking about.

I shall proceed against this position and in favour of my own as follows: first, I shall assume that this position is correct, and try to show the difficulty of finding any interpretation of 479A-B on that assumption. Then I shall draw out the further difficulty that on the assumption that τὰ πολλὰ καλά are particulars this passage seems to have no very obvious relevance to the conclusion Socrates draws from it. After showing, I hope, that there is reason for questioning this assumption, I shall turn to the beginning of the passage and present an alternative interpretation, dealing with certain difficulties on the way. Finally I shall bring forward some positive confirmation from Books VI and VII.

Socrates is about to put a knock-out question to anyone who denies
ἓν τὸ καλὸν εἶναι and who πολλὰ τὰ καλὰ νομίζει, – that is, on this interpretation, to anyone who thinks there is no such thing as the form of
τὸ καλόν, but just thinks that there are many beautiful things. The
question he puts is: "Is there any beautiful object which will not appear
ugly? Or just act which will not appear unjust?" And the opponent is
made to answer, as though it were obvious: "No; it must be the case
that they will appear beautiful in a way and ugly in a way". It is important
that this is taken as obvious viz. that any beautiful object must (seem to)
have the opposite characteristic of being ugly. What we want to know is:
why did Plato think it obvious? It is not so at first sight, so that it is
incumbent on the holder of the view I am criticising to explain what
Plato believed such that he thought it so. What is the background of this
argument? There seem to be two possible interpretations if "τὰ πολλά..."
refers to particular objects and actions.

i. The point might be that there is no beautiful object such that you
cannot conceive of a more beautiful one, in comparison with which it
will seem ugly. This is the point that no particular ever has, perfectly,
the property we attribute to it, and so by the yardstick of perfection it
must appear to have the opposite property. To this I have two objections:
first, it is far less plausible when we come to 479B3: τί δὲ τὰ πολλὰ
διπλάσια; ἧττόν τι ἡμίσεα ἢ διπλάσια φαίνεται;. For what can Plato be
thinking of here? – that there is a perfection of duplicity compared with
which any earthly double is a very half? If he is wanting to make the
point that no particular of any size is ever perfectly double any other
(for more exact measurement is always conceivable by relation to which
it would not be double), then this is not the language in which to make it:
for more exact measurement would never, however exact, tempt us to
think that it was, rather, half the other. What it *might* mean is that there
is no particular of size A which is double a particular of size B which will
not also seem half a particular of size C; this would at least be more
plausible; but it would only show that particulars *can* possess (apparently)
opposite properties, not at all that they *must* possess them both imperfectly.[1] Secondly, even with regard to beauty and justice, it is far from

[1] And it would only show that they *can* possess them: to say that any particular that is a
double must also be a half leads either to vast a priori claims about the necessary existence
of infinitely large objects granted the existence of one double, or very queer views on the
form of the Double. What is true is that any *size* of group or measurement which is
double some other must be half a further one, – but now we are talking of types, no
longer of particulars.

118

being an obvious position which his opponents would accept straight off as ἀνάγκη; – why *must* it be that we can always conceive of an act which in the circumstances would have been more just than repaying this debt? It is hard to believe that, if that was his point, Plato met no opposition; yet he usually draws attention to the fact when he is letting himself off some argument.

ii. Alternatively, the point might be about the identity use of "is". That is, Plato might be treating τὸ διπλάσιον and the rest as names; so just as the same man cannot be Plato and Socrates, just so the same thing cannot be Double and Half; if it can vulgarly be said to be both double and half, then we still have to find the real Double and Half, the proper bearers of the names. This would be a way of making the point that no particular or number of particulars that we give as cases of doubles are in themselves sufficient for teaching the meaning of the terms; for there is nothing in the things themselves to make us take them for doubles rather then halves; instances only help some one in so far as they help him towards a definition which tells him "what a double is" or what "double" means.

Though this interpretation gives some account of doubles and halves, it faces the same difficulty as the other with regard to beauty and justice: that it is far from obvious why opponents should accept the statement that every just act also appears unjust. Indeed, if this is Plato's point it is more easily made without dubious dabbling in contraries: for he could argue from the mere multiplicity of καλά; for if "καλόν" is a name, then like 'Socrates' it must grow increasingly less adequate as a name the larger the number that bear it; but the adequacy of "καλόν" is unaffected by the number of καλά; therefore in calling them καλά we cannot be naming them; therefore we are naming something else, which must surely be καλόν; therefore things in a sense are καλόν, in a sense are not. Would this not even be the more natural way if Plato's troubles had to do with identity and predication?

There is, however, a further objection against any interpretation that takes "τὰ πολλὰ καλά" as referring to particular beautiful objects. It will be remembered that the discussion about τὸ ὄν, τὸ μὴ ὄν and τὰ μεταξύ was introduced as a 'consolation' (476E) to the φιλοθεάμων; – the consolation presumably being that to deny him knowledge is not to attribute downright ignorance to him but to allow him a measure of truth. Socrates, then, first establishes that ἐπιστήμη and ἄγνοια are concerned with τὸ ὄν and τὸ μὴ ὄν respectively and suggests that if anything lies between these two it will be characteristic of it that it both ἔστι καὶ οὐκ ἔστι.

Next δόξα is shown to be a separate ability, half way between ἄγνοια and ἐπιστήμη so that its object must be half way between theirs; finally (479) he claims to show that τὰ πολλὰ καλά are indeed half way, – it is characteristic of them that they ἔστι καὶ οὐκ ἔστι – and so must be "objects" of δόξα. Now taking it that τὰ πολλὰ καλά are genuine objects we have just had something of a lecture on the status of physical objects and our knowledge of them. It is therefore somewhat surprising that when Socrates sums up their findings at 479D he has nothing to say about objects at all; what he does say is: Ηὑρήκαμεν ἄρα, ὡς ἔοικεν, ὅτι τὰ τῶν πολλῶν πολλὰ νόμιμα καλοῦ τε πέρι καὶ τῶν ἄλλων μεταξύ που κυλινδεῖται τοῦ τε μὴ ὄντος καὶ τοῦ ὄντος εἰλικρινῶς. Whatever "νόμιμα" means it does not mean "particulars". Judging from his use of it a few paragraphs later at 484d with τίθεσθαι Plato means something like "customary rules about the beautiful and the just". (cf. also 359A). The question is, what conclusions of this sort follow from the previous discussion? I have no doubt that all sorts of possible conclusions could with ingenuity be devised, but that "ἄρα" suggests that what follows has as good as been said in what precedes. Better would be some interpretation which made it so.

The Context

I hope that I have now shown that at the least it is not obvious that Plato is talking here about particulars. I wish now to turn to the beginning of this passage, and first of all to draw attention to the context of the discussion. In the course of discussing whether the city he has outlined is a practical possibility, Socrates produces the surprising assertion that it will anyway never come about until philosophers rule or rulers are philosophers (473D). He recognises that he must now say whom he is calling philosophers such that it is clearly right for them to rule and for others to follow (474B-C); and their claim to rule is to be based on the fact that they alone can claim to have the truth about what is best to do, they alone *know*. As lovers of learning, however, they are liable to be confused with certain other people whom despite other descriptions I shall refer to just as "οἱ φιλοθεάμονες". As these are the people who are to be shown incapable of ἐπιστήμη though innocent of ἄγνοια it is important to see as clearly as possible what sort of people they are, and first to remember that they are possible candidates that someone might put forward as people who would know what they were about, as those whom Socrates might mean as possible rulers. Secondly, it is clear that the type is well known though apparently taking various forms. They are people

120

with a love of learning, but with no taste for dialectical discussion; their learning is culled, for instance, from attendance at festivals in the case of φιλήκοοι; but they do not attend merely to fill in time, like the Saturday cinema queues; they would be more likely to be found at the Cannes Festival, studying the art: they are οἱ τῶν τεχνυδρίων φιλοσόφοι. When Socrates describes them at 476A10 he calls them φιλοτέχνοι καὶ πρακτικοί: they think in terms of skill, art, technique, of finding out how things are done; but they find out, for instance, about τὸ καλόν just by going to theatres and festivals: these are the things they are enthusiastic about, and so they become authorities in criticism, people who could set up to teach the principles of composition and so forth. They observe in practice the features that make a play a success, and they observe that there is a great variety of such features which account for the successes of different plays and in various ways produce a good effect.

Like most of us when we think we have detected the source of strength or weakness in a play, these people would feel, and in a way rightly, that they were finding the explanation of the beauty of this play, and were on their way to a fruitful study of plays in general; but one of their discoveries will be that there are various ways of producing a successful play, various possible explanations of the success of a play. Consequently they would be understandably impatient of someone who insisted, apparently, on asking for a single explanation: such a request would seem unsophisticated and uneducated; – surely it must be clear to any man of intelligence who has studied the subject that the search for a single account is a wild goose chase?

This seems to me a fair description of the people Plato has in mind, and we are told two interesting things about them to be interpreted in the light of this: first, that they make no distinction between αὐτὸ τὸ καλόν and τὰ μετέχοντα, and cannot grasp it when you introduce them to it (476B-D) and secondly, that they will not allow you to say ἓν τὸ καλὸν εἶναι (479A), – and at 476A we have been told that the participation by things and acts does make each form seem many. So we get this position: as observed in the things around us each form *does* seem many; so it is understandable that οἱ φιλοθεάμονες, who concentrate on the things around them, should make the mistake of thinking they are many; and these people go so far as to deny that there is one form of beauty etc. Now if "τὰ πολλά ..." refers to particulars, then these people are for some reason keen to assert that there is a large number of particular objects of any description; and as they take the assertion ἓν τὸ καλὸν εἶναι to deny this, they must be taken as understanding Plato to say that there

121

are not many beautiful objects but only one. Further, if this is the inter-pretation of this passage, then Plato must take this to be the dispute between them. Yet if this is the dispute it is difficult to see how the multiplicity of particulars would hinder the grasping of the one in any way which was not susceptible of simple explanation. For suppose that "καλός" were used invariably and exclusively for things that were round and red; why should the fact that there were a lot of καλά make it hard for them to see that it was possible to give one answer to "τί ἔστι τὸ καλόν;" viz. that it is the round and red? Thirdly, it should be remember-ed that the people Plato has in mind are πρακτικοί; they want answers and explanations; so it is worth asking just how they could have thought that the assertion that there were many particulars was important or helpful; – it might be all right for a philosopher faced with Parmenides, but not for a theatre-lover who dislikes philosophy. If I am interested in art and what makes a good work of art I shall not be helped by being taken to the National Gallery, shown a catalogue, and told "So you see, there are several thousand beautiful pictures," – this tells me nothing to the point; I could not care less.

What, then, is Plato's point at 476A? Surely this: if we concentrate on objects we shall find, not that there are a good many beautiful ones, but that a good variety of them is beautiful, that objects of very varied descriptions are beautiful. Consequently when we try to give some account of what makes objects beautiful we shall find that we have to give a variety of different accounts; and though we may be sure that what we point to in this case is what accounts for the beauty of *this*, it is undeniably not what accounts for the beauty of this other thing. So the unavoidable outcome of accounting for beauty in terms of observable properties is to think that there is no single account to be given of beauty, – there is not just ἓν καλόν but a multiplicity of καλά: many things are beautiful, not in the sense of many particular objects, but in the sense that gold is beautiful and certain proportions, and certain combinations of colours. As it is impossible to see anything in common between the many things that can in this sense be said to be beautiful, it is natural to deny that there is one thing, beauty, present in all cases, and even to denounce such a suggestion as uneducated. Further, if it was not part of the original thesis it is obviously a consequence of it that some of the things observed to be beautiful will in some cases be ugly: a shape that would suit Helen would not suit Agamemnon; thus there is none of the many καλά which will not also be αἰσχρόν. Similarly, the normal rules of δικαιοσύνη tell us what things are just: the repayment of debts, the

122

telling of the truth; but as Cephalus was shown in Book I each of these things will also on occasion be ἄδικον.

At the risk of interrupting the argument, some account should be given here of τὰ πολλὰ διπλάσια.. As in the case of τὸ καλόν, ὁ φιλοθεάμων will consider "τί ἐστι τὸ διπλάσιον;" a foolish question. His interest in arithmetic will be a practical one, as his interest in geometry etc., and his skill in these fields will be derived from practical experience. "What is the double?", in the void, will seem to him an unprogressive question; but give him a size and he can give you the double; but as any man of education knows there are many doubles and, of course, each size which is a double is also a half. Theories about *the* Double are in his eyes useless if not retrograde: he is πρακτικός καὶ φιλότεχνος; Plato does not pursue the case of doubles, for though we might be curious about a more complete account it is not one of those things that we get upset about. The normal answers to "τί ἐστι δικαιόν;" on the other hand, have an immediate relevance to behaviour, and we ask the question because we want to know how to behave. As the answers, however, at times tell us to do things in conflict with our desires we also want to know what δικαιοσύνη is such that it is worthwhile: Plato is concerned to show that the lawgiver's answer to "τί ἐστι δικαιόν;" is on these grounds inadequate, – each answer also gives something which is ἄδικον, – and so to show that we must look elsewhere or else just abandon indefensible rules.

Τὰ πολλὰ καλὰ ἔστι καὶ οὐκ ἔστι, then, in the sense that the many "things" given in answer to "τί ἐστι καλόν;" all fail as much as they succeed; and unless "καλός" is to be said to be hopelessly ambiguous, or merely subjective, there must be some further account of an all-embracing kind. The philosopher is characterised as one who pursues and is only satisfied with an answer to "τί ἐστι καλόν;" such that what he gives ἔστι and in no way οὐκ ἔστι καλόν. The φιλοθεάμων, by contrast, is one whose main interest is practical, in the manipulation and management of particular things and situations, and his method is such that though his answers are practically helpful, still he has many answers of which each in a sense admittedly οὐκ ἔστι καλόν. He therefore clearly does not know τί ἐστι καλόν (τὸ ὄν), and so does not have ἐπιστήμη: he is said rather to have δόξα, Plato doubtless keeping to Parmenides' name for the way of the senses. Anyone who has not even got so far as the φιλοθεάμων's interest is of course in a state of ἄγνοια on the question. "Τὸ ὄν" (τὸ παντελῶς ὄν) and "τὸ μὴ ὄν μηδαμῇ" (477) are clearly incomplete expressions, to be filled out as "τὸ ὄν καλόν" or "τὸ μὴ ὄν δικαιόν" according to context: this comes out at the conclusion of the passage (479) where τὸ πολλὰ καλά are shown εἶναι καὶ μή in that each ἔστι καὶ οὐκ ἔστι καλόν. Consequently the famous passage about τὸ ὄν, τὸ μὴ ὄν and τὰ μεταξύ is concerned not with a variety of objects but with different types of answer sought and to be attained by two possible methods of enquiry (or by complete lack of interest, in the last case).

Republic VI, 507B

Before bringing forward some final confirmation of this view, I had best mention this passage from Book VI which I presented earlier as a possible support of the view that τὰ πολλά... are particulars. I hope that it is by now clear that this passage presents no real difficulty. True, it speaks of τὰ πολλά as objects of sight, not of thought; but then, οἱ φιλοθεάμονες *are* interested in particulars, and their explanations of τὸ καλόν etc. *are* in terms of visible things, or otherwise observable things; Plato *is* talking of observables, but of types, not of particulars.

Later confirmation

In Book VI the topic of Book V, the distinction between the philosopher and the pseudo-philosopher, is continued, and what is said there may be safely taken as a gloss and elaboration of the earlier passages. I will take only one passage from this book. In the course of censuring the pseudo-philosophers Socrates accuses them (492C) of taking their lead from public approbation or censure and calling the same things noble or base as the populace does. He then accuses the sophists of teaching nothing more than popular views (493A seq.); they make a study of those things which are liked and those which are disliked, acquiring a certain σοφία on the subject, without knowing what of them is δικαιόν, what ἄδικον; οἷς μὲν χαίροι ἐκεῖνο ἀγαθὰ καλῶν, οἷς δὲ ἄχθοιτο κακά, – where, if they are to be teachers, it must mean "calling the *sorts* of thing the beast likes good etc." In this way they work out their various τέχναι, and call themselves σοφοί, – ὡς δὲ καὶ ἀγαθὰ καὶ καλὰ ταῦτα τῇ ἀληθείᾳ, ἤδη πώποτε του ἤκουσας αὐτῶν λόγον διδόντος οὐ καταγέλαστον (493D); The teachings of the sophists are said to be based on observation of popular tastes, and throughout the passage the plurals "ἀγαθά" and "καλά" have been used of kinds of thing taught as good or noble; as these things accord with popular taste any view that there was some one objective account would be unpopular: αὐτὸ τὸ καλὸν ἀλλὰ μὴ τὰ πολλὰ καλά, ἢ αὐτό τι ἕκαστον καὶ μὴ τὰ πολλὰ ἕκαστα, ἔσθ᾽ ὅπως πλῆθος ἀνέξεται ἢ ἡγήσεται εἶναι;

124

(493E). The Sophists have the advantage in practice of relying on taste rather than truth; but the relevant point is that coming at the end of this passage "τὰ πολλὰ καλά" cannot mean other than "the many types of thing deemed καλόν". At the very least, this shows my interpretation of "τὰ πολλά..." to be linguistically possible.

It may still be felt that my account of Plato's worry is far-fetched, that I am reading too much in in suggesting that he is talking e.g. of moral rules, and is worried by the conventionalists' inability to give a full account of behaviour, which does not end in paradox. I shall now, therefore, quote *in extenso* the passage where Plato states it. I would draw attention to the fact that the man here spoken of is one who has always adhered to the rules of behaviour learnt from his parents; that when questioned he gives the answer of the lawgiver, which turns out to be unsatisfactory (compare the language at 538D7 with that at 479B9-10). But I will leave the passage to speak for itself: 538C6:

Τῇδε. ἔστι που ἡμῖν δόγματα ἐκ παίδων περὶ δικαίων καὶ καλῶν, ἐν οἷς ἐκτεθράμμεθα ὥσπερ ὑπὸ γονεῦσι, πειθαρχοῦντές τε καὶ τιμῶντες αὐτά. Ἔστι γάρ. Οὐκοῦν καὶ ἄλλα ἐναντία τούτων ἐπιτηδεύματα ἡδονὰς ἔχοντα, ἃ κολακεύει μὲν ἡμῶν τὴν ψυχὴν καὶ ἕλκει ἐφ᾽ αὑτά, πείθει δ᾽ οὐ τούς γε καὶ ὁπηοῦν μετρίους· ἀλλ᾽ ἐκεῖνα τιμῶσι τὰ πάτρια καὶ ἐκείνοις πειθαρχοῦσιν. Ἔστι ταῦτα.

Τί οὖν; ἦν δ᾽ ἐγώ· ὅταν τὸν οὕτως ἔχοντα ἐλθὸν ἐρώτημα ἔρηται· Τί ἐστι τὸ καλόν, καὶ ἀποκρινομένου ὃ τοῦ νομοθέτου ἤκουεν ἐξελέγχῃ ὁ λόγος, καὶ πολλάκις καὶ πολλαχῇ ἐλέγχων εἰς δόξαν καταβάλῃ ὡς τοῦτο οὐδὲν μᾶλλον καλὸν ἢ αἰσχρόν, καὶ περὶ δικαίου ὡσαύτως καὶ ἀγαθοῦ καὶ ἃ μάλιστα ἦγεν ἐν τιμῇ, μετὰ τοῦτο τί οἴει ποιήσειν αὐτὸν πρὸς αὐτὰ τιμῆς τε πέρι καὶ πειθαρχίας;

Ἀνάγκη, ἔφη, μήτε τιμᾶν ἔτι ὁμοίως μήτε πείθεσθαι.

The answer of the lawgiver would have been in terms of types of action that are right or wrong, and it is hard to believe that Plato's complaint here is not the same as at 479A-B.

τὰ δικαιά, then, are the things that it is just to do, and there is not one that on occasion may not be ἄδικον. Each δικαιόν ἔστι καὶ οὐκ ἔστι. It may be as well to end with a few remarks on τὸ ὄν and τὰ μεταξύ, over which I have so far passed rather rapidly so as not to break up the argument. There are, however, two difficulties that I must try to meet, one a possible misunderstanding, the other deriving from views about Plato's preoccupations.

125

The first, the misunderstanding, runs as follows: "You have made τὸ ὄν and τὸ μὴ ὄν incomplete expressions, to be filled out, according to context, by the addition of καλόν, δικαιόν, or whatever it may be. Yet this is surely to anticipate the *Sophist*, and such a view, to say the least of it, needs defence." Such a view would indeed need defence, but as it is not my view I shall not defend it. My point is this merely: the passage from 477 to the end of the book is closely knit together; it is enough, in order to show that one of the πολλὰ καλά ἔστι καὶ οὐκ ἔστι, to show that it is and is not καλόν (cf. 479A5-C5); what it is between is being and not being καλόν; it is *consequently* the object of δόξα, and cannot claim to yield knowledge, for knowledge is of that which is, which this has just been shown not to be; that is to say, knowledge is of that which is καλόν or whatever it may be. Now on my view this is all, so far, in Plato's eyes, truistic, granted the point that τὰ πολλὰ καλά are and are not. For knowledge, after all, is of the truth, or as the Greek has it, of that which is; but of that which is what? – this has to be supplied according to the case. It seems to me quite clear that on this interpretation Plato might still very well get into the difficulties of the *Sophist*, for he has not yet made any distinction between the 'is' of existence and those of identity and predication. How he would at this time have dealt with that problem cannot be told from this passage, because it is not his concern here, and so he is not so irrelevant as to tell us. That is not to say that there may not be indications of his views which suggest that in fact he did not know the answer, but merely that this passage dᴏes not tackle the problem nor supply the answer. The point is just that for this part of the argument it is only necessary to understand Greek: Socrates' claim is that as οἱ φιλοθεάμονες do not end up with τὸ ὄν (καλόν etc.) they cannot have knowledge. This is not without importance for the second difficulty: for if this were all there were to the argument, it would still be open to Socrates' opponents to retort that indeed it follows that they have no knowledge of justice etc., but then there is no such thing as such knowledge. But Socrates has stopped this hole, not by any argument, but by eliciting the admission earlier (476A) that there is such a thing as justice etc. He then uses this admission in order to distinguish the philosopher from the decoy; but he is especially intent to show that while the decoy's knowledge is useful, and an advance on complete lack of interest, it is in no strict sense knowledge; but this proof is not based on a metaphysical demonstration of the status of particulars, but on an admitted fact about

126

the only results obtainable in certain fields by purely empirical methods together with a logical requirement for anything that is to count as knowledge.

The Eleatics

This leads on to the second difficulty. For surely, it might be argued, this passage must be taken as a contribution to the Eleatic debate. Plato must have realised that he was flouting Parmenides' rule, and must therefore be taking up a position on questions concerning τὸ ὄν and τὸ μὴ ὄν. His very use of the word 'δόξα' recalls Parmeides and his remarks about the world of sense. Now this objection raises a great many points and I can only dogmatically state my position on them.

To begin with, I am sure that Plato would not have forgotten Parmenides when he wrote this passage, and that in consequence he doubtless enjoyed writing such Eleatically shocking things. Also he must have realised that his remarks committed him to the need to give an answer to Eleatic objections and difficulties as Socrates is perhaps represented as doing in the Phaedo, and certainly in the *Parmenides*. Despite all this, however, the fact remains that in the *Republic* Plato is not dealing with Parmenides: in the first instance he is dealing with Thrasymachus, and in this passage with people who are so far from being Eleatic that it is characteristic of them to be interested in and put a premium on beautiful sounds and shapes and colours as the source of knowledge. It is against these people that Plato is arguing; it is from them and against them that he extracts his points about εἶναι καὶ μὴ εἶναι. As I have remarked, in reference to the Δισσοὶ Λόγοι, there were those in Greece from whom it would not be difficult to get admission of such points. With these opponents it would have been unnecessary and irrelevant for Plato to turn and deal with Eleatic arguments. It is, in fact, one result of this interpretation to remove this passage from the number of those which treat of the ontological status of the physical world and suchlike problems.

This involves, of course, a far wider thesis which I cannot argue here, but which it may be as well to admit to. It seems to me quite mistaken to pass from similarity of terminology in Plato to similarity of problem: the terminology should be interpreted in terms of relevance to the particular argument; it should not be expected to provide an answer to problems not raised in the context, just because elsewhere similar terminology has been used to deal with those problems. Thus a paradox on the possession of contrary properties occurs later in the *Republic*, but in the context of a quite different argument; and Plato shows himself (e.g. in

127

the *Philebus* on questions of the One and the Many, and in the *Sophist* on τὸ ὄν) very alive to the variety of problems that one expression may cover, without, apparently, ever devising any elaborate technical terminology, – even the sacred expression 'αὐτὸ καθ'αὑτὸ τὸ ἕν" can be used in the *Republic* (524D10) to refer, not to a form, but to a finger. I therefore think that the first question to ask is: who are his opponents here? (or: what is his problem?), and then: how might this answer be an answer? Only then is it worth asking: what bearing have his answers here on his answers to other opponents and problems elsewhere? And it may by then be clear that the answer is: None. For this reason I think the key to this passage lies in the description of οἱ φιλοθεάμονες. The result of this is that in this book Plato has said nothing to Parmenides.

Wadham and Pembroke Colleges, Oxford.

Knowledge and Belief in *Republic* V

by Gail Fine (Cornell University)

It is often said that Plato distinguishes knowledge and belief by reference to their objects, so that one can have knowledge, but not beliefs, about Forms, and beliefs, but not knowledge, about sensibles. If I know, I can know only a Form; and if I have a belief, it must be directed to sensibles. Call this the two worlds theory (TW)[1].

It is clear that Plato does not always subscribe to this view. Both at *Meno* 98a and at *Theaetetus* 201a—c he clearly allows knowledge and belief to be about the same objects; and he may also there allow knowledge of sensibles. Still, the theory of Forms is not prominent in either of these dialogues, and so it might be argued that even if Plato did not always accept the two worlds theory, he at least did so in the middle dialogues, especially in the *Republic*. Not even this claim is true as it stands: at *Republic* 520c Plato says that the philosopher who redescends to the cave will have knowledge of the things there[2], and at 506c he claims to have beliefs, but not knowledge, about the Form of the Good. But although these are things Plato sometimes says, it might nonetheless be maintained that his explicit theory does not allow these claims, and that

---

[1] TW is defended by J. Brentlinger, "Particulars in Plato's Middle Dialogues", *Archiv für Geschichte der Philosophie*, LIV (1972); F. M. Cornford, *The Republic of Plato* (Oxford, 1941), pp. 180f.; R. C. Cross and A. D. Woozley, *Plato's Republic: A Philosophical Commentary* (London, 1964), pp. 164f.; R. E. Allen, "The Argument from Opposites in *Republic* V", *Review of Metaphysics* XV (1961), p. 165; G. Vlastos, "Degrees of Reality in Plato" in J. R. Bambrough, ed., *New Essays on Plato and Aristotle* (London, 1965); J. Hintikka, "Knowledge and Its Objects in Plato" in J. M. E. Moravcsik, ed., *Patterns in Plato's Thought* (Dordrecht, Holland, 1973); and by G. Santas, "Hintikka on Knowledge and Its Objects in Plato" in Moravcsik. (In what follows, these works are cited by authors' names alone.) Note that by 'the two worlds theory' I do not mean only the thesis that there are Forms as well as sensibles (a thesis I do not dispute) but especially the epistemological claim that there is only knowledge of Forms and only belief about sensibles (a claim I shall dispute). I use 'belief' merely as a counter for *doxa*; 'opinion' or 'judgement' are equally possible translations.

[2] Plato's claim is that the philosopher will "know each of the images, what they are and of what"; *gnōsesthe* plus the *hatta* clause suggest he means 'know' and not merely 'recognize'.

9 Arch. Gesch. Philosophie Bd. 60

that theory comm.its him to the two worlds theory, that there is no
knowledge of sensibles and no belief about Forms.

A crucial passage often adduced in support of this view occurs at
the end of *Rep*. V (473c11−480a13), Plato's only lengthy attempt
to distinguish knowledge from belief, and it is that passage I shall
discuss in what follows. I do not deny that the text can be read so
as to support TW. But if it is, it not only contradicts Plato's explicit
claims elsewhere, but it is also a very bad argument. Plato might,
of course, have offered us such an argument. But if we can find a
better argument consistent with the text, we should prefer it, and
I think such a better reading is available. The best argument consistent with the text, however, fails to support TW.

I shall argue that although Plato in some way correlates knowledge with Forms, and belief with sensibles, he does not say that there
is knowledge only of Forms or belief only about sensibles. All he
argues is the weaker claim that to know, one must, first of all, know
Forms; restricted to sensibles, one cannot achieve knowledge.
This makes Forms the primary objects of knowledge, but not necessarily the only ones; knowledge begins, but need not end, with
knowledge of Forms. This also leaves open the possibility of having
only beliefs, and not knowledge, about Forms.

If this is right, *Rep*. V does not commit Plato to TW. He might still
be committed to it elsewhere, of course, and I do not dispute that
claim here. But if this central passage does not commit Plato to
TW, we should at least be more careful in ascribing it to him elsewhere[3].

I

The general context is Plato's claim that only philosophers
should rule, since only they have knowledge, and knowledge is necessary for good ruling. Only philosophers have knowledge, he argues, because only they know Forms, a knowledge without which no
other knowledge is possible. He argues this claim twice over — once,
briefly, to Glaucon, on the assumption that the theory of Forms is
true[4], and once, at greater length, to certain opponents called

---

[3] *Phil*. 58 e—59 c (although see also *Phil*. 61 d 10—e 4, 62 a 2—d 7) and *Tm*.
28 a—29 c may support TW; but I do not think the *Rep*. is committed to TW.
[4] One might think that the first argument, since it assumes the theory of Forms
at the outset, supports TW; but it does not. Plato argues only that the sightlovers, since they do not recognize Forms, cannot achieve knowledge and so
have only belief. This of course does not imply that no one can ever have
knowledge of sensibles, or that every claim about a Form is tantamount to knowledge of it (cf. 476 c 9—d 3 with 520 c). Plato argues only that there is no know-

sightlovers (*philotheāmones*, 475d2; cf. 476a10, b4), who do not accept the theory of Forms (476c2—7); they recognize that there are many beautiful things, but not that there is one Form, the Beautiful[5].

In the second argument, Plato wants to persuade the sightlovers, on grounds acceptable to them (476e4—8, 478e7—479b2), that they do not have knowledge but only belief. If his argument is to rest on genuinely noncontroversial premises, as he claims it does, it cannot assume the theory of Forms, or any esoteric theory unacceptable to the sightlovers, at the outset. I shall ask later whether or not Plato satisfies this condition of noncontroversiality[6].

Plato's general strategy is to correlate knowledge with what is (knowledge is *epi tō(i) onti*), belief with what is and is not *(epi tō(i) onti te kai mē)*, and ignorance[7] with what is not *(epi tō(i) mē onti)*. He then draws out various implications of these correlations, and concludes that only those who know Forms have knowledge at all; the sightlovers, who are restricted to the world revealed by their senses, can at best have belief.

The force of this argument in large part depends on the reading of 'is' (*'esti'*); but a decision here is not at all easy. Plato's opening moves illustrate the difficulty:

(1) Whoever knows knows something *(ti)* (476e7—9).
(2) Whoever knows knows something that is *(on ti)*; for one could not know a thing that is not *(mē on ti)* (476e10—11).
(3) What completely is is completely knowable; what in no way is is in no way knowable (477a2—4).
(4) If anything is and is not, it lies between what really is and what in no way is (477a6—7).
(5) Knowledge is set over *(epi)* what is; ignorance (*agnōsia*) is set over what is not (477a9—10).
(6) Something between knowledge and ignorance is set over what is and is not (477a10—b1).

---

ledge without knowledge of Forms — that is, all knowledge begins with Forms. So read, the conclusion of the first argument exactly matches that of the second, although the arguments leading there are very different.

[5] For discussion of the sightlovers, see N. R. Murphy, *The Interpretation of Plato's Republic* (Oxford, 1951), pp. 100—105; J. C. B. Gosling, "*Republic* V: *ta polla kala*, etc.", *Phronesis* (1960), pp. 12f. I discuss the sightlovers in IV below.

[6] See Gosling, "*Doxa* and *Dunamis* in Plato's Republic", *Phronesis* XIII (1968), pp. 120—122; Murphy, p. 105. It may be, of course, that Plato's conclusion is controversial; but his opening premises should not be. Cf. n. 22.

[7] I use 'ignorance' to translate *'agnoia'*; see III below.

9*

(1) might mean:

    (1a) Whoever knows knows some existent thing; or
    (1b) Whoever knows has some content of his knowledge.

On (1a) Plato is correlating knowledge with features of the world. I shall call this reading an objects analysis. On (1b) Plato is only claiming that if one knows, there is an answer to the question "What do you know?"; he is correlating knowledge with certain sorts of propositions, saying that there is some content of the cognitive condition. No conclusions about what objects these propositions are about need follow. I shall call this reading a contents analysis; in what follows I defend it[8].

A decision between (1a) and (1b) depends on the readings endorsed for (2)—(6), where difficulties again emerge. As is wellknown, 'esti' can be used in several ways[9]. Three of its standard uses, and the only ones we will consider here, are (a) the existential (is-e), (b) the predicative (is-p), and (c) the veridical (is-v). (2), for example, could thus read:

    (2a) Whoever knows knows something that exists.
    (2b) Whoever knows knows something that is (really) F.
    (2c) Whoever knows knows something that is true.

Here (1a) goes naturally with (2a) or (2b), and (1b) goes naturally with (2c). On either of the first two alternatives, Plato simply repeats the claim made at (1a), that knowledge is correlated with objects. On the third reading, he claims not only that knowledge has content (1b) but also that that content is always true or, in other words, that knowledge entails truth.

---

[8] I use 'contents' where I. M. Crombie, *An Examination of Plato's Doctrines*, vol. II (London, 1962), p. 57, uses 'internal accusative' and where Gosling (1968) uses 'formal object'. 'epi' can range over contents as well as objects, as Crombie, p. 58, recognizes. The point is missed by Allen, p. 165, and by Cross and Woozley, who assume 'epi' must range over objects. For a clear Platonic use of what I call contents, see *Phil.* 37a. Cf. also *Phd.* 75 d 4, 75 a 4, 76 c 15 with D. Gallop, *Plato: Phaedo* (Oxford, 1975), p. 230.

[9] For general discussion of 'esti', see C. H. Kahn, *The Verb Be in Ancient Greek* (Dordrecht: Reidel, 1973). G. E. L. Owen, "Plato on Not-Being" in G. Vlastos, ed., *Plato*, vol. I (New York, 1970), pp. 223—225; G. Vlastos, pp. 1—7, and M. Furth, "Elements of Eleatic Ontology" in *Journal of the History of Philosophy* VI (1968), pp. 114—116 argue that Plato uses, fuses, or confuses various uses of 'esti' in this and other arguments. Although Plato does not explicitly discuss different uses of 'esti' until the *Sophist*, this does not entail that he was confused about them earlier. In what follows, I try to see if we can ascribe to Plato an argument that does not require confusion; if such an argument is available, surely it is to be preferred.

Applying these three readings to the rest of the opening steps reveals the outlines of the interpretations I shall consider here. TW has focused on is-e and is-p, yielding a degrees of existence (DE) and a degrees of reality (DR) interpretation[10]. For DE, the claim is that knowledge is of what exists, that belief is of what half exists or what both exists and does not exist, and that ignorance is of what does not exist or is not anything at all. For DR, knowledge is of what is really F (for some predicate F), belief is of what is F and not F, and ignorance is of what is not F.

Although they are possible readings of the text, both DE and DR provide inappropriate starting premisses, by violating the condition of noncontroversiality. DE sharply separates the objects of knowledge and belief, and consigns the objects of belief to the realm of "halfexistent". Even though no specific objects are so construed at this stage, it would be inappropriate to assume that whatever the relevant objects turn out to be, they cannot be both known and believed, or that they merely half exist.

DR also separates the objects of knowledge and belief. But its characterization of the objects of belief might seem more promising. At least, as we shall see, the sightlovers agree that their objects of concern, the many beautifuls, for example, are beautiful and not beautiful. Moreover, a version of (2b) seems to occur at the close of the argument (479e10—480a4; cf. step (36)). But this is a conclusion Plato argues for, and so it should not be a starting premise. Moreover, if we take (3) to mean that whoever knows knows only what is fully F, and not also what is F and not F, then it violates the condition of noncontroversiality. For why can I not know of a particular action, for example, that it is just and not just? There is no intuitive reason for the sightlovers to accept this claim. DR, like DE, provides Plato with inappropriate starting premisses.

Readings focusing on is-v are more promising. Plato's claim is then that knowledge is of what is true, that belief is of what is and is not true, and that ignorance is of what is false. This claim states familiar conditions on knowledge and belief that the sightlovers can be expected to agree to: knowledge, but not belief, entails truth. And unlike DE and DR, this claim does not force a separation of the objects of knowledge and belief, but only of their contents. But this claim does not entail TW: although knowledge and

---

[10] For a defense of DE, cf. Brentlinger, pp. 149ff., and Cross and Woozley. For a defense of DR, cf. Vlastos; Gosling (1968).

belief differ in their truth implications, the claims that are known or believed can be directed to the same objects.

The is-v reading allows two interpretations of belief. Plato might be claiming that each token belief is "true and not true", in the sense of being partly true and partly false, or near the mark. Call this the degrees of truth reading (DT)[11]. Alternatively, Plato might be characterizing the set of beliefs covered by the capacity, claiming that it contains true as well as false members: some of my beliefs are true, others false. Call this reading T.

For DT, 'belief' acquires a specialized sense, not elsewhere accorded it, as being "near the mark"; false beliefs are not beliefs at all. Moreover, the contents of knowledge and belief will be irreducibly different: knowledge will range over truths, and belief over partial truths. T avoids these unintuitive results. It allows false as well as true beliefs (*Gorg.* 454d), and it allows that the same proposition can be the content of belief and of knowledge — at least not all propositions are such that they can be only believed or only known, for you might know a proposition about which I have only belief (*Meno* 97a—98b, *Tht.* 201a—c).

T is the most intuitively plausible of the suggested readings, and in what follows I see how far Plato's argument fits it. I do not claim that T is ever required; but I do claim that it is a possible reading of the text, and that it provides Plato with a more plausible argument than do any of the proposed alternatives. But in providing Plato with a plausible argument, we also avoid TW. For Plato now distinguishes knowledge and belief not by reference to their objects, but by reference to the truth implications of their contents. This need not rule out every version of TW; Plato might claim that the contents of knowledge and belief are always about different objects. But the argument he presents here, as we shall see, neither requires nor suggests any version of TW.

II

Plato argues next that belief is the middle state between knowledge and ignorance; this entails, by (6), that it is set over what is and is not, but Plato does not reach this conclusion until much later.

His next steps simply state what is to be proved:

---

[11] For a defense of DT, see Gosling (1968); Crombie.

(7) Belief is a different capacity (*dunamis*) from knowledge (477b3—6).
(8) Therefore, belief and knowledge are set over different things, each according to its capacity (477b7—8).
(9) Knowledge is set over what is, to know how what is is (*gnōnai hōs esti to on*) (477b10—11).

(7) introduces belief explicitly for the first time; later stages of the argument look for an analogue to (9) for belief, in accordance with (8). (7) also shows that the capacities of knowledge and belief, and not necessarily every token act of knowing or believing, are being distinguished. Were token acts being considered, Plato might be pressed to DT; the emphasis on capacities at least allows T. Plato can now claim, not that every content of belief is only partially true, but that the set of beliefs collected by the capacity of belief contains both true and false members.

(10) Capacities are a kind of thing by which we are able (*dunametha*) to do what we are able to do, and by which everything else can do what it can do (477c1—4).
(11) Capacities are distinguished by (a) what they are set over (*epi*) and by (b) what work they accomplish. What is set over one thing and what accomplishes one thing is one capacity; those things which are set over different things and accomplish different things are different capacities (477c6—d5).
(12) Knowledge is a capacity (477d7—9).
(13) Belief is a capacity, since it is that by which we are able to believe (477e1—3).
(14) Knowledge and belief are different capacities, since knowledge does not err (*anhamartēton*) but belief may err (477e6—7).
(15) Therefore each of them, being capable of something different, is set over something different (478a3—4).
(16) Knowledge is set over what is, to know how what is is (*to on gnōnai hōs echei*) (478a6).
(17) Belief believes (478a8).
(18) Since knowledge and belief are different capacities, and are set over different things, what is known (*gnōston*) and what is believed (*doxaston*) cannot be the same (478a12—b2).

(19)   Since what is known is what is, what is believed must be
       something other than what is (478b3—5).

(10) provides a general account of what a capacity is. (11) expands
upon (10) by providing two conditions for capacity individuation.
It follows from (10), in (12) and (13), that knowledge and belief are
capacities. Applying (11), it then follows, in (14), that knowledge
and belief are different capacities. (15) follows from (11) and (14).
(16) then specifies (11a) and (11b) for knowledge; and this restates
(9). (17) states (11b) for belief. It then remains, as (18) and (19)
acknowledge, to find what belief is set over (the correlate of belief),
in satisfaction of (11a), and this occupies Plato in the final stage of
his argument.

These steps may well arouse our suspicions. (11) claims that if
two purported capacities satisfy its two conditions in the same
way, they are in fact one capacity; and if they satisfy them differently, they are two different capacities. This apparently leaves open
two additional possibilities, however: (i)x and y do the same thing
to different things, and (ii)x and y do different things to the same
thing.

Now at (14) Plato seems to infer from the fact that knowledge
and belief satisfy (11b) differently that they are different capacities;
that is, he seems to assume that because knowledge and belief
satisfy (11b) differently, they also satisfy (11a) differently and
hence, by (11), are different capacities. But given (ii) above, Plato
does not seem to be justified in assuming that knowledge and belief
satisfy (11a) differently, just from the fact that they satisfy (11b)
differently, even if he is justified in assuming that they are different
capacities. For why should knowledge and belief not be different
capacities with different work on the same things? Husbandry and
butchery, for example, do different work, even if both are set over
domestic animals, and so have the same objects or sphere of operation; a difference in their work does not entail a difference in their
objects.

To see whether or not this suspicion of unfairness is warranted, we need to examine (11a) and (11b) more carefully. (11b) is
explained, at least in part, by (14): knowledge, but not belief, does
not err. That is to say, knowledge knows and belief believes (cf.
(13) and (17)), and the result of this work is that knowledge will
collect only truths, because only they can be known, whereas belief
will collect both truths and falsehoods, since both can be believed.

The result of the different work of knowledge and belief is that knowledge, but not belief, includes only truths, but belief contents include both truths and falsehoods[12].

Our reading of (11a) depends on our interpretation of *'epi'*. For TW, *'epi'* ranges over objects. Plato is then assuming that different capacities (*dunameis*) must have different objects. Not only is this untrue in general, as the earlier example of husbandry and butchery makes clear, but if it is what Plato means here, then his argument is indeed invalid. For, as we have seen, (11b) does not entail (11a), so interpreted. On the TW reading, then, this argument is invalid[13].

The contents analysis, however, can avoid this result. As we have seen, *'epi'* can range over contents as well as objects, and was most plausibly so read in earlier stages. Retaining that reading here has the further advantage of rendering Plato's argument valid. For Plato now claims only that when one knows (11b) one knows a piece of knowledge (11a); and when one believes (11b) one believes a belief (11a). That is how (11b) determines (11a). So read, the argument simply elaborates earlier, and noncontroversial, claims; and the trivial move from (11b) to (11a) does not illicitly preclude (i) and (ii), as TW does. To say that knowledge is set over pieces of knowledge, and that belief is set over beliefs, does not restrict the objects these propositions are about; husbandry and butchery are concerned with different sorts of facts, but these different facts could equally well be about the same domestic animals. The objects of knowledge and belief need not be separated; indeed, they are not relevant to the argument at all. Ascribing to Plato a valid argument, then, goes hand in hand with rejecting TW.

Plato has not only allowed there to be knowledge and belief about the same objects ((ii) is left open); he has also left open the possibility that your token-piece of knowledge could be my token-belief. A given proposition is a belief when it is believed,

---

[12] This interpretation of *'anhamartēton'* is adequate for the argument, whether or not it is all Plato has in mind. Truth is, of course, only a necessary, and not also a sufficient, condition on the content of knowledge. Plato elsewhere also endorses an explanation condition (see, e. g., *Meno* 98a); but that condition need not be invoked here, since the set of contents collected by the capacities of knowledge and belief can be distinguished by the truth condition alone. I follow Crombie, p. 57, and Santas, pp. 45f. in correlating *'anhamartēton'* with (11b).

[13] This problem for TW is also noted by Crombie, p. 57, and our alternative accounts of the argument are the same.

and a piece of knowledge when it is known; that is how (11b) determines (11a)[14].

III

Plato has now specified both what knowledge is set over and what work it does (16). He has claimed that belief is a distinct capacity from knowledge (14), and he has specified what work it does (17). He must now specify what it is set over. First, however, he distinguishes belief from ignorance; this is in order, given (5) and (6).

(20) Whoever believes believes some one thing (478 b 6—10).

(21) What is not is not one thing, but nothing (478 b 12—c 1).

(22) We assign ignorance to what is not, and knowledge to what is (478 c 3—4).

(23) Therefore we do not believe either what is or what is not (478 c 6).

By (19) is has been shown that belief is not set over what is, and this conclusion is repeated at (23), along with the claim that it is not set over what is not, either. That claim evidently implies that belief is not the same capacity as ignorance, since ignorance is said to be set over what is not ((22), (5)).

Now we might expect this argument to be parallel to (14)—(19). There Plato claimed that belief is not set over what is because it does not entail truth as knowledge does. 'What is' is not an adequate account of the content of belief. Similarly here, Plato claims that neither is 'what is not' an adequate account of the content of belief, since belief does not entail falsity, as ignorance does. Still, particular beliefs might be false just as, earlier, they could be true. The claim is only that belief entails neither truth nor falsity.

But the argument seems to say rather more than this. (20) and (21) seem to claim not that all beliefs are false, but that the contents of belief contain no false beliefs. If false beliefs are now assigned to ignorance, belief will no longer be set over true and false beliefs. It then either collapses into knowledge, if it is simply set over what is — a collapse the previous argument had tried to avoid — or is correlated with partial truths, as DT suggests.

But neither does this seem to account for all that occurs here. For (20) and (21) also seem to shift away from is-v to is-e (what does not exist) or to a strong version

---

[14] This is of course consistent with (18). For (18) does not discuss *token* contents but only the *set* of belief contents and of knowledge contents. It says that the set of belief contents is not the same as the set of knowledge contents, since it has one different property: containing true and false members, and not only true members. This of course does not prevent your knowing that justice is psychic harmony while I only believe it.

of is-p (what is not anything); they mention the availability of content, not the truth or falsity of particular contents.

So read (20) may seem plausible: it supplies an analogue to (1) for belief. Belief, like knowledge, has content; when one believes, there is some content of the mental condition. Considering (20) along with (21), however, leads to other problems. For Plato may now seem to be denying the possibility of false belief, along familiar lines; as Crombie suggests, he ''seems to argue from the premise that every belief must have content to the conclusion that the content of a belief cannot be a nonentity, or in other words a falsehood''[15]. Retaining is-v above seemed to restrict the content of belief to true beliefs; ignorance was set over false beliefs. Now, if Plato equivocates between is-v and is-p, he seems to deny that there are any false beliefs. Either way, belief will not be set over true and false beliefs as I claimed it would.

But the argument need not be read in either of these two ways. We can easily avoid the equivocation Crombie suggests by using only is-p here. Plato's claim in (20), as we have seen, is that belief has content; it does not happen that one believes and yet believes nothing. But then (21) may, instead of shifting illegitimately to is-v, simply draw out this consequence of (20). In assigning what is not to *agnoia*, Plato assigns not false beliefs but nothing to it. *Agnoia* is then something like blank ignorance, and there is no determinate content of the mental condition. True and false beliefs are still the correlate of belief, as we claimed; *agnoia* consists not of false beliefs but of ignorance or lack of awareness. If one is ignorant of p, one cognizes nothing true of p; there is no content of the mental condition.

The chief difficulty with this reading is that (22) is then strikingly unparallel to (5), despite their apparent similarity; for (5) uses is-v, whereas (22) uses is-p. Another reading is possible, however, and it will preserve the parallelism. Suppose I claim that justice is a vegetable. Plato might argue that my claim does not amount to a belief about justice at all; it displays total ignorance of justice. We might then read (21) with is-v, after all, while still avoiding the equivocation Crombie suggested. It claims that if what I say is not at all true of justice, it says nothing — that is, it says nothing true about justice. So read (22) and (5) both use is-v. Nor is this line of argument DT. Plato's claim is now only that totally false beliefs are assigned to ignorance, and not that all false beliefs are. If one has *agnoia*, he will have a totally false belief, or ignorance. But Plato has not asserted that every false belief is a content of ignorance. Although ignorance has as its contents only very false beliefs, not every false belief need be assigned to ignorance.

Plato has now proved that:

(24) Belief is neither knowledge nor ignorance (478 c 8).

This makes belief a candidate for being the middle state, set over what is and is not, and he next argues that is satisfies the conditions for being the middle state:

---

[15] Crombie, *op. cit.*, p. 59.

(25) Belief is neither clearer than knowledge nor more obscure than ignorance; it is more obscure than knowledge, but clearer than ignorance (478 c 10—14).

(26) Belief lies between knowledge and ignorance (478 d 1—4).

(27) We said before (in (6)) that what is and is not will be between what is and what is not, and will have some state between ignorance and knowledge set over it (478 d 5—9).

It follows that belief is set over what is and is not; (6) can now be filled in appropriately. If the argument we have sketched is Plato's, he has, as promised, distinguished knowledge and belief on non-controversial grounds, acceptable to the sightlover. He has argued that knowledge, but not belief, entails truth; there may be false beliefs, but there is no false knowledge. We need not appeal to is-e or is-p to understand Plato's main claims; nor need we appeal to a peculiar "degrees of truth" doctrine. The first two options were ruled out on grounds of general plausibility; the argument could be read without them, and was effective only without them. DT, although it may seem plausible initially, is less attractive once Plato makes clear that he is discussing the set of beliefs covered by the capacity; he can then say, as we would like, that although any particular belief is determinately true or false, the set of beliefs contains some true and some false members.

But the argument is not yet complete. The sightlover could accept it so far, and still see no reason to conclude that he has only belief; but showing this was Plato's main aim. In the final stage of his argument he goes further, and argues that the particular claims of the sightlover are at best beliefs.

IV

The final stage of Plato's argument raises more severe problems for my interpretation T than any encountered so far. The first problem arises with the next step:

(28) It remains, then, to find what partakes of what is and is not so that we may say it is believed (478 e 1—4).

(28) is problematic, for it seems to say that every token belief is true and not true, or only partially true, as DT, but not T, holds. Nor are the next steps of Plato's argument encouraging:

(29) Each of the many Fs is no more F than not F (479 e 5— 479 b 8).

(30) Therefore, each of the many Fs is and is not (479 b 9—10).

(31) The many Fs, therefore, are between being and not being (479 c 6—d 1).

(29)—(31) seem to shift away from DT no less than from T, towards one or another version of TW; for it is clear that here 'is' cannot be 'is-v', but must be 'is-e' or 'is-p'. Moreover (28) claims quite generally that whatever is between being and not being is what is believed; (31) asserts that the many Fs are between being and not being. The conclusion seems clear: belief is set over the many Fs. And this implication is in fact explicitly drawn in the last step:

(32) We have found, then, that the many *nomima* of the many about the beautiful and the rest roll about between what is not and what fully is (479 d 3—5).

(33) We agreed that if any such thing appeared it would be assigned to the intermediate capacity and be something believed and not known (479 d 7—9).

(34) Therefore, those who look on the many Fs have only belief, and not knowledge (479 e 1—5).

(35) Those who look on the Fs which always stay the same have knowledge (479 d 7—8).

(36) Knowledge is set over Forms; belief is set over the many Fs (479 d 10—480 a 4).

But it now looks as if Plato has specified Forms and sensibles as the correlates of knowledge and belief; he seems to be concerned with objects and not, as we thought, with contents. This leaves us with two options: either Plato consistently intended one or another version of the objects analysis, so that T is just irrelevant; or else Plato began with the noncontroversial assumptions we have elicited, and now shifts, legitimately or not, to a claim about objects[16].

I argue first that if we use DE or DR here, Plato's argument is either fallacious or unfair. I then argue that although (29)—(31) shift away from is-v, they explain, and do not controvert, T.

(29) clearly uses is-p; the predicate term is in fact explicitly specified ('is no more F than not F'). The claim is the familiar Platonic one, pressed in the first argument addressed to Glaucon, as well as elsewhere, that any observable property adduced to explain

---

[16] It is of course possible that Plato just confuses these various uses so that 'shift' is inappropriate; but I do not think this assumption is necessary. Cf. n. 9.

what makes something beautiful, for example, is no more beautiful than ugly[17]. In some cases, bright coloring explains something's beauty; in other cases, an appeal to bright coloring explains something's ugliness. But then bright coloring is no more beautiful than ugly. Any observable property F is both F and not F, since it collects F as well as not F cases. The sightlovers can be expected to agree, and so (29) does not violate the condition of noncontroversiality: no one explanation of beauty, phrased in terms of sensibles, will account for all cases of beauty; and it is for just this reason that the sightlovers insist on many accounts. No one account will do.

Now (30) and (31) differ from (29) in omitting the predicate 'is no more F than not F'. For DE this indicates that Plato has moved from 'is no more F than not F' to 'does and does not exist'. But the move is of course fallacious, since is-p does not carry existential import in this way. One cannot infer from the fact that x is not F that x does not (fully) exist. The paper on which I am now writing is not green, nonetheless, it exists. Yet DE seems to rest largely on the supposition that Plato is guilty of this crude error[18].

This does not imply, of course, that Plato does not endorse DE. But if we can find a more plausible interpretation, we should prefer it; and it is not difficult to find one. (30) and (31) are easily taken as ellipses of (29); (29) licenses us to read (30) and (31) correspondingly. Is-p is then the only use of *'esti'* we need see here[19].

But now one may wish to argue that, since is-p is relevant here, all preceding unsupplemented uses of *'esti'* be read correspondingly, and that DR therefore best represents Plato's argument. Plato's claim is then that one can know only what is really and fully F, or the Forms; one can at best have beliefs about sensibles which, as (29) explains, are F and not F. As Gosling writes, "Socrates is going to argue that the offerings of the *philotheāmones* are and yet are not just, beautiful, etc. and so must be *doxasta*."[20]

This line of argument, however, either violates the condition of non-controversiality, or is invalid. We might agree to read (2) as

[17] See, e. g., *Phd.* 66a, 74b, 100b; *HMa.* 289cd; *Rep.* 523—4. For discussion, see Gosling (1960) and T. H. Irwin, "Plato's Heracleiteanism" (forthcoming in the *Philosophical Quarterly* (January, 1977)).
[18] At least, Cross and Woozley (pp. 145 and 162) cite no other evidence in favor of DE (aside from the undefended assumption that Plato systematically confuses is-e and is-p).
[19] Cf. Gosling (1960), pp. 123f.; Vlastos, p. 6, n. 4.
[20] Gosling (1968), p. 126. Vlastos also defends this view.

(2b), so that (2), taken together with (3), claims that I can know only what is fully F, and not also what is F and not F. So read, Plato's argument is valid, but in beginning with this assumption, he violates his condition of noncontroversiality. For why should I not be able to know, for example, that sensibles are F and not F? Surely by itself the claim that sensibles are and are not just provides no reason for precluding knowledge of them. Of course, I can know that x is fully F only if x is fully F. But, similarly, I can know that x is F and not F only if x is F and not F. Read this way, Plato's argument is invalid: it begins with the plausible (2c) reading of (2), that knowledge entails truth, but then draws an illegitimate conclusion about the unknowability of sensibles. The underlying reasoning seems to go something like this:

(i) Necessarily (if A knows that x is F, then x is F).
(ii) If x is a sensible, x is F and not F.
(iii) There are sensibles, and therefore things that are F and not F.
(iv) One cannot know that x is F, if x is a sensible, since, (by iii), x is (also) not F.

'Is F and not F' is, however, a perfectly good substitution instance, in (i), for 'is F'; and since sensibles are F and not F, Plato has not shown why one cannot know that they are. This line of defense, then, leaves Plato with an invalid argument. Of course, one might wish to buttress the argument with additional premises that yield the desired conclusion validly. But the fact remains that no such premises are specified here. Again, if a more plausible argument can be found, it is to be preferred.

I agree, then, that (29)—(31) use is-p; but I resist interpreting the preceding argument to suit. Instead, I think Plato uses is-v in preceding stages, and shifts to is-p here. If this is so, we face a problem of a different sort: does Plato simply confuse is-v and is-p? Or is there a plausible connecting link between the two uses of '*esti*'? I think a link between is-v and is-p can be found, and it preserves the veridical reading.

Note first that (32) says not that the many Fs, the concern of (29)—(31), are between being and not being, but that *nomima* about the many Fs are between being and not being. (33), correspondingly, implies that *nomima* are the correlate of belief. What are these *nomima*? '*Nomimon*' is a general word for anything one can *nomizein*; it also conveys a notion of generality, and of custom or convention. It can be complemented with is-p or is-v, depending on whether we take it to mean "customary rules" or "customary beliefs". Now although *'nomimon'* can in general be complemented with is-p, the present context suggests is-v. It is the beliefs of the many about justice and the like — that justice is paying one's debts, for example (*Rep.* 331c) — that are being criticized; since the sightlovers restrict themselves to sensible properties in attempting to say what justice is, they are led to various claims that will be unsatisfactory. Plato's claim is that the sightlovers' beliefs about beauty, justice, and the like are the correlate of belief; (32) than uses is-v[21].

Now to say that (32) assigns only certain beliefs to belief does not yet answer all our worries. For it is still true that (29)—(31) use is-p, and that (36) assigns the many Fs to belief; even if *nomima* are among the correlates specified for belief, Plato's claim seems to go beyond this. Also, we have not yet answered an earlier question, raised about (28), of whether the present use of is-v better fits DT or T. Both problems can, I think, be answered in favor of T.

The sightlovers do not acknowledge Forms; all their accounts or explanations of beauty, justice, and the like, will be phrased in terms of sensibles. They will define beauty, for example, as the brightly colored; their accounts will refer to and be based on such observable properties. But we know from earlier steps, and from elsewhere, that such properties are F and not F; some cases of bright coloring are beautiful, others are not. But if 'bright coloring' picks out cases of ugliness no less than of beauty, no belief like 'the beautiful is the brightly colored' can amount to knowledge — or, in general, no belief based on observable properties can amount to knowledge. The connection between is-p and is-v is then this: reliance on observable properties that are F and not F (is-p) issues in the unsatisfactory *nomima* (is-v); the *nomima* are based on observable properties, and that basis prevents them from being knowledgeable accounts.

---

[21] Many translators use is-v for translating *'nomima'* here: 'beliefs' (Bloom), 'conventional opinions' (H. D. P. Lee, G. M. A. Grube), 'conventional notions' (F. M. Cornford). J. Adam (*Rep.* vol. II, p. 157; cf. I 343) says that *'nomima'* refers to 'popular canons or opinions'. This reading seems suggested by the sense of the argument, although the syntax does not, of course, require it. For other occurrences of *'nomima'*, cf. *Rep.* 484 d 2, 589 e 7, *Gorg.* 488 d 9, e 4, *HMa.* 294 c 4. I should make it clear that my interpretation of *nomima* is not also an interpretation of *ta polla kala*, which I take to be sensible properties, as I explain above. As I read the argument, Plato talks about certain sorts of opinions as well as about certain sorts of objects. Although these concerns are connected in the way I explain above, they are distinct concerns.

This connection also explains (34)—(36). The sightlovers, since they look only to the many Fs, can at best have belief; no account phrased in terms of sensibles can yield knowledge, and so in that sense belief is set over the many Fs. Now this leaves open two possibilities: either there is no knowledge, since there are no entities beyond the many Fs by reference to which one could acquire knowledgeable accounts; or else there is knowledge and, hence, there are other entities beyond the many Fs, that make this knowledge possible. In first explicitly mentioning Forms in these concluding steps, Plato endorses the second option[22].

This reference to Forms and sensibles does not play into the hands of TW. Plato is not claiming that all knowledge concerns only Forms, or that all beliefs concern only sensibles. He does claim that all knowledge requires knowledge of Forms. But this leaves open the possibility that one could be aware of Forms in less than a knowledgeable way; and it also leaves open that once one has knowledge of Forms, it can be extended beyond Forms to sensibles. All knowledge begins with knowledge of Forms, but it need not end with them, too; nor need every grasp of a Form amount to knowledge of it. To understand Plato's claims, the appropriate restrictive clauses must be assumed: restricted to the many Fs, the most one can attain is belief; for knowledge, one needs an account in terms of Forms. But the content of this account need not be restricted to Forms, nor need every claim about a Form be knowledgeable.

I have argued so far that the shift to is-p does not upset, but rather explains, T. But we are still left with another problem: (32) assigns only *nomima* to belief. This supports an is-v reading, but it may seem to support DT rather than T. A *nomimon*, such as that the beautiful is the brightly colored, is, presumably, simply false. *Nomima*, although false, are not, however, contents of ignorance, since they are not totally false; but since they are not true, neither can they be contents of knowledge. But once it is spelled out this way, it looks as if we have supported DT: *nomima* are the contents of belief, since they are only partially true.

---

[22] It may seem that he is not justified in doing so, however, given the first possibility, so that his argument becomes invalid at this stage. I think this is a plausible line to take. But the strategy is a familiar one in Plato (see, e. g., *Pmd.* 135a—c, *Tm.* 51d, where Plato also infers that Forms must exist if knowledge does) and so does not affect my interpretation. In any case this line of argument need not violate the principle of noncontroversiality; if the sightlovers will agree that there is knowledge, they will now accept the existence of Forms. Plato will then have committed them to the existence of Forms on grounds they have accepted. His argument then follows the standard elenctic procedure.

10 Arch. Gesch. Philosophie Bd. 60

I do not think we need to read Plato in this way. There are at least two alternatives. First, although any *nomimon* is simply false, it collects other beliefs, some of which are true, others of which are false. For example, the *nomimon* that courage is endurance leads to the true belief that Socrates is courageous and to the false belief that lions are (cf. *Laches*, 196 e). 'Is and is not' then applies disjunctively to members of a set of beliefs collected by a *nomimon*; but every member of the set is determinately true or false.

Second, it may be that *'nomima'* need not be restricted to the general accounts offered by the sightlovers, but applies as well to the beliefs such accounts collect; that is, not only 'courage is endurance' but also 'Socrates is courageous' may count as a *nomimon*. In that case, we still consider sets of beliefs clustered about a general account, and 'is and is not' still applies disjunctively; but since each member of the set is a *nomimon*, (32) and (33) are not elliptical, as they are on the first reading.

If we do not take 'is and is not' disjunctively, in either of these suggested ways, but instead take it to apply conjunctively to each *nomimon*, then Plato's description of *nomima* does indeed seem close to DT. For he then seems to say that although any *nomimon* is just false, none is false enough to count as a content of ignorance (since, for example, each leads to some true beliefs). But although *nomima*, interpreted this way, do fit DT's specifications for beliefs, we need not interpret the preceding argument to suit. Instead, what Plato does at (32), I think, is to restrict the scope of his argument. His claim there is not that all beliefs are like *nomima*, but only that *nomima* are at best beliefs. That is, being a *nomimon* is a sufficient but not a necessary condition for being a content of belief.

Plato prepares us for the shift. His avowed strategy is to show that, given a general and noncontroversial account of belief, the sightlovers can at best have belief. To show this, of course, he must provide not only the general account but also a description of sightlovers' beliefs. It is not surprising that the specialized account is narrower: it attempts to classify only one sort of claim. Other claims might count as beliefs for other reasons; but what is of immediate concern is *nomima*.

Plato's claim, then, is that *nomima* are not contents of knowledge, since they are not true and knowledge entails truth; but although false, they are not contents of ignorance, either, for they are not totally false. If we want to consider other beliefs, the explanation of their status might differ; not all beliefs are like *nomima*. All Plato has argued here is that *nomima* (*inter alia*) are contents of belief. But the final narrowing of his argument need not infect preceding stages[23].

---

[23] This alternative is not wholly satisfactory, however. For now Plato does equivocate on 'is and is not'. Until (32) it seemed to apply disjunctively to contents collected by the capacity of belief, so that any belief was determinately true or false; but at (32) and (33) 'is and is not' seems to apply conjunctively to a particular *nomimon*. I do not know if Plato does equivocate in this way, or consistently advocates DT, or endorses one of the two more satisfying explanations I suggest above. Any of these alternatives is possible; I prefer the third largely on grounds of plausibility, and because it fits well with the earlier argument, where Plato seems clearly to be considering sets of beliefs collected by the general capacity of belief. Even if we are pressed to DT or to the equivocation

VI

On the traditional two worlds interpretation of Plato's argument in *Republic* V, knowledge and belief are distinguished by reference to their special objects: knowledge is only of Forms, and belief is only of sensibles. One cannot know sensibles or have beliefs about Forms. If this is Plato's argument, it violates his starting condition of noncontroversiality, by requiring strong and implausible premises that his opponents cannot be expected to agree to. Moreover, Plato misuses his criteria for capacity-individuation, and, on at least some of the current interpretations, equivocates on uses of *'esti'*.

I suggested that Plato's argument could be interpreted in another way, so that it is free of controversial premises, involves no equivocation on *'esti'*, and is valid. On this interpretation, knowledge and belief are distinguished not by their different sets of objects, but by their truth implications. Knowledge, but not belief, entails truth. The argument resulting from this claim is nonfallacious; but it fails to support the two worlds theory. On our reading, Plato has precluded neither knowledge of sensibles nor beliefs about Forms. He does argue, at the close of the passage, that whoever knows will know Forms, since it is only by reference to them that correct accounts are forthcoming; if one is restricted to sensibles, like the sightlovers, the most one can attain is belief. But although all knowledge begins with Forms, it need not end with them, too; and, also, one may fail to acquire knowledge of Forms, and have only beliefs about them.

The price of ascribing to Plato a valid argument whose premises are noncontroversial is the loss of the two worlds theory. It is a price I am quite willing to pay[24].

---

interpretation, however, we still avoid TW. For Plato still at most claims that any partially true content is a content of belief; but such contents could be about sensibles or Forms. Nor has Plato said that every claim about a sensible is at best partially true.

[24] I am especially indebted to T. H. Irwin for many helpful criticisms of several drafts of this paper. Earlier versions have also been read and helpfully criticized by J. L. Ackrill, J. C. B. Gosling, A. Nehamas, N. Kretzmann, and G. E. L. Owen.

CANADIAN JOURNAL OF PHILOSOPHY
Supplementary Volume II (1976)

The Contents of the Cave

J.R.S. WILSON, University of Edinburgh

'The similes of the Sun, Line, and Cave in the *Republic* remain a reproach to Platonic scholarship because there is no agreement about them, though they are meant to illustrate.'[1] So wrote A.S. Ferguson in 1934, and so he could write to-day. Four decades have produced at least twenty more substantial contributions to the debate, but no agreement. I shall not attempt to arbitrate between existing interpretations, nor shall I offer an account of the 'simile of light' as a whole. I shall confine my attention to a single point: the significance of the shadows in the cave, and of the objects which cast them. The suggestion I shall make seems an obvious one, but I have not found it in the literature.[2] I hope to show at least that it deserves serious consideration.

---

1 A.S. Ferguson, 'Plato's Simile of Light Again', *Classical Quarterly*, XXVIII (1934), p. 190. Ferguson has been given less than his due recently. I have learnt more about the 'simile of light' from him than from any other writer. I cannot accept his interpretation of the Cave, but the account in the next paragraph of how the three constituent 'similes' interrelate is greatly endebted to his discussion in the article cited, and in its two-part predecessor 'Plato's Simile of Light', *Classical Quarterly*, XV (1921) and XVI (1922).

2 The most common view is that perceiving the shadows stands for the acceptance of second-hand opinions, perceiving the objects which cast them for the state of mind of one who decides for himself, but still within the field of *doxa*. First propounded by R.L. Nettleship (*Lectures on the Republic of Plato*, 2nd ed., London, 1901, Chapters XI and XII), its adherents include J.E. Raven ('Sun, Divided Line and Cave', *Classical Quarterly*, N.S., III (1953) and *Plato's Thought in the Making*, Cambridge, 1965, Chapter 9), R.C. Cross and A.D. Woozley (*Plato's Republic*, London, 1964, Chapter 9), F.M. Cornford, and H.D.B. Lee (in their translations of the *Republic*, Oxford, 1941, and (revised) Harmondsworth, 1974, respectively). Very similar views are advanced by J. Adam (*The Republic of*

117

In the Sun, the difference between seeing in sunlight and seeing in an inferior light[3] symbolises the difference between *epistēmē* and *doxa*. In the Line, Plato distinguishes two kinds of seeing in sunlight in order to illustrate the difference between two kinds of *epistēmē*, *dianoia* and *noēsis*. These two kinds of seeing in sunlight recur in the world outside the cave, where they stand for the same states of the soul. The cave itself is lit by the inferior light that comes from the fire. The two kinds of seeing by that light stand for two kinds of *doxa*, *eikasia* and *pistis*. These were introduced only in the final paragraph of Book VI, after the distinction between *dianoia* and *noēsis* had been established. It was not they that were used to illustrate that distinction, but two related kinds of seeing — related in that what is seen in one way or the other by the eye is also the object of one or the other kind of *doxa* in the soul. Visible things constitute one category of *doxasta*, and once the distinction between *dianoia* and *noēsis* has been illustrated by reference to visual images and originals as objects of sight, these can be used directly to sub-divide the *doxa* of which they are also objects. *Eikasia* and *pistis* are the states of the soul which relate to the visual images and originals of the lower line, but as the field of *doxa* extends beyond the visible, so the fields of its two varieties extend to images and originals in general. If the prisoners in the cave are 'like ourselves' (515A), the shadows they see can hardly stand for visual images. What kind of preoccupation with images, then, is Plato attributing to his contemporaries?

Plato, Vol. II, Cambridge, 1902, Appendix I to Book VII) and I.M. Crombie (*An Examination of Plato's Doctrines*, Vol. I: *Plato on Man and Society*, London, 1962, Chapter 3). Other interpretations are proposed by A.S. Ferguson in the articles cited, B. Jowett (*The Dialogues of Plato Translated into English*, Vol. II, Oxford, 1871, p. 84), L. Campbell (*Plato's Republic: The Greek Text*, Edited with Notes and Essays by B. Jowett and L. Campbell, Oxford, 1894, Vol. II, *Essays*, pp. 16f), H. Jackson ('On Plato's *Republic* VI 509d sqq.', *Journal of Philology*, X (1882), an interpretation recently revived by J. Ferguson in 'Sun, Line, and Cave Again', *Classical Quarterly*, N.S., XIII (1963)), H.J. Paton ('Plato's Theory of *Eikasia*', *Proceedings of the Aristotelian Society*, XXII (1921-2)), N.R. Murphy ('The "Simile of Light" in Plato's *Republic*', *Classical Quarterly*, XXVI (1932), 'Back to the Cave', *Classical Quarterly*, XXVIII (1934), and *The Interpretation of Plato's Republic*, Oxford, 1951, Chapter VIII), J. Gould (*The Development of Plato's Ethics*, Cambridge, 1955, Chapter XIII), D.W. Hamlyn ('*Eikasia* in Plato's *Republic*', *Philosophical Quarterly*, VIII (1958)), J. Malcolm ('The Line and the Cave', *Phronesis*, VII (1962)), and R.K. Elliott ('Socrates and Plato's Cave', *Kant-Studien*, LVIII (1967)).

3 A.S. Ferguson cites Aeneas Tacticus to show that the *nukterina phengē* of 508C are artificial lights such as lamps and watchfires, not the moon and stars, as commonly supposed. See 'Plato's Simile of Light Again', p. 194 n. 2.

The originals of the images are themselves images, and belong to the field of *doxa*, for the objects which stand for them and whose shadows the prisoners see are images of the men, animals, etc. in the upper world, but are lit by firelight. As the men and animals stand for Forms, the objects must stand for images of Forms, and their shadows for images of images of Forms. Now if the Forms in question are moral Forms, an interpretation at once suggests itself. For if we equate the men, animals, etc. with the Forms of moral qualities such as justice, their images will surely be those qualities in the soul, and the shadows the reflections of those qualities in outer appearance or behaviour. The cave, I suggest, represents the human world, not the whole world of sense. The prisoners are those who attend not to the soul but to outer appearance, who identify a person with his body, and who wrongly think of moral qualities in behavioural terms. The initial manner of their release corresponds to the attempt by Socrates to persuade his fellow-citizens to examine themselves and care for their souls.

If I am right, then the fact that the objects are made and carried by men will indicate that they stand for qualities of men; the men who carry them can perhaps be seen as stand-ins for the prisoners themselves, rendered immobile as these are by the requirements of the allegory. Support for this reading comes from the reasons given by Socrates for likening the prisoners to 'ourselves' (515A-B). In the first place, he says, they would have seen nothing of themselves or of one another except the shadows cast by the firelight on the opposing wall. Only after a response from Glaucon does he add that they would have seen as little of the objects carried behind them.[4] The implication is surely that the plight of the prisoners represents a kind of self-ignorance or ignorance of the soul, and that this is closely associated with a mistaken understanding of human qualities.

To render this interpretation more plausible, I shall show, first, and I think uncontroversially, that Plato does often portray the subjects of Socratic interrogation as ignoring the soul, and Socrates as endeavouring to redirect their attention inwards, and secondly, that elsewhere in the *Republic* he does talk of body and soul in terms of image and

---

4 A.S. Ferguson suggests as a translation of the much disputed sentence which follows: 'If then they were able to talk to each other, do you not think that they would consider they were addressing those objects before them, the objects they saw?' ('Plato's Simile of Light, Part II', p. 22). If this were correct, it would fit my interpretation nicely, for Socrates would then mean in this and his next remark that the men whom the prisoners represent, when they talk to one another, take themselves to address and to be addressed by one another's bodies.

119

original. I shall then attempt to meet a possible objection to my claim that the cave represents only the human world.

Considering first the early dialogues, we find that the picture of Socrates in action conforms to his self-description in the *Apology*. He told his hearers at his trial 'that to let no day pass without discussing goodness [*aretē*] and all the other subjects about which you hear me talking and examining both myself and others is really the very best thing that a man can do, and that life without this sort of examination is not worth living',[5] and that in obedience to the god he had spent all his time 'going about trying to persuade you, young and old, to make your first and chief concern not for your bodies nor for your possessions, but for the highest welfare of your souls'.[6] For Socrates the soul is the real person, and its welfare the only thing that matters, but even someone as close to him as Crito could lose sight of this. In the *Phaedo*, when the time has finally come for Socrates to die, Crito asks him how he would like to be buried. Socrates gently chides his friend for thinking that he, Socrates, will be buried at all — Crito has mistaken Socrates for his body.[7] Plato makes Socrates take every opportunity to turn the discussion towards the soul. So when Critias praises the beauty of Charmides' body, Socrates asks if his soul is as beautiful (*Charm* 154D). In the same way he tells his unnamed friend how the physical beauty of Alcibiades had paled beside the wisdom of Protagoras (*Prot* 309). And in the *Laches* it is Socrates who moves the argument away from the merits of fighting in armour, and declares the aim of education to be care of the soul.

When Socrates asks what virtue is, or a particular virtue, the first answer he receives always refers to behaviour. Thus for Meno, a man's virtue 'consists in managing the city's affairs capably, and so that he will help his friends and injure his foes while taking care to come to no

---

5 *Apology* 38A, H. Tredennick's translation in *The Last Days of Socrates*, Harmondsworth, 1954.

6 *Apology* 30A-B, Tredennick's translation.

7 *Phaedo* 115Cff. We hear a much later echo of this when Plato deals in the *Laws* with funeral regulations: 'While I am alive I have nothing to thank for my individuality except my soul, whereas my body is just the likeness of myself that I carry round with me. This means we are quite right when we say a corpse "looks like" the deceased. Our real self — our immortal soul, as it is called — departs, as the ancestral law declares, to the gods below to give an account of itself.' (*Laws* 959 A-B, T.J. Saunders' translation, Harmondsworth, 1970). The description of the body as a 'likeness' of the self obviously supports my thesis in this article.

harm himself',[8] and a woman's virtue is also a matter of the way she behaves. When Socrates asks Laches what courage is, he receives the reply: 'if a man is willing to remain at his post and to defend himself against the enemy without running away, then you may rest assured that he is a man of courage'.[9] Charmides thinks that temperance is 'doing everything in an orderly and quiet way — things like walking in the streets, and talking, and doing everything else in a similar fashion'[10] — in other words, to be temperate is to behave in a certain style.[11] For Euthyphro, piety is 'just what I am doing now: prosecuting a wrongdoer for manslaughter or temple-robbery or any other such crime, whether the offender happens to be your father or your mother or anybody else; and ... not to prosecute such a person is impious'.[12] Socrates, where necessary, guides his interlocutor from particular example to general explanation,[13] but more importantly for our purposes, he shifts attention at the same time from the outward behaviour in terms of which the virtue is initially conceived to the inner state of the soul.[14]

The *Republic* conforms to the same pattern. The accounts advanced in Book I of what it is to be just are all couched in behavioural terms. Cephalus refers to particular rules of behaviour — to be just is to tell the truth and to pay one's debts. Polemarchus attempts to characterise just behaviour more generally: he suggests first that to be just is to render every man his due, and then, when pressed by Socrates to say what this means, that it is to help one's

---

8   *Meno* 71E. W.K.C. Guthrie's translation in *Protagoras and Meno*, Harmondsworth, 1956.

9   *Laches* 190E, R.K. Sprague's translation in *Laches and Charmides*, Indianapolis and New York, 1971.

10 *Charmides* 159B, Sprague's translation.

11 See M.F. Burnyeat, 'Socrates in Action', in G. Vlastos (ed.), *Socrates*, New York, 1971.

12 *Euthyphro* 5D-E, Tredennick's translation in *The Last Days of Socrates*.

13 As Rosemary Sprague points out, Charmides needs no such guidance. (op. cit., p. 66 n. 24.).

14 The *Euthyphro* is an apparent exception, but only apparent, if what Socrates is trying unsuccessfully to make Euthyphro see is that our obligation to the gods is the improvement of our souls, as Taylor and Vlastos claim. See A.E. Taylor, *Plato*, London, 1960, p. 155 and G. Vlastos, 'The Paradox of Socrates', in G. Vlastos (ed.), *Socrates*, p. 14. On the general point at issue, see T. Penner, 'The Unity of Virtue', *Philosophical Review*, LXXXII (1973), and M.F. Burnyeat, op. cit.

121

friends and to harm one's enemies. When Thrasymachus says that to be just is to serve the interest of someone stronger than yourself, to be unjust to serve your own interest, he also thinks of justice in terms of behaviour. Glaucon and Adeimantus point the way in towards the soul, and this is the path that Socrates follows, as indeed he must if he is to show that it is in a man's true interest to be just. In Book IV he identifies justice and the other virtues with conditions of the soul. Justice, he says, 'is not a matter of external behaviour, but of the inward self and of attending to all that is, in the fullest sense, a man's proper concern'.[15] If behaviour is also called just, it is because it preserves and produces justice in the soul.[16] Socrates has earlier encapsulated the behaviour of a just man in the formula 'doing one's own'.[17] He now says that this is a sort of 'image' (*eidōlon*) of justice (443C) — justice itself is not that outer 'doing one's own', but the inner state in which each part of the soul does *its* own. This brings us on to the most crucial point in my argument, that Plato in the *Republic* does speak of outer behaviour as an image or reflection of the inner self.[18]

The most striking instance is sometimes obscured in translation. In Book III, after Socrates has outlined his system of 'musical' education, he sums up its purpose. He draws an analogy with learning to read: we could be said to know the different letters only when we could pick them out wherever they occurred, in small words or in great; to recognise the images of letters in water or in mirrors, furthermore, we must know the originals — the same skill and practice are involved (402A-B). He continues:

> Then, by heaven, am I not right in saying that in the same way we shall never be 'musical', neither we nor the guardians that we have undertaken to educate, until we are able to recognise the qualities [*eidē*] of temperance, courage, liberality and high-mindedness, and those akin to them and their opposites also, wherever they are carried about [*pantachou peripheromena*], and to apprehend the presence both of them and of their images in those they are present in, disdaining them neither in the petty nor in the great, but believing the same skill and practice to be involved?

---

15 443D-E, Cornford's translation.

16 443E and 444C-D.

17 Vlastos' rendering of '*to ta hautou prattein*' in 'Justice and Happiness in the *Republic*', *Platonic Studies*, Princeton, 1973. This article was also published in a slightly different form in G. Vlastos (ed.). *Plato*, II, New York, 1971.

18 Vlastos remarks that 'what a man does is, for Plato, only an "image" of what he is' ('Justice and Happiness in the *Republic*', p. 126). He does not see the full implications of this.

That must be so, he said.

Then, I said, when a beautiful disposition in the soul coincides with a matching and harmonious outward form, cast in the same mould, is not this the fairest sight for one who can see it? (402B-D)

The mention of reflections surely points forward to the simile of light;[19] deciphering the one passage should help us understand the other. Socrates says that as one must know the letters before one can identify the reflection of a letter, so one can recognise the image of a moral quality only if one knows the original. But what here is the original, and what its image? '*Eidē*' is often translated 'forms', but Plato can hardly mean the transcendent Forms, for, as Adam and Raven point out, these are introduced only in Book V.[20] I suggest that the *eidē* are qualities in the soul, and their images the reflections of those qualities in outer appearance. The next question that Socrates asks now follows naturally on, and does so only on this interpretation.[21] We can also understand why Socrates should describe the qualities as 'carried about',[22] anticipating the objects which men carry behind the prisoners in the cave, and which on my reading represent just these qualities. What Socrates is saying here is thus that the ability to recognise the external expressions of moral qualities presupposes the ability to recognise these qualities in the soul.

Elsewhere in the *Republic* also the outer seems for Plato to provide an image of the inner. Socrates explicitly tells us that the external expression of justice is an image of the state of the soul which *is* justice. Are the other virtues not similarly mirrored in behaviour?[23] If temperance is an inner harmony of the soul (432B-C and 442C-D), does it not also give rise to an outward harmony? A brave man surely can endure; the courage which makes him brave is a kind of power of

---

19 Bosanquet saw this, though he missed its significance. See B. Bosanquet, *A Companion to Plato's Republic*, 2nd ed., London, 1895, p. 107.

20 See J. Adam, op. cit., Vol. I, ad 402C16, and J. E. Raven, *Plato's Thought in the Making*, p. 126.

21 Beauty, perhaps unlike the other qualities, will be reflected in physical appearance as well as in behaviour. Socrates could not at this point use a virtue to illustrate his meaning, for the nature of these has yet to be explained.

22 Shorey's 'convey' captures the sense of '*peripheromena*', but Lindsay's 'scattered about', Lee's 'in all their many manifestations' and Cornford's 'wherever they occur' disguise the rather strange description.

23 See my article 'The Argument of *Republic* IV', *Philosophical Quarterly*, XXVI (1976).

123

the *thumos* to endure in the face of pleasure or pain (442B-C). Wisdom is the knowledge, located in the reason, of what is good for each part of the soul and for the soul as a whole (442C); the wise man knows what is good for each part of the polis and for the polis as a whole. In each case the virtue is almost literally reflected in the outer appearance to which it gives rise. The same principle perhaps holds for the inferior types of character described in Books VIII and IX. For can we not say that the relationships, both internal and external, of the timocratic man are based on force rather than on *logos* (547C, 548B-C and 549A-B), that the oligarchic man is characterised by internal and external *polupragmosunē* (551Ef and 553C-D), that the inner anarchy of soul of the democratic man shows itself in an outer anarchy of behaviour (561), and that the tyrannical man treats other men as 'the passion that dwells in him as a tyrant'[24] treats the other elements of the soul (573ff)? Finally, when Socrates argues at the end of Book IX that the only real pleasures are those of the intelligence, he says that the pleasures that derive from the body are mere 'images' of these (586B), and, recalling the Cave, that they are 'shadow pictures' (*eskiagraphēmenai*) (583B and 586B).

There is ample evidence, then, to support my reading. Now I must consider a possible objection to it. I have argued that the Cave alludes only to our apprehension of moral qualities, a view to which 517D-E and 520C lend support. The shadow-guessing of 516C-D refers not to a 'Humean' view of causation, as Shorey and others suggest,[25] but to the superficial understanding of human behaviour possessed by the successful politician.[26] But what of mathematics? I must claim that no stage in the initial story of the prisoner's escape represents the study of mathematics, but that this is introduced only later, as an alternative way of turning the mind's eye to the world of Forms. I must show how certain apparently recalcitrant passages can be reconciled with this interpretation.

The first occurs at 516A. The released prisoner, emerging into the sunlight, must habituate himself by looking at shadows and reflections. Only then can he see the men and other things which are their originals. The stage of looking at images surely represents *dianoia*. But is that not the state of mind of the mathematician? How then can I say that the men and other things stand only for the Forms of moral

---

24   575A, P. Shorey's translation, Loeb Classical Library, London, 1934.

25   See e.g. Shorey, op. cit., ad loc., Bosanquet, op. cit., p. 267, and Hamlyn, op. cit., pp. 20ff.

26   Cf. 426C and 493A-C, and *Gorgias* 465A and 501A.

qualities? Now there is a problem here only if *dianoia* is confined to the mathematician, but Neil Cooper has recently argued for a more generous interpretation of its scope, to include any attempt to understand Forms through images.[27] He suggests, furthermore, that such use of images is characteristic of Plato himself. Besides removing a difficulty for my reading, Cooper's thesis is attractive in itself. Plato's method of argument in Books II to X of the *Republic* is not dialectic, but relies very heavily on images and analogies. He uses the term '*eikōn*' of the comparison of the Guardians to watch-dogs (375D), and of the images of the ship (487E), the Sun (509A), the Cave (515A and 517A), the supposititious son (538C), and the fabulous monster to which the soul is compared at the end of Book IX (588B), but his resort to analogy is much more general than this. His central argument, that justice pays, depends on comparing the soul to a polis. One could cite also the comparison of the Guardians to craftsmen (395B-C, 421C, etc.), the great beast (493Aff), the drones (552C, 554B, etc.), the sea-god Glaucus (612Dff), the references to dyeing (429Dff), to breeding animals (459Aff), to lovers (474Cff), and, for more than one purpose, to health and medicine (e.g. 425Eff, 444Cff, 489Bff) and to painting (e.g. 420Cff, 472D, 500Eff), and many other examples. Again and again Socrates makes his point through the use of such analogies. If this form of argument, like mathematics, gives rise to *dianoia*, our problem is solved. The initial release of the prisoner and his turning to the objects which cast the shadows will correspond the the Socratic method of the early dialogues and *Republic* I, with its consequent bewilderment and confusion, and the perception of real things in the upper world through images to the method employed in the rest of the *Republic*, the apprehension through images of the Forms of moral qualities. The final stage, of apprehending those Forms directly, is one we never reach.[28]

The moral Forms are the ones that matter for Plato, and any system of education must culminate in their study. He had come to feel, however, that the mind must receive a preliminary training before it can safely be let loose on moral questions. The student must first be taught to think abstractly, and this can best be achieved through the

---

27   N. Cooper, 'The Importance of *Dianoia* in Plato's Theory of Forms', *Classical Quarterly*, N.S., XVI (1966). See also R.G. Tanner, '*Dianoia* and Plato's Cave', *Classical Quarterly*, N.S., XX (1970), and, for a useful discussion of Plato's reliance on analogy and imagery in the middle dialogues, R. Robinson, *Plato's Earlier Dialectic*, 2nd ed., Oxford, 1953, Ch. XII.

28   At 533A Socrates says that Glaucon would not be able to follow him further, but that if he could, he would no longer be looking at an *eikōn* of the truth but at the truth itself.

125

study of mathematics. At 518C-D he substitutes for the image of the Cave a simplified picture wherein the soul must be turned around from the world of becoming to the world of being, as the eye from darkness to light. He suggests that there may be an art which would turn the whole soul round most quickly and effectively, and when he takes up the theme again at 521Cff, he identifies this art with mathematics. He is not now elaborating the story of release of 515Cff, but proposing an alternative — one which cannot be represented in terms of the original allegory.

This interpretation, like many others, may appear to founder at 532B-C. Socrates is often understood there to say that the prisoner's whole progress from the initial release from bonds to the perception of shadows and reflections of real things in the sunlit world above can be attributed to the arts he has been describing. Thus Robinson, arguing that the Cave is not parallel to the Line, claims that in this passage Plato 'further unmistakably says that the viewing of shadows and reflections in the real world, and of the puppets in the cave, and everything down to the very moment of unchaining, is "the work of the sciences we have gone through" (which is certainly mathematics ...)'.[29] For Ross, too, 'the turning from shadows to the images that cast them ... and to the firelight, the ascent to the sunlight, and the looking at reflections and shadows of things in the sunlit world, are said to symbolise the study of the mathematical arts'.[30] One way of dealing with this is to deny that the '*technai*' referred to here are the mathematical sciences alone. Thus John Malcolm, reviving a suggestion of Bosanquet's, claims that *mousikē* is included.[31] But that would imply that children in the ideal polis begin life as prisoners, which I am inclined to doubt. Furthermore the release described at 515Cff, with its dazzling and bewilderment and reluctance of the prisoner to advance, cannot represent the educational system of the *Republic*. I believe rather that on a careful reading of the passage, the problem disappears. Socrates summarises the progress of the prisoner up to the perception of shadows and reflections in the upper world, and continues:

> all this study of the arts we have described has this power of leading the best element in the soul up to the contemplation of what is best among realities, as the clearest organ in the body was led up to what is brightest in the material and visible world.

---

29 R. Robinson, op. cit., pp. 183f.

30 W.D. Ross, *Plato's Theory of Ideas*, Oxford, 1951, p. 74.

31 J. Malcolm, op. cit., p. 40. Cf. B. Bosanquet, op. cit., p. 298.

He does not say that the progress of the prisoner 'symbolises' the study of mathematics. Nor, I think, must the phrase 'all this study of the arts' refer to that progress. Socrates is saying merely that mathematical studies of the kind he has described have the power to lead the soul up to a point that corresponds to the point that the prisoner has reached when he looks at shadows and reflections in the upper world. That point is reached by an alternative road to the one represented by the progress of the prisoner in the initial story.

For insofar as Plato's reformed system of higher education was to be introduced into existing society, where men through their childhood upbringing are in bondage and ignorant of the soul, any discussion of moral issues would occur only after a period of mathematical training. The process represented in the Cave by the move from perceiving the shadows to perceiving the objects which cast them, with its attendant distress, would disappear. In the ideal polis, on the other hand, no-one would be in a situation comparable to that of the prisoners. Although those who had received only the first stage of education in 'music' and gymnastics would not yet have emerged from the cave, they would not be bound by neck and legs with their backs to the objects which cast the shadows. They would be able to see both those objects and their shadows, and to identify both correctly. In other words they would be able to recognise moral qualities both in the soul and reflected in behaviour, though they could not yet give a rational account of the nature of these qualities. Those who undertook mathematical and dialectical studies would emerge from the cave, though not in a way that can straightforwardly be represented in terms of the allegory. They would as a result attain knowledge of the Forms of moral qualities, and finally of Goodness itself.

127

13

THE LINE AND THE CAVE IN PLATO'S *REPUBLIC*

THIS reconstruction of Austin's views is based on three sources. There are notes dating from the 1930s for a reply to a paper (so far as I know unpublished) by W. D. Ross on the metaphysics of the *Republic* and the *Phaedo*. These notes are very full and the first half of the printed paper is very faithful to them; alterations are mainly excisions of comments on Ross which cannot be read profitably without Ross's paper and which do not advance Austin's argument. The later parts of these notes rely heavily on the view that Plato, like Aristotle, always used the word 'hypothesis' to mean an existential postulate; Austin came to doubt this at a later date. For the second half of the paper I have therefore made considerable use of Austin's own notes for a class held at Oxford in the late 1940s, and of notes taken at this class by Professor Hugh Lloyd-Jones, with a modified thesis about the nature of hypothesis. I am grateful to Professor Lloyd-Jones for allowing me to see his notes. I transliterate and translate what Austin left in Greek; I, not he, am responsible for the English names given to the segments of the line.

J. O. URMSON

Too much has already been written on the interpretation of the Line and Cave in Plato's *Republic* (509–18). In Britain in the present century, to omit other references, there have been elaborate discussions in Adam's edition of the *Republic*; in Ferguson's articles in the *Classical Quarterly* of 1921, 1922, and 1934; by Stocks in the *Classical Quarterly* of 1911; by Murphy in the *Classical Quarterly* of 1934; by Paton in the *Proceedings of the Aristotelian Society* of 1921–2; and by Hardie in his *Study in Plato* of 1936. In this paper I shall assume that the reader is

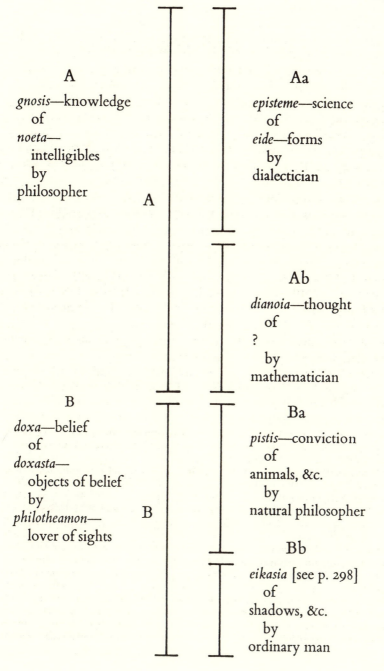

A
gnosis—knowledge
   of
noeta—
   intelligibles
   by
philosopher

A

Aa
episteme—science
   of
eide—forms
   by
   dialectician

Ab
dianoia—thought
   of
?
   by
   mathematician

B
doxa—belief
   of
doxasta—
   objects of belief
   by
philotheamon—
   lover of sights

B

Ba
pistis—conviction
   of
animals, &c.
   by
   natural philosopher

Bb
eikasia [see p. 298]
   of
shadows, &c.
   by
   ordinary man

acquainted with this literature. But I shall not discuss it; rather I shall attempt to present Plato's doctrines as accurately as possible.

We may start by obeying Plato's instruction and drawing the line. It should be vertical, not horizontal, and of a decent length.

The first main segment of the line, A, symbolizes *gnosta* (knowables), *noeta* (intelligibles), or *onta* (realities). The second, B, symbolizes what are variously called *gignomena* (becoming), *aistheta* (perceptible), *doxasta* (objects of belief), or *horata* (visible). Some have made great play with the fact that the objects of B are actually called visible when the line is first drawn (509d8). But a reading of 507a–c shows clearly that 'sight' is used metaphorically to include our belief about the good and the beautiful; the 'visible' is the whole domain of what was distinguished in Book V as *doxa* (belief). Again, in 534a the lower main segment B of the line is explicitly said to symbolize the *doxasta* (objects of belief).

Having divided the line into the two main segments, we are next required to divide each of these segments in the same way as the line was originally divided. It will thus be seen that we have on our hands six segments, grouped in pairs, in every pair a longer and a shorter in the same ratio. It is quite essential to bear this in mind and not to speak casually of the line 'being divided into four segments'. Let us impress this on our minds by using the nomenclature of the diagram, which I think is apt and easy to follow. The large original segments I call A and B: A is subdivided into Aa and Ab: B is subdivided into Ba and Bb. When two segments are in the ratio mentioned I shall say that they are in the AB ratio and that the things they symbolize are in the AB relation: similarly I shall speak of 'an A segment', 'a class of A objects', and 'an A state of mind'.

Let me here mention a point which has often been discussed. If the pairs Plato mentions and is interested in are all to be in the same ratio, it is a simple mathematical consequence that the so-called 'two middle subsections', Ab and Ba, should be equal in length. From this fact, unmentioned by Plato, no inferences should be drawn. No doubt Plato, being a mathematician, noticed the point, but so far as as we know he attached no special importance to it. Some, such as Sir David Ross, have thought this equality a defect which Plato would, if he had noticed it, have wished to eliminate; but this is utterly unwarrantable, for if Plato's symbol were so inadequate he could easily have chosen another. Two reasons advanced for the view by Ross are wrong in important ways. First, he thinks that the 'continuous advance in clearness as we pass from *eikasia* through *pistis* and *dianoia* to *noesis*, and in reality as we pass from the objects of each to the objects of the next', would not be adequately represented in the line unless this equality, which opens a door to Ferguson's heresy, were eliminated.

Now I do not quite understand what this problem is about continuity, but it seems clear that Ross thinks that the continuity is broken if ever we come to a cut in the line which has not got, on either side of it, two segments in the AB ratio. But the line is already satisfactory in this respect, without there being any need for Ab and Ba to stand in that ratio. For the middle cut in the line is the cut between, not indeed Ab and Ba, but A and B. This is emphasized by the 'Cave' allegory which Plato, at 517b, says must be attached to the preceding account, and which I take to be parallel, in the old sense, to the Line: for although the progress in a man's education is continuous enough, it is evident that there is no special relation between the statuettes carried through the cave, which are parallel to segment Ba, and the reflections on the surface of the earth, which are parallel to segment Ab. We must not think of the man, at this stage, passing from looking at statuettes to looking at reflections on the earth's surface, but as passing from the realm of objects illuminated by the fire to the realm of objects illuminated by the sun. The passage is not from conviction (*pistis*) to thought (*dianoia*), but from belief (*doxa*) to knowledge (*gnosis*). In the résumé in Book VII at 534a, just as clearly as in the account of the line in Book VI, the grouping is only into the pairs belief and knowledge, science and thought, conviction and *eikasia*; at 534a, indeed, the relation of thought to conviction is significantly omitted—significantly since here Plato mentions rather the analogy between thought and *eikasia*.

Secondly, Ross has a more specific reason for his view that the equality of Ab and Ba is unfortunate. He seems to think that what Plato actually tells us about the relation between thought and conviction corresponds exactly to what he tells us about the relations between the members of each of the other pairs of states of mind (*pathemata*) which stand in the AB relation. This seems to me false and to have bad consequences. What Plato tells us is that the man in the state of thought (*dianoia*) *uses as* images (*eikones*) those very objects of which the objects in segment Bb *are* images. But we are never told that the man in a state of conviction *uses* the objects of Bb as images, only that they are in fact images. Thus no verbal parallel is here drawn between the relations *thought–conviction* and *conviction–eikasia*. However, I shall not press this point, for the following reason: that I think it very highly probable that Plato did think that the man in an A state of mind (*pathema*) does use the corresponding B objects as images. We shall shortly see that the reason why little prominence is given to this fact is that, in the case of at least two of the three pairs of states of mind in the AB relation, the upper state of mind must be left more or less obscure. Why then does Plato mention the fact that in thought the objects of conviction are used as images? It is not in order to relate thought and conviction, but, as the context makes obvious, in order to contrast science and thought. This is borne out, if that is necessary, by other facts. For example, if Plato had wished carefully to relate thought and conviction in the AB relation, he could scarcely have failed to notice that a Bb object would do just as well as a diagram for the mathematician as would a Ba object. Again at 511d and 533d thought is said to be intermediate between belief and knowledge; but if the AB relation held between thought and conviction he quite clearly should have said 'conviction' not 'belief'.

In short then I see no necessity whatever for supposing that Plato held that Ab and Ba are in the AB ratio or regarded their equality as significant. It is therefore unfortunate that so many people use the relation between these two segments, which seems to them the most easy and familiar, to explain the AB relation itself and so the whole symbolism of the line. This is a fatal error; the relation between these two segments in no way explains the AB relation.

What then is the AB relation? Here it is important to grasp that the AB ratio between each pair of segments of the line has a *double* symbolic significance, as Plato himself says. The segments of the line are of course symbolic both of classes of objects and of states of mind. What we must discover, then, is what the AB ratio symbolizes, first in the case of the objects, secondly in the case of the states of mind. The relation between the A and B objects is comparatively clear: they are related as 'original' to 'copy' or 'image' (*eikasthen* to *eikon*). It is evident that, in the case of each AB pair, this metaphorical language of *eikon* and *eikasthen* will have a different precise meaning, but the positions occupied by the A objects and B objects in respect to each other will be always analogous and recognizably describable as those of 'original' and 'image' respectively. The metaphor is of course most directly applicable in the case of Ba and Bb. At 510a Socrates asks permission to treat the metaphor as applicable also to the relation between the objects in the main segments A and B. Clearly the extension to the case of the objects in Aa and Ab, which are certainly none of them visible, must be more metaphorical still. What these objects all are I shall not discuss at this stage; but the line must make sense here, however we interpret it.

The next problem is what the relation is between the A and B states of mind. It seems to be supposed commonly that this needs no explanation: the A state of mind is that which concerns itself with the A class of objects, the B state of mind that which concerns itself with the B class of objects. But Plato tells us much more and other than that.

In the first place, as Hardie points out in his *A Study in Plato*, we must understand the metaphor, constantly recurring, of dreaming. It was first used and carefully explained in Book V, to which we are later referred back emphatically; it is in Book V that the relation between knowledge (*gnosis*) and belief (*doxa*), symbolized as A and B in the line, was described in detail. What Plato does in Book VI is to subdivide each of them into states of mind related in the same way as knowledge and belief. In Book V that relation is metaphorically named that of waking to sleeping and is carefully described as consisting in this, that the man in the B state of mind makes a certain complicated *mistake*, which the man in the A state of mind does not make. That this relation is intended to apply throughout the Line can be proved by the text throughout: but I shall simply mention enough evidence to clinch the matter.

(1) At 510a8 the main A–B division of the line is described as being in truth as the believed is to the known.

(2) With regard to the two subordinate pairs: Aa and Ab are described, as in Book V, as related as waking to sleeping at 533c, as Hardie notes.

(3) As for the Ba–Bb relation, at 515a–c the prisoners in the cave, who are in the Bb state of mind, are carefully described as making a mistake of just the kind described in Book V as being made by sleepers. Moreover, this sort of mistake is described again, with special regard to sensible objects, in the *Theaetetus* at 158, and called there once again the mistake made in *dreaming*. I shall not use evidence from elsewhere, but shall give reasons later why the *Theaetetus* not only may but should be used in interpreting the *Republic*.

142

What is the mistake in question, which is typical of the man in the B state of mind? It is compound, as carefully described in Book V. Granted that there are two sorts of objects related as originals to copies:

(i) He thinks that there is only one set, namely the one which is most obvious and 'before' him. If it were put to him, he would deny that there was a second set at all.

(ii) He thinks that this set is what we, who distinguished two sets, would call the originals; that is, he ascribes to the set before him, which he thinks is the only set, the properties which we would ascribe to the originals, and which we should refuse to ascribe to the set which he recognizes, as being only copies.

A man in this state is said 'not to understand about' (*noun ouch echein*), a constantly recurring phrase, the objects which he seeks to describe, those that are truly original.

It will be seen then that it is quite incorrect to say that the B state of mind is distinguished as being concerned with the B class of objects. It is in a way concerned with both classes of objects, confusing them in a certain definite manner.

Now what of the A state of mind, called a state of being awake? The man in this state recognizes that there are two classes of objects, related as originals to copies. Further, he recognizes that the objects which are obviously before him are the copies only. And, I *think*, he is *not* then able to turn away from the copies and 'look at' the originals, but what he can do is to use the copies simply as copies in order to infer about that he is really interested in, the originals. But this is not quite certain.

Why does Plato describe the former state as dreaming? Because the mistake made is precisely typified by the mistake we make in dreams, when, having before us dream-images, we not only do not distinguish between them and material things, but take it for granted that what is passing before us is material things. This Plato describes in the *Theaetetus*, when he discusses dreams on page 158.

So then, we have six segments of the line, grouped in three pairs; each pair symbolizes first two sets of objects, related as originals to copies, or as more to less real, secondly two states of mind, related as being awake to being asleep.

We now come to the second main point: the detailed interpretation of the symbolism in the case of each of the three pairs of segments.

About its interpretation in the case of the pair A and B I shall not say much. The classes of objects are those which *are* (*onta*) and those which *become* (*gignomena*), as Plato repeatedly says. The mistake made by the ordinary man is that he does not distinguish perceptible *gignomena* from *onta*, but thinks there is only one set of objects, the visible ones, to which, however, he ascribes properties, such as 'reality', which properly belong only to *onta*. Not much is told us about the two states of mind in detail, because Plato intends to point out later that this is an over-simplification and that each state of mind requires subdivision.

Let us rather consider the pair Ba and Bb, conviction (*pistis*) and *eikasia*. No doubt the purpose of the line is primarily to distinguish between thought (*dianoia*) and science (*episteme*), and that is why not so much attention is devoted to *eikasia* and *pistis* in Book VI. But the distinction between Ba and Bb is none the less important, particularly in connection with the interpretation of the Cave. For it seems to me certain that the Line and the Cave are in the traditional sense parallel; and therefore it is as certain as can be that the ordinary man, in default of philosophical education, lives all his life in a state of *eikasia*, while *pistis* is a merely short-lived and unsatisfactory first stage when he starts his education. Perhaps those who think that the elucidation of the Ba–Bb relation is unimportant do so because they do not realize that there lies ready to hand an interpretation on which it would turn out to be important. But such an interpretation is ready to hand and I shall develop this shortly.

As I intend to use certain doctrines from the *Theaetetus* I shall explain why I think this legitimate, despite the fact that this dialogue is probably later than the *Republic*. The doctrines in question, about sense-data, are doctrines of the Heracliteans, notably of Cratylus. Now Cratylus was Plato's own teacher in his youth, perhaps even before he came under the influence of Socrates. Whatever may be thought of Aristotle's account of Plato's development, that much is surely unquestionable. Therefore these doctrines were certainly known to Plato when, and since long before, he wrote the *Republic*. Moreover they are doctrines which no one, once trained in them, readily forgets. Therefore we may take it as highly probable that Plato had them in mind when he wrote the *Republic*.

In the *Theaetetus* then (153–8) a quite traditional account of sense-data, not unlike that of Descartes, is given: all that we sense is on a level—dreams are on the same level as our waking sensations. Material objects are *perhaps* only groups of sensations (*athroismata*), but no account of them is decided on; what is made clear is that we do not, contrary to our ordinary opinion, sense material objects, since, as far as what we sense goes, it is just the same whether we are awake or asleep. I do not say that Plato was right in this, but merely that he believed it. Similar doctrines are found in the *Timaeus* at pages 45, 61, and 67.

Now let us return to the *Republic*: what are the two sets of objects corresponding to Ba and Bb? Ba consists of animals, trees, &c.—material objects. What of Bb? This consists of shadows, echoes, reflections in smooth objects, and 'everything of that sort'. What is the sort? I say, plainly 'sense-data'. The examples are chosen because they are the very examples which modern philosophers use when they want, if they do, to suggest to pupils that they do not sense material objects! They take as examples hallucinations, noises, mirror images, and the like. That Plato was well aware of the doctrine of sense-data is shown in, for example, Book X, where we are told that the painter does not copy the material bed but only an appearance of it. Now it seems to me that the relation between sense-data and material objects has often been held, especially by those who rely on the argument from dreaming, to be that between copy and original. By such philosophers the ordinary man is thought to live in a state of 'naïve realism', mistaking sense-data for material objects and failing to distinguish between them in precisely the way described as typical of a man in a state of dreaming and represented at 515a–c as awareness only of shadows and echoes, which are taken to be the only reality.

As for the upper state of mind, conviction (*pistis*), there is a difficulty here, in that Plato did not himself believe in the existence of physical objects like the sense-data: hence we have only 'statuettes' in the light of the fire in the Cave; hence, too, no one stays looking at the statuettes, although to distinguish between them and the shadows on the wall is a necessary first stage in education. Certainly Plato does not believe that it is possible to refrain from looking at sense-data and look at material objects instead: even the guardian, when he returns to the Cave, looks at the shadows and not the statuettes. But the fact that the upper state of mind here is not wholly genuine explains why Plato tells us so little about it; but one assumes that the man with conviction does use sense-data as images from which to draw inferences about material objects.

Regarding the names *pistis* and *eikasia*, of which I have translated *pistis* as 'conviction' and left *eikasia* untranslated, it is not reasonable to make too much of the ordinary Greek (or English) meanings of these words. It would be very surprising if ordinary Greek had four words forming just such a scale as Plato means to describe. *Eikasia* does not mean 'conjecture', as is often thought, but is a rare and artificial word, connected with the verb εἰκάζειν, and that does not mean 'to conjecture'; in fact it has no exact English equivalent. The root idea is 'to treat a thing as like another'; it thus can mean 'to compare', and in some contexts, such as the phrase ὡς εἰκάσαι, it can mean 'to conjecture' in the sense of 'to go by likenesses'. The word *pistis* is used elsewhere by Plato, almost in a technical sense. It is nearer to 'faith' than 'belief'. Its use in the *Timaeus* is almost technical; see, for example, the beginning of the account of the physical world in the *Timaeus*, where the account is said to be not knowledge but only *pistis*. At 29c we are told that 'what being is to becoming, that truth is to *pistis*'; at 49c there is a reference to a '*pistos* account'; at 37b we are told that an 'account of the perceptible' yields only 'opinions and *pisteis*', whereas an 'account of the intelligible' yields 'reason and science'. Therefore in the *Timaeus pistis* is the best state about the physical world that we can get ourselves into.

We now turn to the upper segment of the line, where the difficulties are of a very different kind. It is not these difficulties which have led Ferguson and others to deny the parallelism of the Line and Cave. The distinction between the two upper segments Aa and Ab is painstakingly stated at the end of Book VI. But even so Plato finally says that he has not succeeded in making the distinction really clear; in fact he has repeated himself about five times in almost identical terms. He is thus not doing what he ought to do if he is to apply the symbolism of the Line straightforwardly. He ought first to explain the distinction between two classes of objects, and then show how the man in the Ab state of mind confuses and the other distinguishes them. But there is nothing about two classes of objects, and nothing about how the mathematician confuses and the dialectician distinguishes them. What then does he say at the end of Book VI? There are two things that he says again and again about the mathematician: first, that he uses hypotheses in order to proceed from them to draw conclusions; secondly, that he continually makes use of sensible diagrams. By contrast, Plato says that if a man is to gain true knowledge he will have to destroy the hypotheses, using them as starting-points in the search for an *arche anhypothetos*—an unhypothesized starting-point.

First we must explain the word 'hypothesis'. In his *A Study in Plato* Hardie points out that in Aristotle it is a more or less technical term, meaning an existential postulate. When Aristotle sets out the *archai* or starting-points of the sciences he includes *theseis* which are definitions and *hypotheseis* which are postulates to the effect that objects corresponding to certain of these definitions exist. Euclid does not use Aristotle's precise terminology, but does follow his procedure. He does not need to postulate that objects corresponding to all his definitions exist, because he can prove by constructions that some exist when he has assumed the existence of the rest.

I should like to say that the word 'hypothesis' meant the same in *Plato*, and in a way I shall, but it does not have this precise meaning. Plato often uses it in just this way, but in other cases more loosely, so that it means 'an assumption', 'a suggested definition', or something of that kind. The passage in *Meno* (86–7), for example, does not fit the sense of 'existential postulate'. Perhaps it was this imprecision which led to Aristotle and Euclid being so careful in their use of the word 'hypothesis'. Plato's examples are not what we should call hypotheses but 'the odd, the even, and the three kinds of angle'. I believe that he means that the mathematician gives definitions of these three things and then proceeds to his demonstrations. But what Plato wants to point out is that he has assumed and not proved that objects of these three types really exist. The mathematician of Plato's day apparently did not state his assumptions, as Euclid did, but just gave definitions. Presumably it was Plato's criticism here that was responsible for this change.

We can now see the force of Plato's criticism of the use made by mathematicians of sensible diagrams. What he has in mind is that the mathematician says: 'I am demonstrating the nature and properties of the circle', and then says, pointing to his diagram, 'I do not mean this, but it will do to go on with.' The fact that he has the sensible diagram enables him to overlook the necessity of showing that his demonstrations are about something real to a still greater degree. Plato complains that though the mathematician purports to tell us about non-sensible realities, all he, in fact, has to show is his definitions and his sensible diagrams. But nothing is real knowledge except what is about something real. Thus we can see that Plato believed that the mathematician confused the *logos* that he had with an undemonstrated being which he did not have, and was thus dreaming about reality also, but within the realm of the intelligible.

Thus we require another account of the objects of mathematics to supplement the one given by the mathematician. He has only *logos*, definitions, and has no real knowledge, and this we cannot have unless we can show by a new method that supra-sensible objects do really exist. The unhypothesized starting-point is that which requires no existential postulate. How we are to attain it Plato does not profess to see, but he insists that it must be attained if any pursuit designed to acquire knowledge of the supra-sensible is to be justified. The traditional argument for the forms 'from the sciences' assumes that mathematical knowledge is real, and argues that therefore its objects must exist. Plato is here saying, in effect, that this argument puts the cart before the horse. The reality of the objects must be proved first in order to show that mathematics is science.

The mathematician resembles the dreamer in failing to realize the distinction between the *logos* and the form itself. Plato regards the *logos* as the image (*eikon, eidolon*) of the form, and he often uses this language. Nowhere does he speak with such rigour on this subject as here, but one should compare the remarks in the important *Cratylus* at 423–32 and 438–9 on realities (*onta*) and the names (*onomata*) and *logoi* that are their images (*eikones*). In the *Seventh Letter* (343) Plato says that in getting to know about anything there are five factors—the name, the *logos*, the illustration (*eidolon*), the thing itself (*on*), and the science (*episteme*). The circle is his example, one relevant to our present interest. This is a very important passage, partly because it is not in a dialogue but a statement by Plato in his own person.

We can therefore make sense of what Plato says about the Aa–Ab relation in the upper line. My exposition of the Line is thus complete. But there are three other points to be considered.

First, some think that the two sets of objects between which Plato distinguishes in the upper line are the *mathematica*, a belief in which is ascribed to Plato by Aristotle in the *Metaphysics*, and the forms; Hardie and Adam both hold this view. Certainly in the abstract respect of being ontologically between forms and perceptible things, and of being many where the forms are unitary, the *mathematica* seem to fulfil some of the necessary conditions. But there are many difficulties. (*a*) This doctrine is a great deal more obscure and difficult than editors and commentators allow. Cook Wilson and his followers were too hasty, for Aristotle's statements on this subject are very obscure. Cook Wilson says that the *mathematica* were postulated because in mathematical demonstrations we talk, for example, of two circles intersecting, but there is no evidence for this. (*b*) We have no evidence outside this passage that Plato held this doctrine at the time he wrote the *Republic*. Those who try to show that remarks in other dialogues might imply it strain their interpretations. (*c*) If Plato had meant to allude to them he would have been perverse to use in describing the objects of mathematics language at least equally appropriate to the forms themselves. (*d*) How can those who think that Plato was interested in pointing out that the mathematician was concerned only with *mathematica* explain why he says so much about hypotheses and diagrams at the end of Book VI? What have these to do with the distinction between forms and *mathematica*? What is the relation between relying on existential postulates and the doctrine of *mathematica*?

Secondly, when Plato denounces the mathematicians for their reliance on sensible diagrams, he does observe that the sensible diagrams used are from the segment Ba and thus exhibits a relation between the objects of Ab and Ba. This fact is apt to be misleading because people think that the relation between the objects of the mathematician and the objects of Ba ought to be typical of the AB relation. But Plato never implies this. To suppose that we can take the mathematician's use of diagrams as typical of the AB relation is wrong. Plato mentions the point only in order to·bring out the contrast between thinking (*dianoia*) and science (*episteme*).

Finally, I want to point out that other philosophers have felt similar difficulties about mathematics. Descartes, who is the modern philosopher most akin to Plato, says in his account of the method of doubt things closely analogous to what Plato says in the *Republic*. Descartes begins by saying that the testimony of the senses is valueless, and both agree on this. Descartes then turns to mathematics, where at least our ideas are 'clear and distinct'. Descartes says that what is such cannot be doubted as the testimony of the senses can be doubted. But in spite of this Descartes does raise doubts about mathematics; who is to say whether there is any reality corresponding to these ideas? It might be that an arch-deceiver contrives that our ideas differ from reality. Both Plato and Descartes have to find some starting-point whose very nature guarantees the existence of something real corresponding to it; we know where Descartes found it and how he used it to validate mathematics. We know too that Plato held that the starting-point without postulates was the Form of the Good; but in the *Republic* he does not profess to lead us to that starting-point.

IMAGE AND REALITY IN PLATO'S *REPUBLIC*[1]

by D. GALLOP (University of Toronto)

The *Republic* presents a perennial paradox. It disparages imitation and expels the dramatist from the ideal state. Yet Plato is a dramatist and a past-master of imitation himself.

One aspect of this familiar conflict has been freshly emphasised by Mr. Richard Robinson in his book *Plato's Earlier Dialectic*. In a section devoted to Plato's use of images, he writes:

"On the face of it, then, there is an inconsistency between Plato's principles and his practice about images. According to what he says about them, he ought never to use them; yet his works are full of them" (pp. 220—221).

Of the *Republic* in particular he says:

"A dialogue which emphatically condemns imitation (595 C—597 E), and demands a form of cognition that uses no images at all (510—511, cf. *eikones* 510 E), is itself copiously splashed with elaborate images explicitly called 'images' by the speakers" (*ibid.*).

He continues:

"There is no passage in Plato's works which fairly explains or even describes this incoherence. Probably it never struck him nearly so sharply and forcibly as it is here stated."

Plato might, Mr. Robinson goes on to suggest, have justified his use of images as suitable for written works or for teaching purposes. He could thus have removed the incoherence between his principles and his practice if he had thought of it. But the fact remains that he did not do so. "Plato's use of images is condemned by his own views on images and imitation." This, together with other "major incoherences" he finds in Plato, suggests to Mr. Robinson that "a man might discover important new truths and yet be widely mistaken about the method by which he did so" (p. 222).

It will be argued here that the alleged incoherence is more apparent than real; that Plato, in the *Republic* as elsewhere, is fully conscious of the relation between the methods he preaches and those he practises; and that a reappraisal of this issue can shed

[1] Most of this article was written during my leave of absence from the University of Toronto in the spring of 1963. I am grateful to the University, and to the Canada Council, for generous financial aid, which enabled me to visit Oxford, and to many friends in England and Canada for discussion of the paper or its subject matter. I also wish to record my debt to the late J. L. Austin, whose interpretation of the Divided Line suggested its basic idea.

some light upon his philosophic design and political attitude in constructing an "ideal state". This view will be supported by a study of the *Republic's* numerous allusions to images, especially those of painting and sculpture. Plato's use of these images will be seen to have a significant bearing upon the structure of the work as a whole.

One of the commonest uses of images from painting and sculpture in the *Republic*[2] is to illustrate the procedure of Socrates or his friends. Live metaphors from painting and modelling are embedded in the language in which Socrates repeatedly describes the construction of the *polis*. We were, he says, "moulding the city" (374A, 466A), merely "outlining a sketch" of a constitution, and not elaborating it in detail (414A, cf. 548D). Similar metaphors are used for the formation of principles in fiction (*tupoi*), and for the development of moral character by their means (*plattein*, 377B—C, 500D).

In Book II Socrates congratulates Glaucon upon the vigour with which he is cleaning up his figures of the just and unjust man, as if he were getting statues ready for a contest (361D). Much later, when Socrates has completed his own description of the just man, embodied in the philosopher ruler (540C), Glaucon returns the compliment. "A most beautiful finish, Socrates, you have put upon your rulers", he says, "as if you were a statuary". In Book IV Socrates compares the construction of the *polis* with the painting of a statue, to rebut the objection that the rulers would not be happy in their austere way of life. To demand worldly prosperity for them, he says, would be like demanding that the eyes of a statue be painted as attractively as possible, without regard to the colour of real eyes, or to the beauty of the statue as a whole (420C)[3].

Elsewhere, however, the references to painting are less friendly. In Book II Adeimantus says that a young man who is impressed by the arguments of the moral sceptic will conclude that he must cultivate a "façade" of virtue (*skiagraphian aretês perigrapteon*, 365C). In Book VII, when Socrates speaks of unsound perceptions that provoke intellectual reflection (523B), Glaucon takes him to be referring *inter alia* to shadow-paintings. In Book IX non-

---

[2] P. Shorey's translation (Loeb Classical Library) is used throughout with a few slight modifications. References are to the Stephanus pages of the *Republic* unless otherwise noted.

[3] The painting metaphor recurs in the *Timaeus* (19B) where Socrates refers back to the construction of the *polis*.

intellectual pleasures are condemned as "shadow-paintings and illusions" (583 B, 586 B). In such passages[4] paintings typify mere surface appearances, or their reproductions; and it is against a preoccupation with these that the *Republic* is largely directed.

This becomes clear, above all, in the extensive and hostile discussion of imitation in Book X. Socrates there uses painting as an analogy in three different ways, to justify his exclusion of mimetic poetry from the ideal city. First, he argues that the products of the painter are at third remove from reality. This holds true of mimetic art generally, and hence of the poet as well (597 E). Secondly, the painter who imitates objects is contrasted both with the maker and with the user of them. The imitator has neither the user's knowledge nor the maker's correct opinion, derived from association with the user. Hence the poetic imitator will be ignorant as to the value of what he portrays, and will be forced to cater for ignorant popular taste (601 C—602 B). Thirdly, we are told that the painter appeals to that inferior element in the soul which entertains perceptual judgments in conflict with the deliverances of measurement and calculation. The emotional disturbances produced by poetry are analogous to the perceptual conflicts engendered by painting. Poetry, therefore, like painting, appeals to an inferior element in the soul (605 A).

The purpose of these arguments, as has been said, is to impugn the poet; and we may agree with those commentators[5] who have held that the passage contains no "Condemnation of Art" at large. Nevertheless, the treatment of painting *is* derogatory, and since Plato mounts a serious and vehement critique of poetry upon it, he may be presumed to have written it in earnest. If so, we appear to be faced with a special case of the incoherence which Robinson perceives in his work. On the one hand we find Socrates disparaging the painter on three different grounds. On the other hand we find him comparing himself with a painter at frequent points throughout the work. How are these things to be explained?

The answer is simple. Socrates is no ordinary painter, but a philosopher artist. As such, he depicts the Intelligible rather than the visible world, Reality rather than appearances, Forms rather than particulars. Hence his strictures upon the painter do not apply to himself.

---

[4] Cf. especially *Sophist* 234 B—D.
[5] e. g. G. M. A. Grube, *Plato's Thought*, p. 192.

It can, no doubt, be argued that Plato would not altogether deny the capacity to represent Forms even to artists of the ordinary type. In Book III (401A) painting features in the environment of the growing guardians as a source of harmony and good character, and Socrates argues (402A—C) that they must be able to recognise the moral Forms "and their images" if they are to be truly cultured. Since he envisages the reproduction of moral Forms in works of art, it may be inferred that Plato recognized a superior kind of painting, and that he had, after all, a properly exalted conception of the artist's purpose[6].

With this, however, we shall not be concerned. We shall not consider how far Plato regarded the ordinary artist as capable of representing Forms. What matters for our purpose is that he regards himself as doing so. We find this idea expressed in a key passage (472D—E) at the very heart of the *Republic*.

"Do you think, then," [says Socrates] "that he would be any the less a good painter, who, after portraying a pattern of the ideally beautiful man and omitting no touch required for the perfection of the picture, should not be able to prove that it is actually possible for such a man to exist?"
"Not I, by Zeus", he said.
"Then were not we, as we say, trying to create in words the pattern of a good city?"
"Certainly."
"Do you think, then, that our words are any the less well spoken if we find ourselves unable to prove that it is possible for a state to be governed in accordance with our words?"
"Of course not", he said.

In what follows we shall see that Socrates' comparison of himself with a painter makes three closely related points. First, Plato acknowledges his own use of sensible illustrations, and its limitations as a philosophical method. Secondly, he accords the status of a word picture to the *Republic* itself. It is a verbal image of moral and political Forms. Thirdly, he avows the theoretical character of its political doctrine, the gulf between words and deeds, theory and practice. In effect, the painting and sculpture analogies enable him to clarify his own method and purpose, to compare himself with the mathematician, and to contrast himself with the poet and craftsman. If this is borne in mind, the incoherence which Robinson

---

[6] In Book II (377E) the poet who images the nature of gods and heroes badly is compared with a painter whose pictures bear no resemblance to his models. By implication there would be nothing amiss with a faithful portrait. Even Book X, it has been held, does not condemn imitation in general, but only superficial or incompetent work. See J. TATE, *Imitation in Plato's Republic*, *Classical Quarterly* 1928, 1932.

finds in Plato will disappear, and a carefully ordered design will emerge in its place.

1. Sensible Illustrations

To begin with, let us consider a sentence from the Divided Line, referred to by Mr. Robinson in the passage quoted earlier. The allusion to images (*eikones*) which he specifically mentions occurs in that section of the Line assigned to the state called *dianoia*, and associated with the procedures of mathematics. Socrates is drawing the first of two distinctions between mathematics and dialectic. Mathematicians, he says, make use of visible diagrams and models, and base their arguments upon these although they are thinking not of these sensible exemplars, but only of the real entities which they resemble.

"The very things which they mould and draw, which have shadows and images of themselves in water, these things they treat in their turn as only images, but what they really seek is to get sight of those realities which can be seen only by the mind" (510 E).

It is instructive to relate this procedure to that of Socrates himself. For here as elsewhere[7] Plato may be supposed to have mathematics in mind as a model for ethical inquiry. In at least one passage (437 A) Socrates describes his procedure in language appropriate to deductive argument. The discussion in Books V— VII shifts repeatedly to and from between "value" concepts (goodness, justice, beauty etc.) and mathematical ones (double and half, large and small etc., e. g. 479 A—B). It would thus be entirely appropriate that the mathematician's search for the nature of the Square should correspond with Socrates' quest for moral and political Forms.

In one respect they are indeed comparable: namely, in their use of sensible images as aids to conceptual argument. Just as the mathematician "moulds and draws" things in order to argue about the Square, so Socrates moulds and draws images in order to argue about Justice. Thus in Book IX the human soul is compared with a composite creature, part man, part lion, and part many-headed beast.

"Let us fashion in our discourse a symbolic image (*eikona plasantes*) of the soul," says Socrates, "that the maintainer of that proposition [sc. that injustice is profitable] may see what he has said" (588 B).

---

[7] Most conspicuously in the *Meno* (especially 86 D—87 B).

The profusion of sensible images throughout the *Republic* hardly needs to be stressed. Indeed, as Robinson points out, Socrates calls attention to it himself.

"Your question," I said, "requires an answer expressed in an image (*eikonos*)".
"And you," he said, "of course, are not accustomed to speak in images!"
"So," said I, "you are making fun of me after driving me into such an impasse of argument. But, all the same, hear my image so that you may still better see how I strain after imagery. For so cruel is the condition of the better sort [sc. of philosophers] in relation to the state that there is no single thing like it in nature. But to find an image for it and a defence for them one must bring together many things in such a combination as painters mix when they portray goat-stags and similar creatures" (487 E—488 A).

This comparison with painting accurately conveys the purpose of Plato's images. They assist a case which is "hard to prove" (*logon dusapodeikton*) and, in general, they serve to illustrate rather than to demonstrate[8]. Like the geometer's diagram, they suggest truths which remain to be established by independent argument. An account of the virtues based upon sensible images thus falls far short of a demonstration that is philosophically adequate.

Socrates evidently recognizes this in Book IV where he is about to move from the city to the individual. He tells Glaucon:

"In my opinion we shall never apprehend this matter accurately from such methods as we are now employing in discussion. For there is another longer and harder way that conducts to this. Yet we may perhaps discuss it on the level of our previous statements and inquiries" (435 D).

Even if there *were* any failure on Plato's part to practise the method he preaches, it might reasonably be allowed that he acknowledges it in these remarks. But there is in fact no such incoherence as Robinson supposes. True, as he says, the *Republic* "demands a form of cognition that uses no images at all". But for whom does it demand this, and for what purpose? Neither for Socrates' listeners, nor for Plato's readers. It is only for the potential guardians that the present "mere sketch" of Justice will be inadequate. It is for their training that the "longer and harder way" is prescribed (504 D). The nature of their route is, of course, adumbrated in Books VI—VII, but the route itself is not there followed, as Robinson himself has noticed in another connection (*op. cit.* p. 66). When pressed in Book VII to explain the nature of dialectic, Socrates tells Glaucon that he would not be able to follow him further (533 A). For what he would then see would no longer be an image

---

[8] Cf. P. Shorey's note on 375 D: "Plato never really deduces his argument from the imagery which he uses to illustrate it."

but the reality. The Sun, Line, and Cave similes provide sensible images of the Forms, and of the discipline that would enable us to perceive them directly for ourselves. By using such images, the *Republic* consciously apes the mathematician's procedure[9]. It confines itself to the level of *dianoia*.

Enough has been said to dispose of the problem of Plato's use of images as Robinson presents it. The copious use of images which he takes to conflict with Plato's prescribed method is recognized by Plato himself as a *pis aller*. Pure dialectic would dispense with images altogether. They are nevertheless invaluable aids to conceptual thought, and the philosopher may use them as the mathematician does, provided he remains aware of their limitations.

2. Images of the Forms

There remain, however, those images that lie at the core of the *Republic's* argument, Socrates' portraits of the ideal city and ruler. These cannot be treated as mere "sensible" illustrations, parallel with the geometer's diagram, imperfect instances of the Forms they represent. They do not merely *suggest* an account of Justice, as a diagram suggests the definition of the Square. Rather, these pictures *embody* a definition of Justice and the State. One who sees Socrates' picture has *eo ipso* grasped his definition, and has thereby attained the best vision of these Forms that Plato can give his readers. Geometers conduct their arguments with reference to the Form of Square, which they seek to "see" with the mind (*idein tê(i) dianoia(i)*, 510E). Socrates seeks the nature of Justice and Injustice, in order to "look at them" (*apoblepontes*) and discover what they yield of happiness and the reverse (472C). For geometer and moralist alike, the attainment of a definition and the vision of a Form are alternative descriptions of the same experience. The *Republic* records and imparts that experience, much as a painter captures and conveys what he has seen in his model. It reproduces the contents of its author's intellectual vision.

Visual metaphor is rightly regarded as a leit-motif in the *Republic*. At the outset Socrates proposes that they examine Justice writ large in the city, in order to help them to "look upon" (*episkopein*) it in the individual (368D—E). To discover the origin of Justice and Injustice, they "watch" (*theasaimetha*) a city coming into existence (369A, cf. 372E). When the first sketch of the city is

---

[9] The Line itself is a mathematician's diagram *par excellence*.

complete, Socrates tells Adeimantus to procure a light and to call the other speakers to help "see" (*idômen*) where Justice and Injustice may be found within it (427 D). Throughout the ensuing search, visual metaphor recurs again and again (431 B, 432 C—E). The sustained use of it in the central books needs no emphasis, but it is worth recalling that in Book V philosophers are defined through comparison and contrast with lovers of spectacle (*philotheamones*). They are called *philotheamones* of the truth (475 E). The truth about Justice and Injustice is part of the "spectacle" that philosophers desire to behold. Hence the *Republic* is a spectable designed for them, a dramatic enactment of moral and political truths. Within this drama the supremely just and supremely unjust men are protagonists. Thus they are appropriately portrayed as figures in a competitive spectacle to be adjudicated by the speakers in the discussion (580 B—C). Plato, as Werner Jaeger has said, "creates ideal human figures to correspond to all moral attitudes and modes of life; and this mode of personifying a quality in a type personality became a regular part of his thought"[10].

The *Republic*, then, gives us a verbal image of the Forms. With this in mind let us reconsider the treatment of painting in Book X. Socrates first distinguishes between the Form of Bed made by God, the bed made by a carpenter, and the picture-bed made by a painter. He then asks (597 D), with studied vagueness, what is the relation of painter to bed. Glaucon answers that he may most reasonably be termed an imitator of what "those others" (*ekeinoi*), i. e. God and the carpenter, manufacture. Socrates' question and Glaucon's answer leave it open whether it is the Form or the ordinary bed that the painter imitates. Socrates does not raise this question until several lines later (598 A), whereupon Glaucon opts for the ordinary bed. Here for an instant, the possibility of imitating the Form of Bed is entertained, although in the next instant it is denied to be the business of the ordinary painter. We may now suspect whose concern it would be. Between God who

---

[10] *Paideia*, Vol. II. p. 260. It may be added that in treating himself as a dramatist Plato asserts his own claim to supplant the poets. Cf. *Laws* 817 B: "Our whole polity has been constructed as a dramatisation of a noble and perfect life; that is what we hold in truth to be the most real of tragedies. Thus you [sc. ordinary tragedians] are poets, *and we also are poets in the same style, rival artists and rival actors*" (trans. A. E. TAYLOR). Here, no doubt, lies the true answer to the paradox stated in the first paragraph of this paper. This is the view of P. FRIEDLÄNDER in *Plato*, Vol. I. pp. 119—121.

makes the Form of Bed and the carpenter who makes an ordinary bed, there lies the philosopher, who makes the Bed in words.

Socrates has not, of course, made a Bed in words. But he has depicted a City in words, and the Craftsman who would model a city upon it, the philosopher ruler. As T. A. Sinclair has observed[11], "the theory of Forms or Ideas can be applied to the State as to other and simpler products of human activity". Hence in Plato's choice of beds and tables as examples, we should see great subtlety, and not merely the obsession with furniture for which lesser philosophers are well known.

Consider the examples with which Socrates belabours the painter at 598 B—C. He is said to depict a *carpenter*, amongst other craftsmen, and to be able, if he is a good painter, to deceive naive viewers into thinking the carpenter a real one. The painter, we notice, can imitate not only a bed, but the craftsman who makes it, his own superior on the scale of makers. Not only artifacts, but artificers are superficially represented by the ordinary painter. By contrast, the philosopher painter represents the Ideal Artificer and Artifact, Ruler and City, and his portrayal of both is more than skin deep. Unlike the ordinary imitator he represents the truth. His works are not dictated by popular taste or political pressure[12], and their appeal is not to the senses or emotions but to the intellect.

If the status of the *Republic* as a verbal image is recognized, it will throw light upon a much vexed difficulty in the similes of Books VI—VII. The scheme of the Divided Line requires four sets of "objects" (*eph' hois*) corresponding to the four "cognitive states" (*pathêmata*) listed at 511 D—E. Yet no distinctive objects are anywhere unambiguously assigned to the state called *dianoia*. The distinction between the two higher segments of the Line is explained by contrasting not the objects but the procedures of mathematics and dialectic. Mathematics is said to differ from dialectic in its use of images, and in its uncritical adoption of hypotheses. But both alike are, on the most plausible interpretation[13], concerned with Forms.

Nevertheless, it seems clear that Plato did mean to assign a distinctive set of objects to the level of *dianoia*. At 511 E all four of the cognitive states are said to partake of clarity to the same degree

---

[11] *A History of Greek Political Thought*, p. 145.

[12] For the effect of popular demand cf. 493 C—D, 602 B. For political pressure 568 A—C, cf. *Protagoras* 346 A—B.

[13] *i. e.* taking *auta ekeina* in 510 E and *auta* in 511 D to refer to Forms.

that their objects partake of reality. Since *dianoia* unquestionably partakes of less clarity than *noêsis* (or *epistêmê*, as the highest cognitive state is later called, 533 D), it must somehow apprehend objects that are less real than those of dialectic. This is plainly implied again at 534 A, where Socrates, after reiterating the four states and the proportions between them, excuses himself from going into "the proportion between their objects" (*tên d' eph' hois tauta analogian*). Moreover, the Cave simile distinguishes images from realities outside the Cave as well as within. The emerging prisoner looks at shadows and reflections before he can look at the objects that cast them (516 A—B, 532 B—C). *Dianoia* is thus somehow to be associated with objects that are mere shadows or reflections of those grasped by dialectic.

What then can these objects be? The interpretation put forward above suggests an answer. Plato, it has been argued, is a painter of Forms, a maker of verbal images corresponding to the *logoi* of the mathematician. Hence the special objects of *dianoia* will be those *logoi*[14], of which the *Republic* itself provides moral and political examples. *Logoi* are the images through which the emerging prisoner must first perceive the truths of mathematics and morals, the reflections outside the Cave, in which Plato intends his readers to view the Forms of Justice, Man and City.

This treatment of *logoi* as images has parallels in at least two other dialogues. In the *Phaedo* (99 D—100 A) Socrates describes the method of *logoi* to which he turned after becoming dissatisfied with studying the physical world. This method he compares with studying things through their reflections in water or some other medium. He admits that one who studies "in words" (*en tois logois*) is not using images to any greater extent than one who studies "in things" (*en tois ergois*). For sensible objects are themselves mere images. Hence in adopting the method of *logoi* he is using images to a lesser extent than observers of the physical world. Nevertheless, the comparison implies that *logoi are* images in their own way. Secondly, in the *Cratylus* (439 A—B), after a protracted comparison between names (*onomata*) and pictures, the speakers agree that names are images of things; and that it would be better to learn the truth from things themselves than from their images. But how to learn or discover the things themselves will perhaps, Socrates

---

[14] To interpret the objects of *dianoia* in this way is compatible with taking 510 E to mean that the mathematician seeks to see Forms. For the special objects of *dianoia* are media *through* which the Forms are seen at this level.

suggests, prove too hard for Cratylus and himself. Here too, the way of words is treated as an inferior method, a *deuteros plous*, and yet as the best available to the speakers. Like the *Republic*, the *Phaedo* and *Cratylus* are confined to verbal images[15]. Such vision of the Forms as they afford can only be indirect.

If the foregoing suggestion about the Divided Line is accepted, Plato's plan can be schematised in terms of it as follows:

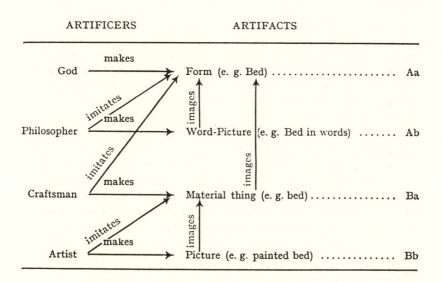

Two comments may be made on this diagram:

(a) The "artifacts" exhibit the ratio holding between "objects" on the Divided Line. The initial division of the Line yields a distinction between the visible and the intelligible (509 D), the opinable and the knowable (510 A). In respect of their reality (*alêtheia*) these are related as likeness to original (*to homoiôthen pros to hô(i) homoiôthê*). This appears in the diagram as the relation

---

[15] In the *Statesman* (277 C) the *Eleatic Stranger* says: "It is more fitting to portray any living being by speech and argument (*lexei kai logô(i)*) than by painting or any handicraft whatsoever to persons who are able to follow argument; but to others it is better to do it by works of craftsmanship." Here although painting and craftsmanship are *contrasted* with "speech and argument", the latter are treated as if they were themselves a superior kind of representation, and the speakers who use them have just previously been compared both with sculptors and painters (277 A—B). For yet another comparison between *logoi* and pictures cf. *Critias* 107 C—D.

between B and A[16]. Forms (Aa) are "more real" than their like-nesses, material things (Ba). The subdivision of each major segment of the line is made in the same ratio (*ana ton auton logon*, 509 D). Thus the ratio of likeness to original reappears in the relation between Forms (Aa) and verbal images (Ab), and again between material things (Ba) and pictures (Bb). In each pair the Bs are images of the As, and the latter are "more real" than the former.

(b) The trio of artificers—philosopher, craftsman, artist — can plausibly be related to the trio of user, maker, imitator, discussed in Book X (601 C—602 B). The user of an object, e. g. a flute, is there credited with knowledge of what constitutes a good or bad one, since he understands the purpose for which it is made. The maker, acting upon the user's instructions, is said to have correct belief, whereas the imitator has neither knowledge nor correct belief. In the *Republic* the "user" is the philosopher. He knows what constitutes a good or bad city[17], since he understands the purpose for which a city is constructed. His grasp of its purpose is embodied in his word-picture of the Form of City. Thus the philosopher and the craftsman both imitate the Form, each in his own way. The philosopher comes closest to the truth, whereas the ordinary imitator is at "third remove" from it (597 E, 599 D). The craftsman comes in second place. His products are "things" (*erga*), as opposed to the philosopher's "words" (*logoi*). The relation between these must now be further explored.

---

[16] I have adapted for my own purpose J. L. Austin's lettering, which displays clearly the ratio holding between the segments of the Line. A complete reinterpretation of the Line cannot, of course, be attempted here. The above remarks aim only to show its bearing upon the structure of the *Republic*. In particular it is not suggested that paintings or poetic images are the sole contents of Bb. These more probably include "appearances" in general, which are reproduced by popular art.

[17] The doctrine that only the user has knowledge may seem disputable in general, and has been felt to have an unfortunate implication for the present argument. N. R. MURPHY observes (*The Interpretation of Plato's Republic*, p. 225, note 1) that the "user" of a city might appear to be not the philosopher but the subject (whom Plato would, of course, credit with no political knowledge at all). However, in the *Cratylus* (390 B—D) the law-giver is treated as a "maker", and the "user" is said to be one who knows how to ask and answer questions, *i. e.* the dialectician. Cf. also *Euthydemus* 289 B: "the sort of knowledge we require is that in which there happens to be a union of making and knowing how to use the thing made." This sounds like a "pre-echo" of the *Republic*'s demand that philosophers ("users") should become rulers ("makers").

3. Words and Deeds

Let us return once again to the attack on poetry in Book X. At 598 E Socrates first raises and then rejects a possible defence of the poet against the charge of ignorance. It might be urged that the good poet must know the various crafts that he represents, or he would be incapable of the fine work that he does. But this will not help him. For he produces only a semblance of his object and not the object itself. He must therefore be ignorant and incapable of producing the real thing.

"If he had genuine knowledge of the things he imitates he would far rather devote himself to real things (*ergois*) than to the imitation of them, and would endeavour to leave after him many noble deeds and works" (599 B).

Homer and the other poets, however, have no practical achievements to their credit. Hence they can have had no knowledge of what they portrayed (601 A).

This invites an analogous criticism of Plato himself. If the doing of things rather than the imitation of them is a necessary condition of knowledge, it might be retorted that no knowledge is attested by the mere painting of a city in words. Sauce for the poetic goose is sauce for the philosophic gander. To prove his worth, the philosopher should not only paint cities and rulers but make them. He should be not only a painter, but a carpenter; a man of action, not merely of words.

This criticism can be answered by elaborating the parallel already drawn between Socrates and the mathematician. In Book VII mathematical disciplines are repeatedly valued less for their practical uses than for their capacity to turn mind away from the sensible towards the intelligible world. Geometers are said to use terms which belie the true nature of their work.

"They speak as if they were doing something and as if all their words were directed towards action. For all their talk is of squaring and applying and adding and the like, whereas in fact the real object of the entire study is pure knowledge" (527 A).

This recalls Socrates' initial reply when he was first challenged to show that the ideal city could be realized in practice. Their primary purpose, he had argued, was theoretical, not practical (472 C). Like the geometer's so-called "constructions" those of the *Republic* are undertaken for the sake of knowledge.

"Is it possible" [he had asked], "for anything to be realized in deed as it is spoken in word, or is it the nature of things that action should lay less hold upon truth than speech, even if some deny it?" (473 A)

Glaucon agrees that this is so, and certainly the remark is of fundamental importance. We are reminded here, as repeatedly (389D, 452A, 501E), of the gulf between making a city in words and making one in fact. But also, as Shorey observes[18], Plato is contradicting the Greek commonplace which contrasts the word unfavourably with the deed. A verbal account of the Form of City brings us closer to the truth than any empirical survey[19]. The city in words, even though it cannot be realized in practice, is a better medium for observing the true city than any actual state. It is, indeed, only that city that is properly so called (422E).

Socrates' city is a model (*paradeigma*) different in kind from anything in the sensible world. Even the stars are imperfect copies of the Forms they reveal. They should be used:

"as patterns (*paradeigmata*) to aid in the study of those realities [the Forms], just as one would do who chanced upon diagrams drawn with special care and elaboration by Daedalus or some other craftsman or painter. For any one acquainted with geometry who saw such designs would admit the beauty of the workmanship, but would think it absurd to examine them seriously in the expectation of finding in them the absolute truth with regard to equals or doubles or any other ratio" (529D—E).

The true astronomer will regard the stars as creations of just such a painter (530A). But if the works even of this divine artist are imperfect, the attempt of a human one to realise the just city on earth may be expected to fail as well. Inevitably it will be further from the ideal than the philosopher's verbal picture.

It is a recurrent complaint against philosophy that its concerns are merely verbal, and hence trivial. The *Euthydemus* and other dialogues show that Plato was deeply sensitive to this charge and to the danger of giving it substance. He recognized logomachy as a constant menace to the progress and prestige of the subject (539B—C). Yet he held that the philosopher's products are, in a sense, all the better for being "merely verbal". In Book VI Adei-

---

[18] Note on 473A. Cf. also his note on 487C: "The commonplace Greek contrast of word and deed, theory and fact, is valid against eristic but not against dialectic."

[19] R. ROBINSON, however, writes: "To get ideas by analogy about the actual human soul it seems that he [Plato] ought to look at actual cities. In particular, to answer his main questions, 'What constitutes a just man?' and 'Is a just man necessarily happier than an unjust one?' *he ought to select actual cities commonly reputed just*, and try to see how they differ from actual unjust cities and whether they are happier" (*op. cit.* p. 211, my italics). To Plato, one imagines, this would sound like telling a geometer to seek the properties of a triangle by selecting actual shapes "commonly reputed" triangular.

mantus objects that Socrates' portrait of the philosopher, although logically unanswerable, is in gross conflict with the facts (487C). His arguments, as Hume said of Berkeley's, admit of no answer and produce no conviction. In answering the objection, however, Socrates makes it clear that he was attempting to define the *true* philosopher, and not the charlatans who have usurped the name. For this purpose a "merely verbal" account is more to the point than any "facts". So Adeimantus' objection shows that he has failed to understand that "action lays less hold upon truth than speech", that words speak louder than actions.

Plato can thus be defended against the objection that mere word-painting, if it disqualifies the poet, should also disqualify the philosopher. Since the latter depicts Forms and not phenomena, the fact that he merely paints need not debar him from pronouncing upon morals and statecraft. For his words, like the mathematician's but unlike the poet's, lay more hold upon truth than action.

Nevertheless, philosophic paintings have their limitations. First, any philosophic work must be liable to those defects that are, according to the *Phaedrus*, inherent in the written word.

"You know, Phaedrus," [says Socrates], "that's the strange thing about writing which makes it truly analogous to painting. The painter's products stand before us as' though they were alive: but if you question them, they maintain a most majestic silence. It is the same with written words: they seem to talk as if they were intelligent, but if you ask them anything about what they say, from a desire to be instructed, they go on telling you the just same thing for ever"[20].

Here, no doubt, it is the etymology of *zôgraphia*, which suggests a comparison between writing and the portrayal of a living thing. Both portrait and script contain the illusion but not the reality of life, the capacity for self-expression that is characteristic of what they represent. This defect can be remedied only in oral dialectic.

Secondly, Plato acknowledges that his painted city is an imaginative construct, virtually unrealisable in practice. The *Republic* is a fantasy[21], a philosopher's fiction. In constructing the *polis* Socrates twice calls himself a "story-teller" (*muthologein* 376D, 501E), and he reminds himself in a heated moment that they are only "playing" (536C). There is, to be sure, a sense in

---

[20] *Phaedrus* 275D—E, trans. R. HACKFORTH. Cf. *Protagoras* 329A.

[21] The *Sophist* (266D) describes a painting as "a man-made dream for waking eyes", a formula which fits the *Republic* in several respects. I hope to pursue Plato's use of the dream figure in a separate paper.

which the theorist who merely talks about cities is only "playing"[22] in comparison with the statesman who builds them. In the *Phaedrus* (276 E) praise is bestowed on the man who can "play in words, telling stories (*muthologounta*) about justice and so forth". This is an apt, and no doubt self-conscious, description of the *Republic* itself. Stories (*muthoi*), it tells us, may serve as speculative approximations to the truth (382 D), and this is its own purpose. But since it is mere make-believe, it lacks the seriousness of genuine action. The painting metaphor points up the unreality of Plato's *polis*, and belittles the achievement of a mere city on paper. Even in this profoundly theoretical work there remains a conflict in Plato between theorist and statesman.

The conflict could be resolved only if the theorist were to *become* a statesman, the one condition represented as necessary for any approximation to the ideal city (473 D). But that condition is highly unlikely to be fulfilled. In existing cities a philosopher's concern for his own integrity will preclude him from entering public life (496 E—497 A). He will be too much preoccupied with watching "the constitution in his own soul".

"If that is his chief concern", [says Glaucon], "he will not willingly take part in politics".
"Yes, by the dog, in his own city he certainly will", [Socrates replies], "yet perhaps not in the city of his birth, except in some providential conjuncture" (592 A).

"His own city" Glaucon interprets correctly as the city in words which exists nowhere on earth, but only as a pattern in heaven. Only in such a city would there be any obligation upon a philosopher to return to the Cave and rule his fellow men (520 A—C). Elsewhere nothing short of "compulsion" (500 D, cf. 347 B—D), or "some miracle" (*theia tis tuché* 592 A), will make him take part in political life.

With these bitterly disaffected remarks in mind we should read two passages in Book VI (484 C—D, 500 E—501 C), in which Socrates compares the philosopher ruler with a painter. The second and more elaborate is worth considering in its context. Socrates'

---

[22] This notion of play (*paidia* as opposed to *spoudé*) is repeatedly linked by Plato with mimetic art, which is treated as one species of it (*Sophist* 234 B). Cf. *Republic* 602 B). For the theorist's construction of a city as play, cf. *Laws* 685 A. For the view of philosophical argument as mere child's-play cf. Callicles' derisive remarks in the *Gorgias* (484 D, 485 B) and Socrates' attempts to forestall criticism in the *Theaetetus* (168 D—E). Even Adeimantus can compare him with a skilled player of draughts (487 B—C).

defence of philosophy has reached an *impasse*. Existing pseudo-philosophers, he allows, are rightly despised as worthless. Yet any philosophically gifted natures there may be are almost inevitably corrupted by their environment. So what hope is there of gaining an ear for the true philosopher's gospel? What chance that the Many would ever give him the doctor's mandate he will need to cure them?

But, he now says (500 E), perhaps they are not after all implacable. They would not be angry if they perceived what philosopher-rulers would do. Like artists, they would start with a clean canvas, sketch the outline of the constitution and then constantly refer to the moral Forms as their model, looking from them to their picture and back again, sometimes deleting and repainting, but continuing until they had made human character as dear to God as it might become (501 C).

A note from J. Adam's commentary brings out, with unconscious elegance, the problem posed by this passage:

"Plato's attempt to conciliate the Many is obviously half-hearted. The Multitude can never be philosophers (494 A), and are not likely to believe in the philosopher-king. But it was necessary to prove or postulate some degree of assent or at least quiescence on their part *in order to demonstrate the possibility of the perfect city*" (Vol. II, p. 44, my italics).

But, we may ask, what sort of a "demonstration" would this be? And why should Plato, if he seriously meant to "demonstrate" the possibility of the perfect city, have done so in a manner which patently begged the question? Obviously he did not suppose that a programme of moral Form-painting would have been a persuasive platform on which to go to the country. All such talk, as Socrates says (494 A), could have meant nothing to the ordinary man.

There is, on a closer view, something suspiciously perfunctory about the whole passage. Adeimantus agrees (501 C—D) that the Multitude will be placated by assurances about moral Form-painting, *if they are sensible (ei ge sôphronousi)*. But we know that they are *not* sensible (492 B—C), and that a false conception of philosophy has prejudiced them violently against it. When Socrates asks if they will still be angry upon hearing the philosopher's gospel, Adeimantus answers: "They will perhaps be less so". To this Socrates replies:

"Instead of less so, may we not say that they have been altogether tamed and convinced, so that for very shame, if for no other reason, they may assent?" (501 E)

Adeimantus at once agrees. But the "conversion" is pointedly

9   Arch. Gesch. Philosophie Bd. 47

artificial. Here as before (375 A—B) Socrates has persuaded his opponents only on paper. By arbitrarily amending Adeimantus' answer so as to render them "altogether tamed and convinced" he emphasizes their intractability in real life. The theorist's *fiat* needs only a stroke of the pen. In practice things are less easy. Socrates has only just (499 C—D) stressed the remoteness of time and place in which a philosopher ruler might exist, if at all. His "demonstration" that the city is "difficult but not impossible" (502 C) amounts to an admission that it cannot be realized here and now. It is a wry appraisal of the prospects for any approximation to the perfect city in Plato's own age and society. Words, as Glaucon remarks later, "are more easily moulded than wax *and other such media*" (588 D), including, we may no doubt add, the minds and institutions of men.

On this view the description of the philosopher's moral Form-painting appears as one of the most moving passages in the work. In effect, Plato here projects his own labour in writing the *Republic* on to the level of political action. Philosopher rulers, *if* they existed, would paint a real city using the same model, and the same painstaking care, that he himself is now using to paint the city in words. But in this day and age there is virtually no chance that they will exist. Hence it is only Plato who is looking to the Forms to fashion a man in the image of God. It is only the city in words that will be outlined, coloured, rubbed out, and revised[23], until it becomes a painting of the greatest beauty (*kallistê graphê* 501 C). This painting is to be found nowhere in reality save in the heart of the philosopher himself, and on the pages of his greatest work.

Thus the painting metaphor here signals Plato's disillusionment and political frustration. The figure of the philosopher artist is all of a piece with the celebrated image of him sheltering under the wall from the dust and hailstorm of social corruption(496 D—E). Both alike are self-portraits, sombre with pessimism and resignation. Those who can, do; those who cannot, paint.

A similar mood is recorded in the Seventh Letter, in a passage describing Plato's state of mind when he visited Syracuse in 367:

---

[23] This reading of the passage is perhaps supported by the contemptuous description in the *Phaedrus* (278 D—E) of the writer "twisting and turning his phrases, pasting them together and pulling them apart". As R. Hackforth says, this may well reflect the impatience of Plato the philosopher with Plato the meticulous literary artist. The process of "touching up" can go on indefinitely (cf. *Laws* 769 A—C).

"Holding this view and in this spirit of adventure it was that I set out from home, — not in the spirit which some have supposed, but dreading self-reproach most of all, lest haply I should seem to myself to be utterly and absolutely nothing more than a mere voice (*logos monon*) and never to undertake willingly any action (*ergou*)"[24].

Plato's misgivings proved, as we know, abundantly justified, and his failure in Syracuse is the more poignant on this account of his motives. In the *Republic* he had charged the poets with imitating only because they could not act. Yet he embarked upon the Sicilian project conscious that this was also a reproach to philosophers, and therefore to himself.

*

Two broad conclusions emerge. First, Plato consciously contrasts the method of images used in the *Republic* with that of dialectic proper. Secondly, he had, when writing it, little hope that its political plan could be implemented or even approximated. It remains, primarily, a theoretical investigation of moral and political concepts.

---

[24] *Epistle* VII, 328 B—C, trans. R. G. BURY.

A REASONABLE SELF-PREDICATION
PREMISE FOR THE THIRD MAN ARGUMENT

I PROPOSE a way of understanding the self-predication premise of the third man argument which Plato used against himself. The way I propose fulfills some of the desiderata for a good interpretation of Plato: it is not unreasonable by itself; it is formally consistent with the other premises of the third man, singly and jointly;[1] it could have seemed that the argument containing the premise was a serious threat to the theory of forms, as Plato evidently feared (*Parmenides* 135A-B). I do not, however, intend to say that therefore my proposal gives what Plato meant. Section VI explains what I do intend.

I. THE THIRD MAN ARGUMENT

The third man argument of *Parmenides* 132A-132B strongly appears to have as premises part of Plato's theory of forms; the argument's conclusion is that there are infinitely many forms associated with each predicate. The conclusion contradicts another thesis of the theory of forms, the thesis that there is just one form associated with each predicate. Obviously, the argument presents a difficulty for the theory.

The following formulation is an instance of the argument for the predicate "large." There is, according to Plato, an analogous argument for every predicate.[2]

---

[1] The desideratum which the feature described in this clause fulfills is that the premises not be obviously formally inconsistent.

I omit ·here the demonstration of the formal consistency of the premises. There is room for argument that some of the premises entail the denial of others, or entail the denial of others in conjunction with some other beliefs Plato had or could or should have had. I am glad there is room for such argument. I do not wish to be constructing an argument Plato could not have evaded. It seems clear to me that at least by the time of the *Sophist* Plato thought that the third man did not vitiate the theory of forms.

[2] My formulation of the argument owes a great deal to the formulations of C. Strang ("Plato and the Third Man," *Proceedings of the Aristotelian Society*,

1. There is a plurality of things that are large (fact).[3]
2. If a plurality of things are all of them large, there is (at least) one form of large things in virtue of which all of them are large (one-and-the-same form).[4]

Supplement, XXXVII [1963], 147-164) and P. T. Geach ("The Third Man Again" in R. E. Allen [ed.], *Studies in Plato's Metaphysics* [New York, 1965], pp. 265-277). Strang's formulation uses something like my 2a, but does not enter it as a premise. My formulation is simpler than Geach's. (Plato's is simpler than mine.)

[3] Numerals with no attached letter label premises which are found in the text of the *Parmenides*. Numerals with attached letters go to premises which I have supplied to fill in gaps in the argument.

Premise 1 occurs as part of an adverbial clause: "Whenever it seems to you there is a certain plurality of large things" (132A2), which amounts to "sometimes it seems to you there is a certain plurality of large things, and then. . . ."

As G. Vlastos points out in his "Plato's Third Man Argument (*Parm.* 132A1-B2): Text and Logic" in *Philosophical Quarterly*, 19(1969), 289-301, hereafter "TMA II," n. 10, p. 298, "it seems to you" (his "you think that") is not intended to cast doubt on what follows. It is safe to take what follows "it seems to you" as Premise 1 of the argument Plato intended.

[4] (*q*) "Whenever it seems to you there is a certain plurality of large things, as you view them, it perhaps seems there is a certain single form, the same over them all" (132A2-3).

The qualification "in virtue of which (by which) all of them are large" does not appear until later in the text (132A7-8 and B1). I have supposed Plato intends it in Premise 2 also.

It is made clear that the certain single form spoken of in (*q*) is a form of large things by the next sentence: (*r*) "For which reason you think that there is a single largeness" ("the large," literally) (132A3-4).

It is controversial whether "a certain single form" means "at least one form (of large things)" as my Premise 2 takes it to mean, or means "a unique form (of large things)"—i.e., "the one and only one form (of large things)" as Vlastos ("TMA II") takes it.

The crux of Vlastos' argument for "unique" is this: "single" or "one" clearly means "unique" at various occurrences within the third man argument of the *Parmenides*, which occurrences make clear that it means "unique" in (*r*); (*q*) is given as a reason for (*r*); if "single" did not mean "unique" in (*q*) the transition from (*q*) to (*r*) would obviously be unsatisfactory, "a transparent fallacy" (Vlastos, p. 293). Therefore, "single" must mean "unique" in (*q*).

I agree with Vlastos' views as I have summarized them up to the "therefore." The "transparent fallacy" seems deliberate to me. One lesson intended by the third man argument is that the observation that various things have one and the same property is suspect as a reason for positing the unique form. One might capture the tone of Parmenides' argument thus: "You give as a reason for there being a unique form of large things (a unique largeness) that there

452

2*a*. Any plurality of large things and a form of large things in virtue of which they are all large is itself a plurality (condition for pluralities).

3. Any form of large things is large (self-predication).[5]

3*a*. Nothing is large in virtue of itself (non-self-explanation).[6]

---

are several large things sharing in one and the same character or form. Well, using that reason, you might as well argue that there are infinitely many forms of the large. Here is how."

H. Cherniss, *Aristotle's Criticism of Plato and the Academy* (New York, 1962), p. 294, describes the "one over many" principle in a way that brings out the transition from "one and the same" to "unique" (without, however, commenting on its doubtfulness). "The principle by which an unique idea is posited to explain the identical attribute observed in a multitude of objects."

To set out the transition that I think is being made: (*a*) a number of things are large; (*b*) they share in one and the same form of large things; (*c*) the form they share in is a unique form of large things. To complicate matters slightly, one might have between (*a*) and (*b*) a step (*a*1): they share one and the same character—being large. See Vlastos' note 16 ("TMA II," p. 298). See 132D9-E1 for a general statement of the move from (*a*) either to (*a*1) or to (*b*): "Is there not a great necessity that a thing which is like share in one and the same thing with what is like [it]?" (Maybe "share one and the same *eidos*" [form? character?] if you read *eidous* in E1.)

Vlastos gives a useful review of many passages in which Plato clearly uses "one" to mean "exactly one" or "the one and only" in the phrase ⌜one form (of F things).⌝ Citing these passages, however, does not establish the sense of "one" in this passage. It is important to notice, I think, that in 132A2-3 "one" (or "single") occurs in connection with "the same"; the phrase is "a certain single form, the same. . . ." I take it that the whole phrase amounts here to "one and the same" and that "one" here amounts to "one" in "one and the same." (In this much I follow Strang, *op. cit.*, p. 150.) It is clear that ⌜one and the same F⌝ does not mean, amount to, or usually suggest ⌜the one and only one F.⌝ E.g., at *Parmenides* 131B3-4 we find "one and the same day," which does not mean "the one and only one day."

I emphasize that I do not claim that "one" in any of its occurrences in the *Parmenides* passage 132A-B is ambiguous.

[5] "[T]he large itself and the other large things" (132A6) certainly suggests that the form of large things generated at the first stage of the argument is large. Since the argument is supposed to go on analogously to the first step infinitely many times, it seems appropriate to summarize the imagined infinity of analogous cases by Premise 3, which is general, and makes a claim for any form of large things.

By "self-predication" I mean to indicate at least claims of the form ⌜the F is F⌝ (e.g., "The camel is a camel") as well as ⌜F-ness is F⌝ and others.

[6] This fills the gap in the *Parmenides* argument which Vlastos' "non-identity premiss" ("TMA II," p. 291) fills. "If anything has a given character by participating in a form, it cannot be identical with that form." Vlastos'

4. There are infinitely many forms of large things (conclusion).[7]

Premises 1, 2, 3, and the conclusion 4, are stated in the *Parmenides*. The premises stated do not even begin the infinite regress. It is assumed that Plato intended the reader to take for granted premises needed to fill in any obvious gaps in the argument.

2*a* and 3*a* are very simple claims whose addition to the given premises, 1, 2, and 3, yields 4, Plato's conclusion.[8]

---

note 37 says that it appears to have been "universally accepted"—that is, everyone agrees that something like it, roughly speaking, must have been used in the argument.

Agreement that something like the premise was used should be distinguished from agreement that what was used is a compulsory tenet in the theory of forms. It is, at the least, not clear (but see Strang, *op. cit.*, p. 158) that non-self-explanation (like Vlastos' non-identity) is an appropriate part of the theory of forms. (I will not here speculate on whether this was the flaw Plato came to see in the argument.)

The reasons to suppose that non-self-explanation is, nevertheless, being used in the argument are two. First, there is a gap which it fills naturally. Second, Plato clearly held that nothing which is not a form is large in virtue of itself; the latter might have been conflated, especially when not stated clearly, with non-self-explanation, from which it differs only in the qualification "which is not a form."

This qualification is important; one might even suppose that it could never have been overlooked by Plato, and that accordingly he would never have felt threatened by an argument that used unstated non-self-explanation.

[7] "And each of your forms will no longer be one, but they will be infinite in number" (132B1-2).

[8] Remarks on pluralities. All together the premises imply that there is no plurality consisting of exactly the things which are large.

The content of 2*a* may be brought out if we notice (as was pointed out to me by John Wallace) how replacing 2*a* by the simpler 3*b* weakens the premises:

3*b*. A single item by itself constitutes a plurality.

If we are to use Premise 2, as Plato does, to generate other forms of large things besides the form (call it "largeness$_1$") provided immediately by Premises 1 and 2, since Premise 2 begins conditionally "if a *plurality* of things. . .," it is natural to expect in addition to 1, 2, 3, and 3*a*, a premise which provides, as 2*a* did, some new pluralities (of large things).

3*b* so provides, but it carries us only as far as a second form of large things: by 3, largeness$_1$ is a large thing; by 3*b*, there is a plurality consisting just of largeness, so by 2, there is a form of large things (call it "largeness$_2$") in virtue of which largeness$_1$ is large; by 3*a* largeness$_2$ $\neq$ largeness$_1$.

By similar reasoning from 3, 3*b*, and 2 we can establish that there is a form

The *Parmenides* (135A-B) gives evidence that Plato held the third man a serious difficulty for the theory of forms; there is no announced answer to the argument in Plato's writings; Plato later—for example, in the *Sophist*—develops the theory as though he thought it had no crippling defects. There is the historical question: what was Plato's answer to the argument?

II. The Self-predication Premise

The historical question would be answered by the supposition that Plato took the third man argument to reduce to absurdity part, but not the whole, of the theory of forms. A version of this supposition which has some advocates is that Plato was reducing to absurdity self-predication.

The self-predication premise for "large" is: a form of large things is large. Largeness, which Plato would say large things shared, is a form of large things. So the self-predication premise contributes to the consequence that largeness is large.[9]

(call it "largeness$_3$") in virtue of which largeness$_2$ is large; by 3a largeness$_3$ ≠ largeness$_2$. But we cannot prove that largeness$_3$ ≠ largeness$_1$. That is, the altered premises are consistent with there being exactly two forms of large things, each large in virtue of the other.

See note 22 for evidence that Plato did not hold that a single form counted as a plurality.

[9] A typical response to "Largeness is large" is that it is neither true nor false unless there is an answer to the question "Largeness is a large what?" This question does not arise for a number of self-predications—for example, "Man is a man," "White is white."

There is some chance that Plato held that for the form largeness the answer was: "Not a large something or other, but just large." For example, at *Phaedo* 74a9-12, which involves "equal," like "large" in need of completion, though of a different kind, Plato perhaps means to say of the form the equal that it is not an equal pair of sticks (equal in length) or an equal pair of stones (equal in weight) but is just equal. (The *Phaedo* remark, understood as a hint of a general view about predicates that are incomplete in one way or another, apparently conflicts with the remark in the *Sophist* at 255 that the different [which includes at least the form of the different] is always spoken of with reference to a different thing.)

I have not considered any special difficulties which may arise for formulating the argument for attributive adjectives and others similarly in need of some supplement, if the above paragraph does not represent Plato's view. If there are insuperable difficulties, then my proposal gives only a way of understanding the self-predications which do not involve the troublesome expressions.

455

In the analogous argument for other predicates, the analogue to the self-predication premise for "large" will help lead to self-predications such as "Justice is just," "Holiness is holy," "Man is a man," "The camel is a camel."

These sentences strike many people as patently false. Faced with "Justice is just," they are disposed to say that it is people and laws and institutions that are or can be just; to say that justice is just is to make a category mistake.[10]

For one who held that in giving the third man argument Plato meant to show need to abandon an absurd, indeed insane, self-predication assumption, there would be the additional historical-medical question: why was Plato temporarily so mad as to hold self-predication?

The self-predication premise seems to me not implausible. If Plato was using the argument to get rid of some part of the theory, I see no immediate reason why self-predication should be what he wanted to discard.

The strongest evidence that Plato ever held something expressible by the general self-predication premise is *Parmenides* 132A-B: for first, it claims that the third man argument will go through for any form; second, it is likely that it contains the self-predication premise for largeness in the remark "What about the large itself and the other large things?"

There are particular claims of the self-predicational syntax in other dialogues.[11] The premise is in Aristotle's report of the argument in the fragments of his *On Ideas*.

---

[10] "Such a view is, to say the least, peculiar. Proper universals are not instantiations of themselves, perfect or otherwise. Oddness is not odd; Justice is not just; Equality is equal to nothing at all . . . not even God can scratch Doghood behind the Ears. The view is more than peculiar; it is absurd." R. E. Allen, in R. E. Allen (ed.), *Studies in Plato's Metaphysics* (New York, 1965), p. 43.

[11] *Phaedo* 100C: "if anything else is beautiful besides beauty. . . ." *Hippias Major* 292 E: "Beauty is always beautiful. . . ." *Protagoras* 330: "Justice is such as to be just . . . nothing else could be holy if we will not allow holiness to be so." *Republic* 597, *Timaeus* 31A, mentioned in note 21 *infra*. *Lysis* 217D, where it looks as though white is white.

III. Some Grammatical Points

In English and in Greek, sentences which count as self-predications are of at least two kinds whose differences are relevant here. Examples of the two are: (1) "Justice is just"; (2) "The camel is a camel."

They differ thus. The first has an adjective as predicate. The second has a sortal predicate, "camel."

I call (self-) predications of the first kind "adjectival (self-) predications" and (self-) predications of the second kind "sortal (self-)predications."

The first has as subject an abstract substantive expression, one kind of expression which Plato used to name forms. The second sentence has as subject a phrase which it is most natural to take in isolation as referring to the species, the camel, if you know that the phrase is not elliptical for "the camel over there." Plato also used such phrases as names for forms, which are presumably not the same as species.

Plato used phrases similar to such species names as "the camel" as names of forms associated with adjectival predicates: the Greek for "the just," a phrase consisting of the neuter singular definite article and appropriate adjective, is as good a name of the form justice as is the Greek abstract substantive for "justice."

IV. Pauline Predication[12]

A customary objection to many self-predications is that the form of words—abstract substantive or species name, for example, in subject position and predicate appropriate only to entities which the subject-expression does not name—is absurd. Or, to direct the objection especially at Plato: self-predications are absurd in attaching to some subject expression which, according to Plato, names a form a predicate which obviously could not be true of the named form.

---

[12] I am grateful to Gregory Vlastos for asking many questions which affected this section particularly and for encouraging me to work on this paper.

There are sentences which are not self-predications which display the allegedly absurd form of words, but which, far from seeming absurd, seem true—for example: "Charity suffereth long and is kind . . . rejoiceth with the truth, beareth all things" from St. Paul's first letter to the Corinthians.[13]

I call "Pauline predications" sentences which (a) attach to some subject expression which Plato would say named a form a predicate which someone might reasonably allege as inappropriate to the named form as "just" is alleged inappropriate to justice and which (b) we naturally take to be true.

If one can accept as true the Pauline predication "Charity suffereth long," despite its having the feature held a defect of self-predications, one should not object immediately to the self-predications "Charity is charitable" and "Justice is just." Adjectival self-predications have at least no more objectionable features than adjectival Pauline predications.

To turn to sortal predications: the disparity between the degree to which sortal self-predications like "The whale is a whale" are tolerated and the degree to which closely related predications like "The whale is an animal" are tolerated[14] is similar to the disparity between the degrees of acceptance of "Charity is charitable" and "Charity suffereth long." People who think the sortal self-predication "The whale is a whale" is obviously false, because the species the whale could not be an individual whale, are willing to say that the sortal predication "The whale is an animal" is true. Consistency does not, however, seem to require that assent to "The whale is an animal" should compel assent to "The whale is a whale" as assent to "Charity suffereth long" should compel assent to "Charity is charitable." One can rather naturally claim a difference between the two sortal predications. One may say that "is an animal" is true both of individual animals and of species of animal, while "is a whale" can be true

---

[13] Compare Lactantius: "Plato and Aristotle said much about justice (*justitia*) bestowing the highest praise on it because it assigns to each man what is his own and preserves equity in all things." *Select Fragments*, vol. XII of *The Works of Aristotle Translated into English*, W. D. Ross (ed.), (Oxford, 1952), p. 101.

[14] Geach, *op. cit.*, has noticed this kind of disparity, p. 270.

458

only of individuals and of varieties of whale, so the whale cannot be a whale, although it can be an animal.

"The whale is an animal" counts as a Pauline predication, however, on the ground that someone might reasonably view its predicate as true solely of individual animals. With the predicate so viewed, the sentence is a Pauline predication.

Given that people accept Pauline predications (and ought not to reject without explanation Plato's self-predications) the question arises: how can they accept them without absurdity? what can they mean by them? It is fruitful to treat the latter question as the question: what semantical roles might the parts of the sentences have?

V. THREE RESPONSES TO PAULINE PREDICATIONS

Here are three ways one might react to Pauline predications and to Plato's self-predications. The last would be appropriate for Plato. In summary, the three are: to recoil, to reparse, and to reinterpret.

(1) To recoil is to declare that locutions like "Charity suffereth long" are irredeemably false, despite popular assent to them.

(2) To reparse is to redescribe the logical structure of the sentences in question. Commentators on Plato have offered two kinds of redescription.

The first kind is Aristotle's: he claims that certain sortal self-predications—for example, "Man is a man"—say no more than or are paraphrasable into sentences in which "man" is not the subject expression but has assumed the role of a predicate. "Man is a man" becomes "Everything which is a man is a man."

Of the unparaphrased sentence Aristotle comments that the word "man" in it does not refer to an individual, as it appears to do. His comment, which occurs in an analysis of why the third man argument arises for Plato's theory, is meant as a criticism of Plato's treatment of the grammatical role of certain expressions like "man" and doubtless "justice." These appear to be names or singular terms—that is, expressions which refer to some

459

181

individual. According to Aristotle, on reflection "man" turns out to be only apparently a referring expression. Sentences in which it is the subject expression do not attribute anything to an entity named by their subject expressions.[15] The Aristotelian course is to treat "Justice is just" like "Man is a man."

Aristotle's recommendation does away with apparent form names as Russell's theory of descriptions does away with definite descriptions: sentences containing them are just short ways of saying something not containing them; form names, like definite descriptions, need not be assigned denotata in giving the semantics of your language; the truth conditions of sentences containing form names (or definite descriptions) will already be determined by your treatment of other expressions.

A second kind of redescription is offered by Allen and perhaps by Cherniss. Allen takes "Justice is just" as a veiled relational claim, an identity claim, "Justice is justice."[16]

(3) A third means of understanding our Pauline predications and Plato's self-predications is what I call "reinterpreting." A reinterpreter does not redescribe the logical structure of such sentences, but takes their grammatical form as their logical form.

---

[15] *Soph. El.* 178*b*36-179*a*5: "Isolation does not produce the third man but agreeing that it [i.e., man] is just what a certain 'this' is does . . . it is apparent that one must grant not that what is predicated in common of them all is a certain 'this' but that it signifies either what it is like or in relation to what or how much or something like that."

Maybe "isolation" means "the using expressions like 'man' (and 'justice' and other abstract substantives)." If so, Aristotle is saying that it is not a mistake to employ such expressions; the mistake is to take their apparent grammar as their logical grammar. Compare *Cat.* 3*a*10. To paraphrase: it appears when one speaks of man or the animal that one is speaking of a certain "this"; but one is not.

[16] Cherniss, *ACPA*, p. 298; Allen, *op. cit.*, p. 44. Allen's view seems to me not as good a possible interpretation of Plato as the one I propose *infra*. To sketch one disadvantage: one would expect the account one gives of Plato's self-predications—e.g., "Justice is just"—to help one understand predications like "Justice is holy." If we suppose the latter to be a relational claim, as is "Justice is just" on Allen's view, "Justice is holy" amounts to "Justice is holiness." Then the argument in *Protagoras* 330 has "Justice is holiness" as a premise to an argument whose conclusion is "Justice is holiness." So *Protagoras* 330's argument turns out to be highly uninteresting. But the participants in it sound as though they find the transitions from step to step in it difficult and not trivial.

460

That is, he agrees that the subject expression "justice" or "charity" is a referring expression, not a device to help say something which could equally well be said without it. "Justice" is to be classified as a singular term referring to justice when one gives the semantics of the language containing "justice."

A reinterpreter aims at consistently holding these beliefs: the apparent referring expression "justice" is an actual referring expression; the sentence "Justice is just" says something about what "justice" refers to—namely, justice; the predicate "just" is true of what the subject expression refers to if the sentence is true; the sentence is true. So the reinterpreter must say that the predicate "just" has justice in its extension. As a gesture of appeasement to the critics who recoil from Pauline predication I use "reinterpretation" for what might equally well be thought of as philosophical discovery.

Here are two quite different ways of reinterpreting. The first—which I call "conservative reinterpretation"—is to hold that the predicate "just" has two extensions.[17] In "Socrates is just," if that is true, it has the extension that those who recoil from Pauline predications claim "just" always has; that is, it is true of people, their characters, acts, institutions. To mark off this role of the predicate, I use "just$_1$." In "Justice is just" or "Piety is just," "just" has the extension of "is such that if anything x participates in it, then x is just." To mark off this role of the predicate, I use "just$_2$." Lest the explanation of "just$_2$" look circular, let me spell it out in two clauses:

x is just$_2$ if and only if

either (i) x is a form and if anything y participates in x, y is just$_1$

or (ii) x is a form and if anything y participates in x, y is just$_2$ or y is just$_1$

For any predicate F, sortal or adjectival, with a recoiler's use

---

[17] This is not the same as saying that "just" has two uses which have different extensions. The latter way of speaking is meant to indicate that "just" is true of widely different kinds of things but meant to be neutral on the question whether "just" is therefore ambiguous.

461

an analogous distinction between F_1 and F_2 can be made, with analogous clauses given for F_2.

This familiar kind of explication is not circular. It gives some initial conditions, devoid of use of "just$_2$" under which certain items are just$_2$. Given these items, you can go on to find others which are just$_2$.[18]

A second way of reinterpreting, which I call "expansive reinterpretation," is to hold that "just" is more widely applicable than one might have thought before reflection on "Justice is just": that is, it is held that "just" has the same extension as "just$_1$ or just$_2$" where "just$_1$" and "just$_2$" are as explained above.

In explaining the extension "just" has in the reinterpreters' use I rely upon there being people who recoil from Pauline predications and who assign to their use of "just" a very narrow extension.

It should be noted that the "if. . . then. . ." within clauses (*i*) and (*ii*) of the definition of "just$_2$" cannot be the material conditional.[19] For I am trying to sketch a position which would be open to Plato; if the "if. . . then. . ." were material, then, on the ground that nothing participates in non-self-identity or the unicorn, "Non-self-identity is just" and "The unicorn is just" would turn out to be true, as Plato would probably not have held.

---

[18] Remarks: clause (*i*) and some other information let us know that legal justice—suppose it a kind of justice which has no subspecies—is just$_2$. Clause (*ii*) and some other information let us know that justice itself is just$_2$.

Evidently, only forms will be just$_2$. Perhaps not so evidently, the two clauses leave open the question whether justice participates in itself. Clause (*i*) is superfluous.

It may look as though it would be simpler to describe the extensions of F_1 and F_2—in particular, "just$_1$" and "just$_2$"—by these clauses: x is just$_1$ if and only if x is just in the way appropriate to non-forms; x is just$_2$ if and only if x is a form and every participant in x is just in the way appropriate to non-forms. But such clauses for "virtuous" would not guarantee that "is virtuous$_2$" was true of virtue, since some of virtue's participants are forms (e.g., charity, justice). The two clauses for the definition of F_2 allow for the latter.

[19] I owe notice of this to a member of an audience at Rochester to which I read this paper.

462

VI. Plato and Reinterpretation

I do not claim that Plato explicitly adopts either way of reinterpreting. He does not.

I have described two extensions—one conservative, one expansive—for the predicates of Plato's self-predicative claims. Given these extensions for the predicates, the self-predicative claims would be true.

Suppose in Plato's use the predicates had one of the described extensions; it would not follow, nor do I claim, that "just$_1$ or just$_2$" gives what "just" meant to Plato, or that Plato would have used the phrase to describe the extension of "just." I am not attributing to Plato an unexpressed belief that "just" has the two roles of, or is to be explained via, "just$_1$" and "just$_2$."[20]

To indicate an extension possible for Plato's predicate "just," I might simply have started a list and put Socrates, justice, and holiness on it. The point of offering a general description of the extension I have in mind instead of merely starting a list is to forestall the objection to the list that there is no way of characterizing generally without incoherence the items on the list.

The most I assume about Plato is that he knew how to use "just" without immediate absurdity. Such an assumption has no interesting consequences for what he might have meant by "just" in the sense of how he might have explained "just." The proposal I am making is that Plato, consistently with the premises of the third man argument, might have meant by "just" something with the extension of, for example, "just$_1$ or just$_2$."

VII. Why Conservative Reinterpretation Does Not Evade the Third Man

Will reinterpreting avoid the third man argument? It may look as though a conservative reinterpreter, holding that a predicate F had *two* extensions, could avoid the regress where the associated form the Φ had no participants which were forms except perhaps for the Φ itself.

---

[20] For the observations in this paragraph I am grateful to Paul Benacerraf.

He would claim that since the predicate F had two extensions, either wholly or largely disjoint, the predicate F was ambiguous. Our notion of ambiguity is captured by Quine, who says of certain ambiguous words that (at the same time) "from utterance to utterance they can be clearly true or clearly false of one and the same thing. This trait, if not a necessary condition of ambiguity of a term, is at any rate the nearest we have come to a clear condition of it."[21] The conservative reinterpreter I am imagining takes the condition as sufficient for ambiguity: the declaration that "just" has two extensions has the result that "just" is ambiguous. Suspending judgment on the question whether Plato could usefully have declared an ambiguity, in our sense, of F, I will explore the consequences of the declaration.

Clearly the one-and-the-same-form premise would fail to generate a common form of the seal over the seals in the Los Angeles Zoo and the Great Seal of the United States: we may describe its failure by saying that the premise is supposed to generate a common form of Φ things only for a plurality of things which are Φ in the same sense. If the Φ and the plurality of things which are Φ do not, on ground of ambiguity of F, count as a new plurality of things which are Φ in the same sense, the claim that F is ambiguous, as "seal" is, will render illegitimate an application of the one-and-the-same-form premise on a mixed batch of Φ things and will avoid the regress[22] in this special sort of case.[23]

But citing the described ambiguity of F is not enough to flaw the argument for most predicates. For example, take "virtuous."

---

[21] W. V. Quine, *Word and Object* (New York, 1961), p. 131.

[22] I mean: will avoid a regress from the premises I have set out. Another regress for any form the Φ could be established using Premises 2, 2a, 3, and 3a, if Plato did not deny that the Φ all by itself counted as a plurality of things which are Φ.

There is some evidence that Plato did not hold that a single form counted as a plurality: at *Republic* 597 and *Timaeus* 31 A Plato gives arguments close in form to the third man. These arguments have a short regress, though nothing prevents the infinite one. The arguments go: if there were two forms of the bed (*Timaeus*: the animal) there would have to be a third. One presumes that Plato did not think the single form the bed (the animal) generated the regress; that may be because the single form did not count as a plurality.

[23] Neil Lubow's insistence on this special case provoked useful reflection on avoidance of the regress generally.

Virtue, charity, justice, and humility are virtuous, all in the same way—namely, virtuous$_2$. The one-and-the-same-form premise, then, requires a common form of virtue over them. So the argument generates a regress for virtue and for any form of the Φ when there are kinds of the Φ.[24]

VIII. Definition and the One-and-the-Same-Form Premise

Turn to the question whether Plato could usefully have claimed ambiguity in our sense for any predicate F with a recoiler's use. It is not crucial to know if Plato would or would not have used a word translatable "ambiguous" to characterize "just" with its two different uses.[25] Our question is whether the dif-

---

[24] It should be noted that self-predications for some predicates are so generally accepted that they could not count as Pauline (they fail the first clause in the description of Pauline predications); e.g., "Self-identity is self-identical" (see Vlastos, "The Third Man Argument in the *Parmenides*" reprinted in Allen, *op. cit.*, p. 241). On its most natural understanding, it seems to contain "self-identical" with the same sense as "self-identical" in "Socrates is self-identical." There seems to be no reason to say that "self-identical" is ambiguous because it is true of both Socrates and self-identity. Doubtless self-identity is self-identical$_1$ as well as being self-identical$_2$.

[25] He would evidently have used a phrase translatable "not ambiguous." See G. E. L. Owen, "A Proof in the Peri Ideon," reprinted in R. E. Allen, *op. cit.*, pp. 293-312. Owen discusses Aristotle reporting on Platonic doctrine, and describes as "what must be intended as an exhaustive analysis of the ways in which a predicate can be used without ambiguity" (p. 295) a list in which item (c) below appears (pp. 293-294). "When the same predicate is asserted of several things not homonymously but so as to indicate a single character, it is true of them either . . . or (c) because one of them is the model and the rest are likenesses, e.g., if we were to call both Socrates and the likenesses of Socrates 'men.' "

The use of "just" for just people and for justice itself would clearly fall under (c). Plato wants to distinguish (c) predication, which he might nevertheless agree was a case where there were somewhat different grounds for application of the same predicate, from cases of enormous difference, as in the case of "seal."

Notice Owen's comment on type (c) predication (pp. 297-298): "The analysis would misrepresent its Platonic sources if (c) were not a type of unequivocal predication. This is implied by the reference in *Republic* 596-7 to a bed in a picture, a wooden bed, and the Paradigm Bed as [three beds] and more generally by such dicta as that nothing can be just or holy or beautiful if the corresponding form is not so. These utterances have no sense unless the predicate applies without difference of meaning to model and likeness alike."

465

ference between the two uses is so great that the one-and-the-same-form premise would be as illegitimately applied to a plurality of just things consisting of, say, Socrates and justice as to a plurality of seals consisting of the seals in the Los Angeles Zoo and the Great Seal.

I offer a brief account, each point in which is controversial and deserving of more detailed treatment, of some reasons which weigh on the side of a negative answer to our question, although they do not compel a negative answer.

"Just" used for just$_1$ things differs from "just" used for just$_2$ things in applying to items that are widely, even categorially, different from what "just" used for just$_2$ things applies to. But we are not entitled to use this difference to establish that there is not one and the same form of justice over just$_1$ things and just$_2$ things, unless we can adequately distinguish (as I cannot) the latter difference from the difference between "just" used for just acts and "just" used for just people; just people and just acts are quite different (even categorially so): yet there is supposed to be one and the same form of justice over them.

A difference useful to find would be a difference between the definitions that Plato would have given "just" in its two uses. I shall assume that failure to find such a difference would be strong reason to say that the employment of the one-and-the-same-form premise on "just" in the recoiler's use and "just" said of justice is legitimate.[26]

A Platonic definition of "just" may be represented as an "if and only if" claim: "x is just if and only if . . . ." Let us label Plato's requirement that the predicate D defining a predicate F

---

[26] In effect this is the assumption that difference in Platonic definition is likely to be necessary for illegitimacy.

Notice, incidentally, that it may not be sufficient. Owen, *op. cit.*, p. 297, suggests cases where different paraphrases (Platonic definitions?) are appropriate to different uses of a predicate, but where Plato would nevertheless not hold the predicate ambiguous (in his sense).

It is awkward to speak of Plato defining a use of a predicate. What I ask you to imagine is: Plato first defining "just" while supposing it true only of non-forms and then defining "just" while supposing it true only of forms.

There is of course something bizarre about imagining Plato agreeing to attempt a definition of a predicate with only a recoiler's use.

must be true of exactly what F is true of by saying that Platonic definitions are to be *adequate*.

Suppose that there is an analysis of "just" which is adequate to a recoiler's use of "just." Let the analysis be "is disposed to allot to each man his due."[27]

The recoiler's analysis will also be adequate to Plato's presently supposed reinterpretive use of "just" for forms since the defining phrase "is disposed to allot to each man his due" has a reinterpretive use. The reinterpreting Plato would hold not only that justice is just. He would hold also that justice is disposed to allot to each man his due.[28] For, on the assumption that the defining phrase in the recoiler's use is adequate as a definition of the recoiler's use, justice is disposed-to-allot-to-each-man-his-due$_2$.

That the recoiler's phrase "is disposed to allot to each man his due" is definitive of the recoiler's "just" seems reason to suppose that Plato's use of the phrase, which is adequate to Plato's use of "just" for forms, will also be definitive of that use.

It might be objected to this supposition that a Platonically acceptable analysis of "just" with the extension of "just$_2$" would state that only forms are what are just in this use of "just" and that a Platonically acceptable analysis of "just" with the extension of "just$_1$" would, in contrast, say that only non-forms are what are just in this use of "just."

Mention of the category of their extensions, however, does not turn up in Plato's definitions of predicates which have a recoiler's use. The absence of such mention is some indication that such mention does not belong there. The differences which Plato certainly recognized between a just person and a just form are not part of what it is for them to be just. If the only differences

---

[27] If this analysis were adequate, it would hold, as it does not, for "just" as said of particular acts, kinds of acts, people, institutions. Perhaps an adequate analysis of "just" would have to be disjunctive to cover all of these. The argument here, however, would not be affected if the definition were disjunctive, so long as it was an adequate definition.

"Is disposed to" is the usual gesture against the suggestion that the just man is in a continual frenzy of activity.

[28] Recall the citation from Lactantius in note 13 *supra*.

467

mentionable between the two uses of "just" are those which amount to a difference whose mention does not belong in a Platonic definition of "just" (or any predicate with a recoiler's use), the same phrase will be definitive of "just" as used for the extension of "just$_1$" and of "just" as used for the extension of "just$_2$."

That the same phrase will be definitive of the recoiler's and Plato's reinterpretive use of "just" is some reason to suppose that the two uses get the same Platonic definition.

It is unsuitable to object here that the alleged sameness of definition is "merely verbal" and that the defining phrase "is disposed to allot" must have two different senses because the two uses of "just" which the phrase defines are said of categorially different items. Unsuitable, because our present question is: will the difference in category of what falls under the two uses of "just" make for a difference in sense that would be revealed by a difference in Platonic definition? In quest of an answer for "just" we are not entitled to assume that for "disposed to allot" the answer is yes.

I said at the beginning of this section that I would notice considerations that weighed on the side of answering negatively the question: if Plato were a conservative reinterpreter, would he hold illegitimate the application of the one-and-the-same-form premise at the crucial stage of the argument? "Weigh on the side of" was to indicate this: the position of a conservative reinterpreter is consistent with those of Plato's views so far mentioned, but for him to take the position—to declare "just" ambiguous by Quine's condition—would not be for him *thereby* to avoid the regress. For it looks as though he would affirm (1) that there is nevertheless no difference in the Platonic definitions of the two uses of "just"; and such an affirmation seems strong reason to affirm as well (2) that an application of the one-and-the-same-form premise to any group of items of which "just" in the two uses was true would be legitimate. Reinterpretation of the kind I have described offers a reasonable hypothesis about how Plato might have used self-predicative claims; but it does not by itself provide a distinction which would block the use of the one-and-the-same-form premise.

In fact, the distinction among uses of any predicate F which is needed in order to fault the argument as relying on an illegitimate application of the one-and-the-same-form premise is a distinction which puts F's self-predicative use on the one side of the distinction and puts all the non-self-predicative uses on the other side,[29] as the discussion in Section VII and note 24 indicates.

To summarize and make general the above points about "just": For any predicate F with a recoiler's use I have provided other predicates F_1 and F_2 such that ⌜the F is F_2⌝ and ⌜the F is F_1 or F_2⌝ is true. It is consistent with the premises of the third man argument to take such a predicate F to have the extension of F_2 when it occurs as a predicate in self-predications, or to have the extension of ⌜F_1 or F_2.⌝

For any such predicate F, if its analysis or definition D for the recoiler's use is adequate, then ⌜the F is D⌝ will be true, when D has the conservative reinterpreter's extension, the extension of D_2. Moreover, D with the extension of D_2 will be definitive, so far as one can see, of F with the (conservative reinterpreter's) extension of F_2.[30] The predicates which define any recoiler's predicate are exactly as able to have the kind of extensions I propose for predicates in Pauline predications and self-predications as "just" is.

---

[29] The Cherniss-Allen account of the uses of "just" is an example of a distinction which does so.

There is some evidence that Plato did make a distinction between self-predicative and non-self-predicative uses of F as a response to the third man argument. I agree with Cherniss (*ACPA*, pp. 308 ff.) that Aristotle's *Metaphysics* 1079a32-b11 is evidence that Plato did make such a distinction; I do not agree with his account of what the distinction is (see n. 16).

[30] Likewise when F and D are taken to have the expansive reinterpreter's extensions of ⌜F_1 or F_2⌝ and of ⌜D_1 or D_2,⌝ respectively.

On the conservative reinterpreter's position, notice, F within the subject expression of ⌜the F is F⌝ is ambiguous also by Quine's criterion. The four ways of understanding ⌜the F is F⌝ have the same truth conditions as (1) ⌜the F_1 is F_2⌝; (2) ⌜the F_2 is F_2⌝; (3) ⌜the F_2 is F_1⌝; and (4) ⌜the F_1 is F_1.⌝ The first way of understanding ⌜the F is F⌝ is the way which is employed in the third man. The first two ways are true; the second two are false.

It is important to notice that if the discussion of sec. VIII is correct, the subject phrases in all four of the ways of understanding ⌜the F is F⌝ designate one and the same form.

If the Platonic analysis D of a predicate F as used in the re-coiler's way is the same for F as for its associated form, there is that much reason for Plato to affirm that the one-and-the-same-form premise generates a common form over participants in the Φ and the Φ itself. The difference between the way the Φ is Φ and the way many of its participants are Φ is best brought out by saying that the Φ is a form which is Φ perhaps[31] solely by bringing about that its participants are Φ. Many of its participants may be Φ without being able to have participants. Such categorial differences, however, do not make a difference to what it is to be Φ and do not get mentioned in the account of what it is to be Φ.

It is not only *self*-predicative claims or their consequences by definition which we can now understand to be true. For any predicate G with an associated form the ψ such that all the participants in a form the Φ thereby (as a matter of entailment) are ψ—that is, thereby have G true of them, the form the Φ will have G_2 true of it. That is, it will have G true of it, if G has the extension of G_2 or of $\ulcorner G_1$ or $G_2,\urcorner$ as the reinterpreter proposes.

SANDRA PETERSON

University of Minnesota

---

[31] Recall note 24.

A CORRECTION TO
"A REASONABLE SELF-PREDICATION PREMISE FOR THE THIRD MAN ARGUMENT"

THE explanation I gave of "$just_2$" in "A Reasonable Self-Predication Premise for the Third Man Argument" in *Philosophical Review*, LXXXII (1973), 451-470, might be circular in a bad way, not merely in the benign way of the recursive definitions to which I had thought it parallel.

I owe realization of the potential circularity to Mr. H. Sarkar, who asked me why I did not include "$y \neq x$" in clause (*ii*) of the explanation. With this inclusion—and with the omission of clause (*i*), which is, as indicated in note 18 of the paper, dispensable—the revised explanation reads:

x is $just_2$ if and only if x is a form and if anything y $(y \neq x)$ participates in x, y is $just_2$ or y is $just_1$

In note 18 I remarked that the earlier definition left open the question whether justice participates in itself. I meant: I do not know whether it does; it does not follow from my explanation of "$just_2$" that it does or that it does not. What I meant was correct; unfortunately it would also have been correct to add that if justice *does* participate in itself the definition of "$just_2$" would be circular. For suppose that justice does participate in itself. Then when one uses the unrevised explanation of "$just_2$" to work out the condition under which justice is $just_2$ one arrives at:

justice is $just_2$ if and only if   justice is a form and if anything y (for example, justice) participates in justice, y (for instance, justice) is $just_2$ or y is $just^1$

Since justice is certainly not $just_1$, it is evident that to know if the right-hand side of the biconditional holds, we need to know if justice is $just_2$: but the right-hand side is supposed to provide the explanatory conditions for justice's being $just_2$, so the explanation is circular.

The revised explanation avoids this circularity. And it leaves open the question whether justice participates in itself.

SANDRA PETERSON

University of Minnesota

96

AMERICAN PHILOSOPHICAL QUARTERLY
Volume 16, Number 2, April 1979

II. SELF-PREDICATION AND PLATO'S THEORY OF FORMS

... τὸ τί ἦν εἶναι ἑκάστῳ τῶν ἄλλων τὰ εἴδη παρέχονται ...
... they furnish the Forms as what it is for each of
the others to be ...

Aristotle, *Metaphysics* A, 988b4–5

ALEXANDER NEHAMAS

CONSIDER this famous passage of the *Phaedo*:
... if anything is beautiful other than the beautiful itself, it is beautiful for no other reason but because it participates in that beautiful; and I mean this for everything. Do you agree with this sort of explanation (*aitia*)?[1]

In its context, this statement suggests that Plato accepts the following three ideas:

(1) Beauty (which is here merely an example) is beautiful.

(2) Whether anything else is beautiful is an open question.

(3) If anything else can be actually considered beautiful, this must be explained in terms of its participation in Beauty, which is itself beautiful in a way which does not seem to require such an explanation.[2]

These are strange ideas, for what strikes us as requiring explanation is not so much why ordinary things are beautiful, or large, or just, but rather why Plato is at all tempted to say that they are not. Plato's view seems to be that, strictly speaking, only Beauty

is beautiful, and that it takes philosophy to show that anything else is. To understand why Plato holds this view we must understand his general view of predication, that is, how he construes the attribution of characteristics to things, how he interprets sentences of the form "*a* is *F*." I think that there is something unusual in his interpretation; otherwise, he should not have been willing to consider as obviously true only those sentences in which the subject-term purports to refer to the very Form of *F*-ness.

By "self-predication" I shall understand simply the idea that Beauty is beautiful—in general terms, that the *F* itself is *F*—independently of any particular analysis we might give to it.[3] So construed, self-predication is clearly part and parcel of the theory of Forms; but it is also clear that it is acceptable in Plato's writings independently both of the theory and of specific knowledge of what the relevant Form is. Thus Protagoras agrees that Justice is just and Piety, pious (*Prot.* 330c3–e2), Hippias, that Beauty "will never appear ugly to anyone anywhere" (*Hip. Maj.* 291d1–3), and Euthyphro, that the *eidos* of Piety is pious (*Euth.* 6e3–6),[4] long before each one of

[1] *Phd.* 100c4–8; and cf. *Parm.* 128e6–129b1, *Symp.* 211b1–5.

[2] See my "Predication and Forms of Opposites in the *Phaedo*," *Review of Metaphysics*, vol. 26 (1973), pp. 461–491, esp. p. 464, and Norio Fujisawa, "Ἔχειν, Μετέχειν, and Idioms of 'Paradigmatism' in Plato's Theory of Forms," *Phronesis*, vol. 20 (1975), pp. 30–49, esp. pp. 35–36.

[3] The term was originally introduced, along with a particular analysis, in Gregory Vlastos' important paper, "The 'Third Man' Argument in the *Parmenides*," in R. E. Allen (ed.), *Studies in Plato's Metaphysics* (London and New York, 1965), pp. 231–263. The term shall also be used to refer to sentences in which self-predication occurs.

[4] It may be possible to find self-predication at *Euth.* 5d1–5 as well, though the sense of the text there is not so clear. On a number of possible translations, such as, for example, as R. E. Allen's, the passage does not contain a self-predication: "Or is not the holy, itself by itself, the same in every action? And the unholy, in turn, the opposite of all the holy—is it not like itself, and does not everything which is to be unholy have a certain single character with respect to unholiness?" (*Plato's "Euthyphro" and the Earlier Theory of Forms* [London, 1970], p. 26). But it is also possible to construe πᾶν/*pan* at 5d4 adverbially and with what precedes it in the text and translate: "Is not whatever turns out to be unholy (i.e. the unholy itself) like to itself and having wholly one character with respect to unholiness?" Cf. Parmenides, DK B8.22 : *epei pan estin homoion*, which has given rise to a similar dispute. G. E. L. Owen ("Eleatic Questions," *Classical Quarterly*, vol. 10 [1960], pp. 84–102, esp. pp. 92–93), followed by Michael C. Stokes (*One and Many in Presocratic Philosophy* [Washington, D.C. and Cambridge, Mass., 1971], pp. 134–135) takes *homoion* adverbially, while A. P. D. Mourelatos (*The Route of Parmenides* [New Haven, 1970], p. 111, n. 30) takes it adjectivally. This debate can be resolved if we follow Owen and take ὅμοιον/*homoion*, as well as *pan*, adverbially, yet not as modifying *estin* (which is why Mourelatos rejects this reading) but, instead, an implicit predicate "*F*": *pan estin homoion* becomes "it is all alike *F*," echoed, if that is true, closely by the *Euthyphro*.

93

them is shown not to know what Justice, Beauty, or Piety is, and without any commitment on their part to the existence of the separate Forms. And when Plato does introduce the Forms, self-predication is still acceptable prior to the successful discovery of what any particular Form is.[5] Self-predication thus preceeds the theory of Forms. In addition, the idea appears in Plato's early dialogues for a reason: it plays an important role in Socratic definition.

When Laches, for example, tries to define being brave as standing one's ground and not retreating, Socrates rejects his effort by arguing that on occasion one may actually be brave in retreating (La. 190e4–191b3, cf. 192b10–193c5). To Cephalus' idea that Justice is returning what one owes, Socrates counters that on occasion one may, in returning what is owed, be unjust (Rep. 331c1–d3), and to Polemarchus' refinement of this proposal he objects that what it implies, namely, harming one's enemies, is actually never just (Rep. 335e5, cf. 334d12–e2). Finally, when Hippias claims that Beauty is being a beautiful maiden, Socrates' response is that being a beautiful maiden is compatible with being ugly and hence "no more beautiful than ugly" (Hip. Maj. 289c5).

What is important for our purpose is Plato's willingness, which is obvious in the last two instances above, to move from the fact that something is compatible both with the possession and with the non-possession of a given characteristic F to its being both F and not F itself. For example, Socrates' attitude seems to be that if people can be brave on some occasion without standing their ground, then standing their ground is on no occasion what accounts for the bravery of those who are brave.[6] These two points are explicitly connected by Plato himself at Phd. 101a5–b1, where he argues that the

explanation of something's being F can never be appealed to in order to account for something's being not-F, and that this explanation must itself be F.[7]

We may express this point by saying that standing their ground is never what makes people (or their actions) brave.[8] Alternatively, we could say that standing one's ground is not itself brave and thus cannot provide a good answer to Socrates' question—a question aiming at knowledge of what being brave is. Anything which can under any conditions be characterized as not-F fails to be itself F, that is, it fails to be the F itself—and Socrates does reject proposed candidates precisely on the ground that they are not-F as well as F.[9] It is this point which Plato makes, in the context of the theory of Forms, at Republic 479c3–5.[10]

With the one exception of Hippias (who is characterized as slow rather than reluctant—Hip. Maj. 287c–291a), Socrates does not find it difficult to convince his interlocutors that the F is F. This is something usually conceded at the very beginning of his discussions. What is difficult is to find out what that, the F itself, is. Many candidates are disqualified because they are no more F than not-F, and this seems to be incompatible with the fact that the F itself is F. Our question is why this should be so, why "the F itself is F" should be incompatible with being in any way not-F, why it should imply being F in every way.

This approach towards self-predication suggests that at least sometimes Socratic definition should follow a particular pattern. The search should begin with an agreement (explicit or tacit) that the F itself is F; a plausible candidate should then be selected, and its name substituted for the subject-term in the self-predication. One should then try to determine

---

[5] For example, Symp. 210c–212a, which is deeply committed to self-predication, does not in fact ever say what Beauty is; the Phaedo, despite its essential reliance on self-predication both in its introduction and in its employment of the theory (74a–75d, 100b–105e), does not contain even a specimen definition of a Form; the self-predication of auta ta homoia is accepted at Parm. 129b1–2 without any statement of what this thing is (and cf. on the use of teras, Phd. 101b1), and so is the self-predication of the one and the many at Parm. 129b6–7.

[6] Socrates' approach is well described by Gerasimos Santas, "Socrates at Work on Virtue and Knowledge in Plato's Charmides," in E. N. Lee, A. P. D. Mourelatos, R. M. Rorty (eds.), Exegesis and Argument: Studies in Greek Philosophy Presented to Gregory Vlastos (Assen, 1973), pp. 105–132. Socrates, Santas writes, "has not been trying to show that the characteristic Charmides hit upon, quietness of behavior, is contrary to the characteristic of temperance, but rather that it is irrelevant to it; some cases of quietness may be cases of temperance— possibly even all—depending on some further characteristic of the performance" (p. 117).

[7] See "Predication and Forms of Opposites in the Phaedo," pp. 465–466 (n. 2 above) and, for discussion of different views of this passage, David Gallop, Plato's "Phaedo" (Oxford, 1975), pp. 184–186. It is significant that Aristotle adopts in a general way the second part of this condition. Cf., for example, Metaphysics a, 993b24–27: ". . . a thing has a quality in a higher degree than other things if in virtue of it the similar quality belongs to the other things as well (e.g. fire is the hottest of things; for it is the cause of the heat of all other things) . . ." (Ross translation).

[8] This relation is expressed variously in Plato's texts: cf. Euth. 6d11 (hōi), Prot. 332c1–2 (hupo + genitive), Hip. Maj. 288a10 (di'ho), Charm. 160d7 (ποιεῖν/poiein).

[9] Cf. Hip. Maj. 289c4–5, c9–d1; Euth. 8a7–8.

[10] The many explanations offered by the "lovers of sights," Socrates says, "play a double game, and we cannot securely think that any one of them is or is not, either both or neither."

whether the resulting sentence is true. This pattern can actually be found—for example, in the second elenchus of Euthyphro (*Euth.* 6eff.). Socrates there expresses the view that Piety is pious by means of his paradigmatic vocabulary at 6e3–6.[11] Euthyphro agrees, and goes on to offer what is just a substitution instance of the self-predication.

What is pleasing to the gods is pious, and what is not pleasing [to them] is impious. (*Euth.* 6e10–7a1)

Socrates then argues that since the gods disagree among themselves, the very same things will be both pleasing and not pleasing to them (8a4–5), and that therefore, on Euthyphro's account,

the same things would be both pious and impious. (8a6–7)

But his question, he continues, was what is itself pious,

not what happens, the very self-same thing, to be both pious and impious. (8a11–12)

The conclusion is that since what is pleasing to the gods is both pious and impious, it cannot be the pious itself.

This pattern is also discernible at *Rep.* 331d4–335e5, as well as in the *Hippias Major*, where Socrates complains that Hippias' answer would have been a good one had his question "originally been what is both beautiful and ugly" (288c9–d5). That we can find it is, I hope, some evidence that we are not completely on the wrong track. In addition, its existence explains a peculiar feature of such elenchi. For to Socrates' question, "What is the F?," the answer often given is not "*a* is the *F*," but "*a* is *F*" (cf. also *Euth.* 9e1–3, *Rep.* 331e3–4). We can now see that such answers, rather than betraying confusion on the part of Socrates' interlocutors, or even on Plato's

own, are perfectly legitimate, since they are just instances of the self-predication which governs the elenchus.[12]

A self-predication, then, is not a *discovery* we make about a particular Form after we have found out what it is, but rather a truth known antecedently, which can even supply a condition of adequacy on the Form's definition: whatever the *F* itself turns out to be, it must be *F* in a suitable sense; and this sense in turn involves always and in every case being *F*. We must now try to capture the sense in which the *F* itself is *F*, accounting at the same time for the fact that Plato did not feel that he had to argue for this strange idea, but that he did feel that every other sentence of the form "*a* is *F*" created a philosophical problem.

My suggestion is that we should accept the following analysis of self-predication:

The *F* itself is *F* = df. The *F* itself, whatever it turns out to be, is what it is to be *F*.

The suggestion actually is that Plato tends to interpret every sentence of the form "*a* is *F*" as "*a* is what it is to be *F*," and that his difficulties with ordinary predication stem exactly from this interpretation. But we will come to this later. For the moment, we should note how such an analysis of "Justice is just" helps to show how both

Returning what one owes is (what it is to be) just

and

Doing one's own is (what it is to be) just

are proper answers to Socrates' question "What is Justice?", since both are instances of the self-predication, though only the second, according to Plato, is true.

So construed, self-predications describe the Forms,[13] but what they describe is the Forms' very

---

[11] If the view supported in n. 4 above is correct, the self-predication has been already accepted by Socrates and Euthyphro at 5d1–5.

[12] I have tried to support such a claim in "Confusing Universals and Particulars in Plato's Early Dialogues," *Review of Metaphysics*, vol. 29 (1975), pp. 287–306.

[13] For list of conditions which successful interpretations of self-predications must satisfy, see Sandra Peterson (subsequently, "Peterson"), "A Reasonable Self-Predication Premise for the Third Man Argument," *The Philosophical Review*, vol. 82 (1973), pp. 451–470, esp. p. 461.

This particular condition is satisfied by Vlastos' original view of self-predication in "The 'Third Man' Argument in the *Parmenides*," a view on which "*F*-ness is *F*" is taken as a bona-fide predication, asserting that *F*-ness is an *F* thing, along with its participants—albeit superlatively so. This interpretation faces a number of difficulties:

(a) It depends on a questionable assumption about the ways in which words are connected with things for Plato; see below, pp. 100 ff.

(b) It has the consequence that no single predicate applies both to the Form and to its participants: "If the Form, Largeness, is superlatively large, while large mountains, oaks, etc., are only deficiently large, it must follow that the single word *large* stands for two distinct predicates ['large₁' and 'large' respectively]. Now since Largeness is, by hypothesis, the Form of the predicate "large," it cannot be the Form of the different predicate "large₁." There must then be two Forms, Largeness and Largeness₁" ("The 'Third Man' Argument in the *Parmenides*", pp. 253–254). But if this is so, then it is not clear that to say that Largeness is large (i.e. large₁) is illegitimately to assimilate it to individuals that are large (p. 252). In addition, it remains obscure why the Forms' possession of their properties can explain their participants' possession of their own, distinct, properties.

nature.[14] They are thus not just ordinary predications, yet they are not pure tautologies either. They are not, on any occasion, absurd: nothing is logically or metaphysically wrong with Justice, doing one's own, being what it is to be just, with Motion being what it is to move, or with Plurality being what it is to be plural.

Now if Plato understands all predication on this model, we can explain why nothing other than the Form can be strictly speaking *F*. For neither Socrates (a "particular") nor returning what one owes (a "universal") is just, since neither is what it is to be just.[15] If Plato thinks that a characteristic can only be attributed to a thing if it constitutes that thing's very nature, nothing but Justice (which simply is that nature) can be just. For, to paraphrase the *Phaedo* (102b8–c4), when we say that Socrates is just we do not say in words what is in fact the case: for Socrates is not just in virtue of being Socrates, in virtue, that is, of his nature, but only in virtue of the justice which he happens to possess.[16] And since being just is not the nature of anything other than Justice, nothing that we know about these things in themselves (that is, nothing we know about their nature) will help us determine whether they can ever be considered just. We can only determine this if we can establish an appropriate relationship (participation) between such things and something else, distinct or separate from them (*chōris, chōriston*).

To learn what Justice is is therefore to learn something very important about those things that make a claim to being considered (but that are not) just: anything can be considered, or said to be, just which can be seen as a doer or as a doing of one's

---

(c) The theory of Forms is burdened by a number of paradoxes, discussed by Vlastos in "The Unity of Virtues in the *Protagoras*" and "An Ambiguity in the *Sophist*", both in *Platonic Studies* (Princeton, 1974), pp. 221–269, 270–322, and in "A Note on 'Pauline Predications' in Plato", *Phronesis*, vol. 19 (1974), pp. 95–101. Vlastos resolves such paradoxes (e.g. that Motion is a thing that moves, though all Forms, according to the theory, are at rest) by arguing that where they result, the self-predication must be interpreted as a distributive statemen' (a "Pauline" predication), true only of the Form's participants and not of the Form itself.

This view still must face the objections raised against taking self-predications as ordinary predications in the cases where paradoxes are not involved. In addition, it *reduces* talk of the Forms to talk about their participants and thus runs the risk of eliminating ontological commitment to Forms. Vlastos' replies to this objection ("An Ambiguity in the *Sophist*," p. 274 n. 13, pp. 320–322; "A Note on 'Pauline Predications' in Plato," pp. 100–101) do not seem to me sufficient, for the only way we can try to secure reference to Forms in Pauline predications is by introducing quantifiers purporting to range over them but which actually do not pick out any free variables in the sentences that follow them. "The relation of *B* to *A* is such that necessarily everything that is *B* is also *A*" is not committed to the existence of anything over and above the values of "everything"; cf. W. V. Quine, "On What There Is," *From A Logical Point of View* (New York, 1968), pp. 1–21, esp. pp. 12–14, and Wilfrid Sellars, "Abstract Entities," in *Philosophical Perspectives* (Springfield, Ill., 1967), pp. 229–269.

(d) To return to Vlastos' original view, we should note that it makes it difficult to account for the asymmetry which Plato finds to exist between, say, "Beauty is beautiful" and "Charmides is beautiful"—an asymmetry indicated by the fact that the latter, and only the latter, needs to be explained according to Plato. On this view, the asymmetry can only be located in the very sense of "beautiful," as we saw in (b) above. But then we are faced with a dilemma: either both Beauty and Charmides are beautiful in the same sense—and Charmides is as perfectly (superlatively) beautiful as Beauty, or Beauty is as imperfectly (deficiently) beautiful as Charmides—or they are beautiful in different senses, and it is not clear why Charmides is beautiful by participating in Beauty, which is beautiful in another sense of the predicate. We shall see below that the asymmetry in question, which allows Plato to deny that Charmides is in fact beautiful, must be located not in the sense of the predicate "beautiful," but by postulating a single, restrictive sense of "is" in which Beauty is, and Charmides is not, beautiful—the predicate itself having the very same sense in both applications.

[14] R. E. Allen, "Participation and Predication in Plato's Middle Dialogues", in Allen, *Studies in Plato's Metaphysics*, pp. 43–60, has insisted on this aspect of self-predication. The main problem with this view is that Allen, assuming that a term true of an object for Plato must be either its proper name or its accidental predicate, and holding against Vlastos that it cannot be the latter, concludes that "Beauty is beautiful" just means "Beauty is Beauty." But:

(a) It is doubtful that "Beauty," "the beautiful itself," and "beautiful" are ever synonymous, as Allen has to claim; cf. Vlastos, "The Unity of Virtues in the *Protagoras*", p. 263 n. 111.

(b) The view cannot account for Socrates' argument at *Prot.* 330b7–332a3; cf. Peterson, "A Reasonable Self-Predication Premiss for the Third Man Argument," p. 460 n. 16.

(c) The view considers the Forms as standards, but construes standards in a disputable manner. To read "Beauty is beautiful" as a tautology on the grounds that this is the proper logical form of "The standard meter is a meter long" while its denial is self-contradictory is dubious. Cf. Colin Strang, "Plato and the Third Man," in Gregory Vlastos (ed.), *Plato I: Metaphysics and Epistemology* (Garden City, 1971), pp. 184–200, esp. pp. 187–191, and, for a systematic attack on this view, Saul Kripke, "Naming and Necessity," in Donald Davidson and Gilbert Harman (eds.), *Semantics of Natural Language* (Dordrecht, 1972), pp. 253–355. And cf. D. Halliday and R. Resnick, *Physics* (New York, 1964), p. 3: "Accurate measurements taken after the standard [meter] was originally determined show that it differs slightly (about 0.023%) from its intended value."

[15] I have argued that the distinction between universals and particulars is not relevant to Socrates' definitional concerns in "Confusing Universals and Particulars in Plato's Early Dialogues," *op. cit.*

[16] An interesting discussion of self-predication and of the questions raised by this passage can be found in Charlotte Stough, "Forms and Explanations in the *Phaedo*," *Phronesis*, vol. 21 (1976), pp. 1–30. Our views are similar, especially in our agreement that Plato's concept of *being* is one which antedates the concepts of identity and predication; cf. Stough, p. 12 with n. 16.

own; it must participate in, or be a case of, doing one's own.[17] In coming to know what Justice is, we come to know the one thing to look for in every case—though discerning it may be so difficult in practice (since nothing is in itself, or purely, a doer or a doing of one's own) that some may despair of its existence:

Each [Form] is in itself one; but by appearing every-where in combination with actions, bodies, and with the others, it appears to be many. (*Rep.* 476a5–7)

On this interpretation of self-predication we need no longer suppose, as has in the past seemed necessary, that the predicate "just" has a different sense when it applies to Justice than it has when it applies to its participants.[18] The predicate has only one sense, and so, unfortunately for sensibles, does the "is" which connects subject and predicate; this is why *only* Justice is just, why, in general terms, the Forms are said to be, in contrast to sensibles, "purely" or "really."[19] The imperfection of the Form's participants does not consist in *what* they are but rather in *how* they can be said to be just.[20]

This interpretation may also help to show that Plato's conviction that each Form is in every case one and the same,[21] that it is always and without change

F,[22] that it is simply and alike F,[23] and that it is F in every possible respect[24] depends not on metaphysical prejudice but on compelling reasons.

Suppose, for example, that we define Justice as X, having characteristics ABC. Having ABC is therefore just, that is, what it is to be just. Now suppose that something else, Y, distinct from X and consisting in having characteristics DEF, makes an equal claim to being the just itself. Having DEF must therefore also be just, in the same way. Given our interpretation of "is" we can now argue validly to the following disjunctive conclusion: either ABC and DEF do not make an equal claim to be the just itself, and only one of them is, or if their claims are in fact equal, neither is successful, and something distinct from both of them is really just. For, by hypothesis, ABC and DEF are distinct, and ABC is just. Hence, DEF cannot be just. For, if it were, then since ABC is not DEF, ABC would not be what DEF is, that is, just. Thus, ABC, which has been defined as the just itself would turn out not to be just. The same argument could also be made for DEF. Given this understanding of "is", and its accompanying principle that the F itself is F (which is, I shall suggest, a special case of Parmenides' notorious principle, "Never shall this be proved, that what is not is"[25]) anything that does

---

[17] Capturing the close relationship between the Form's being F and its participants' being F is the goal both of Vlastos' distributive approach and of Peterson's interpretation of "F-ness is F" as "F-ness makes whatever participates in it F" (though this is a simplified version of Peterson's elaborate view; cf. Peterson, pp. 461–462 for a fuller statement). The problem is that the former approach *reduces* the self-predication to a statement about the Form's participants (see n. 13 (c) above), and thus cannot account for the explanatory function which the Form has. The latter view, by contrast, reduces the self-predication to an assertion of the explanatory connection, and does not attribute to the F-ness anything over and above the second-order property "makes whatever participates in it F." In this way, the fact that Justice is what makes its participants just is taken to be the whole content of the statement that Justice is just, instead of appealing to this latter as the ground for the ability of Justice to provide that explanation. It is interesting, in this connection, to appeal to a distinction recently drawn by Hilary Putnam, "On Properties," in *Mathematics, Matter, and Method* (London, 1975), pp. 305–322, esp. pp. 316–317, between "causal" and "canonical" descriptions of properties. "Justice makes its participants just" is then a *causal* description of Justice, and though it is connected to, it is not identical with, say, "Doing one's own is just," or "Justice is doing one's own," which is the Form's canonical description, and which accounts for the Form's causal or explanatory role.

[18] This is an essential feature of Vlastos' view in "The 'Third Man' Argument in the *Parmenides*" (*op. cit.*), of Allen's identity interpretation, and of Peterson's approach. Vlastos' "Pauline" interpretation avoids this feature, by denying the application of the predicate to the Form altogether when the relevant difficulties arise.

[19] *eilikrinōs, pantelōs, ontōs*: *Phd.* 74d4–7 02a10–103a2 *Rep.* 479a5–d5, 523e3–524a10. For fuller discussion and references, see Gregory Vlastos, "Degrees of Reality in Plato," *Platonic Studies* (*op. cit.*), pp. 58–75, and my "Plato on the Imperfection of the Sensible World," *American Philosophical Quarterly*, vol. 12 (1975), pp. 105–117.

[20] The asymmetry between Forms and their participants, if asymmetry it is, would "belong to the 'being' rather than to the 'F' in 'being F'," as Wilfrid Sellars writes in "Vlastos and the 'Third Man'," *Philosophical Perspectives*, p. 28.

[21] *hen, tauton*: *Euth.* 5d1, 6d9–e1; *La.* 191d10–11; *Me.* 72c6–d1, 74a7–10, 75a6–9; *Rep.* 476a4–7, 479a3–5, 597c1–d2; *Parm.* 131a8–c10, 132a1–b1.

[22] *aei, aei on, hōsautōs aei echei, aei kata tauta echei*: *Phd.* 78d1–2, 79e3–5; *Symp.* 211a1; *Crat.* 439d4–5, e1–5; *Rep.* 479a2–3, 484b4; *Tim.* 48e6, 51a1.

[23] *monoeides*: *Phd.* 78d5; *Symp.* 211b1.

[24] This generic idea is expressed in a number of ways, e.g., at *Symp.* 211a2–5: Beauty is not beautiful (a) only in some respect and not in another (*tēi men . . . tēi de*), (b) only at some time and not at another (*tote men . . . tote d' ou*), which is connected with its being unchangingly beautiful (cf. n. 22 above), (c) in relation to some things and not to others (*pros men . . . pros de*; also *tōi men . . . tōi de*, *Phd.* 74b7–c3, and cf. *Hip. Maj.* 289a1–b7), (d) here but not there, for some but not for others (*entha men . . . entha d'ou, tini men . . . tini d'ou*).

[25] DK B7.1: *ou gar mēpote touto dāmēi, einai mē eonta*. Plato does not explicitly deny this principle until his writing of the *Sophist*: *Soph.* 237a3–b3, 241d1–7, 258c6–e3; for an extended discussion of Plato's Eleatic concerns in that dialogue, see G. E. L. Owen, "Plato On Not-Being," in Vlastos, *Plato I*, pp. 229–267, to whom a serious debt is hereby acknowledged.

not make an *exclusive* claim to being *F* is immediately disqualified. If two things make an equal claim, neither of them is *F*, hence neither of them is the *F*, and there must be something else, distinct from both of them, which is really *F*, and to which the previous two are somehow related:

> a further one would appear whose *eidos* (aspect, form) they, in turn, would both have and that, not these two, would then be what [*F*] is.[26]

It is important to notice that we can construct parallel arguments for the other, equally Parmenidean, characteristics which Plato attributes to the Forms. For example, if *X* is what it is to be just, then *X* must be always and without change just. For if *X* were at any time characterizable as not just, this would violate the Parmenidean principle that "what is must be and cannot not be"[27] and it would show that *X* is indentifiable independently of its being just.[28] But then it follows that *X* cannot be what it is to be just: nothing is identifiable independently of its nature, and a thing's nature is precisely that respect in which a thing never changes.[29] Such arguments all depend on the assumption that what is *F* cannot in any way appear to be not-*F*. And this assumption can make claims to self-evidence (rather than seeming to depend on prejudice or confusion) if we see the "is" of predication in Plato as specifying the very restrictive concept "is what it is to be." In this way, by construing self-predication as a more fully spelled-out version of Parmenides' principle of being, we are enabled to give both theses more plausibility and more of a historical context.

It is widely agreed that the later Presocratics were concerned to show, against Parmenides, that the sensible world has a measure of reality because of the existence of objects (atoms, the elements, or the *homoiomerē*) which meet Parmenides' conditions on being, and which underlie appearance and constitute the reality of which the sensible world is the appearance:[30]

> The Parmenidean logic had rudely checked the course of Greek thought . . . it determined the subsequent course of Presocratic philosophy which was in the main a series of attempts to save the world of nature without transgressing the rules of the new logic.[31]

It is also agreed that in the *Sophist* Plato tries directly to refute the Parmenidean principle to the effect that unless something is *F* in every way it is not *F* in any way. Yet

> few students of ancient philosophy would expect to find in the earlier dialogues . . . arguments or passages recalling the verses of Parmenides.[32]

If the argument of the preceding pages is correct, however, then it may be plausible to suppose not only that Plato's vocabulary echoes Parmenides', but that he, along with his contemporaries, worked within a Parmenidean framework for a large part of his life—until he turned to overthrow that framework in his later works. His generalization of Socrates' moral concerns into the theory of Forms represents, ironically, one of the last Presocratic systems—broader and more magnificent, to be sure, than Atomism or Empedocles' system of cycles, but still their competitor: a first among equals.

Thus the Forms, and only the Forms, are *F* in a way which seems to satisfy Parmenides' conditions on being, and thus they constitute reality. If this is so, however, what are we to say of the many other things which we want to, which we even have to, consider beautiful, or large, or just? My suggestion has been that Plato follows Parmenides to the extent of thinking that there is, strictly speaking, only one way of having a characteristic, namely, being that characteristic itself. This is precisely what the interpre-

---

[26] *Rep.* 597c7–9, replacing Plato's term "bed" with a variable. In this way, perhaps, we can supply Plato with an argument for his conclusion that there can only be one Form for each relevant predicate, and thus provide an answer to Strang's question: ". . . the first two Beds, simply *qua* a plurality, require a further Bed above them. But why are we obliged to deny that the first two Beds are Forms?" (Strang, pp. 192–193). The reason is that if two things are equally *F*, neither of them is strictly *F*, and thus neither can be the Form. In the same way, we may also provide a justification for Plato's pervasive "One-Over-Many" Assumption (cf. Strang, "Plato and the Third Man," pp. 186–187).

[27] Parmenides DK B2.3: . . . *estin te kai . . . ouk esti mē einai.*

[28] I use "identifiable" here in the sense of Malcolm Schofield, "Plato On Unity and Sameness," *Classical Quarterly*, vol. 24 (1974), pp. 33–45, esp. p. 39.

[29] Cf. Mourelatos, *The Route of Parmenides*, p. 107: "What a thing *gets* to be (or *comes* to be) is not what the thing really is, i.e. in its essence or nature."

[30] A recent discussion of this idea can be found in David J. Furley, "Anaxagoras in Response to Parmenides," in Roger A. Shiner and John King-Farlow (eds.), *New Essays on Plato and the Presocratics* (Guelph, 1976), pp. 61–86.

[31] Harold Cherniss, "The Characteristics and Effects of Presocratic Philosophy," in David J. Furley and R. E. Allen (eds.), *Studies in Presocratic Philosophy*, Vol. I (London, 1970), pp. 1–28, p. 22.

[32] Friedrich Solmsen, "Parmenides and the Description of Perfect Beauty in Plato's *Symposium*," *American Journal of Philology*, vol. 92 (1971), pp. 62–70, p. 62.

tation of "*a is F*" as "*a is what it is to be F*" implies; and, of course, it also follows from the interpretation that only the *F*, and nothing else, is *F*. Plato, that is, follows Parmenides in not distinguishing clearly between having a property and being a property, between being *F* and "receiving" *F*, to use Aristotle's expression from *Physics* A 3. Aristotle, in fact, denies that the conclusion that only the *F* is *F* follows from this interpretation of "a is *F*": the argument, he says, is inconclusive (*asumperantos*), for "the being of [*F*] will be different from that which has received it."[33] Not having made this distinction, Parmenides seems to have argued that what constitutes reality is not things but rather the nature of such things; he also seems to have concluded that everything other than this nature, everything other than what-is, is in no way, that everything other than being is "deceptive appearance" (B8.52,60, cf. B1.30).

Plato, it seems to me, was unwilling to follow Parmenides in denying all reality to sensible objects. Though he does not think that, for example, Charmides, or being a beautiful youth, is beautiful (since such claims, by means of the arguments which we rehearsed above, can be shown to entail contradictions of the form "The *F* is not *F*"), he tries to preserve a measure of these things' claim to being considered beautiful by showing that they bear an appropriate relationship to Beauty, to what is itself beautiful. Thus he offers as a second-best alternative to—and *not* as an analysis of—such things' being beautiful the idea that, rather than *being* beautiful, they *participate* in, or that they resemble, or that they in some way possess, the one thing which alone really is beautiful.[34]

Before we go on to examine this aspect of the theory of Forms, and its semantical implications, we should stop to consider a serious objection to this general interpretation of self-predication. This objection contends that given this interpretation, Plato's argument to the effect that the Forms are distinct (ἕτερα/*hetera*) from their participants at *Phaedo* 74a9–c6 is a failure.[35] In that argument, Plato tries to show that the equal itself is distinct from all sensible equals on account of the fact that though equal things are unequal, the equal itself is never unequal.[36] Let us now use "the *F*" as a term referring to the Form, and "this *F*" as a term referring to any participant in that

Form. Plato's point can now be put as follows: though it is always and without exception true that the *F* is *F*, it is not always and without exception true (in fact, he seems to believe, it is never true) that this *F* is *F*.

The objection now is that if we interpret

(1) The *F* is *F*

as

(2) The *F* is what it is to be *F*,

Plato's argument fails, in that it can be shown that this *F* is in fact *F*. For it is quite true that

(3) The *F* is not what it is to be not-*F*,

and it is equally true that

(4) This *F* is not what it is to be not-*F*,

since no unequal thing, for example, is what it is to be unequal, that is, inequality. But, given our interpretation of "is," (4) is equivalent to

(5) This *F* is not not-*F*,

which is, in turn, equivalent to

(6) This *F* is *F*,

and, therefore, sensibles, no less than the Forms themselves, turn out to be *F*, which contradicts our approach to self-predication.

I would reply to this objection that what Plato is trying to point out is that *F*-things can be considered no more *F* than not-*F*, and that this characteristic is what distinguishes them from the Forms. That is, Plato believes that though "This *F* is not-*F*" has a claim to being true, so does the claim

(7) This *F* is not *F*,

and the problem with sensible objects is that neither claim is better supported than the other. And precisely because both (6) and (7) are equally true, Plato concludes that neither of them is true, and that sensibles cannot be said "either to be or not to be, either both or neither" (*Rep.* 479c3–5). Plato concludes that sensibles are never *F* on account of the fact that there is as good reason for saying that they are *F* as there is for saying that they are not-*F*. The objection is correct in pointing out that given our interpretation of "is," it follows from Plato's argument that we can say that *F*-things are *F*. It overlooks the fact, however, that, given that same interpretation, it is equally true to say that *F*-things are not *F*, and that it is the contradiction generated by these statements (given, again, this interpretation of "is") that forces Plato to separate Forms from sensibles, and to limit the application of "being" to the Forms.

---

[33] *Phys.* A 3, 186a28–29. Aristotle's criticism of Parmenides in this chapter, and some of the similarities between Parmenides' view and the theory of Forms and between this criticism and Plato's own attack on Eleaticism at *Soph.* 244b–245d, are discussed by W. Charlton, *Aristotle's "Physics" I, II* (Oxford, 1970), pp. 59–62.

[34] Cf. *Phd.* 100d4–6, 102b8–c4, and, on the construal of the latter passage, Stough, "Forms and Explanations in the *Phaedo*," *op. cit.*, p. 17, n. 24.

[35] This objection was made to me by M. F. Burnyeat.

[36] I have discussed the structure of this argument in "Plato on the Imperfection of the Sensible World."

However, though Plato is unwilling to speak of sensibles as being (either F or not-F), he is not willing to stop talking altogether of their having characteristics. And it is this unwillingness on his part which prompts him to introduce the relation of participation, a relation which is, to repeat, an alternative to, and not an analysis of, being F. It is, then, for this reason that Plato feels that·he must explain why ordinary things are beautiful, large, or equal: why, as he puts it, they are "named after" the Forms (*epōnumian ischein, Phd.* 102b2). Just as, on the ontological level, only the beautiful itself is beautiful, so, on the semantical, the word "beautiful" is strictly speaking only the name (*onoma*) of the beautiful itself and of nothing else. The word, we may say, is only "derivatively" the name of beautiful things.[37]

It is important to notice, however, that in this context a "name" (*onoma*) cannot be construed either as an arbitrary identifying tag, conventionally (or even causally) associated with an object, or as a term denoting its referent through any set of characteristics which that object happens to possess.[38] Rather, Plato seems to think that "beautiful" names only the beautiful because he thinks of an *onoma* as revealing the nature of what it names, and that it is only if this very strong semantical relation obtains that a word can pick out an item in reality. An *onoma*, therefore, is only in a strictly literal sense a *proper* name for Plato. This attitude towards language seems to me to be presupposed by the many commonplace puns on proper names in Greek literature,[39] as well as by the following statement attributed to Pericles by Thucydides:

... and it has been called by the name "democracy" because it has been set up not for the few but for many,[40] which suggests that the characteristic on account of which democracy is given its name (*onoma*) is not a chance property of the system, but something that determines it in an essential manner. More specifically, this attitude is presupposed by Plato's willingness to speak of names as something which things in the world do or do not *deserve* (*axiousthai,* Phd. 103e3).

On this view, the predicate "just" is the name (*onoma*) only of what it is to be just, and not of anything which merely happens to be just. The catch-all semantical term *onoma* involves this very strong relationship between word and thing, and, for this reason, I disagree with an assumption which governs much recent discussion of predication and sélf-predication in Plato. This is the assumption that an *onoma* is either a proper name (and thus has a conventionally grounded relation to its referent) or a predicate construed along the lines of class-membership.[41] If we accept this assumption, then when Plato says that "beautiful"· is a name of the beautiful, we are faced with a dilemma; either "beautiful" is a proper name of the beautiful and the self-predication reduces to the tautology "The beautiful is the beautiful"; or, to avoid this result, "beautiful" is a bona-fide predicate of the beautiful, and Beauty turns out to be, with serious consequences for the theory of Forms, a member of the class of beautiful things.[42] Yet, I think that Plato's discussion of the way in which sensibles are named after the Forms at *Phd.* 102–104 shows that instead of

[37] The term, but not its analysis, is taken from Allen, "Participation and Predication in Plato's Middle Dialogues," *op. cit.*, pp. 45–47.

[38] Different attempts to attribute to Plato contemporary theories of reference, and the difficulties they encounter, are discussed by J. M. E. Moravcsik, "Recollecting the Theory of Forms," in W. H. Werkmeister (ed.), *Facets of Plato's Philosophy* (Assen, 1976), pp. 1–20. An interesting discussion of Plato's approach to reference can be found in Gail Fine, "Plato on Naming," *Philosophical Quarterly*, vol. 27 (1977), pp. 289–301. Fine and I agree that "for '*n*' to name *x*, it must reveal the *tupos* or outline of the essence of *x*; that is, it must correctly describe *x*'s essence," (p. 298), though Fine goes on to compare Plato's view with John R. Searle's theory of proper names ("Proper Names," in P. F. Strawson (ed.), *Philosophical Logic* [Oxford, 1967], pp. 89–96). However, Searle does not require the cluster of descriptions associated with a name to concern the essence of that referent, and his view is therefore not parallel to Plato's.

[39] Among the most notable of these is the pun of *Prometheus Bound*, pp. 85–86: *pseudōnumōs se daimones Promēthea kalousin*: "the gods call you 'Prometheus' pseudonymously". See also *Odyssey* 1.62, 5.340, 19.407–409 for puns connected with the etymology of "Odysseus." Needless to say, one should also think of the *Cratylus*, and cf. J. V. Luce, "Plato on Truth and Falsity in Names," *Classical Quarterly*, vol. 19 (1969), pp. 222–232, esp. 225–226.

[40] Thucydides B II. 37.1.

[41] This assumption, generally implicit, has recently been stated by Vlastos, "The Unity of Virtues in the *Protagoras*," p. 238 with n. 46; cf. p. 225, n. 8. The interpretation of predication as expressing class-membership is given by Vlastos, "A Note on 'Pauline Predications' in Plato," *op. cit.*, p. 98. Plato usually employs the copula, Vlastos writes, as "it is most commonly used in Greek (as in English) subject-predicate sentences, sc. to indicate that the individual named by the subject-term is a member of the class of those possessing the attribute expressed by the predicate-term." But though Plato may well *employ* the copula in some such manner, it does not follow that he would analyze its employment in the way which Vlastos accepts. Though Plato uses the copula (it is difficult, in fact, to imagine how he might not have) he may not have arrived at a correct theory of how the use is to be construed. And his philosophical problems stem not from his *employment* of predication, but of his *analysis* of what it is to say of something that it is beautiful, just, or large.

[42] Cf. notes 13 and 14 above. Allen's identity view, we can see, accepts the first horn of this dilemma, while Vlastos' original view chooses the second. Vlastos' distributive interpretation preserves the assumption by construing "beautiful" as a bona-fide predicate of beautiful things, rather than construing it as a term true of the Form.

assuming that an *onoma* can ever specify an accidental property of a thing, he introduces the notion "being named after" precisely in order to capture this linguistic operation. By contrast, he retains *onoma* and *onomazein* (naming) for cases where a word expresses the nature or essence of its referent.[43]

Semantic vocabulary does not play a major role in Plato's early dialogues. As far as we can tell, Socrates, concerned with the question of the nature of virtue, did not stop to consider what we are to say about the rejected candidates for the *F* itself—things which, though not *F* strictly speaking, are still in a way *F*. In the *Meno*, however, we meet with semantic terminology. Socrates there argues that though both being round and being straight "are called by some one name" (*heni prosagoreueis onomati*), that is, the name "shape," there must be something else

which occupies the round no less than the straight . . . that which you name "shape" indeed . . . (74d7–e1)

He then goes on to ask:

What on earth, then, is that of which this word, "shape", is the name? (74e11)

His argument seems to be that since neither being round nor being straight is what it is to be a shape, neither is what the name "shape" names. And we cannot possibly construe "names" as "is true of" (the relation expressed by class membership) in this context, since this is precisely the sense in which both the round and the straight are "called by some one name" and this sense is being contrasted with

naming. The correct sense of "names" here must be that of specifying the very nature of what being a shape is.

We should notice two points. First, that once this semantical relation is openly employed, the question, what to say about all the things which we call "*F*" but which are not really (are not actually named) *F* comes to the fore, inconspicuous as it may have previously been. And with its emergence (which occurs in the *Meno*, a dialogue independently acknowledged to signalize the beginning of Plato's middle period) is associated the introduction of the theory of Forms. For the theory aims to answer exactly this question, by appealing to participation on the ontological, and to "being named after" on the semantical level.[44]

The second point to notice is that on this construal of *onoma*, it follows that if something has any name, it can only have one name. For if a name specifies what a thing is, no two distinct names can apply to the same thing, since nothing can have two natures.[45] Conversely, no name can name more than one thing, for these two, by hypothesis, distinct things would then have to have the same nature, and thus be one. Interestingly, the arguments for this position would parallel, on a semantical level, the arguments we rehearsed above in relation to the ontological status of the Forms, and which derive from Eleatic assumptions. The basic semantical principle which governs naming, and which we might call the One-Name Assumption is this:

If *w* is the name of *a*, then *w* is the only name *a* has, and *a* is the only object named by *w*.

---

[43] Vlastos finds Plato making the distinction between proper names and descriptive predicates at *Phd.* 104a5–7 ("The Unity of Virtues in the *Protagoras*," p. 238). Plato writes: "Don't you think that [Three] may always be called both by its own name and by the name of the odd, though [the odd] is not identical with Three?" Vlastos glosses this as follows: "Here 'names' is evidently used in the two different senses I have specified. In '"Three" names Three' to 'name' is to refer. In '"odd" names Three' to name is to describe" (p. 239). We should remark:

(a) Plato does not write that three *may* be called by its own name, but rather that it *must* be called by its own name (*prosagoreutea*), which brings us closer to the idea of things deserving, or having a claim to, their own name, and away from the conventional associations of "reference."

(b) Plato has been distinguishing between Forms and their participants by saying that while the tall itself is (and is named) tall, Simmias, who *is not* tall, is named after it (*epōnumian echei*) because he participates in it (102c10–d2; cf. Aristotle, *Metaphysics* A, 987b7–10). "Being named after" seems to be Plato's term for Vlastos' "qualifying predicate." When Plato comes to discuss three and odd, he does not seem to draw a distinction between names on the one hand and predicates on the other (since "odd" is not an accidental predicate of three). Rather, he seems to be distinguishing two ways of naming within the strong sense of "name" which we have been discussing: Three is not only (what it is to be) three, but is also (essentially) odd.

[44] Cr. Stough, "Forms and Explanations in the *Phaedo*," *op. cit.*, p. 21, with n. 30.

[45] If this is true, it may have some interesting implications for Socrates' theory of the Unity of Virtue. For if Virtue is truly one thing for Socrates (so, recently, Terry Penner, "The Unity of Virtue," *The Philosophical Review*, vol. 82 [1973], pp. 35–68), then its names ("justice," "virtue," "temperance," etc.) must also be one name. Though Socrates does not discuss this, I think we could justify this claim by arguing that all these names, insofar as they have the same *logos*, that is, knowledge of good and bad, are in fact the same name. The same name can, on this account, be embodied in different words, i.e. sounds. Cf. *Cratylus* 389–390, and Charles Kahn, "Language and Ontology in the *Cratylus*," in *Exegesis and Argument*, pp. 152–176. I have discussed this point with Alan Code, Marc Cohen, and Michael Wedin; they remain unconvinced.

The One-Name Assumption can be located in the presentation of the theory of Forms in the *Parmenides*, when Socrates contrasts Forms and sensibles by characterizing the latter as *talla ha dē polla kaloumen* (129a3). The expression can be translated as "the others, which we call 'many'"; "many," however, can function either as a referring expression, as a term by which sensibles are collectively denoted, or as a place-holder for the predicate, in which case the phrase should be taken as "the others, which we call many things" or "the others, which we call by many names." On the latter reading, which I prefer, the Forms' participants are things which can be denoted by more than one name (the possibility being grounded in their participation in many Forms, after each of which they are named); by contrast, the Forms are things which can be called only by one name.[46]

This last idea, the One-Name Assumption, is, of course, too restrictive; the Forms, too, must be capable of bearing more than one name. This is why the attack on Parmenides in the *Sophist* contains as its integral part the theory of the blending of Forms. For this latter theory asserts that the Forms, too, participate in one another, and its purpose, significantly, is to show

in what manner we call in each case the very same thing by means of many names. (*Soph.* 251a5–6)

This dual attack on Parmenides, semantical no less than ontological, supports the idea that the One-Name Assumption goes hand-in-hand with the ontological principle which we discussed above, and that both spring from an Eleatic approach to language and reality.

The overall consequence of this discussion is that Plato turns out to be both more naive and more sophisticated than we sometimes suppose. He is not concerned with the more contemporary problem of universals, but then neither does he make elementary errors about it. He is concerned with articulating the very concept of predication; this is, if I am right, one of the central purposes of the theory of Forms. He does not begin with an antecedently existing understanding of predication; there was no theory about how a single thing can have many

characteristics, or how a single thing can be denoted by more than one word. Certainly, Plato did not start out believing that to say that something is large is to say that a general term, true of objects in general, is true of some given individual, and end up with a strange notion of being, according to which each general term must also function as the proper name of an abstract entity, which is more real than the objects with which he began.[47]

Rather, Plato begins with a peculiar notion of being, stemming from Parmenides and, as far as we can tell, broadly accepted in his time. According to this conception, nothing is which is not what it is to be something, and each word can pick out at most one thing in the world, the very nature of what the word names. Beginning with this, Plato concludes with a very sophisticated justification of predication, an operation with which this notion of being is, strictly speaking, incompatible. He assumes that "being" has only one sense, and that nothing is which does not meet in every way a set of very stringent conditions. Yet we do say that many other things also are: the theory of Forms aims to show that though this is not strictly speaking correct, neither is it just delusion.

The main weakness of the theory is its very commitment to Parmenides' principle, according to which nothing is *F* is any way that is not *F* in every way. It is not until he writes the *Parmenides* and the *Sophist* that Plato questions this assumption and concludes that everything that is in some way *F* will also not be *F* in some other way, that "being" does not have only one sense, and that even being itself, without contradiction, is not. During Plato's middle period, the *F* itself (which is in every way *F*) competes with the many *F* things for the appellation "*F*", and is the only thing which deserves it: it is another thing, distinct from them, whose claim to being *F* is the only one acceptable.

The *Parmenides* rightly emphasizes this separation between Forms and their participants in its first part, and the principles which underlie it in its second. It is not a little to Plato's credit that he realized that the explanatory value of the postulation of the Forms ultimately depends on denying that principle, and that he was willing and able to overhaul the very framework on which his theory originally depended.

---

[46] One part of this assumption is exhibited at *Parm.* 147d1–e6, where it is said that no matter how many times a name is said (that is, to however many things in however many occasions it is applied) what it names is "that . . . of which it is the name" (d4), and that we "always apply it to that nature (*phusis*) of which it is the name" (e5–6). I think we can find this denied at *Phil.* 18b–d, where Theuth is said to apply the name "element" to each and every sound of the human voice: *heni te hekastōi kai sumpasi stoicheion epōnomase*. Linguistically, at least, this echoes *Parm.* 147e1–2: *ouk ep' allōi oude allo ti onomazeis ē ekeino houper ēn onoma*.

[47] This common approach to Plato, can be found very clearly in Anders Wedberg, "The Theory of Ideas," in Vlastos, *Plato I*, pp. 28–52, esp. pp. 28–29.

In his "parricide" of Parmenides (*Soph.* 241d3), Plato conceived predication; and without the theory of Forms, which made him Parmenides' intellectual offspring, his parricide could never have occurred.[48]

University of Pittsburgh

Received May 5, 1978

[48] Too many friends and colleagues to name here have discussed these issues with me during the past few years. A special debt is owed to Gregory Vlastos, whose ideas have inevitably shaped my own. An earlier version of the paper was read at Ohio State University, and yet another version was presented to the Pacific Divison of the APA in March of 1978. Acknowledgement is also thankfully made to the National Endowment for the Humanities for their financial support.

THE LOGIC OF THE THIRD MAN

THE MAIN PROBLEMS facing the interpreter of the Third Man Argument (*TMA*) in Plato's *Parmenides* (132a1-b2) arise not so much from what Plato says as from what he does not say. Gregory Vlastos, in his famous paper of 1954,[1] points out that the argument is formally a *non sequitur* and sets out to discover the suppressed premises of the argument. The literature dealing with the *TMA*, already large in 1954, has become enormous since then, and all of the authors I have read have followed Vlastos at least this far. But beyond a shared belief that the *TMA* as written is formally invalid and that in order to understand the argument we must identify its suppressed premises, there has been little agreement among the commentators. What *are* the suppressed premises? Is Plato committed to holding them? Is the argument, with the addition of such premises, valid? Did Plato think it was? What does it prove? What did Plato think it proves? Radically different answers have been offered to these questions, and I do not expect to offer definitive answers to any of them in this paper. What I hope to do is to show in what way the main lines of interpretation offered to date are inadequate, and to advance a formalization of the *TMA* which avoids these inadequacies and seems to me better to reveal the logical structure of the argument. On the basis of my examination of the logic of the *TMA* I conclude that the philosophical point of the argument is different from what it has been generally supposed to be.

I

The text, in Cornford's translation, reads as follows :

I imagine your ground for believing in a single form in each case is this. When it seems to you that a number of things are large, there seems,

---

[1] "The Third Man Argument in the *Parmenides*," *Philosophical Review*, LXIII (1954), 319-349; reprinted with an addendum in *Studies in Plato's Metaphysics*, ed. by R. E. Allen (London, 1965), pp. 231-263. Subsequent references will be to the reprinted version, which will be cited hereafter as "*TMA* I."

I suppose, to be a certain single character which is the same when you look at them all; hence you think that largeness is a single thing. . . . But now take largeness itself and the other things which are large. Suppose you look at all these in the same way in your mind's eye, will not yet another unity make its appearance—a largeness by virtue of which they all appear large? . . . If so, a second form of largeness will present itself, over and above largeness itself and the things that share in it, and again, covering all these, yet another, which will make all of them large. So each of your forms will no longer be one, but an indefinite number.

Vlastos, in his original account of the *TMA*, transcribes what he identifies as the first two steps of the argument in the following way:

(A1) If a number of things, *a*, *b*, *c*, are all F, there must be a single Form F-ness, in virtue of which we apprehend *a,b,c*, as all F.

(A2) If *a*, *b*, *c*, and F-ness are all F, there must be another Form, F-ness$_1$, in virtue of which we apprehend *a*, *b*, *c*, and F-ness as all F.[2]

It is obvious that (A2) does not follow from (A1), and so Vlastos concludes that "there must have been something more in Plato's mind than the information supplied at (A1)"[3] to make the inference to (A2) seem plausible. Now the question of what was in Plato's mind at this point is admittedly a difficult one; but Vlastos is content to raise "a more modest question : What are the simplest premises, not given in the present Argument, which would have to be added to its first step, to make (A2) a legitimate conclusion?"[4] In answer to this question he produces two premises, one to justify the antecedent of (A2) and one to justify its consequent. The two premises are the well-known self-predication (*SP*) and non-identity (*NI*) Assumptions :

(*SP*) Any Form can be predicated of itself. Largeness is itself large. F-ness is itself F.[5]

---

[2] *TMA* I, pp. 232-233.
[3] *TMA* I, p. 236.
[4] *Ibid.*
[5] *Ibid.*

449

(*NI*) If anything has a certain character, it cannot be identical with the Form in virtue of which we apprehend that character. If x is F, x cannot be identical with F-ness.[6]

Given (A1), these two premises are supposed to yield (A2) in the following way. It is a commonplace that there are *F* things—say, *a, b, c.* (A1) tells us that there is a Form, *F*-ness, in virtue of which we apprehend these as *F.* (*SP*) tells us that this Form, *F*-ness, is another *F* thing. But (*NI*) tells us that the Form in virtue of which we apprehend all of *a, b, c,* and *F*-ness as *F* things cannot be *F*-ness. Hence, it must be a second Form, *F*-ness$_1$. And this amounts to an assertion of (A2).

But, as Vlastos himself noticed, there is something strange about the way in which these new premises operate. For it is obvious that (*SP*) and (*NI*) are inconsistent; together they entail that *F*-ness is not identical with *F*-ness, which is self-contradictory. Indeed, they are formal contradictories, as Peter Geach pointed out;[7] (*SP*) is the assumption that *F*-ness is an *F* thing, and (*NI*) amounts to the assumption that *F*-ness is not an *F* thing. But this does not discourage Vlastos from insisting upon (*SP*) and (*NI*) as being the *TMA*'s implicit premises. For they are surely *sufficient* to generate (A2) (and hence the entire regress) just because they are inconsistent and can generate any conclusion we like. But since they are inconsistent, Vlastos feels he must conclude that Plato did not realize that these were the argument's implicit premises : "If Plato had identified all the premises which are necessary (and sufficient) to warrant the second step of the Third Man Argument, he would not have produced the Third Man Argument at all."[8] That the premises necessary to generate the *TMA* are inconsistent is thus a cornerstone of Vlastos' interpretation—for it is on this basis that he concludes that Plato did not know what premises he was using, on the charitable assumption a philosopher—or Plato, anyway—will not produce an argument whose premises are inconsistent unless he is unaware of the inconsistency of the

---

[6] *TMA* I, p. 237.

[7] "The Third Man Again," *Philosophical Review*, LXV (1956), pp. 72-82; reprinted in Allen, *op. cit.*, pp. 265-277. Subsequent references will be to the reprinted version.

[8] *TMA* I, p. 241.

premises. And in the case of a premise set consisting of the formally contradictory pair (*SP*) and (*NI*), the only way to be unaware of the inconsistency of the premises is to be unaware of one or both of the premises.

It seems to me to be a matter of some importance for our understanding of the *TMA* to determine whether these premises *are* necessary to generate the regress. Let us be clear that we understand what is involved in the claim that (*SP*) and (*NI*) are indispensable premises. If (*SP*) and (*NI*), as formulated, were required as *TMA* premises, the conclusion of the argument would itself have to be logically inconsistent. A proposition is itself inconsistent if the *only* premise set from which it will follow is an inconsistent one. But, worse still, if the conclusion were inconsistent, then it would make no sense to say that (*SP*) and (*NI*) in particular are *required* as premises—for any other inconsistent set of premises would do just as well. But is the conclusion of Plato's argument inconsistent? The conclusion, we recall, is this : "Each of your forms will no longer be one, but an indefinite number." I suppose there may be some inclination to regard this conclusion as logically inconsistent, for it seems to say of the Forms that each *one* is *not* one, but many. But this inclination finds no real support in Plato's text and is fostered only by a peculiarity in Cornford's translation.[9] The conclusion of the *TMA* (οὐκέτι δὴ ἓν ἕκαστόν σοι τῶν εἰδῶν ἔσται . . . .) is explicitly the contradictory of that thesis (ἓν ἕκαστον εἶδος) of the Theory of Forms which Parmenides cites at 132*a1* and then sets out to refute in the regress argument. And the thesis that Parmenides sets out to refute is not the triviality that each Form is one (Form), but rather, as Cornford correctly puts it, that there is "a single Form in each case." (I will have more to say later about how the phrase ἓν ἕκαστον εἶδος should be taken.) So the conclusion of the argument should read : "And so there will no longer be *one* Form for you in each case, but infinitely many."[10] So formulated, the conclusion no longer has even the look of a logical inconsistency.

---

[9] Cornford's reading is, of course, grammatically possible. My point is that it is not the only possible reading, and that the only reasonable way to understand the conclusion is as the denial of the ἓν ἕκαστον εἶδος thesis.

[10] Vlastos' translation in his most recent *TMA* paper ("Plato's 'Third Man'

Thus it simply cannot be true that an inconsistent premise set
— {(*SP*), (*NI*)} or any other, for that matter—is *necessary* for generating the infinite regress of Forms that the *TMA* purports to
generate; the proposition that there are an infinite number of
Forms of Largeness, for example, may be a most peculiar proposition, but it is not an inconsistent one. And if these assumptions are
not necessary for generating the regress, there can be no good
reason for trying to foist them on Plato. For (*SP*) and (*NI*) were
introduced in the first place on the basis of their logical, not
textual, credentials. And even if texts can be found which show
that Plato was, after all, committed to each of these inconsistent
assumptions, this will still not justify their introduction as premises
of the *TMA*. The *TMA* intrigued Plato as it has countless of his
readers; and Vlastos' reconstruction of it has the defect of robbing
the regress of its interest.

II

None of what I have said so far is really new. Vlastos' critics
from the first have been dissatisfied with his reconstruction of the
TMA for just this reason. The first and one of the most powerful of
these critics, Wilfrid Sellars, proposed a formalization of the
argument with a consistent premise set.[11] Since I have argued that
such a formalizaton is a desideratum, a look at the Sellars version
will be in order.

Sellars' main point is that the self-predication and non-
identity assumptions do not have to be understood as contradictories. His argument turns on the question of how we are to
treat the expression "*F*-ness" in the formalization of the argument.
More precisely, his question is this : to what syntactic category do

---

Argument [*Parm.* 132a1-b2]: Text and Logic," *Philosophical Quarterly*, 19
(1969), 289-301, henceforth cited as "*TMA* II"), p. 293. Interestingly, nowhere
in *TMA* I does Vlastos actually produce a translation of the *TMA*'s conclusion,
although there are numerous allusions to it.

[11] "Vlastos and 'The Third Man,'" *Philosophical Review*, LXIV (1955),
405-437; reprinted in *Philosophical Perspectives* (Springfield, Ill., 1967), pp. 23-54.
Subsequent references will be to the reprinted version.

we assign the substituends for "*F*-ness"?[12] One possibility is to regard substituends for "*F*-ness" as proper names of Forms : "Largeness," for example, or "Redness." In this case "*F*-ness" would be what Sellars calls a *representative symbol* or *representative name*. Another possibility is to regard substituends for "*F*-ness" as variables proper. To do so entitles us to quantify with respect to the substituends for *F*-ness and say, "There is a Redness such that . . ." or "For all Largenesses . . .," and so forth, which would be syntactically inappropriate if "Redness" and "Largeness" were names. Now the expression "*F*-ness" combines what Sellars calls these "modes of variability," and is a *representative variable*. That is, "*F*-ness" stands in place of, or represents, not a class of names but a class of variables.

Looked at in this way, (*SP*) and (*NI*) are defective in that they contain free occurrences of the representative variable "*F*-ness."[13] The defect can be remedied with the aid of quantifiers; the result is the Sellars version of the two assumptions :

(*SP'*) All *F*-nesses are *F*.

(*NI'*) If x is *F*, then x is not identical with *the F*-ness by virtue of which it is *F*.[14]

And, as Sellars correctly points out, "the inconsistency vanishes."

Sellars is now able to generate the regress from a consistent premise set containing, in addition to (*SP'*) and (*NI'*), the following two premises :

---

[12] I use "substituends for '*F*-ness' " here as short for the more appropriate expression: "expressions which result from '*F*-ness' when '*F*' is replaced by one of its substituends."

[13] Strictly speaking, the defect is this: every substitution instance of each of (*SP*) and (*NI*) contains free occurrences of the variables represented by "*F*-ness."

[14] Sellars' formulation, (*NI'*), is not quite right as it stands. For (*NI'*), together with the other assumptions, will not generate the regress as Plato envisages it. Plato thinks of the particulars a, b, c as being *F* in virtue of the first Form, *F*-ness I, and *all* of these, in turn, as being *F* in virtue of a second Form, *F*-ness II. But (*NI'*) disallows this, since it requires that there be, for each *F* thing, such a thing as *the F*-ness by virtue of which it is *F*. Hence *F*-ness II cannot cover any of the particulars that *F*-ness I covers, and the regress will not develop. The formulation of the non-identity assumption that Sellars requires would be, rather, this: If x is *F*, then x is not identical with any of the *F*-nesses by virtue of which it is *F*.

453

(G) If a number of entities are all *F*, there must be an *F*-ness by virtue of which they are all *F*.

(P) *a*, *b*, *c*, and so forth, particulars, are *F*.

The proof is a non-terminating sequence which proceeds in this way : (P) provides us with a stock of *F*'s, (G) generates a Form by virtue of which they are all *F*, (*NI'*) establishes that none of the *F*'s in the stock is identical with the Form (G) has generated, and (*SP'*) establishes that the Form just generated is an *F*. Thus our stock of *F*'s is increased by one, and we are ready for new applications of (G), (*NI'*) and (*SP'*) which will generate fresh Forms, ad infinitum.

This argument Vlastos himself regards as "incomparably better"[15] than an argument whose premise set is inconsistent, as all versions Vlastos has produced have been. The only thing wrong with it, according to Vlastos, is that it is not supported by the text and so cannot be regarded as a version of the argument Plato presented. The reason it does not fit the text, according to Vlastos,[16] is that (G) represents Plato as saying that there is *at least one*

---

[15] *TMA* II, p. 293.

[16] Vlastos has located the difficulty in Sellars' account in different places at different times. In his 1955 reply to Sellars ("Addenda to the Third Man Argument: A Reply to Professor Sellars," *Philosophical Review*, LXIV [1955], 438-448) he claimed that substituends for "*F*-ness" are not variables but proper names of Forms. This takes us back to (*SP*) and (*NI*) as Vlastos originally formulated them: an inconsistent pair. He now maintains that the self-predication and non-identity assumptions were defectively formulated in *TMA* I, that they are not, when properly formulated, an inconsistent pair, but that the *TMA* premise set is *still* inconsistent since it must contain a version of (G) according to which "the Form corresponding to *F* is unique" (*TMA* II, p. 300, n. 39; cf. p. 292).

That the *TMA* premise set is an inconsistent triad (rather than an inconsistent pair) was first put forward, to my knowledge, by Anders Wedberg (*Plato's Philosophy of Mathematics* [Stockholm, 1955] Ch. III, esp. pp. 36-37). Wedberg's premise set is this:

(*i*) A thing is *Y* if and only if it participates in the Idea of *Y*-ness.

(*ii*) An Idea is never one among the objects participating therein.

(*iii*) The Idea of *Y*-ness is (a) *Y*.

This premise set has (*ii*), a non-self-participation assumption, in place of Vlastos' (*NI*). And while (*ii*) and (*iii*) are consistent (i.e., self-predication is compatible with non-self-participation) the addition of (*i*) produces an inconsistent set. On the inconsistency of { (*SP'*), (*NI'*), (G1) }, see n. 20 below.

Form corresponding to a given character, whereas Plato's own words, both throughout the *TMA* and elsewhere in the dialogues, make clear that he means to be saying that there is *just one* Form corresponding to a given character. The word "one" (ἕν or μία) occurs five times in the *TMA*, and at each occurrence, Vlastos argues, it means "*just one*" and not "*at least one.*" And, as Vlastos further argues, in numerous other places[17] where Plato uses the phrases ἓν εἶδος or μία ἰδέα (or their equivalent) he means "*one* Form," "a *single* Form," not "at least one Form." Here Vlastos is surely correct :[18] when Parmenides concludes that there is not *one* Form in each case, but rather an infinite number, he means to be denying the ἓν ἕκαστον εἶδος thesis. So that thesis must surely be that there is *exactly* one Form in each case; if ἕν meant "at least one," the conclusion of the *TMA* would not contradict that thesis. It seems to me that the best reason for trying to read ἕν here as "at least one" would have been this : if ἕν means "exactly one," then (*G*) cannot be correct as a formulation of the *TMA*'s first premise. Rather, that premise would apparently have to be, as Vlastos suggests,

(*G*1) If a number of entities are all *F*, there must be exactly one Form corresponding to the character, *F*; and each of those entities is *F* by virtue of participating in that Form.[19]

and it is easy to see that (*G*1), (*SP'*) and (*NI'*) form an inconsistent set.[20]

---

[17] *Rep.* 476*a*, 507*b*, 596*a*; *Parm.* 131*a*8-9, 132*b*5, 132*c*3-4, 133*b*1-2.

[18] Another possible interpretation has been offered by Colin Strang ("Plato and the Third Man," *Proceedings of the Aristotelian Society*, supp. vol. XXXVII [1963], 147-163). Strang argues that although the occurrences of ἕν in *a*1 and *b*2 must be taken to mean "exactly one," the occurrences of μία and ἕν in *a*2, *a*3, and *a*7 need only be taken to mean "at least one." But why should we assume that Plato is using ἕν equivocally in the *TMA*, shifting senses from one line to the next? Strang's only reason seems to be that the assumption of such a shift in senses enables him to reconstruct the *TMA* as a valid argument with consistent premises and a conclusion which is the denial of the uniqueness thesis. But, as I hope to show below, it is possible to produce such a reconstruction without assuming any equivocation on ἕν. If I am right in this contention, Strang's interpretation should lose much of its appeal.

[19] Adapted from Vlastos, *TMA* II, p. 290.

[20] Given the assumption that there are *F* things. For suppose there are;

III

We seem to be faced with the following dilemma : when Plato introduces a Form for the "many large things" with the words μία ἰδέα, we must interpret him as meaning either "at least one" or "exactly one." If we take the former reading we can generate the regress from a consistent premise set but only at the cost of misreading the text; if we take the latter reading, we will be fair to the text but only at the cost of leaving the argument's premise set inconsistent. Neither of these alternatives is very attractive.

Fortunately, there is a way out of the dilemma. It is to show that the second horn contains a mistake, and that we can read μία and ἕν throughout as "exactly one" and still have a consistent premise set. We can make a beginning in this direction by noticing that, even if we agree that μία means "exactly one," Vlastos' (G1) is not the only alternative to Sellars' (G). Another alternative would be

(G2) If a number of entities are all *F*, there must be exactly one Form by virtue of which they are all *F*.

Two points should be noted about (G2). First, it is a more reasonable alternative to (G) than is (G1), since it differs from (G) *only* in that it replaces "*an F*-ness" with "exactly one Form," which is really all one is entitled to if one's only objection to (G) is that (G) is based on a misreading of μία ἰδέα. Second, (G2) does not assert that there is a unique Form corresponding to the character *F*, as (G1) does, but only that, given a number of *F*'s, there is a unique Form corresponding to *them*, in virtue of which *they* are all *F*. Thus (G2) leaves open the possibility, as (G1) does not, that there is more than one Form corresponding to the character *F*. It does not *assert* this—for, after all, that is the *conclusion* of the argument, and we should hardly expect the conclusion itself to be baldly asserted in a single premise—but it does not rule it out, either. And

---

then by (G1) there is exactly one Form—call it "*F*-ness"—corresponding to the character *F*. By (SP') *F*-ness is itself an *F* thing and by (NI') *F*-ness is not identical with the Form by virtue of which it is *F*. But according to (G1) *F*-ness is the Form by virtue of which *each F* thing is *F*, so *F*-ness is, after all, identical with the Form by virtue of which it is *F*. So *F*-ness both is, and is not, identical with the Form by virtue of which it is *F*.

456

it leaves this possibility open in spite of the fact that it reads μία as "exactly one" and not "at least one."[21]

But are there not difficulties with (*G*2)? (*G*2) seems to tell us this: (1) if *a*, *b*, and *c* are all *F*, then there is exactly one Form by virtue of which they are all *F*, and (2) if *h*, *i*, and *j* are all *F*, then there is exactly one Form by virtue of which they are all *F*. The question whether the Form introduced in (2) is the same Form introduced in (1) is left open. But not for long; for (*G*2) also tells us that (3) if *a*, *b*, *c*, *h*, *i*, and *j* are all *F*, then there is exactly one Form by virtue of which they are all *F*. And now our option to treat the Forms introduced at (1) and (2) as distinct seems to be canceled. For the Form introduced at (3) must be identical with the Form introduced at (1), for it is by virtue of just *one* Form that *a*, *b*, and *c* are *F*. But, by parity of reasoning, the Form introduced at (3) must be identical with the Form introduced at (2). So we have one Form after all, and not two or three. And now it seems that (*G*2) has been reduced to (*G*1), with the result that we are still faced with the dilemma that (*G*2) was supposed to get us out of.

This is one way of reading (*G*2), but it is not the only way. As we have been reading (*G*2) it comes to this. If, say, *F*-ness 1 is the one Form corresponding to a given set of *F*'s, then *F*-ness 1 is the one Form corresponding to any subset of that set; members of that set participate in *F*-ness 1 and are *F* by virtue of that participation and they participate in no other *F*-ness. But it is possible to read (*G*2) differently; we can suppose it comes to this: if *F*-ness 1 is a Form corresponding to a given set of *F*'s, then *F*-ness 1 is the *only* *F*-ness corresponding to precisely *that* set. Other Forms

---

[21] There are good logical reasons for insisting that (*G*1) simply *cannot* be an indispensable premise. For (*G*1) embodies (in part) the *uniqueness* claim:

(*U*) There is exactly one Form corresponding to each character or property

which is precisely what the conclusion of the *TMA* denies. Since not-(*U*) is the conclusion, (*U*) cannot be required as a premise. Vlastos' reply to Sellars ("Addenda to the Third Man Argument," p. 440) suggests that he would justify the inclusion of (*U*) in the premise set on the ground that the *TMA* is a *reductio*. But this would be to confuse the argument with its proof. If not-(*U*) is a consequence of a set of premises which includes (*U*), then it is a consequence of that set with (*U*) deleted. Indeed, this is the leading principle of *reductio* proofs. Hence (*G*1), which entails (*U*), cannot be *required* as a *TMA* premise.

457

might correspond to subsets of that set, but no other Form will correspond to that set itself. If we read $(G2)$ this way, the argument of the preceding paragraph designed to show that $(G2)$ reduces to $(G1)$ will fail; for that argument depended on the assumption that the Form corresponding to a given set of F's is the Form corresponding to each of its subsets.[22]

Put another way, our difficulty so far has been this : (G) and $(G2)$, the two versions of Plato's one-over-many principle that we have been considering,[23] make reference to F's but not to sets of F's. Since they make no reference to sets of F's, the force of (G) and $(G2)$, respectively, can be given in these two quantificational versions :

$(G3)$ For any x, if x is F then there is at least one F-ness in which x participates.

$(G4)$ For any x, if x is F then there is exactly one F-ness in which x participates.

But neither of these is acceptable. $(G3)$ is unacceptable for Vlastos' reasons : Plato's one-over-many principle is meant to introduce *exactly* one, not (merely) at least one, Form. $(G4)$ is unacceptable because it is inconsistent with the introduction of a second Form

---

[22] Sellars seems to be making substantially the same point when he writes ("Vlastos and 'The Third Man,' " pp. 29-30):

> [A]s being large by virtue of participating in a given Largeness, an item is a member of a certain class of large items. Thus, *a*, *b*, *c*, etc., would be members of the class of large *particulars* by virtue of the fact that each participates in the *first* largeness. On the other hand, *a*, *b*, *c*, etc., *together with this first Largeness* are members of a more inclusive class by virtue of their common participation in the second Largeness, and so on. Thus it does *not* follow from Plato's premises that the members of *one and the same class* of large items, e.g., the class of large particulars, are members of *that* class by virtue of two different Largenesses. The latter would indeed be a gross inconsistency. ... [T]he regress as Plato sets it up requires that it be incorrect to speak of *the* Form by virtue of which an item, *x*, is large, without going on to specify the class of large things with respect to which it is being considered.

Even though his reasoning here commits him to saying that there will be *exactly* one F-ness for a given set of F's, however, Sellars goes on to formulate his one-over-many premise as (G), thus leaving himself open—unnecessarily—to Vlastos' objection.

[23] $(G1)$ has already been dismissed. Cf. n. 21.

458

216

into the *TMA* : the second Form introduced has all of the participants of the first, plus one. If we are going to come up with an adequate formulation of (*G2*), then, we will have to shift to a version which quantifies over sets of *F*'s as well as over *F*'s.

IV

We might try to formulate our set-theoretic version of (*G2*) in this way :

(*G5*) For any set of *F*'s, there is exactly one Form over that set.

But there is something intuitively unsatisfactory about (*G5*); for it introduces a new relation, the "over" relation, which holds between Forms and sets of *F*'s, and we have, thus far, no idea of what that relation might be. It is natural to suppose that the relation of a Form to the set it is "over" can be analyzed in terms of the participation relation between that Form and members of that set. Unfortunately, there is no easy way of doing this. Suppose we try :

(*G6*) For any set of *F*'s, there is exactly one Form in which all members of that set participate.[24]

Clearly this will not do. (*G6*), like (*G4*), conflicts with the second step of the *TMA*. All members of the set {Mt. Everest, Mt. Mc-Kinley} participate in Largeness 1; but they both, together with Largeness 1, participate in Largeness 11, . . . and so on. There may be more than one Form in which all members of a given set of *F*'s participate. We might alter (*G6*) to read :

(*G7*) For any set of *F*'s, there is exactly one Form in which *only* members of that set participate.

---

[24] (*G6*) is essentially identical to Colin Strang's (*loc. cit.*) "strong *OM*," the strong version of the one-over-many thesis. Strang agrees that strong *OM* is inconsistent with the *TMA* premises (giving roughly the same argument I give), but he is content to rest the *TMA* on "weak *OM*" (essentially [*G6*] with "at least" in place of "exactly").

459

This will not do either. (G7) tells us that, given a set of F's, there will be one Form all of whose participants are members of that set. But this seems a most unlikely assumption. Consider the set {Everest, McKinley}. There is *no* Form of Largeness whose participants are limited to the pair {Everest, McKinley}. Hence there may be no Form in which only members of a given set of F's participate.

Perhaps we should combine (G6) and (G7), yielding :

(G8) For any set of F's, there is exactly one Form in which all and only members of that set participate.

But this is no better. For while the objection to (G6) will not work against (G8), the objection to (G7) will; nothing in Plato's theory tells us that there should be one Form of Largeness over the set {Everest, McKinley} and *another* Form over the set {Everest, Kilimanjaro}. Plato's one-over-many principle will have to allow for more than one Form corresponding to the predicate "F"; but it should not require as many Forms corresponding to "F" as there are sets of F's. Some sets of F's, such as the ones mentioned above, are just not interesting enough to require their own special Forms.

But some sets are—the set of F particulars, for example. So perhaps something like (G8) would do as a formulation of the one-over-many principle if there were some way of specifying *which* set of F's is involved. As a start, we might try :

(G9) For any set which is the set of F particulars, there is exactly one Form in which all and only members of that set participate.

But (G9), while unobjectionable as a Platonic truth, is too weak to be of much help in generating a regress. For (G9) is equivalent to :

(G10) There is exactly one Form in which all and only members of the set of F particulars participate.

And (G10) is silent about sets containing things other than F particulars, whereas it is just such a set that pops up in the second step of the *TMA*.

460

Clearly what is wanted is a more restricted version of ($G8$) that is not so restricted, as ($G9$) is, that it defuses the infinite regress. It will be my aim in the next section to produce such a version of the one-over-many principle.

V

Let me begin with a series of definitions. These definitions will be given in terms of a single undefined relational predicate, "participates in," and the schematic letter "F," which will serve as a dummy predicate and will play the role that "large" does as a sample predicate in the TMA.

($D1$) By an F-*object* (hereafter "object," for short) I will mean any F thing (anything, that is, whether a particular or a Form, of which "F" can be truly predicated).

($D2$) An F-*particular* (hereafter "particular," for short) is an object in which nothing participates.[25]

($D3$) A *Form* is an object that is not a particular.

($D4$) I will also speak of a particular as an *object of level 0*.

($D5$) An object is an *object of level one* if

(a) All of its participants are particulars, and

(b) all particulars participate in it.

($D6$) In general, an object is an *object of level n* ($n \geq 1$) if

(a) All of its participants are of level $n - 1$ or lower, and

(b) all objects of level $n - 1$ or lower participate in it.

I will define the level of a set of objects as the level of its highest-level member. Thus,

($D7$) A set of objects is a *set of level n* if it contains an object of level n and no higher-level object. Finally,

---

[25] Strictly, this should be modal: a particular is an object in which nothing *can* participate. For the subsequent definition of a Form as a non-particular should have it that a Form is an object in which something *can* participate, in order to leave open the possibility of there being a Form which lacks participants. But no harm is done here by simplifying the definitions, since the TMA assumes the existence of particulars, which, in turn, guarantees that no Form (in this discussion) will go unparticipated in.

461

(D8) A set of level n will be said to be a *maximal set* if it contains every object of level m for every $m \leq n$. In other words, a maximal set contains every object on every level equal to or less that the level of its highest-level member.

The one-over-many principle that seems to be operative in the *TMA* can now be stated. I will lablel it "*OM*-axiom" to try to emphasize its deductive power, since it turns out to be the only assumption needed to generate not only the *TMA* but a number of important theorems as well.[26]

(*OM*-axiom) For any maximal set there is exactly one Form in which all and only members of that set participate.

(Thus [*OM*-axiom] is simply [*G8*] restricted to maximal sets.) That the infinite regress of the *TMA* is a consequence of (*OM*-axiom) can be proved formally; the proof will proceed in roughly the following way. Assume the existence of the set of particulars— that is, the set of non-Forms of which "*F*" can be truly predicated; since this is a maximal set, (*OM*-axiom) gives us one Form over that set;[27] the addition of this Form to the set of particulars gives us a new maximal set; (*OM*-axiom) then gives us a new Form; and so on. Now two questions arise about the proof as just sketched. (1) How do we know that each application of (*OM*-axiom) gives us a "new" Form—that is, one not identical with any of the objects introduced up to that point in the proof? (2) How do we know that the addition of a Form to the set it is over produces a maximal set? It is clear that we must have answers to these questions; if we cannot answer (1) we cannot guarantee that there will be a regress, and if we cannot answer (2) we cannot guarantee that we will keep producing sets to which (*OM*-axiom) will be applicable. Before setting out the *TMA* formally, then, it will be useful to mention two consequences of the axiom and definitions which will enable us to answer these questions. They are the following two theorems :

---

[26] Except, of course, the assumption that there are particulars; we must be given a non-empty set of particulars to which to apply the *OM*-axiom.

[27] "Over" will be used (until further notice) to abbreviate "participated in by all and only the members of."

(T1) No object is on more than one level.

(T2) There is exactly one object on each level (greater than O).

(T1) is derivable from (G2), (D4) and (D6); (T2) is derivable from (D6), (D8), and (OM-axiom). The proofs will be omitted.[28] Our formalization of the TMA can now be sketched more fully.

THE TMA (FIRST VERSION)

1. Let α be the set of all particulars.
2. α is a maximal set (level O).   (1), (D4), (D7), (D8)
3. There is exactly one Form over α,   (2), (OM-axiom)
   call it "F-ness 1."
4. F-ness 1 is of level one.   (1), (3), (D5)
5. F-ness 1 is not a member of α.   (2), (4), (T1), (D7)
6. $\alpha \cup \{F$-ness 1$\}$ is maximal   (2), (4), (T2), (D7), (D8)
   (level one).
7. There is exactly one Form over   (6), (OM-axiom)
   $\alpha \cup \{F$-ness 1$\}$, call it "F-ness 11."
8. F-ness 11 is of level 2.   (6), (7), (D6)
9. F-ness 11 is not a member of   (6), (8), (T1), (D7)
   $\alpha \cup \{F$-ness 1$\}$.
10. F-ness 11 $\neq$ F-ness 1.   (9)

---

[28] Roughly, the proofs would run as follows.

For (T1): Suppose an object, y, to be on more than one level, say levels i and $i + j$, for some $i \geq O$ and $j \geq 1$. Then, by (D6), y participates in itself, since an object of level $i + j$ is participated in by every lower-level object and hence by any object of level i. But then y must also be on a level *lower* than i, since, by (D6), all participants of an object of level i are on a level lower than i. Iteration of this reasoning will show that y must also be on level O. But then, by (D4), y is a particular; and by (D2) nothing participates in y. Hence y does not participate in itself. But this contradicts the assumption that y is on both of levels i and $i + j$.

For (T2): To show that, for any $n \geq 1$, there is exactly one object of level n, let α be a maximal set of level $n - 1$. (This assumption is justified by the fact that it is provable that, for every n, there is a maximal set of level n.) Then by (OM-axiom) there is exactly one Form over α. But, by (D8), the members of α are all and only those objects of level $n - 1$ or lower. Hence there is exactly one Form participated in by all and only objects of level $n - 1$ or lower, which means, by (D6), that there is exactly one object of level n.

463

11. $\alpha \cup \{F\text{-ness } 1, F\text{-ness } 11\}$ is   (6), (8), ($T2$), ($D7$), ($D8$)
maximal (level 2).

12. There is exactly one Form over   (11), (OM-axiom)
$\alpha \cup \{F\text{-ness } 1, F\text{-ness } 11\}$, call it
"F-ness 111."

Etc.   Etc.

The sequence, of course, is non-terminating; but since this is where Parmenides left off we, too, can stop at this point and examine the results.

The most important point about the argument whose proof is sketched above is the absence of explicit self-predication and non-indentity assumptions. This is not to say that self-predication and non-identity are not involved in the TMA as I have presented it; they are, but not as explicit premises in the argument. This seems to me to mark the point of greatest similarity between Plato's statement of the argument and my formalization of its proof. Self-predication is *presupposed* in the definitions of "Form" and "object"; non-identity comes in not as a premise but (at step 10) as a consequence of the line which is an instance of the theorem that a Form is not a member of the set it is over. It may be felt that it is perverse deliberately to conceal just those "assumptions" that some have argued are really the ones responsible for the TMA. On the contrary, I feel that it is a virtue of this way of looking at the TMA that it directs our attention to the one-over-many principle, which has been the least discussed of the TMA's assumptions, even though it was the only one Plato explicitly formulated.

But how well does (OM-axiom) represent the one-over-many principle Plato employs in the TMA? The most glaring difference is this : Plato does not say anything that suggests that the "many" to which the one-over-many principle will be applied must be (what I have called) a maximal set. Quite to the contrary, the text suggests that Plato is prepared to apply the principle to non-maximal sets; it is applied to πόλλ' ἄττα μεγάλα, "some plurality of large things" (Vlastos)—that is, *some* set of many large things. If Plato is prepared, as he seems to be, to start the TMA with *any* set of large things, then (OM-axiom) cannot be adequate as a formulation of the relevant one-over-many principle.

464

So our problem is this : if we think of the *TMA* as starting with some non-maximal set, we do not yet have a principle which will provide us with exactly one Form over that set, in some suitable sense of "over." Given (*OM*-axiom), the best we can do for a general one-over-many principle would be this : no matter what set we start with, there will be exactly one Form over the lowest-level maximal set which includes that set—that is,

(*G*11) For any set α, there is exactly one Form participated in by all and only members of the lowest-level maximal set which contains every member of α.

The Form (*G*11) generates will not, however, be said to be *over*, in the sense given to that term above, the set to which (*G*11) is applied. For "*x* is over α" has been abbreviating "*x* is participated in by all and only the members of α." And so unless α is a maximal set, the Form (*G*11) introduces will not be *over* α.

It should now be apparent that "participated in by all and only the members of" does not, after all, capture the intuitive sense of "over" (ἐπί) in "the one over the many." For one thing, the *over* relation ought to be understood to be a one-many relation; for another, the one which is over a set of many things ought to be understood to be over each of them. Yet the *over* relation, as defined thus far, has neither of these features; it is a relation that obtains between a Form and a maximal set, and hence is a one-one, not a one-many, relation; consequently a Form cannot be said to be over each of the members of the set it is over.

VI

The formalization of the *TMA* proposed in the last section suffered from the defect of requiring a maximal set at step one. Since it is at precisely that point that it seems to diverge from Plato's argument, I shall try to remedy the defect in the present section.

I shall begin by providing a definition of the *over* relation which will be closer, I think, to Plato's notion of that relation:

(*D*9) *x* is over *y* = *df* *y*, or, if *y* is a set, every member of *y*, participates in *x*.

465

The *over* relation will clearly not be a one-one relation. But it will not be a one-many relation, either. For to suppose it is would be to assume ($G6$) once again, and ($G6$) has already heen rejected as inconsistent with the second step of the *TMA*. The *over* relation must—unhappily, it seems—be a many-many relation.

The *over* relation is many-many because not only is F-ness I over each of the particulars a, b, c, but so is F-ness II, and so forth. But still, it is F-ness I and *not* F-ness II (or any of the others in the hierarchy) that makes the first appearance in the *TMA*. That is, it is not just *any* Form over the initial set that appears at the first step of the *TMA*; it is, one might say, the Form *immediately* over the initial set that appears first. The Form immediately over the particulars a, b, and c will be the Form whose participants are particulars only; it ·may be over other particulars, but it will not be over any Forms. We can make the sense of "immediately over" more precise:

(D10) x is immediately over y = df x is over y and x is over all and only those sets whose level is equal to or less than that of y.

Thus, while F-ness I and F-ness II are both *over* particulars a, b, c, only the former is *immediately* over them, for the latter is not over sets of level 0 only, being over the level one object F-ness I. So while the *over* relation may be many-many, the *immediately over* relation is one-many. And since it is, the one-over-many principle required for the *TMA* can be stated in terms of it :

(IOM-axiom) For any set of F's, there is exactly one Form immediately over that set.

This axiom, it turns out, is equivalent to ($G11$) and entails (OM-axiom);[29] hence by using it in place of (OM-axiom) we can pro-

---

[29] That (IOM-axiom) entails (OM-axiom) can be seen as follows. Let α be a maximal set of level n (cf. n. 28); by (IOM-axiom) there is exactly one Form, say x, immediately over α; by (D10) x is over all and only sets of level n or lower; hence x is over α and over no higher-level set; by (D9) x is participated in by all members of α, and, by the previous step, participated in by nothing else; hence x is participated in by all and only members of α. Therefore, if α is a maximal set, there is exactly one Form participated in by all and only members of α—which is (OM-axiom).

duce a formalization of the *TMA* which is not open to the objections raised against that of the previous section. Once again it will be helpful if we can make use of an additional theorem in our proof :

> ($T3$) If x is immediately over y, then the level of x is one greater than the level of y.

($T3$) is derivable from ($D6$)–($D10$).[30] The formalization of the *TMA* follows.

THE *TMA* (FINAL VERSION)

1. Let α be any set of F's (of level n).
2. There is exactly one Form   (1), (IOM-axiom)
   immediately over α, call it "F-ness 1."
3. F-ness 1 is of level $n + 1$.   (1), (2), ($T3$)
4. F-ness 1 is not a member of α.   (1), (3), ($T1$), ($D7$)
5. $\alpha \cup \{F\text{-ness 1}\}$ is of level $n + 1$.   (1), (3), ($D7$)
6. There is exactly one Form   (5), (IOM-axiom)
   immediately over $\alpha \cup \{F\text{-ness 1}\}$, call it "$F$-ness 11."
7. F-ness 11 is of level $n + 2$.   (5), (6), ($T3$)
8. F-ness 11 is not a member of   (5), (7), ($T1$), ($D7$)
   $\alpha \cup \{F\text{-ness 1}\}$.
9. F-ness 11 $\neq$ F-ness 1.   (8)
   Etc.   Etc.

Once again, self-predication and non-identity assumptions are built in but not made explicit. The difference between this version of the *TMA* and the first lies in the different ways in which the one-over-many principle is formulated. The main advantage of (IOM-axiom) over its predecessor is that it makes clearer Plato's

---

[30] Proof of ($T3$): let y be of level n, and let x be immediately over y; then by ($D10$) x is over all and only sets of level n or lower; hence x is over the maximal set of level n, and over no higher-level set; by ($D9$) every member of the maximal set of level n participates in x, and nothing else does; hence all of x's participants are of level n or lower and all objects of level n or lower participate in x; thus by ($D6$) x is of level $n + 1$.

4⁶7

inclination to think that while the one-over-many principle yields exactly one Form for the set under consideration at each step, that principle is consistent with there being more than one Form over the set with which we start. This inclination comes out, I think, in Plato's use of verbs like δοκεῖ and φαίνεται to introduce the Forms at each step. Over the first set of large things *just* one Form "appears" or "comes into view," even though, as it turns out, there will be others. The one which appears will be the one immediately over that set. There may be more than one Form over a given set, but there would not *appear* to be to someone asked to pick out the one over the many. Clearly, Plato thinks of the Form introduced at each step as just overtopping, as it were, the set of things over which it is introduced. Over the set of particulars with which, presumably, we begin there will be *just* one object of the next level. But the uniqueness of the Form on each level is insufficient to prove the uniqueness thesis in which Plato is interested—namely, that there is exactly one Form corresponding to each predicate.

All of this fits perfectly the over-all structure of the *TMA*.[31] Plato offers the one-over-many principle (at 132a2-3) as a *reason* for holding that the Forms are unique (ἓν ἕκαστον εἶδος, 132a1).[32] The reasoning, presumably, would go like this : when you consider a set of large things, exactly one Form of Largeness will come into view, immediately over that set; so there is exactly one Form of Largeness. What Parmenides sets out to show is that this reasoning is inconclusive; indeed, it is the point of the *TMA* to show that the

---

[31] The only part of my reconstruction for which there is no direct textual support is the division of objects into levels. Plato does not, of course, have a word for "levels," nor does he explicitly divide objects in the way I have in my reconstruction. But I would defend this division on the grounds that it gives a fairly precise formulation of the logical structure implicit in Plato's argument. Any account of the *TMA* must, it seems to me, take very seriously the one-over-many principle, and part of doing this is to say what is involved in the claim that a Form can be "over" its participants. It is clear that Plato thought of Forms as being on a higher "ontological level" than particulars (cf., e.g., *Rep.* 515d, 477a ff.; *Tim.* 28a, 49e; *Phdo.* 74a, 78d ff., *et passim*). The *TMA* seems to extend this notion by assuming, in general, that a Form is on a higher level than its participants.

[32] The importance of this line has not, I think, been sufficiently appreciated. It seems to me to show conclusively that the *TMA* is not, as has been generally supposed, a *reductio* argument directed against the uniqueness thesis.

one-over-many principle, far from supporting the uniqueness thesis, leads to its denial.[33]

VII

If my account of the *TMA* is, at least in its essentials, correct, then the difficulty in the Theory of Forms that is being shown up lies in the one-over-many principle. The argument of one over many, thought to be a safe route to the uniqueness thesis, has been shown to be defective. This diagnosis of the *TMA*, however, will be unacceptable to those who think that in *Republic* X Plato has shown us that he knows very well how to disable objections to the uniqueness thesis.[34] There (597c-d) Plato argues in the following way. There is just one Form of Bed (literally, "bed in nature," ἐν τῇ φύσει κλίνην); for suppose there were two; immediately, another would crop up whose εἶδος they would both have, and it, not they, would be the Form of Bed (literally, "what [a] bed is," ὃ ἔστιν κλίνη). The crucial move in this "Third Bed Argument" (*TBA*) is a one-over-many move;[35] as soon as a second Form

---

[33] I have been arguing that the *TMA*'s premise set is consistent; hence, I am commited to the consistency of (*IOM*-axiom). But of course the consistency of this axiom is not independent of the sort of set theory we assume. In particular, the set theory my formalization presupposes cannot include the principle of abstraction—namely, the principle that, for any predicate, there is a set consisting of all and only objects to which that predicate applies—in formal notation:

$$(\exists\alpha)\ (x)\ (x \in \alpha \equiv Fx)$$

For if there were such a set (the universal set of *F*'s) it would contain no highest-level member (there being no such thing as the *last* Form in the infinite regress) and hence it would not be a set of *any* level (cf. [*D*7]). But then no Form could be immediately over that set (cf. [*D*10]), contradicting (*IOM*-axiom). Even though the principle of abstraction has its own difficulties (cf. Quine, *Methods of Logic*, p. 249) we may still wish to retain it. In this case (*IOM*-axiom) would have to be altered to read:

> For any set α, if α is a set of level *n*, for some *n*, then there is exactly one Form immediately over α.

[34] E.g., Cherniss, "The Relation of the *Timaeus* to Plato's Later Dialogues," *American Journal of Philology*, LXXVIII (1957), 225-266; reprinted in Allen, *op. cit.*, pp. 339-378. Subsequent references will be to the reprinted version. Cf. also Cornford, *Plato and Parmenides* (New York, 1957), p. 90.

[35] But cf. Vlastos, "Addendum (1963)" (to *TMA* I), p. 263, who cites the *TBA* as an instance where Plato employs the full-strength non-identity

threatens, it is an application of one over many that saves the day. The two beds we thought were both Forms are not Forms after all; it is the Third Bed which is the *one* Form.

If the *TBA* shows that one-over-many reasoning does yield the uniqueness thesis, then either the *TMA* is invalid or my account of it is mistaken. Fortunately, the *TBA* does not establish the uniqueness thesis; hence it cannot provide an answer to the *TMA*, although *TMA* and *TBA* reasoning will jointly produce a surprising but important conclusion. The *TBA* shows that there cannot be as many as two Forms of Bed, for the supposition that there are two demands the existence of a Third Bed, which, the *TBA* assures us, is *the* Form of Bed. But suppose we add our Third Bed, *TMA* style, to the beds already collected. The one-over-many principle will produce a Fourth Bed, and it, not the Third, will be the Form. Clearly what the *TBA* shows is that there is not *more* than one Form of Bed; it cannot show that there is exactly one unless it can show that the regress described above will stop. But, according to the *TMA*, this is precisely what it cannot do. So while the *TBA* shows only that there is not more than one Form, the *TMA* shows that there is not exactly one Form. And if neither exactly one nor more than one, then none. The surprising conclusion of the *TMA* together with the *TBA* is that there are no Forms.[36] But Plato never put the two arguments together in this way, and hence apparently never realized that they produce this conclusion.

---

assumption; Cherniss, pp. 371-373, who sees Plato here denying self-predication (on the grounds that the ἐστι in ὃ ἐστι x means "="); and Strang, p. 157, who correctly points out, *contra* Cherniss, that (*a*) if a denial of self-predication is involved in the *TBA*, Plato cannot have clearly seen it and (*b*) the *TBA* is "itself ripe for the *TMA* treatment."

[36] This conclusion can be obtained formally by altering (*D3*), in light of the *TBA*, to read:

> (*D3'*) A *Form* is an object that is not a particular *and does not participate in any object*,

and by substituting "object" for "Form" in (*OM*-axiom). But since every object generated by (*OM*-axiom) will belong to at least one maximal set, every such object will participate in a higher-level object. Then none of the objects generated by (*OM*-axiom) is a Form. But from this it follows that

> (*T3'*) For any *n*, if *x* is an object of level *n*, then *x* is not a Form.

470

The one-over-many principle will not yield the uniqueness thesis. And the *TBA* will not safeguard that thesis from the threat of the *TMA*. But that principle provides only one among many routes to the uniqueness thesis that Plato might have employed. I shall briefly consider one such route, suggested by the language in which the Forms are introduced in the *Phaedo*.[37]

In that dialogue Plato claims that there is something beyond sensible *F* things, something he calls "The *F* Itself" (74*a*11-12).[38] The *F* Itself is *F* without qualification (74*b*7ff.);[39] it can never seem non-*F* (74*c*1-3);[40] other *F* things fall short (ἐνδεῖ) of The *F* Itself (74*d*6-7), they are like (οἷον) it but inferior (φαυλότερον) to it (74*e*1-2); they are called by the same name (ὁμωνύμων) as The *F* Itself (78*e*2). Later in the *Phaedo*, Plato starts calling such things as The Beautiful Itself and The Large Itself "Forms" and says that other things are named after the Forms by participating in them (102*b*1-2).

Now this way of referring to a Form (schematically) as "The *F* Itself" is striking in several ways. To refer to a Form as "The *F* Itself" is, first of all, to *name* the Form (to say just which Form

---

[37] I owe a number of points both in the remainder of this section and elsewhere in this paper to discussions with Gareth B. Matthews.

[38] The sample predicate Plato uses is "equal"; the phrase he uses, αὐτὸ τὸ ἴσον.

[39] Suggested by Plato's claim that the "sensible equals" (sticks, stones, etc.) may appear to be "equal to this but not to that" (τῷ μὲν ἴσα φαίνεται, τῷ δ᾽οὔ, 74*b*8-9). Presumably, The Equal Itself cannot appear equal to this but not to that; it is just Equal, pure and simple—the *qualifications* "to this," "not to that" are inappropriate. (On the reading of the datives in *b*8-9, cf. G.E.L. Owen, "A Proof in the PERI IDEON," in Allen, *op. cit.*, p. 306, whose interpretation I follow. Even on the traditional reading of the datives as masculine rather than neuter and governed by φαίνεται rather than ἴσα it is still possible to see Plato here announcing a certain qualification on the *F*-ness of *F* particulars which does not apply to The *F* Itself. But I think Owen's reading is better.) Cf. also *Symp.* 211*e*; *Hip. Maj.* 289 ff.; Vlastos, "Degrees of Reality in Plato," in *New Essays on Plato and Aristotle*, ed. by R. Bambrough (London, 1965), pp. 1-19.

[40] The question whether αὐτὰ τὰ ἴσα can ever seem unequal is raised and answered in the negative. But it is a matter of dispute among recent commentators whether the phrase αὐτὰ τὰ ἴσα ("the equals themselves") does, in fact, refer to the Form—i.e., αὐτὸ τὸ ἴσον. I am assuming that it does, and that the (somewhat unexpected) plural can be satisfactorily explained. Cf. Geach, "The Third Man Again," p. 269; Vlastos, "Postscript to the Third Man Argument: A Reply to Mr. Geach," *Philosophical Review*, LXV (1956), 83-94, reprinted in Allen, *op. cit.*, pp. 279-291 (esp. pp. 287-288, 291).

471

it is). But it is also to name the Form in such a way as to make
clear how it is that participants in the Form are homonymous
instances of it—that is, named after it. Third, and most important,
is this : to refer to a Form as "The F Itself" makes it perfectly clear
that there is just *one* Form after which F things are named. After
all, it is *The F* Itself. So built into this way of referring to the Forms
by their proper names are two other features : that of homonymy
—particular F's get their (common) name from the Form's (proper)
name—and that of uniqueness—corresponding to the deficient,
changeable, qualifiedly F things there is just *one* thing that is
unchangeable and does not fall short of being F, which is hence
unqualifiedly F : *The F* Itself.

What I have been suggesting is not an argument for the uniqueness thesis. That thesis is not so much argued for in the *Phaedo*
as simply built into Plato's way of referring to the Forms. To
refer to a Form as "The F Itself" does not *prove* the thesis—but it
does, or should, forestall any objections to it. Thus, when Parmenides, at the second step of the *TMA*, claims to have proved the
existence of a *second* Form, what one would expect from Socrates
is not a counterargument but a charge of unintelligibility. (*Another*
The Large Itself? *Two* The Larges Themselves? Whatever do you
mean? That doesn't make any sense!) But no such charge is to be
found in the text. Perhaps, then, Plato's willingness to press on
with the *TMA* should indicate to us that the sort of difficulty for
the uniqueness thesis which he envisaged was not one which could
be palliated by appeal to a way of referring to the Forms. The
text seems strongly to support this point, for, despite the fact that
the *TMA* includes, *inter alia*, *Phaedo*-style reference to the Forms,
Plato seems to take special pains to avoid having to say anything
like "another The F Itself." The Form first introduced by the
one-over-many principle is referred to canonically at 132a6 as
"The Large Itself" ($a\vec{v}\tau\grave{o}\ \tau\grave{o}\ \mu\acute{\epsilon}\gamma a$), but the second Form is introduced
in a specially cautious way. Parmenides asks (literally) "will not
some one [thing] once again large appear?" ($o\vec{v}\chi\grave{\iota}\ \acute{\epsilon}\nu\ \tau\iota\ a\vec{v}\ \mu\acute{\epsilon}\gamma a$
$\varphi av\epsilon\hat{\iota}\tau a\iota$). It is only after he gets assent to this, which is ambiguous
as between The Large Itself making a second appearance and a
second (something) making its first appearance, that Parmenides
makes clear, for the first time, that the Form which has just appeared

472

230

is *another* Form (Ἄλλο ἄρα εἶδος μεγέθους, a10). According to the reasoning of the *Phaedo* this should be unintelligible (*Another* Form of Largeness? How could it be different from the first?) but Plato does not seem to be interested in making that point. Plato, it seems, just turns his back on the sort of reasoning which could save the uniqueness thesis.

VIII

I think it is safe to conclude that Plato in the *TMA* is interested not so much in the uniqueness thesis per se as in its relation to the one-over-many principle. What the *TMA* shows is that to keep uniqueness the one-over-many principle will have to be abandoned[41] or modified,[42] for it is an application of that principle to the set consisting of large particulars and The Large Itself that generates a second Form. Well, this does not seem too high a price to pay; simply modify the principle in such a way as to make it applicable only to sets of particulars. It will thus generate one Form for each predicate (which we want it to do) but no more than one. But there is no indication that Plato himself ever tried to restrict the principle in this way.[43] We can best understand and

[41] As Plato himself seems to have done. Cf. *Politicus* 262a-63d.

[42] As some members of the Academy apparently did, restricting the principle, according to Aristotle, to sets of particulars (καθ᾽ ἕκαστα). Cf. *Alex. in Met.*, 80.8 ff.

[43] There is an almost overwhelming temptation to think that the *TBA* depends upon a restricted one-over-many principle, for it appears that Plato is assuming, in that argument, that anything which requires a Form over it (to make it what it is) is not a Form. And does this not amount to the assumption that the one-over-many principle cannot be applied to Forms? I think this temptation should be resisted. For if the *TBA* really *assumed* that the one-over-many principle cannot be applied to Forms, Plato would have had to show that the two alleged Forms of Bed were not really Forms *before* he could apply the one-over-many principle to deduce the existence of the Third Bed—i.e., the genuine Form of Bed. But how could Plato show this without undercutting his own argument? If the *TBA* really assumed a restricted one-over-many principle, the argument would collapse. ("Suppose there are two Forms of Bed; since we can't apply the restricted one-over-many principle to Forms, we can't deduce the existence of the Third Bed; so we're stuck with two Forms of Bed!") I conclude that whereas the unrestricted one-over-many principle entails the denial of the uniqueness thesis, the restricted principle is compatible with that thesis but does not entail it.

appreciate his failure thus to restrict the principle, I think, by looking at his most famous formulation of it (at *Rep.* 596a6-7):[44]

We are in the habit of assuming one Form for each set of many things to which we give the same name.

But now recall the *Phaedo's* doctrine of the homonymy of Forms and their participants. The things falling under a Form are *homonymous* instances of it. The general term which is applied to the many is *borrowed* from the name of the Form : they are called after the Form. That is, what makes it correct to call each particular *F* "*F*" is that it is correct to call the Form under which the particulars fall "*F.*" So the set of things to which we give the name "*F*" will contain a Form. Yet according to 596a, the principle of collection for a set of many things to which the one-over-many principle is to be applied is that they be things "to which we give the same name." So it seems inevitable that Plato would ultimately include Forms in sets to which the one-over-many principle is applicable.

It is still possible to read 596a in a harmless way, even if we waive the restriction to particulars : we assume one Form for each set of many things to which we give the same name; and among those will be one thing which does not participate in that Form—namely, the Form itself. Of course, the principle could then no longer be appropriately called the "one-over-many" (perhaps the "one-over-all-but-one-of-the-many" would be more appropriate). This objection is not a frivolous one; for the one-over-many principle is supposed to provide an answer to questions like "What makes it correct for many things all to be called '*F*'?" The answer is supposed to be that the many things all stand in a certain relation (participation) to a certain Form—the one over the many. And according to the suggested reading of 596a not all of the many things correctly called "*F*" will stand in that relation. Hence the idea will have to be given up that predicating "*F*" of something is, quite simply, a matter of asserting that a relation obtains between that thing and a certain Form. It is the

---

[44] εἶδος γάρ πού τι ἓν ἕκαστον εἰώθαμεν τίθεσθαι περὶ ἕκαστα τὰ πολλά, οἷς ταὐτὸν ὄνομα ἐπιφέρομεν.

474

one-over-many principle which is the metaphysical embodiment of that idea, and in the *TMA*, I have argued, Plato is pointing out the logical shortcomings of that principle. In so doing he has taken an important step toward liberating himself from an initially compelling but overly simple and ultimately unsatisfactory theory of predication.[45]

S. Marc Cohen

Indiana University

---

[45] An earlier version of this paper was presented to the philosophy department of the University of Massachusetts in April, 1970, as part of a symposium on Plato's *Parmenides*, and to the Institute in Greek Philosophy and Science held at Colorado College in July, 1970. Among the many people of whose helpful criticism I have been the beneficiary I wish especially to thank Aryeh Kosman, Gareth B. Matthews, and Gregory Vlastos.

475

PLATO AND ARISTOTLE ON FORM AND SUBSTANCE

I. Introduction

Plato and Aristotle give different answers to the question 'What are the substances (*ousiai*)?'. One way Aristotle defends his answer is by arguing that his candidate substances – particulars such as Socrates or Callias – better satisfy the criteria for substance than do Plato's candidates – eternal, unchanging, nonsensible universals called 'Forms'.[1] This defense goes along with another. For Aristotle disagrees with Plato, not only about the candidates, but also about the criteria for substance: one reason Plato fastens on to the wrong candidates is that he focuses on some of the wrong criteria.

Aristotle mounts his defense in different ways in the *Categories* and *Metaphysics*. In both works he defends the priority of particulars. In the *Cat.*, however, their nature is left unanalysed; and their priority is defended largely by appeal to unPlatonic criteria. In the *Met.*, by contrast, Aristotle analyzes particulars into compound, form, and matter. Socrates, for example, may be viewed as a compound of his form (his soul) and his matter (his body); or he may be viewed as his form or soul. Further, Aristotle now invokes additional, Platonic criteria for substance; and this leads him to argue that it is Socrates as form that counts as primary substance; the primary substances are individual forms.[2]

By the time of the *Met.*, then, Aristotle agrees with Plato that the primary substances are forms; but Platonic and Aristotelian forms are quite different. Platonic Forms are universals; Aristotelian forms are particulars; where there can be at most one Platonic Form corresponding to a given predicate, there may be several Aristotelian forms; and many Aristotelian forms, though no Platonic ones, are sensible, perishable, and changeable.

Why, and with what justification, does Aristotle prefer his candidates and criteria to Plato's? Is he right to believe that his candidates (ASs, for 'Aristotelian substances') fare better than do Platonic Forms (PFs)? And are his criteria plausible? I shall suggest that where Plato's and Aristotle's criteria converge, PFs if anything fare better than do ASs; Aristotle can defend his candidates only by significantly weakening his own criteria, a weakening Plato need not countenance. Where their criteria diverge, PFs fare badly; but this is not obviously to PFs' discredit, since such criteria are not plausible necessary conditions on substance.

II. *Substance and Essence*

First we need a more detailed account of what substances (*ousiai*) are, and of Plato's and Aristotle's candidates for that role; so let me begin with that.

'*Ousia*' is a verbal noun from the Greek verb 'to be'. As Aristotle uses the word, it occurs in two distinct grammatical constructions. We can say that x is an *ousia* – a being, reality, or substance; or we can say that the *ousia* of x is F, where 'F' answers the 'What is it?' question about x. In the first construction, we are talking about substances, full stop; in the second, about the substances *of* things – here '*ousia*' carries a dependent genitive.[3]

On the first use, *ousiai* are the basic beings there are, whatever these turn out to be. To call something an *ousia*, in this sense, is to confer basicness; but there is no antecedent restriction on what sort of thing fills the bill. Let us call this sort of *ousia*: *primary substance*. Any entities one takes as basic or fundamental are one's primary substances. For the Presocratics, the primary substances are various sorts of material stuff – water or air or fire; for Plato, they are eternal, unchanging, nonsensible universals called 'Forms'; for Aristotle they are particulars such as Socrates or Callias.

In its second use, Aristotle often identifies a thing's *ousia* with its essence or nature (e.g. *Met.* 1017b21–21; 1031a18); so let us call this sort of *ousia*: *essence*. If you think everything is essentially watery, you think water is the *ousia*, essence, of things; if you think living a certain sort of life is the human essence, you think living that sort of life is the *ousia* of human beings.

It is natural, but not necessary, to identify these two sorts of *ousiai* – to believe, that is, that the essences of things are the primary substances. That, I take it, is Plato's view: his primary substances are his Forms; and he takes Forms to be the essences of things. We specify a thing's essence, say what it is, by suitably relating it to the relevant Form or Forms. It is, indeed, in part *because* he believes that Forms provide answers to the 'What is it?' question – are the essences of things – that he takes them to be the primary substances.[4]

In the *Cat.*, by contrast, Aristotle resists the Platonic identification of primary substance and essence. There he argues that the primary substances are not universals of any sort, but such entities as an individual man or horse or tree. He does not say that such entities are primary substances because they are essences; indeed, they do not appear to *be* essences at all, although they *have* essences. Their essences are their species and genera – universals in the category of substance; and these are Aristotle's secondary substances. Hence, although no universal is a *primary* substance, Aristotle concedes to Plato that at least some universals – the species and genera of primary substances – are *secondary* substances. One reason they count as secondary substances is that they tell us what the primary substances are – that is, are their essence.[5] Aristotle thus sees *some* connection between being a substance and being an essence. But what the *primary* substances are is not determined by appeal to essence; and essences are demoted to the status of (at best) secondary substances.[6]

In the *Met.*, on the other hand, Aristotle is newly sympathetic to Plato's identification of primary substance, form, and essence. He now argues that each primary thing is identical to its essence (Z. 6), and that the form of each thing is its essence, and so is primary substance (1032b1–2). This claim is liable to misinterpretation, however, so let me say a bit more about the *Met.*'s view of things before proceeding further.

In the *Cat.*, some entities called '*eidē*'[7] – substance species – are allowed to be secondary substances and essences. When Aristotle, in the *Met.*, argues that *eidē* – forms – are primary substances, is he arguing that the *Cat.*'s secondary substances (or their universal forms or essences) are primary substances after all – that, as for Plato, certain universals are the primary substances? So it is sometimes thought. G. E. L. Owen, for example, in 'The Platonism of Aristotle', writes that in *Met. Z*, Aristotle argues that:[8]

> if we take any primary subject of discourse and say just what it is, we must be producing a statement of identity, an equation which defines the subject. And this in turn helps to persuade him that the primary subjects of discourse cannot be individuals such as Socrates, who cannot be defined, but species such as men. In the *Categories*, on the other hand, the primary subjects are still the individual man or horse or tree. Aristotle seems at this early stage to be much more hostile than he later becomes to Plato's treatment of the species as a basic and independent subject of discourse. So it becomes tempting to think of this element in *Metaphysics* VII as a return to, or a renewal of sympathy with, Plato.

But I believe that the *eidē* that now count as primary substances are not species, or universals of any sort, but individual forms; it is, e.g., Socrates' individual form or essence, his soul, that now counts as a primary substance. This goes beyond the *Cat.*, insofar as the *Cat.* does not analyse particulars; it does not invoke the notions of compound, form, and matter, nor argue that individual forms are the primary substances. But Aristotle still maintains the *Cat.*'s view that particulars are the primary substances. Hence, when he suggests that Socrates is identical with his form, he does not, as is sometimes said,[9] mean that he is identical with the species man (or to the universal form of that species), but that he is identical with his soul, which is proprietary to him. Aristotle's promotion of form and essence, then, is not a concession to Plato about the priority of universals; there is no 'renewal of sympathy with' Plato on this score. Indeed, the *Met.* is, if anything, more hostile to universals than is the *Cat.*; for it revokes the *Cat.*'s concession that at least some universals are secondary substances. In the *Met.*, no universal is a substance at all (see esp. Z. 13 at, e.g., 1038b8–16, b34–1039a2). though Plato is right to identify primary substance, form and essence, he proposes the wrong candidates for playing these roles.

The claim that the primary substances of the *Met.* are individual forms is, to say the least, highly controversial, and I shall not mount anything like a complete defense of it here. But in the next section I argue that Aristotle's criteria for substance require that all substances be particulars; and in subsequent sections I argue that Aristotle can escape his criticisms of Plato only if his substances are particulars. Aristotle may, of course, be inconsistent, and other evidence might pull us in a different direction. But if we focus on his criteria for substance, and on his criticism of Plato, we are pulled towards individual forms. To defend individual forms is not, however, the main purpose of this paper; the main purpose is to assess the plausibility of Aristotle's criticisms of the claim of PFs to substancehood, and his success in defending his alternative. The first stage in such an analysis must be consideration of Aristotle's criteria for substance, so I turn next to that.

III. *Criteria for Substance*

Although criteria can be culled from many sources, I shall focus on criteria Aristotle commends in the *Cat.* and *Met.*

(1) *Substances persist through change.* In the *Cat.* Aristotle proposes the following *idion* – special feature or distinguishing mark – of substance: 'It seems most distinctive of substance that what is numerically one and the same is able to receive contraries. In no other case could one bring forward anything, numerically one, which is able to receive contraries' (4a10–13). Although (1) is proposed as distinctive of substance, strictly speaking it is distinctive only of primary substance. Aristotle is concerned, not with the fact that, for example, the species man can be pale and dark – that there can be pale and dark men – but with the fact that an individual man can be pale at one time, dark at another. (1) thus requires of (primary) substance that it be able to sustain change through time; (primary) substances are the basic subjects of change.[10]

(1) is necessary and sufficient for being a *primary substance*. But it is not necessary for being a *substance*, since there are secondary substances, and they do not satisfy (1) (except, of course, insofar as their members do).

(2) *Substances are (basic) subjects.* In the *Cat.*, something is a *subject* just in case something can be predicated of it; and something is a *basic* subject just in case it is a token of a type such that tokens of that type are not predicated of anything, but all other sorts of things are ultimately predicated of tokens of that type. In the *Met.*, by contrast, Aristotle explicates the notion of a *subject* (and not just of a basic subject) in terms reminiscent of the *Cat.*'s notion of a *basic subject*. In Z.3 for example, he says that a subject is 'that of which other things are predicated, while it itself is no longer <predicated> of anything' (1028b36–7; but cf. Δ. 8, 1017b23–4, τό θ' ὑποκείμενον ἔσχατον).

In the *Cat.*, being a subject is necessary but not sufficient for being a substance;

and being a basic subject is both necessary and sufficient for being a primary substance (2a11–14; a34–5; b36–3a1). Correspondingly, in the *Cat.*, particulars such as Callias count as basic subjects; but one reason secondary substances are adjudged substances is that they are the next best subjects – they are secondary subjects (2b15–22; b36–3a6).

In the *Met.*, by contrast, being a subject (that is, being one of the *Cat.*'s basic subjects) is apparently both necessary and sufficient for being a substance *tout court* (1029a1–2; 17–19; 1038b15). Since every universal is, in Aristotle's view, necessarily predicated of something (e.g., 1038b15–16), no universal (and so no secondary substance) is a subject. (2) thus requires that the *Met.*'s substances all be particulars.

(3) *Substances are thises* (*tode ti*). In the *Cat.* (3b10–18), Aristotle takes it to be both necessary and sufficient for being a this that something be a particular. Thus he first claims that whatever is indivisible and one in number – that is, is a particular – is a this (3b10–13); he then argues that secondary substances are not thises, because they are said of many things (3b13–18) – that is, are universals. This leaves open the possibility that nonsubstance particulars are thises, and so the *Cat.* seems to allow. In the *Cat.*, then, being a this – that is, a particular – is necessary but not sufficient for being a primary substance; but it is neither necessary nor sufficient for being a substance.

In the *Met.*, the status, explication, and application of the thisness criterion change. First, it is now necessary and sufficient for being a substance;[11] in contrast to the *Cat.*, there are no longer any nonsubstance thises. Second, thisness is no longer explicated in terms of particularity. In truth, Aristotle never provides a clear explanation of the notion; but it seems to convey the idea of determinateness, perhaps of countability, and of being a stable object of reference. And at 1030a4, he suggests that a this must not essentially involve one thing's being said of another. Third, although thisness is no longer explicated in terms of particularity, it still applies only to particulars – though not to *all* particulars, at least not in the primary way. Now every universal, in Aristotle's view, is necessarily said of something; hence none is a this (1038b15–16; b35–1039a2). If no universal is a this, but every substance must be, then, once again, it follows that Aristotle's substances in the *Met.* are all particulars.

Aristotle uses the notion of thisness, not only to exclude universals from the ranks of substance, but also to restrict the range of particulars that so count. In Z.4, for example, he argues that a white man is not a this, since it essentially involves one thing's being said of another – white of the man. Aristotle also seems to believe (a point which perhaps emerges most clearly in Z.11) that a man considered as a compound is not a this, since his form is essentially said of his matter. It is individual forms that count as thises in the primary way, and so they are the primary substances.

*

(1–3) are all present in the *Cat.*; and at least (2–3) are present in the *Met.* as well, though they are there handled differently and used to different ends.[12] In particular, they are all used to show that all substances are particulars. The *Met.* also highlights further criteria, either absent or muted in the *Cat.*:

(4) *Substances are separate (chōris, chōriston).*[13] In *Met.* Z. 1, Aristotle says that substances are naturally prior to nonsubstances, because only they are separate (1028a33–4).[14] 'Separate' is not explained here; but in Δ.11, Aristotle says that substances are naturally prior to other things because they 'can be without the other things, while the others cannot be without them' (1019a1–4). A is separate from B, then, just in case A can exist without B. Aristotle believes that substances are separate from other things, though not conversely. Like (2–3), (4) appears to be a necessary and sufficient condition for substance in the *Met.* Since only substance is separate, it is sufficient; and since all substances must be separate, it is necessary.

In both the *Cat.* (2b3–6) and *Met.* (e.g. 1086b3–5), Aristotle denies that universals (and so the *Cat.*'s secondary substances) are separate.[15] In the *Cat.*, the species and genera of substance, though not separate, are nonetheless allowed to be secondary substances. In the *Met.*, however, the fact that universals are not separate debars them from the ranks of substance altogether. Once again, then, the substances of the *Met.* must all be particulars.

Notice that although the *Cat.* denies that universals are separate, it does not say that (primary) substance is separate. In contrast to the *Met.*, the *Cat.* contents itself with the weaker claim that everything else is dependent on the primary substances; but this leaves open the possibility that primary substances are similarly dependent on, and so are not separate from, other things. In the *Met.*, the separation of substance is stressed, and used against universals.

(5) *Substances are prior in definition.* In Z.1, Aristotle says that substances are prior in definition because 'in the definition of each thing there must be a definition of the *ousia*' (1028a35–6). The force of (5) might be:

(5a) For all x, to define x, one must define its essence.

Or it might be:

(5b) For all x, to define x, one must include a definition of a relevant substance.

Aristotle believes that definitions state essences (e.g., 1017b21–2; 1036a6–7); so he believes (5a). But (5) is a criterion for *substance* only if read as (5b). These two readings are connected, however, since Aristotle argues that to state the essence of anything, one must state the definition of (or at least mention) a relevant substance; hence (5a) implies (5b). Aristotle also argues (in Z.4) that the primary substances are the primary definables; and that the primary definables are identical to their essences (Z.6). Hence the essences mentioned in (5a) will be identical to the substances mentioned in (5b), in the case where x is a primary substance. Notice that one result of this is that primary substances are essences.

Commitment to (5) is at best muted in the *Cat.*; but insofar as it is present, it appears to favor secondary over primary substances. For one reason secondary substances are adjudged substances is that they answer the 'What is it?' question about primary substances – they tell us what they are, are their essences (2b7–14; 2b29–37). (Some) definitions state, or are of, secondary substances; though the content of such definitions applies to, or is true of, primary substances, primary substances are not themselves definable nor, though they have essences (their secondary substances), are they themselves essences.

In the *Met.*, by contrast, (5) is explicit; and it too now appears to be necessary and sufficient for substance.[16] Now if, in the *Met.* as in the *Cat.*, (5) favors universals, then Aristotle is in difficulty. For as the discussion in (2–4) reveals, Aristotle now denies that there are any universal substances; yet (5) is supposed to determine substance. To be consistent, then, he must argue that (5) determines particular substances.

(6) *Substances are prior in knowledge.* In Z.1, Aristotle argues that substances are prior in knowledge because 'we think we especially know each thing when we know what it is – what man or fire is – rather than when we know $<$ what $>$ quality or quantity or where $<$ it is $>$; since we also know each of these $<$ only $>$ when we know what the quantity or quality is' (1028a36–b2).

Aristotle does not explicitly use '*ousia*' in stating (6); and his use of '*ti estin*' suggests he is making a point analogous to (5a): to know something is to know what it is, that is, its essence. This point is relevant to the epistemological priority of substance, however, since Aristotle argues that to know the essence of anything, one must know a relevant substance. For to know something is to know its definition; and we saw, in discussing (5), that an adequate definition of anything must include a definition of a substance. Hence to know anything, one must know a definition of a substance. This again suggests that primary substances are essences. For presumably the primary knowables are the primary definables; and the primary definables, as we have seen, are essences.

In the *Cat.*, commitment to (6) is muted; but insofar as it is present, it, like (5), appears to favor secondary over primary substances. In the *Met.*, by contrast, (6), like each of (2–5), is a necessary and sufficient condition for substance; and, again, since universals no longer count as substances, Aristotle must, to avoid contradiction, show how particular substances satisfy it.

*

Our survey of criteria has brought to light some interesting differences between the *Cat.* and *Met.* The *Cat.* uses fewer criteria, at least explicitly; and different criteria enjoy different statuses–some are necessary but not sufficient for being a primary substance, some are necessary and sufficient, and so on. Further, different criteria favor different candidates: (1–3) favor certain particulars as the primary substances; (5–6) (insofar as they are present) favor certain universals as secondary substances – though the favor is not so great as to challenge the primacy of particulars. (4) is not used at all.

In the *Met.*, by contrast, each of (2–6) (where some of these are now explained differently) is apparently both necessary and sufficient for being a substance *tout court*. Moreover, all substances are now particulars; there are no longer any universal substances.

Contrary to Owen and others, then, the *Met.* does not display increased sympathy with Plato on the status of universals; it is if anything more hostile to them. For it revokes the *Cat.*'s concession that at least some universals count as secondary substances; the criteria for substance debar all universals from the ranks of substance.

In other respects, however, the *Met.* is more sympathetic to Plato. For the particulars that now count as primary substances are individual forms; Aristotle, like Plato, now promotes forms and essences (though non-Platonic ones) as primary substances. Further, his use of criteria owes something to Plato too. (1–3), the criteria highlighted in the *Cat.*, are unPlatonic; in the *Cat.*, Aristotle fights Plato on foreign territory. But (4–6) are Platonic criteria (or so at least Aristotle believes): the battle now moves to home turf; the *Met.* engages in a dialectical debate absent in the *Cat.* But although this in a way displays increased sympathy with Plato, in a way it does not. For Aristotle argues that even if we give Plato his criteria, PFs do not qualify as substances. Let us see how well he prosecutes his case.

IV. *Platonic Substances*

(1) Since PFs cannot sustain change through time, they obviously fail (1) – just as do the *Cat.*'s secondary substances. But I doubt that Plato would be much worried; he would challenge the criterion. To be sure, he might argue, it might be reasonable to insist that the basic entities in the universe be stable, persist from one moment to the next. But of course PFs are stable, indeed, eminently so. If (1) is weakened to stability, it is plausible; but then PFs satisfy it. If it is strengthened in Aristotle's way, it is not plausible.

Aristotle might reply that stability is not enough; the stable entities must explain changes objects in the world undergo – yet PFs cannot explain change (991a 8–11; 991b). Now it might be reasonable to require explanatory relevance to change; but I think Plato could fairly insist that PFs are explanatorily relevant to change. To be sure, they do not *initiate* change; they are not efficient causes of change.[17] But as Aristotle should be the first to agree, efficient causes are only one sort of explanation of change. Not would Aristotle be reasonable to require that whatever explains change must itself change; indeed, his own prime mover explains at least some changes but does not itself change. PFs, being properties, are relevant – indeed necessary – to explaining some changes, even though they themselves do not change; for explanations of change require reference to the properties involved; and PFs are among the properties there are.

Aristotle may be right, then, to require that substances be stable and explanatorily relevant to change; if (1) is so weakened, it is at least a reasonable necessary condition on substance – but one PFs satisfy. If, however, it is strengthened so as to require that substances be capable of sustaining change through time, then it is not a reasonable necessary condition on substance, and so PFs' failure to satisfy it is not to their discredit.

Aristotle might, however, fairly protest (though Plato would no doubt reject the protest) that (1) is a reasonable sufficient condition for substance – for it seems reasonable to assume that among the entities explanatorily relevant to change are those that undergo and sustain change. PFs' failure to satisfy a sufficient condition for substance does not show that they are not substances at all; but if other entities than PFs satisfy (1), that would show that PFs are not the *only* substances.

(2) Just as Aristotle denies that PFs satisfy (1), so he denies they satisfy (2); PFs are not basic subjects. Indeed, in the *Met.* they are not subjects at all.

Plato would probably agree that PFs are not basic subjects; in the *Timaeus* he seems to accord the receptacle that role (see, e.g., 49e7ff; 50b5ff). But Plato would again simply reject the criterion. To be sure, he might argue, it might be reasonable to insist that the basic entities be subjects in the following sense: 'those subjects of discourse to which all our descriptions of the world must, at any rate when properly analysed in canonical form, make direct or indirect reference'.[18] But PFs are basic subjects in this weakened sense; for to call something a basic subject in this sense is only to call it a fundamental explanatory entity. It is only by tightening (2) up and restricting it to (basic) subjects of properties, that Aristotle can use it against Plato; but since (2) so construed is an implausible criterion for substance, this does not harm Plato.

I think Plato would be right to protest against (2), construed as a necessary condition on substance. What, after all, makes subjects prior to their properties? Perhaps Aristotle would say, appealing back to (1): the fact that subjects can sustain change of property through time. But even if this is so, I have suggested that properties are equally necessary to explaining change – we should not be forced to choose between them. Or perhaps Aristotle would say that subjects are favored over properties because properties depend on, cannot exist without, their subjects. But it is far from clear that properties are dependent on their subjects; perhaps they can exist uninstantiated.[19] It is difficult to see, however, how subjects can exist without properties; do not properties then have the edge? Or are not properties and their subjects at least mutually dependent? (See further, IV (4) and V (4).) Or perhaps Aristotle would say that we invoke properties to explain particulars, and that explananda are prior to explanantia. But why are not explanantia at least as basic or fundamental as explananda?

(2), then, is not a plausible necessary condition on substance. but Aristotle might with more reason defend its sufficiency – for subjects, no less than their properties, seem necessary to explaining change; explananda seem as fundamental as explanantia. And although this would not dislodge PFs as substances, it would show, if other things satisfy (2), that PFs are not the only substances.

(3) In contrast to (1–2), Aristotle seems to believe that PFs satisfy (3). At least, he insists that Plato treats PFs as thises (*S.E.* 22; *Met.* Z.13). This might be thought an advantage of PFs; but in Aristotle's view, it is not. He argues that because PFs are thises, they are vulnerable to the TMA – a vicious infinite regress. Though PFs satisfy (3), this leads to severe difficulties; satisfaction of (3) is thus no boon.

Aristotle in effect levels a dilemma against Plato: either (*a*) PFs are thises, and so are vulnerable to the TMA; or else (*b*) they are not thises, and so cannot be substances. On the face of it, this is an odd criticism for Aristotle to press. For (3) is an Aristotelian criterion. If PFs are vulnerable to this dilemma, how can Aristotle escape it?

The answer, in brief, is as follows: PFs are not vulnerable to the TMA merely because they are thises, but because (so Aristotle believes) they are *also* universals; it is because they are allegedly universals and particulars at once that the TMA threatens. Aristotle can avoid the dilemma, then, if ASs are thises but not also universals. Here is one reason to doubt that ASs are universals of any sort – for if they were, they would succumb to Aristotle's dilemma.[20]

Whether or not Aristotle can escape his dilemma, I believe Plato can: he would protest against both (*a*) and (*b*). As to (*a*): if we think of the *Cat.*'s account of thisness, in terms of particularity, then I doubt that PFs are thises; they are universals but not particulars.

Why does Aristotle disagree? Later (in IV (4)) I shall sketch an argument of Aristotle according to which the separation of PFs implies their particularity; but this argument fails. Of course, even if separation does not imply particularity, PFs might nonetheless be particulars. Some (perhaps including Aristotle) believe that self-predication has this result; but this is unclear. First it is unclear that Plato even accepts self-predication, as that notion is traditionally construed.[21] But second, even if he does, it does not, in general at least, imply particularity. The Form or property or universal of immobility, e.g., can be immobile without thereby being a particular; all universals are immobile, but they are not thereby all particulars. It is not clear, then, that PFs are particulars, and so not clear that they are thises, as the *Cat.* conceives them.

If we turn, on the other hand, to the *Met.*'s account of thisness, in terms of one thing's not being essentially predicated of another, and determinacy, then I think Plato would say that PFs are thises, and so satisfy (3): for since they can exist uninstantiated, they are not what they are in virtue of being said of anything; and they can also be stably referred to.[22] But this does not, *pace* Aristotle, turn them into particulars; not only particulars satisfy (3), understood in the *Met.*'s way. Since I am sympathetic to the possibility of uninstantiated universals, this reply seems reasonable to me.

Either, then, PFs fail (3), construed in terms of particularity; or else they satisfy it, construed in the *Met.*'s way, but do so without thereby becoming particulars.

If PFs are not thises, are they not vulnerable to (*b*)? Here I think Plato would follow a by now familiar ploy: (3), construed in terms of particularity, is not a plausible criterion for substance, and so PFs' failure at (3), so construed, does not impugn their status as substances. And since even Aristotle does not believe that (3), so construed, is a sufficient condition for substance, the fact that other sorts of entities than PFs satisfy (3) would not even lead us to question PFs' status as *the* substances.

If, on the other hand (3) is instead construed in the *Met.*'s way, then, as Aristotle believes, it may well be at least a plausible necessary condition for substance; for we expect substances to be determinate, stable objects of reference. But as we have seen, PFs (despite Aristotle's view to the contrary) satisfy (3) so construed.

PFs fail (3), then, only if it is implausible; they satisfy (3) on its more plausible reading – but they do so without being particulars, or succumbing to the TMA.

(4) Just as Aristotle insists that PFs are thises, so he insists they are separate (see, e.g., 1078b30–31; 1086a32–b13); and he appears to be correct. At least, in the *Timaeus*, Plato seems committed to the separation of at least some PFs. For there he commits himself to the following two claims:

(*a*) Forms have always existed.

(*b*) Sensibles have not always existed.

(*a*) and (*b*) imply:

(*c*) There was a time at which Forms, but no sensibles, existed.

And (*c*) implies that at least some Forms are separate. For if, as (*c*) says, there was a time when some Forms, but no sensibles, existed, and if separation is just the capacity for independent existence, then obviously at least some PFs are separate. Here, then is one criterion for substance Aristotle correctly says PFs satisfy.

Although Aristotle is correct to say that Plato is committed to the separation of some PFs, he is wrong to suggest, as he seems to, that (4) is a Platonic criterion for substance, a criterion Plato argues his PFs satisfy. It is in fact surprisingly difficult to find any commitment to separation in the dialogues; the issue is never explicitly broached, and Plato certainly never offers (4) as a criterion for substance. Aristotle could thus have prosecuted his dialectical case against Plato quite fairly without invoking (4); and in view of the difficulties he himself has with (4) (see V (4) below), this would have been to his advantage.

Although Aristotle concedes that PFs satisfy (4), he argues that their satisfaction of it is not to their credit, since severe difficulties then ensue. For if PFs are separate, they are thises, and so particulars; but since they are also universals, they are incoherent entities – both universals and particulars at once.[23] This charge, however, fails; for the separation of PFs does not imply their particularity. (Notice, however, that since *Aristotle* believes that separation implies particularity, and since he insists that his substances are separate, he presumably believes that his substances are particulars.) If separation is just the capacity for independent existence; and if PFs are universals; then to say that they are separate is just to say that they can exist uninstantiated; and this does not turn them into particulars.

Why does Aristotle disagree? I can think of only one explanation. In *De Int.* 7, Aristotle defines universals as follows: 'by universal I mean that which by its nature is predicated of many things' (17a39–40). One might suppose he means only that universals *can* be predicated of many things; but he seems to mean instead that they must *actually* be predicated of many things. If, then, one countenances the possibility of uninstantiated universals, one countenances the possibility of something that can exist that is not actually predicated of many things. This cannot, by definition, be a universal; what else can it be, then, but a particular? Hence allegedly separate universals must actually be particulars.

This is not, however, so much an argument against separate universals as a definitional fiat that they cannot exist. Unless Aristotle can provide plausible reasons for his definition – and I cannot find any – his argument simply begs the question against the Platonist. And since I am myself sympathetic to the possibilty of uninstantiated universals, I am inclined to believe that PFs can be separate, while still retaining their status as universals. I conclude, then, that PFs nonproblematically satisfy (4).

(5–6) I believe Plato would argue that PFs satisfy (5–6). In the *Meno*, he argues that knowledge is true belief plus an explanatory account (an *aitias logismos*) (98a). In *Phaedo* 100, he argues that PFs are *aitiai*, basic causes or explanatory entities. Hence, adequate accounts must refer to PFs; all definitions, and so all knowledge (since knowledge requires definitions, *logoi*), involves reference to PFs. Similarly, in *Rep.* 5, Plato argues that knowledge involves appropriate reference to PFs. To know or define PFs, however, one need not – indeed, one cannot – first know or define other things; knowledge and definition of PFs is a precondition for knowledge and definition of anything. Hence, PFs are prior in knowledge and definition.

Further, Plato presumably believes that PFs are thus prior because he accepts the connection between knowledge, definition, and essence; it is because he believes that PFs are the essences of things, and that knowledge and definitions are of essences, that he believes that PFs are prior in knowledge and definition. Hence, for Plato as for Aristotle, constraints on knowledge and definition suggest that the primary substances are essences.

We have seen that Aristotle allows that PFs satisfy (4); does he also believe they satisfy (5–6)? Since he reject the existence of PFs, he of course does not believe they are really thus prior; still, does he believe Plato has a plausible case here?

One might believe he should. First, he agrees that PFs are at least universals; and he sometimes says that universals are prior in definition – perhaps, more strongly, that they are the only objects of knowledge and definition (see, e.g., *Met.* 1018 b32–3; Z.15; *An. Po. passim*). Second, he agrees that PFs are at least intended to be the essences of things (e.g. *Met.* 991b1–3 = 1079b35–1080a2); and so again he should concede that they are plausibly said to be prior in knowledge and definition. Aristotle sometimes seems to suggest that at least Plato would reason in this way. In *Met.* A. 6, M. 4 and 9, for example, he suggests that Plato introduced PFs as stable objects of knowledge and definition; the possibility of knowledge and definition requires the existence of unchanging, nonsensible universals that the Platonists call 'Forms'. And in H.1, he says that PFs are thought to be substances for the same reasons that universals and genera are (1042a15–16) – presumably because they are all thought to be the essences of things, and so basic objects of knowledge and definition.

But Aristotle protests that this line of thought is implausible; he argues that, to the contrary, PFs are unknowable and indefinable. If so, they are not prior in knowledge and definition. Thus, in *Met.* Z.15, he argues that definitions are of universals and so PFs, being particulars, cannot be defined. In M.10, a parallel point is pressed for knowledge: since knowledge is of universals, and PFs are particulars, PFs are unknowable.

We have already seen why Aristotle believes PFs are particulars: because they are separate, and separation, Aristotle believes, implies particularity. Aristotle thus in effect now levels the following dilemma against Plato: (*a*) If PFs satisfy all of (4–6), they are incoherent entities, both universals and particulars at once – for satisfaction of (4) requires particularity, whereas satisfaction of (5–6) requires universality; (*b*) If PFs satisfy only (4) (and so are particulars), or only (5–6) (and so are universals), they fail to satisfy at least one necessary condition for substance. Either way, PFs cannot be the primary substances.

Once again, it is puzzling to see Aristotle levelling this dilemma. For (4–6) are not just criteria Plato, perhaps confusedly, commends; they are Aristotle's own criteria. If Plato is vulnerable to this dilemma, is not Aristotle vulnerable to it as well? Later we shall need to ask whether Aristotle escapes this dilemma and, if so, if he does so in a way that leaves intact his criticism of Plato.

For now it is worth noting that Plato has an easy escape route: he would simply reject (*a*). Separation does not imply particularity; hence PFs can satisfy all of (4–6), without incoherence, as universals. Since Aristotle believes that separation implies particularity, however, the same escape route is not open to him.

Aristotle might argue that even if all of this is so, there is another way in which the separation of PFs is incompatible with their being prior in knowledge and definition. If PFs are separate from sensible particulars, they cannot be their essences; and if they are not their essences, they are 'no help towards knowledge of them' (*Met.* 991a 12–13 = 1079b 15–16). Even if PFs can be known, then, such knowledge would be useless; and so, again, they are not prior in knowledge and definition.

Thus in *Met.* Z.6 Aristotle argues that the essence of a primary thing is identical to that thing; if PFs are separate from sensible particulars, they cannot be identical to them and so, if sensible particulars are primary things, PFs cannot be their essences. Further, in Z.13 Aristotle insists that the essence of x must be peculiar to x; but the PF of man, e.g. (if there is one), is not peculiar to Socrates and so cannot be his essence. (Notice that these arguments again pull us in the direction of individual forms. At least, if Socrates has an essence at all (and he seems to), his essence must be peculiar to him; since no universal is peculiar to any particular, his essence must be a particular. But since essences are forms, there are individual forms; and they must be Aristotle's primary substances.)

Neither of these arguments depends on the dubious claim that separation implies particularity; and both strike me as more promising. Nonetheless, Plato is not without his resources. To the argument in Z.6, he would no doubt reply that sensible things are not primary things, and so need not be identical to their essences. On the other hand, PFs are primary things, and they are identical to their essences. Either way, Plato can accept the claim in Z.6 – that primary things are identical to their essences – without abandoning the claim that PFs are the essences of sensibles.

The argument of Z.13 is in effect an argument for individual essences; whereas Plato, in putting forth PFs as the essences of things, opts for general or universal essences – as had Aristotle in the *Cat.* Since I do not know whether there are individual essences, I do not know who has the better position here; certainly both views have serious philosophical credentials. But even if Aristotle is right on this score, it shows only that PFs cannot be the whole essence of any sensible; it does not show that they cannot be part of their essence,[24] or that they are not knowable or definable. Indeed, unless we agree with Aristotle about the primacy of particulars, it does not even show that PFs are not prior in knowledge and definition.

If we accept the view Aristotle himself often advocates – that universals are prior in knowledge and definition – and agree, against Aristotle, that PFs are universals but not particulars, then PFs fare quite well on (5–6). The most Aristotle can persuade us of is that PFs cannot be the whole essence of any sensible; but that falls short of showing failure at (5–6).

To summarize so far: Aristotle is correct to say that PFs fail (1–2); but this does not impugn their status as substances, since (1–2) are not plausible necessary conditions on substance. The most Aristotle can fairly argue is that (1–2) are plausible sufficient conditions, so that if other things satisfy them, PFs are not the only substances. Aristotle is probably wrong, on the other hand, to argue that PFs satisfy (3) (if, that is, (3) involves particularity); but this does not even disqualify them as *the* substances, since (3) so construed is not, even by Aristotle's lights, a necessary or sufficient condition on substance. PFs do, however, satisfy (3) construed in the *Met.*'s way.

Aristotle believes PFs satisfy (3) because he believes they satisfy (4). They do satisfy (4); but this does not turn them into particulars – PFs can satisfy (4) as universals. Aristotle argues that PFs fail (5–6), again largely on the grounds that they are particulars; this argument fails, since PFs are universals, not particulars – and Aristotle himself (sometimes) believes universals satisfy (5–6). Perhaps PFs are inadequate as the whole essence of particulars; but this is insufficient to show failure at (5–6).

PFs, then, fail the unPlatonic criteria (1–3) – the only criteria pressed in the *Cat.*; but this does not disqualify them as substances. On the other hand, they fare quite well on the allegedly Platonic criteria (4–6) highlighted in the *Met.* Though the dialectical project of the *Met.* is more impressive than is the quick attack in the *Cat.*, it too fails to dislodge PFs from the ranks of substance.

Aristotle's offensive attack thus fails: he has not succeeded in persuading us that PFs are not substances. But a defensive strategy might still be successful: for perhaps Aristotle can persuade us that even if PFs are substances, they are not the only substances. And this might be accomplished in a variety of ways. If, for example, (1–2) are plausible sufficient conditions on substance, and if ASs satisfy them, this should persuade us to add ASs to the list of substances. Or if ASs do at least as well on (4–6) as PFs do, that too should persuade us to accept ASs along with PFs–if, that is, (4–6) are plausible criteria for substance.

V. *Aristotelian Substances*

(1) Aristotle is surely correct to say that the *Cat.*'s primary substances can persist while changing;[25] and since PFs do not satisfy (1), ASs fare better here. Since (1) is only plausible construed as a sufficient condition this should not lead us to prefer ASs to PFs; but it does give us some reason to add ASs to the list of substances.

It is worth noting, however, that although the *Cat.*'s primary substances fare better on (1) than PFs do, various difficulties nonetheless arise. For example, Aristotle claims that *only* his primary substances satisfy (1). Yet by the time of the *Physics*, he acknowledges that matter appears to satisfy it as well – a lump of bronze, e.g., can sustain the change of shape that results in its constituting a ring. Perhaps this is one reason why (1) is muted in the *Met.*

(2) To be a (basic) subject, recall, is to be a token of a type none of whose members is predicated of anything, and is such that all other sorts of things are predicated of tokens of that type. We have seen that PFs (in common with all universals) fail (2). But, again, this is not to their discredit, since (2) is not a plausible necessary condition on substance. Still, we have agreed that (2) is a plausible sufficient condition on substance; if Aristotle's substances satisfy it (in which case they must be particulars), then once again we have reason to add them to the list of substances.

In the *Cat.*, Aristotle claims that his primary substances are basic subjects; everything else is predicated of (said of or in) them, and they are not predicated of (said of or in) anything. But unlike *Met.*, the *Cat.* does not wrestle with the notions of form and matter; and in the *Met.*, where Aristotle wishes to promote individual form as primary substance, it appears that forms are predicated of matter. How, then, can they satisfy (2)? Indeed, it looks as though matter (or prime matter) is the only subject. For only matter is not predicated of anything; and everything else is ultimately predicated of it (Z.3, 1029a7–27). (2) thus threatens to dislodge not only PFs, but also Aristotle's favored candidates. (Notice, though, that the threat is from *matter*, not universals.) Plato is unmoved; he rejects the criterion, perhaps because of the difficulties just adverted to. But Aristotle retains the criterion; so he needs to confront the difficulties.

And of course he does. He attempts to resist the descent to matter by arguing that, for example, matter does not do so well on other criteria for substance, such as separation and thisness (Z.3, 1029a27–30). This is not to the present point, however, which is that Aristotle's alleged primary substances do not do as well as he would like on the subject criterion.

A better argument is this one: that the *way* in which form is predicated of matter is importantly different from the way in which other things are predicated of form. To be a (basic) subject is to be a token of a type (i) none of whose members is predicated of anything but matter; and (ii) such that all other sorts of things than matter are predicated of tokens of that type.

This may allow individual forms to be (basic) subjects. But it does so by modifying the criterion. That might look like cheating – altering the criterion so that it picks out the desired candidates. But it is not cheating if Aristotle can produce a good argument to show that his modified subject criterion is preferable to the initial one – preferable, that is, not just because it yields the candidates he would like, but for reasons of general appeal. Perhaps Aristotle means to signal that this is his justification for the revision when he remarks (Z.3, 1029a9–10) that the initial criterion is inadequate and unclear. Whether or not Aristotle has a good argument here is, of course, another question, and not one I shall try to answer here. Here the main point is that, although PFs fail (2), so too may Aristotle's favored candidates; but however well ASs fare here, this does not give us a reason to prefer them to PFs, since the criterion is not a plausible necessary condition on substance. Insofar as ASs satisfy (2), however, and insofar as it is a plausible sufficient condition, that gives us reason to believe that ASs, as well as PFs, are among the substances.

(3) We have seen that PFs are not thises, as the *Cat.* conceives of thises, but are thises – though not particulars – as the *Met.* conceives of them. Are ASs thises? They certainly are on the *Cat.*'s construction; for they are particulars. This, however, is no reason to count ASs as substances, since (3) so construed is not a plausible necessary or sufficient condition for substance.

Are ASs thises on the *Met.*'s understanding of that notion? So Aristotle claims (1030a3ff.), and I am not concerned to dispute the point. Though many individual forms are predicated of some matter, they are not what they are in virtue of being so predicated – in contrast to compounds, or to such accidental unities as a white man: here no doubt is one reason for opting for individual forms over compounds as the particulars that count as primary substances. And it is also, as we have seen, a reason for preferring them to universals since, in Aristotle's view, universals are necessarily predicated of many things.

Notice, though, that the fact that ASs are thises does not render them vulnerable to the TMA, as Aristotle urged PFs would be, if they were thises – for ASs are only particulars, and not also universals. Here is another reason to believe that Aristotle acknowledges individual forms; for the forms that are thises (and so primary substances) cannot be universals, on pain of the TMA.

ASs, then, do better on (1–2), and on (3) construed in terms of particularity, than do PFs. The best Platonic defense in the face of this fact – and I have argued that it is a good one – is to argue that (1–2), and (3) so construed, are not plausible necessary conditions on substance, so that ASs' success over PFs does not impugn PFs' status as substances. On the other hand, insofar as at least (1–2) are plausible sufficient conditions, Aristotle can fairly insist that PFs are not the only substances; ASs qualify as well. This is, to be sure, a more hospitable conclusion than Aristotle wishes to endorse; but it nonetheless involves a significant criticism of Plato, for whom PFs appear to exhaust the ranks of substance.

What, now, of (4–6)? I shall suggest that PFs satisfy (4–6) at least as well as, perhaps better than, ASs – as Aristotle himself should (in some moods) agree (at least in the case of (5–6)). Of course, this gives us no reason to prefer PFs to ASs, unless (4–6) are plausible criteria for substance; so that too needs to be investigated.

*

(4) In the *Cat.*, Aristotle wisely does not insist that his primary substances are separate, though he less wisely insists that no universals are – less wisely because, as we have seen, universals may well enjoy the capacity for independent existence. In the *Met.*, Aristotle retains his belief that universals are not separate; but he now insists that substance is separate. This insistence, however, is not clearly justified.

Consider compounds first – say Socrates, considered as a compound of form and matter. Socrates, on Aristotle's view, cannot exist and fail to be a man. But then, the secondary substance or species man must exist if Socrates does. (This is so even in the *Met.*, where man no longer counts as a secondary substance.) But if Socrates cannot exist unless man does, he is not independent of, and so is not separate from, man. Similar remarks apply in other cases. For example, although Socrates can of course exist even if he is not tan, he cannot exist if he is not colored in some way; hence he is not independent of color or, therefore, of nonsubstance generally. Nor are individual forms separate. Just as the compound Socrates cannot exist unless man does, so no individual form of man can exist unless man (the universal, however conceived) does. PFs, however, are separate from particulars; and so they, but not ASs, satisfy (4).[26]

One might argue that this is no reason to prefer PFs to ASs, since (4) is not a plausible condition on substance. All that is plausible is the weaker claim of ontological basicness, that the basic entities in the universe be such that other things depend on them. (This claim is weaker because it allows mutual dependence.)

This is a reasonable claim: separation may be sufficient for basicness; but it does not seem to be necessary. It does seem reasonable, however, to suppose that basicness involves other entities being dependent on the basic ones; indeed, this seems constitutive of ontological basicness.

Weakening (4) in this way turns it into a plausible condition on substance. But does this help Aristotle? notice first that Plato would of course argue that PFs satisfy not only (4) but also the weaker claim of ontological basicness; sensibles depend on PFs.[27] But do ASs also satisfy our new version of (4)? Can Aristotle plausibly argue that they are ontologically basic? If, as I have suggested, universals are separate, then of course they are not dependent on ASs, and so ASs are not ontologically basic with respect to them. But if other sorts of things are dependent on ASs, ASs might nonetheless count as ontologically basic. One might argue, for example, that individual nonsubstances (Callias' whiteness, as opposed to the universal, whiteness) or events depend on ASs; if so, ASs are ontologically basic at least in that *some* other sorts of things depend on them. This is, however, a weaker version of ontological basicness than Aristotle himself defends for ASs in the *Cat.* (2b3–6), where he claims that *all* (and not just some) other sorts of things depend on ASs. Still, this weaker version of ontological basicness gives a reasonable sense to the notion, and allows ASs to satisfy it. Hence both PFs and ASs can be allowed to satisfy the new version of (4).

Aristotle himself seems to see the need to modify (4) – though not in the way I have suggested, in terms of ontological basicness. In H.1 (1042a28–31), he distinguishes between being separate without qualification (*haplōs*) and being separate in definition (*logō*(i)). He claims that although compounds are separate without qualification – that is, can exist without other things – some forms are only separate in definition – that is, can be defined without reference to other things. It is now apparently sufficient for satisfying (4), then, that something be separate in definition.

This suggestion, however, involves at least four difficulties. First, Aristotle in effect concedes that some of his own substances do not satisfy (4), but at best a weakened or modified version of it. To be sure, we earlier urged, on Plato's behalf, that Aristotle's criteria (1–3) are plausible only if modified or weakened. But this involved Plato rejecting Aristotle's criteria; whereas now Aristotle is rejecting his own criteria.

Second, Aristotle still insists that compounds are separate without qualification; but that seems false.

Third, if to define other things one needs to include a definition of substance, then the modified version of (4) collapses into (5); but as we shall shortly see, it is unclear that Aristotle's primary substances satisfy (5). If this is so, then the retreat from (4) to (5) is of no help.

Fourth, the retreat threatens to undermine one of Aristotle's criticisms of Plato.

We saw before that Aristotle argued that PFs cannot satisfy all of (4–6) without incoherence – for (4) requires particularity, whereas (5–6) require universality. Yet if Aristotle now collapses (4) into (5), he can no longer argue that joint satisfaction of (4) and (5) is incoherent; for to satisfy (5), now, just is to satisfy (4). (To this, I suppose Aristotle could reply that although satisfaction of (5) is sufficient for satisfying (4), PFs are in fact separate without qualification, so incoherence still threatens. But we have seen that Plato has an effective reply to this argument.)

PFs, then, fare better on (4) than ASs do. If, however, (4) is altered to a weak version of ontological basicness – which yields a more plausible condition than (4) – then PFs and ASs both satisfy it. Aristotle, however, apparently modifies (4), not in terms of ontological basicness, but in terms of being separate in definition. Let us see, then, how well ASs fare on (5), and its close companion (6).

(5–6) Aristotle begins *Met.* M.10 by raising a dilemma that, he says, threatens both himself and the Platonist: substances must be separate; whatever is separate is a particular; particulars are unknowable; but substances must be knowable. This is just the dilemma we earlier saw Aristotle force on Plato (IV (5–6)); now he acknowledges that he faces it as well. How does he avoid the dilemma? And does he do so in such a way as to leave intact his criticism of Plato?

Aristotle's solution is to insist that substances must be separate, and so particulars;[28] but he insists that particulars – or at least some particulars – are knowable after all. Hence Aristotle, like Plato, rejects (*a*) of the dilemma (see IV (5–6)); but he rejects it by insisting that particulars can be known and defined, whereas Plato rejects it by insisting that universals are separate, but not thereby particulars. We have seen that Plato's response is effective; is Aristotle's?

He distinguishes between actual and potential knowledge; he then claims that actual knowledge, being definite (*horismenon*), is of something definite – a particular; whereas potential knowledge being universal and indefinite, is of what is universal and indefinite, or indefinable (*ahoriston*, 1087a17). One sees color coincidentally, by seeing this token color; or studies the letter A by studying a particular token of the letter-type A.

Aristotle is claiming at least that one can recognize individual objects as tokens of types, or as instances of universals. If this were all he were arguing, one might protest that this recognitive ability is not sufficient to make particulars prior in knowledge or definition; indeed, it is not even sufficient to make them knowable or definable, as Aristotle normally understands those notions. But Aristotle seems to go further, and to insist that particulars are definite or definable, universals indefinite or indefinable (1087a16–18). This stronger claim allows particulars to be knowable and definable; but it is inconsistent with other claims Aristotle makes, such as the claim in Z. 15, that particulars are indefinable. The claim in M.10 thus seems to be either too weak, or else to contradict other central Aristotelian claims.

Even if this could be resolved, is there a point against the Platonist here? Has Aristotle argued that his own substances satisfy (5–6), but that PFs cannot? If we focus on the weak point about recognition, then perhaps Aristotle would argue as follows: we can come to know various universals, or acquire general concepts, only by first learning to recognize and identify various particulars. But these must be this-world particulars, such as compounds and their forms, and not other-worldly particulars, such as PFs. Hence forms and compounds are prior in learning and recognition, whereas PFs cannot be.

In reply, I think Plato would appeal to his doctrine of Anamnesis, and argue that PFs are prior in learning; we can identify objects in this world only because we knew PFs in another world. Aristotle seems to believe that there are two neatly separable stages in learning, as though one first identifies particulars, and only later acquires general concepts.

Though I think Aristotle is right to attack parts of the doctrine of Anamnesis, as he does, for example, in the *An. Po.*, Plato at least sees that we do not first identify particulars, and only later apply general concepts to them; to identify anything, one must already possess general concepts. That is the core of truth in the doctrine of Anamnesis that Aristotle's simple account of concept acquisition ignores.[29]

To learn about properties, however, it is not clear that we need first, or as well, to have access to sensible particulars. Certainly, as even Hume agrees, we can form the idea of a shade of blue we have never seen; so we can at least form ideas of properties independently of particulars that instantiate those very properties.[30] But perhaps, as Leibniz may believe, we need experience of *some* particulars to become aware even of our innate ideas.[31] If so, perhaps the best conclusion to draw, in the case of learning and recognition, is the hospitable one we have suggested in other cases: neither sensible particulars nor PFs (universals) are prior to the other; both are necessary to learning and recognition, to the way we view the world.

What if we turn, then, to scientific-knowledge and definition? If we explicate these notions in Aristotle's usual way, such that there is scientific-knowledge and definition only of universals, then PFs, but not ASs, satisfy (5–6); for PFs, but not ASs, are universals.

One might again argue that this is no reason to prefer PFs to ASs, since (5–6) so construed are at best plausible sufficient conditions for substance. That may well be true, and I shall shortly consider various modifications of (5–6). But notice first that there is a difficulty in *Aristotle*'s pressing this argument; for it involves conceding that his substances do not satisfy his own criteria but, at best, modified versions of them.

Still, how might (5–6) be modified so as to yield more plausible criteria? One might argue that the best sort of knowledge and definition must at least concern permanent features of the universe. From this point of view, PFs, being eternal or everlasting, are better off than many Aristotelian forms, which are perishable. But perhaps Aristotle could insist that at least the prime mover, or god, or the stars, fare as well as do PFs; for they too are imperishable.

One might argue that (5–6) are still too strong to be reasonable criteria for substance. Surely the best sort of knowledge and definition will refer, not just to universals or to permanent features of the universe, but also to various sublunar phenomena, not all of which are permanent. After all, we are concerned to understand the world around us, and hence definitions and knowledge must be about it; otherwise we just have an arid deductive system that does not constitute genuine knowledge. If we weaken (5-6) in this way, then it constitutes a plausible criterion for substance; but it is then also one both PFs and ASs satisfy.

PFs and ASs, then, fare equally well on (5-6), if they are construed in terms of learning and recognition. If (5-6) are instead interpreted in terms of scientific-knowledge and definition, then PFs fare better than do ASs – unless Aristotle significantly weakens his usual views about the nature of scientific-knowledge and definition. Such modification might yield a more plausible conception of such knowledge and definition; but it is noteworthy that it is required, not to argue against Plato, but to allow his own candidates to satisfy (5-6). In any case, none of the interpretations of (5-6) that we have considered favors ASs over PFs.

It is worth noting, however, that Aristotle's new focus on (5-6) is probably one reason for his advocacy of individual form. First, forms are identical to their essences, as primary substances must now be. Second, though individual forms, being particulars, may not be strictly scientifically-knowable or definable, they are closer to being knowable and definable than are such particulars as compounds. At least, since they do not include matter as compounds do, they are 'purer' instances of universal laws, and so subject to fewer vagaries. This goes along with a point noted before (V (3)): that individual forms, in the *Met.*, are better thises than are compounds; for they are not what they are in virtue of one thing's being predicated of another, and so are more determinate objects of secure reference.

And it is worth noting too that although Aristotle may not easily be able to defend his claim that individual forms satisfy (5-6), he does try to argue this; he does not, at this point, slide back to the *Cat.*'s view according to which universals better satisfy (5-6). (5-6) may indeed raise difficulties for Aristotle; but he does not attempt to resolve them by turning to universal substances.

VI. *Conclusion*

What can we say, by way of conclusion, about the debate between Plato and Aristotle on what the substances are?

In the *Met.*, Aristotle argues that PFs cannot be substances, because they satisfy none of (2-6) – at least, they satisfy none of them nonproblematically: no universal can be a subject or a this; none can be separate; none is the essence of any particular; none is prior in knowledge or definition. Though Plato would of course protest against most of these claims, Aristotle believes the protest is implausible and, in some cases, that it leads to incoherence, making PFs both universals and particulars at once. ASs, on the other hand, nonproblematically satisfy (2-6), and so are the substances. As we have seen, the details of his argument require that his (primary) substances be individual forms.

If our argument has been correct, a different verdict should be returned. Though PFs are not subjects or (*Cat.*) thises, this does not impugn their status as substances, since these are not plausible necessary conditions on substance; and PFs do satisfy associed weaker, and more plausible, conditions. On the other hand, PFs satisfy (4–6) (in Plato's view; but also, he appears to have a reasonable view here); nor does this require them to be universals and particulars at once. If we focus on (2–6), then, we have been given no reason to reject PFs, and some reason to look on them favorably.

Though Aristotle goes too far in barring PFs from the ranks of substances, he can reasonably press a weaker claim: that ASs belong in the ranks as well. To be sure, ASs satisfy (4–6) only if Aristotle significantly weakens them – a weakening Plato need not countenance. But such weakenings may be welcome, since they yield more plausible criteria for substance than do the initial strong readings. Further, ASs also satisfy (1–2) which, I have conceded to Aristotle, are at least plausible sufficient conditions on substance; and they also satisfy (3), on both of its constructions.

Our argument suggests that we should not accept as legitimate the presupposition? of Plato's and Aristotle's question 'What are *the* substances?' – namely, that there is some one sort of entity that has privileged status, or alone satisfies all the criteria for substance. Different sorts of entities – both universals and particulars – are indispensable features of the way the world is, and so of our understanding of the world.[32]

CORNELL UNIVERSITY   GAIL FINE
BRASENOSE COLLEGE, OXFORD

NOTES

1. Some dispute that Forms are, or are only, universals; with Aristotle, I assume that Forms are at least universals. Though all Forms are universals, the converse is not true; Forms appear to be a subclass of universals – non-sensible ones. (I assume that not all universals are nonsensible – redness, e.g., is not.) I discuss some features of Forms in more detail in my 'The One over Many', *Philosophical Review* 89 (1980) 197–240; and in 'Relational entities', *Archiv für Geschichte der Philosophie* (1983).

2. I thus align myself with those who believe that in the *Met.* Aristotle acknowledges individual forms, and counts them as his primary substances. This view is, of course, highly controversial; and my defense of it here is at best partial. That the primary substances of the *Met.* are individual forms is also defended by E. Hartman, *Substance, body, and soul* (1977), esp. chapter 2; and W Sellars, 'Aristotle's Metaphysics: an interpretation', in *Philosophical perspectives* (1959) 73–124. If this view is rejected, then many of the things I say about Aristotle's criticism of, and alternative to, Plato would need to be revised. On the other hand, if I sketch Aristotle's criticisms correctly, that supports the picture I paint of his alternative. I do not deny, by the way, that Aristotle countenances forms (or entities called '*eidē*') other

than individual forms (see esp. n. 7). But unless otherwise noted, whenever I speak of Aristotelian forms, I shall mean the individual forms that count as primary substances.

3. D. R. Cousin, 'Aristotle's doctrine of substance', *Mind*, n.s. 42 (1933) 319–37; 43 (1935) 168–85; R. Dancy, *Sense and contradiction: a study in Aristotle* (1975) 95ff.

4. It is, of course, sometimes disputed that Plato accords sensibles essences or that, if he does, their essences are Forms. For a partial defense of the view assumed here, see 'Relational entities'.

5. *Cat.* 2b7–14; 2b29–37. A second reason they count as secondary substances is that they are the second best subjects. I discuss both reasons further below, in III and V.

6. I say 'at best' because not all essences count as secondary substances; only the essences of primary substances do. Redness, or color, are the essences of various nonsubstances; but they are not substances at all.

7. '*eidos*' is one word Plato uses for PFs. Aristotle uses '*eidos*' in at least the following ways: (*a*) for individual forms (e.g. Socrates' soul); (*b*) for species (e.g. man); and (*c*) for the universal form or essence of that species (e.g. rationality). This multiple usage need not import any confusion. The distinction between (*b*) and (*c*) is made much of by J. Driscoll, in 'EIDE in Aristotle's earlier and later theories of substance', in *Studies in Aristotle*, ed. D. J. O'Meara (1981) 129–159. He argues that in the *Met.*, the primary substances are *eidē* of sort (*c*); I favor (*a*). Driscoll is right to argue that (*a*) is not the only alternative to (*b*), which he agrees is not primary substance in the *Met.*; but there are other reasons for preferring (*a*) to (*c*).

8. G.E.L. Owen; 'The Platonism of Aristotle', *Proceedings of the British Academy* 51 (1965) 125–50, 136–7. In a later article, 'Particular and General' *PAS* 79 (1978–79), esp. 14–15, however, he seems to have retracted this view in favor of individual forms, though the claim is not pressed.

9. By, e.g., M. J. Woods, 'Substance and essence in Aristotle', *PAS* 75 (1974–5) 167–80; cf. also C. Kirwan, *Aristotle's Metaphysics: Books* Γ, Δ, *and* E (1971), esp. 100–101.

10. Cf. J. L. Ackrill, *Aristotle's Categories and De Interpretatione* (1963) 89–90. The translation is also Ackrill's; all other translations are my own.

11. Thus, in Z.4 (1030a5–6) he says that *only* substances are thises; and in Z.3, matter is ruled out as (the sole) substance on the grounds that, *inter alia*, it is not a this (1029a28–30). The notion of a *tode ti* is difficult, and has been explicated in many different ways. Cf., e.g., J. A. Smith, 'TODE TI in Aristotle', *CR* 35 (1921) 19; Owen, 'Particular and general', 2; J. Barnes, *Aristotle* (1982), 43. Barnes remarks that *tode ti* is 'an unorthodox phrase which Aristotle nowhere explains'.

12. I am unsure whether (1) is tacit in the *Met.* Perhaps it plays a role in the restriction Aristotle sometimes makes of substances to natural substances, i.e. to those with internal sources of change. In any case, I shall largely ignore (1) when speaking of the *Met.*

13. I take both '*chōris*' and '*chōriston*', as used in connection with substance and PFs, to indicate *actual*, and not merely *possible*, separation; and I take actual separation to be the *capacity* for independent existence. Most of the claims I make in this paper about separation are defended in detail in 'On the separation of Platonic Forms', forthcoming in *Oxford Studies in Ancient Philosophy* (1984).

14. At 1028a32–3, I read: *kai physei kai logō(i) kai gnōsei* – adding '*physei*' to, and deleting '*chronō(i)*' from, Jaeger's text. This emendation is not essential to my view.

15. I say that in the *Cat.*, Aristotle denies that universals are separate. To be sure, this follows from his remark that universals are ultimately dependent on primary substances; but it is interesting to note that Aristotle does not use '*chōris*' or its cognates in pressing this claim. Notice, in this connection, the

account of natural priority in *Cat.* 14b10–22. Here, in striking contrast to *Met.* Z.1, A can be naturally prior to B without being separate from B; indeed, separation is actually precluded, since natural priority is defined so as to obtain only between items that reciprocate as to existence. In general, the *Cat.* has considerably less to say about separation than the *Met.* does. '*Chōris*' and its cognates occur only once, at 1a25.

16. Such, at any rate, appears to be the implication of Z.1. Even if (5) is only necessary, however (and it is clearly at least that), the problems I raise for Aristotle over (5) would remain (see below, V (5)). One might find it tempting to weaken (5) so that it requires only that *ousiai* be mentioned (as opposed to defined) in every definition. I know of no place where priority in definition is explicated in this weaker way, however. But even if it is, neither would this remove the difficulties canvassed below; for substance must still be definable, even if its definition need not actually occur in definitions of other things, and that is sufficient for the worries I later air. Analogous remarks to those made in this note apply to (6).

17. Aristotle, of course, believes that Plato intends PFs to be efficient causes of change (*Met.* 991b3–9 = 1080a2–8; cf. *G.C.* 335b7–15, 18–24), and he criticizes them on that score. Aristotle has recently been defended by J. Annas, 'Aristotle on inefficient causes', *Philosophical Quarterly* (1982) 311–326. But I was unpersuaded by her argument, which seems to assume that if Plato does not explicitly distinguish between efficient and other sorts of causes, he must be confused about their differences. A more sympathetic reading of Plato is provided by G. Vlastos, 'Reasons and causes in the *Phaedo*', *Philosophical Review* 78 (1969) 291–325.

18. Owen, 'Particular and general', 2. This is Owen's explication of what Aristotle means by 'subject'. If Owen is right, then PFs are subjects in Aristotle's sense; but I doubt that Owen is right.

19. The issue is disputed; but for one plausible defense of the possibility of uninstantiated universals, see P. Butchvarov, *Resemblance and identity* (1966) 186–97.

20. See Owen, 'Particular and general', 14; contrast the passage cited above from 'Platonism'.

21. 'Self-predication', as traditionally construed, is the claim that the Form of F is itself an F thing, a member of the class of F things; the Form of Large, e.g., is itself large. If S. Peterson's account of self-predication is accepted, there would be even less reason to suppose that self-predication implies particularity. See S. Peterson, 'A reasonable self-predication premise for the Third Man Argument', *Ph. R.* 82 (1973) 451–470.

22. Indeed, the *Met.* account of thisness has Platonic antecedents: cf. *Crat.* 439c6–440c1; *Tht.* 181–3; *So.* 261–3; *Tm.* 48e2–52d1. For some discussion, see D. Zeyl, 'Talk of a world in flux', *HSCP* 79 (1975), esp. 146–8; J. Driscoll, 'The Platonic ancestry of primary substance', *Phronesis* (1979) 253–269. Interestingly, Plato never seems explicitly to say that PFs are thises, so conceived; and like Aristotle he at least sometimes uses similar phrases of sensible particulars. But his notion of being a this is not defined in terms of sensible particulars; and PFs satisfy his notion, even if he does not himself explicitly make the point.

23. See esp. *Met.* M.9; I discuss the passage in detail in 'Separation'.

24. Aristotle may, however, intend to foreclose this possibility in *Met.* Z.13.

25. I assume mereological essentialism is false.

26. Notice that this problem for ASs is not alleviated by claiming that they are universals, not particulars; for as we have seen, Aristotle consistently denies that universals are separate, and he consistently associates separation with particularity. On the other hand, T. H. Irwin has suggested to me that ASs – conceived as individual forms – are, contrary to my suggestion, separate, at least from universals: whenever Aristotle defines universals, he defines them in terms of being predicated of *many* things. Suppose that only Socrates – one man – exists. Then the universal, man, does not exist; its

existence requires the existence of *many* men. But if Socrates exists, and the universal, man, does not, then Socrates is separate from man. A parallel argument shows that Socrates is separate from all universals. He is not, of course, independent of, e.g., his individual pallor or height; but perhaps these are not *other* than him, and so he need not be separate from them. (An analogous argument might be used to show that neither is he separate from his matter; for he is not other than it in the requisite way.) But if Socrates is separate from all universals so, too, is every other man and, analogously, every other AS.

I am unpersuaded by this argument, however. Even if it is accepted, it gives us no reason to prefer ASs to PFs; it shows at most that universals and particulars are on an equal footing.

27. This might actually be disputed. Suppose, as is sometimes believed, that there are Forms only corresponding to the accidental properties of things. Then even if Socrates is, e.g., tan, in virtue of participating in the Form of Tan, he is not dependent on the Form, since he can exist without it; he would of course then cease to be tan, but that would not impugn his continued existence. However, at least in the *Timaeus* there are Forms corresponding to some of the essential properties of things (there is, e.g., a Form of Man), and so at least there sensibles do depend on (some) Forms: Socrates could not exist if he were not a man; hence he is dependent on the Form of Man, since he can be a man only by participating in it. I discuss this issue more fully in 'Relational entities'.

28. Notice that if separation here is *definitional* separation (and not IE), then Aristotle apears to believe that even definitional separation implies particularity. And at least one line of thought does yield this result: in Z.1, Aristotle argues that every definition must include a definition of *ousia*. If all *ousiai* are substance particulars, then definitions of everything else, including universals, must include definitions of them. But then no universal can be definitionally separate; each must include a definition of a substance particular. Hence if something is definitionally separate, it is a particular. I rather suspect, however, that separation here is IE.

29. This is, of course, a controversial account of Aristotle that I do not have the space to defend here.

30. D. Hume, *A treatise of human nature*, ed., L. A. Selby-Bigge (1888), Book I, Pt. 1; *Enquiry concerning human understanding*, ed. L. A. Selby-Bigge (1902), section 2.

31. G. W. Leibniz, *New essays on human understanding*, translated and edited by P. Remnant and J. Bennett (1981), Book I, chapter 1, *passim*.

32. An earlier version of this paper was read at the Oxford Philosophical Society in November, 1982; I thank the audience on theat occasion for a number of helpful comments. I especially wish to thank my commentator, Professor J. L. Ackrill, for generous and helpful written and oral comments; and also Terry Irwin, M. M. Mackenzie, and Jennifer Whiting. I am also grateful to the National Endowment for the Humanities for awarding me a fellowship for 1982-3, and to the Principal and Fellows of Brasenose College, Oxford, for electing me to a Visiting Fellowship for 1982-3.

BEING IN THE *SOPHIST*:
A SYNTACTICAL ENQUIRY*

LESLEY BROWN

PLATO'S *Sophist* presents a tantalizing challenge to the modern student of philosophy. In its central section we find a Plato whose interests and methods seem at once close to and yet remote from our own. John Ackrill's seminal papers on the *Sophist*,[1] published in the fifties, emphasized the closeness, and in optimistic vein credited Plato with several successes in conceptual analysis. These articles combine boldness of argument with exceptional clarity and economy of expression, and though subsequent writers have cast doubt on some of Ackrill's claims for the *Sophist* the articles remain essential reading for all students of the dialogue. I am happy to contribute an essay on the *Sophist* to this volume dedicated to John Ackrill.

Among the most disputed questions in the interpretation of the *Sophist* is that of whether Plato therein marks off different uses of the verb *einai*, 'to be'. This paper addresses one issue under that heading, that of the distinction between the 'complete' and 'incomplete' uses of 'to be', which has usually been associated with the distinction between the 'is' that means 'exists' and the 'is' of predication, that is, the copula.

I

Those who hold that there is a sharp distinction in ancient Greek between the complete and the incomplete *esti* may take one of the following stances *vis-à-vis* the *Sophist*:

(1) The *Sophist* contains a clear statement of the distinction, which is just what is needed to help solve the philosophical problems raised in the dialogue.

(2) The *Sophist* needs a statement of the distinction (since it contains at crucial points both complete and incomplete uses), but, alas, it lacks it.

* © Lesley Brown 1986.
[1] '*ΣΥΜΠΛΟΚΗ ΕΙΔΩΝ*' (1955) and 'Plato and the Copula: *Sophist* 251–59' (1957), both repr. in *Plato I*, ed G. Vlastos (New York, 1971), 201–9 and 210–22.

(3) The *Sophist* lacks a statement of the distinction, but this is no ground for lamentation since it would be irrelevant to the philosophical issues addressed by the dialogue.

(3) represents Owen's position in his 1971 article, which has received widespread acceptance.[2] His central claims are the following:

(i) that the *Sophist* is an essay in problems of reference and predication [and *not* of existence] and in the incomplete uses of the verb *to be* associated with these and

(ii) that the argument neither contains nor compels any isolation of an existential verb.

It is on the first claim that this article will focus, though some discussion of the second will naturally be involved. I argue that the distinction between syntactically complete and incomplete uses of the verb *einai* needs careful examination before dispute about Plato's overall position or about individual passages can be fruitfully pursued.[3] I distinguish two different ways of characterizing a complete use, and argue that the one that Owen presupposes, in his *Sophist* article, is the less plausible. In its place I offer an alternative characterization of a complete use, whose effect is that the distinction between the syntactically complete and incomplete uses is less sharp than it has traditionally been conceived to be. With the new understanding of *complete*, many centrally important uses of *esti* in the *Sophist* can be reinstated as complete. Provided that we recognize the continuity between the complete and the incomplete (predicative) uses, there will be no harm in regarding the complete use as weakly existential in force. But it is a consequence of the continuity between the two that distinguishing one from the other is not and could not be part of Plato's answer to the problems he inherited from Parmenides. To this extent, then, I accept Owen's thesis, but I believe that a misconception of the nature of the complete use of *esti*

---

[2] G. E. L. Owen, 'Plato on Not-Being', in *Plato I*, ed Vlastos.

[3] R. Heinaman, 'Being in the *Sophist*', *Archiv für Geschichte der Philosophie*, LXV, No. 1 (1983), 1–17, disputes Owen's claim that Plato's discussion in *Sophist* (*Sph.*) concerns syntactically incomplete uses of *einai*. Though some of his points against Owen are well-taken, he appears to accept the traditional account of the distinction, which I shall dispute, and does not pause to define the crucial terms *complete* and *incomplete*. Some of Heinaman's arguments are discussed in V below. For a critique of Heinaman see now J. Malcolm, *Arch. Gesch. Phil.*, LXVII (1985), 162–5.

led Owen to the implausible views that the problems of the *Sophist* do not concern existence and that the central uses of *esti* in the dialogue are to be construed as incomplete.

II

In this section I outline those parts of Owen's position which are relevant to my discussion. Those familiar with his paper may proceed direct to section III.

Owen opens with a rehearsal of some—up to that time—accepted commonplaces (223-4). These include two theses about the Greek language and a third about the *Sophist*. The theses about Greek are

(*a*) a distinction between two syntactically distinct uses of the verb *to be*: a complete, substantive use in which it determines a one-place predicate, and an incomplete use determining a two-place predicate;

(*b*) answering to the syntactic distinction, a semantic one: in its substantive, complete, use the verb signifies *exist*; in its incomplete use it is the copula or identity sign.

(*c*) The commonplace about the *Sophist* is that here Plato marks off the first use of *esti*—complete, existential—from its other, incomplete uses, and similarly for the negative construction represented by *to mē on*; for (the commonplace runs) the problems which dominate the central arguments of the *Sophist* are existence problems, so that disentangling the different functions of the verb *to be* is a proper step to identifying and resolving them.

Owen's paper confines its attack to commonplace (*c*); he explicitly accepts the first point, the syntactic distinction.[4] In place of (*c*), Owen's central theses include the two quoted above in section I. He accepts that there is a distinction (which he does not define) between a complete and an incomplete *esti*, but argues that Plato's interest in the *Sophist* is exclusively in the incomplete uses.

Owen's reasoning for the desirability of his interpretation can be reduced to four main steps. (1) It is agreed on all hands that the

---

[4] 'The general syntactic claim will not come into question: we can accept a distinction between the verb's complete and incomplete uses provided we are wary of confusing the first with elliptical occurrences of the second' (225). Thus Owen accepts that *esti* has complete uses, but he argues that putative candidates in *Sph.* are incomplete elliptical. His attitude to the second commonplace, the semantic distinction, is not clear from the article, for he does not make clear what semantic force (whether existential or some other) a 'complete' use of *esti* would have.

troublesome concept Not-being or *to mē on*, whose discussion was
forbidden by Parmenides' strictures, and which gave rise to a clutch of
paradoxes at the beginning of the central section (236–41), is
legitimized in the following way. Far from being disallowed as not true
of anything (as had at first appeared) *to mē on* is reinstated as true of
everything, for everything *is not* countless other things. Not-being is
thus equated with difference and shown to be one of the all-pervasive
kinds which occupy so much of the central section of the *Sophist*.
Everything, then, *is not* countless other things: the vindication of *to mē
on* is squarely of its incomplete use—not being is always not being
something or other: there is no trace of a legitimization of not-being as
a negative existential. (2) That being so, it would be feeble of Plato to
raise puzzles about not-being in its other, complete, use, given that his
'solution' ignores such a use. (3) It would be worse still, if we should
find him explicitly pointing to such a distinction among 'is'es, when (as
established at step (1)), he forgets or suppresses the distinction as
applied to 'is not'. (4) What is more, Plato explicitly tells us that (in
Owen's words) 'any light thrown on either being or not-being will
equally illuminate the other' (230). This dictum, which he dubbed the
'Parity Assumption', Owen derived from 250e, and made it a governing assumption of his interpretation. Now it is accepted (step (1)) that
the only illumination cast on Not-being, on 'is not', is on its incomplete
use: by the Parity Assumption, then, we should expect to find only the
incomplete use (or uses) of 'is' illustrated. So not only would it be
unfortunate if Plato were to allow a use of 'is' while disallowing the
corresponding use of 'is not', here he explicitly tells us (if we press the
so called Parity Assumption) that he will not do so.

   So much, then, for the broad canvas of Owen's argument, which
might be described as tailoring Plato's problem to fit the solution
offered. In addition, of course, Owen examines the text passage by
passage, hoping to show that in each case where a complete or existential 'is' had been assumed, or argued for, an incomplete 'is' was either
mandatory or at least possible. Some of these passages I review in
section V below.

                                  III

First a closer look at the 'complete/incomplete use' distinction.
Neither of the pair of terms is explicitly defined by Owen, though he
uses (in the passage quoted in II under (*a*)) the terms *one-place* and

two-place predicate as apparently equivalent to *complete* and *incomplete*.[5] I therefore take as the definition of an incomplete use that in McDowell's commentary on *Theaetetus*,[6] which seems to state in an admirably clear and precise way what Owen intended by his use of the term:

> ... an incomplete use, i.e. a use in which a subject expression and the appropriate form of the verb requires a complement in order to constitute a complete sentence, though in an elliptical sentence the complement may be omitted.

Two crucial points emerge: (1) in an incomplete use a complement is *required*, and (2) an 'is' lacking an explicit complement may yet be an incomplete 'is'. In such a case, presumably, the hearer or reader has not correctly understood the sentence unless he is able to supply the missing complement. A clear example of such a use occurs at *Sophist* 233c6–8 in the course of the attempt to define the sophist as an image-maker who imparts false beliefs to his pupils. Sophists, says the Eleatic Stranger, appear to their disciples to be wise in all things: *panta ara sophoi tois mathētais phainontai*. (*Theaetetus*: Yes, indeed.) *ouk ontes ge*: though they are not ⟨wise⟩. Here the reader has not understood the phrase *ouk ontes ge* unless he supplies *sophoi*, wise, from two lines before. Let us acknowledge the existence of such uses and dub them IE, for incomplete elliptical. How important and frequent they are in the *Sophist* remains to be seen (section V).

How should we characterize a *complete* use? I offer two possibilities: a complete use of *esti* is

C1 a use which neither has nor allows a complement
C2 a use where there is no complement (explicit or elided) but which allows a complement.

I believe that commentators have, implicitly or explicitly, assumed a C1 characterization of *complete*, but that C2 is preferable.

I illustrate the difference between the two, and in particular the meaning of 'allows a complement', with a comparison with verbs other than the verb *to be*. (Naturally the definitions C1 and C2, with their reference to a complement, cannot be applied directly to other verbs,

---

[5] Owen also employs the contrast between a 'substantive' and a 'connective' use. I believe this terminology is misleading, for the complete use (as I define it) is *potentially* connective, and the incomplete use is often *substantive*, if by this is meant that it can have semantic force over and above its role as a copula (see sec IV, 59).

[6] J. McDowell, *Plato, Theaetetus* (Oxford, 1973), 118.

but I hope the point of the comparison will be obvious.) Consider these pairs of sentences:

1*a* Jane is growing tomatoes.
1*b* Jane is growing.
2*a* Jane is teaching French.
2*b* Jane is teaching.

It is, I hope, uncontroversial to say that in 1*a* we have a transitive, in 1*b* an intransitive use of 'is growing'; equally that 1*a* contains a two-place or dyadic use, 1*b* a one-place or monadic use. Since this latter terminology is standardly used to explicate the incomplete/complete distinction it would be natural to say that 1*a* contains an incomplete, 1*b* a complete use of 'is growing', between which there *is* a sharp syntactic and semantic distinction. Pair 2 is clearly rather different, in the following ways (*inter alia*): (i) while 1*a* neither entails nor is entailed by 1*b*, 2*a* does entail 2*b*; (ii) while 2*b* entails 'Jane is teaching something', 1*b* does not entail 'Jane is growing something'; (iii) (a corollary of (ii)) one who heard 1*b* and asked 'growing what?' would reveal misunderstanding of 1*b*, while the follow-up question to 2*b*, 'teaching what?', is perfectly proper. Though 2*b*, like 1*b*, contains an intransitive, complete use of its verb (for 'is teaching' in 2b is certainly not elliptical, though the use no doubt derives from 2*a*-type uses), it is far closer semantically to its transitive, incomplete partner than 1*b* is to its partner.

Returning to the rival characterizations, C1 and C2, of a complete *esti*, the meaning of 'allows a complement' is, I hope, clear from these analogies: just as 'is teaching' in 2*b* is complete but allows an object (it would not be a solecism to ask 'is teaching what?'), so a C2 complete *esti* is one that allows a complement, that is, it is not a solecism to ask 'is what?'. An incomplete and a C2 complete *esti* would bear a closeness analogous to that between the uses of 'is teaching' in pair 2. Many other verbs have complete and incomplete uses like those in pair 2: *fight, eat, breathe*. As Kenny has shown,[7] verbs, unlike relations, can exhibit variable polyadicity; it is therefore misleading to assimilate verbs to relations and characterize their uses as one-place, two-place,

---

[7] A. Kenny, *Action, Emotion and Will* (1963), ch VII. I am indebted to Kenny's chapter, and to discussions with Michael Woods, for suggesting an account of *einai* along the lines of Kenny's verbs of variable polyadicity. Kenny correctly insists that sentences such as 'Plato taught' are not elliptical.

etc. If we compare the Greek verb *to be* with verbs of variable poly-adicity, we shall avoid the pitfalls that arise from this practice.[8] My suggestion, then, is that the complete *esti* should be characterized as C2 rather than C1, that is, as complete but allowing further completion.

That Owen understood C1 as his characterization of 'complete' is shown by his discussion of 259a6–8, one of the passages where Plato uses *esti* without explicit complement, and offers the paraphrase or analysis *dia to metechein tou ontos*, 'because it shares in being'. It was the glossing of 'is' by 'shares in being' that earlier commentators (e.g. Ackrill)[9] had taken to be Plato's way of marking off the existential *esti* from other uses of *esti*, which do not receive this paraphrase. In several places in the *Sophist* it is said of one kind or another that it is, because it shares in being, and it was perhaps natural to see this as marking off an existential, complete use. (These passages are discussed in section V(*c*) below.) At 259a6–8 the Eleatic Stranger sums up his argument about the Different thus: partaking in being, it is by virtue of that partaking—but not the thing of which it partakes but something different:

τὸ μὲν ἕτερον μετασχὸν τοῦ ὄντος ἔστι μὲν διὰ ταύτην τὴν μέθεξιν, οὐ μὴν ἐκεῖνό γε οὗ μετέσχεν ἀλλ' ἕτερον.

'The verb in the last clause' (Owen continues—namely 'but not the thing ...') 'must be supplied from its predecessor, and the verb supplied is the incomplete "is"' (253).

Owen argues that since a subsequent clause adds a completion, the verb in the clause to which it is added cannot be complete. And this piece of reasoning shows that Owen must understand by a 'complete' use one which (not only does not require but also) *does not allow* further completion. The success of Owen's argument at this point thus depends on understanding 'complete' as C1. If we define it, as I shall argue that we should, as C2, it will not follow from the fact that a completion is added in the second clause that the verb in the first was not complete, so that we could read 259a6's first clause as containing a complete *is* (glossed as *metechei tou ontos*) notwithstanding that the

---

[8] Witness, for instance, M. Matthen 'Greek Ontology and the "Is" of Truth', *Phronesis*, XXVIII (1983), 122: 'Let us call a use of "is" *monadic* if it must be completed by exactly one term to form a sentence, *dyadic* if it requires exactly two.' Such regimentation fails to do justice to the nature of verbs in general, and of *einai* in particular.

[9] Above n 1, 212.

second clause promptly specifies what *heteron* is, or rather, is not. Compare 'My sister is still teaching, but not French these days, only Spanish'.

The effect of understanding the complete *esti* as C2 rather than C1 is that the distinction between the incomplete and complete uses is far less striking and clear-cut. In suggesting that it should be so understood, I take issue not only with Owen but also with Vlastos, who in his important article, 'A Metaphysical Paradox',[10] writes of 'the difference between the "is" in *Troy is famous* and in *Troy is*' implicit knowledge of which 'even a Greek child would have had'. (Vlastos's chief interest is in the question how we should understand Plato's descriptions of the forms as *ontōs on*, 'really real', and so forth; he insists that these uses of 'to be' are to be sharply distinguished from those in which 'to be' means 'to exist'.) His choice of example suggests that he takes as one aspect of the distinction the fact (presumably supposed to be well-known to the Greek child) that

3a Troy is famous   does not entail
3b Troy is,   hence, is consistent with
3c Troy is not (i.e. does not exist).

Vlastos's remarks suggest that he believes there is a sharp syntactic and semantic distinction waiting to be articulated, such that only a paradox-monger could trade on an equivocation between them. I discuss this further in the next section, but remark here on a difficulty which must strike all readers of the *Sophist*: if so sharp a distinction existed (as sharp as that between the use of 'is growing' in 1a and 1b) and if, as Vlastos insists, Plato faithfully *observed* it, then the *Sophist* of all places was the dialogue where the distinction ought to have been explicitly stated. But not only does Plato not, according to present consensus, explicitly mark the distinction, he does not even *observe* it to the extent of allowing that a sentence of form 3a can be true while one of form 3b is false. He nowhere allows that X is F does not entail X is but is consistent with X is not. Indeed he allows no role to the complete *is not*, and this is what prompted Owen to deny that Plato's problem concerned existence (i.e. the complete *esti*) at all, for if it had done, Plato could not have failed to delineate both the 'is' of existence and the 'is not' of non-existence. But if, as I shall suggest, the syntactic

---

[10] G. Vlastos, 'A Metaphysical Paradox', repr. in his *Platonic Studies* (1st edn, Princeton, 1973), 47. Vlastos agrees with Owen that the *Sophist* does not contain an explicit statement of the distinction between the 'is' of existence and other uses of 'is'.

distinction (at least) is not as sharp and clear-cut as Vlastos assumes, then Plato's failure to exploit it is more explicable.[11]

IV

But it may be claimed that we *do* find paradox-mongers exploiting precisely this equivocation on the two distinct *esti*s. I now consider the little sophism at *Euthydemus* 283c–d. Socrates and his friends want young Kleinias to get an education, that is, they want him to become wise, which he now is not. So, they are told,

(1) ʽ Ὑμεῖς δέ, ἔφη, βούλεσθε γενέσθαι αὐτὸν σοφόν, ἀμαθῆ δὲ μὴ εἶναι;

(2) Οὐκοῦν ὃς μὲν οὐκ ἔστιν, βούλεσθε αὐτὸν γενέσθαι, ὃς δ' ἔστι νῦν, μηκέτι εἶναι.

(3) ἐπεὶ βούλεσθε αὐτὸν ὃς νῦν ἐστὶν μηκέτι εἶναι, βούλεσθε αὐτόν, ὡς ἔοικεν, ἀπολωλέναι;

A standard diagnosis of the fallacy would be to see an equivocation on *esti*: in (2), which is *true*, it is the two-place copula; in the *false* protasis of (3), it is the one-place existential. But the correct diagnosis is different; it is that the fallacy depends on a syntactic ambiguity in the clauses *hos esti nun* and *hos nun estin*. In (2) it means ʽ(you want him no longer to be) *what he now is*ʼ, where *hos* is the equivalent of *hoios* and the complement of *estin*. But in (3), ʽyou want him, *who now is*, no longer to beʼ *hos nun esti* is a relative clause dependent on *auton*; *hos* is the subject of *esti* which is left without a complement, as is the infinitive *einai*. Now it is true that the effect of lopping off the complement of *einai* is to make ʽyou want him no longer to be aliveʼ, or ʽ. . . to existʼ a natural translation. But I do not think we are forced to postulate a radically different use of ʽisʼ or ʽbeʼ here.

To show this I suggest the following, parallel, argument. Socrates and his friends try to rescue a child from a smoke-filled room; that is, they want him no longer to breathe what he is now breathing (namely smoke). The wily sophists exclaim ʽYou want him no longer to be breathing what he's now breathingʼ, (Yes), ʽSo you want him, who is now breathing, no longer to be breathingʼ. Once again Socrates and friends want the child to die—they want him no longer to be breathing.

Now no one, I think, would try to argue that the fallacy involved

[11] In V(*d*) below I concede that the proof at 255c–d does invoke a distinction between the complete and incomplete uses of *einai*, but, though it can be used for that purpose, it did not form a major plank in Plato's answer to Parmenides.

a shift in uses of the verb 'breathe', simply because in one clause an object is specified and in another it is not. Whenever 'X is breathing' is true, it will also be true that X is breathing something—oxygen normally. Conversely 'X is not breathing' will normally mean the same as 'X is not breathing anything'. But for all that, we should not say either that 'X is breathing' is elliptical, or that the use of the verb where it has an object is significantly different from the use where it has no object. Of course, that in itself is a difference, but not involving an important shift in the verb's sense. And exactly the same may be said of the original argument with the verb *to be*: lopping off the complement produces a falsehood but need not be seen as yielding a sharply different ('one-place, existential') use of *esti*. Rather, 'They want him not to be' will be equivalent to 'They want him not to be anything at all', just as 'They want him not to breathe' will be equivalent to 'They want him not to breathe anything at all'. Contrast the lopping off of the object in 'You want her to stop growing tomatoes', which yields 'You want her to stop growing': here the effect of lopping off the object *is* to produce a sharply different use of the verb.

The sophism in the *Euthydemus*, then, need not be understood as relying on an illicit shift between two uses of the verb *to be* which are syntactically and semantically distinct. The inference from X *is not* F to X *is not* (the move which results from the change in role of the subordinate clause in the sophist's argument) is illicit whether the complete *is* is understood as C1 or as C2, that is, whether or not a 'new' use results. It is only in connection with an inference from X *is* F to X *is* that the two characterizations give divergent answers: with a C2 use, the inference is as straightforward as that from 2*a* to 2*b*, while a more complex story has to be told if a C1 use is envisaged. So the *Euthydemus* passage cannot be used as evidence for a sharp syntactic/semantic distinction known implicitly to all Greek speakers and exploitable by paradox-mongers. For all that that little argument shows, the continuity between the complete and the incomplete *esti* is as strong as that between complete and incomplete uses of the variably polyadic verbs listed above (54).

It is, I believe, this continuity between the apparently complete and the incomplete uses of *esti*, *on*, etc. in the *Sophist* that has led Owen and others to claim that (contrary to appearances) only incomplete uses play any important role in the dialogue, and to interpret those uses without explicit complements (which I read as C2 complete) as incomplete but elliptical. They may urge that this IE use has been found in a very important role elsewhere in Plato, in his discussion of the Form *F* and the many *F*s, where claims about the being of the Form and the being-cum-not-being of the many *F*s require us to supply a complement: the Form *F* is perfectly, unqualifiedly ⟨*F*⟩, the many *F*s are and are not ⟨*F*⟩.[12] If the IE use is well-attested and important elsewhere in Plato, why should I baulk at Owen's detection of it in the *Sophist*?

My answer is this: that if we take the notion of an ellipse seriously, we may detect an ellipse in the assertion that *X is* only where the context supplies the elided complement. In English these uses are extremely common: 'Is he tall? Yes, he is', 'Who is coming? Jane is'. But such 'everyday' ellipses are far from commonplace in ancient Greek.[13] Only in a narrow range of contexts do we find a true ellipse of the complement after 'is', and these are the well-known contrasts, between being and becoming (*F*); between being and merely seeming (*F*); or the comparison between a thing's *being* so and so, and what it is *said* by some speaker or *logos* to be. In all of these cases the verb *to be* is more than the mere copula, but gets a meaning of its own by contrast with its partner: *becoming*, *appearing*, etc. We should be chary of detecting an ellipse unless the context supplies it, or gives us reason to look for one. And though this is sometimes the case in key passages in the *Sophist*, there are very many other central passages which both Owen and Frede[14] have read as incomplete uses where no elided complement can be supplied from the context. These are, I submit, best understood as what I have called C2 complete uses.[15]

[12] This way of understanding claims about the being of the forms derives from Vlastos's influential articles, 'A Metaphysical Paradox' (above n 10) and 'Degrees of Reality in Plato', also repr. in *Platonic Studies*. Though I have reservations about aspects of Vlastos's position (see 56 above and V(*b*) below), accepting it will not affect my argument that the *Sph.* passages discussed in V(*c*) below are *not* elliptical.

[13] It appears that in Plato, at least, the interlocutor's reply *esti* never echoes the *mere* copula; the plain *esti*, as opposed to the very frequent *esti tauta* ('that's so'), may mean 'it is possible' (*Cratylus* 430c1, *Sph.* 225a7). An interesting case, where what we have is the *is* of definition and not the plain copula , is *Theaetetus* 152b12: ΣΩ. Τὸ δέ γε "φαίνεται" αἰσθάνεσθαί ἐστιν; ΘΕΑΙ. "Εστιν γάρ.

[14] M. Frede, 'Prädikation und Existenzaussage', *Hypomnemata*, XVIII (1967).

[15] C. H. Kahn, in *The Verb 'be' in Ancient Greek* (Dordrecht and Boston, 1973), 240, draws the syntactic distinction between an absolute and a predicative construction of the verb *be*. (His well-known thesis is that the absolute construction of *einai* by no means always bears an existential meaning; indeed he suggests the Greeks did not have our notion of existence.) The absolute construction is defined as one where 'there is no nominal or locative predicate and no other complement such as the possessive dative, nor even an adverb of manner. An absolute construction may however admit adverbs of

V

I now turn to the *Sophist* and examine selected parts of the central section (236–64) in the light of the foregoing discussion.

(*a*) *The paradoxes of Not-being (*to mē on*), 236—41*

Though the topic gets introduced by the description of the sophist as a pedlar in illusions and falsehood—both of which seem to call for description involving *to mē on*—the scrutiny of the phrase that follows does not confine itself to a scrutiny of its role in the description of images and falsehood. Rather the phrase *to mē on* itself comes under scrutiny in the opening section of the paradoxes, 237b–239c: what can we apply it to? and what can be applied to it?—with the paradoxical result that it has no application, nor can anything that is—number, for example—be applied to it. So it is unsayable, unthinkable, etc.—but in so saying we contradict ourselves—we apply being and number to it.

Confining my attention to this opening paradox (237b–239c, labelled stages i–iii by Owen (241)), I argue for understanding *to mē on* as a C2 complete use, and proceed by examining Owen's position and Heinaman's arguments against Owen. In brief, Owen claims that *to mē on*, here equated with *to mēdamōs on* (237b7, cf. c2) cannot mean the non-existent, and cannot be a complete use, but means 'that which isn't anything at all', that is, that which for no *F* is *F* (see below). Heinaman counters that it cannot mean the latter but must mean 'the non-existent', and must be a complete use. I argue that their shared assumption, that we must choose between the two interpretations, depends on a faulty understanding of the contrast, and that no such choice is necessary if *to mē on* represents the negation of a C2 complete use, for as such it will be equivalent to 'that which isn't anything at all' without being elliptical or incomplete. If we take *to mē on* to be the negation of a C2 complete *esti*, we can understand it as *both* 'that which isn't anything at all' *and* 'the non-existent' and we are not forced to treat these as rival interpretations.

First, Owen's position: the paradoxes, he writes, arise from the assumption that *to mē on* is the *contrary* of *to on* (231 n 18); that is, they treat the phrase *to mē on* as one that attempts to pick out a subject time'. In a later article ('Some Philosophical uses of "to be" in Plato', *Phronesis*, XXVI (1981), 131 n 20) he emends the above to allow expressions such as *to pantelōs on* to count as absolute, adding 'perhaps the notion of an absolute construction has a clear sense only by contrast with the nominal and locative copula, and does not admit of more precise definition'.

'which for every predicate *F* is not *F*'. Following Heinaman, let us call this 'that which is predicatively nothing'.[16] We may agree with Owen that the paradox, as sketched two paragraphs above, proceeds by stipulating that nothing that is may be applied to what is not (*to mē on*), nor may the latter expression apply to anything that is (238a7–8, 237c7–8), which amounts to treating *to mē on* as that which isn't anything at all, that of which no statement of the form 'It is . .' is true.[17] But we can accept this point and still read *to mē on* as a C2 complete use, for, as I have argued in IV, the negation of the C2 complete *esti* is equivalent to 'is not anything at all'. And there are good reasons for doing this, and for saying that *pro tanto* the paradox is about *to mē on* in the sense of the non-existent. For (i) when a puzzle is raised about the applicability of the term *to mē on*, about whether *to mē on* can be thought about etc., it is natural to take this as an early member of that long-lived and far-flung family of puzzles about how one can think of, speak of, or refer to the non-existent. Not the earliest, of course: and in recalling Parmenides we have another reason to expect a puzzle about non-existence. (ii) When in the course of the argument it is said that nothing that is, no *on*, can be applied to *to mē on*, with the result that number, which is *in primis* an *on*, cannot be applied to it (238a7–b1), what is here said about number is surely that it is a thing that is, i.e. exists, not that it is ⟨some unspecified complement⟩, which is how the incomplete reading would have to take it if it is to treat *on* and *mē on* in the same way.

Heinaman attacks this interpretation of *to mē on* as what is predicatively nothing, correctly pointing out that it does not fit 240e.[18] His

[16] cf. J. Malcolm, 'Plato's Analysis of τὸ ὄν and τὸ μὴ ὄν in the *Sophist*', *Phronesis*, XII (1967) , 137: '[*to mē on*, here = *to mēdamōs on*] may be read, literally, as 'that which "is not" in all possible respects' or 'that which in no way at all may be said to be. . . . On this reading *to mēdamōs on* is stronger than "non-existence".' I take it that what Malcolm means is this: Plato refuses to allow anything the description *to mēdamōs on*, while he would have had to allow that, e.g., Pegasus qualifies for the description 'non-existent'. But this shows only that *to mēdamōs on* is 'stronger than' *our* notion 'non-existent'. It remains possible, and indeed likely, that Plato's failure to make the 'Pegasus point' is due not to a lack of interest in 'existence problems' (as Owen would have it), but to the fact that he cannot distinguish non-existence from not being anything at all.

[17] See McDowell, above n 6, 200, for this formulation.

[18] I here abbreviate Heinaman's argument (above n 3, 4–6): at 240e false judgement is described as (*a*) one which judges *pōs einai ta mē onta*, (or, the line before, *ta mēdamōs onta*), (*b*) one which judges *mēdamōs einai ta pantos onta* (describing positive and negative false judgements respectively). If *ta mē onta* (= *ta mēdamōs onta*) = that which is predicatively nothing, then by parity of reasoning *ta pantos onta* would have to be things which are predicatively everything, an absurdity.

argument does indeed show that Owen's interpretation of *to mē on* and *to mēdamōs on* as *that which is predicatively nothing* does not fit the 240 passage, but Heinaman concludes that Owen's reading must be wrong *passim* and that the only alternative is to read *to mē on* as the non-existent.[19]

But while Heinaman does show that Owen cannot claim support for his interpretation of *to mē on* at 237 from the 240 passage, he, like Owen, is assuming that the phrase has the same role in the two passages, which need not and indeed cannot be so.[20] In fact Heinaman's own candidate, 'the non-existent', fits 240e no better than Owen's, while in the original paradox (Owen's i–iii) we do not need to choose between them. We can say both (*A*) that a complete (C2) use figures in that paradox and (*B*) that the heart of the paradox is an understanding of *to mē on* as that which isn't anything at all. This yields a reading which is more satisfying both than Owen's which denies (*A*) and Heinaman's which denies (*B*). And if it be objected that on this reading we can draw no distinction, on Plato's behalf, between the non-existent and that which isn't anything at all, I reply that this is merely to be faithful to Plato. Had the possibility of the distinction been implicit in his knowledge of Greek, his failure to avail himself of it (by saying that 'does not exist' has a legitimate application, while 'isn't anything at all' has none) would be inexplicable. However we should understand his 'solution' to the paradox concerning Not-being,[21] it is clear that it dismisses as a wholly absurd notion that Not-being which is the simple *negation* of the complete *X is*,[22] allowing only *X is different from being* and *X is not F, ⟨G, etc.⟩* as

---

[19] Heinaman (20) dismisses another possibility, the veridical *esti*. I agree that *to mē on* and *to mēdamōs on* in 237–9 cannot consistently be read as veridical, in spite of the introduction of the topic of not-being at 236e via the mention of falsehood, and the allusion at 237a3–4 to the characterization of false speaking as *legein to mē on*, cf. 260c3–4.

[20] Malcolm, above n 3, 164 n 3, concedes that he was wrong to invoke the 240e passage in support of his interpretation of *to mēdamōs on* as absolute (predicative) non-being. He continues to defend the latter as an interpretation of 237–9; my only disagreement with him is over his insistence that this is to be distinguished from an interpretation in terms of non-existence.

[21] A question too complex to be considered here. For some recent discussions see D. Keyt, 'Plato on Falsity', in *Exegesis and Argument* (*Phronesis*, supp. vol. I), ed Lee, Mourelatos, and Rorty (Assen, The Netherlands, 1973), 285–305; F. A. Lewis, 'Plato on Not', *California Studies in Classical Antiquity*, IX (1976); J. McDowell, 'Falsehood and not-being', in *Language and Logos*, ed M. Schofield and M. Nussbaum (Cambridge, 1982), 115–34; D. Bostock, 'Plato on "is not"', in *Oxford Studies in Ancient Philosophy*, ii (1984), 89–119.

[22] 258e7–259a1.

acceptable.[23] As noted above (in II), it was because Plato's *solution* does not countenance the negation of the complete *esti* that Owen reconstructed the original *problem* to exclude it. But, as I have argued, we can preserve Owen's insight that the original paradox gets its force by treating *to mē on* as 'that which isn't anything at all' within a framework of seeing it as a (C2) complete use; and, as I am about to argue, the complete use is prominent also in the sequel to the paradoxes.[24]

(b) The theories about being (to on), 242–50

I shall discuss this section briefly and dogmatically, extracting some points important to my thesis.[25] (1) Plato discusses philosophers who had something to say about being (*to on*, or *ousia*; used interchangeably, e.g. compare 248c2 with 247d6). The assertions he ascribes to them, (that hot and cold are, that only one thing is, that only that which offers resistance to touch is, etc.) must for the most part be construed as containing syntactically complete uses of *esti*. (2) Most of the theories discussed are about *what there is*, and most of the relevant uses of *einai* look exceedingly like existentials, and call for the translation *exists* (see e.g. 246a10, 247b1, 247e3). (3) However, while the theories of the dualists, monists, and materialists are naturally described as theories about what exists, about what there (really) is, in that each can be seen as offering a reductive account of all existents to their favoured candidate(s), the Idealist theory, ascribed to 'Friends of the Forms' is rather different. In allowing *ousia* only to forms, and relegating perceptible, changeable objects to the status of *genesis*, it is *not* reducing all things to forms, but rather according forms a special

---

[23] For the former, *X is different from being*, see 256d5–8, d11–e2; for the latter, *X is not F, G, etc.*: this may be either a negative identity statement or a negative predication. Whether and how Plato distinguishes these is a vexed question, since he appears to have but one analysis, '*X* is different from *F*'. For denials of identity see 257a3–5, but 256e6 may mean to include negative predications as well as negative identities in the 'countless not being with respect to each form', i.e. the countless truths of the form '*K* is not . . .'.

[24] The puzzle that immediately follows, 239d–240d, where an image is defined as that which οὐκ ὄν ὄντως ἐστὶν ὄντως ἦν λέγομεν εἰκόνα ('something which is not really but really is what we call an image'), does seem to contain (elliptical) incomplete uses of *esti* and cognates. That this is so is shown by the context: the contrast between the genuine, *alēthinos*, (e.g. horse) and the thing that is like, *eoikos*, but isn't really (a horse). The difficulty with this little puzzle is to see how it could be thought to engender paradox once the missing complements are supplied.

[25] The whole section on theories of being is virtually ignored by Owen. Malcolm, above n 16, holds that in this section *to on*, *einai*, etc. may but need not be taken as complete and therefore existential.

status among things that exist. Thus Plato does not hesitate to include among theories of *to on both* theories about what exists *and* the 'Friends of the Forms' theory about what is real. This casts further doubt on Vlastos's claim (above 56) that Plato observed a sharp distinction between the two senses of *esti*. (4) In places (e.g. 246e–247b) the argument uses the absolute *einai* interchangeably with *einai ti*, to be something, which is just what is to be expected if the former is a C2 complete use (as illustrated in III). (5) Though the discussion makes heavy use of the complete *esti* ((1)), which is by and large to be understood as existential ((2)), one of Plato's chief interests in this whole section is in scrutinizing the role of a predicate expression, preparatory to his discussion of the late-learners' difficulty. (The late-learners refuse to admit statements which predicate one thing of another (an *other*)—they won't allow you to say that a man is good or to apply anything except 'man' to man. And this position, the refusal to take seriously the role of a predicate expression, lies behind the fallacious refutation of the dualists at 243d–244a, cf. 250a–e). The predicate expression chosen for scrutiny, *esti*, is to that extent representative of all predicates, and Plato need not be interested in pursuing the complete *esti* for its own sake, but in order to draw some morals about the correct understanding of an ascription of one thing to another. Once again we can accept this without having to accept that the complete *esti* has no role in this section. It is important for what follows that we have in this section just what we seem to have: theories about what is, where that 'is' is a complete use.

(c) The communion of kinds (252–9)

We have finally arrived at the heart of the *Sophist*, the section in which five *megista genē*, greatest kinds, are identified and proved to be distinct from one another, and their interrelations plotted. Our path lies through a minefield of difficulties, which cannot be here discussed. I shall concentrate my attention on those passages where Plato asserts of some form or other that it *esti dia to metechein tou ontos*, that it is because (or, in that) it shares in being, and argue for a traditional understanding of them as containing complete uses. However this is not to dispute that Plato's chief interest in this section is the investigation of the *megista genē*, and in particular his insistence on the possibility of saying truly that a given kind is what it also is not. He argues that, for some values of K_1 and K_2, K_1 *is* K_2 and K_1 *is not* K_2 are both true, and we naturally understand these as a positive predication and a negative identity respectively. Which distinctions Plato is himself drawing attention to is a matter of controversy,[26] but for present purposes it is enough to concede that his major interest is in the above sample sentences, which admittedly contain incomplete uses of 'is'. We may also agree that where complete uses are found, they are not seen as importantly distinct from the incomplete ones. Indeed, this is part of my thesis about the complete, C2, use. Nevertheless, it is important to argue, against Owen and Frede,[27] that the locution *esti dia to metechein tou ontos* offers an analysis of a complete use of *esti*.

There are three main passages to be considered:

(i) 256a1
(ii) 256d8–e6
(iii) 259a4–b1

Owen considers these passages in reverse order, arguing that since neither (iii) nor (ii) can be construed as containing a complete use of *esti*, (i), despite appearances, cannot either (253–5).

I shall take them in their natural order. (i) forms part of a series of propositions about the sample kind *kinēsis*; it comes in the pair *Kinēsis is not stasis* but *Kinēsis is, because it shares in being.*[28] How should we understand the claim that *Kinēsis is, because it shares in being*? One would have to have very good reason for rejecting the view that this is a syntactically complete, existential 'is', given what has led up to this. Kinēsis is one of five distinct kinds. It was one of the first to be postulated. In the course of the proof of the non-identity of the kind *being* with either *kinēsis* or *stasis* (254d10) we have the premiss *to de ge on meikton amphoin*, being mixes with (i.e. is predicable of, as it transpires) both: *eston gar amphō pou*: for both, presumably, are. Again, one would

---

[26] Ackrill (1957) in Vlastos (ed), above n 1, 212–13, argued that Plato distinguished the 'is' of identity from that of predication in 256a–e, esp. 256a10–b4. Doubters include Owen (251 n 47, 257–8); F. A. Lewis, 'Did Plato discover the *estin* of identity?', *California Studies in Classical Antiquty*, VIII (1975), 113–43; D. Bostock, above n 21. Owen's position on this seems to me correct: he agrees with Ackrill that here Plato succeeds in distinguishing *predications* from *statements of identity*, but denies that he does so by marking off different senses of *esti* (251 n 47).

[27] Frede (above n 14) argues that all three passages to be discussed contain *incomplete* uses.

[28] This pair of statements has a different form from the next three (*K* is and is not *tauton*, is and is not *heteron*, is and is not *on*), because Stasis is not even predicable of Kinēsis.

have to have good grounds for denying that this is a complete, existential use. And this is reinforced by going back again to 250a–b where it is agreed that kinēsis and stasis both are (250a11). Now 250a–b is the culmination of the discussion of theories of being, discussed above ((b), 63). I insisted that these are theories of what there is, while conceding that ontological questions were not, for all that, Plato's chief target.

A connection can be traced between the three passages, 250a11, 254d10, and 256a1, which all make the same assertion but with increasing technicality of expression: at 250a11, we have simply, kinēsis and stasis *are*; at 254d10 the same assertion, accompanied by the claim that being mixes with both (*to de ge on meikton amphoin*); finally at 256a1 the fully technical version: *kinēsis esti, dia to metechein tou ontos*. This, then, is the argument for taking 256a1 as analysing a complete use of *esti* and *pro tanto* making an existence claim: it is naturally connected with the two earlier passages, each of which contains a complete use.[29]

(ii) 256d8–e6. This much discussed passage has often been cited to show that *esti, dia to metechein tou ontos* cannot analyse a complete use.[30] I argue that if we take a complete use to be C2, the argument has no force.

The passage is the culmination of the discussion of the interrelations of *kinēsis* with the other kinds. It is here said that *kinēsis* is not being (since it is different from being) but *kinēsis* is being, since it shares in being (*epeiper tou ontos metechei*). The result is then generalized for all the kinds, and the following conclusion drawn:

Περὶ ἕκαστον ἄρα τῶν εἰδῶν πολὺ μέν ἐστι τὸ ὄν, ἄπειρον δὲ πλήθει τὸ μὴ ὄν.

[In the case of each of the forms, then, there is much that it is and indefinitely much that it is not.[31]]

[29] Frede, above n 14, 56, claims that 256a1 is contained in 255e11: *Kinēsis is altogether different from stasis* (1). (1), he argues, contains both subsequent assertions; both (2) *(Kinēsis) is not stasis* (a14) and (3) *Kinēsis is, because it shares in being*. If this means that (3) is an *ellipse* of (1), this cannot be right. That would be to treat like the exchange 'Courage is different from foolhardiness'. 'It is indeed.' Here we have true incomplete elliptical use, but such a use would, I submit, not be permissible in Greek. If it means that (3) is an *inference* from (1), then we need not hold that because *is* in (1) is incomplete, so must *is* in (3) be. We need not, because we have an alternative account, in terms of a C2 use (in (3)), and an analogy with the inference from 'Caesar is fighting the Gauls' to 'Caesar is fighting'.

[30] e.g. by Owen 254, Malcolm, above n 16, 143; cf. Malcolm, above n 3, 165.

[31] I prefer this to the alternative translation proposed, for his own reasons, by McDowell: 'in the case of each of the forms, what is (it) is multiple and what is not (it) is indefinite in number' (above n 21, 125).

There is thus an inference from

(1) Each kind shares in being (256e3) to
(2) There is much that each kind is (e5).

And this, in Owen's view, shows that

> the use of the verb [*to be*] on which the ES rests his conclusion is the connective use, distributed between identity and predication. . . . So to extract any express recognition of a substantive or existential use of *is* from this passage would not square with the argument. (254)

With the second sentence we may agree, if by 'a substantive or existential use' is intended a use seen as discrete from the incomplete use. The passage does indeed show that Plato saw an intimate connection between (1) and (2), but this is quite consistent with taking (1) to contain a complete, C2, use. Compare the inference from *Jane is teaching* to *Jane is teaching something*. Once again, we can preserve an important insight, in this case into Plato's perception of the relation between (1) and (2), while rejecting the implausible view that (1) is an incomplete (i.e. elliptical) use.[32]

(iii) 259ab. This passage has already been discussed, in III (55). Owen's argument against this passage containing a complete use was there shown to depend on understanding a complete use as one which *does not allow* a completion. If we understand a complete use as one which allows but does not require a completion, the sentence presents no difficulty for the view that *esti, dia to metechein tou ontos* (and the variant here found: *metaschon tou ontos*, 259a6) represent a complete use.

To sum up my discussion of the passages containing the key phrase *esti, dia to metechein tou ontos*: there is every reason to take passage (i) as containing a complete use. Since passages (ii) and (iii) repeat the phrase, this gives us good grounds for interpreting them in the same way. But passages (ii) and (iii) suggest a C2 understanding of complete, rather than C1; that is, a use connected to the incomplete use in the manner explained in III. This being so, we can agree with those who deny that distinguishing the complete from the incomplete use was an important part of Plato's strategy, while insisting that the

---

[32] Heinaman, above n 3, 7–8, suggests that in this passage Plato either 'slides from' *Each form is, (i.e. exists)* to *each form is (predicatively) many things*, or infers the latter from the former. My view is the second; the inference is a straightforward one if a C2 use is involved in (1). Malcolm, above n 3, 165, resists this interpretation on the grounds that such an inference would be 'flagrantly fallacious'.

phrase in question does analyse a complete (C2) use. Plato has no idea of solving the problem of not-being by allowing that *X is F* need not entail *X is*, no wish to allow that only a subclass of things that are *F* are things that are (i.e. exist). But though it is not part of his overall strategy to draw a distinction between the complete and the incomplete use, he does, I believe, employ it as an occasional tactic, to wit, in his proof of the non-identity of the kinds *being* and *different*.

(d) 255c–d: the proof of the non-identity of being and the different

This proof proceeds by invoking a distinction, said to be familiar to Theaetetus (255c12), in the way things that are are said to be:

Ἀλλ’ οἶμαι σε συγχωρεῖν τῶν ὄντων τὰ μὲν αὐτὰ καθ’ αὑτά, τὰ δὲ πρὸς ἄλλα ἀεὶ λέγεσθαι.

[But I think you agree that some of the things that are are said to be 'themselves by themselves', while some are said to be in relation to other things.]

In contrast, that which is different is always said to be different in relation to something different (*to de ge heteron aei pros heteron*).

What is the distinction alluded to? One line of interpretation, A, takes it to be between uses of *esti*: according to A, the proof points out that *esti* has both a *pros allo* use and an *auto kath’ hauto* use, while *heteron* has only the former. The other line, B, denies this.[33] Those who favour A differ over whether the distinction is, Ai, between the complete (*auto kath’ hauto*) and the incomplete (*pros allo*) uses,[34] or, Aii, between distinct incomplete uses which these labels pick out.[35] I refer the reader to Bostock's recent discussion of the passage, which argues for the natural interpretation Ai, and against recent advocates of the alternatives.[36] Assuming that interpretation Ai is correct, we may ask: is the complete (*auto kath’ hauto*) use to be understood as C1 or as C2?

There seems to be no objection to taking the distinction to be

[33] Heinaman, above n 3, 14, '.. the passage is standardly interpreted as drawing a distinction between non-relative or complete predicates such as *man* and relative or incomplete predicates such as *equal*'. See, e.g., Á. E. Taylor, 'The *Sophist* and the *Statesman*' (London, 1961), 161 for this view.

[34] e.g. J. M. E. Moravcsik, 'Being and Meaning in the *Sophist*', Acta Philosophica Fennica, XIV (1962), 48.

[35] Owen, above n 2, 255–8; Frede, above n 14, 12–29.

[36] Above n 21. To Bostock's arguments against Owen and Frede, who insist that Plato's phrases *pros allo* and *pros heteron* are not to be equated with the standard formula *pros ti*, one may add that in *Philebus* 51c–d (on beauty) Plato himself uses *pros ti* and *pros heteron* interchangeably to make the contrast with *autas kath’ hautas (kalas)*.

between an incomplete (*pros allo*) use and a use which *does not need* a completion, that is, a C2 use. Plato's point would then be that every use of *heteron* requires a completion while some uses of *esti* do not require a completion. To make his point Plato needs only the C2 understanding of an *auto kath'hauto* use: he does not have to claim that there are some uses of *esti* which additionally do not *allow* a completion (C1). Indeed the traditional explication of the *auto kath'hauto/ pros ti* distinction is phrased in precisely C2 terms (Diogenes Laertius III. 108: 'things which are said *kath' heauta* are such as do not need anything additional in their interpretation').

I believe that this proof does invoke a distinction between a C2 complete and an incomplete use of *esti*. But there is no inconsistency in maintaining both of the following; (i) in this passage, 255cd, to achieve a proof of the non-identity of the kinds *being* and *different*, Plato points out that *esti*, unlike *heteron*, has a complete (C2) and an incomplete use; and (ii) the relation between the complete (C2) and the incomplete use is such that the distinction between them cannot form part of his overall strategy in solving the problems of not-being.

Conclusion

I have argued for a new understanding of the distinction between the syntactically complete and incomplete use of *esti*, supplanting the traditional understanding in terms of *monadic* and *dyadic*. A consequence of the proposed characterization, which I labelled C2, is that the complete and incomplete uses are related as follows: *X is* (complete use) entails *X is something* and *X is F* entails *X is*. *X is not* (complete use) is equivalent to *X is not anything at all*. Understanding the complete *esti* thus allows us to say (*contra* Owen) that the *Sophist*'s problems about not being are stated in terms of the complete *esti*, but also to see why Plato found no role for *to mē on/to mēdamōs on* where that is the negation of the complete *esti*. We can also agree that at 255c–d Plato draws attention to the distinction between the complete and incomplete uses of 'is', while denying that this amounts to the discovery of a fundamental distinction between existence and the copula.

I hope to have shown that understanding the relation between the complete and incomplete uses of *esti* in the way proposed yields a satisfying reading of the *Sophist*. I believe that this proposal for the *Sophist* can be extended to, and supported by consideration of, other works of Plato and indeed Aristotle. Aristotle's well-known insistence (*Analytica Posteriora* 92b4–8) that it is necessary to know *that* a thing is in order to know *what* it is (in other cases, as with 'goatstag', one can know only what the name signifies) is well explained if we pursue the analogy between *einai* and verbs such as *teach*: compare 'it is necessary to know that X is teaching in order to know what X is teaching'. And though Aristotle explicitly recognizes that *what is not is thought about* does not entail *what is not is* (the very point which the *Sophist* requires but which Plato fails to make), his discussion of the point does not suggest that he finds a clear semantic and syntactic distinction between the *esti*s in that pair of sentences.[37] *Sed haec hactenus*.[38]

Somerville College, Oxford

---

[37] *de Interpretatione* 21a31–2; *Sophistici Elenchi* 166b37–167a4, cf. 180a32–4. In the second passage the fallacious inference is put under the general heading of fallacies παρὰ τὸ ἁπλῶς τόδε ἢ πῇ λέγεσθαι καὶ μὴ κυρίως and is treated analogously to that from *the Indian is white in the tooth* to *the Indian is white*. Each involves the illicit removal of a qualifier (is white *in the tooth*, is *thought about*). Far from showing that Aristotle has here recognized two distinct senses of *esti*, his discussion of the fallacy suggests that he assumed a single sense to be involved, as with *white*. His point would then be that just as being white in the tooth is not really a way of being white, being thought about is not really a way of being, (as being an expectant mother is not necessarily being a mother). So that although he points out that 'it is not the same thing to be something and to be *haplōs*' this does not seem to be an express recognition of a clear-cut distinction such as Vlastos believed to be latently known to every speaker of Greek.

[38] An earlier version of this paper was given to the Southern Association of Ancient Philosophy in Oxford in September 1983. I am grateful to those who participated in the discussion then, and to Michael Woods and Christopher Kirwan, for helpful comments.

Lesley Brown, "The verb 'to be' in Greek Philosophy: Some Remarks" in S. Everson (ed.), Language (Cambridge, 1994)

6 Falsehood and not-being in Plato's *Sophist*

JOHN MCDOWELL

1. For me, G. E. L. Owen's 'Plato on Not-Being'[1] radically improved the prospects for a confident overall view of its topic. Hitherto, passage after passage had generated reasonable disagreement over Plato's intentions, and the disputes were not subject to control by a satisfying picture of his large-scale strategy; so that the general impression, as one read the *Sophist*, was one of diffuseness and unclarity of purpose. By focusing discussion on the distinction between otherness and contrariety (257B1–C4), Owen showed how, at a stroke, a mass of confusing exegetical alternatives could be swept away, and the dialogue's treatment of not-being revealed as a sustained and tightly organised assault on a single error. In what follows, I take Owen's focusing of the issue for granted, and I accept many of his detailed conclusions. Where I diverge from Owen – in particular over the nature of the difficulty about falsehood that Plato tackles in the *Sophist* (§§5 and 6 below) – it is mainly to press further in the direction he indicated, in the interest of a conviction that the focus can and should be made even sharper.

2. By 256E5–6 the Eleatic Stranger (ES) can say 'In the case of each of the forms, then, what is is multiple and what is not is indefinite in number.' Yet it is only at 258B6–7 that Theaetetus is allowed to announce the availability, at last, of the application for 'what is not' that was needed in order to flush the sophist from his refuge. Why was it not available already at 256E5–6? What is the relation between the application for 'what is not' vindicated in the earlier passage and the application vindicated in the later passage?

1 In *Plato, I: Metaphysics and Epistemology*, ed. Gregory Vlastos (Garden City 1971), 223–67.

We can make the question more pressing. What was needed in order to capture the sophist was a non-paradoxical characterisation of the sort of unreality a semblance has, and of falsehood (236D9–237A9, 239C9–240C6, 240C7–241B3). Ultimately the first task is merged into the second (264C10–D5).[2] Now when the ES tackles the second task, the backward reference (263B11–12) with which he seeks to justify his use of the expression 'what is not' is to 256E5–6: the *earlier* of our two passages, not the one in which Theaetetus notes the participants' acquisition of the equipment necessary for their project of pinning down the sophist. But if the project required the ES to go beyond 256E5–6, how can the reference back to the earlier passage be appropriate in its execution?[3]

I shall deal with this composite difficulty by dividing it. First (§3 below) I shall consider the relation between the passages in which 256E5–6 and 258B6–7 are embedded, in abstraction from the question how either is related to the final characterisation of falsehood. Then (§4 below) I shall return to the latter question.

3. 256E5–6 expresses a generalisation of the results of 255E8–256D10. So its employment of 'what is not' must be warranted by the fact that each form or kind *is not* indefinitely many others, as change is not rest (255E14), the same (256A5), other (256C8), being (256D8); that is, in that it is other than – non-identical with – each of them. If, then, we were to consider the expression '(is) not beautiful' within the framework constructed in this passage, we should find ourselves understanding it so as to be true of anything other than the form or kind *beautiful*; no less true, then, of Helen or Aphrodite than of the snub-nosed Socrates, and hardly a plausible reading for day-to-day uses of the expression (cf. 257D10). So it would be unsurprising to find the ES moving beyond 255E8–257A7 – where we are supposed to have been made comfortable with the use of 'is not' in statements of non-identity – in the direction of making room for the use of 'is not' in statements of negative predication.

2 Owen, 250, 259.
3 See Edward N. Lee, 'Plato on Negation and Not-Being in the *Sophist*', *Philosophical Review*, 81 (1972), 267–304, at p. 299 n. 53. (The difficulty is more serious than Lee allows: the treatment of falsehood is not just 'one of [Plato's] major "analytic" problems', but the very problem alluded to at 258B6–7.) James P. Kostman, 'False Logos and Not-Being in Plato's *Sophist*', in *Patterns in Plato's Thought*, ed. J. M. E. Moravcsik (Dordrecht 1973), 192–212, acknowledges inability to explain the reference to 256E5–6 (197, 210 n. 11).

And I believe that is indeed what we are meant to find in the passage that starts at 257B1.[4]

Not that the enterprise of 257B1 ff. is to be conceived as disconnected from that of 255E8–257A7. Together the two passages constitute a careful step-wise response to Eleatic doubts about 'is not'. The first does not merely assume that 'is not' is acceptable in statements of non-identity, but painstakingly works for that conclusion. And the second, in arguing that 'is not' is acceptable in statements of negative predication, employs a strategy essentially involving the materials that have proved useful in the first.

(1) It has been accepted that the nature of *the other* is all-pervasive (254D4–E7). The ES begins the first passage with particular exemplifications of that conclusion: not (brazenly) statements like 'Change is-not rest', but (cautiously) statements like 'Change is not-rest' (the negative particle is ostentatiously annexed, by word order, whose effect I have tried to capture by hyphenating, to the name of the kind than which change is being said to be other, not to the verb). We may be hard pressed to see a real distinction here. But it was the negating of the verb 'to be' in particular, not negation in general, that Parmenides found unintelligible. The ES is starting with something that should be uncontentious: something against which, as it stands, no Parmenidean strictures apply. The upshot, indeed, will be that the puzzling distinction marks no real difference; but in the dialectical circumstances this needs to be argued, not assumed.

The ES proceeds innocently through a series of examples of the form presumed uncontentious: 'Change is not-rest' (255E14), 'Change is not-the-same' (256A5), 'Change is not-other' (256C8). Then he unsheathes his knife. Being was one of the five kinds of which it was agreed, at 254D4–255E2, that each is other than all the others; so anyone who has allowed the first three examples to pass, as true in virtue of the fact that change is other than rest, the same, and other, has no ground for protest when, in virtue of the structurally indistinguishable fact that change is other than being, we insist on what is in fact another example of the same form: 'Change is not-being' (256D8). Moreover, the same can be said of

---

4 A *caveat*: when I write, as I shall, of the 'is not' of non-identity and the 'is not' of negative predication, I do not mean to imply that Plato aims to distinguish senses of 'is not' (and correspondingly of 'is'). See Owen, 257–8.

any other kind (other than being itself) (256D11–E2). It is clear now that we must abandon any hope of accepting the negative statements that constitute the natural expression for the pervasiveness of otherness, while divesting them of counter-Eleatic significance by insisting that being is not what is negated; and the ES now takes himself to be entitled to relocate the 'not' in statements of non-identity like the first three examples – statements other than those in which one term is being itself. The puzzling distinction vanishes, shown up as empty; and, on the strength of 255E3–7, the ES can conclude that each kind or form is-not all of the indefinitely many others.[5]

(2) The second passage also attacks (on a less restricted front) a Parmenidean refusal to make sense of 'is not'. The ES diagnoses the refusal as based on a mistake about negation: that of supposing that the addition of 'not' yields an expression for the contrary of what was meant by the original expression (257B1–C4).[6] In the case of, say, 'not beautiful', the mistake does not have the effect of depriving the negative expression of meaning altogether. The meaning of 'ugly' is a perfectly good meaning, even though it is wrong to assign it to 'not beautiful'. But in the case of 'is not', the mistake is destructive. An expression that meant the contrary of what 'is' means would mean, if it meant anything, the same as what would be meant, if anything could be, by 'in no way is'; and this is an expression for which no use (as distinct from mention) can be found, even in attempts to formulate in the material mode the thought that it has no application (237B7–239C8, on 'in no way being'; recalled, in terms of 'contrary of being', at 258E1–259A5).[7]

The ES works up to the destructive form of the mistake from a consideration of the non-destructive form. What makes it possible to say significantly of something that it is not-beautiful – what

---

5 Cf. Owen, 233–4, n. 21. The 'both . . . and . . .' construction is strained, on Owen's construal of 256C11–12; and the strain is unnecessary, given the evident intelligibility of the line of thought I have set out.

6 See Owen, *passim*: e.g. 231–2. (It seems perverse to take 257B1–C4 as anything but an introduction, no doubt partly promissory. to what follows. Cf. Lee, 268–9; and, differently, Frank A. Lewis, 'Plato on "Not"', *California Studies in Classical Antiquity*, 9 (1976), 89–115, at pp. 111–12, n. 19.)

7 The mistake would undermine statements of non-identity too: (1) has dealt piecemeal with that application. Note that it would not help to protest that we should be considering not 'is not', but 'is not . . .' If to negate being is to deny all being to one's subject, thereby defeating one's attempt to speak of it, then it cannot make any difference if one writes (say) 'beautiful' after the incoherent 'is not'.

ensures that the expression 'not beautiful' is not condemned, whenever uttered, to fly out vainly into a void, so much empty chatter – is not (as the erroneous view might have it) that, should the statement be true, the negative expression would strike home against the subject's being *ugly* (for such statements can be true even though their subjects are not ugly); but rather that the negative expression, if uttered in a true statement, would strike home against some attribute *other* than *beautiful*, possessed by the subject (257D10–11). (It is not that the erroneous view, applied to 'not beautiful', generates a worry about idle chatter; that it does not is precisely what is meant by describing this application of the view as non-destructive. But an adherent of the view would be saddled thereby with an account of why admittedly 'safe' examples of negative expressions are safe, as 'not beautiful' is, which could not but make 'is not' problematic.)

I intend the phrase 'strike home against' as a counterpart, coloured in the interest of conveying a feeling for what I take to be the ES's point, for drabber terms that Plato uses: 'indicate' (relating expressions and things, 257B10) and 'utter . . . of' (relating utterers, expressions, and things, 257D10). We should not, I believe, commit Plato to the view that the relation in question, between negative expressions and things (specifically, something like attributes) other than those meant by the words negated, is in any strict sense a semantic or meaning-determining relation.[8] Compare the tolerance of phrases like 'true in virtue of'. Sometimes we should decline to fill the gap, in ' "Socrates is not beautiful" is true in virtue of . . .', with anything that would not count as displaying the sense of the quoted sentence. But this does not mean that we necessarily reject, for all purposes, such claims as this: ' "Socrates is not beautiful" is true in virtue of Socrates' being snub-nosed'; and it is at least not wrong to say that the form or kind, *snub-nosed*, is other than the form or kind, *beautiful*. Of course such remarks do not begin to look like a determination of the sense of 'not beautiful'.

It can be tempting to elaborate them into such a determination – either reconstruing 'other than' as 'incompatible with', and analysing 'Socrates is not beautiful' as 'Socrates has some attribute incompatible with being beautiful', or leaving 'other than'

8 For this crucial point, see Lewis, 112 n. 27.

meaning what it does in 255E8–257A12, and using a universal quantifier: 'All Socrates' attributes are non-identical with being beautiful.' Commentators have not been reluctant to succumb to these temptations on Plato's behalf. But an interest in either sort of elaboration is, to say the least, not obviously present in the text.[9] (Incompatibility figures in accounts of the *Sophist* only because its proponents cannot see how Plato can achieve his purpose without it; and I think the same goes for the universal quantifier imported by those who rightly jib at an unannounced shift in the sense of 'other than', but take the same view of the purpose.) This unconcern with analysis need not seem a defect, if we see the ES's project as what it is: not to give an account of the sense of phrases like 'not beautiful', but rather to scotch a mistake about what entitles us to our confidence that they are not idle chatter, that they do indeed have the precise sense that we take them to have. (No need, in executing this project, to produce any substantive theory about what that sense is.)[10] The mistake is worth scotching here, not for its own sake, but because if it is allowed to pass in this case it can be carried over to undermine our confidence in the intelligibility of 'is not'.

We might put the ES's point about 'not beautiful' thus: 'not beautiful' is to be understood, not in terms of the contrary of *beautiful*, but in terms of that part of the nature of otherness that is set over against it. My suggestion is that 'understood in terms of' (at least in the affirmative component of this thesis) is best not taken as promising an analysis. 'Not beautiful' means exactly what it does, *viz. not beautiful*; the role of the notion of otherness is in an explanation, at a sub-semantical level, of why we do not need to fear that such a semantical remark is condemned to vacuity.[11]

9 See Lewis, 105–6; 113 n. 40.
10 An attribute can be other than *beautiful* without being (ever) appropriately mentionable as that in virtue of which something is not beautiful. In order to *guarantee* that what is true in virtue of some fact expressible in terms of otherness is that something is *not* beautiful, Plato would need the commentators' extra apparatus. But he does not need extra apparatus for his different purpose. His point is this: what the attributes that *can* be cited in the role in question have in common is that they are *other* than *beautiful*. (See Lewis, 104.) This suffices without further ado to correct the error about contrariety, which is what threatens the intelligibility of 'is not'. (It is not to the point to object that someone who is, e.g., long-haired has an attribute other than *beautiful*, but is not necessarily not-beautiful on that account. This contradicts no thesis of Plato's. Cf. David Wiggins, 'Sentence Meaning, Negation, and Plato's Problem of Non-Being', in Vlastos, op. cit., 268–303, at pp. 291, 294.)
11 Here I diverge from Lee's thesis that otherness plays a novel, 'constitutive' role at 257C5 ff. What seems correct is this: 255E8–257A12 yields nothing that could be called 'the nature of the not beautiful' (in the sense which that passage could countenance, the not

The ES proceeds to the case of negating being by generalising his point about 'not beautiful' (258A1–2, 4–5, 7–9), and then representing the case of 'is not' as a further instance of the generalisation (258A11–B3). But the inference by instantiation can be understood also as a matter of reformulating the generalisation:[12] 258A11–B3 introduces the idea, not of a part of the nature of otherness contrasted with being as such (whatever that might mean), but of a part of the nature of otherness contrasted with being . . . (e.g. with being beautiful). We can capture the movement of thought as follows. The thesis from which the ES generalises – that *not beautiful* is to be 'understood in terms of' (see above) otherness than *beautiful* – could be written thus: (*being*) not beautiful is to be 'understood in terms of' otherness than (*being*) *beautiful*. When the ES instantiates the generalisation with respect to being, what happens is, in effect, that 'not' shifts back to the hitherto implicit verb, and the complement recedes out of focus. The point becomes this: *not being* (*e.g. beautiful*) is to be 'understood in terms of' otherness than *being* (*beautiful* – to stay with the same example).[13] Only the mistake about contrariety – which has been adequately refuted by the discussion of the case, presumed uncontentious, in which 'not' does not go with the verb 'to be' – could make it seem that the change in the placing of 'not' makes a difference.

4. If I am right, the not-being welcomed at 258B6–7, as what was needed in order to pin down the sophist, is the not-being that

beautiful – e.g. the attribute *snub-nosed* – is rightly so called, not by virtue of its own nature, but by virtue of partaking in the form of otherness: cf. 255E4–6); whereas 257C5 ff. is concerned with something of which it can be said that its nature is being not beautiful (258B8–C4). But Lee's 'constitutive' role for otherness seems problematic. He explains it in remarks like this: 'The determinate sense of "*x* is not tall" . . . lies precisely, but lies entirely, in saying that tall is what *x* is not' (295); but this would scarcely cut any ice with Parmenides. It seems preferable to relocate Lee's distinction: 255E8–257A12 equips us to understand a supervenient role, and 255C5 ff. a constitutive role, for the notion of *being not beautiful*; the notion of otherness plays a semantical role in the former passage and a sub-semantical role in the latter. (The only semantical thesis suggested by the second passage is to the effect that 'not beautiful' means *not beautiful*; I believe this captures in semantical terms the point of the implicit thesis that the nature of the not beautiful is being not beautiful.)

12 See Lee, 282 n. 21.

13 Owen (239 n. 33) objects to supplying 'part of' with 'the nature of being' at 258B1, on the ground that it implies the reductive thesis (i.e. insistence on detaching 'not' from the verb 'to be': Owen, 236–41). But if the notion of a part of the nature of being were established, as applying to such items as *being beautiful*, the reading Owen objects to could make the point in my text, precisely without implying the reductive thesis. A better reason against 'part of' is that the notion of parts of the nature of being has not been established (see Lee, 283–4).

figures in *negative* predications like 'Socrates is not beautiful.' (That statement attributes not-being to Socrates in that it says that he is not – beautiful.) When the sophist's escape is blocked (cf. 264B9–D9) by the production of a non-paradoxical characterisation of falsehood, the point, in the example chosen, is evidently that a false *affirmative* predication attributes what is not to its subject (263B9). Part of our composite problem (§2 above) was to explain why pinning down the sophist requires the materials of 258B6–7, not just those of 256E5–6. So we need to explain how the ES's description of a false affirmative predication, in 263B, can be seen as an application of the conceptual equipment established in the discussion of negative predication.

This component of the problem is easily solved if we understand the 'is not' of 263B as arrived at by a 'converse' reformulation of the 'is not' of 258B6–7. The earlier passage signals vindication of the legitimacy of 'is not' in statements like 'Socrates is not beautiful'; that statement can be reformulated as claiming that *beautiful* is not in relation to Socrates, and now we have the terminology of 263B (capturing the falsity of 'Socrates is beautiful').[14] This answers the question why we have to wait until 258B6–7 before being told we have what is needed for pinning down the sophist: what 263B requires is (a 'converse' version of) the 'is not' of negative predication, which is not yet available at 256E5–6.[15]

The other component of our composite problem was to explain why it is appropriate for the treatment of falsehood to refer back to 256E5–6, even though the conceptual equipment it needs was not yet established in that passage. We can now see at least the outline of a solution to this problem too. The ES's vindication of the 'is not' of negative predication builds essentially on the fact that, whatever attribute one takes, there are plenty of attributes other than it – the negative part of what was said at 256E5–6. If the use of 'is not' at 263B is nothing but a transformational derivative of the 'is not' of negative predication, the ES's entitlement to the

---

14 On the 'converse' idiom, see Michael Frede, *Prädikation und Existenzaussage* (Göttingen 1967), 52–5, 80, 94–5; Owen, e.g. 237–8. As will emerge, I think there is less of this idiom in the *Sophist* than is commonly thought.
15 No doubt the equipment of 256E5–6 would serve for an account of falsity in identity statements. But it would not be generalisable to cover false predications, whereas the account of false predications could be applied to identity statements ('*The same as Socrates* is not about Theaetetus').

former must be justified by precisely what justifies his entitlement to the latter. So it is exactly to the point for 263B11–12 to hark back, past the treatment of negative predication, to the foundation on which that treatment builds.[16]

There is a complication, resulting from the usual way of understanding 263B11–12 and 256E5–6. What we find at 263B11–12 is this: 'For we said that in the case of each (thing) there are many (things) which are and many which are not.' On the usual view, this relates to its context as follows. Universal instantiation of its negative part, with respect to Theaetetus, is supposed to yield, as something the ES could address to Theaetetus, 'There are many (things) which are not in relation to (in the case of) you.' Then '*In flight* is not in relation to you' (263B9, with 'in relation to you' supplied from 263B4–5, 11: the ES's account of the falsity of 'Theaetetus is in flight') is an exemplification: it cites one of the many such things which the instantiation assures us there are. On this view, then, 263B11–12 is taken to contain 'converse' uses of 'is' and 'is not', with the universal quantifier 'each (thing)' binding what would be in the subject place in a more straightforward formulation. The force is: in the case of everything (including Theaetetus), there are many things that it is (e.g. seated) and many that it is not (e.g. in flight). Since 263B11–12 purports simply to repeat 256E5–6 ('we said', 263B12), the standard view imposes a structural parallel in the interpretation of 256E5–6: again, 'converse' uses of 'is' and 'is not', with the universal quantifier binding what would be in the subject place in a more straightforward formulation. Here, then, the force is: in the case of each form, there are many things that it is and an indefinite number that it is not (that is – this is all that 255E8 ff. has licensed – an indefinite number with which it is non-identical).[17]

These interpretations evidently raise a difficulty about 'we said', at 263B12. On this reading, 263B11–12 does not simply restate what was said at 256E5–6; it makes two tacit modifications – modifications which, in view of its bland claim to be a repetition, we should be constrained to regard as surreptitious. First, the range of the universal quantifier is extended, from forms to

16 In fact, as we shall see, 256E5–6 is more straightforwardly relevant to the 'converse' use of 'is not' than this outline explanation suggests: not just obliquely relevant through its bearing on the non-'converse' basis of the transformation.
17 See, e.g., Owen, 235.

everything (including Theaetetus). Second, the negative part of the generalisation is extended from denials of identity to cover negative predications as well.

Can these modifications be incorporated into an overall interpretation that solves our problem: that is, one that gives 257B1 ff. the sort of importance in the final characterisation of falsehood that 258B6–7 would lead us to expect, and accounts for the fact that 263B11–12 refers back to 256E5–6? It could be claimed, plausibly enough, that the modifications are licensed by 257B1 ff., given that that passage extends the scope for acceptable uses of 'is not' precisely from statements of non-identity between kinds or forms to statements like 'Socrates is not beautiful' (§3 above). But the surreptitiousness is still a mystery. It constitutes, in effect, a pretence that nothing of importance for the project of 263B has happened since 256E5–6. Thus, even if *we* can see 257B1 ff. playing the role we have been led to expect, we find *Plato* unaccountably refusing to acknowledge it.[18]

18 Owen (260) conspicuously fails to appeal to 257B1 ff. in explaining the tacit modifications. What Owen explains is not the extension in the later passage, but the restriction to non-identity in the earlier. The idea seems to be as follows: Plato wants to be able to say, of *any* attribute, that it is not (in relation to some subjects) (259); this desideratum can be met for pervasive forms like being, identity, and difference only if the 'is not' is understood as that of non-identity; hence that is what figures in 256E5–6. But: (1) Why the putative desideratum? Not for 263B: Plato would hardly be at pains to secure that '*In flight* is not about Theaetetus' should seem an example of a general kind of truth (examples of which hold about all forms, including the pervasive ones), when the move needed to construct the general kind of truth (understanding the 'is not' as that of non-identity) actually renders problematic the status of the 'exemplification' (in which the 'is not' is precisely not to be so understood). (2) The putative desideratum is not enunciated by 256E5–6 as Owen interprets it; he takes 256E5–6 to say, not that any attribute is not in relation to something, but that an indefinite number of attributes are not in relation to every form. Of course the indefinite number, in any case, will be all the attributes other than the topic form itself, including the pervasive ones. But we have no reason to suppose Plato wants to be able to say 'an indefinite number' because he *anyway* wants to be able to say 'all' (to include the pervasive forms), and *consequently* has to understand 'is not' in terms of non-identity; rather than that he finds himself able to say 'an indefinite number' (or 'all', if he had felt like it) because he is *anyway* understanding 'is not', at this stage, in terms of non-identity. (3) It is not the restriction to non-identity in 256E5–6 that needs explaining. If we do not believe that Plato unpardonably helps himself in mid-argument to a new construal of 'other' (as we should not: Owen, 232 n. 19), we must regard non-identity as fundamental in his anti-Eleatic strategy. What more natural, then, than that he should begin on 'is not' by making room for its use in statements of non-identity? As for what does need explaining: against Parmenides, it takes more than the mere observation that *beautiful, in flight*, etc., are non-pervasive kinds to justify going beyond 256E5–6 so as to allow oneself the use of 'is not' in negative predications (or 'converse' counterparts thereof). Owen's suggestion that the observation is enough to explain the 'tacit extension' leaves no room for 257B1 ff., understood as a careful defence of the use of 'is not' in negative predications.

Is it possible, then, to eliminate the tacit modifications: to understand 263B11–12 as nothing but a repetition of 256E5–6? This requires us to suppose that 'in the case of each (thing)' at 263B12 can be glossed, from 256E5, as 'in the case of each of the forms', and that the negative part of 263B11–12 involves nothing but statements of non-identity. It would follow that the relation between 'There are many (things) that are not about (in the case of) each (thing)' – the negative part of 263B11–12 – and '*In flight* is not about (in relation to) Theaetetus' – the ES's account of the falsity of 'Theaetetus is in flight' – cannot be one of exemplification. However, so long as 'about each (thing)', in the generalisation, is understood as supplementing 'converse' uses of 'is' and 'is not', it seems impossible to see what else the relation could be, and the tacit modifications seem unavoidable. The key to an alternative reading is the possibility that the 'about' phrases function differently. As before, 'about Theaetetus' supplements a 'converse' use of 'is not', in '*In flight* is not about Theaetetus'; but we can take 'about each (thing)', at 263B12, to constitute a simple quantifier phrase (like 'concerning everything' in, at least, logician's English), binding what the subjects of *non*-'converse' uses of 'is' and 'is not' are said to be and not to be; and similarly with 'about each of the forms' at 256E5.[19]

The force of 256E5–6, on this alternative reading, will be as follows: in the case of each of the forms, what is (it) is multiple and what is not (it) is indefinite in number. There is no problem about understanding this as a conclusion from what precedes it, so long as we see that the generalisation ('each. . . (it). . . (it)') picks up, not the role of *change* in the preceding demonstrations, but the role of, for instance, *the same*. In the case of the form, *the same*, change both is it (256A7–8) and is not it (256A5 'is not-it', convertible to 'is-not it' after 256D8–9: §3 above).[20] Just so, in the case of every form, there are many things (or at any rate many forms; forms are all that the ES's variables have so far ranged over) that are it and an indefinite number that are not it.[21]

The meat of the remark, in the context of Plato's anti-Eleatic project, lies in its negative component; and of course I do not

---

19 The preposition '*peri*' governs different cases in 263B11 and 263B12, and the same case in 263B12 and 256E5.

20 We are likely to suppose that 'is' functions differently in its two occurrences; but Plato seems to suggest, rather, that the difference of function is in what replaces 'it' (256A10–12). See Owen, 258 n. 63. (Cf. n. 4 above.)

21 R. S. Bluck, *Plato's Sophist* (Manchester 1975), considers taking 256E5–6 this way round, but rejects it on the ground that on this interpretation the passage does not have the right inferential relation to 256D11–E3 (158). But as regards the negative part,

pretend that it makes any doctrinal difference whether we suppose the ES to say that in the case of each form it is not an indefinite number of others, or that in the case of each form an indefinite number of others are not it. The point of the second reading is not that the substance is different, but that it permits us to extract an appropriate sense from the text without understanding 'in the case of each of the forms' as supplementing 'converse' uses of 'is' and 'is not'. This way we can take 263B11–12 to say, as it purports to, the very same thing, without threatening the intelligibility of its relation to the claim that *in flight* is not in relation to Theaetetus.

The claim that the form, *in flight*, is not in relation to Theaetetus is a claim on whose availability, to capture the falsity of 'Theaetetus is in flight', the ES insists. He needs to defend the claim against an Eleatic objection to the effect that its use of 'is not' makes it undermine itself, offering, so to speak, to deprive itself of a topic. Not at all, says the ES. That which is not, in the relevant sense, is not that which utterly is not (long since dismissed), but that which *is* other[22] (than that which is in

whatever we can say to explain the inferential relation which, taken one way round, it bears to 256D11–E3 (or, better, 255E8–256E4) – and Bluck says something (158–9) – will serve equally well for the inverted reading; and the positive part, on either view, needs generalising beyond anything said in 256D11–E3 (my view makes it a perfectly intelligible extension of the results of 255E8–D10). Two further possible objections: (1) If 256E5–6 said (as Owen implies: 235, 254) that about each form what is not is more numerous than what is, it would be an objection that, taking the passage my way, this would be false of pervasive forms: all the forms that are not *the same* are *the same* – in the relevant senses – and there is one more form that is *the same*, viz. the same itself. But 'many' does not exclude 'indefinite in number', and the text leaves it open that in some cases the many may be *more* than the indefinite number. The distinction is adequately explained by the fact that with non-pervasive forms there are fewer exemplifications of the 'is . . .' component. (In the case of each form, what is it is – at least – multiple, and what is not it is indefinite in number.) (2) On my view, 257A4–6, where *being* is the *subject* to 'is . . .' and 'is not . . .', cannot be (as is often said: see, e.g., Lee, 282, n. 21) an instantiation of the generalisation of 256E5–6, where the quantifier binds what *follows* 'is . . .' and 'is not . . .' But the affirmative part of 257A4–6 ('being is its single self') never looked, on any view, like an instantiation of 256E5–6. (And, given the reversibility of statements of non–identity, the negative part follows by instantiation from 256E5–6 taken either way round.)

22 *'Onta hetera'* ('things that are other'), 263B11. Cf. Wiggins, 295: he renders the relevant sentence thus: '[i.e. it says] things which are[2], but different things which are[2] from the things which are[1] respecting Theaetetus'; and he takes 'are[2]' as synonymous with 'are[1]' – 'In *Theaetetus is flying* the kind Flies is[1] because it applies to *something* even if it does not apply to Theaetetus.' It must be on this foundation that Wiggins bases the idea that Plato 'persists in seeing Socrates' being able to purport that "Flying is respecting Theaetetus" as explained by there being such a *genos* as Flying (rather than vice versa)' (298); there being such a *genos* being for Plato, Wiggins thinks, a matter of its having an extension (cf. also 287). But where Wiggins has Plato (deplorably) insisting that the meaningfulness of 'Theaetetus is in flight' requires that *in flight* be *instantiated*, what Plato in fact insists is that *in flight* is *other* (than what is in relation to Theaetetus); this is not Wiggins's dubious condition for the statement to be *meaningful*, but a perfectly correct condition for it to be *false*.

relation to the subject[23]). And the 'is' I have stressed, which emphasises that the claim does not deprive itself of a topic, cannot now be queried; for it has been accepted, at 256E5–6, that for every form there *are* plenty of forms that are not (because they *are* other than) it. This fills out our outline answer to the second component of our composite question; it shows how it can be that, although 263B uses 'is not' in a way that is established only in the course of 257B1 ff., it is nevertheless entirely appropriate for it to justify its doing so by a restatement (just that, not a surreptitious improvement) of 256E5–6.[24]

5. It may seem back to front to broach only now the question of what puzzle about falsehood the sophist is supposed to hide behind. But this way we can let our interpretation of the problem be influenced by the desirability of finding Plato saying something to the point in response to it.

Many commentators suppose that the puzzle about falsehood is on these lines: the falsity of a false belief or statement would have to consist in the fact that the *situation* or *state of affairs* it represents is an utter nonentity, something totally devoid of being; but there is no coherent way to express such a 'fact' (237B7–239C8), so no coherent way to formulate a characterisation of falsehood made inescapable by a correct understanding of what falsehood would be (if there were any such thing).[25] However, when the ES comes to use the dangerous phrase 'what is not' in the characterisation of falsehood, his point, as we have seen, seems to be that the falsity of 'Theaetetus is in flight' consists in its attributing what is not to its subject, in that *in flight* is not in relation to Theaetetus. And if the puzzle was the one about situations or states of affairs outlined above, this response (on its own at least) seems irrelevant. The sophist might reasonably object:

23 This would translate *!ontōn . . . peri sou'* at 263 B11. But *'ontōn'* is very dubious: in favour of the manuscripts' *'ontōs'*, see Frede, 57–8. Even so, it is natural to supply *'tōn ontōn'* ('than the things that are') between *'hetera'* and *'peri sou'*.

24 Owen (260) gives a clear statement of the relevance of non-identity between attributes to the justification of the 'is not' of 'converse' negative predication, but does not see that this removes the need to interpret 263B11–12 as modifying 256E5–6.

25 See especially Wiggins. For a variant, Owen, 245: he uses the word 'situation', but what he has in mind, as missing from reality when the statement 'Theaetetus is in flight' is false, is the flight of which the statement accuses Theaetetus. (This is in an account of *Tht.* 188C9–189B9. But the difference on which Owen insists (243) between that passage and the *Sophist*'s puzzle lies not in the content of the puzzle but rather in Plato's attitude to its materials.)

Attributes, like *in flight*, are not the sort of thing that I thought a description of falsehood in beliefs and statements would have to represent as not being. And it was not in the sense you exploit – not being in relation to something – but in precisely the sense you agree is problematic – not being anything at all – that I thought a description of falsehood would have to represent my different items, situations or states of affairs, as not being. You have not shown that the description of falsehood I found problematic is not compulsory, dictated by the nature of the concept of falsehood; and you have certainly not shown that it is not problematic.

Some commentators are sensitive to the vulnerability of 263B, considered as a response to the puzzle about situations; and they shift attention to the passage (261C6–262E2) that leads up to the explicit discussion of truth and falsity in statements. There the ES distinguishes (in effect) between a kind of sentence-constituent whose function is to make clear what is being talked about and a kind of sentence-constituent whose function is to make clear what is being said about it. The commentators draw the obvious moral: a sentence (one of the simple kind Plato considers, at any rate) gets its purchase on reality through its possession of a sentence-constituent of the first kind. And they suggest that any inclination to protest against 263B, on the lines envisaged above, would stem from a failure to grasp this point. Worrying about the apparently total absence from reality of states of affairs answering to false statements, or of what would be components of such states of affairs, answering to the predicates of false statements, would manifest a lack of enlightenment about the localisation, within sentences, of the relation that gives them their bearing on the world.[26]

But the puzzle about situations is a deeper puzzle, and the objection to 263B, considered as a response to it, is a better objection, than Plato's strategy, on this view of it, gives them credit for being. The puzzle turns on the thought that the falsity of 'Theaetetus is in flight' should consist in the fact that the state of affairs that the sentence offers to represent, or perhaps the flight in which an utterer of the sentence would accuse Theaetetus of being engaged, is nothing at all. And that thought, properly understood, is absolutely *correct*; it needs no support from a half-baked conception of how speech has its bearing on reality, such as would

26 See Owen, 263–5.

be undermined by the distinction drawn at 261C6–262E2. In conjunction with 237B7–239C8, the thought threatens to undermine the possibility of falsehood; what we should need in order to neutralise this destructive effect is, not the considerations of 261C6–262E2 (which are powerless for this purpose), but something to show us why a description such as 'dealing, in thought or speech, with what is in fact nothing at all' (which might figure in a characterisation of falsehood on the lines of what this puzzle represents as problematic) does not incoherently represent the thought or speech it applies to as (genuine thought or speech, but) possessing no subject matter. And the *Sophist* contains no trace of the necessary distinction.[27] Of course it is possible that Plato simply fails to deal adequately with the difficulty he tackles – fails to see its full depth; but charity recommends that we credit him, if possible, with better success at a different project.

261C6–262E2 does indeed, obliquely and inexplicitly, undermine a paradoxical argument for the impossibility of falsehood. But it is an argument distinct both from the commentators' puzzle about situations and from the difficulty about falsehood that is the *Sophist*'s main concern.

What the passage's differentiation of functions would correct is a position indifferent to, or ignorant of, the distinction between mentioning something and saying something; and such a position does make appearances elsewhere. The idea might be expressed on these lines: the unit move in the language-game of informative discourse (occupying a position analogous to that which we might ascribe to statements; but that term carries a burden of logical theory that includes at least the missing distinction) is the putting into words of some thing. A dim perception that the minimal informative performance must have some complexity (the point of which 261C6–262E2 evinces a clear, if partial, perception) can, in the absence of the distinction, yield only the requirement that

---

27 For the distinction, see Wiggins, 274–5. Owen suggests (246) that in the *Sophist* Plato does not want to deny that 'we can speak of mythical centaurs or chimerical flights' (such items are not wholly devoid of being, since we can say that they are). But on Owen's own account (229) the dialogue contains no direct evidence of hospitality to the chimerical. And there is nothing in the *Sophist* (or in *Prm.* 160B6–161A5, also cited by Owen) to show how the acceptability of reference to the chimerical, on the ground that its target is not devoid of being, might be reconciled with the thought – surely acceptable on some construal – that such 'items' as the flight of which Theaetetus is falsely accused are in fact nothing at all. So long as this thought is not disarmed, it must remain unclear how 237B7–239C8 can fail to have its full destructive effect.

the thing put into words must be constituted of parts, so that the putting of it into words can be a complex performance by virtue of consisting in the successive mentioning of the parts.[28] This position would undermine the possibility of contradicting another person's remark: the best one could hope to achieve would be a change of subject.[29] Equally, it would undermine the possibility of speaking falsely. Failure to put a certain thing into words cannot constitute false speech: for either one will have put a different thing into words, and so spoken truly (though with a different topic); or else one will have failed to put anything into words, which is the nearest we can come, in the terminology I have adopted to express the position that lacks the crucial distinction, to the conclusion that one will not have said anything at all.[30]

This crude position makes no explicit appearance in the *Sophist*.[31] But 261C6–262E2 says exactly what is needed to correct it. And it seems plausible that some terminological apparatus, introduced at 262E5 and used at 263A5, A9–10, C5, C7, is meant to signal Plato's awareness of the bearing of 261C6–262E2 on the crude position. The crude position lends itself to a slogan on these lines: 'A thing can be put into words only by its own form of words.'[32] This slogan encapsulates the destructive effect of inability, or refusal, to distinguish mentioning and saying: any attempt to formulate the notion of error in a form of words succeeds in describing only idle chatter, or else a flawless capturing in words of some other thing. Having drawn the necessary distinction, Plato continues to use the possessive to express the 'about' relation, now safely localised, between (what we can now without risk of misleading describe as) statements and things (263A5, A9–10; 'about me' and 'mine' are interchangeable). The terminology irresistibly suggests an echo of the old slogan,

28 See *Tht.* 201D8–202C5; cf. Aristotle, *Metaph.* 1024b26–1025a1.
29 Cf. *Euthd.* 285D7–286B6.   30 Cf. *Euthd.* 283E7–284C6.
31 *Pace*, apparently, Owen, 241, claiming that '237B7–E7 is a version of the familiar paradox'. In fact (as Owen immediately concedes) that passage does not purport to undermine the notion of falsehood. There is no reason to take it as addressing anything except the *Sophist*'s question: how is it possible to mention or speak of (not 'say') what is not?
32 See *Tht.* 202A6–8; cf. *Metaph.* 1024b32–3. ('Form of words' here represents '*logos*', the noun cognate with '*legein*'. Ordinarily these might be translated 'statement' and 'say'; but as '*legein*' here expresses the notion, straddling those of mentioning and saying, that I am rendering by 'put into words', I use a term similarly free of unwanted theoretical connotations for '*logos*'.)

verbally almost unaltered, but now rendered quite innocuous: 'A thing can be talked about only by a statement of its own.'

The puzzle about falsehood thus obliquely disarmed by 261C6–262E2 is perceptibly less sophisticated than the difficulty about situations or states of affairs outlined above. The notion of a state of affairs is the notion of something with a complexity of a different kind from that of a mere composite thing; it is the notion of a chunk of reality with a structure such as to mirror that of the proposition or statement it would render true. Anyone who could genuinely be credited with possession of this notion would already have advanced beyond a stage at which he could be instructed by 261C6–262E2. And, as I urged above, this would not immunise him against a worry, should he conceive it, about the utter absence from reality of the states of affairs represented by false statements or beliefs. Something similar holds for the notion of a component of a state of affairs answering to the predicate of a statement (the crude position precisely lacks the equipment to effect any such singling out); and for a worry about the total absence of such an item from reality when a statement or belief is false.

Although the difficulty about falsehood generated by the crude position (unlike the puzzle involving situations or states of affairs) is cogently answered in the course of the *Sophist*, the crude position cannot easily be read into the passage in which the dialogue's official problem about falsehood is set out in detail (240C7–241B3). Not-being figures in the crude position's difficulty in that one of the candidate descriptions of falsehood it suggests and portrays as problematic (the other being, irrelevantly for present purposes, in terms of change of subject) is: a form of words such that what it puts into words is not (is nothing at all). The problem about this is that in the attempt to characterise the form of words as false we undermine its bearing on reality. Now the *Sophist*'s paradox is directed against both of two distinguished kinds of falsehood: both falsehoods that represent what is not as being (240E1–4, understanding '*doxazein*' at E3), and falsehoods that represent what is as not being (240E5–9). The threat to the former of these, if this were all that we had to consider, might perhaps be assimilated to the problem posed by the crude position. But this will hardly do for the latter, where the fact that what is represented (as not being) is *what is* ensures that whatever difficulty there is about the falsehood's purchase on reality does not arise in a comparable way. No doubt the fact that what is is represented *as not being* generates a difficulty that could be expressed as one about the falsehood's hold on reality. It remains the case, however, that the *Sophist*'s problem evidently arises in rather different ways for affirmative and negative falsehoods; there is a complexity here for which the crude position has no counterpart.[33]

6. What, then, is the *Sophist*'s difficulty?

Bearing in mind the desirability of finding something to the point in 263B, we should understand the disjunctive characterisation of falsehood at 240C7–241B3 in terms of attributes. Thus an example of the kind of falsehood that represents what is as not being might be 'Theaetetus is not seated', uttered when Theaetetus is seated. This represents *seated*, which is, as not being; that description correctly captures the statement's falsity if we take 'is' and 'not being' as 'converse' uses and supply 'in relation to Theaetetus'. The other kind of falsehood is illustrated by the example actually discussed in 263B, 'Theaetetus is in flight'. This represents *in flight*, which is not, as being; again, that description correctly captures the statement's falsity if we take 'is not' and 'being' as 'converse' uses and supply 'in relation to Theaetetus'.

Why should the sophist find these characterisations of falsehood problematic, so that their putative incoherence affords him a hiding place? Because he makes the mistake we have seen that the ES devotes himself to correcting: he cannot see how 'is not' could be anything but a synonym for 'has the contrary of being' or 'utterly is not' (note how these latter expressions figure in the problem-setting passage: 240D6, E2, E5), and he can find no coherent   significance   for   it   under   that   interpretation

---

33 Owen's remark (265) 'Falsehood had appeared an abortive attempt to mention something' appears to miss this complexity. I am taking it that 236D9–237A9 announces, without precise detail, the difficulties about images and falsehood spelled out in 239C9–240C6 and 240C7–241B3. (237A3–4 might be taken to imply a simpler paradox, turning on the idea that a falsehood itself – sc. the content of a false belief – is not. But all that the lines say is that we are committed to the being of what is not when we claim that falsehood occurs: a commitment we can understand 240C7–241B3 as explaining.) Cf., e.g., Wiggins, who extracts a puzzle to which Owen's remark would be appropriate from the earlier passage together with 237B7–E7 (cf. n. 31 above), ignoring the complexity of the later passage (268–71); and I. M. Crombie, *An Examination of Plato's Doctrines*, II (London 1963), who suggests (505–7) that the later passage introduces a new (and spurious) difficulty.

(237B7–239C8). So it seems to him that when we try to capture the falsity of 'Theaetetus is in flight' by saying that it represents *in flight*, which *is not* (in relation to Theaetetus: given the mistake, the addition does not help),[34] as being, we must be talking nonsense; and when we try to capture the falsity of 'Theaetetus is not seated' by saying that it represents *seated*, which is (in relation to Theaetetus), as *not being*, we describe the statement as talking nonsense, and hence contradict ourselves if we also describe it as significant.

This paradox is utterly disarmed by the ES's painstaking demolition of the Eleatic mistake about negation. Once the mistake has been corrected, it suffices simply to restate the characterisation of falsehood that had seemed problematic; this time carefully avoiding the erroneous equation between 'not being', on the one hand, and 'opposite of being' or 'in no way being', on the other.[35]

If we understand the *Sophist*'s problem about falsehood on these lines, we can see Plato's response to it as an unqualified success. (Contrast the interpretation in terms of situations or states of affairs: §5 above.) What makes this possible is that – to stick to the less complicated case of affirmative falsehoods – we regard the sheer unavailability of anything answering to the words 'in flight', in the false statement 'Theaetetus is in flight', not as a *premise* in an argument purporting to show that a description that captures the statement's falsity is incoherent (an independently obvious reformulation, that is, of the claim that the statement is false); but rather as an *inference* from the claim (which does, in fact innocuously, capture the statement's falsity) that what answers to the words is not (in relation to Theaetetus). The former problematic unavailability (the unavailability of the flight of which the statement accuses Theaetetus) is indeed a concomitant of the statement's falsity; and it is not something with which Plato shows us how to cope. (See §5 above.) The latter unavailability (the unavailability of the attribute or kind, *in flight*) is simply a mistake, and one which Plato definitively corrects.

It may seem a cost of this reading that it separates Plato's concern in the *Sophist* from the deep philosophical difficulty raised by Wittgenstein when he writes: 'How can one think what is not the

34 See n. 7 above.
35 This is actually done only for the affirmative kind of falsehood; once the diagnostic point is clear, the other kind can be left as an exercise for the reader.

case? If I think that King's College is on fire when it is not, the fact of its being on fire does not exist. Then how can I think it?'[36] But it is surely not a cost but a gain that we find in the *Sophist*, not an unconvincing attempt on that interesting difficulty, but a wholly successful solution to a different one.

It is true that we cannot easily find the different difficulty pressing. Indeed, there may be an inclination to protest: how could anyone suppose that the claim '*In flight* is not in relation to Theaetetus', by trying to describe its subject as not being, incoherently represents itself as lacking a subject altogether? Is it not obvious that not being . . . (for instance not being in relation to Theaetetus) is not the same as utterly not being? But the fact is that it was not obvious to Parmenides, if Plato's diagnosis is correct. According to Plato's suggestion, it was precisely by equating 'not being' with 'being in no way' that Parmenides excluded plurality, qualitative diversity, and change from what can sensibly be affirmed to be the case. The *Sophist*'s puzzle, on the present interpretation, applies the same method in order to cast doubt on the concept of falsehood: an intriguing employment of Parmenides' destructive elenchus at a meta-linguistic level, which would impose limitations (for instance) on the strictures available to Parmenides himself against failures to take his point. But what the puzzle elicits from Plato is a move which, by destroying the foundation, has the effect of dismantling the entire Eleatic position.

36 *The Blue and Brown Books* (Oxford 1958), 31.

CONFLICTING APPEARANCES[1]

By M. F. BURNYEAT

Read 1 February 1979

My incapacity to extend the boundary of my 'this', my inability to gain an immediate experience of that in which it is subordinated and reduced—is my mere imperfection. Because I cannot spread out my window until all is transparent, and all windows disappear, this does not justify me in insisting on my window-frame's rigidity. For that frame has, as such, no existence in reality, but only in our impotence.

F. H. Bradley.

I

'FROM the fact that honey appears bitter to some and sweet to others Democritus concluded that it is neither sweet nor bitter, Heraclitus that it is both.' This report from Sextus Empiricus (*PH* ii. 63) testifies that arguments from conflicting appearances came early to the repertoire of philosophy. Democritus' purpose was to establish the view summed up in a famous fragment: 'Sweet exists by convention, bitter by convention, colour by convention; in reality atoms and the void exist' (frag. 125). If we speak of honey as sweet, it is because this is the response sanctioned by custom and convention, especially linguistic convention, to the way certain atoms impinge on our organs of taste, but there is no more to it than that: no more than a response to atomic stimuli. Terms like 'sweet' and 'bitter', 'white' and 'black', correspond to nothing in the collections of atoms which constitute the things in the world around us. Our attributions of what were later to be called secondary qualities are a projection on to that world of our own, merely subjective affections.

Heraclitus' message was quite different: not the empty subjectivity of sensible appearances but their one-sided partiality. It may be questioned whether he actually used the honey example, but there is no doubt that his strange gnomic utterances include others to the same or similar effect.

[1] I am grateful for advice from Jonathan Lear, Gisela Striker, David Wiggins, and Dr G. Berrios.

Sea is the most pure and the most polluted water: drinkable and salutary for fishes, but undrinkable and destructive for men.

(frag. 61)

Again, 'Donkeys would choose chaff rather than gold' (frag. 9), 'Pigs enjoy mud rather than clean water' for washing in (frag. 13 with Sext. Emp. *PH* i. 56). Are they right or we? The implied answer is that each is right—from his own point of view. It follows that the different but equally valid points of view are one-sided, partial reflections of reality. At some deeper level, from as it were an absolute god's-eye vantage-point, the opposition and contrast is overcome. The sea is both pure and impure; mud is both clean and dirty; rubbish is wealth. It sounds like a contradiction, and so it is—within our human language. Our language is so structured that to call something pure is to imply that it is not impure and vice versa. But that only raises the question, a generalization of the question we met with in Democritus, whether the oppositions and contrasts encoded in our language correspond to anything in reality. Maybe the language which makes us treat the conflict of appearances as a conflict, which makes us say that where appearances conflict both cannot be right, is itself an aspect of our anthropocentric partiality.

But we began with Sextus Empiricus, and Sextus, as a good Pyrrhonian sceptic, has his own moral to draw from the fact that honey appears bitter to some and sweet to others. The sceptical conclusion is that there is no saying which it is; one must suspend judgement on whether it is really sweet or really bitter (*PH* i. 101, 213–14). And Pyrrhonian scepticism extends this pattern of reasoning beyond the field of sensible appearances to every subject of inquiry. In morals, for example, because to some societies or individuals it appears right, to others wrong, for a man to marry his sister or have sexual intercourse in public, the sceptic suspends judgement on whether it is right or wrong (*PH* i. 145–63). Similarly with any question about how things really are—there is always a conflict of appearances and always the sceptic finds himself unable to decide between them.

We now have three different, actually three incompatible conclusions from a single premiss. Which might seem more than enough. But we have yet to reckon with Protagoras. It was probably Protagoras, with some precedent in Heraclitus, who gave currency to the extended notion of appearance whereby one speaks of conflicting appearances not only in the field of sense-perception but wherever there is disagreement and one view is opposed to another. And the moral Protagoras drew was that each of the conflicting appearances is true *for* the person whose appearance it is. His doctrine that man is the measure of all things recommends a relativistic account of truth which allows the honey to be both sweet and bitter, subject to the qualification that it is sweet *for* (in relation to) some palates and bitter *for* others. By relativizing the attributions of sweet and bitter Protagoras avoids the contradictions embraced by Heraclitus. Similarly in morals, the doctrine that man is the measure of all things asserts that marrying one's sister is right for one individual or society, wrong for another.

So far we have four ancient characters on the stage. We should bring on some of their modern-dress counterparts. And first Berkeley. You do not have to read far into the first of Berkeley's *Three Dialogues* before you find the following:

> That which at other times seems sweet, shall to a distempered palate appear bitter. And nothing can be plainer, than that divers persons perceive different tastes in the same food, since that which one man delights in, another abhors. And how could this be, if the taste was something really inherent in the food? (p. 180)[1]

Berkeley agrees with Democritus in concluding from the conflict of appearances that the food is not inherently sweet or bitter. On the other hand, he sides with Heraclitus and Protagoras against Democritus in wanting to count both appearances veridical. There really is something sweet and something bitter. But since (contrary to Heraclitus) nothing can be both sweet and bitter, the sweet thing and the bitter thing are separate and distinct. The sweetness belongs to an idea perceived by or in the mind of one person, the bitterness to an idea perceived by or in the mind of another (or the same person at another time). This looks like Protagoras, since sweet and bitter alike exist only for one who tastes it, and we shall see that it does have a lot in common with a theory of perceptual relativism which Plato developed out of Protagorean materials in the *Theaetetus*, which theory Berkeley himself thought was exactly like his own (*Siris*, § 311). But there is in fact a difference. When Protagoras says that something exists for the person to whom it appears, he does not intend Berkeley's idealist conclusion that sensible

---

[1] References to the *Three Dialogues* are by page number in *The Works of George Berkeley*, ed. A. A. Luce and T. E. Jessop, vol. ii (London, 1949).

qualities exist in the mind which perceives them.[1] In this lecture I shall be more concerned with the resemblances than with the differences between Berkeley and Protagoras, but in view of the difference just noted we should in principle count Berkeley's a fifth conclusion from the premiss of conflicting appearances. The conclusion, namely, that each appearance reveals a distinct but mental existence.

The issue between Berkeley and Protagoras breaks out again in twentieth-century disputes about whether sense-data are mental or merely dependent for their existence on a mind perceiving them. For in the twentieth century arguments from conflicting appearances have frequently been used to establish that what we perceive is sense-data rather than physical objects. Russell, for example, in *The Problems of Philosophy*, chap. 1, argues that because a table appears to be of different colours and of different shapes from different points of view, as the result of variations in lighting and perspective, therefore we do not see the real colour or the real shape of the table. We may say, for the purposes of ordinary practical life, that the real colour of the table is brown and its real shape rectangular, but all we actually see is a series of appearances (sense-data) no one of which has more right than its competitors to stand as the table's real colour or shape. Other theorists introduce sense-data by way of 'the argument from illusion', but often, in Ayer for example (*The Foundations of Empirical Knowledge*, p. 3), this is just the same argument under another name. The only difference is that it is presupposed—our more sceptical characters might say gratuitously presupposed—that we know which appearance is correct and which the illusion.

Conflicting appearances continue to be popular in moral philosophy also. Most recently, J. L. Mackie (*Ethics: Inventing Right and Wrong*, chaps. 8 and 10) has appealed to the radical divergences between the moral codes of different groups and societies as support for the thesis that values are not part of the objective fabric of the world. If they were objective, he thinks, it would be hard to explain the divergences and disagreements. Whereas if they are in fact subjective, we can explain the erroneous claim to objectivity which seems to be built into moral language. It is a projection of subjective preferences and local practices which are felt to be in need of external validation.

[1] See my 'Idealism and Greek Philosophy: What Descartes Saw and Berkeley Missed', in G. N. A. Vesey ed., *Idealism Past and Present* (Royal Institute of Philosophy Lectures 13 [1978/9], forthcoming).

We are back, it seems, with Democritus, except that the scene has shifted to the moral sphere. And that is no novelty either. For Democritus probably modelled his reasoning on a pattern of argument which originated in fifth-century debates about whether justice and other values are natural or conventional. In one form or another, ancient drama is still being repeated.

That more or less completes my cast of performers. The minor roles can be filled as they are needed. It remains to spotlight the critic in the audience. In *Sense and Sensibilia*, well aware that he is attacking a tradition of thought which goes back to Heraclitus (pp. 1–2), Austin writes:

What is wrong, what is even faintly surprising, in the idea of a stick's being straight but looking bent sometimes? Does anyone suppose that if something is straight, then it jolly well has to *look* straight at all times and in all circumstances? Obviously no one seriously supposes this. (p. 29)

The fact is, as we have seen, many philosophers have supposed exactly this. They have appealed to cases of conflicting appearances in order to call in question the unqualified language in which we ordinarily attribute sensible qualities, moral properties, and so on, and they have done so in a manner plainly presupposing that it would only be correct to say without further qualification that honey is sweet and the stick straight, or that marrying one's sister is wrong, if it appeared so to all alike.

II

What emerges from this brief historical review is a typical philosophical problem. I do not mean the problem of deciding what does follow from the premiss that appearances conflict. For the answer to that question, I believe, is that nothing follows: nothing of any epistemological significance at all. The problem rather is to discover why so many conflicting conclusions have been thought to follow. Why have some philosophers been so impressed, while others like Austin remain unimpressed, by the familiar fact that appearances conflict? What assumptions, spoken or unspoken, are at work to make the familiar fact seem problematic?

That the answer is to be sought, at least sometimes, at the level of unspoken assumptions may begin to look likely if we return to Austin's remark that no one seriously supposes that if something is straight, then it jolly well has to *look* straight at all times and in all circumstances. We have already seen that, taken as a claim about the historical record, this is wrong. It has to be wrong because the following two propositions are equivalent by the rule of contraposition:

(1) If something appears F to some observers and not-F to others, then it is not inherently/really/in itself F.

(2) If something is inherently/really/in itself F, then it appears F to all observers or it appears not-F to all.

And for the purposes of the present discussion we may simply bracket off as irrelevant the second disjunct in (2). For no one, or no one except possibly Berkeley's Hylas in a moment of dialectical desperation (*Three Dialogues*, pp. 181–3, 187), is going to propose that for a thing to be really F it must appear otherwise to every observer. To be sure, Democritus claims that the real properties of things are hidden, i.e. do not appear to any of us: 'Man must know by this rule, that he is cut off from the real' (frag. 6), 'In reality we know nothing; for the truth is in the depths' (frag. 117). But Democritus claims this, I take it, not from Hylas' motive but because he accepts (1), hence also (2), and he cannot find any instance within human experience where something appears F to everyone.[1] Honey and the stick have no properties which appear the same to all observers, so they themselves are merely phenomenal, the effect on human sensibility of the motions of atoms: 'In reality we know nothing of anything, but belief is a flowing in upon each of us' (frag. 7; cf. frag. 9).[2] Thus within the macroscopic world of human experience the second disjunct of (2) is not operative for Democritus either. And (2) without its second disjunct is the very thing that Austin said no one seriously supposes to be the case.

What is true is that a totally explicit text for (2) is remarkably hard to find. In one version or another formulation (1) abounds. The arguments cited from Democritus and Protagoras, Berkeley and Russell, all rest on (1), while Sextus quite frequently applies its epistemic counterpart

(1′) If something appears F to some observers and not-F to others, then we do not know (cannot determine) whether it is inherently/really/in itself F.

(1′) in turn transposes to

[1] See Diels–Kranz, *Die Fragmente der Vorsokratiker*[6] 68 A 112, A 135 §§ 63–4, 69–70.

[2] See further Diels–Kranz, 67 A 32, 68 A 37, A 57.

(2′) If we know whether something is inherently/really/in itself *F*, then it appears *F* to all observers or it appears not-*F* to all.

But I can find no clear instance of (2′) in the lengthy epistemological disquisitions of Sextus' *Outlines of Pyrrhonism* and *Adversus Mathematicos*. Once or twice we catch a glimpse of (2) (*PH* i. 177, iii. 179, ? *M* viii. 37), but it is the exception rather than the rule. Similarly with Berkeley, I count some eight instances of (1) in the first *Dialogue*,[1] as against a mere couple of instances of (2), and these last are in any case confused with something different (see V below). As for Russell's treatment of these issues in *The Problems of Philosophy*, it is all based on (1) with not so much as a hint of (2).

We may wonder why people should be shy of taking their stand on formulation (2). And why, for that matter, Austin should seemingly have failed to notice that what he says no one would seriously suppose is just a reformulation of the sort of view he has been shooting at all along. Perhaps the reason is that (2) is *manifestly* implausible in some way that (1) is not. That would imply that (1) has been persuasive because it wraps things up a bit, keeps hidden an influence which comes closer to the surface in (2). I am going to propose that the hidden influence is a certain undeclared picture or model of what perception is or ought to be like. It is an inappropriate picture, even more inappropriate when carried over into the moral sphere, and for that reason it is not something a philosopher will readily acknowledge, even to himself.

There are, I fear, obvious pitfalls in the way of a diagnosis such as this. The history of philosophy must respect its texts and the arguments in those texts, and if one is going to suggest that there is more to an argument than appears in the text one needs to have good grounds in the text itself. We have all known occasions when it was reasonable to say of someone, 'He only maintains that *p* because at some level he thinks that *q*, although he might not accept *q* if he was explicitly asked about it.' But we also know that this type of diagnosis can be abused, and in the history of philosophy it has sometimes been abused. Being mindful, therefore, of the dangers ahead, I propose to set out from a detailed textual examination of one of the arguments from conflicting appearances where, if I am right, the influence of an inappropriate model of perception can be discerned.

[1] pp. 180, 181, 185,? 186, 189 (3 times), 191.

But at once we face a historical problem. We cannot go directly to Protagoras or Democritus, since their arguments survive only in second-hand reports; and Heraclitus preferred gnomic paradox to the mundane process of getting from premises to conclusions. The earliest reasoned argument on our subject which we can study in the original words is an argument in Plato's *Theaetetus* on behalf of Protagorean relativism, occurring in a passage (153 D–154 B) which has never, I think, been given the extended discussion it deserves. Protagoras is the beneficiary of the argument, not its author: there is every reason to think that the argument is a dialectical construction by Plato himself, rather than something extracted from Protagoras' own writings. Consequently we must bear in mind that we shall be viewing the argument in a double perspective, our own and Plato's. This is Plato's attempt to bring out the kind of thinking which leads to a relativistic account of sensible qualities, so it already contains an element of diagnosis. I believe, however, that Plato's diagnosis is on the right lines, and that all we need do is complete the job he began.

III

153 D   SOCRATES. Well then, you must think like this. In the case of the eyes, first, you mustn't think of what you call white colour as being some distinct thing outside your eyes, or in your eyes either—in fact
E you mustn't assign any place to it; because in that case it would, surely, be at its assigned place and in a state of rest, rather than coming to be.

THEAETETUS. Well, how can I think of it?

SOCRATES. Let's follow what we said just now, and lay it down that nothing is one thing just by itself. On those lines, we'll find that black, white, or any other colour will turn out to have come into being, from
154 A the collision of the eyes with the appropriate motion. What we say a given colour is will be neither the thing which collides, nor the thing it collides with, but something which has come into being between them; something private to each one. Or would you be prepared to insist that every colour appears to a dog, or any other living thing, just the way it appears to you?

THEAETETUS. Certainly not.

SOCRATES. And what about another man? Is the way anything appears to him like the way it appears to you? Can you insist on that? Or wouldn't you much rather say that it doesn't appear the same even to yourself, because you're never in a similar condition to yourself?

THEAETETUS. Yes, I think that's nearer the truth than the first alternative.

B   SOCRATES. Surely then, if what we measure ourselves against or touch had been large, white, or hot, it would never have become different by bumping into a different perceiver, at any rate not if it didn't undergo any change itself. And on the other hand, if what does the measuring or touching had been any of those things, then again, it wouldn't have become different when another thing came up against it, or the thing which came up against it had something happen to it: not if it hadn't, itself, had anything happen to it.[1]

Socrates' aim in this passage is to establish on behalf of Protagoras that sensible qualities like hot and cold, white and black, are essentially relative to the individual perceiving subject. This thesis is expressed in two connected ways. (a) The colour white, for example, is not to be located in (153 D 9–E 1) or identified with (154 A 1–2) either the object perceived or the eye of the perceiver. It is not a distinct thing existing anywhere at all, but when an eye lights on[2] what we would ordinarily describe as a white stick or a white stone,[3] something occurs between them and it is in this transaction that the colour white arises or comes to be. In other words, the colour is a relational happening or occurrence, essentially involving both parties to the perceptual encounter (153 D–154 A). (b) Neither the object seen nor the perceiving subject is in itself white (154 B). Indeed, nothing is in itself any one thing at all (153 E 4–5, referring back to 152 D).

These two formulations add up to a proposal to treat terms like 'hot' and 'cold', 'white' and 'black', as incomplete or relational predicates. From formulation (b) in its Protagorean context we may gather that no sentence of the form 'x is white' is true as it stands, without a qualifying clause specifying a perceiver for whom it is true. This gives us the result that the colour white is essentially relational and its occurrences should

[1] Quoted in the translation of John McDowell, *Plato—Theaetetus* (Oxford, 1973), with the following modifications: (a) Socrates' last speech at 154 B 1 ff. should begin with an inferential 'Surely then', not McDowell's 'Well now' (the Greek is οὐκοῦν), and should not be spaced off from 154 A as a separate paragraph designed to set a puzzle (McDowell, pp. 19, 131). (b) At 154 B 2 McDowell has 'bumping into a different person', where the Greek is not so specific and where we should allow for the animal perceivers cited in 154 A. (c) For ἴδιον at 154 A 2 McDowell has 'peculiar', but it is not misleading to use the epistemologically loaded term 'private' (cf. 161 D, 166 C).

[2] I choose this English expression to counterbalance the exaggeratedly somatic overtones of McDowell's translation in terms of colliding and bumping. προσβάλλειν is used of the sun's rays striking the earth and in similar cases.

[3] For the examples, cf. 156 E.

canonically be represented in sentences of the form '*x* is/becomes white for so-and-so'. But now, if that is so, there is no unqualified predicate 'white' to be abstracted from its predicative position and made the subject of the definitional question 'What is white?'. There is no such thing as (being) white *simpliciter*, only white for you and white for me.[1] Hence, finally, formulation (a): white is not a distinct thing existing in the subject or in the object of perception.

We now have a thesis: sensible qualities like hot and cold, white and black, are essentially relative to perceivers. What are the grounds for accepting it? They are not, as commentators sometimes suggest,[2] grounds pertaining to a theory of the mechanism of perception. The thesis is meant to be established independently of any detailed understanding of the commerce between perceiver and perceived;[3] indeed, the thesis will shape the theory of perception to be elaborated in the dialogue (156 A ff.) rather than being shaped by it. The argument for the relativity of sensible qualities is entirely general, and its leading premiss is the conflict of sensible appearances.

Socrates in 154 A mentions three types of variation or conflict between appearances, in a classification that was to become traditional. Colour appearances vary between man and other animals, between one man and another, and between one time and another within the experience of a single man.[4] Socrates actually implies the strongest possible claim, that no two colour appearances are alike, but I want to leave that aside for the moment. It will be sufficient for the argument Socrates has in view to start from the more modest claim that variations do occur. For he asserts at 154 B that this is incompatible with attributing sensible qualities either to the object or to the subject of perception.

We may elucidate his claim as follows. Take, as before, an

---

[1] The abstraction-move underlying ὃ δὴ ἕκαστον εἶναί φαμεν χρῶμα (153 E 7–154 A 1) is standard in Plato: see G. E. L. Owen, 'Dialectic and Eristic in the Treatment of the Forms', in G. E. L. Owen ed., *Aristotle on Dialectic* (Oxford, 1968), pp. 114–15.

[2] e.g. F. M. Cornford, *Plato's Theory of Knowledge* (London, 1935), p. 40, McDowell, op. cit., p. 131.

[3] Witness the difficulty (adverted to by McDowell, pp. 130–1) of fitting the language used to describe perception here into the more detailed story that comes later.

[4] The first two types of variation correspond to the first two of the Ten Modes of Pyrrhonian scepticism, the third is expanded in a number of the remaining Modes (Sext. Emp. *PH* i. 36 ff.).

event of the kind we would ordinarily describe as the seeing of a white stone ('measuring ourselves against' is Protagorean for perceiving of any kind). Then, first, the stone cannot be white in itself or else, so long as it suffered no change, it would appear white to any other perceiver. Second, the subject of perception cannot itself be white either, or else, so long as it suffered no change, it would see everything white: including the stone we started with, supposing that to have been painted red.[1] More generally, if sensible qualities inhere in the objects of perception, they ought to make themselves apparent to every perceiver alike, regardless of differences between perceivers or changes in the condition of a single perceiver; if, alternatively, they inhere in the perceiving subject, then conversely their appearance should not be affected by differences and changes in the objects perceived. But it is a fact of experience familiar to us all that sensible appearances vary with differences and changes on either side of the perceptual encounter. So we are invited to draw the desired conclusion: sensible qualities are essentially relative to the individual perceiver.

That is the argument, and at first reading it may not seem a significant advance. The words 'Or would you be prepared to insist . . . ' at 154 A 2–3 indicate that it is the conflict of appearances which is to show that colours are not inherent in the object or the subject, but relational. That is, in 153 E–4 A the argument rests on (1). But then Socrates proceeds in 154 B to spell out his argument in terms of (2). And we have already seen that (2) is just a reformulation of (1); it provides no additional support for the conclusion he wishes to draw.

But this dismissive judgement is premature. In the first place, we should be grateful to Plato for putting the emphasis on formulation (2), the thing Austin said no one would seriously suppose. Given the rarity of (2) in later philosophers, it is not to be assumed that it was prominent in earlier presentations of the line of thought which Plato is reconstructing. We can also thank Plato for making absolutely explicit the important point that with either formulation the argument only applies on the assumption that the thing we are talking about remains unchanged (cf. Ayer. pp. 14–15). Second, (1) and (2) as formulated concern only the object of perception, while Socrates' argument for a relativistic account of sensible

[1] It was, I think, R. Hackforth, 'Notes on Plato's *Theaetetus*', *Mnemosyne* series 4, 10 (1957), p. 130, who first made sense of ἥ τι παθόντος (154 B 5), construing it as a genitive absolute rather than with ἄλλου.

qualities comes in two halves. One half attends to the object of perception, the other tackles the curious-sounding suggestion that the thing which is white in itself, or the thing where the whiteness is to be found, is the perceiving subject. Why should anyone suppose that? And, if he did, what on earth would he mean by it?

In his admirable commentary on the *Theaetetus* John Mc-Dowell suggests[1] that the issue is not whether the perceiver is coloured white but whether he is seeing white. A perceiver cannot be said, in the ordinary unqualified way, to be seeing white unless, so long as he undergoes no change, he sees everything white; i.e. it is a condition of his seeing white at all that he sees only white, not also other colours. I do not think this can be the right reading of the text. For one thing, it involves understanding 'any of those things' (154 B 4) as taking up 'measuring or touching', i.e. perceiving, rather than 'large, white, or hot', which is the obvious reference for the phrase. McDowell only makes the suggestion because he finds it obscure 'why anyone might be thought to want to say (except for obviously irrelevant reasons) that an eye is white'; why, in other words, there should be an issue as to whether the subject of perception, as opposed to its object, is in itself coloured. Why indeed? This is exactly the sort of hermeneutic puzzle in the face of which it becomes reasonable to probe for unspoken assumptions underlying the surface text.

With this in mind I want to bring to bear on our text two passages from later writers, one ancient and one modern. In the first chapter of *Appearance and Reality* Bradley presents the following argument against the reality of secondary qualities:

We assume that a thing must be self-consistent and self-dependent. It either has a quality or has not got it. And, if it has it, it cannot have it only sometimes, and merely in this or that relation. But such a principle is the condemnation of secondary qualities.

It matters very little how in detail we work with it. A thing is coloured, but not coloured in the same way to every eye; and, except to some eye, it seems not coloured at all. Is it then coloured or not? And the eye—relation to which appears somehow to make the quality—does that itself possess colour? Clearly not so, unless there is another eye which sees it. Nothing therefore is really coloured; colour seems only to belong to what itself is colourless. And the same result holds, again, with cold and heat. A thing may be cold or hot according to different parts of my skin; and, without some relation to a skin, it seems without any

---

[1] op. cit., pp. 131–3.

such quality. And, by a like argument, the skin is proved not itself to own the quality, which is hence possessed by nothing. (pp. 9–10)

The resemblances are striking. Whether Bradley had the *Theaetetus* passage in mind I do not know. If he did, he preferred to change the argument, for Bradley's reason for denying colour to the eye is that it is only coloured when seen by a second eye, which seems to assume the conclusion to be proved. But at least here is one serious philosopher witnessing to the relevance in this sort of context of the thought that the colour of the eye might be the source of the colour we see. And there is another resemblance. Although Bradley endorses the argument, and will later (pp. 12 f.) say that it applies equally to primary qualities, his attitude to it has none the less a certain detachment;[1] his presentation, like Plato's, is mixed with diagnosis. So it is not without interest that he starts off with that rare thing, a clear and explicit version of (2): 'A thing . . . either has a quality or has not got it. And, if it has, it cannot have it only sometimes and merely in this or that relation.'

The second passage for comparison is Sextus on the subject of perception:

Sufferers from jaundice say that things which appear white to us are yellow, and those whose eyes are bloodshot say they are blood-red. Since, then, some animals also have yellow eyes, others bloodshot eyes, others albino, and others eyes of yet another colour, it is likely, I think, that they have a different perception of colours. (*PH* i. 44)

Why is it likely? Do things really look blood-red when you wake up from a heavy drinking-bout with bloodshot eyes? I want to suggest that anyone who thinks it likely is in the grip of a certain picture or model of perception. If one thinks of visual perception as a matter of looking out through the eyes as through a window, then coloured eyes will be like the tinted spectacles favoured by modern philosophers of perception, only further in; just so, on Sextus' explanation of the phenomenon (*PH* i. 126) yellow or red in the eye is an admixture of colour within the field of vision. Some animals look out through a yellow or a blood-red window-pane, and so will you too if your eyes go yellow with jaundice or blood-red from drinking too much. I forbear from quoting Sextus' further remarks

---

[1] Because he thinks that at the common-sense level it is perfectly correct to say that secondary qualities, no less than primary, are 'an actual part of the physical world' (p. 247). What he is most opposed to is the metaphysical bifurcation of primary and secondary qualities.

(*PH* i. 47) about the shape things must look to animals whose eyes have slanting or elongated pupils.

It should not be thought that this is just a piece of antique physiology. Descartes, no stranger to optics, cites the example of a man with jaundice to whom things look yellow because his eye is tinged with yellow (*Regulae*, XII), and so does Berkeley (*Three Dialogues*, p. 185), who couples it with the example of animals with eyes of a different texture from ours. Russell broadcast the jaundice example from the BBC in 1948.[1] It was still going strong in 1963 when Professor Roderick Chisholm used it in a paper on 'The Theory of Appearing',[2] and it gave evidence for both sides of an Aristotelian Society symposium in 1968.[3] Yet it is quite false that people with jaundice see (white) things yellow. Of this I am assured both by medical authority and by those who have had the condition. As a matter of fact, we all have yellow inside our eyes. In humans and a range of other animals the lens of the eye is yellow. But so far from making things look yellow, this enhances colour contrast and eliminates blur from the differential refractive properties of different wavelengths of light. Red can help too: turtles have red oil droplets in their eyes to improve their vision over the glary surface of the water. But these are relatively recent discoveries.[4] What we have to ask is why for centuries the myth about jaundice should continue to be believed, as it evidently still is believed. (Someone actually said to me, 'But surely, they have yellow eyes', and appealed to the phrase 'a jaundiced view of things'.) For that matter, according to Austin (p. 49), it is equally false to say, with Ayer (p. 6),[5] 'When, as the result of my putting on green spectacles, the white walls of my room appear to be green, my experience is qualitatively the same as if I were perceiving walls that really were green.' Austin does not say why it is false, but I think

---

[1] See Bertrand Russell, *Why I am not a Christian and other essays on religion and related topics* (London, 1957), pp. 161–2.

[2] Cited from Robert J. Swartz ed., *Perceiving, Sensing, and Knowing* (New York, 1965), p. 183.

[3] F. N. Sibley and Michael Tanner, 'Objectivity and Aesthetics', *Arist. Soc. Suppl. Vol.* 42 (1968), pp. 39 and 60.

[4] Gleaned from the fascinating store of empirical detail in Gordon Lynn Walls, *The Vertebrate Eye and Its Adaptive Radiation*, Cranbrook Institute of Science Bulletin No. 19 (Michigan, 1942), pp. 191 ff. More recent still is knowledge of picrotoxin. Picrotoxin intoxication, I am informed, yellows the skin (but not the eye) and does make things seen assume a yellowish look.

[5] But Ayer is actually retailing examples from other people.

it would be correct to insist that the experience of looking *through* green and the experience of looking *at* green are importantly distinct. So those who cite the jaundice example are committing a double error of fact if they say without qualification that the condition makes things look yellow. First, there is no such yellowing effect; second, if seeing through yellow eyes really were like seeing through yellow-tinted glass, it would still be distinguishable from the experience of seeing a yellow object. But the important point is that the manner in which philosophers through the centuries have repeated this type of example, in defiance of ascertainable fact, is evidence that at some level people are powerfully drawn to the thought that we look through our eyes as through a window.

That we are dealing with an implicit picture or model of perception, not an explicit inference from outmoded physiology, is clear even in antiquity. One early citing of the jaundice example is by Lucretius (iv. 332–6), and on the atomist assumptions of Lucretius' official physiology of perception one might well think that the example should be nonsense. For remember that for an atomist yellow is nothing but the effect of certain atoms impinging on the eye, not a characteristic of the eye or of anything else. Lucretius, however, has an answer. The eyes and body of the jaundiced person emit numerous atomic effluences of the type requisite for him to appear yellow to other people and some of these 'seeds of yellow' return to his own eye mixed up with the effluences from outside objects, with the result that those objects look yellow to him. It is an obvious difficulty for this explanation that it should imply that if someone whose eyes appear a normal healthy white puts on a clean white toga, he will see everything white. Lucretius offers nothing to ease this difficulty, and seems not to have noticed it. Clearly, his belief that yellow eyes produce yellow appearances is not a deduction from physiological theory but a notion independently acquired, which physiology is then made to accommodate. And the influence of the window model shows itself when he adds a reference to 'seeds of yellow' in the eye itself (335)—as if the eye were within the field of vision and the man were looking through it.

This evidence from Lucretius is the more remarkable because at iii. 359–69 he attacks a view which explicitly compared the eyes to windows through which the mind looks out at things.[1]

---

[1] Lucretius actually says 'doors' (*fores*), not 'windows', but the parallels at Cic. *Tusc.* i. 46, Philo fr. (p. 615 Mang.), Sext. Emp. *M* vii. 129, 350, 364

The point at issue is whether it is the eyes themselves or the mind within which is the proper subject of perception. The window comparison comes from someone advocating a version of Plato's view (see VIII below) that it is a unitary mind, not the separate sense-organs, which does our perceiving.[1] Lucretius disagrees, for it is Epicurean doctrine that the body is endowed by the soul with a perceptual sensitivity of its own. That is, he disavows the window model when it is put to him. But, I claim, he would not have said what he later says about the jaundice example unless at a less concious level he was still susceptible to its influence.

It is not unlikely that similar examples were already current by the time Plato wrote the *Theaetetus*. Perhaps the earliest attested appeal to the jaundice example—the earliest, at any rate, that I have found, and it has a blood-red example to go with it—is due to the Cyrenaic school, who developed a hard-line sceptical epistemology in the second half of the fourth century B.C. By Sextus' account (*M* vii. 192, 197–8), they used these and other examples to argue that we have no knowledge of or access to anything beyond our own experiences. For in such cases it is true that we are 'yellowed' or 'reddened' (the curious terminology for the experience of something's appearing yellow/red is revealingly suited to the examples), but false—as anyone will agree—that the objects seen are yellow or red. So how on any other occasion can we be sure of more than that we are thus 'yellowed' or 'reddened'? It would be interesting to be better informed than we are about the Cyrenaic epistemology,[2] but for present purposes the important thing is that the examples

(quoted by Cyril Bailey, *Lucreti De Rerum Natura* [Oxford, 1947], ii p. 1052) make it likely that *fores* renders θυρίδες, 'windows'.

[1] Who was this someone? Bailey, loc. cit., says, 'The theory which Lucretius here refutes is quite definitely that of the Stoics', and cites the Cicero passage—but Cicero does not name his source. Sextus traces the comparison to Strato of Lampsacus and to Aenesidemus' work on Heraclitus. Sextus wishes to think (*M* vii. 364) that the point of the comparison is to make a claim that the mind can get a direct, unmediated perception of things, in contrast to a view of the senses as obstructively 'in front of' the mind (*M* vii. 352–3). Lucretius and Cicero, however, make it clear that the issue is the one discussed at *Theaet.* 184 B ff., about the subject of perception and its unity; Tertullian, *De Anima* 14 confirms that this was Strato's and Aenesidemus' concern also. To get back from this evidence to Stoic doctrine (whether Posidonius or earlier) is a matter of unravelling the tangled knots of Aenesidemus' work on Heraclitus: see Ulrich Burkhard, *Die angebliche Heraklit-Nachfolge des Skeptikers Aenesidem* (Bonn, 1973).

[2] For a few suggestions, see 'Idealism and Greek Philosophy', op. cit.

would only serve to illustrate and recommend so extreme a theory if they were of a type which the audience was ante-cedently disposed to accept as familiar and uncontroversial.[1]

I hope this is enough justification—I do not think it is more than enough—for a diagnosis of what is going on in the second half of the argument before us. In terms of the window model, Socrates' point is that if the white were in the eye of the per-ceiving subject, then he would be looking out, as it were, through a white-tinted pane and so should see everything white.

Now apply the window model to the first half of the argument. If the white were out there in the stone, not in the eye of the beholder, and one looks through the eye as through a window, then one's view of the white must be unobstructed. The window-pane should be transparent, without spot or blemish. Or better, since classical Greek windows were unglazed, the eye should be an open aperture with no pane at all. There is as it were nothing between the perceiver and the thing he perceives. In that case the stone should appear white to every perceiver.

My suggestion, then, is that the window model makes sense of an argument which otherwise is no argument at all. The next step is to look for confirmation of this diagnosis in the wider context of the dialogue as a whole.

IV

The passage under discussion is part of an elaborate dialectical construction designed to unravel the implications and commit-ments of Theaetetus' definition of knowledge as perception (151 E).[2] The question at issue is this: if we accept that know-ledge is perception, what must we suppose about perception and the world for the definition to hold good? The answer, in broad outline, is that we must accept a Protagorean epistemo-logy and a Heraclitean account of the world. Protagoras said, 'Man is the measure of all things, of those that are, that they are, and of those that are not, that they are not', meaning by this that whatever appearances a person has, they are true for him—things really are, for him, as they appear to him to be—and, conversely, the only things that are real for him are those that appear to him. For the present we can confine our-selves to sensible appearances and to the first half of the double

---

[1] νενόμισται at *M* vii. 193 reports precisely that the examples are common currency.

[2] For a more textual justification of this reading than I can offer here see 'Idealism and Greek Philosophy', op. cit.

thesis contained in the measure doctrine: whatever sensible appearances a person has, they are true for him. If we adopt this principle, we will postulate a state of affairs matching every sensible appearance, to render that appearance true, and then, if perception is construed in Protagorean terms as the having of sensible appearances (cf. 152 B 11– C 1), every perception will be the unerring apprehension of a particular state of affairs: the state of affairs which consists in something's really being, for the perceiver, as it appears to him to be. By this line of argument every case of perception is a case of knowledge and Theaetetus' definition is so far vindicated.

It is at this point that the argument we have been puzzling over becomes relevant, and we can now see why Socrates makes the very strong suggestion that no two colour appearances are alike. The theory he is elaborating is committed to the view that, if this were so, each appearance should still yield knowledge of a real state of affairs. If the theory is to hold good, it must be able to take in its stride the most extreme variation imaginable in the course of appearances. So we had better suppose, for the sake of the argument, that extreme variation actually obtains. Each appearance is independent of every other appearance, yet each is knowledge.

But now, if each appearance is independent of every other, yet each is knowledge, there must be a matching variation in the states of affairs which correspond. Everything I know and perceive must be characterizable independently of what is the case for any other perceiver, including myself at another time, and indeed independently of what is the case for my other senses at the present time. So we are left with such items as a thing's being white for my eye now. Nothing can be white in itself and white is not a distinct thing in itself, only white for me/my eye now.

Thus the argument is plain sailing if we put it back into its context in the dialogue and add to the premiss of conflicting appearances the Protagorean principle that each and every perceptual appearance is the measure or criterion of what is the case for the perceiver; or, more briefly, that every perception is knowledge. From this combination of premisses it does follow that sensible qualities cannot inhere either in the object or in the subject of perception. But now: what is the Protagorean principle but a cool theoretical formulation of the window model (transparent version)? As Plato puts it elsewhere in the dialogue, what the principle claims is that every perception is 'clear' (179 c).

I think this diagnosis is correct. The Protagorean principle does not challenge the assumptions of the window model but confirms them. It embodies a thesis that perceptual experience is transparent and saves it from the objection raised against transparency at 154 B by making the white private to the eye which sees it (154 A 2) and by denying the distance which separates the eye from its object. The colour white is not in me nor out there but in between, something private to me and the object I see (153 DE, 154 A)—the spatial language may be metaphorical but conflicting appearances are often effects of the intervening medium. The choice of metaphor reveals that the window model is still dominant. Protagorean windows provide a flawless close-up view of the contents of a private world.

Someone may object that this evidence from the wider context of the dialogue actually cuts the other way. To say that a philosopher is in the grip of an inappropriate picture of perception makes it sound as if something rather disreputable is going on. But it has now turned out that, on the contrary, Plato's argument is guided by an entirely explicit, coolly theoretical principle which is quite sufficient to get us from the conflict of appearances to the relativity of sensible qualities. If so, it seems not only rude but unnecessary to bring in this talk of the window model. Never mind that the Protagorean principle can be seen as itself an exemplification of the window model. The question is, why should it be?

But here we must recall the double perspective I spoke of earlier. It is Plato who has contrived that the argument from conflicting appearances comes after the definition of knowledge as perception and after the formulation of the Protagorean principle which supports it. The whole passage, as I noted earlier, is part of an elaborate working out of the implications and commitments of the initial definition. The trouble is that nothing has been said so far as to why anyone would be tempted to think that knowledge is perception, and no motivation has been given for adopting the Protagorean principle except that it is necessary to do so if the definition is to hold good. And even this consideration is not right out into the open yet. The discussion starts from the definition, as Socratic discussions typically do, and Socrates turns at once to argue, in the manner described, that the definition requires to be supported by a Protagorean epistemology and so is effectively equivalent to the doctrine that man is the measure of all things; 'Protagoras said the same thing as Theaetetus but put it a different way' (152 A). Only later, as the discussion develops, is there an opportunity to go into the philosophical motivations for holding a relativistic view. And 'later' means, in the first instance, the passage we are looking at. That passage plays a double role. Considered as a development of the position already premissed for examination, it may be allowed to pre-suppose the Protagorean principle that every perceptual appear-ance is the measure or criterion of what is the case for the perceiver; in which case the argument goes through. But con-sidered as Plato's attempt to bring out the kind of thinking which motivates perceptual relativism, it must stand on its own feet.[1] If, then, we raise the question how Protagoras himself came to the doctrine that man is the measure of all things, if we ask why he maintained that every appearance is the measure or criterion of what is the case for the person whose appearance it is, Plato's answer is that it was his solution to the problem of conflicting appearances. In the *Theaetetus*, indeed, the measure doctrine is initially introduced and explained in terms of what Protagoras would say about an example of conflicting appearances, the example of the wind which feels cold to one person and does not feel cold to another (152 B). And there can hardly be any serious dispute that Plato's answer is right. No philosopher who was not antecedently worried about conflicting appearances would propose a thoroughgoing relativism of the Protagorean kind.

But this means that the window model is not otiose. If we do ask the argument from conflicting appearances to stand on its own feet, it stumbles. Hence it is legitimate to suggest that anyone who finds it persuasive is leaning on some extra support, whether or not he is aware of the fact.

V

Interestingly—and this may help my diagnosis—we encounter a rather similar problem of double perspective in Berkeley's first *Dialogue*. Here we find a whole series of arguments from conflicting appearances: the case of sweet and bitter quoted earlier, the famous example of the water which feels warm to

[1] That the passage has this additional role is confirmed by comparing it with the immediately preceding 153 AD, which performs a parallel function for the Heraclitean component of Plato's dialectical construction. This is a light-hearted collection of Heraclitean considerations, capped by a joking inter-pretation of Homer, the whole making no contribution to the serious business of developing the implications and commitments of Theaetetus' definition.

one hand and cold to the other, and many more. But before embarking on these and other arguments Berkeley has laid down a notion of immediate perception which turns out to embody a version of the Protagorean principle we have been discussing. Immediate perception is knowledge (cf. Theaetetus' definition), what is immediately perceived must really be as it appears to be, hence the states of affairs (ideas) apprehended in perception must vary to match each and every change in sensible appearances. Or better, where the Protagorean theory has reality change to keep pace with the changing appearances, for Berkeley the states of affairs apprehended in immediate perception simply are the appearances. This notion of immediate perception defines a Berkeleyan perspective granted which the ensuing arguments are impeccable. The trouble is that at the start of the first *Dialogue* the full implications of the notion of immediate perception are not brought into the open, and if we ask why we should accept the notion, why we should adopt the Berkeleyan perspective, the answer is that it is Berkeley's solution to the problem of conflicting appearances. As in the *Theaetetus*, so in the *Three Dialogues*, the notion which comes first in the order of exposition should, in the order of argument, come last.

This is clear if we compare the *Three Dialogues* with Berkeley's earlier work, *The Principles of Human Knowledge*. In that treatise arguments from conflicting appearances are much less prominent, the reason being that they are now not Berkeley's own weapon but part of the armoury of the sceptic whom he takes as his opponent. The conclusion from the premiss of conflicting appearances is not the *Three Dialogues* conclusion but the sceptical conclusion urged by Sextus Empiricus: 'It must be confessed that this method of arguing doth not so much prove that there is no extension or colour in an outward object, as that we do not know by sense which is the true extension or colour of the object' (*Princ.* § 15). (The echo of Sextus is no accident: there is evidence that Berkeley's project for refuting scepticism was connected with his reading of the Pyrrhonian arguments transmitted by Bayle's *Dictionary*.)[1] In Berkeley's view, then, the (Pyrrhonian) sceptic has a good argument to show that 'Things remaining the same, our ideas vary, and which of them, or even whether any of them at all represent the true quality really existing in the thing, it is out of our reach to

[1] Richard Popkin, 'Berkeley and Pyrrhonism', *Review of Metaphysics* 5 (1951/2), pp. 223–46.

determine' (*Princ.* § 87). The only answer is to deny the contrast between how things appear and how they really are: 'Colour, figure, motion, extension and the like, considered only as so many *sensations* in the mind, are perfectly known, there being nothing in them which is not perceived' (*ibid.*) But now: to say there is nothing in the idea which is not perceived and thereby perfectly known is to make explicit, in a cool theoretical formulation, the prime desideratum of the window model—transparent, close-up version (Berkeley is famous for his denial that sensible qualities are at the distance we take them to be). The thesis is that, whatever else may go on in what we would ordinarily describe as the seeing of a white stone, at the core of the process is a transparently clear 'immediate' awareness of white, a white which is not at a distance from the eye.[1] Instead of looking through the eye, we enjoy a more satisfactorily transparent view of the contents of our own minds. To them we look through—nothing at all. This is Berkeley's solution to the challenge of the sceptical use of conflicting appearances.

But the *Three Dialogues* tries to recommend that solution from the perspective of the ordinary man. It is a popular exposition, written to take readers into the principles of Berkeley's philosophy 'in the most easy and familiar manner' (Preface, p. 168). To that end Berkeley appropriates the sceptic's arguments from conflicting appearances and tries to make them prove directly that sensible qualities do not inhere in outward objects. They would prove this if they could call on the notion of immediate perception and the Protagorean principle it embodies. But these, of course, are no part of the ordinary man's perspective. And without that assistance the arguments do no more than assert proposition (1) for a succession of different values of F. Once or twice Berkeley transposes (1) into (2). Thus after citing the jaundice example and animals with differently textured eyes to show that colours are not inherent in any outward object, i.e. after an argument which rests on (1), he continues:

The point will be past all doubt, if you consider, that in case colours were real properties or affections inherent in external bodies, they could admit of no alteration, without some change wrought in the very bodies themselves. (p. 185)

But that transposition, as we have seen, is no help to the cause. And perhaps it only looks as if it might help because Berkeley's formulation is ambiguous as between (2) and the quite different

[1] At *Siris* § 317 Berkeley endorses the *Theaetetus* account of white.

principle that if the colour of something were a real property of it, the colour could not actually change (as opposed to: it could not appear to change) without a change in the thing itself. This principle could well seem plausible, but it is irrelevant here, since the examples Berkeley is talking about are examples of apparent changes in the colour of a thing. The same goes for a later passage on primary qualities:

No real inherent property of any object can be changed, without some change in the thing itself. . . . But as we approach to or recede from an object, the visible extension varies, being at one distance ten or an hundred times greater than at another. Doth it not therefore follow from hence likewise, that it is not really inherent in the object? (p. 189)

The principle of the argument talks about real change, the illustration about apparent change in size, so what is claimed to follow does not follow at all.

There is no getting away from this distinction. It is one thing to say that the real or inherent features of an object cannot be among those that are affected by changes external to the object, e.g. in the surrounding environment or in the perceiver. This means, roughly, that the real inherent features of an object must not be relational (cf. Sext. Emp. *M* viii. 453–7). It is quite another to suggest that the real inherent features cannot be among those that *appear* to vary with changes outside the object. The latter principle is the one whose persuasiveness we are trying to diagnose; confusion with the former occurs too seldom to explain its pervasive influence in the first *Dialogue*. In the end, I think, if Berkeley or his reader is led by the argument from conflicting appearances to accept the conclusion that sensible qualities do not inhere in outward things, it is in good measure due to the supporting influence of the half-formulated thought—half-formulated because it is suggested but not fully spelt out when the notion of immediate perception is first introduced—that every perceptual experience contains within it a direct awareness of something. Which is to say that Berkeley's rebuttal of scepticism in the first *Dialogue* only works to the extent that an internalized version of the window model is implicitly present all along.

VI

Is it just coincidence that the ambiguities of the *Theaetetus* argument and of Berkeley's first *Dialogue* run parallel? I have already mentioned that Berkeley himself thought the *Theaetetus* theory exactly like his own. Perhaps, then, the common features can tell us something about why relativistic views have exercised such a strong hold on the philosophy of perception.

Our inheritance from Protagoras and Berkeley is modern sense-datum theory, which has reworked the old materials in a manner which may tend to disguise their essentially relativistic character. But it is quite profitable, I think, to read the seemingly sterile disputes about whether sense-data can exist unsensed, or whether they can be identified with parts of the surfaces of things, as disputes about the possibility of restoring some independence and externality to one term of the Protagorean relation. Better still, we can recognize a rather explicit expression of the window model in the notion, central to sense-datum theory, of sensing or acquaintance or direct awareness—the terminology varies but most theorists are agreed that the relation we have to the object or sense-datum which is presented to us in perceptual experience is a relation of unmediated non-inferential knowing (cf. Theaetetus' definition).[1]

Predictably, it is G. E. Moore who gives the most 'window-like' account of the matter:

When we refer to introspection and try to discover what the sensation of blue is, it is very easy to suppose that we have before us only a single term. The term 'blue' is easy enough to distinguish, but the other element which I have called 'consciousness'—that which sensation of blue has in common with sensation of green—is extremely difficult to fix. That many people fail to distinguish it at all is sufficiently shown by the fact that there are materialists. And, in general, that which makes the sensation of blue a mental fact seems to escape us: it seems, if I may use a metaphor, to be transparent—we look through it and see nothing but the blue. ('The Refutation of Idealism', *Philosophical Studies*, p. 20.)

So nearly explicit a picture of an internal window may help to make plausible what I said about an internalized version of the window model in Berkeley. Moore comes back to it later:

When we try to introspect the sensation of blue, all we can see is the blue: the other element is as if it were diaphanous. (p. 25)

This 'other element', the sensation or consiousness, Moore says is in fact a 'knowing' or 'being aware of' or 'experiencing' something, viz. blue (p. 24). Admittedly, Moore does not here

[1] See, for example, H. H. Price, *Perception* (London, 1932), pp. 3, 31; C. D. Broad, 'Some Elementary Reflexions on Sense-Preception' (1952), cited from Swartz, op. cit., p. 44.

talk his usual sense-datum language about blue, but his dia-phanous awareness of blue is a good preparation for it.

If other sense-datum theorists are less candidly revealing about the pictures which guide their thinking, they tell us more about the philosophical motivation for bringing in the notion of sensing or acquaintance. Russell sums up the results of the first chapter of *The Problems of Philosophy* in these terms:

What the senses *immediately* tell us is not the truth about the object as it is apart from us, but only the truth about certain sense-data which, so far as we can see, depend upon the relations between us and the object. Thus what we directly see and feel is merely 'appearance', which we believe to be a sign of some 'reality' behind. (p. 16)

This direct seeing and feeling of appearances or sense-data is what he later calls acquaintance or direct awareness, where this is one kind of knowledge of things (p. 46). But remember that chapter 1 of *The Problems of Philosophy* begins with the arguments from conflicting appearances which I cited at the outset of this lecture. So in Russell's case also it is reflection on conflicting appearances which is supposed to lead us to adopt the notion of acquaintance.

The examples of conflicting appearances bring to our atten-tion the fact that, as Russell puts it in the passage just quoted, 'sense-data . . . depend upon the relations between us and the object'. And it is clear from the discussion which precedes that what Russell means by this is that the way things appear to us at a given moment from a given point of view is causally dependent on the state of our sensory apparatus, the condition of the inter-vening medium, on perspectival effects and so on. All of which is undeniably correct. But unless (1) is true, for which Russell offers no independent argument, none of this shows that the colour or the shape which the table appears to have is not its real colour or shape. It shows only that if and when the table does appear the colour or the shape it really is, it does so thanks to the causal interaction of our sensory apparatus with a variety of environmental factors. And this, I think, is what at bottom Russell is getting at when he invokes the notion of what we directly or immediately see and feel. His idea is that if, *per impossibile*, the senses could tell us about 'the object as it is apart from us', they would have to do so directly or immediately, where 'directly' and 'immediately' can only mean: not by way of a causal interaction between us and the environment.

No doubt Russell would not like this way of putting it. The idea only works because it remains half-formulated. But that it is the idea which guides his thought is confirmed when he says that we do directly and immediately see and feel the sense-data or appearances which themselves depend upon the relation between us and the object. All the causal aspects of the perceptual process having been assigned to the production of sense-data, to the bringing about of the relation of acquaintance, that relation itself is left free of causality.

We are back at *Theaetetus* 154 AB. Causality makes the appearances relative to the conditions of perception, and that wrecks the hope of a transparent view of the external object with its real (inherent) properties. But we can save transparency by making the 'immediate' object of perception private to the perceiver and by abolishing the distance between subject and object; thus Russell locates sense-data in the private (apparent) space of the individual perceiver, again on grounds having to do with conflicting appearances (pp. 29–30).

Notice, therefore, that if there were such a thing as perception without causality, proposition (2) would very likely be true. A great many, at least, of the cases where a thing which is really *F* appears to someone not to be *F* are cases of interference or breakdown in the causal process by which we obtain information through the senses. Moreover, (2) does hold for sense-data. A sense-datum of necessity really is as it appears to be to the one observer who has access to it; (2) holds here just because causality does not get in the way. But Russell's argument rests on (1), which we saw to be equivalent to (2). So the argument has the same ambiguity as we found in Berkeley and the *Theaetetus*. What is supposed to come out of it is a cool theoretical formulation of the window model: the thesis that we have knowledge by acquaintance or direct awareness of sense-data. But the argument only works to the extent that a half-formulated version of the window model is present from the start. It is present because (1), which is formulated, reduces to (2), which contains (in its first disjunct) the unformulated demand for transparency.

I will not venture to assert that what I say three times is true. But at least, if it is true, it can hardly be coincidence that it is true. That is one gain from following the *fortuna* of the window model in modern times. Another gain is that we have come to see that the appeal of the window model is connected with worries about causality. Perception, it is felt, ought not to be mediated by a causal process.[1] But alas, that cannot be. The truth is that the window model is utterly inappropriate to the real facts of perception. But instead of coming to terms with reality, our theorists find a place for the window model within perception. Let causality do its worst: at the core of the perceptual experience there will still be an unmediated knowing, like Moore's diaphanous awareness of blue, and when a suitable story has been told about the objects of this knowing, the problem of conflicting appearances is solved. It is a phantasy solution, in a quite proper sense. For if my efforts at diagnosis have hit the mark, the conflict of appearances only ever became the problem these theorists took it to be because this was going to be the solution.

VII

At this point, now that we have connected the window model with a desire to cut free from the trammels of causality, we should turn aside briefly to the field of morals. On the face of it, if conflicting appearances are a problem here, it should be a different problem. We do not ascribe moral properties to things, as we ascribe sensible qualities, on the basis of a causal transaction between us and them. That may hold sometimes of predicates like 'nice' and 'nasty', predicates which merely express a reaction to things. But it certainly does not hold of terms like 'right' and 'wrong' or 'loyal', 'honest', 'charitable', and 'brave'. True, the cruder form of emotivist theory assimilates moral predicates to predicates of reaction, but the very implausibility of that assimilation is strong evidence that moral conflict ought

---

[1] The day after this lecture was delivered, there arrived on my desk a copy of *Mind* 88 (Jan. 1979), containing Maurice Charlesworth's paper, 'Sense-impressions: A New Model'. The 'new model' is none other than the window model, recommended as a means of picturing a role for sensations in perception which does not make them representative of external things. Roughly, if we can perceive the world *through* sensations as through a transparent window-pane, we will not be stuck with the traditionally problematic notion that we perceive sensations *instead of* the world outside (which they merely represent), and by this means we can avoid the dilemmatic choice between representative realism and phenomenalism. It is most instructive to see how, to make the model work, Charlesworth eventually finds it necessary to abandon simple transparency and imagine a *physics* for the glass we look through, a physics which makes its own contribution to the way things appear to us. In other words, he has to make the window a properly causal medium. Just this is what Berkeley and Russell are unwilling to do for immediate awareness.

to be a quite different type of issue, with difficulties of its own and peculiar to itself.

All too often, however, what one finds in the philosophical literature is a repetition of the debate about sensible qualities. The same form of argument is used (in Sextus, as we saw earlier, the parallel is deliberate and explicit, and it was almost certainly that way in Protagoras also); often there is the same reliance on a mythical example which for some reason people want to believe (those distant tribes who have sexual intercourse in public are a recurring presence in Greek literature from Herodotus onwards, and they are still at it in Montaigne).[1] But over and above these parallels with the debate about perception, there is also in the moral debate a preoccupation with perception itself, and it is this that we need to scrutinize.

When Mackie presents 'the argument from relativity' for the thesis that moral values are not objective, not part of the fabric of the world (note the initial choice of metaphor [p. 15]), he starts off by acknowledging that the divergence in moral beliefs between one group and another is in itself merely 'a fact of anthropology which entails neither first order nor second order ethical views' (p. 36). Nevertheless, such divergence requires explanation. The next step is to argue that the divergences in belief would be difficult to explain on the assumption that moral values are objective, whereas on the opposite assumption that values are not objective the divergences can quite reasonably be explained as due (and Mackie must mean they are *all entirely* due) to local or personal differences in the ways of life which give rise (by a process of projection or objectification) to the conflicting value-systems. How, then, is it to be shown that the objectivist will find it difficult to explain moral conflict and disagreement?

For this key step in the argument Mackie offers just two models for understanding disagreement. One is disagreement between scientific investigators in cases where the issue is objective but the evidence is insufficient to decide between the speculative hypotheses favoured by different investigators (p. 36). This, we may agree, is not a plausible parallel for the moral case. The other model is divergence in perception:[2]

---

[1] *Apologie de Raimond Sebond, Essais* ed. Pierre Villey (Paris, 1922), ii. p. 341. Montaigne also retails, as we would expect, both the honey and the jaundice examples (pp. 348, 362).

[2] Cf. Gilbert Harman, *The Nature of Morality* (New York, 1977), chap. 1, who asks whether moral principles can be tested and confirmed and proceeds

The argument from relativity has some force simply because the actual variations in the moral codes are more readily explained by the hypothesis that they reflect ways of life than by the hypothesis that they express perceptions, most of them seriously inadequate and badly distorted, of objective values. (p. 37)

But why would the objectivist have no choice but this? Why must he treat moral divergence, like perceptual divergence, as a straightforward indication of error on somebody's part, and then explain moral error on the analogy of perceptual error? Mackie says, and this is his second argument against the objectivity of values, 'the argument from queerness'—

If there were objective values, then they would be entities or qualities or relations of a very strange sort, utterly different from anything else in the universe. Correspondingly, if we were aware of them, it would have to be by some special faculty of moral perception or intuition, utterly different from our ordinary ways of knowing everything else. (p. 38)

It is Mackie who introduces the perceptual model, not his objectivist opponent, Mackie who claims that objectivism must sooner or later turn into intuitionism: 'Intuitionism merely makes unpalatably plain what other forms of objectivism wrap up' (*ibid.*). Not only should the objectivist dispute this assertion, but he should notice that the only substantive argument Mackie offers for it is the following: when people judge that some things are good or right, and others bad or wrong, for the most part they do so 'not because—or at any rate not only because—they exemplify some general principle for which widespread implicit acceptance could be claimed, but because something about those things arouses certain responses immediately in them, though they would arouse radically and irresolvably different responses in others. 'Moral sense' or 'intuition' is an initially more plausible description of what supplies many of our basic moral judgements than 'reason'. With regard to all these starting points of moral thinking the argument from relativity remains in full force' (p. 378) It is the emotivist assimilation to predicates of reaction,[1] overlaid by a perceptual gloss. That is why the argument from relativity to inquire whether they can be tested and confirmed *by observation*, only to find that 'there does not seem to be any way in which the actual rightness or wrongness of a given situation can have any effect on your perceptual apparatus' (p. 8).

[1] Cf. p. 42 where, to illustrate our projection or objectification of moral attitudes, Mackie uses the analogy of someone who calls a fungus foul because it fills him with disgust.

remains in full force. Moral predicates express an immediate response or reaction to things, so if the objectivist is to make intelligible the notion of a mistaken application of such predicates, he must say that something goes wrong in the transaction between us and them. And for this it is no doubt true that the only decent model we have is the model of misperceiving.

Thus Mackie's whole case rests on the premiss that, for the most part at least, we apply moral predicates to things, as we apply sensory predicates, on the basis of a transaction between us and them. At this point Mackie's account of morals really is parallel to Democritus' account of secondary qualities.[1] Any sensible objectivist who denies the premiss gets off scot free. But what is of interest here is the way Mackie argues that a perceptual model for the supposed transaction breaks down, and can be seen to be absurd, as soon as one tries to fill in a certain amount of as it were 'causal' detail to explain what happens when things go wrong. In effect, Mackie first projects upon the objectivist his own attachment to the window model, transparent distance version (an intuition of non-natural qualities out there in the fabric of the world), and then he complains that the model is unrealistic because it cannot cope with the conflict of appearances. Hence values are subjective. And this does seem remarkably like Democritus concluding that honey is neither sweet nor bitter on the grounds that, while it appears sweet to you and me, it also appears bitter—so Sextus assures us (*PH* i. 101), and Sextus was a doctor—to people with jaundice.

VIII

None of this shows, of course, that moral values are objective or that the objectivist can in fact give a plausible account of moral disagreement. Likewise, my earlier discussion did not attempt to prove that sensible qualities are inherent in the things we ascribe them to. I have not argued that there is no truth in relativism or in subjectivism, whether these are taken as theories about values, about secondary qualities or about primary qualities as well. I have criticized what may in full propriety be called the classical arguments for relativism and subjectivism, but I have criticized them chiefly with a view to understanding their appeal. Anyone who teaches outside the walls of a conventional

---

[1] Cf. also Mackie's remarks on the extent to which moral values exist by convention, pp. 36, 42 ff.

university philosophy department soon finds that these arguments are a potent force in the wider culture of our society: as potent as they were in ancient Greece. They seem to come naturally, of their own accord, to many people untutored in philosophy, as soon as they engage with Heraclitus' question, how far our language and the ways we ordinarily speak about things can claim absolute validity. Arguments which have that kind of appeal call for diagnosis as much as for straightforward logical appraisal.

I shall return to this matter of diagnosis, but first, to prevent misunderstanding, there are several further points I should mention, if only to make it clear where they fit in and what I do and do not want to say about them.

(1) I have not said, nor do I believe, that the window model is an aberration of philosophers whose worries about conflicting appearances take a relativist or subjectivist turn. Another adherent of the picture is Plato himself.

Plato sets up relativism in the *Theaetetus* in order to argue that when its implications and commitments are followed through it will be seen to lead to multiple absurdities, not the least of which is that in the end those private, relative occurrences of white and other sensible qualities cannot be identified or described as, e.g., white rather than anything else; perceptual relativism makes language impossible. What Plato most objects to in the kind of empiricism represented by Theaetetus' definition and Protagoras' epistemology is that it covertly assigns to perceptual experience as such those functions of thought which are required for the perceiver to identify what his experience is of. His target in this polemic is the Berkeleyan view that one has only to sense white to know it for what it is. Accordingly, when the *Theaetetus* goes on (184 B–7 A) to give Plato's own account of the matter, a very sharp distinction is drawn between perception and judgement. It is one thing to perceive a colour, quite another to judge or be aware that it is the colour white. However, in thus arguing that perception as such cannot be knowledge, because perception on its own has no power of judgement or conceptualization, Plato himself makes heavy use of the window model in the interests of an important thesis about the unity of the perceiving consciousness.[1]

---

[1] See my 'Plato on the Grammar of Perceiving', *Classical Quarterly* NS 26 (1976), pp. 29–51, to which I must refer for a detailed defence of the interpretation sketched out here.

Plato's contention is that we cannot make sense of perception (whether as philosophers or as perceivers) except in terms of a unitary mind or soul which can think and reason about the objects of different senses and make comparisons between things perceived at different times. It must be one and the same enduring soul which perceives all the objects of the several senses and it must be that same part of ourselves which applies thought to what we perceive. For this thesis Plato offers cool theoretical argument, rather good argument, but in addition he helps the argument along with models and metaphors. If there were no unitary consciousness, the several senses would be like the band of warriors in the wooden horse at Troy, each carrying on his perceptual activity independently of the others and of the whole which contains them. In place of this picture Plato puts another, better one. Colours and other sensible qualities are out there, with a (non-relative) nature or essence of their own; the soul gains access to them through the senses or sense-organs; and we are encouraged to take the preposition 'through', on which much emphasis is laid, as a spatial metaphor.[1] The metaphor of organs or senses as apertures for the soul to perceive through conjures up a picture of a unitary soul which, because it stands back as it were from the individual senses, is able both to perceive the objects of more than one sense and to think about what it perceives in general terms. In a word, a unitary soul, and only a unitary soul, can be *conscious*.

All this stands in powerful contrast to the empiricism initiated by Theaetetus' definition. If the empiricist were to reply by pressing Plato with his own argument at 154 AB, the answer would be that it does not work because the notion of appearing already incorporates the perceiver's thought or judgement (cf. *Sophist* 264 B), and it is thought which applies the predicates '*F*' or 'not-*F*' to things; the perceptual element in appearance can be described in causal terms but that is all there is to say about it.

I give this very summary sketch of Plato's own position, not because I think his final answer satisfactory, but because I think that his use of the window model brings out an important point. So far from being an aberration of certain empiricist philosophers, the picture associated with the model is one compellingly natural expression of the difficulty of coming

[1] It was this, presumably, that inspired the explicit window comparison attacked by Lucretius (III p. 84 above).

to terms with what it is to be both in the world and cognizant of the world. The eyes and the remaining sensory apparatus of the body are entangled in the causal mechanisms which are necessary to perception. In certain philosophical moods it may strike us that they are too much in the world to be cognizant of it. To explain perceptual consciousness it is then tempting to imagine oneself standing off, as it were, from one's own body and its causal involvements, looking through it (to use Plato's ambiguous preposition) at the world beyond. And here too, as in the empiricists, the metaphorical looking is free of causality, because the causality gets used up, so to speak, in the body's interaction with the enviroment.

(2) I have not said anything about the inappropriateness of the window model to senses other than sight. I have not done this because what is interesting and revealing about the model is the way in which it is inadequate to the specific mode of perception, namely sight, by which it is inspired. It has often been remarked that the philosophy of perception has tended to give the primacy to sight, allowing the other senses to provide useful examples of illusion or conflicting appearances but otherwise leaving them to tag along. Perhaps the window model has something to do with this tendency.

In this connection the *Theaetetus* passage we started from is quite revealing. It sets forth its thesis in terms of colour predicates, and when it does come to mention others, the examples given are 'large' and 'hot'. Now 'large' is clearly suggested by the Protagorean image of perceiving as measuring. We are to think of a situation in which we literally measure ourselves against an object in order to estimate its size by comparison with our own. That is, the example invites a visual interpretation again. What is more, it invites us to picture our own body as within the visual field.

It would, however, be perfectly possible to take one's inspiration from a sense other than sight. C. D. Broad once presented the argument from conflicting appearances in images of jumping and grasping:

In its purely phenomenological aspect *seeing* is ostensibly *saltatory*. It seems to leap the spatial gap between the percipient's body and a remote region of space. Then, again, it is ostensibly *prehensive* of the surfaces of distant bodies as coloured and extended, and of external events as colour-occurrences *localized* in remote regions of space. ('Some Elementary Reflexions on Sense-Perception', op. cit., p. 32.)

Given this imagery to work with, Broad's conclusion from the usual survey of conflicting appearances is that the phenomenology is misleading, the distance to those remote regions cannot be jumped, so we have to say that perceptual experiences are 'prehensions' of non-physical particulars which do really have the qualities of redness, squeakiness, hotness, etc., which they appear to have (p. 42). It is the *Theaetetus* argument again, conducted in terms of movement and the modality of touch.

Now Broad's 'prehensions' have a more embodied precedent in the hand-gestures with which Zeno of Citium illustrated the Stoic theory of the cataleptic or 'grasping' impression (Cicero, *Academica* i. 41, ii. 145), a truth-guaranteeing experience which the Stoics also imaged as a perfect picture of its object (Sext. Emp. *M* vii. 248) and as a clear and distinct impression of it (Diogenes Laertius vii. 46). The difference is that, where Broad has to content himself with a non-physical grasp of a non-physical particular, the Stoics have enough faith in the natural adaptedness of our faculties to the universe we live in to be whole-hearted physicalists. Their grasping, picturing or clear and distinct impression is a causally determined, wholly physical process in which one body, the perceiver, achieves certain truth about another body. What links the bodily grasp of the Stoics to Broad's etherial prehensions is our word 'perception'. It comes from the Latin 'perceptio', meaning 'a taking hold of', which was one of Cicero's translations of the Stoic term 'catalepsis', grasp (cf. Cic. *Acad.* ii. 17). It looks very much as though the idea of perception as a firm grasp of an object is some sort of antithesis to the window model, and perhaps a different, if rather less common, way of coping with the same ultimate problem.

(3) I have not so far said anything about arguments in which the premise of conflicting appearances is overtly and deliberately combined with further premisses. Most of the sceptical arguments in Sextus are of this kind. In his better moments Sextus knows that Berkeley was wrong to say it follows just from the conflict of appearances that 'we do not know by sense which is the true extension or colour of the object'. Of course, if we are told that something appears F to one person and not-F to another, we cannot decide on that basis alone whether the thing is F or not-F. But this does not prove that it cannot be determined at all, nor that it cannot be determined by sense.

It is important here not to confuse the perceiver's question 'Is it F or not-F?' (answer: 'It appears to be F') with the outsider's question 'Is it really F as it appears to him to be?' It is easy to confuse the two because of course the perceiver himself can step back and ask about himself the outsider's question in the form 'Is it really F as it appears to me to be?' Now, in a conflict case the outsider needs a reason to prefer one person's appearances to another's. Nothing has been said so far to show he cannot have it. Suppose he does. Then certainly, *his* knowledge that the thing is really F is not based on sense alone. But for all that has been shown so far to the contrary, he is now entitled to say of the person to whom it appears F that *he* knows it is F because and simply because he perceives it to be so. That is, the outsider may very well reach the conclusion that the conditions are right for the insider to gain knowledge from his perception. Hume's assessment of the sceptical argument from conflicting appearances has it exactly right:

These sceptical topics, indeed, are only sufficient to prove, that the senses alone are not implicitly to be depended on; but that we must correct their evidence by reason, and by considerations derived from the nature of the medium, the distance of the object, and the disposition of the organ, in order to render them, within their sphere, the proper *criteria* of truth and falsehood. (*Enquiry concerning Human Understanding* XII. 117.)

What is true is that if as outsiders we become convinced that there is never reason to prefer one person's appearances to another's, we shall conclude that under no circumstances does knowledge result when the insider judges that something is F because it appears so to him. But, contrary to Berkeley, this cannot be proved by the conflict of appearances alone. Accordingly, much of Sextus' effort goes into arguing, explicitly and in detail, that there is never reason to prefer one appearance to another; or as he puts it, that there is no criterion of truth— neither the senses nor anything else are 'the proper criteria of truth and falsehood'. Add that to the premiss of conflicting appearances and the sceptical argument goes through. For if there is no criterion of truth, all appearances are of equal strength, equally worthy and equally unworthy of belief, and we are forced to suspend judgement.

So put, the sceptical challenge seems to me to deserve something better than the phantasy solutions it has so often received. It calls for a detailed examination and appraisal of the grounds on which we ordinarily prefer some appearances to others.

It is not enough, for example, to talk in a general promissory way about healthy minds in healthy bodies under normal conditions of perception. The justification for taking these as the measure or criterion of what sensible qualities things have must lie in a detailed understanding of the interaction between perceiver and perceived. The question of the reliability of the processes by which we obtain information about the world must be squarely faced in causal terms, not avoided by taking refuge in the window model and its illusory alternative to the causal medium in which perception is immersed.

(4) I have not so far called attention to differences among the three categories of variation or conflict between appearances which Socrates sets out at *Theaetetus* 154 A. But clearly, there are important differences both between and within these categories. In morals, for instance, they are different sorts of difference of outlook and judgement which distinguish a man in his maturity from that same man in adolescence, a man hungry and oppressed from that same man when he has become the leader of his people, and a man inflamed with passion from that same man reflecting next day. And these differences should themselves be contrasted, not equated, with the differences between one man and his contemporaries, which are different again from the differences between him and people of other times and places. Similar points could be made about differences in the import of conflicting appearances for the different sense modalities. But where perception is concerned, it seems to me that the interesting category is the one least attended to in modern discussions, the variation between man and other animals. The interesting problem is not relativity or subjectivity in general, but Heraclitus' problem of anthropocentricity.[1]

Suppose we have been able to justify our practice of preferring the appearances enjoyed by healthy humans in normal conditions of perception over those of human subjects affected by jaundice and other disadvantages. Sextus will argue, and he has both Heraclitus and Protagoras behind him, that even so it is arbitrary to prefer human appearances, however carefully selected, to the conflicting appearances which other animals get from the same things. There is no need to resort to

---

[1] Compare David Wiggins, 'Truth, Invention, and the Meaning of Life', *Proc. Brit. Acad.* lxii (1976), pp. 331–78, at pp. 348–9; Thomas Nagel, 'What is it like to be a Bat?', *Philosophical Review* 83 (1974), pp. 435–50.

quaint examples like Heraclitus' pigs enjoying the mire.[1] We know, or have good reason to believe, that a table which normally looks brown to us looks very different to a normal healthy cat, who has only black and white vision and sees everything in gradations of grey. Is it not a kind of epistemological 'speciesism' (cf. *PH* i. 59) to prefer our own perceptions to the cat's?[2]

As it stands, this is not a good argument. We do not in fact prefer in a completely general way our own perceptions to those of other animals. We readily accept, and so does Sextus (*PH* i. 62 ff), that animals are often more sensitive to smells than we are, and in some ways more sensitive to sound. Even in the case of colour, we could believe, and it may actually be the case, that some animals have a spectrum wider than ours. In sum, we have a notion of better or worse perceptual equipment and that notion is not species-specific. It is an empirical question, who is best at perceiving what, and the citing of variations in perception between us and other species does nothing to show that the question cannot ever have a well-grounded answer.

Thus Sextus' argument fails. But Heraclitus will come back to make the charge of anthropocentric partiality at a higher level. It is our human language in which all this has been said, our language in which the scientist's empirical investigation is carried out. The interesting case would be one where it is not just that the other animal is missing something we can pick up or vice versa, but rather that he has an experience of colour, say, which is through and through different from that of any human.[3] Then some of Heraclitus' paradoxes could begin to bite.

[1] Though Berkeley did: *Three Dialogues*, p. 181.

[2] Another way of getting to the problem is by changing human beings. For ways of doing this, see Jonathan Bennett, 'Substance, Reality and Primary Qualities', *Amer. Phil. Quart.* 2 (1965), pp. 1–17, who is concerned to draw a moral about the distinction between primary and secondary qualities. Bennett shows that the objectivity of primary qualities is more fundamental, in a certain clear sense, than the objectivity of secondary qualities, but it would be wrong to conclude that this makes my problem disappear. We still have to explain what type of objectivity the secondary qualities can enjoy. And here the variety of animal perceptions (the first Mode of Pyrrhonian scepticism) offers a more radical challenge than, for example, limited colour blindness in human beings.

[3] If I mention here Gerald H. Jacobs and Robert L. Yolton, 'Visual Sensitivity and Colour Vision in Ground Squirrels', *Vision Research* 11 (1971), pp. 511–37, it is without confidence that they intend to describe such a case.

Suppose we had elaborated a scheme of colour predicates to describe the other animal's experience from his point of view. Let one of these predicates be 'huey'. Would it be a contradiction for one and the same thing to be both blue and huey all over at the same time? Must we oppose the colour-qualities things have for us (the Protagorean idiom seeming inescapable as the only alternative to paradox) to those they have for the other creature, insisting that 'blue' and 'huey' be regarded as contraries in the same way as 'blue' and 'red' within our own colour vocabulary? Many will prefer the Democritean solution that the object in itself, absolutely considered, is neither blue nor huey, all colour being equally subjective. But Heraclitus himself was not so despairing.

Heraclitus' version of the absolute god's-eye vantage-point is not designed to show us the world 'as it is apart from us'. On the contrary, when he talks of the god's-eye view, he projects into it all our opposing, relativity-conditioned predicates:

To god all things are fair and just: but men suppose some things just and others unjust. (frag. 102)[1]

I interpret this to mean that our human contrast between justice and injustice has no absolute validity, even though it is necessary to the very meaning of the terms in our language:

For [men] would not know the name of *Dikē* [= Justice] if these things [sc. injustices] did not exist. (frag. 23)

From an absolute vantage point everything is just—but not in a way that contrasts with injustice. For at that level it is equally true that justice is strife, i.e. what men think of as injustice:

What one ought to understand is that war [sc. that which separates] *is* common [sc. that which connects] and justice *is* strife, and that all things which come to pass do so in accordance with strife and what ought to be. (frag. 80)

And what holds for moral predicates holds for the rest of our language:

God is day night, winter summer, war peace, hunger satiety: he changes [sc. becomes many opposite things] in the way that fire [sc. the fire at a sacrifice], when it is mixed with spices, is named according to the scent of each. (frag. 67)

No matter. We can still try to imagine a case and consider what we could say about it.

[1] Text as in M. Marcovich, *Heraclitus*, Editio Maior (Mérida, 1967), pp. 480–2.

In sum, the absolute viewpoint, far from being different from every partial viewpoint, would be one which saw that every partial viewpoint is correct.

All this may seem indulgent mystification, even if I am pardoned for thinking that we might apply what Heraclitus says about opposed predicates within language as it is to the imagined case of 'blue' and 'huey'. What possible alternative to Democritus can Heraclitus offer unless he explains what the overcoming of opposition and contradiction within the god's-eye vantage-point amounts to? But reasonable as it may seem to ask for such an explanation, to expect Heraclitus to say that the predicates are not really opposed, the strife image tells us that of course they are opposed (so too frags. 102 and 23, quoted above); and many other fragments convey the same message with unmistakeable force. Heraclitus' solution to the problem of conflicting appearances is not an explanation but a certain kind of awareness:

To those who are awake the world-order is one, common to all; but the sleeping turn aside each into a private world. (frag. 89)[1]

The world as we ordinarily understand it is from a god's-eye view relative to us and the categories of our language, as a dreamer's world is to him. The trouble is that people are not aware of this. Most men 'fail to notice what they do after they wake up, just as they forget what they do when asleep' (frag. 1). A true awakening would remember the dream world and be aware that it was a private world.

For those who have heard not me but the *Logos* wisdom is agreeing that all things are one. (frag. 50)

Wisdom is becoming aware of the relativity of one's categories and experience, not thereby denying its (partial) validity but putting it into perspective along with other viewpoints. The *Logos* which connects things that our language separates and opposes is itself still language, our own language. The god's-eye view for Heraclitus is simply this: seeing that the human view is the *human* view and no more. One carries on as before—one speaks and can only speak from within one's own language. But the wise man is awake to what he is doing. That is how Heraclitus could sum up his whole philosophy in the words 'I searched out myself' (frag. 101).

---

[1] For a defence of the authenticity of this fragment see Marcovich, op. cit., pp. 99–100.

What this account of Heraclitus suggests as his answer to our earlier problem is the following. The inclination to regard 'blue' and 'huey' as incompatibly opposed is not to be suppressed but rather recognized for what it is, namely, a manifestation of the fact that we cannot absorb the other creature's colour scheme into our own. To recognize this is to recognize that it lies in the nature of a viewpoint—any viewpoint—to claim the absolute allegiance of the one whose viewpoint it is. Heraclitean wisdom is thus comparable to the stance of a man who recognizes that his morality is one among others, yet does not on that account feel, nor think that he ought to feel, its values to be any the less absolute or binding. There may be difficulties in expressing and maintaining this stance, but it is really no less difficult to conceive a Protagorean or Democritean life which seriously attempted to treat first-order experience and concerns as relative or subjective.[1] And this brings me to the question of diagnosis.

IX

When I was discussing the relation of the *Theaetetus* argument to the Protagorean principle laid down at the beginning of the dialogue, I considered the objection that my window-model diagnosis was both rude and unnecessary. I have, I hope, dealt sufficiently with the claim that it is not necessary. But I have not addressed the complaint that I make it sound as if something rather disreputable is going on in the *Theaetetus* argument and the others we have been looking at. I am very far from thinking this to be so. I have indeed emphasized the pictures and the metaphors, but so that we may see them for what they are. Whether it is the flawless close-up vision or the prehensive grasp, whether it secures a whole object or only some part of the surface of one or just a non-physical substitute for these, such pictures have their origin in our earliest and deepest experience. If they have elicited a smile, it should have been a smile of recognition, not contempt. For if, as Heraclitus advised, we remember our dreams, we will recognize that there was a time in our own lives when the problem of conflicting appearances engaged our strongest feelings; a time, moreover, when perception and valuation were not yet distinguished. We know too little about the psychic roots of creative philosophy to turn our backs on these sources of inspiration. If they are found disreputable, the fault really is, for once, in

[1] For valuable discussion of this and related issues, see Wiggins, op. cit.

the eye of the beholder. Of course the arguments must be criticized. But the point is that the criticism must be joined by respect and understanding.

It is that element of respect, so necessary for real understanding, which I miss in Austin's work as a critic of the tradition which he rightly saw as stemming from Heraclitus. Austin is a third case of double perspective. In his first chapter he explains that he cannot go back to the very earliest texts from before Plato, since they are no longer extant. So he chooses Ayer as his 'chief stalking horse', with subsidiary references to Price and to Warnock's book on Berkeley. These works seem to him 'to provide the best available expositions of the approved reasons for holding theories which are at least as old as Heraclitus—more full, coherent, and terminologically exact than you find, for example, in Descartes or Berkeley' (p. 1). But unfortunately, this was a serious historical mistake on Austin's part.

It was a mistake because the reasons Ayer provides for the introduction of sense-data are *not* the traditionally approved reasons, though Ayer himself claims that they are:

What the advocates of the sense-datum theory have done is to decide to apply the word 'see' or any other words that designate modes of perception to delusive as well as to veridical experiences, and at the same time to use these words in such a way that what is seen or otherwise sensibly experienced must really exist and must really have the properties that it appears to have. No doubt they also use these words in other, more familiar, senses. But it is this usage that leads them to the introduction of sense-data. (p. 24)[1]

This was wrong as history—neither Protagoras nor Berkeley nor Russell relied on a novel sense of 'see' or 'perceive'—but correct as an account of what Ayer himself wished to do, which was to make the whole issue a question of which language one chooses for the purposes of philosophical theory. On the reading I have offered in this lecture, the traditional argument from conflicting appearances sets up a private substitute object to be perceived in the very same sense of the verb as that in which we originally wanted to perceive whole objects out there in the world. What is changed by adding the relativistic qualifiers

[1] A footnote on the next page refers to G. A. Paul, 'Is there a Problem about Sense-Data?' (1936), in Swartz, op. cit., pp. 271–87, as clearly bringing out the point that the sense-datum theorist is simply recommending a new verbal usage. But Paul denies that the sense-datum theorists themselves would represent their procedure in such terms (pp. 227–9).

'for me', 'immediately', 'directly', and the like, is not the sense of the verb 'perceive' but its object. What guarantees that something really is as it appears to be is not a special sense of the verb but its taking as object something which is itself (an) appearance.[1] And this is completely at variance with Austin's diagnosis in terms of linguistic sleight of hand (cf. pp. 3–5) or the unjustified invention of a special sense of 'perceive' (chap. IX). It is true that Austin tempers his diagnosis from time to time with an acknowledgement that it was Ayer who gave the subject a linguistic turn (cf. p. 102). But that acknowledgement is itself modified by Austin's view that the new linguistic clothing is really just a disguise for the old traditional arguments for an ontological dichotomy between sense-data and material objects (pp. 59–61, 84, 105–7). And despite these qualifications, he continues to discuss the arguments and diagnose their mistakes in predominantly linguistic terms, taking it that Ayer does give 'the approved reasons' for the old theory.[2] The effect, as many readers of *Sense and Sensibilia* have felt, is that Austin's objections fall unhappily between two stools. They neither get to the bottom of the traditional arguments, which require a diagnosis deeper than linguistic methods can achieve, nor are they appropriate to the essentially stipulative, constructive character of Ayer's own enterprise.

It seems to me, then, that as a critic Austin falls short because he did not properly sort out the double perspective he adopted when he decided to look at the history through Ayer's spectacles. He would have done better to go back to the original sources, which he was of course well equipped to handle. Even the earliest sources, prior to Plato, are not completely beyond the reach of historical understanding—as I hope to have shown. In trying to show this, my essential claim has been that a

---

[1] Let me add that I have nothing to say in this lecture about phenomenalism. Considered as a theory about the analysis of material object statements in terms of statements about perceptual experience, phenomenalism is a separate issue from the introduction of sense-data (just one approach to perceptual experience) with which it has historically been associated.

[2] To mention just one of the historical distortions that result, Price, who really belongs to the prelinguistic phase, gets landed with Ayer's account (as quoted above) of how sense-data are introduced (Austin, p. 103). A footnote seeks to make amends, but it does not make clear that Price only raised the matter of the senses of 'perceive' in chapter 2 of *Perception* (pp. 22 ff.), *after* introducing sense-data in chapter 1 on the basis of an entirely epistemological argument from what we can and cannot doubt (though cf. p. 5 n.).

respectful historical understanding of the original sources is a first step towards realism in our own philosophy.

X

It is only fitting that the epilogue be given to the founder of the series of lectures in which I have the honour to speak. In a philosophically judicious and historically informed paper on 'Appearance and Real Existence'[1]—a paper which treats ancient and modern philosophy as a single continuing story, with equal honours for Plato, Kant, and Hegel—Dawes Hicks has this to say about Russell's version of the argument from conflicting appearances in *The Problems of Philosophy*:

> It is obvious, I think, that this argument is fallacious, and that the conclusion does not follow from the premises. For, in order to test it, suppose that colour of some kind *is* inherent in the table, that the table *has* a specific colour. Then, surely, there would be nothing to conflict with this supposition in the circumstances that such real colour will present a different aspect if another colour be reflected upon it, or if a blue pair of spectacles intervene between it and the eyes of the observer, or if it be enveloped in darkness rather than in daylight. The reasoning would only be valid on the assumption that if the table is really coloured, the real colour *must* appear the same in darkness and in daylight, through a pair of blue spectacles and without them, in artificial light and in the sun's light—an assumption which, on the view I am taking, is at once to be dismissed as untenable. If the colour did appear to be the same in these varying circumstances, then certainly there would be reason, and sufficient reason, for doubting the reliability of visual apprehension.[2] For obviously the conditions mentioned—real, objective conditions, as I take them to be—cannot be without influence upon any real colour the table may be said to possess. (p. 42)

This is where we came in. Russell's argument rests on proposition (1), (1) is equivalent to (2), and (2) is manifestly false. There it is—the logical refutation neatly laid out, clear and conclusive, just one year after the publication of *The Problems of Philosophy*. Why did it make no difference? Why, if straightforward logical refutation is enough, do the arguments from conflicting appearances live on?

[1] *Proc. Arist. Soc.* 14 (1913/14), pp. 1–48.
[2] Compare Augustine, *Contra Academicos* iii, 26: 'If an oar dipped in water looked straight, I would rather accuse my eyes of false testimony'—so far as I can discover, the point is original with Augustine, one of several that make the *Contra Academicos* a pioneering work.

Protagoras and Inconsistency: *Theaetetus* 171 a6—c7[1]

by Sarah Waterlow (Edinburgh)

'He [Protagoras], for his part, allowing as he does that all men believe what is so, agrees, I suppose, that his opponents' opinion of his own opinion is true — their opinion being that he is mistaken . . . So he would agree that his own view is false, if he allows to be true the view of those who take him to be mistaken . . . But the others do not agree that they themselves are mistaken . . . Whereas he again agrees that this view of theirs is also true, from what he has written . . . So everyone beginning with Protagoras will question his view, or rather, he will agree to his opponent's point; for whenever he agrees with his opponent that the latter's opinion is true, Protagoras himself will be agreeing that neither a dog nor anyone you please is a measure of even a single thing of which he has not knowledge. So since it is doubted by everyone, to no one will Protagoras' "Truth" be true, neither to anyone else nor to Protagoras' himself.' (*Theaetetus* 171 a6—c7.)

So runs the argument said by Socrates[2] to be the 'most ingenious' of all those marshalled in the *Theaetetus* against Protagoras' doctrine that all beliefs are true. The general purpose of the argument is clear: to show that the doctrine is in some way self-refuting[3]. But it is not so clear precisely how the refutation is effected or even whether it is validly effected at all. The question of validity cannot be decided until it is known what kind of argument Plato has constructed here. This latter question is the subject of this paper. I shall be concerned in particular with one commonly accepted view according to which Plato is trying to show that Protagoras' doctrine, when held in conjunction with a premiss which no one could deny, entails its own contradictory[4]. In Section I, it will be argued that this interpretation is implausible since it fails to take

---

[1] I am indebted to Alexander Broadie for discussion of many points of this paper.
[2] *Theaetetus* 171 a6. All references are to the *Theaetetus* unless otherwise specified.
[3] Sextus Empiricus called the argument a 'περιτροπή' (Adv. Math. vii 389).
[4] For such an interpretation, see Grote, *Plato* vol, 2, pp. 352—3; A. E. Taylor, *Plato: the Man and his Work*, p. 334; Bochenski, *Ancient Formal Logic*, p. 16; Sayre, *Plato's Analytic Method*, pp. 87—91; Hussey, *The Presocratics*, p. 113; McDowell, *Theaetetus*, pp. 169—171.

full account of the Protagorean position as presented by Plato.
But it cannot be denied that the reasoning of 171 a6—c7 looks in
some respects remarkably like an attempt to prove the position
inconsistent. In Section II, a different interpretation is proposed,
which avoids the defects of the common one, but which nevertheless accounts for the latter's initial plausibility.

I

Protagoras' position as attacked by Socrates in 171 a6—c7
consists of (a) the doctrine (D) that all beliefs or opinions are true,
and (b) the admission of the undeniable fact that most men hold
that some opinions are false, and hence hold (or would, if the matter
were put to them) that Protagoras' opinion that all opinions are
true is itself a false opinion. If the reasoning of 171 a6—c7 is intended
to show that this position is logically inconsistent, then certainly
the reasoning fails. The position entails no contradiction, as several
commentators have remarked[5]. If Protagoras means D to apply to
all opinions without restriction, and in the *Theaetetus* this is how he
is presented[6], then he is commited to accepting that the opinion
of D's falsity is true. But since presumably he himself believes in D,
he must at the same time regard D too as true. This may look self-
contradictory, but is not so in reality. At no point does Plato succeed (assuming this to be Plato's intention) in showing that Protagoras is committed to asserting that the same thing both is and is
not the case. Nor could he succeed, given the grounds on which he
himself presents Protagoras as holding that all opinions are true.
Protagoras holds this because, in his view, whatever anyone believes
to be the case *is* the case relatively to the believer at the time of
his belief. Thus if one man holds that p and another that not-p,
the two opinions are on Protagoras' view both true, since their
both being true does not entail that the self-same fact or reality
both holds and does not hold, but only that there are two different
realities each existing relatively to one and the other believer and
so making each belief true. Thus the reality corresponding to Protagoras' D does not have to give way to that corresponding to his

---

[5] For analyses of the failure of the argument as a proof of inconsistency, see Grote,
Sayre, McDowell, 11. cc.

[6] Throughout this paper, 'Protagoras' means the Protagoras that appears in the
Theaetetus. I shall not be concerned with the question whether this character is a
fair portrayal of the historical Protagoras.

opponents' denial of D, or *vice versa*, since it is as if each holds good in a separate world contained within each believer. Protagoras' D and his opponents' denial are therefore not mutually inconsistent.

This conclusion holds good whether or not we suppose that Protagoras assumes that the realities making true his own opinions, have, in every case, the same metaphysical status as those making true the opinions of others. In the preceding paragraph I took this to be the case: i. e. that Protagoras would be willing to allow that what makes true an opinion of his own, for instance D, is no more of an absolute reality than what makes true the opinion of another. On this view there is clearly no inconsistency involved in his holding that D and his opponents' denial of it are both true. But it may be that Protagoras does not intend his relativism to apply to himself, its proponent, or at any rate not to his own belief that all opinions are true. This is perhaps the more natural interpretation of his position[7]. On such a view, what makes true his belief that all beliefs are true is a reality absolutely and *simpliciter*. Thus it would be a fact *simpliciter* that all beliefs are true. For it would be a fact *simpliciter* that all beliefs except for the Protagorean belief expressed as D, are true because made true by facts that exist relatively to the believers. And it would be another fact *simpliciter* that Protagoras' belief in D is true because made true by a fact *simpliciter*. On this view, 'true' means something different when applied by Protagoras to his own opinion D and when applied to all other opinions. No doubt this position could be shown to be conceptually incoherent on some level. But it clearly does not entail any straightforward logical inconsistency. On this view, when Protagoras claims that while he himself truly holds D, other men truly deny it, he merely claims that whereas the fact corresponding to D is a fact *simpliciter*, there also exist, relatively to other men, certain relative facts corresponding to their denials of D. And this claim is not self-contradictory.

Since, then, Protagoras' position is logically consistent, Plato's argument in 171 a6—c7 is fallacious if interpreted as a demonstration of inconsistency. This fallaciousness is not by itself a sufficient reason for rejecting the interpretation. But there are other grounds for doing so which will become apparent if we consider more closely the context and implications of the position itself. I shall argue

---

[7] See 170 e6—171 a3, where Socrates produces the conclusion that what Protagoras declares is so, is so only for himself. It seems to come as unwelcome surprise to Protagoras' pupil.

that even if it *were* logically inconsistent, and seen to be so by Plato, it is highly implausible that he would have attempted to refute it by proving the inconsistency.

Let me begin by asking what, after all, is wrong with an inconsistent position. Why is it to be avoided, and why, if a man proves his opponent's position to be of this character, should he be said to have refuted him? In showing it up as inconsistent, he shows it up as untenable, but what is the basis of the untenability? This cannot be explained simply by pointing to the syntactical fact that the position contains elements one of which is the negation of another. We have to look further for an explanation, to the concepts of meaninglessness and falsity. On the one hand, the fault of an inconsistent position may be said to lie in its failure to express any determinate meaning, taken as a whole. On the other hand, the position may be condemned as necessarily false or unsatisfiable. Apart from these two defects, there would appear to be nothing wrong with inconsistency. Thus a man who seeks to refute another by proving him inconsistent may be supposed to be operating under the assumption that inconsistency renders the position meaningless or under the assumption that it renders it unsatisfiable. We have now to consider whether in 171 a6—c7 Plato is likely to be operating under either of these assumptions.

There is no positive evidence that Plato would have assumed that by proving Protagoras' position inconsistent he would thereby prove it meaningless. At no point does he explicitly accuse the latter of saying nothing, or nothing meaningful. It might be thought that explicit accusation would hardly be necessary once inconsistency had been shown: that Plato would take it for granted that the implication was obvious. But this is implausible for several reasons. If the point is so obvious, why should Aristotle have given it so much care and attention in *Metaphysics* Γ and K ?[8] After all, the connection between inconsistency and meaninglessness is not entirely clear even to ourselves, equipped with all the apparatus of modern logical and semantic theory. One need only allude to such problems as how, if an inconsistent statement lacks determinate meaning (which lack would seem to put it beyond the bounds of logical treatment), it can be made the subject of *reductio ad absurdum* proof. But whether or not we view such difficulties as constituting serious obstacles in the way of any inference from inconsistency to meaning-

---

[8] 1006 a11—25; 28—1007 a8; 1062 a11—19.

lessness, it is certain that no philosopher would make such an inference or expect his audience to make it, unless he possessed in some form or other the conception of determinate meaning. But there is little reason to think that when Plato wrote the *Theaetetus* he had arrived at such a notion. Up until *Sophist* he hardly distinguishes problems of meaning from problems of truth and knowledge. In the *Cratylus*, which most writers group chronologically with the *Theaetetus*, names are considered simply as true or false. In the *Theaetetus* itself, Plato shows no interest in the concept of meaningfulness as such. For instance, the paradox of false belief figures primarily as a paradox in epistemology: (How is error possible?), rather than in the theory of meaning (How can a false belief have meaningful content?). In one passage[9] the latter question seems to rise to the surface, but Plato does not pursue it. And even in the *Sophist* Plato does not consider the problem of meaningfulness except in relation to the simplest λόγος or unit of discourse, which is shown to require a certain internal structure if it is to be a λόγος at all[10]. There is no discussion of complex λόγοι, and no hint therefore that meaningfulness in their case might depend on the preservation of certain relations (e. g. that of mutual consistency) between the simpler λόγοι of which they are composed.

Let us now consider whether in *Theaetetus* 171 a6—c7 Plato is arguing on the assumption that by proving Protagoras' position inconsistent, he will prove it untenable because necessarily false or unsatisfiable. Now if he aims to show that it is necessarily false, he flagrantly begs the question against Protagoras. For the issue is, precisely, whether opinions can be false. To argue on the assumption that a position of a certain nature (viz. an inconsistent position) is necessarily false, is already to have assumed that such a position even can be false, which is exactly what Protagoras denies concerning *all* positions that are actually held as opinions. And there can be no doubt that the Protagorean position under attack is being held as an opinion by Protagoras.

Perhaps, however, we should take Plato to be aiming to show this position to be inconsistent in order to prove it necessarily unsatisfied in some sense of 'unsatisfied' that does not mean simply 'false'. In that case he would not be begging the question. But what further sense of 'unsatisfied' would be relevant here? Not that in which a command or an intention may be said to be unsatis-

---

[9] 189 a6—14.
[10] *Sophist* 261 d1—262 e1.

fied, since Plato is concerned not with Protagoras' commands and intentions, but with his opinions. The logical concepts of 'satisfaction' and its contradictory are used to delineate something analogous to truth-value for commands etc., which cannot possess truth-value proper. An opinion therefore cannot be in this sense unsatisfied since it does have truth-value — even if Protagoras is right, and there is only one effective truth-value, i. e. True. One might equally say that in the case of opinions, satisfaction and its opposite *are* truth and falsity. Thus Protagoras' doctrine could be re-expressed as: All beliefs are satisfied (because true). Any attempt then on Plato's part to show that this doctrine is unsatisfied would as much beg the question as would an attempt to prove it false.

It is true, of course, that for Protagoras, opinions have a dimension of value other than truth-value; for they may also be good and bad[11]. The meaning of 'good' and 'bad' in this context seems to fluctuate between 'pleasant', 'healthy' and 'expedient', and their contraries, but the question of Protagoras' precise meaning need not concern us here. We are concerned with reasons why Plato might have thought it worthwhile to prove Protagoras inconsistent. We have seen that neither the concept of meaninglessness nor that of falsity provides an adequate answer to this question. However, might it not be that Plato assumes that to prove a position inconsistent is to prove it 'bad' in some sense of 'bad' that Protagoras himself would recognise? But if this is what Plato is doing, why does he not make it clear? If this is his assumption, and if 171 a6—c7 is his argument for inconsistency, why does he make no display of Protagoras being forced to acknowledge the badness of his own position? This is unlikely to be one of those conclusions that Plato leaves us to infer for ourselves, if only because it cannot be taken for granted that an inconsistent position is, as such, a bad one in any sense that Protagoras would accept. We do of course normally take it for granted that inconsistency is bad, or at least that consistency is preferable, but only because we take it for granted, normally, that what is inconsistent is necessarily false, and that a possibly true position is preferable to one that cannot be true. But on this view, the badness can only be explained in terms of falsity, so that we are not here dealing with a sense of 'bad' that Protagoras would acknowledge or that Plato can assume him to acknowledge without begging the question in the way already discussed.

---

[11] See e. g. 166 d5—167 c7.

It would be useless, then, to show that Protagoras holds an inconsistent set of beliefs. By his lights, whatever is believed is true. It follows that even what is inconsistently believed is true, even when the inconsistency occurs in beliefs held by the same subject, e. g. Protagoras himself[12]. Only those who accept the intellectual obligation to avoid inconsistency have any reason to give up a set of inconsistent beliefs. But this obligation rests upon the obligation to avoid, so far as possible, meaninglessness and falsity. But this latter obligation is real only for those who allow that beliefs *can* be otherwise than true. But if there is never any chance of this being so, then by abiding by the laws of logic we do not reduce our chances of falling into false or incoherent beliefs, and respect for those laws is no more than an idle fetish. No more, that is, unless it can be shown that inconsistency is to be avoided on grounds independent of falsity or meaninglessness: on account of being unaesthetic, say, or unpleasant or impractical, etc. Even if this could be shown, the point would need to have been established *before* any attempt is made to refute a Protagorean on grounds of inconsistency.

We cannot leave this matter without touching on the question whether it is even possible for a man to hold inconsistent beliefs knowing them to be so. For it might be suggested that Plato assumes it to be in some sense impossible. In that way, if he can prove that Protagoras' beliefs are inconsistent, he will get the latter to give up the claim to have those beliefs. For Plato will have shown that the Protagorean position is one that no one is *able* to hold, and that Protagoras only *seemed* to himself to be holding it. Protagoras, of course, has a ready reply: if he seemed to himself (believed himself) to hold it, then he did hold it. Moreover, even assuming that it is in some sense impossible knowingly to hold inconsistent beliefs, it may be argued that the impossibility rests on the subject's prior belief that inconsistent beliefs cannot both be true. In that case, the subject's inability to believe what he knows is inconsistent is due to the fact that no one can believe what he believes cannot be true. Even Protagoras cannot do that. But then the impossibility of holding inconsistent beliefs is an impossibility only for most men, not for Protagoras, since it depends on the prior assumption that

---

[12] For a discussion of Protagoras' position as involving a denial of the law of contradiction, see Kerferd, 'Plato's Account of Protagoras' Relativism', *Durham University Journal* v. xlii, N. S. v. xi, 1949—50.

inconsistent beliefs cannot both be true. This assumption we have
no reason to expect Protagoras to share.

I do not mean to imply by these arguments that Protagoras'
position would in fact be a tenable one if it were inconsistent, or
even that it could properly be called a position at all. My purpose
is to show that a simple proof of inconsistency is by itself ineffective
against him. We know from Aristotle[13] that there were philosophers,
'the followers of Protagoras' among them, who denied or at any
rate sincerely claimed to deny the law of non-contradiction. I suggest that the views which Plato ascribes to Protagoras in the *Theaetetus* entail the same denial, and that Plato could hardly have been
unaware of the entailment. In fact there are two indications in the
dialogue that Plato saw that Protagoras would not stop short of
maintaining contradictory beliefs. Firstly, in 166b4—5 Protagoras
is made to say: 'ἢ αὖ [δοκεῖς τινὰ] ἀποκνήσειν ὁμολογεῖν οἷον
τ'εἶναι εἰδέναι καὶ μὴ εἰδέναι τὸν αὐτὸν τὸ αὐτό;' It is true that
in the next sentence Protagoras mentions a manoeuvre whereby
someone who did fear to say ('ἐάνπερ . . . δείσῃ') that the same
man both knows and does not know the same thing could avoid
saying it. We shall consider this manoeuvre in a moment. But there
is no suggestion that for Protagoras, the saying of it is to be avoided
at all costs. Secondly, in 167a7—8 Plato alludes to the traditional
crux of false belief as if it were one source of the doctrine he attributes to Protagoras. False belief is thinking what is not, and thinking what is not is impossible. It follows that all beliefs are true,
even mutually inconsistent ones. It is arguable that some thinkers
accepted this paradox as less intolerable than the alternative, viz.
the admission on a theoretical level that false belief is possible. If,
as seems likely, Plato saw Protagoras in this light, he would not
have attempted to refute any Protagorean doctrine by merely proving its inconsistency.

But there is another reason why such a refutation would be ineffective against the Theaetetan Protagoras. This reason cannot
have escaped Plato, since it is Plato himself who provides his Protagoras with the means to avoid ever being caught in self-contradiction. For Protagoras, a contradiction can occur only when it is
the same subject that holds both contradictory beliefs. But the
Theatetan Protagoras is a Heraclitean. He professes to hold that
a subject is never the same from one instant to another[14]. He can

[13] *Met.* 1005 b35—1006 a3; 1009 a6—1010 a15; 1062 b13—24.
[14] 166 b5—c1.

argue, therefore, that even if it seems that he, Protagoras, is guilty of inconsistency, the expression 'he, Protagoras' denotes a fiction. Really, there is only a succession of momentary subjects each with a belief of its own. We ought to regard each side of what appears to be a contradiction as a separate belief belonging to a different subject. Before one has finished thinking 'p and q' (where 'q' entails 'not-p'), the "one" has been replaced. But if each belief belongs to a different subject, each is made true by a separate relative reality, and therefore no belief genuinely contradicts another.

This Heraclitean reply leads eventually to the abandonment of the concept of belief altogether. A belief that is continually splintering into ever more momentary beliefs held by subjects of vanishing duration cannot properly be said to be anything at all, let alone a belief. But we are concerned here not with the general viability of the Heraclitean move, but with Protagoras' relation to Heracliteanism. That relation may for present purposes be summed up by saying that until Heracliteanism has been refuted, no charge of inconsistency can be made to stick. Thus we should expect an argument proving Protagoras' inconsistency to follow, not precede, an attack on Heracliteanism. Plato does in the end undertake this attack, but only after he is well clear of the argument of 171a6—c7.

I have argued that only if Plato possessed a conception of meaninglessness which there is no reason to suppose him to have possessed, or if he missed obvious implications of his own account of Protagoras' philosophy, would he imagine a proof of inconsistency to be effective against Protagoras. If we assume that he would not have propounded an argument which from his point of view would be useless, it follows that 171a6—c7 is not a proof of inconsistency. Normally we take such an assumption for granted in interpreting any philosopher, but in this case it may seem that there is cause for hesitation. Some commentators have supposed that Plato himself shows signs of not being entirely content with the argument. For almost immediately after completing, it, Socrates says: 'καὶ εἰ αὐτίκα ἐντεῦθεν ἀνακύψειε [ὁ Πρωταγόρας] . . . πολλὰ ἂν ἐμέ τε ἐλέγξας ληροῦντα, ὡς τὸ εἰκός . . . καταδὺς ἂν οἴχοιτο ἀποτρέχων' (171d 1—3). Perhaps, then, the argument *is* put forward as a proof of inconsistency even though Plato had good reason to think that it could not, as such, succeed? In that case, there would be no need to look for a different interpretation, such, for instance, as I propose in the following section.

But why in that case should Plato have included the argument at all? It is not as if he had no ammunition still in reserve against Protagoras (see 177d2—179b5). If the realisation of the argument's inadequacy struck him only as an afterthought, why did not the same afterthought lead him to cancel Theodorus' later remark: '[ἁλίσκεται ὁ λόγος] καὶ ταύτῃ, ᾗ τὰς τῶν ἄλλων δόξας κυρίας ποιεῖ, αὗται δὲ ἐφάνησαν τοὺς ἐκείνου λόγους οὐδαμῇ ἀληθεῖς ἡγούμεναι (179b7—9)? And in any case, some of the reasons why an inconsistency proof must fail are so intimately bound up with Protagoras' position as already presented that their striking Plato only as an afterthought is about as unlikely as their failing to strike him at all.

These unlikelihoods apart, 171d1—3 does not in fact express dissatisfaction, as is clear from the following sentence, 'ἀλλ' ἡμῖν ἀνάγκη οἶμαι χρῆσθαι ἡμῖν αὐτοῖς ὁποῖοί τινές ἐσμεν, καὶ τὰ δοκοῦντα ἀεὶ ταῦτα λέγειν'. Socrates is not retracting the conclusion reached in 171c7. Why then does he say that 'likely enough (ὡς τὸ εἰκός)' Protagoras, if he could appear, would show him up as talking a lot of nonsense? No doubt this is not merely a logically pointless sarcasm. It does not follow, however, that it must be meant as a sincere expression of doubt. The logical point of the remark is to *reinforce* the conclusion already reached, by means of an ironic illustration. 171d1—3 is to be taken closely with the preceding sentence 'εἰκός γε ἄρα ἐκεῖνον πρεσβύτερον ὄντα σοφώτερον ἡμῶν εἶναι' (171c10—d1). 'Probably Protagoras is wiser than we are . . . Indeed (καί), if he were to stick his head out of the ground, he would likely enough show me up as talking a lot of nonsense . . . before running away'. But 171c10 —d1 is not set *in opposition* to what immediately precedes it, viz. "Ἀλλά τοι . . . ἄδηλον εἰ καὶ παραθέομεν τὸ ὀρθόν' (171c9—10), an expression of Socrates' refusal to soften the conclusion of 171a6—c7 despite Theodorus' protests. For the connective relating 171c10—d1 to what precedes is 'ἄρα', an informal expression of inference or, more generally, of the focussing on a new or interesting factor in a situation already presented (see Denniston, *The Greek Particles*, pp, 32—43)[15]. Accordingly, the line of thought in 171c9—d3 as a whole, is as follows:

---

[15] Cornford (*Plato's Theory of Knowledge*, p. 79) and McDowell (op. cit., p. 47) translate the 'ἄρα' by 'Of course', which has a mildly concessive (hence opposing) force, being equivalent to 'Not that we are forgetting that p' where 'p' is a consideration that might be expected to bring the speaker up short. But Denniston reports on no such concessive use of 'ἄρα'.

'We cannot get away from the conclusion that Protagoras' position (in some sense) refutes itself. So (ἄρα) (since in that case some men may be wiser than others in the ordinary sense of 'Wiser', not the Protagorean) probably Protagoras is wiser than we are. Why, if he could appear, he would probably show us to be talking nonsense (i. e. expressing *opinions that fail to be true*)'.

In short, Socrates suggests that Protagoras might rebut his argument not because he himself suspects any actual fault in it, but because even a rebuttal (which he ironically supposes Protagoras quite capable of) would drive home the conclusion that it is absurd to hold that all men are equally wise (in the ordinary sense).

There is therefore no reason to think that Plato himself doubts the effectiveness of the argument in 171 a6—c7. And 179 b7—9 proves his confidence in it. The confidence may or may not be justified. But at least it shows that if there is any weakness in 171 a6—c7, it is a weakness of which Plato is unaware. This, I have argued, could hardly be the case if 171 a6—c7 were what it is so often claimed to be, an attempt to prove inconsistency.

II

It is now time to examine the argument itself in more detail. Plato exhibits Protagoras as forced by his own doctrine into *agreeing* (the verbs repeatedly used are 'ὁμολογεῖν' and 'συγχωρεῖν') to his opponents' assertion that the doctrine is false and that not every sentient being 'is a measure'. Judged by standard logical principles, Protagoras would certainly appear to be contradicting himself by so agreeing. It is, however, to be noted that Plato does not show Protagoras actually *asserting* that his doctrine is false, or as *asserting* its contradictory. He presents him as simply agreeing to the *opponents'* assertions. But how can this make any difference to the logic of Protagoras' position? For we ordinarily suppose that if A agrees with an opinion of B's, then A too holds an opinion of identical content. And if this opinion is inconsistent with another which A already holds, then A, by agreeing, has contradicted himself. So it would seem that Plato in 171 a6—c7 is, after all, arguing that Protagoras' position is inconsistent, even though the argument is both illegitimate and pointless for the reasons we have discussed.

But we must consider more carefully whether A's agreement with B's assertion necessarily implies that A holds, and would himself be prepared to assert, an opinion of the same content as that asserted by B. For only if this is the case would it follow from Protagoras' agreement with his opponents that he too shares their view and so contradicts his own thesis. Consider the conditions under which A may properly be said to agree with B on B's opinion O. A may be described as so agreeing if, given that B holds O, A holds, and would be prepared to assert, an opinion of identical content to O. But it would also be proper to describe A as agreeing if, given that B holds O, A holds (and would be prepared to assert) the higher order opinion that O is true. Ordinary logic dictates that we should take these two modes of agreement as equivalent, on the ground that we cannot hold an opinion without holding that it and any other opinion of identical content are true; and that we cannot hold an opinion to be true without either holding it or some opinion of identical content. Thus I cannot opine that p without also opining that my own and all other opinions that p, are true; and I cannot opine A's opinion that p to be true unless either (if I myself am A)I hold that very opinion, or (if I am not A) I myself hold an identical opinion that p.

But Plato has made it clear that Protagoras' relativism releases him from the second of these two entailments. Protagoras holds that all beliefs are true, but he does not himself subscribe to all beliefs. That is to say, it is not the case that for every opinion held by anyone else, Protagoras holds an opinion of identical content. His admission that another's belief is true, is the admission that there is, relatively to that other, a reality that makes the latter's belief a true one. But if he himself were to hold an identical belief of his own, there would have to be a further relative reality, relative this time to Protagoras himself, and making true *Protagoras'* belief. And the essence of his relativism is this: that the existence of one believer's relative reality does not entail the existence of a similar or qualitatively identical relative reality for any other believer. Thus when Protagoras agrees with his opponents' opposing view, by holding, as he must, that it is true, it does not follow that he shares in that view. But unless he shares in it, he does not contradict himself, for he does not *hold* any view that conflicts with his doctrine.

So long, then, as Protagoras is presented as simply agreeing with his opponents, he is not shown contradicting himself. See, for example, 171 b1—2 and 171 c1—2. But there is one passage, 171 c5—7, in which Plato seems to suggest that Protagoras actually shares the opponents' view. This is the concluding sentence of the argument, in which Socrates says: '. . . ἐπειδὴ ἀμφισβητεῖται ὑπὸ πάντων, οὐδενὶ ἂν εἴη ἡ Πρωταγόρου 'Αλήθεια ἀληθής, οὔτε τινί ἄλλῳ οὔτ' αὐτῷ ἐκείνῳ'. The datives here are most naturally taken as datives of 'person judging'[16]. If they are so taken, then Socrates would appear to be saying that in the judgment of Protagoras as well as in that of his opponents, the doctrine of the 'Truth' is not true. But I would suggest that the dative in Protagoras' case is not intended to indicate that the latter literally makes the judgement in question. The fact that someone agrees with an opinion would normally be taken as ground for ascribing the opinion *to him*, as his. But the normal rules do not apply in Protagoras' case, and I would suggest that here Plato grounds his use of the dative 'αὐτῷ ἐκείνῳ' simply on the fact that Protagoras agrees, even though agreement here does not imply a sharing of the judgment. It is also possible to view the standard dative of 'person judging' as indicating something like possession or ownership. If we bear in mind that ownership is a public concept in the sense that a man can be said to own something only so far as he is a member of a community in which his ownership is publicly acknowledged, then the 'αὐτῷ ἐκείνῳ' applied to Protagoras does not really mean that Protagoras' inner belief-state is of identical content with that of his opponents, since the dative is not being used to ascribe an inner state at all. Instead, it means that his opponents' position is one which he too would be publicly taken to represent. For this is just what would, by normal public standards, be said of him, given that he answers 'True' to his opponents' every assertion.

The above interpretation of Protagoras' agreement in 171 a7—c6 has, I believe, been commonly overlooked through a misunderstanding of the exact nature of Protagoras' relativism. Many commentators have regarded this as a relativism of *truth*: 'Each man's opinions are *true for him*'[17]. On this view it becomes impossible to see how Plato can legitimately say that Protagoras *agrees* with his opponents. For someone who says simply that their opinion is true *for them* cannot be described as *agreeing* with them. Thus in saying that Protagoras agrees, Plato, on this view, would appear to be quietly ignoring that very relativism of Protagoras' which earlier in the dialogue he has been at such pains to expound. But then if Protagoras no longer

---

[16] See e. g. Matthiae, *Greek Grammar*, vol. ii, para. 389.

[17] E. g. Grote, l. c., Burnet, *Early Greek Philosophy* Part I, p. 244, Cornford, *Plato's Theory of Knowledge*, p. 80, Sayre and McDowell, ll. cc, Vlastos, *Plato's Protagoras* p. XIV, Tigner, *Mnemosyne* S. IV, vol. XXIV, 1971 p. 366 ff.

figures as relativist, he no longer figures as someone who can hold that all beliefs are true without contradicting himself. Thus Plato, it seems, is simply displaying this self-contradiction in 171 a6—c7, having enabled himself to do so by means of a cheap *ignoratio elenchi*.

But Protagoras' relativism as Plato presents it is a relativism not of truth but of fact. What is relative to the believer is the reality that makes the belief true. Protagoras' dictum is '[Each] man is the measure', not '[Each] man is the measure-for-himself'. It is *what* is measured that exists only for, or relatively to, the man that is its measure. For statements of this factual relativism, see e. g. 157 b1, 158 a7, 160 b8—c2, 162 d1, 166 d4 and d7—e4, 167 c5. The view has its basis in a theory of perception according to which there is no ontological distinction between an appearance and the quality of which it is an appearance. This doctrine is then tacitly extended to include under 'appearance' opinion as well as sense perception. As a result, the facts, situations, etc. which are the objects of opinion, are made to stand in the same relation to opinion-'appearances' as do sense qualities to sense-appearances on the original theory. In both cases, what the appearance is of, is nothing beyond the appearance. Since the appearance exists only relatively to the subject, the same applies to what the appearance is of. The question of truth can only arise once a conceptual distinction is made (not that Protagoras considers how, if his theory is true, we could ever have come to make it) between what are really only aspects of the same thing, the appearance and its object. All appearances are true precisely because the object cannot fail to exist when the appearance exists. But while both appearance and object depend for their existence on the subject, it is not the case that the relation "between" them (namely their ultimate identity, which ensures that the appearance can never not be *of* the object) is itself something *further* that also depends for its existence on the subject. The being true of the appearance simply follows from the appearance's existing at all. Thus Protagoras can, and does, say that a belief is true (*simpliciter*), not true-for-a-subject. This unqualified use of 'True' cannot be taken to imply that there is independent truth in the sense that an appearance could fail to be true; or that there is a single body of truth to which different subjects could have access, for each subject has his own set of appearances and objects making them true. But the unqualified use is justified in that Protagoras is saying that if an appearance exists, its relation to the object *is* one of necessary accompaniment or correspondence (based on their identity).

Protagoras must eventually admit that this doctrine of his concerning appearances and truth is itself only an appearance to him, Protagoras, and hence is made true by a fact that exists only relatively to himself (170 e7—171 a1). But although the reality of what the doctrine asserts exists only relatively to its proponent, *what* the doctrine asserts is a relativism of fact and not in any extra sense a relativism of truth. Thus while admitting that the reality that makes his own theory true exists only relatively to himself, Protagoras can quite properly on his own terms maintain that since that relative reality exists (so that his appearance *has* an object), the theory is true (*simpliciter*).

I would argue then that the sentence 'S's belief B is true for S' has no distinct function to perform in an exposition of Protagoras' system. The sentence can mean (1) no more than 'S has the belief B', a meaning which is of no philosophical interest. Or it can mean (2) 'What makes S's belief B true is a fact existing only in relation to S'. This is of interest, but it is a statement of *factual* relativism. Or it can mean (3) 'S has a belief (B') that his belief B is true'. In this case, Protagoras' view entails that there exists relatively to S a fact making true his higher order belief B'. This is the fact that the lower order B is true. But what is relative to S is not the truth of B considered as a *relation* between the appearance B and the fact (relative to S) to which B corresponds. Nor is the truth-relation between B' and the relative fact to which *it* corresponds something relative. What is relative is the being-true-of-B considered as a *fact* corresponding to the higher order B' and making it true *simpliciter*[18].

---

[18] Commentators who use 'True for S' in expounding Protagoras' view are, I suggest, drawn to this locution because they assume that propositions are bearers of truth-value. In terms of propositions, Protagoras' view that if A holds that p and B that not-p, both A and B are right, seems to amount to the view that one and the same thing (the proposition that p) both has and has not a certain property (truth). But Protagoras certainly does not mean to say anything as blatantly self-contradictory as this. (Even if inconsistency cannot destroy his position, as I have argued, a contradiction that is glaringly obvious from the outset can hardly *recommend* it). It therefore seems as if he must really mean to be saying that the proposition is true-for-A and not true-for-B. Thus Plato's use of 'True' (unqualified) in his account of Protagoras' view seems no more than a careless abbreviation. But the concept of the proposition is alien to Protagoras, and to Plato (in the *Theaetetus* at least). It is beliefs or opinions that have truth-value (cf. Hintikka, *Time and Necessity* ch. iv). And beliefs are differentiated not merely by content but by subject and occasion of being held. Thus if A holds that p and B

There is no space here to pursue the problem that arises in this connection. For does not Protagoras contradict himself if he holds that the *fact* (which makes true B') of the truth of B is only a relative fact, while the *relation* in which B's being true consists is not in the same way relative? But whatever difficulties may be found in Protagoras' theory, the point which concerns us here is that the theory as it appears in the *Theaetetus* is a factual relativism, in which the use of 'True' *simpliciter* has a proper place. This should be clear from Plato's own language, as well as from the demands of the theory itself. Plato states the doctrine sometimes in terms of beliefs, sometimes of perceptions, and in both cases he almost always uses 'True' (or some equivalent word) *simpliciter* and without a relativising dative. For beliefs, see e. g. 161 d7, 161 e8, 167 b1, 170 c3, 171 a8, 171 b2, 171 b11, 172 b5 and 160 d1 (where the subject is said to be 'ἀψευδής' *simpliciter* (not 'ἑαυτῷ')). For perceptions, see 152 c5, 160 c7, 167 c2. It is to be noted that when Plato speaks of relative *fact*, he is extremely careful to add the dative. The only passages I have found where he omits it are 152 c5 and 171 a9. Since he is not therefore in the habit of dropping a relativising dative when he means it to be understood, we should hesitate to assume that when he uses 'True' unqualified, he nevertheless intends us to supply an implicit dative.

Sometimes, however, 'ἀληθής' does occur with a dative, but in almost all these cases there is no need to take it as expressing a special concept of relative truth. For instance, in 161 d3 'ἑκάστῳ' need mean no more than 'in the case of each man'. In 170 d5 and 171 c6—7 the datives can naturally be taken as of 'person judging': i. e. 'For you it is true that . . .' is equivalent to 'You hold it to be true that . . .'. (See above for a discussion of the second of these passages). In 170 e7—171 a1 ('ἆρ' οὐχὶ ἀνάγκη, εἰ μὲν μηδὲ αὐτὸς ᾤετο μέτρον εἶναι ἄνθρωπον, μηδὲ οἱ πολλοί . . . μηδενὶ δὴ εἶναι ταύτην τὴν ἀλήθειαν ἣν ἐκεῖνος ἔγραψεν'), we should expect 'μηδενὶ δὴ εἶναι ἀληθῆ ταύτην τὴν ἀλήθειαν . . .' if relative *truth* were in question. The second 'εἶναι' is existential, and 'ταύτην τὴν ἀλήθειαν' refers to Protagoras' book. Clearly Plato is not making the trivial point that if Protagoras had not held his theory, that literary work would not exist. He is saying 'What Protagoras in his book asserted

---

that not-p, there are two beliefs, not one proposition affirmed and denied by one and the other subject. Protagoras' factual relativism ensures that both beliefs are true, and there is no need of a further relativising of 'True' in order to avoid contradiction.

to be the case would be the case (or: would be a fact or reality) for no one.' Thus the point here concerns relativity of fact. The one passage in which there seems to be a genuine use of the notion of relative truth is 170e4—5 ('βούλει λέγωμεν ὡς σὺ τότε σαυτῷ μὲν ἀληθῆ δοξά-ζεις, τοῖς δὲ μυρίοις ψευδῆ'). Yet even this can be disputed. Socrates is considering the case in which Theodorus (here representing Protagoras) holds an opinion which others believe to be false. Since they believe it to be false, it follows on Protagoras' view that it is for them a fact that it is false. But what of the statement that Theodorus' opinion is true for Theodorus? It is not impossible that the 'σαυτῷ' has no logical function here but has crept in for stylistic reasons to balance 'τοῖς μυρίοις'. In that case, if Plato had been writing regardless of style he would have said simply 'σὺ μὲν τότε ἀληθῆ δοξάζεις, τοῖς δὲ μυρίοις [δοξάζεις] ψευδῆ'; On the other hand, Socrates may be addressing Theodorus not merely as one who has an opinion rejected by the multitude, but as having in addition the higher order opinion that his original opinion is true. In that case, it is a *fact* relative to Theodorus (making true *simpliciter* the higher order opinion) that his lower order one is true.

I have argued that Protagoras' relativism is such as to allow him to say of all opinions that they are true *simpliciter*; and that the text supports this interpretation. But, as we have seen, this use of 'True' does not imply that when X holds that Y's opinion O is true, X himself holds an opinion identical to O. X can therefore be described as agreeing with Y (or Protagoras as agreeing with his opponents) in that he holds the latter's opinion to be true, without its being implied that X also shares the opinion himself. Thus even if Y's opinion is the contradictory of an opinion already held by X, X can be said to agree without its being implied that he contradicts himself. Seen in this light, the argument of 171 a6—c7 is not a demonstration of Protagoras' inconsistency, especially since, as I previously argued, even if such a demonstration were valid it would be powerless against Protagoras.

What then is Plato seeking to show in this argument? Not that Protagoras' position ought for reasons of logic to be rejected by those who accept it; but that those who reject it can have no reason even to consider accepting it. Protagoras rejects nothing that they assert in opposition. He cannot even reject any doubt in his own thoughts, should any arise, nor consider whether the doubt might be ill-founded, since that would imply that an appearance might be false. Nor can he hold that his external opponents even might be wrong. Thus an opponent confronting Protagoras' position confronts, so to speak, a dialectical nothing, offering no resistance[19]. For there is nothing that can lead him to alter, defend, reconsider or even re-affirm his own opinions, since all he encounters is the instantaneous concession of their truth.

---

[19] At the smallest pressure, Protagoras' thesis ʻοἴχεται ἀποτρέχων' (cf. 171 d3).

Plato on Sense-Perception and Knowledge
(*Theaetetus* 184-186)

JOHN M. COOPER

I

Plato's argument in the *Theaetetus* (184 b - 186 e) against the proposal that knowledge be defined as αἴσθησις[1] has, I think, not yet been fully understood or rightly appreciated. Existing interpretations fall into two groups. On the one hand, F. M. Cornford[2] and others think that Plato rejects the proposal on the ground that the objects which we perceive are not the sort of objects of which one could have knowledge: only the unchanging Forms can be known. On the other hand, there are those[3] who think Plato's argument has nothing to do with Forms but instead turns on a distinction between sensation and judgment which has the consequence that the thinking we do *about* the deliverances of the senses, and not the mere *use* of the senses, is the source of our knowledge. The interpretation which I advance in this paper belongs to the second of these two broad classes, but differs from others in providing a more careful account of the distinctions which Plato seems to be making in this passage. Much of the interest of the argument lies, I think, in the analysis of the process of perception which Plato produces by distinguishing carefully the contribution of the senses from that of the mind; but this analysis has not been given the attention it deserves.

The complexities of the argument can be usefully indicated by a brief examination of Cornford's interpretation. According to Cornford Plato's argument proceeds in two stages. In the first (184 b - 186 a 1) Plato concludes that there is knowledge which is not a matter of per-

---

[1] An expression that might be translated by either "perception" or "sensation." I shall mostly say "perception", but the other sense should constantly be borne in mind; the ambiguity becomes important below, pp. 130ff.

[2] In his *Plato's Theory of Knowledge*, pp. 102-109. Subsequent references to Cornford's views are to this book.

[3] Cf. G. Ryle, "Plato's *Parmenides*", *Mind* 48 (1939) p. 317, reprinted in *Studies in Plato's Metaphysics*, ed. R. E. Allen – hereafter abbreviated *SPM*– p.136; I. M. Crombie, *An Examination of Plato's Doctrines*, II, p. 14.

123

ception, i.e., that "percepts cannot be the only objects of knowledge" (p. 106). In the second (186 a 1 - e 12), it is further concluded that the additional objects of knowledge referred to in the first stage are in fact the *only* objects of true or real knowledge.

In the first stage Plato appeals to the distinction between, on the one hand, the use of the faculty of sensing as such, i.e., the mere presentation of an object in sensation, and, on the other hand, the making of judgments. The point of this appeal is not, however, to suggest that since only judgments are true, judging does, but mere sensing does not, exhibit a sufficient order of logical complexity to count as knowing. Rather, this distinction is introduced in order to bring out the fact that there are other objects besides sense-objects with which we are "acquainted" (p. 106). In judgments we use such words as "is" and "similar", and the thought that something we are sensing exists or is similar to something else is not an achievement of mere sensing; we must bring in, and apply, the notions of existence and similarity, as well as use our senses. From this it is inferred that even if the presentation of an object of sense in sensation is an instance of knowledge, our power of making judgments shows that there is another way of being presented with objects, namely the intuition of Forms, here instanced by Existence, Similarity and the other so-called κοινά. We could not apply the notion of existence to anything if we were not acquainted with Existence; and the knowledge of these (and other) Forms is not acquired by using the senses but by thinking – by an activity of the soul "all by herself" (185 e 1), without reliance on sensation.

The argument of Cornford's second stage (186 a 2 - e 10) is apparently meant to run as follows. Existence (οὐσία) is one of the κοινά mentioned in stage one. Hence both our acquaintance with the Form Existence and our ability to formulate judgments with the help of this notion are functions of the mind independent of sensation. But it is only in attaining to existence that truth is reached; so that knowledge too first occurs at the level of the mind's independent activity, and there is no knowledge in the use of the senses at all. Cornford admits that given the context the most natural way of understanding this last point would be that sensing does not involve the use of "is" and therefore does not amount to judging or asserting anything, so that since knowledge is necessarily knowledge of truths, sensing is in no case knowing. On this view Plato denies that to use the senses is to know anything by arguing that knowledge is the achievement of the

124

mind's capacity to formulate judgments, which is an activity which goes beyond sensing itself. But Cornford thinks that the real point being made here relies on the other "independent activity" of the mind referred to above – that by which it becomes *acquainted* with Forms. The Forms, taken as a group, constitute in Plato's metaphysics the realm of οὐσία and he elsewhere associates knowledge with these objects; so here too he must be making the point that since no object of the senses is a Form nothing the senses give us belongs to the realm of οὐσία. It follows that no activity of the senses, or of the mind through the medium of the senses, can amount to knowledge.

There are obvious difficulties with this interpretation. For example, οὐσία is interpreted in the first stage as naming just one Form among others, but in the second, without any textual warrant for the change,[4] it becomes the collective name of all the Forms or of the metaphysical status of the Forms as a group. Again, although Cornford finds in the passage a distinction between judging and sensing, he represses this distinction at every turn in favor of the distinction between objects we are acquainted with in sensation and objects grasped by intuitive thought: with good reason, since as Cornford admits, the former distinction points towards the activity of judging as the area where knowledge is to be found, while the Forms-sensibles dichotomy leads to the quite different, indeed incompatible, suggestion that knowledge is not a matter of judging truly, but of intuitive awareness of a certain kind of object. Cornford's attempt to combine his distinction between sensation and judgment with a reaffirmation of the doctrine that only

---

[4] No doubt Cornford thinks there is *some* warrant in the fact, as he thinks, that throughout this part of the dialogue Plato assumes that sense objects are in Heraclitean flux: Plato would seem, given this assumption, to invite the interpretation of οὐσία at 186 d 3 and e 5 as indicating the realm of Being as opposed to that of Becoming. But nothing of the kind is being assumed here about the objects of the senses: Heracliteanism is defined at 156 a ff. (cf: 157 b 1, τὸ δ'εἶναι πανταχόθεν ἐξαιρετέον) as involving the refusal to say of anything that it *exists*, but at 185 a precisely this *is* said by Socrates (and accepted by Theaetetus) about the objects of the senses. Cf. G. E. L. Owen, "The Place of the *Timaeus* in Plato's Dialogues", *Class. Quart.* N. S. III (1953), p. 86 (= *SPM* p. 324). Cherniss' attempted rebuttal of this point in "The Relation of the *Timaeus* to Plato's Later Dialogues", *American Journal of Philology* 78 (1957) p. 244 n. 71 (= *SPM* p. 357 n. 1), shows that he has understood neither Owen nor Plato: in saying that Plato "goes on to ascribe οὐσία to objects of perception," Owen obviously meant that Plato says about objects of perception that they exist, and (as just noted) Plato certainly does say this.

125

the intuition of Forms deserves the name "knowledge" produces a confused and inadequate line of thought.

Nonetheless, Cornford's interpretation has met with approval in certain quarters just because it does yield the conclusion that perception cannot be knowledge because the objects of perception are not knowable. Thus H. F. Cherniss, so far as this general conclusion is concerned, enthusiastically adopts[5] Cornford's interpretation, as supporting his view concerning the unity of Plato's thought. Cherniss, indeed, goes well beyond Cornford when he suggests[6] that not merely the general conclusion of the passage, but even the *argument* supporting it, is borrowed from the *Republic*. In Cherniss' view *Republic* 523-525 is "parallel" to *Theaetetus* 184-186 in assigning to the senses the task of "stimulating" the mind to engage in pure thought by turning away from the sense-world toward that of the Forms. Later on I will comment briefly on the alleged parallelism of these two passages, but for the moment I want to concentrate on what Cornford's and Cherniss' interpretations have in common.

Both Cornford and Cherniss think (rightly) that the main point being argued is that knowledge is achieved by the mind operating somehow independently of the senses. But both interpreters think that the mind's independent activity, when it produces knowledge, consists in acquaintance with Forms. This latter point is however not to be found in Plato's text at all, as I shall show in the next section. The only independent activity of the mind discussed by Plato is that in which it applies the κοινά to the objects of the senses, judging that some thing seen exists, is self-identical and so on. He never alludes to our mode of awareness of Existence, Sameness, and so on, and does not locate our knowledge in any such awareness. Cornford is right to emphasize the importance here of some distinction between sensation and judgment; he goes wrong when he brings in the intuition or contemplation of Forms in explicating what Plato says about "judgment".

II

The passage begins (184 b 4 - 185 a 3) with an account of what perception (αἴσθησις) actually is and how it comes about. If Plato is to refute the claim that perception is knowledge he must first mark off

[5] *Aristotle's Criticism of Plato and the Academy*, p. 236 n. 141.
[6] *AJP*. 1957, p. 244 n. 71 (= *SPM* p. 357 n. 1).

126

the activity of perception from other supposed "cognitive" activities, so that he can then enquire whether perception, so understood, amounts to knowledge. Earlier in the dialogue (156 a ff.) the process of sense-perception was represented as something occurring between the sense-organ and the external object perceived, and no account was taken of the fact that a person's *mind,* and not merely his bodily organs, is active in perception. So Plato points out (184 d 1-5) that our sensations (αἰσθήσεις, d 2) are referred to the mind (ψυχή), and that it is not the sense organs (or the sense faculties) which perceive colors and sounds but the mind itself, operating *through* the organs, or, as he also says (e 8, 185 b 8, e 7), through the senses. The organs are parts of the *body* (184 e 5-6, 185 d 3), and the power of sight, touch and the rest are capacities of the *body* (185 e 7). It is quite incorrect to say, as Plato himself had said in the *Republic,*[7] that the senses see this or that, or say or report this or that: it is the subject himself who perceives things *with* his mind *through* the organs and powers of the body, who says or thinks this or that on the basis of his sense-experience. In perception, then, the mind is active through the medium of the senses. Furthermore, though without arguing the point, Plato seems to limit perception to what may be called elementary sense-perception, i.e., the perception of the "proper objects" of the five senses: colors, sounds, tastes, smells and a supposed analogue for touch. He does not indicate how he regards seeing or otherwise perceiving a physical object, but presumably he would wish to say that this is not perception, strictly conceived, but already involves some of those higher reflective activities of mind to be introduced in a moment.

There are problems of interpretation here (particularly concerning how Plato understands the use of the mind in perception) but they are best put off until after the next section of the argument has been outlined. Here (185 a - 186 e) Plato contrasts with the perceptual use of the mind, in which it operates through the medium of the bodily senses, a further and higher use, in which the mind works independently of the body and its senses (αὐτὴ δι' αὑτῆς, 185 e 1, 6). Socrates shows that such an independent use exists by reminding Theaetetus that in some cases we have one and the same thought about the objects of several senses. Thus we can think that a color, a sound, and a taste are each of them the same as itself and different from the others; *what* we think about each of these things, namely *that it is the same as*

[7] Cf. 523 c δηλοῖ, d 5 ἐσήμηνεν, e 4 ὁρᾷ, 524 a 3 παραγγέλλει, a 7 σημαίνει, a 8 λέγει.

127

itself and *that it is different from the others*, is the same in each case. What we are doing here is thinking something common to the objects of several senses, and Plato calls the predicates of such judgments κοινά, "common terms".⁸ Plato explicitly includes among the κοινά existence, identity, difference, similarity, dissimilarity, being one, odd and even, good and bad, beautiful and ugly; all of these are properties of the objects of several, perhaps all, of the senses. Plato argues that in applying common terms to the objects of the senses the mind is not perceiving but doing something else, which we may call reflecting and comparing (a term which is meant to cover what the mind does when it is ἀναλογιζομένη, 186 a 10, ἐπανιοῦσα καὶ συμβάλλουσα, b 8, and συλλογιζομένη d 3). His reason for saying this is that acts of perception are always performed through one sense or another, and what can be perceived through one sense cannot be perceived through any other. Thus only colors can be seen, and no color can be heard or tasted. Hence we cannot be merely perceiving in thinking that a sound and a color exist: what we are then noticing about the objects, their existence, cannot be either an auditory or a visual property, since it belongs equally to the sound and to the color, and it is obvious that there is no further sense through which we could perceive such common properties. Judgments of this kind are made by the mind by itself and without the aid of any sense or organ of sense.

It is important to realize that in his discussion of the higher, reflective employment of the mind Plato is exclusively alluding to the activity of judging *that* something exists, is self-identical, etc.; he nowhere raises the question of how we become acquainted with

⁸ Cornford, at one place (p. 105), notices that the word κοινόν here is to be understood by contrast with what is peculiar to the objects of a single sense. Yet further down the page he says κοινόν is to be understood "in the sense in which a name is common to any number of individual things," and hence that the κοινά are "the meanings of common names," i.e. Forms. Κοινόν is fairly frequently used in this way in Aristotle (e.g. *EE* 1218 a 8, *Met.* Z 1040 b 25, *NE* 1180 b 15), where the contexts show that it is to be understood as meaning τὸ κοινῇ κατηγορούμενον or τὸ καθόλου. But it is obvious that this is not how Plato uses the word here: since the κοινά are predicates belonging to objects of more than one of the senses, such predicates as *white* or *hard* will not qualify as κοινά. Yet they are certainly κοινῇ κατηγορούμενα. I know of no place in Plato where κοινόν is used in this Aristotelian sense: strictly not *Tht.* 208 d 7-9 and 209 a 10-11, to which Cherniss (*ACP* p. 236 n.) refers. By κοινόν in our passage Plato certainly does not mean to refer to Forms generally. The κοινά may be Forms, though Plato does not say so; but they do not include any predicates except those which are common to objects of *several* senses.

128

Existence and the other terms we apply to sense-objects in so judging. For the moment I will take this for granted, leaving the proof until later.

In the first part of our passage, then, Plato draws two distinctions. He distinguishes between the role played by the mind in perception and that played by the senses, and he contrasts this use of the mind with a higher reflective use in which it works independently of the body and its sense-faculties and judges that the objects of the senses exist and that they possess other κοινά. Several points call for comment.

First, it should be noticed that in distinguishing between the senses (αἰσθήσεις) as powers of the bodily organs and the mind as that which[9] perceives (αἰσθάνεται) Plato is in effect using the notion of αἴσθησις in two ways. For the perceptual acts of the mind – the acts of seeing, hearing, smelling, etc. – can be called αἰσθήσεις (cf. 186 d 10 - e 2), as can the powers of the body which Plato says make these acts possible. Αἴσθησις as act is located in the mind, but αἴσθησις as power in the body. Now there is an awkwardness in saying that the *mind* sees, hears and so on, (ὁρᾶν, ἀκούειν, 184 c 6-7, etc.) while locating the *power* of hearing, sight, etc. (ἀκοή, ὄψις, 185 a 2, c 1-2) in the body and its organs: if the mind sees and hears, and not any bodily part, then surely the mind and not any part of the body is the possessor of the power of sight and hearing. But the awkwardness is particularly acute because the thesis which Plato hopes to refute by the analysis of perception being carried out here is put as the identification of αἴσθησις and ἐπιστήμη (184 b 5). Since αἴσθησις, in the analysis, can refer either to a power of the body or to an action of the mind, there is an initial doubt as to what Plato is going to deny in denying that αἴσθησις is knowledge. It might be suggested, for example, that by emphasizing that the senses are powers of the body Plato means to be saying that the *senses* do not contain knowledge: they do no more than provide material for the mind to act upon. It is the mind that does the knowing, and the senses are altogether dumb and devoid of thinking: in using the senses we are not, *per se*, even thinking anything, much less knowing anything. If this is going to be his argument, Plato will only be denying that knowledge lies in the sensory powers of the body; he will not be saying that perceptual acts of the mind are themselves not acts of knowledge. Yet, one might object, this last is precisely what

[9] Plato finds it natural to shift from saying that the person perceives through the sensory powers of the bodily organs (184 b 9, c 6-7, 8, etc.) to saying (185 c 8, e 6-7, 186 b 3) that the mind perceives through the senses.

129

ought to be proved. But owing to the vagueness of Theaetetus' original definition and to the use of the word αἴσϑησις to stand for the body's powers of sensory affection, Plato might fairly claim to have shown that on one plausible interpretation of the thesis it is false. This possibility should certainly be borne in mind, although I think that in the end it is reasonably clear that Plato means to reject even the claim that perceptual acts of the mind are acts of knowledge.[10]

The second remark to be made at this point concerns the nature of perceptual acts, as Plato conceives them, and the distinction between these and the higher acts of reflective judgment. Perception, as something the mind does through the senses, is contrasted both with the sensory affection of the bodily organs and with the higher reflective use of the mind. On close examination of the text, however, it appears that the perceptual use of the mind is conceived of rather differently in the two contrasts. Plato does not seem to have made a clean decision whether by perception he means mere sensory awareness, which does not involve any application of concepts to the data of sense, or sensory awareness plus the restricted use of concepts which is involved in labelling the colors, sounds, etc., presented in sensation with their names – "red", "hard", "sweet", "loud", and so on. This indecision on his part is of the greatest importance for the interpretation of the argument, if, as I just remarked, Plato intends to reject the claim of perceptual acts to be instances of knowing. To the extent that Plato is unclear what he includes under the notion of perceptual acts, both what he is denying and perhaps also why he is denying it will remain unclear. What he says about perceptual acts must therefore be very closely scrutinized.

In drawing the contrast between bodily affection and perception Plato is naturally interpreted as understanding by "perception" sensory awareness by itself. Though he limits the objects of awareness to the proper objects of the five senses, saying that we perceive warm, hard, light and sweet things (184 e 4-5), and even the hardness of a hard thing (186 b 2), through our senses, this need not imply that perception involves the awareness *that* these things are hard, light, and so on. And at one place he seems very clearly to be thinking of perceptual acts as acts of awareness only; he says they are common to

[10] This seems to follow, for example, from 186 d 2, where knowledge is said not to reside ἐν τοῖς παϑήμασιν, which, as 186 c 1-2 shows, is to be understood as a reference to perceptual acts of the mind.

130

men and beasts and can be performed already at birth (186 b 11 - c 2).[11] Presumably he does not imagine that beasts and day-old babies are capable of using concepts. Now if "perception" is here sensory awareness, then one would expect the higher, independent activity of the mind to be the application of concepts to what we perceive. The line between "perception" and reflection would then separate simple sensory awareness from the thinking, of whatever complexity, that one does *about* whatever one is presented with in sensation. On this view, the application of the concept *red* to a perceived color would require some independent action of the mind quite as much as the application of the concept *existence*. In fact, the concepts of existence, identity and so on (the κοινά) would be in no way specially associated with the mind's independent activity[12]; the κοινά would have to be interpreted as mere examples, whose place could be taken by any other terms of any other class or category.

The fact remains, however, that the independent use of the mind is illustrated *exclusively* by the application of concepts which are applicable to the objects of more than one sense. This suggests that the independent use does not include judgments applying concepts peculiar to the objects of a single sense. And in fact, in contrasting perception and the higher use of the mind Plato does seem to contrast the application of the κοινά to objects of sensory awareness, not with sensory awareness itself but with the application of *other* concepts, namely the concepts required for the labelling of the data of sense. Not only does he not illustrate the reflective-judgmental use of the mind by the application of a concept which, like *red*, belongs to only one type of sense-object; he very clearly indicates that thinking with such concepts is not a matter of reflective judgment at all. He says (185 b 4-5)

---

[11] Cf. also 186 d 2-3: παθήματα here too is naturally interpreted to mean acts of (passive) awareness.

[12] It might be suggested that οὐσία, at any rate, does occupy a special position. For, one might say, it is the one concept that is employed on every occasion on which any other concept is applied: every judgment is of the form "A is (or is not) B". One might attempt to argue that all application of concepts involves the use of the other κοινά as well: this is plausible for identity, difference, similarity and dissimilarity. But it is not plausible for "two", "good" and "beautiful". In fact, however, the principle of selection for the κοινά is not their implication in all judgments, but their applicability to objects of different senses. So the supposed special position of at least some of them as regards the power of judgment is not Plato's reason for illustrating the independent activity of the mind by judgments involving them.

131

that we are capable of investigating (ἐπισκέψασθαι) and deciding (cf. κρίνειν, 186 b 8) whether a color and a sound are similar or not, and that we do so with our minds independently of any bodily power. The same point is put (185 c 4-7) by saying that the mind does not operate through any sense in applying the words (ἐπονομάζεις, c 6) "exists" and "does not exist" to things. By contrast, Plato says (185 b 9 - c 3), we investigate whether a couple of things are bitter by means of a bodily power, namely the sense of taste. This clearly means that in operating through the senses the mind applies the words "bitter", "red", "hard", etc. to sense-objects: "investigation about existence" involves the applying of the words "exists" and "does not exist", so "investigation about bitterness" involves the application of the words "bitter" or "not bitter". That this is so is made certain by the remark with which Socrates concludes his exposition of the contrast between the perceptual and the reflective uses of the mind: φαίνεταί σοι τὰ μὲν αὐτὴ δι᾽ αὐτῆς ἡ ψυχὴ ἐπισκοπεῖν, τὰ δὲ διὰ τῶν τοῦ σώματος δυνάμεων (185 e 6-7). In order to decide whether something exists, is similar to something else, etc., one has to reflect; in order to decide whether something is red one does not need to reflect, but to use the mind at the perceptual level only.

There is thus good evidence for each of two different views as to what Plato thinks is involved in what I have called the perceptual use of the mind. He sometimes seems to have in mind sensory awareness without the application of concepts to what is perceived, but in contrasting the perceptual and the reflective uses he seems to think of the labelling of the data of sense with elementary color, taste, etc., descriptions as itself taking place at the perceptual and not the reflective level. I do not think the evidence on either side can be explained away; the most one can do is to try to render the inconsistency palatable. The difficulty arises because Plato tries to combine two rather different distinctions, and this can be made understandable by considering how closely these distinctions are related to one another. We may begin by asking why Plato thinks that different powers of the mind are called on in deciding whether a κοινόν such as self-identity belongs to a sensed color, than are exercised in deciding whether the sensed color is, say, red. The latter operation, the classification or labelling of the data of sense, does not indeed involve the application of a concept which belongs to objects of different senses, but why should that make any difference? In labelling a color, surely, one is, implicitly at least, engaged in reflecting, remembering and comparing – activities which

132

Plato represents as distinctive of the "independent" use of the mind (186 a 9 - b 1, b 6-9). Indeed, it might be said that labelling the seen color calls upon the power to apply some of the κοινά themselves: to recognize the color as red one has to remember past colors, both red and non-red, and think this one *similar* to some and *dissimilar* from others. How can Plato have thought that the application of the elementary perceptual concepts could proceed without this sort of associative activity? And even if this can be managed without the use of the κοινά, why did Plato think it involves quite a different power of the mind from that exercised in thinking about existence, similarity, and so on?

A partial answer can be found, I think, in the view of thinking (διανοεῖσθαι) which Plato puts forward just a few pages later in the *Theaetetus*. Here (189 e 4 ff.) Plato defines the process of thinking as discourse carried on by the mind with itself.[13] On this model one might think of perceptual thought as a matter of saying to oneself, as one experiences various sensations, "red", "warm", "sweet", and so on. And employing the κοινά in thought will be represented as saying to oneself "That (i.e., that color just labelled 'red') exists", or "that color is the same as itself and different from this one", and so on. Now even if recognizing a color as red requires comparison and involves the *implicit* use of various of the κοινά, it is clear that one need not *explicitly* say to oneself "This color is like such and such other colors I've seen and unlike such and such others, so it's red". Anyone who possesses the color concepts is (normally) able to apply them without any explicit process of reasoning at all. But it is an essential feature of Plato's model of what thinking is that only things which one explicitly says to oneself are counted as things that one thinks. Hence all such implicit mental activities must go unnoticed and unaccounted for so long as one retains this model. The contrast Plato draws is between labelling sense data and *explicitly* thinking that, e.g., some given color exists, is the same as itself, different from something else, like or unlike it, beautiful or ugly, and so forth. The point seems to be that the color of a thing can simply be, as it were, read off it once one has the color concept in question; whereas noticing the similarity of one thing to another requires explicit thinking about the other thing and overt

---

[13] The same account appears in *Soph.* 264 a-b, and the different image of writing in a mental book, which appears in the *Philebus* (38 e - 39 a) along side the idiom of discourse with oneself (38 d 1-2, 6, e 1-4), is not significantly different from the present point of view.

133

comparison, just as in Plato's view judging that something is good requires sifting past and present against the probable future (186 a 1 ff.). These judgments, and all judgments involving κοινά, require that one engage in more or less elaborate *explicit* reflection.[14] It is the immediacy of the labelling function that seems to have impressed Plato, and to have distinguished it in his mind from thought employing the κοινά.

But even if Plato can by some such reasoning as this be justified in his separation of labelling and reflective judgment, what can be said in defense of his assimilation of the labelling power to simple sensory awareness? To begin with, it should be noted that the immediacy of the labelling operation is a consequence of the fact that, as it seems, one has in sensory awareness itself all the evidence one needs to justify the application of the appropriate label: I know that the color I see is red just because I can see it. On the other hand, in order to judge that it is beautiful, just seeing it is not enough; as Plato implies, I need in addition to call to mind other objects seen on other occasions and conduct a comparison to see if this color measures up to the appropriate standard of beauty. This means that the exercise of the labelling capacity, though of course it is different from sensory awareness, is very closely related to it. By labelling the data, it is natural to think, one merely makes explicit what was already contained in sensation. But in judgments of existence, usefulness, and so on, one goes beyond the data of sense themselves to consider their relations to one another, their probable consequences and so on. From this point of view, then, the labelling function goes together with sensory awareness and is reasonably grouped together with it in contrast with reflective judgment. And when one adds that one crucially important step in the advance of knowledge is that from the labelling of sense-contents to explicit comparative reflection about them, one sees even more clearly why Plato, with his interest in knowledge, should tend to assimilate or confuse with one another sensory awareness and the labelling of its objects.

---

[14] Is this true of judgments of existence and self-identity? The case of existence is hard to decide because of the obscurity of Plato's examples. If "this color exists" means "this is the real color of something", then I suppose explicit reflection is required. The thought that something is identical with itself is such an unnatural thought that I have no confidence in any conjecture as to what Plato conceived was involved in thinking it: perhaps he is guided here by the thought that self-identity is not a feature of a thing that can simply be read off it in the way colors can.

134

Now Plato's ambivalence in his characterization of perception complicates the interpretation of the remainder of the passage. The reason he gives for making knowledge the outcome of acts of reflective judgment but not acts of perception turns out to lend itself to different interpretations depending on which view of perception is assumed.

But before showing how this is so, I must justify the assumption made in the preceding discussion that in discussing the higher reflective employment of the mind Plato has in view only the power of formulating judgments involving the κοινά and not also or instead the contemplation of the objects Existence, Identity and so on. To do this will require a close analysis of the passage in which the reflective employment of the mind is contrasted with the perceptual.

The relevant section opens at 185 b 7 with the question, "Through what do you think all these [i.e., the common terms] about them [viz., about sound and color]?" As Socrates explains, he has in mind that if you perceive that something is red, or sweet-flavored, you perceive these things through the medium of a sense and a sense-organ; and he wants to know whether one perceives something's existence or self-identity or unity through any analogous organ. At c 7-8, having given this explanation of his question he repeats it: τούτοις πᾶσι ποῖα ἀπο-δώσεις ὄργανα δι' ὧν αἰσθάνεται ἡμῶν τὸ αἰσθανόμενον ἕκαστα; ("What sort of organs do you assign for all of these, through which our sense-perceptory part perceives them?") Here commentators begin to translate and comment as if what is in question were, "How do we become acquainted with the entities Existence, Identity, Unity, etc.?" But it is evident that the question in Plato's text merely restates the question at b 7 and that therefore nothing is said about our becoming acquainted with Existence; the question concerns rather our perceiving or judging that a thing exists. This is overlooked only because the restatement omits the phrase περὶ αὐτοῖν from the earlier statement, (b 8) which would make it clear that it is not a question of becoming acquainted with the meanings of these common terms,[15] but rather one of perceiving or judging *that* they do or do not apply to something.

That the περί phrase is to be understood with the restatement at c 7-8 is made certain by Theaetetus' reply. He adds in his answer the περὶ αὐτῶν (d 1) which was only implicit in the question: "You mean *their* existence and non-existence, similarity and dissimilarity, sameness and difference, unity and other number." But he then goes on to

[15] So Cornford, p. 105.

omit the phrase, in the same idiomatic way, later in his reply when he in turn reformulates the question: διὰ τίνος ποτὲ τῶν τοῦ σώματος τῇ ψυχῇ αἰσθανόμεθα [αὐτῶν]; (d 3-4) ("Through what bodily part do we perceive these with our minds?") And here again translators unaccountably omit the περί phrase and misunderstand Theaetetus to be asking himself whether we become acquainted with Existence and the rest, in themselves, through any agency of the body. Cornford compounds this error by misconstruing in Theaetetus' next answer (d 7 - e 2) the force of the phrase περὶ πάντων which he again reimports. Theaetetus says, "The mind itself through itself, as it appears to me, examines (ἐπισκοπεῖν)[16] for every object [whether it possesses] these common attributes" (αὐτὴ δι' αὑτῆς ἡ ψυχὴ τὰ κοινά μοι φαίνεται περὶ πάντων ἐπισκοπεῖν). But Cornford takes περὶ πάντων with τὰ κοινά, and translates "the common terms that apply to everything", presumably thinking the phrase a variation of τὸ ἐπὶ πᾶσι κοινόν above (c 4-5); but even if this is possible Greek it is obvious that περὶ πάντων ἐπισκοπεῖν is parallel to περὶ αὐτοῖν διανοῇ in the original statement of the question (b 7), so that we have once again the same question about the application of these words to things and not a new question about how we become acquainted with their meanings. Other translators (e.g., Diès) take περὶ πάντων here with the verb, as its position surely dictates, but they have not, I think, seen the consequence of so doing. The consequence, to repeat, is that Theaetetus says nothing about how we become acquainted with Existence and Sameness, but rather tells us that judgments of the existence and identity of a sense quality are not made by the mind through the agency of any sense but rather by the mind independently.

It is, then, quite clear that περὶ αὐτοῖν (185 b 7) is to be supplied right through to 185 e whenever there is mention of grasping, thinking or investigating κοινά. Plato himself repeats it (or a variant) as often as he decently can: the commentators' shift from the question whether we use a bodily organ in applying the κοινά to things, to the question how we become acquainted with Forms, is sheer invention.

Nor does Plato subsequently raise this other question. In what follows (186 a-c) he consolidates his position by running through the

[16] Ἐπισκοπεῖν need not mean "contemplate" (so Cornford, cf. Cherniss SPM p. 6 and W. G. Runciman, Plato's Later Epistemology, p. 15): cf. ἐπισκέψασθαι, which is the aorist used to meet the defect in ἐπισκοπεῖν, just above, 185 b 5. Cf. also 161 d 5, e 7, where both ἐπισκέψασθαι and ἐπισκοπεῖν appear and neither means "contemplate."

136

list of κοινά, adding some new ones and obtaining Theaetetus' agreement that these are all applied to things by the mind independently of perception. Here again translators confuse the issue by taking Plato to be discussing how we arrive at our acquaintance with these common entities; and again there are very clear signs that nothing of the sort is in question.[17] Thus when Socrates inquires whether καλὸν καὶ αἰσχρὸν καὶ ἀγαθὸν καὶ κακόν are among the κοινά about the οὐσία (existence)[18] of which the mind judges all by itself, Theaetetus replies in the affirmative (186 a 9 - b 1). But he goes on to add that when the mind judges about these matters it calculates within itself past and present against the future. Now this is a pretty good brief account of how one judges whether a particular person or action or situation is good or bad or honorable or disgraceful: one does have to weigh past experience and present circumstances in order to get a reasonable judgment as to a person's future behavior or the consequences of an action, and so on. But it is precisely the *wrong* sort of thing to do in order to become acquainted with the existence and nature of a Platonic Form. Consideration of phenomena and phenomenal events is notoriously the main *obstacle* to becoming acquainted with these. It seems clear, therefore, that Socrates and Theaetetus are not discussing the question how we arrive at our knowledge of the Forms Honorableness, Disgracefulness and the like; they are, rather, inquiring how one goes about making particular judgments about the goodness or badness, etc. of particular things.

The general point is reaffirmed once more with complete clarity in the immediately following lines (186 b 2-10). You perceive the hardness of a hard thing, Socrates says, through the sense of touch, and likewise the softness of a soft thing. But the existence of this hardness and this softness (or perhaps of hardness and softness in general), and their opposition to one another, and the existence if this opposition, are not discoverable by the use of the senses. For these, the mind compares things together and keeps going back over them within itself to answer its questions. Once again it is obvious that what

[17] Only 186 a 4 even remotely imports an interest in how we become acquainted with the κοινά; and its immediate sequel is quite evidently concerned not with this but with how to employ them in making judgments about αἰσθητά.

[18] Throughout the passage οὐσία seems to mean (something like) the existence of this or that: cf. 186 b 6 where καὶ ὅτι ἐστόν is epexegetical of τὴν οὐσίαν. At any rate, it never means the *nature* of a thing. (See below pp. 140 f. for a needed qualification).

137

interests Plato is the contrast between two operations of the mind, perceiving through the senses, and reflection, comparison, prediction and in general the interpretation of the *significance* of what one perceives. Neither here nor elsewhere does he raise the question how the mind acquires its knowledge of the common terms which it employs in its interpretative activity.

Thus the difficulty noticed above (p. 125) in the first stage of the argument as Cornford interprets it is eliminated. There is no longer a conflict between the obvious implication of the sensing-judging distinction to which he appeals and the contrast between the perception of sense-objects and the contemplation of thought-objects: the latter contrast is not drawn in the argument at all. The contrast, as I have argued above, is that between elementary sensory awareness together with the labelling of its objects, on the one hand, and the supposedly more sophisticated level of thought attained in thinking that sense-objects exist, are different from one another, and so on.

III

So far, then, I have argued that Plato draws two distinctions, that between the role of the senses and the role of the mind in perception, and that between the use of the mind in perception and its use in reflective judgment involving the notions of existence, identity, and so on. The material thus provided is the basis on which Plato relies in rejecting the definition of knowledge as αἴσθησις.

The refutation Plato produces (186 c 6 - e 10) is characteristically brief and cryptic. He points out that one cannot be knowing anything when he does not grasp οὐσία (being, existence?) and truth, and then relies on the preceding analysis to show that in αἴσθησις one does not grasp οὐσία and truth. We have already seen that Cornford interprets this as meaning that it is not through the use of the senses that one becomes acquainted with the Forms, the only truly real and knowable entities. But since, as I have shown above, there is no reference in what precedes to Forms,[19] or to the process of becoming acquainted with Forms, there is absolutely no excuse for any interpretation of this kind. What Plato means by "grasping being and truth" must be

---

[19] Even if the κοινά are Forms Plato does not say they are, and for the very good reason that it nowhere matters to his argument what their metaphysical status is. See note 8 above.

138

gathered from the account he has just given of perception and the employment of the κοινά in thought.

Clearly, Plato means to argue that the mind in perception does not acquire or evince knowledge, on the ground that knowledge is attained only when οὐσία is grasped, and that it is only in reflective judgment that the power to judge about the οὐσία of anything is evinced. But, because of the uncertainty about what Plato understands by "perception", two different lines of thought, both, I think, plausible and interesting, may be proposed as interpretations of his argument here.

Let us assume first that "perception" means sensory awareness, without conceptualization. Then it is natural to interpret Plato as pointing out that knowing involves, at least, thinking *that* so-and-so is the case. Knowledge therefore involves the applying of concepts and since sensory awareness is a mental power not involving conceptualization it must be wrong to equate knowledge with sensory awareness.

There are several points in favor of such an interpretation. Foremost is the fact that Plato says that knowledge involves "grasping truth". This is very naturally interpreted as meaning that there is no knowledge where there is no formulation of truths, i.e. where there is no thinking *that*, no conceptualization. Secondly, Socrates in stating the conclusion of the argument seems to suggest just this contrast between sensory awareness and thinking that so-and-so is the case: he says, "So there is no knowledge in the experiences we undergo (παθήμασιν), but rather in the reasoning (συλλογισμῷ) we do concerning them" (186 d 2-3). Here nothing indicates that the reasoning envisaged is restricted to any particular subject matter (not, for example, to questions about the application of κοινά); there seems to be a blank contrast between bare seeing, hearing, etc., and thoughts, of whatever sort, about what one is seeing, hearing, and so on.

But if Plato means to say that αἴσθησις occurs without the formulation of judgments, this point must somehow be found in his assertion that in perception we do not "grasp οὐσία". What has the failure to grasp οὐσία to do with the non-judgmental character of perception? Throughout the argument so far οὐσία seems to have meant existence:[20] at its first introduction in the context (185 c 9, cf. a 9 and c 5-6) it seems to mean this and it does not appear to alter in meaning thereafter. Perception's failure to grasp οὐσία should therefore mean that

[20] So Lewis Campbell (*The Theaetetus of Plato*) insists: cf. his note *ad* 186 c 3, and p. liv n. Cf. also my note 18 above.

the thought that something exists is not an act of perception. This is no doubt true, but how does this failure imply that perception is altogether non-judgmental? Judgments of existence are just one class of judgments. Does Plato mean to suggest that somehow we must always be making existential judgments whenever we make judgments of any other type? Or does he mean that before we can make judgments of other types we must be able to make existential judgments? Neither of these alternatives is at all attractive; but the mention of οὐσία here certainly seems not to be an arbitrarily chosen example illustrating a thesis which any other concept would have illustrated equally well.

Is it however correct to insist that grasping οὐσία must mean thinking that something exists? Even although οὐσία (and its cognates) in its earlier appearances in the passage is naturally *translated* "existence", "exists", etc. (as in 185 a 9, ὅτι ἀμφοτέρω ἐστόν), it does not follow that this is what the word *means* there or elsewhere in the passage. English sharply distinguishes the "is" of existence from the copula, but Greek does not; and it is arguable, and has been argued,[21] that the Greek verb εἶναι does not have "senses" corresponding to this distinction. It represents rather an undifferentiated concept straddling this particular distinction. If this is so, one can easily see how Plato might have thought that thinking with the concept οὐσία has a position of priority vis-à-vis all other conceptual thinking, and that to fail to grasp οὐσία is to fail to formulate judgments altogether. To grasp the οὐσία of something is not necessarily to think that it *exists*, but may be no more than to think that it *is* F for some predicate F.[22] In that case to be deprived of the use of εἶναι would mean that one was incapable of predicating anything of anything else, since the copula, which is indispensable to predication, would be unavailable. Hence, without the use of εἶναι one could not have the power of judgment, and therefore one could not have the use of any concepts at all.

In this way, assuming that by "perception" Plato means just sensory awareness, a good and interesting argument can be found

[21] Cf., e.g., C. H. Kahn, "The Greek Verb 'To Be' and the Concept of Being", *Foundations of Language* 2 (1966), 245-265. Cf. also G. E. L. Owen, "Aristotle on the Snares of Ontology", *New Essays on Plato and Aristotle* (ed. R. Bambrough, London 1965), p. 71 n., for salutary remarks on Plato's use of the notion of τὸ ὄν in the *Sophist*.

[22] At 186 a 10, to consider the οὐσία of καλόν, etc. quite clearly means to consider whether some given thing *is* beautiful, good, etc. Here the being of a predicate is its attachment to a subject; likewise the being of a subject is (in part at least) its bearing of a predicate.

140

behind his assertion that since perception does not grasp οὐσία, it does not arrive at truth, and therefore cannot constitute knowledge. But although, as I have indicated, such an argument fits the text quite well in several respects, doubt must remain whether it expresses Plato's meaning. For, as I have argued in the preceding section, the neat distinction, on which this interpretation depends, between perception as sensory awareness and the higher conceptualizing power of the mind, is not everywhere in the context adhered to by Plato himself. The higher power of the mind is restricted to the application of only certain concepts, namely the κοινά (which includes, besides those mentioned, also all others which belong to objects of different senses, or involve reference to objects of different senses); perception, then, includes sensory awareness and the minimum interpretation of its objects which is involved in labelling them "red", "sweet", and so on. The labelling process certainly amounts to using certain concepts, namely what might be called minimal perceptual concepts; and since this is envisaged as taking place without the use of εἶναι, which only comes in with the addition of the higher power of the mind, Plato cannot mean to suggest that all use of concepts requires the use of εἶναι. So one must look further to find an interpretation that will fit this way of understanding the distinction between perception and reflection.

If, then, "perception" means sensory awareness plus the supposedly immediate classification of its objects, what reason can Plato be understood to be giving against the claim of perception to be knowledge? On this view, what would it be to grasp οὐσία, and why would the failure to do this entail that perception is not knowledge? The refutation of Protagoras earlier in the dialogue seems to offer a clue. Plato argues (177 c - 179 c) against Protagoras that thinking a thing does not make it so, at least whenever prediction is involved, because in such cases the truth or falsity of the thought depends on the event; and even if each man is his own infallible judge of how the event turns out, when it occurs, the prediction, once made, is true or not depending on how things turn out (or seem to have turned out) (cf. 178 d 4-6). In making predictions, then, there is room for mistakes; not everyone can claim to have *knowledge* of how things *will* turn out (or even how things will *seem* to himself to have turned out). It is the expert physician who knows whether I will come down with a fever tomorrow (178 c); the expert musician, and not just any layman, knows whether a lyre will be put in tune by loosening its strings (178 d); and in general when

141

one man can claim to *know* better than others how things will turn out, this claim must be based on his possession of an expertise which makes him wiser and more skilled than others in his particular subject area (179 a 10 - b 5). His prediction is not then a mere guess, as the layman's would have to be; it is founded on objectively valid principles of science or art and constitutes knowledge precisely because it is supported by such principles.[23]

This argument against Protagoras is recalled in our passage when Socrates adds καλὸν καὶ αἰσχρὸν καὶ ἀγαθὸν καὶ κακόν to the list of subject matters about which perception is incompetent to judge (186 a 8 - b 1). Judging here involves prediction, Socrates says; and in so saying he clearly refers back to what was said against Protagoras. In the argument against Protagoras, special emphasis was placed on the fact that questions of ὠφέλεια involve prediction, so that some πόλεις are wiser and more expert than others (172 a, 179 a 5 ff., etc.); and in our passage Socrates joins ὠφέλεια with οὐσία as the two most significant matters in thinking about which we employ the higher reflective power of the mind – those of us, at any rate, who are capable of having thoughts on such subjects at all (186 c 2-5). The suggestion is that Plato bases his rejection of perception's claim to be knowledge on the ground that knowledge implies expertise and the appeal to objectively valid principles and standards; while perception does not go beyond subjective reports of the contents of sensory experience and therefore makes no judgments to which such standards and principles are relevant. There are no experts at perception; no one can claim that his perceptual reports, as such, are more true than anyone else's; no one subjects his own or anyone else's reports to criticism by appeal to the sort of standards Plato implies are operative in the doctor's prediction of fever and the pastry-cook's of pleasure to the palate. Precisely because perception is purely subjective, because it is not open to criticism or correction (cf. ἀνάλωτοι, 179 c 5), perception cannot claim to be knowledge. Knowledge is always the result of directing one's thoughts in accordance with principles and standards; hence any claim to knowledge must be open to criticism by appeal to the appropriate standards. Because in perception there is no room for such criticism, perception cannot constitute knowledge.

On this interpretation the failure of perception to grasp the οὐσία

[23] Compare Socrates' refutation of Thrasymachus' claim that ἀδικία – and not δικαιοσύνη – is a virtue and a sign of intelligence, *Rep.* 350 a-c.

142

of its objects would be taken to mean that in perception one notices only the color (etc.) a thing appears to have and says nothing about what its real color is. As I remarked above, οὐσία is an undifferentiated concept of being; but it seems naturally interpreted in this passage (at e.g. 185 a 9) as expressing existence. To judge that a color exists one must engage in the kind of calculation of past and present perceptions with a view to the future which Theaetetus mentions in connection with judgments of value; and just as Plato insists that judgments of value imply the existence of objective standards which experts constantly use to guide their thought, so one must be guided by objective standards in saying how things in the world *are*. This is the work not of perception but of reflective judgment.

But if perception fails to attain to objectivity it also fails to "hit the truth" (186 c 9). A thought is pronounced true or false by appeal to the standards valid for the subject matter. Hence perception, as something altogether subjective and unguided by standards, yields neither truths nor falsehoods. Knowledge, then, must lie elsewhere; in fact, it is to be looked for in reflective judgment, where the notions of existence, identity, similarity and so on, with their associated objective standards, enter for the first time.

I think this interpretation has much in its favor. The fact that it reads quite a lot into Plato's remark that perception fails to grasp οὐσία, and therefore misses truth too, is no objection against it; any interpretation must do the same. What matters is how one brings the context to bear on the interpretation of this final argument. In appealing to the notions of expertise and objective standards this interpretation makes good use of undoubtedly Platonic doctrines undoubtedly expressed in the context; and in understanding perception to include the classification of the contents of sensory experience it adopts what appears to be the correct interpretation of the contrast between αἴσθησις and the independent employment of the mind. And in bringing these two views together it provides a reasonable sense for the final argument.

Crombie[24] appears to reject an interpretation rather close to this one on the ground that it cannot accommodate the examples Plato gives of judgments involving κοινά other than οὐσία. Crombie thinks that on this view the "contribution which the mind makes" consists in "referring our sense-data to the external world"; and the difficulty then arises that one contribution of the mind mentioned by Plato is to

---

[24] *Op. cit.*, pp. 15-16.

notice that a color and a sound are different, a contribution not plausibly interpreted as consisting in the referral of "sense-data" to the external world. On the view I have been expounding, however, the contribution of the mind is not limited in this way. Its contribution is the appeal to objective standards, and it is only in connection with the existence of the objects of sensory awareness that the appropriate objective standards involve the referral of "sense-data" to the external world. In other cases, e.g. those of self-identity and unity and the difference of a sound from a color, it would seem to be a law of logic that the mind invokes, and the fact that it is *applied* to objects of sensory awareness does not make it any the less something objectively valid. One cannot (let us suppose) dispute a man's report that what he sees in his visual field is a red color and what he hears is a bang. But if he goes on to say about the color and the noise that they are the same thing he's enunciating a falsehood; what he says at this level is subject to criticism.

Thus the upshot of the argument, on this second interpretation, is that knowledge brings with it objectivity and appeal to the sort of standards which experts employ. "Perception" fails to be knowledge because one need not be an expert in any sense or have the use of objective standards of any kind in order to be as good at perceiving as anyone else. On this reading, Plato arrives, by way of his assimilation of knowledge to expertise, at a position which gives to empirical knowledge the honorific title of ἐπιστήμη; and the emphasis which he places in this connection on objectivity has the very interesting consequence that Plato's conception of empirical knowledge has a definite Kantian flavor.

Plato, therefore, rejects the claim of "perception" (αἴσθησις) to constitute knowledge on one of two grounds, depending on which of two understandings of "perception" is adopted. If "perception" means mere sensory awareness, then it cannot be knowledge because knowledge involves discursive thought while "perception" is at a lower level of logical complexity. If "perception" means awareness of "sense-contents", explicitly labelled, then it fails to be knowledge because it makes no claims to objective validity. As I have already indicated each of these interpretations is plausible, and neither, I think, can be definitely ruled out. But on the whole I prefer the second interpretation, because it accounts better for Plato's emphasis on thought about κοινά in particular as marking an advance beyond "perceptual" thinking and into the area where we can first speak of knowledge.

144

But whichever of these interpretations is correct, the *Theaetetus* turns out to contain points of great originality – points completely ignored by interpretations which, like Cornford's and Cherniss', attempt to make the *Theaetetus* merely repeat things already said in the *Republic*. The distinction between the senses as bodily powers and perception as a power of the mind, and the identification of what is known with some sub-class of judgments, constitute noteworthy philosophical achievements. They also mark distinct advances over Plato's way of thinking about perception and knowledge in the *Republic*. Cherniss' claim that *Republic* 522-525 is parallel in argument to *Theaetetus* 184-186 can now be seen to be an entirely superficial view. The *Republic* passage is so far from being parallel that it actually makes mistakes which the *Theaetetus'* analysis is intended to show up. These are: (1) The *Republic* passage constantly speaks of the *senses* as saying this or that, whereas (as noted above) the *Theaetetus* scotches this misleading inaccuracy. (2) The *Republic* allows as judgments of perception things which the *Theaetetus*, in distinguishing perception from the mind's power of independent thought, insists belong to a level of intellectual activity entirely beyond perception. Thus at 523 a 3 Plato speaks of the perception that the same thing is both hard and soft, which seems to involve a judgment of identity and so cannot be a matter of perception in the *Theaetetus'* scheme. Cf. also 523 c 11 ff. (perceiving a finger), 524 d 9 - e 6 (perceiving something as a unit). Further important differences between the two passages include: (3) The *Republic* counts both the question whether something is hard or soft, light or heavy (524 a), and the question whether it is one (524 b), as forcing the mind up to its highest level of operation: on either subject the senses are untrustworthy witnesses (523 b 3-4). But the *Theaetetus* distinguishes between the two cases, and actually allows that the mind operating through the senses does judge without recourse as to hard and soft, light and heavy and the other elementary perceptual properties (185 b 9 ff.; 186 b). It is only with respect to *other* questions than these that the mind's higher capacities are called into play. Hence (4) there is no resemblance at all between the function of the senses as stimulative of thought (*Republic*) and the *Theaetetus'* distinction between perception and the higher functions of the mind. Finally, of course, (5) these higher functions of the mind have nothing to do with the contemplation of Forms, as νόησις in the *Republic* does.

145

Furthermore, and importantly, the *Theaetetus* avoids altogether the *Republic's* misleading analysis of knowledge by reference to the objects to which it is directed; the objects about which Plato assumes we have knowledge in the *Theaetetus* include αἰσθητά,[25] and knowledge is distinguished from other states of mind not by its objects but by how the knower is related to them. Plato's views on perception and knowledge in the *Theaetetus* are fortunately much more sophisticated than traditional interpretations make them appear. Scholars do Plato no service by trying to read into the *Theaetetus* epistemological doctrines they think they find in the *Republic*.[26]

Harvard University.

---

[25] This assumption is not abandoned subsequently in the *Theaetetus*; it is very clearly reaffirmed in 201 a-c (cf. Runciman, *op. cit.* p. 37).

[26] The novelty of the *Theaetetus* is made to seem greater than it probably is by those who, like Cornford and Cherniss, think that Plato in the *Republic* and other middle period dialogues firmly denies that one can *know* anything about anything in this imperfect world. It is true that certain arguments and ways of speaking of the *Republic* imply that the things we perceive or have beliefs about are different things from those we can have knowledge about. But Plato certainly thinks that after undergoing the education he outlines his rulers will be able to govern with knowledge, and this surely means that they will *know*, e.g., that a proposed course of action is right or wrong. The difference between the man who has δόξα and the man of ἐπιστήμη must, despite appearances, not entail a total difference of objects thought about. A more plausible view is that the ἐπιστήμων, because of his acquaintance with the Forms, is in a position to know things about the same objects about which the man of δόξα, because of his ignorance of the Forms, can only have beliefs. This view is in accord with the distinction between ἐπιστήμη and ἀληθὴς δόξα in *Meno* 98 a, and has much else to be said for it. If this is the substance of Plato's position in the *Republic* then the *Theaetetus* in allowing knowledge of αἰσθητά does not subvert anything but unwanted implications of misleading arguments in the *Republic*; the *Theaetetus* can then be seen as offering a corrected and more adequate attempt to say some of the things Plato wished to say in the *Republic*.

146

1

Observations on Perception in Plato's Later Dialogues

Ast, in his *Lexicon Plantonicum,* gives the following as the general meaning of the verb "aisthanesthai" in Plato: "to sense, to perceive by a sense, and hence generally to perceive by the senses." This not only seems to me to be wrong, it also seems to be seriously misleading if one wants to arrive at an understanding of what Plato has to say about perception. For it suggests that in general when Plato uses the verb "aisthanesthai," he is relying on a common notion of sense-perception, a notion which Plato just tries to clarify. This suggestion seems natural enough. Surely, one will say, the Greeks even before Plato must have had a notion of sense-perception, and "aisthanesthai" must have been the verb they commonly used when they wanted to talk about sense-perception. And yet it seems to me that one fails to understand what Plato is trying to do, in particular in the *Theaetetus,* unless one understands that it is only Plato who introduces a clear notion of sense-perception, because he needs it for certain philosophical purposes. What he has to say about perception has to be understood against the background of the ordinary use of the verb "aisthanesthai" and against the background of the philosophical intentions with which Plato narrows down this common use so that it does come to have the meaning "to perceive by the senses."

Though "aisthanesthai" presumably is formed from a root which signifies "hearing," its ordinary use is quite general. It can be used in any case in which one perceives something by the senses and even more generally in any case in which one becomes aware of something, notices something, realizes or even comes to understand something, however this may come about. There will, of course, be a tendency to use the word in cases in which it is particularly clear that somebody is becoming aware of something or noticing something, as opposed to just venturing a guess, making a conjecture, learning of something by hearsay. These will be cases of seeing, but then also cases of sense-perception quite generally. But the use of the verb is not restricted to these cases. It is used whenever someone becomes aware of something. And up to Plato's time, and often far beyond it, there is no clear recognition that there are two radically different ways in which we become aware of something, one by way of sense-perception and the other in some other way, e.g., by a grasp of the mind. Thus, there is no reason to suppose that the verb "aisthanesthai," strictly speaking, refers only to sense-perception, but is also used metaphorically in other cases. It, rather, seems that all cases of becoming aware of something are understood and construed along the lines of the paradigm of seeing, exactly because one does not see a radical difference between the way the mind grasps something and the way the eyes see something. Both are supposed to involve some contact with the object by virtue of which, through a mechanism unknown to us, we become aware of it.

But in addition to this very general use of the verb "aisthanesthai," we find in Plato a second, narrower use of the term, e.g., in the *Phaedo* and in the *Republic*. In this use the term is restricted to cases of awareness that somehow involve the body and that constitute an awareness of something corporeal. But even now it would be rash to assume that the verb means "sense-perception." For in these cases it is used almost interchangeably with "dokein" and "doxazein," "to seem" and "to believe." The realm of belief, as opposed to the realm of knowledge, is the bodily world with which we are in bodily contact as a result of which this world appears to us in a certain way, as a result of which we have certain beliefs about it. There is no "doxa," no belief about the ideas, because ideas are not the kinds of things with which one could have the kind of contact that gives rise to a belief or a perception. But, just as it would be a mistake to infer from this that "doxa" means "sense-perception," so there also is no need to assume that "aisthesis" means "sense-perception," though standard cases of "aisthesis" will be cases of sense-perception.

It is also in the later dialogues that we clearly have an even narrower use of "aisthanesthai," in which it, indeed, does mean "to perceive by the senses." And it is this third sense of "aisthesis" whose introduction I want to discuss.

Unfortunately, our main evidence for this very narrow notion of "aisthesis" is contained in a passage of the *Theaetetus*, 184–187, whose interpretation has become highly controversial, since it involves basic claims about Plato's philosophy and his philosophical development.

In this passage Plato tries to show not only that perception is not identical with knowledge, but that no case of perception as such is a case of knowledge. The argument assumes that if we perceive something, a bodily sense-organ is affected, and that through this change in the sense-organ a change is brought about in the mind (186 Cff.; 186 D). What the argument, as I want to interpret it, mainly turns on is that if we have a clear and precise notion of perception, we see that perception is a purely passive affection of the mind and that for that very reason it cannot constitute knowledge, since knowledge minimally involves true belief and since any belief involves an activity of the mind.

If this is correct, then it would seem that Plato's point in introducing this very narrow notion of perception is to untangle the conflation of perception, appearance, belief, and knowledge with which the main discussion of the dialogue begins in 151 D ff. There perception is first identified with knowledge in Theaetetus' first definition of knowledge as perception, and perception gets quickly identified with appearance (152 C 11), which then throughout this section of the dialogue is treated as if it were the same as belief (cf., e.g., 158 A 1 with 158 A 2 and 185 B 2). But, obviously, it is useful to distinguish between these cognitive states: to perceive is not the same as to believe (though in the middle dialogues we had not paid much attention to the distinction); neither is the same as to be appeared to, and to know is yet a fourth thing. But it is not only useful to make these distinctions, as Plato tries to make them in the *Theaetetus* and the *Sophist* (264 A-B). It is necessary to make these distinctions if we want to combat a certain philosophical view that we first encounter in Protagoras, but that, in one version or another, will later be espoused by some rhetoricians, Skeptics, and the so-called Empiricists, namely the view that the beliefs which we have are just a matter of how things appear to us, how they strike us, of what impression, given the contact we have with them, they leave on us. Plato and the philosophical tradition that depends on him, on the other hand, think that we should not rest content with how things strike us, that we have to go beyond that to find out how they really are, quite independently of how they appear to us. The opponents, like Protagoras, question or deny the possibility that we ever get beyond appearance, seeming, belief. And, hence, they doubt or deny that there is any point in reserving the term "knowledge" for something that goes beyond belief. It is in this context that I want to see the argument of the *Theaetetus,* and in particular the section from 184 to 187. Plato thinks that our beliefs and our knowledge about the physical world involve a passive affection of the mind, but he also thinks that they go much beyond this passive affection. And he wants to reserve the term "aisthanesthai," or "to perceive," for this passive element in our beliefs, which he was willing to grant the opponents. It is in this way that the term came to have the meaning of sense-perception.

With this as a background let us turn to the details of the argument. The conclusion that perception and knowledge are two different things is drawn in 186 E 9-10 on the basis of the argument in the preceding lines, 186 E 4ff. It is assumed that to know is to grasp the truth and that to grasp the truth is to grasp being. But in perception we do not grasp being, hence we do not grasp truth. Therefore, to perceive is not to know. This argument has two crucial assumptions: (i) to grasp the truth is to grasp being, and (ii) to perceive is not to grasp being. It is difficult to understand and to evaluate these assumptions, since we do not know what is meant by "to grasp being." There is no argument for the first assumption that can shed light on the meaning of the phrase. But the second premise is supposed to have been established by the argument that extends to 186 C 6. Hence, we can look at this argument to see whether it gives us a clue to what is meant by "to grasp being."

Now, if we look at the argument, it seems that the reason given for the assumption that in perception we do not grasp being is that the mind considers questions concerning the being of something by itself, rather than by means of one of the senses. This would suggest that the mind grasps or gets hold of being in the relevant sense when it manages to settle the question concerning the being of something which it has been considering by itself. This seems to be confirmed by the final comments on the argument in 187 A 1ff. There Plato says that we have learned from the argument at least that we have to look for knowledge not in perception, but in what the mind does when it considers questions concerning being by itself (187 A 5–6), when it forms beliefs (187 A 7–8). It is because we are supposed to draw this moral from the argument that the dialogue proceeds to discuss the suggestion that knowledge is true belief (187 B 4–6). It is in belief that we grasp truth, if the belief is true, though, as the further argument will show, this is not yet a sufficient condition for knowledge, since knowledge requires that this truth be grasped in a particular way.

But if it is in true belief that we grasp truth, it is also in true belief that we grasp being. This suggests that by "grasping being" Plato here means no more than that the mind in forming a true belief manages to settle the question of the being of something correctly. And it is easy to see how Plato could think this, given his views on being. For he assumes that any belief, explicitly or implicitly, is of the form "A if F," and he thinks that in assuming that A is F one attributes being both to A and to F-ness. To assume that Socrates is just is, on this view, to attribute being to Socrates and to justice. Hence, any true belief will presuppose that one has correctly settled questions concerning the being of something.

One may, of course, think that by "grasping being" Plato here means something much stronger than settling the question whether being should be attributed to something in this way. One may think that Plato wants to distinguish two kinds of grasps or intutions, a perceptual grasp or intuition and an intellectual grasp or intuition. Thus, one may think that Plato, having distinguished two kinds of features, perceptual features and nonperceptual or intelligible features, wants to claim that knowledge involves the intellectual grasp of intelligible features and hence that perception will never give us knowledge. But even if this should be Plato's view, this is not the way he argues in this passage. Instead of distinguishing two kinds of features and correspondingly two kinds of grasps or intuitions, he distinguishes two kinds of features and correspondingly two kinds of questions the mind considers and tries to settle (cf. 185 E 6ff.). If F-ness is a perceptual feature, then, when the mind considers the question whether something is F, it draws on the testimony of the senses (cf. 185 B 10–12). If F-ness is a nonperceptual feature like being, then the mind considers the question whether something is F by itself. What little Plato has to say about how the mind goes about doing this makes no reference to some intellectual grasp. Plato is referring to comparisons and to reasonings the mind goes through to come to a judgment (186 A 10ff.; 186 B 8ff.; 186 C 2ff.), the kinds of things the mind does when it tries to decide a matter. And the fact that Plato is 187 A 5ff. characterizes what the mind does when it considers questons by itself as "doxazein," i.e., as coming to form a belief, certainly should warn us against assuming that some special power of the mind to grasp intelligible entities is appealed to here. All that seems to be appealed to is what the mind has to be able to do to form beliefs. And this is a great deal, though Plato here does not care to spell it out in any detail. To be able to form the belief that A is F, the mind has to have arrived at some idea of what it is to be for A and what it is to be for F-ness, or what it is to be for an F and it has to find out whether A is such as to be an F. What Plato here wants to emphasize is the mere fact that the perception is a purely passive affection (cf. 186 C 2 and 186 D 2), whereas the simplest belief even if it concerns a perceptual feature, requires and presupposes a great deal of mental activity. And he infers from this that since all this activity is needed to arrive at truth, perception itself does not give us truth and, hence, cannot be knowledge.

Now one may want to interpret the argument of 184–187 differently and argue thus: Plato distinguishes two kinds of questions, those the mind settles by itself and those the mind settles by relying on a sense. Since there are questions the mind has to settle by itself, and since, presumably, the answer to these questions can be known, we here have an argument which shows that knowledge is not to be identified with perception. But we do not have an argument, nor does Plato intend to argue, that perception never gives us knowledge. After all, there are questions for whose solution the mind relies on a sense. The answer to these questions seems to be provided by perception. It seems to me that this interpretation is wrong. Plato is quite careful never to say that some questions are settled by perception or by a sense. All questions are settled by the mind, though for some it does rely on perception. Thus, I take it that Plato wants to argue that even the question whether A is red is not settled by perception. We may be passively affected by the color red, but to form the belief that something is red presupposes and takes a great deal of activity on the part of the mind. Hence, we perceive the color red, but we do not, strictly speaking, perceive that A is red. Hence, knowledge, since it always involves belief, never is just a matter of perception.

The only textual evidence that seems to stand in the way of this interpretation is the following. In 186 B 11-C 5 we are told that whereas animals and we as children perceive many things right from birth, there are other things that it takes us a long time, much trouble, and some education to grasp. Surely, one will say, to see that something is red does not take much trouble and a lot of education. It is something any infant can do. But, it may be worth remembering that even the Stoics later will deny that children, properly speaking, perceive that something is red. For perception in this wider sense presupposes a state of the development of reason that allows us to articulate a visual impression in terms of concepts and that allows us to accept such an impression as true. Thus, even the simple judgment that something is red presupposes some notion of what it is to be and some notion of what it is to be red. And this we do not have right from birth. Nor is it given to us by perception, but only by reflection on what we perceive. What we perceive, strictly speaking, are just the proper objects of the different senses, e.g., colors in the case of sight (184 E 7ff.). Thus, strictly speaking, we do not even perceive the object of which we come to believe that it is red. And if this is so, it is even more difficult to see how we could be said to perceive that something is red, given this very narrow notion of perception.

Now, Plato, in restricting perception to a passive affection of the mind and in emphasizing the activity of the mind in forming beliefs, thinks of beliefs as something we deliberately arrive at after a good deal of consideration and ratiocination. As Plato puts it later in the dialogue (189 E-190 A), belief is the result of a silent discussion one leads with oneself. In the *Sophist* (263 Eff.) and in the *Philebus* (38 C-E), we get a similar view of belief. Thus, belief is conceived of as something that is actively espoused on the basis of some conscious, deliberate activity. This, no doubt, is an idealization of how we come to have beliefs. For many beliefs we just find ourselves with, and in their case there is no reason to suppose that we ever went through a process of deliberation as a result of which we espoused the belief. The Protagorean view, on the other hand, and the other views alluded to in the beginning, which are like it, assume that beliefs normally are something we just find ourselves with, which have grown on us, which we have just come by by being struck by things in a certain way. And they try to assimilate all beliefs to what they take to be the normal case. Hence, they emphasize the passive element in belief-formation. Thus, one can see why Plato should be interested in emphasizing how small the passive element in belief-formation is. To do so, he restricts the general notion of perception to sense-perception in such a narrow sense and, moreover, to such a narrow notion of sense-perception that we cannot even any longer be said to perceive that something is red. It is this philosophical motivation that underlies Plato's introduction of a narrow use of "aisthanesthai" in the sense of "sense-perception," a sense which the word did not have ordinarily and which it did not have in Plato's earlier writings.

PLATO AND TALK OF A WORLD IN FLUX: *TIMAEUS*
49a6–50b5

Donald J. Zeyl

FEW passages in the Platonic corpus have been subjected to scholarly analysis as extensively and exhaustively as has the passage of the *Timaeus* considered in this paper: the passage in which Plato introduces a problem whose solution requires the postulation of the "receptacle." The Greek of the passage is notoriously difficult to construe, and frequently ambiguous; indeed, Plato himself is conscious of the difficulty of properly articulating the problem and its solution (cf. 49a3,4; a7–b1; 50a4,5). My excuse for reexamining the passage is the fact that some recent studies of it have proposed a construction of the Greek and with it an interpretation of Plato's argument which, I am convinced, is demonstrably untenable, and part of my purpose is to forestall or undermine a consensus of interpretation of the passage not justified by the text.

All commentators agree that Plato intends to show (a) that the constituents of the physical world ("phenomena") are caught up in constant change (as is forcefully argued in the case of the "elements" at 49b7–c7) and (b) that this fact necessitates a reform in the use of certain locutions as referring expressions. But just what is the reform? The traditional view, as expressed by, e.g., Taylor[1] and Cornford,[2] took Plato's point to be one about our references to phenomena. They maintained that Plato proposed a new way of referring to phenomena, represented by the expression τὸ τοιοῦτον in favor of the intuitively natural τοῦτο, on the ground that the latter mode of reference could not be maintained in the face of the continual change characterizing phenomena. Their interpretation was vigorously contested, however, by Cherniss in a thorough, critical review of the older commentators.[3] Cherniss argued that Plato did not intend to recommend a new, adequate manner of

---

[1] A. E. Taylor, *A Commentary on Plato's Timaeus*, Oxford, 1928, p. 316.
[2] F. M. Cornford, *Plato's Cosmology*, London, 1937, pp. 178–180.
[3] H. Cherniss, "A Much Misread Passage in Plato's *Timaeus* (*Timaeus* 49C7–50B5)," *AJP* LXXV, 1954, pp. 113–130. Hereafter I shall refer to this paper and the ones mentioned in nn. 4 and 5 merely by the author's name.

referring to phenomena and to prohibit an old, inadequate one. According to Cherniss, Plato is outlawing references to phenomena as such, and is introducing things of another sort to which our expressions must refer. In other words, in Cherniss's view of the argument, expressions like πῦρ and ὕδωρ are not to be applied to phenomena at all, but should be assigned to certain "distinct and self-identical characteristics" represented by the locution τὸ τοιοῦτον ... Cherniss's interpretation was subsequently criticized by Norman Gulley,[4] who charged that it was "incoherent and self-refuting." Gulley's defense of the traditional interpretation and his criticisms of Cherniss were in turn attacked by E. N. Lee,[5] who undertook to reinstate Cherniss's position, though differing with him on several details.

In the following pages I shall present an interpretation which, though not, I think, the same as the traditional one, follows the traditional construction of the Greek in broad outline. My discussion will progress with reference to the above-mentioned parties to the dispute, and, where relevant, to some other commentators as well. Although the crucial passage begins at 49c7, proper methodology requires that the argument be interpreted in context,[6] and so I begin at 49a6:

Now what has been said is true, but we must speak more clearly about it. This, however, is difficult, particularly since it requires the raising of a preliminary problem about fire and its consorts in order to do so. For it is difficult to say of each of these which one is the sort of thing one must really call "water" rather than "fire," and which any one thing, rather than just any and everyone of them, in such a way as to employ some reliable and stable account. How then, and in what sense are we to speak of this very thing[7] and what is the problem about them that we must first properly work through? First, what we have just now[8] been calling "water" we see — so we think — condensing and turning into stones and earth; again, we see this same thing dissolving and dispersing, turning into wind and air, and air, when kindled, into fire, and fire upon being condensed and quenched, turning back again into the form of air, and air, coming together and thickening, cloud and mist, and from these when they are compressed still more, flowing water, and from water earth

---

[4] "The Interpretation of Plato, *Timaeus* 49D–E," *AJP* LXXXI, 1960, pp. 53–64.

[5] "On Plato's *Timaeus*, 49D4–E7," *AJP* LXXXVIII, 1967, pp. 1–28.

[6] As Lee rightly insists, pp. 2, 3, 15–17, 20ff. It will be seen that my view of the context differs sharply from his.

[7] τοῦτ' αὐτό must, I think (pace Lee, n. 5), refer to the receptacle itself. Cf. αὐτοῦ at a7. For λέγειν, "to speak of, to call" see *LSJ* s.v. λέγω III3,4.

[8] νῦν, i.e., in the immediate past, as ὠνομάκαμεν shows; *not* "now," i.e., in our present state of ignorance, as Lee (n. 7) seems to imply.

and stone once more, thus in a cycle passing on their becoming, so it seems.

Plato picks as his paradigm examples of items in the flux the celebrated four στοιχεῖα[9] although he clearly intends his argument to extend to all phenomena whatever (see 49e7). Nevertheless, his choice of the elements as paradigms must be significant, and its significance becomes apparent, I think, once the role of these four in previous cosmologies is recognized. The "elements," whether all four of them together (as Empedocles held) or only one of them (as, e.g., Anaximenes thought) were the basic stuffs of which the universe was made. All things consisted of, and could be resolved into, these "elements," but they themselves did not consist of, nor could be resolved into, anything else. In other words, the elements were the *basic substrata*. Plato's choice of the elements as his paradigms and his emphatically expressed point that they *do* resolve into something else — into each other, in fact — suggests that he means to challenge this privileged role of the elements. This observation will have some bearing on our overall interpretation of the argument.

Now the sentence in this passage which is crucial to the interpretation of 49c7ff is b2–5, and it must be understood correctly if Plato's solution to the problem there stated is to be properly interpreted. The crucial part of this sentence is the clause οὕτως ὥστε τινὶ πιστῷ καὶ βεβαίῳ χρήσασθαι λόγῳ. Lee comments on this sentence that "the difficulty is that our present ordinary ways of speaking cannot measure up to Plato's requirements of strictness and reliability . . . Since none of the elemental stuffs is free from change, no λόγος about any of them can be strictly secure."[10] He proceeds to connect the sentence, thus understood, with what Plato, on his reading, is saying at 49d3ff: ". . . in order to speak 'most securely' of the elements, we must not (as we do now) refer the term 'fire' (or whatever) to phenomenal stuff," adding in a note (n. 7) which clearly exhibits his construction of Plato's Greek in d5,6 that "we must renounce our ordinary way of speaking (and of thinking) about the world."

I do not think that Plato says or even implies in b2–5 or elsewhere in 48e2–49d7 that our "ordinary ways of speaking cannot measure up" to his requirements or that "no λόγος about any phenomena can be strictly secure." Nothing said in this sentence or paragraph, it seems to me, is

[9] Significantly, Plato does not use this term here. For his explicit rejection of its appropriateness, see 48b5–c2.

[10] Lee, pp. 2, 3.

compatible with, let alone an anticipation of, Plato's alleged later point that "we must not refer the term 'fire' . . . to phenomenal stuff." The first thing to be noticed about b2–5 is its last word, χαλεπόν. Plato is drawing our attention to something that is *difficult*, not something that is impossible or illegitimate. In view of the constant transformation of the elements (b7–c7) it is difficult to pick out any specimen of any one of the elements and call it "fire," "water," etc. *in such a way as to* (οὕτως ὥστε) *make use of a reliable and stable* λόγος.[11] This evidently does not mean that since such a λόγος is not employable in our references to phenomena, those references cannot legitimately be made. What it means is that it is difficult to make such references in a way that will satisfy a certain requirement which nevertheless must be satisfied if the references are to be justified. This requirement is the employment of a πιστὸς καὶ βέβαιος λόγος. Thus the solution to the difficulty will be the discovery of such a λόγος. In what follows I will argue that Plato announces it in 49d–e.

If this is right, then Plato is not getting ready to attack, but to defend our ordinary references to phenomena. He realizes that the flux poses a grave threat to our ordinary references to phenomena: since the water that filled my pond last spring has turned to air in the summer's heat, what right did I have in calling it "water" in the first place? Instead of capitulating to the force of this argument, I take Plato to be developing a strategy against it: we *can* go on happily referring to phenomena by their usual names, with one very crucial proviso. And the proviso is given at 49d7ff.

The λόγος that Plato must find if our ordinary references to phenomena are to saved must be trustworthy and stable in a way in which the λόγος of his predecessors was not. For on the old λόγος, i.e., on the old way of construing our references to phenomena and to the elements *in primis* we involve ourselves in absurdities and contradictions, since this λόγος construes the references as *identifying* references. On its terms, when I call the stuff in my pond "water" I do not *predicate* "water" of the stuff I am referring to (as I would if I described it as "cold" or "wet"); rather, I *identify* it as water. And, in the cosmologies of Plato's predecessors, the ultimate bearers of identity references, the ultimate or basic subjects (the linguistic counterpart to their ontological role as

---

[11] The term "account" by which I have translated λόγος above is almost as semantically versatile as the word it translates. In the present context I take it to mean "rationale," "theory," or, more precisely, "manner of construing," i.e., in this case of construing our references to phenomena. *Tim.* 38a1 furnishes an exact parallel. See *LSJ* s.v. λόγος III2.

basic substrata), were the elements. But now, when I, on the terms of this λόγος, *identify* the stuff in my pond as water, what am I going to say when it has turned to air? Shall I now identify it as air? But it's the same stuff! If I do, what happens to my former identification?[12] Am I not forced (at least) to contradict myself? Perhaps I might give it both (or, given the cycle, all four) names. But then how do I distinguish the "water" of my pond from the "air" into which it has evaporated? Maybe Anaximenes was right: it's all air. But why air? What sufficient reason is there to pick one element rather than another?

This λόγος, then, is neither reliable nor firm. It cannot be relied upon as adequate for our references to the elements (or to phenomena in general). Its use entails that if we want to continue to refer to them as we ordinarily do, we are forced to shift from one identification to another. Plato requires a λόγος which is free from these devastating consequences.

I now propose to turn to 49c7–50a4, of which I give a deliberately literal, annotated translation.[13] The notes will immediately follow the translation. I reserve for later comment the "gold" illustration of 50a–b5.

Since these severally thus never appear the same, of which of them would one not be ashamed of firmly asserting that it is some definite *this*, and not another thing (*i*)? It is not possible, but by far the safest course in making up our minds about them is to speak in the following way: what we always (*ii*) see coming to be at different times in different ways, such as fire, [it is safest] not to refer to fire as "this" but as "what is on each occasion such-and-such" (*iii*), nor to water as "this" but as "what is always such-and-such," nor to anything else as though it possessed some stability, of all the things at which we point, using the expressions "this" and "that" and think we are indicating something (*iv*). For it escapes, not awaiting the locutions "this" and "that" and "for this" and every locution which indicts them of being stable (*v*). But [it is safest] not to refer to them severally by these expressions (*vi*); rather, [it is safest] to call what is such-and-such, always recurring as similar in each and every case, just so (*vii*), and specifically, [it is safest to call] fire "what is such-and-such throughout," and so the whole of what has becoming (*viii*). But that in which each of them appears, continually coming to be in it,

---

[12] The natural reply that what was water is now air, is, of course, precluded by the view of water and air as στοιχεῖα. In fact, as will be seen, it is only on the supposition of Plato's new λόγος that this reply is at all coherent and helpful.

[13] Following established precedent. To prevent confusion with footnotes, the parts of the translation requiring annotation will be indicated by Roman numerals.

and out of which they perish again, that alone [it is safest] to refer to by the use of the terms "this" and "that"; however, that which is of a certain sort — hot or white or any one of the opposites — and all things composed of these, we must not call *that* any of these things (ix).

i

Cherniss (p. 114) insists that τοῦτο cannot be taken predicatively here but must be construed as the subject of ὄν, its antecedent being ποῖον (αὐτῶν). He translates: "concerning which of them could one without shame firmly assert that this is any particular thing and not another?" He bases his construction on a comparison with 49b4, which, he says, "indicates that in the present passage τοῦτο is the subject of ὄν, and ὁτιοῦν καὶ οὐκ ἄλλο the predicate." I do not see how 49b4 (where τοῦτο does not appear) sheds any light whatever on the syntactical role of τοῦτο in d2.[14] All that Cherniss's comparison with b4 can justify is taking ποῖον as subject of ὄν, and this is not disputed. There is another feature of Cherniss's translation that is troubling. By translating ποῖον αὐτῶν as "*concerning* which of them" (my italics), he dislodges this accusative from the syntactical role it most naturally and obviously has, that of being the subject of ὄν, in order to assign τοῦτο to that role. But there is no accusative of reference involved here, and if ποῖον is the subject of ὄν, τοῦτο can hardly be pressed into identical service.[15]

The general sense of the sentence is thus the following: Since the phenomenal elements never retain their identity (a résumé of the whole of b7–c7, as οὕτω shows), which of them can, without embarrassment, be declared to be some one specific thing, as distinct from something else? The job of τοῦτο which thus emerges is that of referring to something that is (thought to be) stable and identifiable, with permanent

[14] K. W. Mills, "Some Aspects of Plato's Theory of Forms," *Phronesis* XIII, 1968, pp. 145–170, esp. pp. 152–161, commenting on Cherniss's construction, writes: "What particularly commends Cherniss's method of construing this question is the way in which it brings it into relation with what Plato had already said at 49b2–5. Plato's exposition is thus given a coherence which on other interpretations it lacks" (p. 154, n. 13). I fail to see the coherence. Mills's own translation of the sentence (p. 154) neglects the τοῦτο altogether.

[15] On ὡς followed by the participle after a verb of saying (or thinking), see Kühner-Gerth, *Grammatik der griechischen Sprache*, 3d ed. 2, p. 94, n. 5; Smyth, *Greek Grammar*, par. 2120f; and Cherniss's comments on the construction at 50b3 (p. 126). The construction aptly suggests that the unwarily asserted belief that a phenomenal instance of one of the elements *is* some thing is, in Plato's view, questionable, to say the least.

characteristics which at any and all times distinguish it from other things. The ὅν, I think, is emphatic. Plato is as anxious here as he was at 38b to prohibit talking of γιγνόμενα as though they are ὄντα.[16]

ii

I take ἀεί with καθορῶμεν, as Cherniss does. It is tempting to take it with ἄλλοτε ἄλλῃ γιγνόμενον, as Gulley evidently does,[17] but I doubt that their relative positions in the text will allow it.

iii

We now come to the heart of the controversy. There is, as Lee notes, an ambiguity in the schema μὴ X ἀλλὰ Y προσαγορεύειν Z[18] which governs d5,6 (and, according to Lee, d7–e8 as well).[19] Thus it could be construed *either* as *A*:

μὴ "X" ἀλλὰ "Y" προσαγορεύειν Z, i.e., not to call the thing Z by the name "X" but by the name "Y" (hereafter called the *A*-reading),

---

[16] This is pretty clearly the point of 38b, a point that follows consistently from Plato's opening remarks at 27d6–28a1. He is concerned to point out that even such seemingly innocuous expressions as τὸ γιγνόμενον εἶναι γιγνόμενον are "inexact" (οὐδὲν ἀκριβές, b3) because they couple εἶναι with γιγνόμενα and thus speak of the latter as ὄντα. The argument has been read differently, however, by Cherniss ("*Timaeus* 38a–b5," *JHS* LXXVII, 1957, pp. 18–23), who interprets the "inaccuracy" to consist of the equivocality of the component expressions in the sentences under fire at b1–3, taken separately. But this breaks the continuity of 38b1–3 with the preceding argument at 37e1–38a8, where Plato has argued that ὄντα may not be talked about in terms which imply γένεσις (cf. a6, "which becoming has attached to what wanders in perception"). Plato makes the converse point in b1–3: we must not speak of γιγνόμενα in terms that are actually "attached" to ὄντα.

[17] See Gulley's translation, p. 53.

[18] Lee, p. 4 and n. 9. But Lee opts without prior argument for *B*, his only proffered reason being "to avoid the ambiguity." His actual reasons seem to emerge in the course of his criticism of Gulley (pp. 15–20), and it may be that the "parallelism" between d5,6 and d7–e6 is also a reason. See next note.

[19] A major point of Lee's in his discussion of these and the next lines of the text is that on his (*B*) reading of the schema, the schema is employed not only in the case of fire (d5,6) and of water (d6,7) but also in making the general point covering all phenomena (d7–e6). See his "analytic translation," p. 5 and nn. 10 and 11, p. 4. It is not clear, however, whether he intends to use it as support for a *B*-reading of the schema (as well as use it to show that Cherniss's interpretation of ἕκαστα [e4] is wrong).

or as *B*:

μὴ Χ ἀλλὰ Υ προσαγορεύειν "Ζ," i.e., not to call the thing Χ, but the thing Υ by the name "Ζ" (hereafter called the *B*-reading).

In what follows, I intend to defend the *A*-reading.[20] For the sake of clarity and brevity, I shall proceed in three stages by examining respectively (1) Cherniss's rejection of *A*, (2) Lee's rebuttal of Gulley's defense of *A*, and (3) the general framework of the argument, which, I shall argue, requires *A*.

1. Cherniss's objections to *A* are all listed on p. 116 of his paper. I shall examine them in the order in which they are raised.

a. His objection to the article in τὸ τοιοῦτον when this expression is construed as *secondary* object of προσαγορεύειν can be met by showing that in fact the *A*-reading (which so construes the expression) requires the article: it is needed to remind us of the fact that the expression is to refer to some *thing*, a *subject* which is temporarily qualified in a certain way (the "what" in "what is such-and-such"). This subject is the one announced in e7ff.

b. The construction of τοῦτο as taking up ὃ καθορῶμεν . . . γιγνόμενον on the basis of an alleged parallel at 49e7–50a1 (a considerable distance away) is weak, if not question-begging.

c. The "correspondence" of τοῦτο here to τοῦτο at d2 (as previously construed by Cherniss) has no argument value for one who rejects that previous construction (as I have done in *i* above).

d. Finally, the πῦρ in d6 is alleged to be "worse than redundant" on the *A*-reading (cf. Mills, p. 154, n. 14). This deserves closer scrutiny. Suppose we take Cornford's advice[21] and delete it from the text. Now the ὡς πῦρ of d5 has no syntactical connections with anything else in the sentence. Thus, on the *A*-reading the primary object of προσαγορεύειν must be the ὃ of two lines earlier — a considerable distance from this verb. Moreover, if Plato is operating with the schema μὴ Χ ἀλλὰ Υ προσαγορεύειν Ζ (as he clearly appears to be in these lines), then we *do* have definite values for Χ and Υ, but none for Ζ other than the ὃ (which cannot be considered a value in any case), and although ὡς πῦρ may *suggest* a value for it, it cannot supply one grammatically because of its isolated position. And for this reason, I suspect, Plato puts in πῦρ in d6 as the primary object of προσαγορεύειν. It is true

[20] Gulley (pp. 57–62) has offered some very trenchant criticisms of Cherniss's construction (especially as it introduces an intolerable ambiguity in the use of τοῦτο) to which this defense may be taken as supplementary.

[21] P. 179, n. 1.

that a slight anacolouthon thus results, but this is a small enough price to pay for the clarity gained.

2. I now turn to Lee's criticisms (pp. 15–20) of Gulley insofar as they are pertinent to a defense of *A*.

a. Gulley had argued (p. 58) that Plato's point in e2,3 (and by implication in e1 also) is obviously about our application of locutions like "this" and "that" to phenomena, and that Plato prohibits such applications. Consequently "consistency seemingly requires" that this should have been his point at d5 and 6 as well. Lee's reply to this ("all that consistency requires is *consistency*, not repetition!") shows that he has failed to see that the function of e1–4 is *explanatory*. What is wrong with calling phenomena "this?" Plato's answer is: to do so is to imply that what is so designated is stable *(ὥς τινα ἔχον βεβαιότητα)*, whereas in fact phenomena are not stable *(φεύγει γάρ . . .)* and so cannot be referred to by "this." What Plato is saying can be put into the following form: do not do X (1), for doing X (2) implies a state of affairs Y which is incompatible with doing X (3). Now it is true that (2) and (3) do repeat (1), but it will be readily seen that, given the explanatory context, such repetition is not at all unnatural.

b. Lee further argues (pp. 18, 19) that it is in fact unlikely that Plato's concern in d5 and 6 has been about the *word* τοῦτο since when he *does* explicitly wish to make a point about this word, he is ready (in the absence of quotation marks) to indicate this by some locution such as he employs at e1; e2,3; and 50a1,2. In this context Lee invokes the logician's distinction between "use" and "mention" and interprets Gulley's construction (with its quotation marks around τοῦτο in d5 and 6) as implying that Plato already *mentions* τοῦτο in d5 and 6, as well as in e1 and 50a1,2 (p. 18), and Lee thinks it strange that only the latter set of lines contain Plato's mentioning-devices, if Gulley is right. This makes it unlikely, according to Lee, that τοῦτο in d5 and 6 should be construed the way Gulley construes it. In reply, it can be said that it is not the case that Plato, even on Gulley's construction, *mentions* τοῦτο in d5 and 6; the mere appearance of quotation marks around a given expression does not suffice to show this. What Plato is doing with τοῦτο here is *using* this term, but using it *as a term*.[22] And so it is quite natural

[22] The difference between *mentioning* a word and *using* it *as a word* is indicated by the fact that in cases where a word *w* is mentioned, *w* can always be expanded into "the word *w*," whereas this is impossible in cases where *w* is merely used as a term. The following might serve as an illustration: in teaching my child good manners, I might say, "Don't call anyone 'dummy,' for 'dummy' is a nasty word." It should be obvious at once that only in the second case "dummy" can be expanded into "the word 'dummy.'"

that Plato, after *using* τοῦτο as a term (as in Gulley's translation and mine), goes on to *mention* it with a view to criticizing its use.

c. Another charge against Gulley is the "self-refuting character" of his interpretation. Lee finds the alleged new mode of referring to phenomena by τὸ τοιοῦτον difficult to reconcile with the fact that phenomena are "fugitive." But his question ". . . if they are as fugitive as all that [as described in e2–4], how can they offer any foothold even to the designation τοιοῦτον?" is answered by the mere observation that τὸ τοιοῦτον, unlike τοῦτο, just is *not* one of those terms the application of which implies the stability of its subject. Plato is not here arguing that the application of *any* term indicts its subject(s) of being stable; *that* is his point at *Theatetus* 182d–183b. What is said here at e2–4 is *not* that a phenomenon does not "abide" any description whatever; only that it just doesn't abide those that imply stability.[23]

3. There are several more general reasons for objecting to the B-reading. First, it does not provide a solution to the problem stated at b2–5. For this problem was *not*: what sort of things provides adequate references for terms like "fire," etc., but: how can we in a satisfactory manner use terms like "fire," etc., to refer to *these* (τούτων, b2), i.e., to the phenomenal elements. It is no solution to say: don't use these terms to refer to phenomena at all, but to something else. Second, as Gulley has observed, the B-reading introduces a *fourth* basic item into the economy of Plato's universe, a class of things which Cherniss calls "distinct and self-identical characteristics" (p. 128) and Lee speaks of as "recurrent, stable and determinate characters" (p. 27), thus making Plato's basic ontological framework consist of four instead of the three constituents which he himself allows at 48e–49a and 52a. Mills, who adopts the B-reading, has noticed the force of this objection and attempts to argue for the compatibility of the B-reading with the professed tripartite ontology. His solution is to take Plato's talk of τὸ τοιοῦτον as "referring to Forms, not to copies of Forms" (p. 154). This involves him, as he sees, in maintaining that Forms enter the

---

[23] Lee's subsequent question, "And even if that term could somehow get a grip on the phenomenon, how could it possibly satisfy Plato's demand for a πιστὸς καὶ βέβαιος λόγος?" rests upon his misinterpretation of this phase (see p. 127 above). On my interpretation of the phrase, the very application of τὸ τοιοῦτον to phenomena illustrates the employment (cf. χρήσασθαι, b5) of the λόγος. And further, to call a phenomenon τὸ τοιοῦτον is precisely "the most sure and certain by far (ἀσφαλέστατα μακρῷ)" manner of speaking about phenomena (cf. περὶ τούτων, d4, which, though strictly governed by τιθεμένους, is most naturally understood to go with λέγειν as well).

receptacle, which is clearly in conflict with what Plato actually says. His way around this is to suggest that "Plato assimilates the way in which Forms are received by space into the way people are reflected in mirrors."[24] As a statement about Plato's procedure here, this is patently false: there is no talk of mirrors in the entire passage. In any case, given the analogy, then just as people themselves don't really enter mirrors (but their reflections do), so Forms themselves don't really enter the receptacle (but their imitations do). But what is a reflection anyway? It is "a queer sort of object, and on examination is discovered not to be an object at all." Reflections are not things in their own right. The conclusion that Mills apparently wishes us to draw is that we cannot single out reflections or imitations of Forms as a distinct class of things at all; if anything, they are simply appearances of Forms. But surely this line of reasoning overreaches itself. For its result is that Plato now has only *two* basic ingredients in his cosmology: the Forms (including their images) and the receptacle. But the three items listed by Plato in both passages cited above are: (1) Forms, (2) imitations of Forms, and (3) the receptacle. Plato clearly *does* draw an ontological line between Forms and their imitations; they are distinguished as two of the three εἴδη.

Third, and in consequence of the last point, what is the role of the τό τοιοῦτον objects in terms of the division of labor outlined at 50b–d? Cherniss identifies the "self-identical characteristics" with the μιμήματα of the Forms. But the μίμημα of 48e6 is explicitly said to "possess becoming" (γένεσιν ἔχον, 49a1; cf. e7), and its counterpart in the repetition of the division at 50c7–d2 is τὸ γιγνόμενον, i.e., the phenomenal, becoming thing. Further, the position that "fire" may not refer to phenomenal stuff but to such a characteristic is implicitly refuted at 51b4–6, where the names of the elements are unhesitatingly given to the appropriately modified parts of the receptacle.[25] Lee has also rejected Cherniss's assignment of the μιμήματα; in his view[26] the μιμήματα are the particular occurrences of the stable characters, and

[24] I wish to record my protest against the tendency among commentators to exegete the passage by means of a "mirror" analogy. The receptacle *receives* and mirrors *reflect*, and the analogy here escapes me. The mirror certainly never assumes the momentary shapes of its "reflections." Surely Plato's own "gold" analogy is much more apposite.

[25] In his discussion of these lines on p. 129 Cherniss does not appear to have noticed that they jeopardize his thesis.

[26] "On the Metaphysics of the Image in Plato's *Timaeus*," *The Monist* L, 1966, pp. 367–368.

not those characters as such. But it is not clear where he would locate the "characters" themselves in Plato's threefold scheme.[27]

iv

The construction of the clause ὅσα . . . ἡγούμεθα τι has also divided the commentators. As one might expect, the *A*-readers, who take ἄλλο μηδὲν (τούτων)[28] as *primary* object of a supplied προσαγορεύειν, will consequently take ὅσα to refer to the phenomena which we are not allowed to call "this." The *B*-readers, who construe it as *secondary* object, will take ὅσα to refer to the "things" to which such predicates as "fire" (as in "this is fire") refer.[29]

The division is, moreover, carried over into the syntax within the clause itself. Thus Taylor, Cornford, and Gulley (the *A*-readers) construe ὅσα as the object of δεικνύντες, and Cherniss, Lee, and Mills (the *B*-readers) construe it either as object (Cherniss, Mills) or as subject (Lee) of δηλοῦν. Now this difference of construction is the consequence of consistently carrying through their constructions of the preceding lines. Thus, on the *A*-reading, we point to phenomena, call them "this," and in so doing we think (mistakenly) that we are pointing

[27] Moreover, it is not clear to me how Cherniss's interpretation of these lines and the moral he draws from it (p. 128, suppl. remark 1) can be consistent with his own interpretation of an argument in the *Theaetetus*, the argument against the "Fluxers" (181bff) which he takes as an "indirect proof" for the theory of Forms (see "The Philosophical Economy of the Theory of Ideas," reprinted in R. E. Allen, ed., *Studies in Plato's Metaphysics*, New York, 1965). The hypothesis of Forms is necessary if the phenomena are to be saved. The threat to phenomena here is a consequence of the flux ontology: references to phenomena are impossible under its conditions. Now surely, if the hypothesis is to avert this consequence, the least it must do is somehow guarantee our references to phenomena. But then why is it that in the *Timaeus*, where the Forms are present with all their metaphysical power, they are not invoked for that purpose?

[28] The τούτων is (happily, for the *A*-readers) not expressed.

[29] This at least seems to be the role which Cherniss gives to ὅσα as secondary object. And thus it is inaccurate to say, as Gulley does (p. 58), that on Cherniss's reading the reference of the clause is the *predicates* "fire," etc. (What kind of "things" these referents must be will be discussed momentarily below.) But Gulley's charge does go home against Lee, whose interpretation of δηλοῦν (elaborately defended on pp. 9–12) necessitates the construction of ὅσα as referring to *predicates*, i.e., to the units of language themselves, and not to the "things" to which they supposedly refer. But this is surely anomalous, and the anomaly is akin to Lee's failure to distinguish *mentioning* a word from *using* it *as a word* (n. 22 above). On Lee's interpretation Plato is forbidding us to call certain things *predicates*. (Lee's rendition of ὅσα as ". . . by any other of the terms which . . ." in his analytic translation (p. 5) obscures this anomaly.)

at what is something in its own right. Now it is pretty clear (and apparently agreed by all) that what we are pointing to must be phenomena, whether this actually said in the text or not. But, on the B-reading, the ὅσα cannot be actual phenomena (cf. Cherniss, p. 117, n. 5 sub fin.) since ὅσα is a sort of variable for *secondary* objects. And what would these secondary objects be? They are the fictitious "entities" which we naively think exist, and can be referred to by predicates such as "fire." In other words, they are putatively stable phenomena. But since Plato does not countenance such entities, he cannot very well say that we in fact do point to them. Hence, on this reading, ὅσα is not a suitable object for δεικνύντες. (For Lee's different way of taking this clause, see above, n. 29).

Now from a purely syntactical point of view, I think that the construction given to this clause by the A-readers is the easier and the more natural one (though the other is not impossible). First, ὅσα goes more naturally with δεικνύντες, the word that immediately follows it in the text, than with δηλοῦν, which is a considerable distance from it. Second, the B-readers leave δεικνύντες hanging by itself (the dative that follows is clearly governed by προσχρώμενοι), as their translations show.[30]

v

All commentators are agreed that φεύγει . . . ὑπομένον describes a fleeting phenomenon. Consistently with his reading of the previous lines, Cherniss takes a supplied τοῦτο (in d7) as the grammatical antecedent of φεύγει (p. 117, n. 5). Lee rejects such a grammatical connection (p. 6) and claims that the subject of φεύγει is just such a thing at which we point and about which we talk, as in e1. I think Lee is right in locating the subject of φεύγει where he does, but this does not rule out any grammatical connection with what has preceded. Consistently with my previous reading, therefore, I take ἄλλο μηδέν (τούτων) as the grammatical antecedent of φεύγει. Since the ἄλλο is itself any specimen member of the whole class ὅσα δεικνύντες, and the subject of φεύγει is itself also any specimen member of the same class, there is no reason, on the A-reading, to deny φεύγει a specific grammatical antecedent.

The switch from the singular φεύγει . . . ὑπομένον to the plural αὐτά (e4) has also arrested the commentators. Cherniss accounts for it by

---

[30] See the translations of Cherniss and Lee. I find Mills's translation, which apparently construes τι as the object of δεικνύντες, impossible.

attributing to Plato an immediate and unexplained switch from talking about the "phenomenon" to talking about the "multiple and transient phases of the phenomenal flux" (n. 7). Gulley criticizes this explanation and accounts for the switch by suggesting that ὅσα is the antecedent of αὐτά, an interpretation which is closed to Cherniss since he does not believe that ὅσα refers to actual phenomena. Although the interruption of the singular φεύγει ... ὑπομένον does make such a grammatical connection difficult, I believe that the reference of αὐτά is in fact the same as that of ὅσα. For the subject of φεύγει, as we saw, is any specimen member of the ὅσα class, and therefore represents that class as a whole; thus whatever locutions are inappropriate to such a representative member of the class are accordingly inappropriate to all members.

vi

I take ἕκαστα as primary object of λέγειν and ταῦτα as secondary object. Cherniss and Lee, understandably, reverse this (Mills takes ταῦτα ἕκαστα together as secondary object). But ἕκαστον and its plural elsewhere in the passage refer consistently to momentarily distinguishable phenomena. (As in d1; see my translation above. Also, I believe, at e5 and again at e8, where, I am sure, the reference is to phenomena as such, and not to "characteristics," whether distinct and self-identical or recurrent and episodic. See n. 40 below.) This suggests a similar reference here, and if this is right, the role of ἕκαστα as secondary object is precluded.

ταῦτα, then, is secondary object of λέγειν. For the reason noted by Taylor,[31] I doubt that ταῦτα is simply the plural of τοῦτο, the secondary object of the previous line. Accordingly, with Taylor I take ταῦτα as *referring* to the various τοῦτο expressions whose legitimate application to phenomena Plato denies, and not as itself the plural of those expressions.

vii

The construction of e5 and 6 has presented a problem for those who adopt the *A*-reading. The οὕτω is awkward and in need of an apology

---

[31] P. 318. Also noted by Cherniss, p. 119. It may, however, be possible that the presence of ἕκαστα justifies such a construction of ταῦτα: just as ἕκαστα collectively designates a group of things each of which is a ἕκαστον, so ταῦτα may collectively designate a group of things each of which may (properly or improperly) be called τοῦτο.

if τὸ τοιοῦτον . . . συμπάντων (either in part or in its entirety; Cherniss has presented good reasons for the latter alternative, pp. 120–121) is, like the previous occurrences of τὸ τοιοῦτον to be construed as a secondary object (in this case, of καλεῖν). But on this interpretation, the role of οὕτω is far from clear. Cherniss is right in insisting (against Taylor)[32] that the function of οὕτω is to refer backward, not forward (p. 121). Cornford takes οὕτω as "resuming the long phrase that precedes,"[33] a construction endorsed by Gulley (p. 54, n. 4). But this is awkward, to say the least.

The problem is resolved if we take τὸ τοιοῦτον as *primary* object of καλεῖν, and translate the οὕτω as "just that," i.e., as referring to the primary object and giving it the role of secondary object as well. Thus X οὕτω καλεῖν means X καλεῖν "X".[34] Plato's point is then simply the following: Each and every phenomenal thing is something that recurrently turns up similar to what it has been on a prior occasion and to what it will be again on some later occasion as it passes through the cosmic cycle again and again. Thus what is fire now, has previously been, and will later be again, fire. But it is only intermittently fire, never permanently. Consequently, this is how we should speak of it: not as a permanent "this," but as a recurrent "such-and-such."[35]

viii

The clauses καὶ δὴ καὶ . . . γένεσιν apply the general point just made, first to fire, and second, to all phenomena in the realm of becoming whatever. Thus all instances of phenomenal fire, and all phenomena in general, should be described each as τὸ τοιοῦτον . . .

It is curious to note that both Taylor and Cornford at this juncture

[32] P. 318.

[33] P. 179, n. 4.

[34] I owe this construction to a suggestion of Professor G. E. L. Owen. It may be that Eva Sachs has anticipated it (see Cherniss, p. 122). It is different in sense from the interpretation which Hackforth gave to his similar construction (*CQ* XXXVIII, 1944, pp. 36–37). Hackforth translates οὕτω as "accordingly" and glosses: "the right way to indicate a quality is by an adjective, such as πυρῶδες or ὑδαρές." But not only does this recommendation find no support elsewhere in the passage; it also contradicts Hackforth's own general interpretation of the argument, viz., that "the purpose of the whole context is not to correct our ordinary *reference* of the terms fire, air, etc." (p. 36).

[35] The use of οὕτω with the passive of καλεῖν is well recognized; see the reference in *Thesaurus Linguae Graecae* IV 871, with example in Diodorus. Although this does not *necessarily* justify the use with the active, it gives some plausibility to it.

slip into a *B*-construction of this clause. In Taylor's case this is due to his interpretation of οὖτω as referring forward to secondary objects of καλεῖν such as "fire," "water," "stone," etc.[36] This leads him to construe καὶ δὴ καὶ as an epexegetic connective (a sense that it does not naturally have) and πῦρ as a specimen secondary object of καλεῖν, thus pushing τὸ διὰ παντὸς τοιοῦτον into the role of primary object. Cornford, who does not share Taylor's interpretation of οὖτω, nevertheless follows him in his construction of the καὶ δὴ καὶ clause.[37]

The anomaly was noted by Hackforth,[38] who proposed a colon after καλεῖν and understanding ἐστίν in the καὶ δὴ καὶ clause, with πῦρ as its subject and τὸ διὰ παντός τοιοῦτον as its object. The argument would then proceed as a syllogism. But a syllogism would be rather stilted in this context. In fact, as Cherniss saw (n. 10), the conclusion of the supposed syllogism is not even expressed. Moreover, Hackforth's proposal also entails a deviation from the usual sense of καὶ δὴ καὶ.

Gulley has avoided both the anomaly of Taylor and Cornford and the pitfalls of Hackforth's attempt to correct it. He translates the clause in much the same way as I have done. This translation has drawn the fire of Lee, who objects to it, not on argued grounds, but by appealing to the authority of "Hellenists of stature" and to an intuitive sense of "the force of the Greek." He does not attempt to show *how* the force of the Greek is violated by this translation (pp. 19–20).

The construction of the clause καὶ ἅπαν ὅσονπερ ἂν ἔχῃ γένεσιν provides another opportunity to test the viability of the *B*-reading. The ἅπαν ... is clearly parallel to πῦρ of the preceding clause (cf. Cherniss, n. 12) and thus, on the *B*-reading, secondary object of καλεῖν. But now, since πῦρ on this reading designates one of the "distinct and self-identical characteristics," it follows that ἅπαν designates the class, not of phenomena, but of "distinct and self-identical characteristics" that belong to generation.[39] It is essential, on this interpretation, that the subject of ἔχῃ γένεσιν should not be any phenomenal thing(s). But this is surely questionable. The expression γένεσιν ἔχον occurs at 49a1 and refers to one of the three classes in the economy of the

---

[36] P. 318.

[37] P. 179.

[38] P. 36.

[39] Cherniss writes (n. 12): "The *only* factors *in generation* that can properly be called by the distinct names, 'fire,' 'air,' 'water,' etc. are the characteristics which being perpetually identical are severally distinct ..." (my italics). The expression "in generation" is apparently invoked to give some force to the ἔχῃ γένεσιν in the text. Certainly Cherniss's "only," which supposedly picks out a subclass of "factors in generation," ill accords with Plato's ἅπαν.

universe. Its equivalent in the repetition of this classification at 50c7–d2 is τὸ γιγνόμενον, which in the *Timaeus* is used regularly to refer to (the realm of) phenomena. The reference of the καὶ ἅπαν clause, then, is unmistakably to phenomena. Thus either the parallel with πῦρ must be given up (an impossibility) or it must be recognized that πῦρ itself refers to phenomenal fire.

ix

In the first part of this sentence Plato declares that only the receptacle, in which phenomena[40] appear as "coming to be" and out of which they "perish," is entitled to the reference of τοῦτο. It is not quite clear what he is saying in the second part of the sentence. He is *either* (a) prohibiting the application of "this" and the like to things that are qualified in some way (these are, in my view, phenomena, similarly described at 49e5), or (b) prohibiting the attribution of qualitative terms to the receptacle. Cherniss insists on (b), condemning (a) as "perverse."[41] Although (b) is just as plausible grammatically, I have opted for (a); the sentence is clearly parallel to 50b2–3, τὸ δὲ τρίγων-ον . . . ὄντα, and thus the construction given to the present sentence depends on the viability of the construction to be given to that sentence in the "gold example."

I turn now to the "gold example" (50a4–b5):

But we must venture to speak of this yet once again, and more clearly. If someone were molding all shapes in gold and went steadily on remolding each one into every other, then if someone (else) were to point at one of them and were to ask "what is it?", it would be far the safest with regard to truth to say "gold," but as for "triangle" and whatever other shapes came to be in it, [it would be far the safest] never to say that they are these (x) since in fact they change while one makes the statement, but should he be willing to accept, with some degree of safety, "what is such-and-such," to be content (xi).

---

[40] That ἕκαστα must refer to phenomena and not to the "perpetually identical characteristics which are severally distinct" (Cherniss, n. 13) is suggested by ἐγγιγνόμενα, a compound of ἐν and γιγνόμενα — thus virtually describing the ἕκαστα as γιγνόμενα — and proved by ἀπόλλυται, which means "perish," "cease to exist" (cf. Cebes' fears about the soul at *Phd.* 70a and 87d), and not merely "pass away," as Cherniss translates it. See *LSJ* s.v. ἀπόλλυμαι.

[41] For a sound criticism of Cherniss's procedure here, see Gulley, p. 60.

x

As Lee has noted,[42] the "gold example" is framed around three possible replies to the "what is it?" question at b1. The first (the "safest") reply is to say, "It's gold." No one disputes that this is the answer, but the significance of the question, and hence that of the answer, requires some comment. For the reference of "it" in the question is not simply to the lump of gold as such, but to the gold as now having some particular shape, as the αὐτῶν ἕν of the previous lines makes clear. This means that the questioner would expect a different reply if the lump had a different shape, or again, that as soon as the shape changed he could ask the question all over again. But the "safest" answer undercuts this expectation. For when full weight is given to the question (which asks for an *identification* of what the goldsmith has in his hands: surely there is some emphasis on the ἐστί) it is seen that such replies as "triangle," "square," etc., fail to satisfy the requirements of the question since they μεταξὺ τιθεμένου μεταπίπτει. As what does the lump *remain*, as gold or as a triangle? Surely if the requirements of the "what is it?" question are to be most securely met, the reply must be: "gold,"

How does the analogy apply to what has preceded?[43] The "gold-as-such" is the analogue to the receptacle, and the "gold-shaped-in-a-particular-way" is the analogue to a phenomenon (or perhaps to the world of phenomena in general). Thus when we point to a phenomenon, e.g., a flame of fire, and ask "what is it?" the safest answer would be to say, "it is [part of (cf. 51b4–6)] the receptacle." For it may come and cease to be fire but it remains permanently (part of) the receptacle.

This leads to the second possible answer (b2–3). The difficulty here is the interpretation of ταῦτα ὡς ὄντα. Cherniss translates: ". . . that these are," and interprets the prohibition as an injunction "never to say 'this is triangle,' 'this is square,'" etc." (n. 17). This interpretation is governed by his view of Plato's earlier injunction not to apply "this" to phenomena, which he takes to come to an injunction not to say "this

[42] In another paper, "On the 'Gold-Example' in Plato's *Timaeus* (50A5–B5)," originally given at the 1965 meeting of the Society for Ancient Greek Philosophy and now printed in *Essays in Ancient Greek Philosophy*, ed. John P. Anton with George L. Kustas, Albany, N.Y., 1971, pp. 219–235; here p. 219. Further references to this paper will be indicated by "Lee*".

[43] Lee's interpretation of the "gold-example" leads him to reject the view (held by Cherniss) that the example parallels (better: illustrates) the whole of 49d–e. But surely Plato *intends* it as an illustration of his previous point; cf. αὐτοῦ πέρι at a5. See Lee*, p. 222.

is fire" of phenomenal fire.[44] Lee's construction of the phrase is more plausible. He takes the ταῦτα as referring back to the various σχήματα of b2 and construes: "never to speak of those — which alter even while one speaks — as being" (Lee*, p. 224), and gives a very plausible defense of his interpretation. But he rejects the view that τὸ τοιοῦτον at b4 takes up the τὸ τοιοῦτον locutions earlier in the argument, and rejects the view that Plato is drawing a contrast between τὸ δὲ τρίγωνον ... ὄντα and ἐὰν ἄρα καὶ ... ἀγαπᾶν. I believe that the contrast is nevertheless there, and that the latter phrase *allows* τρίγωνον, etc., as an answer to the "what is it?" question, with a certain proviso, and so I take it that the former *forbids* this answer without it: the proviso being that the subject so described (by, e.g., "triangle") should be viewed not as a τοῦτο but as τὸ τοιοῦτον. Hence in the present clause I believe that we are given the prohibition to speak of the triangularly shaped gold as "this." Thus I take ταῦτα in b3 as playing a role similar to ταῦτα in 49e4 and τούτων in 50a4, viz., as referring to the various τοῦτο expressions (or else, if n. 31 has successfully justified a precedent, as itself being the plural of those expressions).

The presence of quotation marks around "triangle" in my translation shows that I take τρίγωνον as already an alternative reply to the "what is it?" question. The situation we are thus to envisage is this: suppose the goldsmith *doesn't* give the "safest" reply, but instead answers "triangle." Is this an acceptable answer? I take Plato to be saying: no and yes. It all depends on how you construe the logical job of "triangle."

xi

So far, then, we have learned (1) that the "safest" answer to the "what is it?" question is "gold" and (2) that the answer "triangle," etc., where the triangle is considered a "this" is unacceptable. The last clause, ἀλλ' ἐὰν ... ἀγαπᾶν, tells us that the answer "triangle" where the triangle is considered as "what is such-and-such" *is* acceptable. It is an answer which, while not as safe as the safest, nevertheless can be given "with some degree of safety" (μετ' ἀσφαλείας τινος).

But though we must be content if the questioner will accept it, this does not mean, as Lee holds, that the answer itself is a "second-best" answer (Lee*, p. 223; cf. pp. 226–228). Nor can I accept Lee's view

[44] Cf. Lee, who characterizes the whole of *Timaeus* 49–50 as "concerned with the logic of statements involving ostension" (Lee*, p. 231).

of τὸ τοιοῦτον. His main reason for rejecting the standard view that τὸ τοιοῦτον is simply a further instance of the τὸ τοιοῦτον locutions earlier and now brought into the gold example is the absence of the adverbs and adverbial phrases that had accompanied all the previous appearances of the expression. But surely the very variety of the modifiers used suggests that no one of them has been christened as a technical component of the τὸ τοιοῦτον formula, and thus that each is dispensable. In fact, in only one of the four previous occasions is the adverbial modifier encased within the locution (at 49e6,7), thus justifying some doubt as to whether the adverbs were really meant to be part of the formula at all. Further, it is arguable that τὸ ὁποιονοῦν τι in a2 is itself an echo of τὸ τοιοῦτον[45] and here the adverbs are wholly lacking. More seriously, however, if τὸ τοιοῦτον in b4 has the function which Lee assigns to it, we must attribute to Plato a rather violent change in the sense given to an expression which, on any reading, is a key expression in Plato's argument.

But there are further difficulties. If τὸ τοιοῦτον in b4 means merely something like "such an answer," i.e., one in terms of "triangle," etc., then just why is it that "triangle" is an answer forbidden by the criteria of "safest" answers but *allowed* by the criteria of the moderately safe answers? Lee suggests that the difference lies not in the logical nature of the answer itself but in the degree of philosophical sophistication of the questioner. Thus he is led to interpret ἀσφάλεια as "an inward feeling of security or confidence," i.e., as subjective assurance (Lee*, p. 226),[46] and to sketch the questioner as someone who is apparently not able to grasp the significance of the safest answer. It follows from this that, had the questioner the requisite philosophical astuteness, the answer in terms of τὸ τοιοῦτον (on any interpretation of that phrase) would be one which he would *not* be entitled to accept, Lee goes to some length to support this interpretation by citing other passages in which Plato recommends different teaching procedures for pupils of different philosophical ability (Lee*, pp. 228-230). But in these cases it is clear just how the procedure recommended for the less

---

[45] The reference of τὸ ὁποιονοῦν τι must surely be to some qualified *thing* (as the article shows) and not to some quality. Thus θερμόν and λευκόν are specimen qualities that this thing might have. The expression is thus a sort of variable for phenomena; and on the *A*-reading defended above, τὸ τοιοῦτον has an identical function.

[46] As Lee recognizes, there is clearly a contrast between the μακρῷ ἀσφαλέστατα answer and the μετ' ἀσφαλείας τινος answer (Lee*, pp. 223-224). But if the "safety" of the latter is subjective, that of the former must be likewise — an interpretation that can hardly be sustained by the context.

gifted is appropriate to their state of enlightenment. In the *Timaeus*, however, if Lee is right, this is lacking. We are not told, nor can we guess, just *why* the answer "triangle" *is* suitable for someone less philosophically able. We are apparently simply told that an answer which, strictly speaking, is wrong, is nevertheless right in some cases *only* because the person to whom it is given is a certain sort of person. This seems to me hardly plausible. To be sure, we *are* told that an answer which, strictly speaking, is wrong, is, on a not so strict view, right. But this has nothing to do with the state of the questioner, and everything to do with the nature of the answer.[47]

On my view, the τὸ τοιοῦτον takes up the previous τὸ τοιοῦτον phrases and provides the necessary and sufficient condition for whatever "safety" the answer "triangle" might possess. It is precisely because we refer to what is τὸ τοιοῦτον when we point to the triangular lump of gold and call it "triangle" that the answer is viable at all. And the questioner may well be reluctant to accept his, not because he is philosophically naive, but because he has been trained on the old λόγος (see my comments on 49a6–d4 above). For he is wont to construe all answers to the "what is it?" question as identifications, i.e, as implying that the answer permanently describes the subject in question. Thus he might insist that what he is pointing to either is or is not (to be identified as) a triangle; that we can't have it both ways. Plato's recommendation then is that we must try to persuade him to see that his basic assumption is wrong; that to call the triangularly shaped lump of gold a triangle is after all a justifiable procedure in spite of its transience. It is justifiable precisely because it is not an identification of a permanent object.

It should be noted that the answer recommended in this clause is just as philosophically legitimate as the first answer considered. Its lesser safety must not be sought here.[48] But where must it be sought?

---

[47] Lee has carefully analyzed the meanings of ἐθέλειν, δέχεσθαι, and ἀγαπᾶν as here used in order to support his interpretation. But even if we accept the meanings of these terms for which Lee plausibly argues, given his general interpretation, an anomaly comes to the surface. We are to be content if the questioner is willing to accept a certain sort of answer to the "what is it?" question, i.e., we must not expect anything *more* than that. This suggests that we might well expect the questioner to be reluctant to accept this answer, and we need only overcome his reluctance. But why should the questioner be reluctant to accept the answer "triangle" to his question? What *other* answer might he have preferred?

[48] Cf. the fact that in the *Phaedo* Plato distinguished a "safe" hypothesis (100d8; 101d1–3; 105b7–c1) and a "cleverer" hypothesis (105c2), the latter being, by implication, less safe than the former. But in this case, the less safe of the two is also the philosophically more sophisticated. It is the "safest"

Why is the answer "triangle" less safe than the answer "gold?" Because it does not fulfill the requirements of the "what is it?" question in its obvious, straightforward sense, the sense in which it asks for the identification of the given subject and carries with it the requirement of permanence (cf. 37e3ff). The answer "gold" satisfies those requirements; the answer "triangle" does not. But then the answer "gold" does not satisfy all our "what is it?" questions. To be told that the gold triangle at which he is pointing is "gold" and then to be told that the gold square at which he subsequently points is also "gold" is not likely to satisfy the questioner, who asked the "what is it?" question expecting a different answer in each case. He will feel that his question has been misunderstood. Thus the question must also bear a sense in which "triangle" and "square" can be offered as different and both acceptable answers to it. And this sense is one which doesn't require an identification of the subject, but a description of how it is presently qualified.

Having looked at the argument, we are now in a position to determine its overall meaning. We saw that Plato's discussion began with the statement of a difficulty, viz., that of referring to phenomena (represented by the "elements") by their usual names and thus distinguishing them in a way that would be guaranteed by a πιστός καὶ βέβαιος λόγος. Plato presents his solution to this problem in the passage just analysed, *Timaeus* 49c7–50b5. That is, he provides the logical condition by which references to phenomena by their usual names will be justified. And the condition is this: when we refer to a given phenomenon by the term "fire," we must not think that we are referring to what is τοῦτο, but rather to what is τὸ τοιοῦτον.

But just how does the description τὸ τοιοῦτον satisfy the conditions of a πιστὸς καὶ βέβαιος λόγος in a way in which the description τοῦτο does not? Because τοῦτο decribes a thing as being an entity in its own right, a permanent subject which, while possibly undergoing various modifications, yet retains its identity. And nothing in the phenomenal world is entitled to such status. The description τὸ τοιοῦτον, on the other hand, merely describes its referent as being an *attribute* of some-

---

(100d8) one that is also called "ignorant" (105c; cf. 100d3–4). If Plato's usage of "safe" here is at all a clue to his usage of this notion in our passage, then the "safest" answer is *less* philosophically sophisticated than the answer that has "some degree of safety," a conclusion quite the reverse of Lee's position.

thing *else*. Thus Plato's justification for the reference of "fire," etc., to phenomena is the new logical role that he assigns to those terms: they are to be viewed as picking out a recurrent attribute of something else. In other words, these terms are to be construed as logically (though not grammatically) *adjectival*. And this is precisely what the πιστὸς καὶ βέβαιος λόγος is: the construction of our nominal references to phenomena as adjectival descriptions of some basic, permanent subject worthy of that status. This subject is the receptacle, for only *it* can be designated as τοῦτο.

It should be apparent that this interpretation of the text shows Plato as introducing (or using) a quasi-technical sense of the expressions τοῦτο and τόδε and τὸ τοιοῦτον. The first two denote what is an ontological or logical subject, the last denotes what is an ontological or logical attribute. Now the explicitly technical use that Aristotle makes of these expressions and similar others corresponds to the use Plato is giving them. Aristotle uses these terms ubiquitously in his logic and metaphysics (τόδε τι or some variant and τοιόνδε or some variant) to make precisely this distinction. Thus already in the *Categories* (3b10–23) Aristotle uses them to distinguish primary substance from secondary substance: the former τόδε τι σημαίνει, whereas the latter μᾶλλον ποῖον τι σημαίνει, and this corresponds to his view that primary substance is not, whereas secondary substance is (in relevant instances) "said of a subject." The point is made in the *Sophistici Elenchi* (178b37–38) that "man," since it refers to a κοινόν, is not τόδε τι, ἀλλὰ τοιόνδε. "Coriscus" refers to a τόδε τι, and it is clear that there, as in the *Categories*, the distinction is valid because Coriscus, unlike man, is a basic subject. In *Metaphysics* Z-13 (1039a1–2) none of the "common predicates" indicate a τόδε τι, but a τοιόνδε. This is no doubt due to the fact that anything that can be predicated of a plurality cannot itself be a *basic* subject. In Z-8 (1033b22–25) Aristotle uses the terms in this technical sense, not indeed to distinguish here what he called primary and secondary substance, but to provide an analysis of what he had called primary substance. Here it is the εἶδος which, though it is itself not an individual, is necessary to the individuality of particular things. This εἶδος is τὸ τοιόνδε and its presence in the individual allows us to call the latter now not simply τόδε τι but τόδε τοιόνδε, i.e., an individual basic subject qualified in a particular way, making it the individual it is.

Thus it appears that Plato's use of τοῦτο, τόδε, and τὸ τοιοῦτον is the direct ancestor of Aristotle's admittedly technical use of such locutions. Whether or not Plato was the first to put these terms to such use,[49] he certainly fixes their currency as technical, and prepares them for employment in Aristotle's logic and metaphysics.[50]

UNIVERSITY OF RHODE ISLAND

[49] Simplicius (*In de caelo*, 294.23–295.26) quotes Aristotle *(Περὶ Δημοκρίτου)* as attributing to Democritus a term that may well be τόδε as a name for his "substances" (besides ὄν and ναστόν).

[50] I wish to thank especially Professor G. E. L. Owen for his suggestions and encouragement. Thanks are also due to Professors John M. Cooper and Stanford Cashdollar for discussion of various points. I alone am responsible for the defects that remain.

ACKNOWLEDGMENTS

White, Nicholas P. "Inquiry." *Review of Metaphysics* 28 (1974): 289–310. Reprinted with the permission of Catholic University of America. Courtesy of *Review of Metaphysics*.

Irwin, T.H. "Plato's Heracleiteanism." *Philosophical Quarterly* 27 (1977): 1–13. Reprinted with the permission of Basil Blackwell Ltd. Courtesy of Yale University Sterling Memorial Library.

White, Nicholas P. "Forms and Sensibles: *Phaedo* 74B–C." *Philosophical Topics* 15 (1987): 197–214. Reprinted with the permission of the University of Arkansas, Department of Philosophy. Courtesy of Yale University Sterling Memorial Library.

White, Nicholas P. "Perceptual and Objective Properties in Plato." *Apeiron* 22 (1989): 45–65. Reprinted with the permission of *Apeiron*. Courtesy of *Apeiron*.

Taylor, C.C.W. "Forms as Causes in the *Phaedo*." *Mind* 78 (1969): 45–59. Reprinted with the permission of the Oxford University Press. Courtesy of Yale University Sterling Memorial Library.

Gosling, J. "*Republic* Book V: τὰ πολλὰ καλά etc." *Phronesis* 5 (1960): 116–28. Reprinted with the permission of Van Gorcum en Co. B.V. Courtesy of Yale University Sterling Memorial Library.

Fine, Gail. "Knowledge and Belief in *Republic* V." *Archiv für Geschichte der Philosophie* 60 (1978): 121–39. Reprinted with the permission of Walter de Gruyter, Inc. Courtesy of Yale University Sterling Memorial Library.

Wilson, J.R.S. "The Contents of the Cave." In Roger A. Shiner and John King-Farlow, eds., *New Essays on Plato and the Presocratics: Canadian Journal of Philosophy* Supplementary 2 (1976): 117–27. Reprinted with the permission of the University of Calgary Press. Courtesy of Yale University Sterling Memorial Library.

Austin, J.L. "The Line and the Cave in Plato's *Republic*." In J.O. Urmson and G.J. Warnock, eds., *J.L. Austin: Philosophical*

Papers 3rd. ed. (Oxford: Oxford University Press, 1979): 288–303. Reprinted with the permission of Oxford University Press. Courtesy of Yale University Cross Campus Library.

Gallop, D. "Image and Reality in Plato's *Republic.*" *Archiv für Geschichte der Philosophie* 47 (1965): 113–31. Reprinted with the permission of Walter de Gruyter, Inc. Courtesy of Yale University Sterling Memorial Library.

Peterson, Sandra. "A Reasonable Self-Predication Premise for the Third Man Argument." *Philosophical Review* 82 (1973): 451–70; v.84 (1975): 96. Reprinted with the permission of AMS Press, Inc. Courtesy of Yale University Sterling Memorial Library.

Nehamas, Alexander. "Self-Predication and Plato's Theory of Forms." *American Philosophical Quarterly* 16 (1979): 93–103. Reprinted with the permission of the *American Philosophical Quarterly*. Courtesy of Yale University Sterling Memorial Library.

Cohen, S. Marc. "The Logic of the Third Man." *Philosophical Review* 80 (1971): 448–75. Reprinted with the permission of AMS Press, Inc. Courtesy of Yale University Sterling Memorial Library.

Fine, Gail. "Plato and Aristotle on Form and Substance." *Proceedings of the Cambridge Philological Society* 209 (1983): 23–47. Reprinted with the permission of the Cambridge Philological Society. Courtesy of the Cambridge Philological Society.

Brown, Lesley. "Being in the *Sophist*: A Syntactical Enquiry." *Oxford Studies in Ancient Philosophy* 4 (1986): 49–70. Reprinted with the permission of the author. Courtesy of Yale University Sterling Memorial Library.

McDowell, John. "Falsehood and Not-Being in Plato's *Sophist.*" In Malcolm Schofield and Martha Craven Nussbaum, eds., *Language and Logos* (Cambridge: Cambridge University Press, 1982): 115–34. Reprinted with the permission of Cambridge University Press. Courtesy of Yale University Cross Campus Library.

Burnyeat, M.F. "Conflicting Appearances." *Proceedings of the British Academy* 65 (1979): 69–111. Reprinted with the permission of the British Academy. Courtesy of the British Academy.

Broadie, Sarah Waterlow. "Protagoras and Inconsistency: *Theaetetus* 171a6–c7." *Archiv für Geschichte der Philosophie* 59 (1977): 19–36. Reprinted with the permission of Walter de Gruyter, Inc. Courtesy of Yale University Sterling Memorial Library.

Cooper, John M. "Plato on Sense-Perception and Knowledge (*Theaetetus* 184–186)." *Phronesis* 15 (1970): 123–46. Reprinted with the permission of Van Gorcum en Co. B.V. Courtesy of Yale University Sterling Memorial Library.

Frede, Michael. "Observations on Perception in Plato's Later Dialogues." In Michael Frede, ed., *Essays in Ancient Philosophy* (Minneapolis: University of Minnesota Press, 1987): 3–8. Copyright 1987 by the University of Minnesota. Published by the University of Minnesota Press. Courtesy of the University of Minnesota Press.

Zeyl, Donald J. "Plato and Talk of a World in Flux: *Timaeus* 49a6–50b5." *Harvard Studies in Classical Philology* 79 (1975): 125–48. Reprinted with the permission of Harvard University Press. Courtesy of Yale University Sterling Memorial Library.

SERIES CONTENTS

CLASSICAL PHILOSOPHY

Collected Papers

Series Editor

TERENCE IRWIN

Professor of Philosophy
Cornell University

A GARLAND SERIES